SPEECH PRODUCTION

Macquarie Monographs in Cognitive Science

Series Editor: MAX COLTHEART

The Macquarie Monographs in Cognitive Science series will publish original monographs dealing with any aspect of cognitive science.

Each volume in the series will cover a circumscribed topic and will provide readers with a summary of the current state-of-the-art in that field.

A primary aim of the volumes is also to advance research and knowledge in the field through discussion of new theoretical and experimental advances.

Titles in the series

Routes to Reading Success and Failure: Toward an Integrated Cognitive Psychology of Atypical Reading, Nancy Ewald Jackson & Max Coltheart

Cognitive Neuropsychological Approaches to Spoken Word Production, Lyndsey Nickels (Ed.)

Rehabilitation of Spoken Word Production in Aphasia, Lyndsey Nickels (Ed.)

Masked Priming: The State of the Art, Sachiko Kinoshita & Stephen J. Lupker (Eds.)

Individual Differences in Theory of Mind: Implications for Typical and Atypical Development, Betty Repacholi & Virginia Slaughter (Eds.)

From Mating to Mentality: Evaluating Evolutionary Psychology, Kim Sterelny & Julie Fitness (Eds.)

Cognitive Neuropsychology *Twenty Years On*, Max Coltheart & Alfonso Caramazza (Eds.)

Forthcoming titles

Subsequent volumes are planned on various topics in cognitive science including visual cognition and modeling of visual word recognition.

Macquarie Monographs in Cognitive Science

SPEECH PRODUCTION
Models, Phonetic Processes, and Techniques

Jonathan Harrington
University of Kiel, Germany

and

Marija Tabain
La Trobe University, Australia

Psychology Press
Taylor & Francis Group
NEW YORK AND HOVE

Published in 2006 by
Psychology Press
270 Madison Avenue
New York, NY 10016
www.psypress.com

Published in Great Britain by
Psychology Press
27 Church Road
Hove, East Sussex BN3 2FA
www.psypress.co.uk

Psychology Press is an imprint of the Taylor & Francis Group, an informa business

Typeset by Macmillan India, Bangalore, India
Printed and bound in the USA by Sheridan Books, Inc., Ann Arbor, MI, on acid-free paper
Cover by Hybert Design

10 9 8 7 6 5 4 3 2 1

Library of Congress Cataloging-in-Publication Data

Speech production : models, phonetic processes, and techniques / edited by Jonathan Harrington & Marija Tabain.
p. cm.–(Macquarie monographs in cognitive science)
Includes bibliographical references and index.
ISBN 1-84169-437-1 (hardback : alk. paper) 1. Speech. 2. Phonetics. 3. Speech processing systems. I. Harrington, Jonathan, 1950– II. Tabain, Marija. III. Series.
P95.S6463 2006
414'.8 – dc22

2005030577

ISBN13: 978-1-84169-437-5 (hbk)
ISBN10: 1-84169-437-1 (hbk)

Contents

About the Editors

Jonathan Harrington is a Professor of Phonetics and Digital Speech Processing at the University of Kiel, Germany. He has previously held positions at Macquarie University, Australia and at the University of Edinburgh, Scotland. His current research projects include: the phonetics of Australian Aboriginal languages, socio-phonetics and sound change, and the intonation of German.

Marija Tabain is a Lecturer in Linguistics at La Trobe University in Melbourne, Australia. She has held research positions in linguistics, psychology, and electrical engineering centres in Australia, France, and the U.S. Her research is focused on articulatory and acoustic phonetics, with particular emphasis on cross-language comparisons. Her work is published in the *Journal of the Acoustical Society of America*, the *Journal of Phonetics*, the *Journal of the International Phonetic Association*, *Language and Speech*, and *Phonetica*.

Contributors

Denis Autesserre
Laboratoire Parole et Langage,
Université de Provence, France

Pierre Badin
Institut de la Communication Parlée,
Institut National Polytechnique
Grenoble, France

Gérard Bailly
Institut de la Communication Parlée,
Institut National Polytechnique
Grenoble, France

Maxime Bérar
Institut de la Communication Parlée,
Institut National Polytechnique Grenoble,
France

Louis-Jean Boë
Institut de la Communication Parleé,
Université Stendhal, France

Andrew Butcher
Department of Speech Pathology
& Audiology,
Flinders University, Adelaide, and
Research Centre for Language Typology,
La Trobe University,
Melbourne, Australia

Daniel E. Callan
Human Information Science Laboratories,
ATR Brain Activity Imaging Center,
Japan

Matthieu Chabanas
TIMC Laboratory,
Universite Joseph Fourier, France

Jianwu Dang
Graduate School of Information
Science,
Japan Advanced Institute of Science and
Technology, Japan

Michel Desvignes
Laboratoire des Images & des Signaux,
Université Joseph Fourier, France

Frédéric Elisei
Institut de la Communication Parlée,
Institut National Polytechnique
Grenoble, France

Olov Engwall
Centre for Speech Technology,
Royal Institute of Technology, Sweden

Melissa A. Epstein
Department of Biomedical Sciences &
Orthodontics,
University of Maryland Dental School,
USA

Veronique Ferbach-Hecker
Institut de Phonétique de Strasbourg,
Université Marc Bloch,
France

Susanne Fuchs
Department of Phonetics,
ZAS – Centre for General Linguistics,
Germany

Christian Geng
Department of Phonetics,
ZAS – Centre for General Linguistics,
Germany

Jean-Michel Gérard
Nanophysics & Semiconductors Laboratory,
Division of Physical Sciences (DRFMC),
CEA, France

Satrajit S. Ghosh
Speech Communication Group,
Massachusetts Institute of Technology,
USA

Hiroaki Gomi
Communication Science Laboratories,
Nippon Telegraph & Telephone Corporation, Japan

Frank H. Guenther
Department of Cognitive & Neural Systems,
Boston University, USA

Jonathan Harrington
Institute of Phonetics & Digital Speech Processing,
University of Kiel, Germany

Jean-Louis Heim
Laboratoire d'Anthropologie du Museé de l'Homme,
Muséum Nationale d'Histoire Naturelle,
France

Fabrice Hirsch
Institut de Phonétique de Strasbourg,
Université Marc Bloch, France

Kiyoshi Honda
Department of Biophysical Imaging,
ATR Human Information Science Labs,
Japan

Phil Hoole
Phonetics Institute,
Munich University, Germany

Gregoire Jozan
Human Information Sciences Labs,
Advanced Telecommunications Research Institute Int'l (ATR), Japan

Chandra Kambhamettu
Department of Computer & Information Sciences,
University of Delaware, USA

Patricia A. Keating
Linguistics Department,
University of California, USA

Harlan Lane
Department of Psychology,
Northeastern University, USA

Hélène Lœvenbruck
Institut de la Communication Parlée,
Institut National Polytechnique Grenoble, France

Min Li
Department of Computer & Information Sciences,
University of Delaware, USA

Nicole Marrone
Department of Communication Disorders, Boston University, USA

Shinobu Masaki
Department of Biophysical Imaging, ATR Human Information Science Labs, Japan

Melanie L. Matthies
Department of Communication Disorders, Boston University, USA

Lucie Ménard
Département de Linguistique et de Didactique des Langues, Université du Québec à Montréal, Canada

Christine Mooshammer
Institut fuer Phonetik und Digitale, Christian-Albrechts-Universität zu Kiel, Germany

Kevin G. Munhall
Department of Psychology, Queen's University, Canada

Alfonso Nieto-Castanon
Department of Cognitive & Neural Systems, Boston University, USA

Jyunichi Nozoe
Interdisciplinary Graduate School of Science & Engineering, Tokyo Institute of Technology, Japan

Matthias Odisio
TIMC Laboratory, Université Joseph Fourier, France

Daniel Pape
Department of Phonetics, ZAS – Centre for General Linguistics, Germany

Hugo de Paula
Center for Research on Speech, Acoustics, Language & Music, Federal University of Minas Gerais, Brazil

Yohan Payan
TIMC Laboratory, Université Joseph Fourier, France

Joseph S. Perkell
Speech Communication Group, Massachusetts Institute of Technology, USA

Pascal Perrier
Institut de la Communication Parlée, Institut National Polytechnique Grenoble, France

Rachid Ridouane
Laboratoire de Phonétique et Phonologie, Université Paris 3, France

Johanna-Pascale Roy
Institut de Phonétique de Strasbourg, Université Marc Bloch, France

Christophe Savariaux
Institut de la Communication Parlée, Université Stendhal, France

Douglas Shiller
Speech Perception & Production Laboratory, Queen's University, Canada

Rudolph Sock
Institut de Phonétique de Strasbourg, Université Marc Bloch, France

Ellen Stockmann
Speech Communication Group,
Massachusetts Institute of Technology,
USA

Maureen Stone
Department of Biomedical Sciences & Orthodontics,
University of Maryland Dental School,
USA

Marija Tabain
Linguistics Program,
La Trobe University, Australia

Sayoko Takano
Department of CREST, Research Management Group,
Japan Science & Technology Corporation, USA

Mark Tiede
Haskins Laboratories,
Yale University, USA

Jason A. Tourville
Department of Cognitive & Neural Systems,
Boston University, USA

Eric Vatikiotis-Bateson
Communication Dynamics Project,
ATR Human Information Science Labs,
Japan

Beatrice Vaxelaire
Institut de Phonétique de Strasbourg,
Université Marc Bloch, France

Hani Camille Yehia
Center for Research on Speech, Acoustics, Language & Music,
Federal University of Minas Gerais,
Brazil

Majid Zandipour
Speech Communication Group,
Massachusetts Institute of Technology,
USA

Wolfram Ziegler
Clinical Neuropsychology Research Group,
City Hospital Munich,
Germany

Introduction

JONATHAN HARRINGTON AND
MARIJA TABAIN

The topic of this book, speech production, is about how a speaker makes use of the vocal organs to transmit both linguistic and nonlinguistic (e.g., emotional) meanings to the listener. It is also about building machines to represent some of the stages of human speech production, and it includes both normal and disordered aspects of speech production in its various forms. Some of the chapters use speech production research techniques to measure and to model phonetic differences across languages. These themes represent sometimes overlapping, but usually complementary, ways of understanding speech production that draw upon knowledge from many different disciplines.

These general themes give rise to more specific areas of enquiry that have been current in the speech production literature for many decades and that have also been dealt with in publications arising from the earlier Speech Production Seminars. At the same time, the book reflects some of the many ways in which the field has developed in recent years. In particular, advances in technology have produced more realistic and more sophisticated biomechanical simulations of speech production. There is also now a greater emphasis on modelling speech production in relation to other modalities (auditory and visual) rather than in isolation. The range of data in speech production research, which in earlier years was often restricted to nonwords produced by English speakers, has broadened in the last 10–20 years to include analyses of different types of prosodic structures and of languages whose structures are very different from that of English.

We now consider some of the key topics in speech production that are taken up in this book.

FEEDBACK AND FEEDFORWARD CONTROL OF SPEECH PRODUCTION

In several chapters, evidence is provided that speech production is under adaptive feedforward control. The central idea here is that during language acquisition a child learns about auditory–articulatory relationships under feedback control: A child detects auditorily the discrepancy between the words she/he produces and those that she/he has heard, and uses this auditory feedback (of listening to his/herself speaking) to make a better match to the word(s) heard in the community. Moreover, during language acquisition these auditory–articulatory relationships are learned (internalised) so that with the development of speech motor control, they can be used to make a prediction about the accuracy of speech production prior to articulation: This type of predictive "forward" model is therefore much more rapid than any type of external (auditory, tactile, or proprioceptive) feedback control which can only have direct effects towards the end of the movements in which it arises. In this type of model, speech is planned in terms of its expected sensory consequences, and if there is a discrepancy between this internalised auditory trace and the intended speech production, the neuromuscular commands can be adjusted so that the discrepancy is avoided in subsequent movements. Since such a model does not rely on auditory feedback for the closed-loop control of ongoing movements, it constitutes a type of feedforward control. Feedforward control can also be achieved in the absence of a forward model, by continually updating feedforward commands to incorporate corrective commands generated under auditory feedback control. In both cases, early use of auditory feedback control is gradually replaced by feedforward control, thus allowing the speaker to generate rapid speech without suffering instabilities related to auditory feedback delays. This type of model is discussed in the following chapters:

- Guenther, Ghosh, Nieto-Castanon, and Tourville describe a computationally based adaptive model of speech production, DIVA (Directions Into Velocities of Articulators)—that incorporates both feedforward and feedback control mechanisms—and they relate its various components with regions of the brain.
- Perrier provides evidence from experiments in which the lip rounding is perturbed in the production of [u] of how speakers can rapidly update an internalised model, i.e., learn new relationships between articulatory commands and their acoustic consequences. Perrier also raises the important issue about the extent to which the details of the physical properties of the speech motor system should be represented in internal models. He argues that not all information about the dynamics of speech needs to be included in an internal representation, and he provides evidence that complex dynamics arise from the biomechanical properties of the tongue.

- Compatibly with the DIVA model, Callan makes use of fMRI brain-imaging studies to show differences in brain activity associated with native and second language productions: Whereas Japanese speakers' productions of an English /l~r/ contrast are accompanied by a greater activity in regions of the brain associated with feedback control, there is evidence for a predominantly feed-forward mechanism in native speakers' productions of the same contrast.

DOMAIN IN WHICH SPEECH PLANNING TAKES PLACE

As discussed in Perrier, models of speech production are concerned with the domain in which speech planning takes place—i.e., whether the goals for speech production are in terms of articulatory gestures (Browman & Goldstein, 1992), or whether they are auditory or somato-sensory, or are some combination of these. The starting point for the analysis by Perkell, Guenther, Lane, Marrone, Matthies, Stockmann, Tiede, and Zandipour is that variability is an inherent and necessary aspect of speech production. This is predicted both from quantal theory (Stevens, 1989) in which there are regions of the vocal tract in which a high degree of articulatory variability results in only a small acoustic change; and from Lindblom's (1990) hyper- and hypo-articulation model in which articulatory precision is varied in relation to the listener's requirements for clarity. If, as predicted by the DIVA model, speech production goals are auditory and learned from auditory–articulatory mappings, then there should be a correspondence between a speaker's hearing acuity on the one hand and speech production variability on the other. Compatibly, Perkell et al. use perception and production techniques to argue for auditory targeting by establishing a relationship between speakers' ability to hear and to produce differences both between different vowel categories and between two fricatives, /s/ and /ʃ/.

In one of the analyses described in Guenther et al., the DIVA model learned to drive an articulatory synthesiser that had been matched to a speaker's vocal shape using MRI scans. The output of this articulatory synthesis resulted in a close match to the very many different possible tongue configurations that the speaker had used for /r/ production, thereby providing both a validation of the DIVA model and further evidence that speech is planned in terms of auditory targets.

IS SPEECH SPECIAL?

The idea from the motor theory of speech perception that speech is special is founded on three main principles: Firstly, that there is a specialised phonetic module in the brain with which listeners reconstruct the speaker's intended gestures of phonetic categories; secondly, that the same phonetic module is invoked in speech production; and finally, that the type of processing in the phonetic module is unique, i.e., different from any other type of (nonspeech) activity (Liberman & Mattingly, 1985).

Ziegler argues for the existence of a specialised neural system in speech production on the basis of clinical observations showing a dissociation between involuntary acts that make use of the vocal organs such as breathing, smiling, crying, and voluntary acts such as speaking. For example, patients with certain types of brain lesions may have no difficulty in performing involuntary acts such as breathing and yawning, but cannot perform any voluntary motor control including speech; conversely there is also clinical evidence showing that involuntary movements can be impaired without volitional acts being disrupted. Similarly, and as is very apparent from studies of intonation and prosody (Gussenhoven, 2004; Ladd, 1996), although linguistic information and emotion are communicated by the same speech production mechanisms (e.g., vocal fold vibration), Ziegler points to clinical evidence for their dissociation, i.e., for a motor network for emotional expressions that is autonomous from processes that control the production of speech.

The research of Boë, Heim, Autesserre, and Badin is concerned with the origins of speech and whether the vocal tract capabilities that make speech possible are unique to humans. Their analysis is relevant to Lieberman and Crelin's (1971) hypothesis that Neanderthals became extinct because they did not possess the anatomical basis of speech. In their study, Boë et al. use X-ray images of 22 speakers producing vowels to define statistically the optimum set of bony landmarks for predicting the shape of the vocal tract between the lips and the glottis. For each bony landmark that is defined to be optimal for predicting vocal tract shape, they create an ellipse distribution in the sagittal plane using measurements from a further 91 skulls taken from around the world. They then show that the Neanderthals fall within and near the edge of these ellipses (i.e., the probability that the Neanderthals and these 91 skulls form part of the same population is greater than 95% for each optimal bony landmark), suggesting that Neanderthals did possess the basis for speech.

THE ARCHITECTURE OF A SPEECH PRODUCTION MODEL

Studies of performance errors as well as latency data from reaction time studies have been used to provide evidence that speech production is derived from processing in a number of autonomous modules: In the Weaver model of Levelt, Roelofs, and Meyer (1999), there are separate modules for grammatical encoding, phonological encoding, the lexicon, and phonetic encoding. Levelt et al. (1999) are explicit about defining both what these components consist of and what information is passed between them. The research by Keating is relevant to these types of architectural issues and in particular to how prosody interacts with segmental planning. The electro-palatographic studies in several languages by Keating and her colleagues have shown that segments are highly sensitive to prosodic structure: In particular, a domain-initial consonant that is lower down in the prosodic hierarchy (e.g., one that begins a syllable but not a word or a phrase) tends to be lenited and/or shorter in comparison with a consonant that is higher up in the prosodic hierarchy (e.g., one that begins an utterance, and therefore at the same time begins a phrase, a word, and a syllable). This result, and indeed many other phonetic studies of prosody, is not consistent with the model of Levelt et al. (1999) in which prosodic structure is computed after phonetic segments are specified.

Ziegler's paper is relevant to the notion expressed in the so-called 'translation models' of speech production that there is a dissociation between the plan (the abstract symbolic representation of speech) and its execution (the physical, neuromuscular stages of speech production). Fowler (1984) has for a long time taken a strong view against this position, and further arguments that the plan is not independent of the motor programming are presented in Ziegler. He shows, firstly, that there are some disorders of speech that cannot be neatly categorised into those involving a disorder of abstract planning stages as opposed to those that arise at a physical motor programming stage; and secondly that a model in which the plan is independent of, and hence blind to, its execution is not compatible with the evidence that speech and other oral motor behaviours differ in their underlying motor organisation.

THE PRODUCTION OF PROSODY

As discussed above, Keating provides articulatory evidence from various languages that consonants in initial position higher up in the prosodic hierarchy are strengthened. The question of whether this is a language-specific or universal phenomenon has not yet been resolved, although Keating does suggest that strengthening might not occur to the same extent in Japanese (Onaka, 2003). Butcher's acoustic and articulatory analyses of various Australian Aboriginal languages point to another way in which the type of strengthening is language specific. He shows that domain-final consonants in Australian languages are as strong, or stronger than, domain-initial ones, and he discusses compatible synchronic and diachronic evidence that consonants in many Australian languages are more likely to be deleted and lenited word-initially than word-medially. Perhaps then Australian languages would tend to pattern with Japanese in not showing the effect of domain-initial strengthening that has been found for the languages analysed by Keating and her colleagues.

The study by Ménard, Loevenbruck, and Savariaux is concerned with the production of focus and accent in young children. Their analysis of supra-glottal articulation using EMA shows that children aged 4 have not yet acquired the contrasts in prosodic prominence that signal the distinction between focused and unfocused words. They explain this as a consequence of hyper- and hypo-articulation: That is, young children are less able to hypo-articulate speech at points that are semantically more predictable from context. Their results also suggest that the association between segments and prosody is likely to be a learned aspect of speech production.

ARTICULATORY CORRELATES OF SEGMENTAL FEATURES

Many papers are concerned with the long-standing interest in phonetics of defining the articulatory correlates of segmental contrasts, and in this book a range of data are presented that are relevant to this issue.

- Butcher considers the possibility that there is a relationship between the almost ubiquitous middle ear infections in Australian Aboriginal children and the dominance in Australian languages of segments whose acoustic cues are mostly in the mid-frequency range (i.e., Australian languages are unusual in that almost none include fricatives or a voicing contrast, whereas some have up to seven contrasting places of articulation in stop and nasal consonants).
- Pape, Mooshammer, Hoole, and Fuchs study the interaction between devoicing and various vocalic and consonantal features in German using EMA. They show that devoicing is context specific and more prevalent in low and in lax vowels. They suggest that the main distinction between voiced and voiceless stops in German is dependent on voice onset time rather than on differences of pharyngeal expansion during the closure.
- Sock, Vaxelaire, Roy, Ferbach-Hecker, and Hirsch make use of X-ray and movement data to investigate the interaction between speaking rate and the vowel quantity contrast in Gambian Wolof. They show firstly that there are acoustic and articulatory durational contrasts between long and short vowels, and secondly that these durational distinctions are reinforced by various vowel-dependent articulatory manoeuvres, such as a wider lip opening in long vowels and greater jaw lowering in long /a/.
- Ridouane, Fuchs, and Hoole use transillumination to investigate laryngeal articulation in the production of obstruent clusters in Tashlhiyt Berber, a variety of Berber that is spoken in Southern Morocco. This language is unusual in that entire words, and therefore entire utterances, can be completely voiceless. Their analysis shows how laryngeal and oral gestures are temporally tightly coupled: That is, a sequence of voiceless consonants does not show a single glottal opening gesture at the beginning and end of the voiceless sequence, but rather separate glottal opening movements for each voiceless fricative that are unaffected by the presence of any intervening word boundaries.

- In a study of tongue tip and palatal contacts using a combination of electro-palatography and electro-magnetometry, Fuchs, Perrier, Geng, and Mooshammer show different control strategies for the production of stops and fricatives in German. Both exhibit lateral palatal contact, but whereas fricatives are produced with a planned target at the palate's lateral margins, the target for stops is beyond the palate (which ensures a tight seal between the tongue tip and the alveolar ridge in producing alveolars).
- Takano, Honda, and Masaki are concerned with the physiological mechanisms that underlie differences in intrinsic pitch. Their MRI study of two subjects producing sustained /a/ and /i/ vowels is the first to show how intrinsic pitch differences arise as a result of a tight connection between the hyoid bone and the thyroid cartilage. In the production of /i/, advancement of the hyoid bone due to contraction of the genio-glossus and genio-hyoid muscles can apply a force on the thyroid cartilage causing it to advance, perhaps with a concomitant horizontal translation of the crico-thyroid joint, in the direction that stretches the vocal folds (and hence raises *f*0). But since they do not find any consistent pattern in the movement of the jaw in relation to *f*0 changes, they conclude that the mechanical connection between the hyoid bone and the thyroid cartilage is tighter than between the jaw and the hyoid bone.

TECHNIQUES

Research in the speech sciences is influenced considerably by the development of new algorithms and the invention of new techniques and in the last 10 years, the incorporation of data from magnetic resonance imaging (MRI) has extended the types of research questions and models in speech production—especially as far as three-dimensional (3D) vocal tract modelling (see the section below) is concerned.

- Engwall's study of some of the artefacts that can be introduced by the nature of the recording in MRI is therefore timely. In many MRI studies, subjects have to produce long, sustained articulations. He shows that sustained articulations can induce a backward movement of the tongue and a lack of velum control and that they can be hyperarticulated compared with real-time productions, especially as far as coarticulation is concerned. He also shows that in MRI recordings from the supine position, the shape and position of the tongue can be affected by an associated decrease in the width of the pharyngeal passage.
- In their investigation of the relationship between fundamental frequency and the movement of hyoid and thyroid cartilages, Takano, Honda, and Masaki develop a custom MRI coil for imaging the larynx together with a synchronised scan method that lets them collect data only during phonatory cycles.

- Stone, Epstein, Li, and Kambhamettu make use of ultrasound in their analysis of the shape of the tongue surface and its relationship to coronal sections. As argued elsewhere (Stone, Parthasarathy, Iskarous, NessAiver, & Prince, 2003), ultrasound has some advantages over MRI. Ultrasound is inexpensive; is easy to use for the experimenter and subject; is collected in upright position allowing more typical tongue patterns than supine data; and does not require multiple repetitions to create a high-quality, high-speed dataset (30 Hz).

3D MODEL OF SUPRA-LARYNGEAL ARTICULATION

With the advent of MRI and the continued development of ultrasonic techniques, it has become possible to obtain accurate images of the vocal organs in three dimensions.

One of the main issues dealt with in Stone et al. is that a 3D-model of the tongue's surface can be derived from a small number of cross-sectional or coronal shapes of the tongue sampled at various points from the tip to the root. However, as the literature shows, there is very little data available on coronal tongue. But there is on the other hand a considerable amount of data on the mid-sagittal shape of the tongue (e.g., from EMA). Therefore, if it can be shown that there is a predictable relationship between the tongue's mid-sagittal contour and its coronal shape, then mid-sagittal data can be used to model the 3D surface of the tongue. Stone et al. establish such a relationship and show that the midline height in the sagittal plane is related to whether the coronal shape is arched or grooved.

Gérard, Perrier, and Payan are concerned with developing a 3D biomechanical model of the tongue. In a biomechanical model, the aim is to explain not just the displacement of the vocal organs, but also the way in which motor commands bring about articulatory displacements—this in turn requires a model of the force generation principles and mechanical properties of the articulators. They note the limitations of two-dimensional biomechanical models of the tongue: For example, it is not possible to account for lateral contacts of the tongue that contribute to the deformation of the tongue surface. The data for their 3D tongue model, represented as a mesh with embedded muscular structures within a geometrical model of the jaw and vocal tract walls, is partly derived from an analysis of the mechanical properties of a human tongue obtained from a cadaver. They show a strong relationship between tongue movements caused by applying forces to various muscles in their model and data from X-ray images in the mid-sagittal plane.

The study by Gomi, Nozoe, Dang, and Honda is concerned with developing a 3D model of the oro-facial system in order to account for tissue deformation in lip movement. They model the lips as a mass–spring meshed network, and synthesise various lip shapes from nine oro-facial muscles. They also model the constraints on lip deformation, which come about through passive contact of the inside of the lip with the teeth. By activating various muscles in their model, they show that the marginal and peripheral parts of the orbicularis oris superior and inferior make very different contributions to lip deformation: Whereas lip protrusion is formed by activation of the peripheral orbicularis oris, activation of the marginal muscle results in a tight shutting and pursing of the lips. They also use the model to show that lip rounding is likely to result from a complex interaction between several lip muscles and possibly also jaw muscles.

AUDIO-VISUAL SYNTHESIS

Developing 3D models of the vocal tract is closely related to research on the facial synthesis of speech and on building a talking head. Two chapters are directly concerned with these issues. In the study by Bérar, Bailly, Chabanas, Desvignes, Elisei, Odisio, and Payan, the main aim is to develop a generic talking head that can be modified with a small set of parameters in order to reproduce the anatomy and facial deformations that result from speech movements in a number of different speakers. Another aim is to encode speaker-specific variability. They derive a shape of the skull and jaw that is specific to each speaker by adapting a static generic model to speaker-specific motion capture data. Using statistical analyses, they develop a linear model of shape variation between speakers that separates speaker-independent articulation parameters from the facial shape and appearance that is specific to the speaker.

de Paula, Yehia, Shiller, Jozan, Munhall, and Vatikiotis-Bateson are concerned with how much information is needed by viewers of Japanese and English in order to extract phonetically relevant visual information from dynamic audio-visual speech. They show that faces can be filtered to remove all information above the vocal tract rate without degrading the perception of visual speech information. The finding that perception is tuned to the spatiotemporal resolution of vocal tract events has an important application: Above all, it can be used to define the degree of accuracy that is required to construct models for the production and perception of audio-visual speech.

Beyond these general themes, the reader will find treatments of many of the other "classic" issues of speech production throughout the book, such as speaker variation (e.g., Bérar et al. and Fuchs et al.), coarticulation (e.g., Engwall and Pape et al.), and motor equivalence (e.g., Guenther et al.; Perkell et al. and Perrier). Taken together, the chapters show that we cannot hope to understand speech communication in humans and machines without also understanding how the symbolic level of speech is related to the fine details of vocal organ movement and control. The various studies in this book show how much progress has been made in the last 10 years in our knowledge of speech production, while also pointing to many new and exciting research directions and challenges for the future.

ACKNOWLEDGMENTS

We would like to thank everyone who contributed to this book: The session chairs, who helped us to choose which papers from the conference would form a cohesive whole for this volume; the reviewers, many of whom were not at the conference itself, but who undertook the task of reviewing with as much enthusiasm as those who were; the Macquarie Centre for Cognitive Science, Macquarie University, Sydney for hosting the 6th Seminar on Speech Production in December 2003 (Palethorpe & Tabain, 2003) from which the chapters in this book are derived; and the publisher, Psychology Press, for its continued support.

REFERENCES

Browman, C., & Goldstein, L. (1992). Articulatory phonology: An overview. *Phonetica*, *49*, 155–180.

Fowler, C. (1984). Segmentation of coarticulated speech in perception. *Perception & Psychophysics*, *36*, 359–368.

Gussenhoven, C. (2004). *The phonology and tone of intonation*. Cambridge: Cambridge University Press.

Ladd, D. (1996). *Intonational phonology*. Cambridge: Cambridge University Press.

Levelt, W. J. M., Roelofs, A., & Meyer, A. S. (1999). A theory of lexical access in speech production. *Behavioural and Brain Sciences*, *22*, 1–75.

Liberman, A., & Mattingly, I. (1989). The motor theory of speech perception revised. *Cognition*, *21*, 1–36.

Lieberman, P., & Crelin, E. (1971). On the speech of the Neanderthal man. *Linguistic Inquiry*, *2*, 203–222.

Lindblom, B. (1990). Explaining phonetic variation: A sketch of the H&H theory. In W.J. Hardcastle & A. Marchal (Eds.), *Speech production and speech modelling* (pp. 403–439). Dordrecht: Kluwer.

Onaka, A. (2003). Domain-initial strengthening in Japanese: An acoustic and articulatory study. *Proceedings of the 15th international congress of phonetic sciences*, Barcelona (pp. 2091–2094).

Palethorpe, S. & Tabain, M. (Eds.). (2003). *Proceedings of the sixth international seminar on speech production*. Sydney, Australia: Macquarie University (ISBN 1 86408 871 0).

Stevens, K. (1989). On the quantal nature of speech. *Journal of Phonetics*, *17*, 3–45.

Stone, M., Parthasarathy, V., Iskarous, K., NessAiver, M., & Prince, J. (2003). Tissue strains and tongue shapes: Combining tMRI and ultrasound. *Proceedings of the 15th international congress of phonetic sciences*, Barcelona.

PART 1

Models

1

About Speech Motor Control Complexity

PASCAL PERRIER

ABSTRACT

A key issue in research about speech motor control is the one of the level of complexity that is required for the internal models: have these models to account accurately for all physical properties of the speech motor system, including the complex tongue–jaw biomechanics? Or would more simple internal representations be sufficient, which model only the static characteristics of the peripheral speech apparatus or which give a rough account of articulatory dynamics? On the basis of experimental and modeling studies of speech movements and human limb movements published in the literature, the adequacy of simplified internal representations for speech motor control is analyzed.

INTRODUCTION

In the past two decades, the analysis of speech motor control and its modeling were basically inspired by investigations and models of other skilled human movements, such as reaching, pointing, or grasping. This research approach has been proved to be efficient and it allowed the emergence of a number of speech control models which served as theoretical backgrounds for numerous studies (see among others Guenther, 1995; Laboissière, Ostry, & Feldman, 1996; Ostry, Gribble, & Gracco, 1996; Perkell et al., 1997, 2000; Perrier, Lœvenbruck, & Payan, 1996; Saltzman, 1986; Saltzman & Munhall, 1989). Consequently, the issues raised today in the domain of motor control research are very important for future studies of speech motor control, and addressing them is a prerequisite for the improvement of the current models. Among these issues, two questions are of particular interest: (1) How complex are the acquired internal representations of the motor system, built up during the acquisition of the motor task, and used to plan and achieve the movement? and (2) What role does low-level, short-latency feedback play in achieving an accurate and stable movement control? In this paper, contributions to these issues are proposed, while taking into account some important peculiarities of the speech production task.

SPEECH PRODUCTION: A COMPLEX MOTOR TASK

Compared to many other human motor tasks classically studied in motor control research, speech production has a number of peculiarities that make it particularly complex. Some findings suggesting such a complexity were already frequently discussed in the literature:

1. Because of its semiotic nature, the goal of speech production is actually defined in an abstract domain. Hence, its physical characterization is not straightforward, and this has two consequences. First there is no unique physical correlate for a given elementary speech sound and a large variability of patterns can be observed in the neurophysiological, articulatory, and acoustic domains (see Perkell & Klatt, 1986). Second the issue of the physical space in which the motor task is planned becomes particularly complex, since the distal space can be defined either by articulatory positions, or by spectral properties of the speech signal, or by perceptual characteristics of this signal (see Browman & Goldstein, 1990; Guenther, Hampson, & Johnson, 1998; Savariaux, Perrier, & Orliaguet, 1995; Stevens, 1989; Tremblay, Shiller, & Ostry, 2003), or a multimodal space associating orosensory, auditory, and even visual characterizations.
2. Speech production has a large number of degrees of freedom that confer a many-to-one characteristic on the relationships between motor commands, articulatory positions, and acoustic or auditory properties. This characteristic, together with the above-mentioned intrinsic variability of the physical correlates of the production of a given sound, has the consequence that a large set of motor equivalence strategies can be used to implement a range of coarticulation strategies or to deal with artificial perturbations (such as a pipe or food in the mouth), or pathological perturbations (such as tongue or mandible surgery) or peripheral perturbations (Guenther, Espy-Wilson, Boyce, Matthies, Zandipour, & Perkell, 1999; McFarland, Baum, & Chabot, 1996; Perkell, Matthies, Svirsky, & Jordan, 1993; Savariaux, Perrier, Orliaguet, & Schwartz, 1999). These multiple strategies obviously contribute to the complexity of speech motor control.
3. Compared to other skilled human motor activities, speech movements in normal conditions can be very short, since vowels have a mean duration of

> approximately 80 ms and consonants have mean durations around 40 ms (O'Shaughnessy, 1981). These characteristics seem to exclude any potential online contribution of long-latency orosensory feedback that would be processed by the cortex, and to limit the role of auditory feedback to a suprasegmental level and to an *a posteriori* monitoring used to correct segmental aspects of speech after it was produced (Perkell et al., 1997). The absence of online use of auditory feedback to control speech at a segmental level is well supported by experimental work showing that speakers can produce intelligible speech even after hearing loss (Lane & Wozniak, 1991; Manzella, Wozniak, Matthies, Lane, Guiod, & Perkell, 1994). Compatibly, work on stutterers and normal speakers shows that delaying auditory feedback in the range of 50–200 ms affects prosodic (speaking rate, fluency, rhythm, intonation, and stress) rather than segmental features (Hargrave, Kalinowski, Stuart, Armson, & Jones, 1994; Stager & Ludlow, 1993). At the same time, speech gestures have to be accurate enough in order to ensure that the associated acoustic signal can be correctly perceived by a listener. How accuracy can be obtained without the use of long-latency feedback that would be processed by the cortex, is a key issue for speech production research, but not for other human motor tasks except for eye saccades.

To deal with the complexity and the multimodality of speech task representations, with the numerous motor or auditory equivalence strategies and with the accuracy requirements in the absence of long-latency feedback going through the cortex, the large majority of speech motor control models published in the literature assume the existence of *internal representations* of the speech apparatus, called *internal models* (Guenther, 1995; Hirayama, Vatikiotis-Bateson, Kawato, & Jordan, 1992; Jordan, 1990; Jordan & Rumelhart, 1992; Kawato, Maeda, Uno, & Suzuki, 1990; Laboissière, Schwartz, & Bailly, 1991; Perkell et al., 1997, 2000; Perrier, Payan, & Marret, 2004).

INTERNAL MODELS AND SPEECH PRODUCTION CONTROL

A Useful Concept to Deal with the Control of Complex Motor Tasks

The *internal model* concept was proposed in the research domain to deal with the nonbiunivocity between motor commands and position of the final effector, and with the delays associated with the processing of long-latency feedback. The basic hypothesis is that copies of the motor system, or of subsets of it, could be learned in the brain during the acquisition of the motor skill (in our case in the speech learning phase). Once they are learned, these models could be used to estimate predictions of the consequences of motor command changes on the trajectory of the final effector. According to different existing models of human motor control published in the literature, the role of *internal models* in the execution of the motor task could take different forms.

A first hypothesis suggests that internal models' predictions could be the basis of task-planning strategies aiming at ensuring that the final effector moves along a specific desired trajectory in the task space. This is the so-called *desired trajectory hypothesis* (Kawato, 1999). Since human motor systems have usually an excess of degrees of freedom, many different motor command sequences are likely to allow the achievement of the specified trajectory. The basic idea of the *desired trajectory hypothesis* is that the central nervous system would use internal models prior to the execution of the movement, in order to select an optimal one from all possible motor command sequences that would both generate the required trajectory and minimize a motor criterion, classically related to the concept of effort. This kind of internal model is classically called *inverse internal model*, since it permits to go from the desired output to the motor commands.

For target-oriented movements, an alternative hypothesis suggests that the central nervous system would use internal models as *direct* models during the planning to optimize the positioning accuracy of the final effector at the target in presence of neural noise (Harris & Wolpert, 1998). From this perspective, internal models would also be used prior to the execution of movement, but the trajectory of the final effector toward the target would be a consequence of the planning strategy rather than the specification of the task itself. Another, more recent use of direct internal models was proposed by Todorov and Jordan (2002) in the framework of their *optimal control feedback* model. According to this model, the motor control strategy would not consist in specifying a desired trajectory in the task space and in selecting the appropriate commands for the motor system to follow this trajectory. It would instead make use of feedback information during the execution of movement to selectively modify motor commands in an optimal way, when deviations in the task space occur that would endanger the achievement of the task goal. The proposed use of feedback would require long-delay loops that are known to generate instabilities in closed-loops servo-mechanisms and that would consequently induce inadequate corrections from the controller. To overcome these problems, Torodov and Jordan (2002) have proposed using the outputs of the internal models as afferent signals.

Thus, from the perspective of motor control models such as the *desired trajectory hypothesis*, or Harris and Wolpert's (1996) proposal, or the *optimal control feedback* model, internal models are very powerful tools for dealing both with the many-to-one nature of the relations between motor commands and vocal tract configurations or spectral characteristics of the acoustic signal, as well as with the long latency of feedback processed by the cortex, and with the possible multimodality of the speech task representations. And there is considerable experimental evidence to suggest that internal models are set up and used in the control of speech production control.

Experimental Findings Support the Existence of Internal Models for Speech Production Control

Most of the data supporting the internal model hypothesis for speech production were obtained in perturbation experiments where a noticeable change was artificially introduced either in the speech production apparatus or in speech perception feedback.

Savariaux et al. (1995, 1999) perturbed the production of the French [u] by introducing a 2-cm-diameter tube between the lips of their subjects. None of the subjects could compensate for the perturbation without a training phase where they could listen to their acoustic speech production. However, immediately after the insertion of the tube, the large majority of the subjects showed articulatory changes that tended to partly compensate for the perturbation by reducing the acoustical and perceptual gaps between their normal and their perturbed [u]'s. In addition, none of them provided changes in a direction that would have been incompatible with a compensation. These observations support the idea that prior to their first production with the lip tube, speakers would use an internal representation to indicate in which direction articulatory changes should be provided to compensate for the perturbation.

Perkell et al. (2000) reported results about the spectral characteristics of speech produced by cochlear-implanted patients according to whether the cochlear implant was turned on or off. It was shown that the degradation of speech without the auditory feedback was very slow, and that it was perceptually noticeable only in alveolar fricatives that require accurate tongue positioning. This supports the hypothesis of the existence of internal representations of the relations between motor commands and spectral characteristics of the signal, which would allow the subjects to predict their speech signals in spite of the absence of auditory feedback. Note that Perkell et al. (2000) suggested that auditory feedback would be necessary to maintain these representations.

Houde and Jordan (1998) set up an original experimental protocol where subjects were asked to produce whispered steady-state vowels, while listening via headphones to acoustic feedback that had been distorted by slightly shifting the formants. Subjects were asked to compensate for the auditory perturbation so that they no longer perceived any perturbation. All subjects could compensate after training, and an after-effect was also systematically observed once the auditory feedback perturbation was removed. These findings support the idea that due to the distortion of the auditory feedback, subjects learned new relations between their articulatory commands and the associated spectral characteristics of the speech signal, i.e., a new internal model, and that they relied after training on this new representation to control their speech production.

The three experimental paradigms described above could in fact be explained by static internal models describing the link between steady-state articulatory configurations of the vocal tract and spectral patterns. However, a recent experiment carried out by Tremblay et al. (2003) suggests that a more complex internal representation could be required for speech motor control. Subjects were asked to produce vowel-to-vowel transitions while a velocity-dependent perturbing force was applied to their jaw. Thus, perturbations modified the dynamical state of the speech apparatus and not only the static relations between articulation and perception. After training, the subjects were able to compensate for this perturbation in such an accurate way that the jaw moved along the same articulatory path as under normal conditions. In addition, an after-effect was observed once the perturbation was removed. This suggests that the subjects were able to learn a new internal model taking into account the modified dynamical properties of their jaw, and to use it in their speech production. Interestingly, the learning was not observed, when the task only consisted of moving the jaw from a closed to an open position without speaking.

What Kind of Internal Models for Speech Production Control?

As shown in the preceding section, different sources of evidence show that the control of speech production could incorporate and make use of internal models. These models could be purely static, as suggested in the first three examples, or could require a more complex description of the physics as shown by Tremblay et al. (2003). This raises the question of the level of complexity of the internal models of speech production. This is a key issue not only for speech production research, but also for motor control research in general as illustrated by the controversy between Kawato and colleagues and Ostry and colleagues in their respective attempts to explain arm trajectories in pointing tasks (Gomi & Kawato, 1996; Gribble, Ostry, Sanguineti, & Laboissière, 1998). Does the motor control system need internal models that describe the motor system in its whole complexity, including dynamical and biomechanical aspects (Kawato et al.'s hypothesis), or could a rough description be sufficient (Ostry et al.'s assumption)?

In the case of speech motor control, this question becomes particularly acute, since the physical properties of speech apparatus are particularly complex:

1. The tongue is a hydrostat, i.e., a soft body with highly complex, typically nonlinear, physical properties and deformation capabilities (see Gérard, Perrier, & Payan in this volume for more details). This articulator is carried by the mandible, a hard body with dynamical properties that differ strongly from the ones of the tongue. Hence, the mechanical coupling between these two articulators cannot be described by simple mechanical laws.

2. The tongue moves in a narrow space delimited by the pharyngeal walls, the palate, the teeth, and the cheeks. Consequently, the tongue is often in contact with external structures. The amount of contacts as well as their location vary during speech production, and this induces over time changes in the physical constraints on tongue movements (damping, limitation of movement amplitude in a given direction, etc.).

Thus, the mechanical and dynamical properties of the peripheral speech apparatus are not only very complex, but also vary during the movements, since they depend on the positions of the articulators in relation to each other and on the strain of the soft tissues. Consequently, building up accurate internal models of this apparatus means, first, accounting for a strong mechanical and dynamical complexity, and, second, making the models sufficiently flexible in such a way that they can adapt based on information about the internal structure of the soft tissues and about their relations to solid structures. Recent publications have shown evidence for the very good capacity of the central nervous system to learn adaptable internal models of complex and time variable dynamics to control accurately the arm or the limb (Dingwell, Mah, & Mussa-Ivaldi, 2002; Flanagan & Lolley, 2001; Wainscott, Donchin, & Shadmehr, 2005). However, in the case of speech articulators, things seem to be even more complex, since, in this case, to be accurate, internal models would have to adapt very quickly and on the basis of short-latency proprioceptive afferent signals. Hence, it seems reasonable to assume that internal models of speech production are inaccurate functional descriptions of the speech motor system. From this perspective, different levels of complexity, from a pure static model to a sophisticated dynamical one, can be considered. In this context, an important challenge consists in collecting evidence supporting one hypothesis or the other. In the following sections, results will be presented that support the hypothesis that simplified internal representations could be efficiently used for speech motor control.

SIMPLIFIED INTERNAL MODELS COULD BE SUITED TO THE CONTROL OF SPEECH PRODUCTION

Complex Trajectories Do Not Necessarily Require Complex Internal Models

The hypothesis that planning of skilled movement sequences would be based on cost minimization principles using dynamic variables such as jerk (Hogan, 1984) or torque change (Kawato et al., 1990) is often proposed to explain specific kinematic characteristics of human movements such as the curved path observed for the finger in pointing tasks (Gomi & Kawato, 1996) or for the tongue in speech tasks (Löfqvist & Gracco, 2002). However, our recent work carried out with a 2D biomechanical model of the tongue does not support this point of view (Perrier, Payan, Zandipour, & Perkell, 2003).

We simulated tongue movements in Vowel–Velar Stop–Vowel sequences with a 2D biomechanical model of the tongue, which includes the main muscles responsible for shaping and moving the tongue in the midsagittal plane (posterior and anterior parts of the genioglossus, styloglossus, hyoglossus, inferior and superior longitudinalis, and verticalis). Tissue elastic properties are accounted for in finite-element (FE) modeling. Muscles are modeled as general force generators, which (1) act on anatomically specified sets of nodes of the FE structure and (2) modify the stiffness of specific elements of the model to account for muscle insertions into tongue tissues. The model was controlled via a target-based model using Feldman's Equilibrium Point Hypothesis (Feldman, 1986). In our simulations, each sound was specified within a given speech sequence by a set of motor commands that determine a static equilibrium position of the tongue. The transition from one sound to the next was produced by shifting the motor commands at a constant rate of shift. Hence, the temporal paths of the motor commands were strictly dependent on the time of occurrence of discrete sets of motor commands specifying the successive equilibrium positions associated with the phonemes of the sequence. These paths were not determined by any requirement on the articulatory trajectory itself. Under these conditions, the simulated tongue trajectories replicated nicely the well-known curved aspect observed in real speakers (see Perrier et al., 2003, for details). Consequently, there is no need to hypothesize any cost minimization based on dynamical variables, nor on dynamical internal models, to explain the curvature of the articulatory paths. It could be simply due to biomechanical properties of the tongue, i.e., passive tongue elasticity, muscle arrangements within the tongue, and force generation mechanisms. These results do not disprove the hypothesis of complex internal representations, since jerk or torque minimization principles could act in combination with biomechanical factors. However, our simulations suggest that this hypothesis is not a necessity to explain curved articulatory trajectories in speech.

We do not want to discard the possibility that internal representations could include some knowledge about the dynamics of the speech apparatus. It is well known that time control is a major issue in speech production, since phone durations can carry a significant part of the linguistic information. Since time is strongly dependent on the dynamics of the motor system, it is very unlikely that the dynamics could be excluded from the internal representations that the brain builds up to control the movements. Now, the question is whether coarsely specified dynamical internal models could be sufficient to reach the time and positioning accuracy required for speech production.

Inaccurate Dynamical Representations are Compatible with Movement Accuracy

Inaccurate internal models of the speech production apparatus will induce errors in the estimation of motor commands from the specification of the desired gestures. Consequently, they will induce gesture and acoustic inaccuracy, unless motor commands can be corrected during the execution of movement. To deal with this problem, Kawato and colleagues (e.g., Gomi & Kawato, 1992; Kawato, 1999; Kawato et al., 1987) proposed to use a combination of a *feedforward controller*, inferring motor commands from the desired output by using inverse dynamics, and of a *feedback controller* taking into account the output errors of the motor system to correct the motor commands *on line*. This is definitely a good framework to further think about how to deal with internal model inaccuracy. Still, there are two important problems remaining: (1) How to deal with feedback delays? (2) Is such a feedback controller compatible with a sparse description of the desired output, in which only target points are specified?

As explained above, Todorov and Jordan (2002) proposed a solution to the first problem, by suggesting using the outputs of the internal model as feedback signals. However, it is not clear how their control model would behave, if the feedback signals taken into account are inaccurate owing to internal model inaccuracy. An alternative, very interesting, contribution to this issue was proposed by Hanneton, Berthoz, Droulez, and Slotine (1997), who analyzed hand movements in visuomanual-tracking tasks. Instead of providing a gradual correction of the motor commands based on the continuous comparison between the actual position of the motor system and a desired trajectory, their feedback controller generates from time to time a very strong change to the motor commands in order to push the motor system back to the right track.

Hanneton et al.'s subjects were seated in front of a computer screen on which a point moved continuously along a random trajectory. By moving a joystick commanding a simulated second-order mechanical system, the subjects had to drive another point on the screen, so that it followed as accurately as possible the first point. Hanneton et al. (1997) observed that hand movements were made of a number of small successive submovements associated with high-velocity peaks and separated from each other by short periods in which velocity was small. Spectral analysis of these trajectories showed that the dynamical system controlled by the subjects and consisting of the joystick and the simulated mechanical system had nonlinear dynamical properties.

The authors could reproduce the observed movement patterns with a control model based on the processing of an intermediate *sliding variable* (Slotine & Li, 1991), while assuming linear characteristics for the dynamical system controlled by the subjects:

> A sliding variable is a specific combination of the instantaneous error and its successive time derivatives. [...] Sliding variables can be viewed either as a

> prediction about the error or as a criterion to be minimized by an algorithm adapted to the dynamics of the system being controlled. [...] In the dynamic case, [...] control mechanisms are built based on arrangements of feedforward and feedback components: the feedforward part provides an estimate of the inverse dynamics of the controlled system while the feedback part compensates for uncertainties about this estimate. (Hanneton et al., 1997, p. 382)

Thus, these authors proposed that the submovements associated with high-velocity peaks could be produced in a ballistic-like way by the central nervous system when the absolute value of the sliding variable exceeds a constant threshold. Once triggered, these parts of the movements would be independent of any feedback (*open-loop* movements). The role of these rapid open-loop movements would be to bring rapidly the sliding variable value back below the threshold. The other parts of the movement, those having a small velocity, would correspond to the classical *closed-loop* response of the dynamical system to the motor commands.

This approach is very appealing, because it makes it possible to reach gesture accuracy in spite of internal model inaccuracy, and because it seems to be compatible with a target-based model of control, since a sparse description of the output based on discrete target sequences would not allow a continuous feedback correction. Hanneton et al. (1997) have demonstrated that system stability is possible, even if feedback corrections to the inputs are not continuous and strong. However, it should be noted that Hanneton et al.'s (1997) experiment involved long-latency visual feedback, since according to their model, the delay time of this feedback control would be 290 ms. This would be obviously far too long for speech production. However, the corrective movements proposed by Hanneton et al. (1997) do not seem to require a cortical processing of the feedback, since they are ballistic and fully determined by the initial impulse. Hence, it seems possible that this model could be applied to speech by taking into account low-level short-latency feedback, such as orosensory afferences. Further work is obviously needed to test this hypothesis for speech production.

CONCLUSION

In this paper, we have provided various types of evidence in support of the hypothesis that internal models of the speech production apparatus, from the motor commands to the articulatory patterns or to the spectral characteristics of the acoustic signal, could exist and be used in the planning and/or the execution of speech production. We have also shown that complex articulatory patterns would not necessarily require complex internal models, since a part of the measured complexity could arise from the physical characteristics of the speech production system.

Nevertheless, the necessity for speakers to control temporal events in speech production with accuracy raises the question of the level of complexity that is required for the internal models to take into account dynamics. The sliding variable hypothesis offers a robust framework to think about inaccurate dynamical descriptions of the speech production system, without the need to specify the complete desired articulatory paths. However, a role for short-latency feedback needs to be considered given that in speech production movement durations are shorter than long-latency feedback delays.

Very sensitive mechanoreceptors have been found in the human tongue (Trulsson & Essick, 1997). Neural linkages between the upper lip and the jaw have also been hypothesized (Gracco & Abbs, 1985), in order to explain compensatory movements of the upper lip in case of a sudden perturbation applied to the jaw. [Note that Gomi, Honda, Ito, & Murano (2002) have suggested that, in addition to the neural linkage, a dynamical coupling between lips and jaw could contribute to the compensatory movement.] Hence, short-latency reflexes exist in the neural circuitry of the speech articulators, and they seem to contribute to the stability of the speech output. Hence, it is worthwhile looking further for general neurophysiological evidence that short-latency reflexes could be used in combination with a sparse description of the desired articulatory paths and simplified internal representations to produce accurate speech movements.

REFERENCES

Browman, C. P., & Goldstein, L. M. (1990). Gestural specification using dynamically-defined articulatory structures. *Journal of Phonetics*, *18*, 299–320.

Dingwell, J. B., Mah, C. D., & Mussa-Ivaldi, F. A. (2002). Manipulating objects with internal degrees of freedom: Evidence for model-based control. *Journal of Neurophysiology*, *88*, 222–235.

Feldman, A. G. (1986). Once more on the equilibrium-point hypothesis (λ model) for motor control. *Journal of Motor Behavior*, *18*, 17–54.

Flanagan, J. R., & Lolley, S. (2001). The inertial anisotropy of the arm is accurately predicted during movement planning. *Journal of Neuroscience*, *21*(4), 1361–1369.

Gérard, J.-M., Perrier, P., & Payan, Y. (2006). 3D biomechanical tongue modeling to study speech production. In J. Harrington & M. Tabain (Eds.), *Speech production* (pp. 85–102). New York: Psychology Press.

Gomi, H., & Kawato, M. (1992). Adaptive feedback control models of the vestibulocerebellum and spinocerebellum. *Biological Cybernetics*, *68*(2), 105–114.

Gomi, H., & Kawato, M. (1996). Equilibrium-point control hypothesis examined by measured arm stiffness during multijoint movement. *Science*, *272*, 117–120.

Gomi, H., Honda, M., Ito, T., & Murano, E. Z. (2002). Compensatory articulation during the bilabial fricative production by regulating muscle stiffness. *Journal of Phonetics*, *30*, 261–279.

Gracco, V. L., & Abbs, J. H. (1985). Dynamic control of the perioral system during speech: Kinematic analyses of autogenetic and nonautogenic sensorimotor processes. *Journal of Neurophysiology*, *54*, 418–432.

Gribble, P. L., Ostry, D. J., Sanguineti, V., & Laboissière, R. (1998). Are complex control signals required for human arm movement? *Journal of Neurophysiology*, *79*, 1409–1424.

Guenther, F. H. (1995). Speech sound acquisition, coarticulation and rate effects in a neural network model of speech production. *Psychological Review*, *102*, 594–662.

Guenther, F. H., Espy-Wilson, C. Y., Boyce, S. E., Matthies, M. L., Zandipour, M., & Perkell, J. S. (1999). Articulatory tradeoffs reduce acoustic variability during American English /r/ production. *Journal of the Acoustical Society of America*, *105*, 2854–2865.

Guenther, F. H., Hampson, M., & Johnson, D. (1998). A theoretical investigation of reference frames for the planning of speech movements. *Psychological Review*, *105*, 611–633.

Hanneton, S., Berthoz, A., Droulez, J., & Slotine, J. J. E. (1997). Does the brain use sliding variables for the control of movements? *Biological Cybernetics*, *77*, 381–393.

Hargrave, S., Kalinowski, J., Stuart, A., Armson, J., & Jones, K. (1994). Effect of frequency-altered feedback on stuttering frequency at normal and fast speech rate. *Journal of Speech and Hearing Research*, *37*, 1313–1319.

Harris, C. M., & Wolpert, D. M. (1998). Signal-dependent noise determines motor planning. *Nature*, *394*, 780–784.

Hirayama, M., Vatikiotis-Bateson, E., Kawato, M., & Jordan, M. I. (1992). Forward dynamics modeling of speech motor control using physiological data. In R. P. Lippman, J. E. Moody, & D. S. Touretsky (Eds.), *Advances in neural information processing systems* (Vol. 4, pp. 191–198). San Mateo, CA: Morgan Kauffmann Publishers.

Hogan, N. (1984). An organising principle for a class of voluntary movements. *Journal of Neuroscience*, *4*, 1745–2754.

Houde, J. F., & Jordan, M. I. (1998). Sensorimotor adaptation in speech production. *Science*, *279*, 1213–1216.

Jordan, M. I. (1990). Motor learning and the degrees of freedom problem. In M. Jeannerod (Ed.), *Attention and performance* (pp. 796–836). Hillsdale, NJ: Erlbaum.

Jordan, M. I., & Rumelhart, D. E. (1992). Forward models: Supervised learning with a distal teacher. *Cognitive Science*, *16*, 316–354.

Kawato, M. (1999). Internal models for motor control and trajectory planning. *Current Opinions in Neurobiology*, *9*, 718–727.

Kawato, M., Maeda, Y., Uno, Y., & Suzuki, R. (1990). Trajectory formation of arm movement by cascade neural network model based on minimum torque-change criterion. *Biological Cybernetics*, *62*, 275–288.

Laboissière, R., Ostry, D.J., & Feldman, A.G. (1996). Control of multi-muscle systems: Human jaw and hyoid movements. *Biological Cybernetics*, *74*, 373–384.

Laboissière, R., Schwartz, J. L., & Bailly, G. (1991). Modelling the speaker–listener interaction in a quantitative model for speech motor control: A framework and some preliminary results. *PERILUS XIV* (pp. 57–62). Institute of Linguistics, Stockholm, Sweden.

Lane, H., & Wozniak, J. (1991). Speech deterioration in postlingually deafened adults. *Journal of the Acoustical Society of America*, *89*, 859–866.

Löfqvist, A., & Gracco, V. L. (2002). Control of oral closure in lingual stop consonant production, *Journal of the Acoustical Society of America*, *111*, 2811–2827.

Manzella, J., Wozniak, J., Matthies, M., Lane, H., Guiod, P., & Perkell, J. (1994). Speech production before and after deafening. *Journal of the Acoustical Society of America*, *95*, 3012(A).

McFarland, D., Baum, S. R., & Chabot, C. (1996). Speech compensation to structural modifications of the oral cavity. *Journal of the Acoustical Society of America*, *100*, 1093–1104.

O'Shaughnessy, D. (1981). A study of French vowels and consonant durations, *Journal of Phonetics*, *9*, 385–406.

Ostry, D. J., Gribble, P. L., & Gracco, V. L. (1996). Coarticulation of jaw movements in speech production: Is context-sensitivity in speech kinematics centrally planned? *Journal of Neuroscience*, *16*, 1570–1579.

Perkell, J. S., Guenther, F. H., Lane, H., Matthies, M. L., Perrier, P., Vick, J., Wilhelms-Tricarico, R., & Zandipour, M. (2000). A theory of speech motor control and supporting data from speakers with normal hearing and with profound hearing loss. *Journal of Phonetics*, *28*, 233–272.

Perkell, J. S. & Klatt, D. H. (1986). *Invariance & variability in speech processes*. Hillsdale, NJ: Lawrence Erlbaum Associates, Inc.

Perkell, J., Matthies, M., Lane, H., Guenther, F., Wilhelms-Tricarico, R., Wozniak, J., & Guiod, P. (1997). Speech motor control: Acoustic goals, saturation effects, auditory feedback and internal models. *Speech Communication*, *22*, 227–250.

Perkell, J. S., Matthies, M. L., Svirsky, M. A., & Jordan, M. I. (1993). Trading relations between tongue-body raising and lip rounding in production of the vowel /u/: A pilot "motor equivalence" study. *Journal of the Acoustical Society of America*, *93*, 2948–2961.

Perrier, P., Lœvenbruck, H., & Payan, Y. (1996). Control of tongue movements in speech: The Equilibrium Point hypothesis perspective. *Journal of Phonetics*, *24*, 53–75.

Perrier, P., Payan, Y., & Marret, R. (2004). Modéliser le physique pour comprendre le contrôle : Le cas de l'anticipation en production de parole. In R. Sock & B. Vaxelaire (Eds.), *L'anticipation à l'horizon du Présent* (pp. 159–177). Sprimont, Belgium: Pierre Margala (Collection Psychologie et Sciences Humaines).

Perrier, P., Payan, Y., Zandipour, M., & Perkell, J. (2003). Influences of tongue biomechanics on speech movements during the production of velar stop consonants: A modeling study. *Journal of the Acoustical Society of America*, *114*, 1582–1599.

Saltzman, E. L. (1986). Task dynamic coordination of the speech articulators: A preliminary model. *Experimental Brain Research Series*, *15*, 129–144.

Saltzman, E. L., & Munhall, K. G. (1989). A dynamical approach to gesture patterning in speech production. *Ecological Psychology*, *1*, 1615–1623.

Savariaux, C., Perrier, P., & Orliaguet, J.-P. (1995). Compensation strategies for the perturbation of the rounded vowel [u] using a lip-tube: A study of the control space in speech production. *Journal of the Acoustical Society of America*, *98*, 2428–2442.

Savariaux, C., Perrier, P., Orliaguet, J. P., & Schwartz, J. L. (1999). Compensation strategies for the perturbation of French [u] using a lip tube. II. Perceptual analysis. *Journal of the Acoustical Society of America*, *106*, 381–393.

Slotine, J. J. E., & Li, W. (1991). *Applied nonlinear control*. Englewood Cliffs, NJ: Prentice-Hall.

Stager, S. V., & Ludlow, C. L. (1993). Speech production changes under fluency-evoking conditions in non-stuttering speakers. *Journal of Speech and Hearing Research*, *36*, 245–253.

Stevens, K.N. (1989). On the quantal nature of speech. *Journal of Phonetics*, *17*, 3–45.

Todorov, E., & Jordan, M. I. (2002). Optimal feedback control as a theory of motor coordination. *Nature Neurosciences*, *5(11)*, 1226–1255.

Tremblay, S., Shiller, D. M., & Ostry, D. J. (2003). Somatosensory basis of speech production. *Nature*, *423*, 866–869.

Trulsson, M., & Essik, G.K. (1997). Low-threshold mechanoreceptive afferents in the human lingual nerve. *Journal of Neurophysiology*, *77*, 737–748.

Wainscott, S.K., Donchin, O., & Shadmehr, R. (2005) Internal models and contextual cues: Encoding serial order and direction of movement. *Journal of Neurophysiology*, *93*, 786–800.

2

A Neural Model of Speech Production

FRANK H. GUENTHER, SATRAJIT S. GHOSH, ALFONSO NIETO-CASTANON, AND JASON A. TOURVILLE

ABSTRACT

This paper describes the Directions Into Velocities of Articulators (DIVA) model, a neural network model of the brain computations underlying the acquisition and production of speech sounds. The model, which is implemented as a set of equations representing neural activity and synaptic strengths, is designed to account for the results of functional magnetic resonance imaging (fMRI) and electromagnetic midsagittal articulometry (EMMA) experiments in the production of speech. Computer simulations of the model have been performed to illustrate its ability to account for speaker-specific articulator movements in different phonetic contexts, as well as fMRI activations seen during normal and perturbed speech. The model is also used to generate predictions that guide new fMRI and EMMA experiments aimed at achieving a better understanding of the neural bases of speech. The results of these experiments are in turn used to further refine the model.

INTRODUCTION

Controlling speech movements for producing the syllables that make up a spoken utterance requires a complex integration of many different types of information by the brain, including auditory, tactile, proprioceptive, and muscle command representations. This chapter addresses these representations and their interactions with reference to a model of the neural processes involved in the production of speech sounds such as phonemes and syllables. The model, called the DIVA (Directions Into Velocities of Articulators) model, has been developed to account for a wide variety of experimental data concerning articulator movements in adults and the development of speaking skills in children. Neural correlates of the model's components have been identified, thus allowing the model to serve as a framework for interpreting and organizing the accumulating mass of data from functional imaging studies of the human brain.

Several aspects of the DIVA model differentiate it from other models in the speech production literature. Whereas the Levelt and Roelofs model (e.g., Levelt, Roelofs, & Meyer, 1999) focuses on linguistic and phonological computations down to the syllable level, the DIVA model focuses on the sensorimotor transformations underlying speech production from the syllable level down to the level of coordinated articulator movements. The task dynamic model of Saltzman and Munhall (1989) is a computational model that provides an alternative account of the control of articulator movements. However, unlike the DIVA model, its components are not associated with particular brain regions, neuron types, or synaptic pathways. Of the current biologically plausible neural network models of speech production (e.g., Morasso, Sanguineti, & Frisone, 2001; Westermann & Reck, 2004), the DIVA model is the most thoroughly defined and tested. It is unique in using a pseudoinverse-style control scheme (from which the model's name is derived) that has been shown to provide accurate accounts of human articulator kinematic data (e.g., Guenther, Hampson, & Johnson, 1998; Guenther, Espy-Wilson, Boyce, Matthies, Zandipour, & Perkell, 1999). [Prior treatments of pseudoinverse control in robotics can be found in Klein & Huang (1983) and Liégeois (1977).] It is also unique in using a combination of feedback and feedforward control mechanisms (as described in the current article), as well as embodying a *convex region theory* for the targets of speech that has been shown to provide a unified account of a wide body of speech acoustic, kinematic, and electromyographic data (Guenther, 1995). Finally, the model has been used to systematically investigate the development of speech motor skills in infants (Callan, Kent, Guenther, & Vorperian, 2000).

The next section provides an overview of the DIVA model. This is followed by a description of the model's components and their corresponding equations. Subsequent sections are concerned with tests of the model using articulometry and functional magnetic resonance imaging (fMRI). The chapter concludes with a discussion of brain regions involved in speech production that are not treated by the model in its current form.

OVERVIEW OF THE DIVA MODEL

Figure 2.1 provides an overview of the DIVA model. The model consists of a neural network controller whose cells correspond to boxes and whose synaptic weights correspond to arrows in the figure. The input to the model is a string

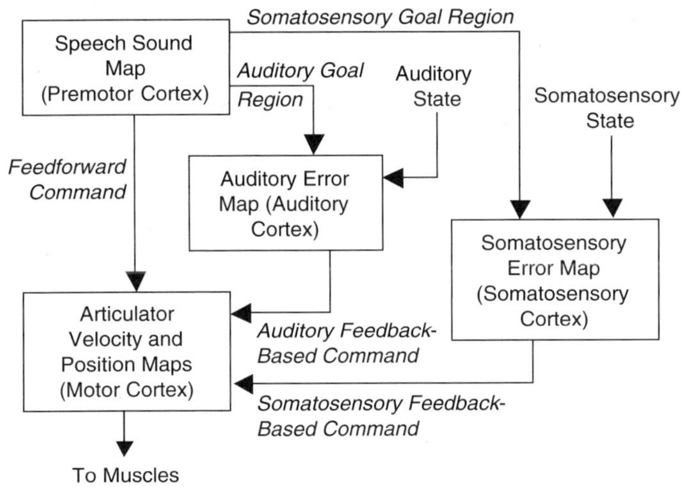

FIGURE 2.1. Overview of the hypothesized neural processing stages involved in speech production according to the DIVA model.

of speech sounds that activate the model's speech sound map cells. The model's output consists of muscle commands (labelled "to muscles" in Figure 2.1) that control the positions of eight articulators that determine the vocal tract shape of an articulatory synthesizer (e.g., Maeda, 1990). This synthesizer then generates an acoustic signal. The model utilizes a babbling stage to learn the neural mappings (arrows) necessary for controlling the movements of the articulatory synthesizer in order to produce desired sounds.

In the model, production of a phoneme or syllable starts with the activation of a speech sound map cell corresponding to the sound to be produced. These cells are hypothesized to correspond to "mirror neurons" that have been found in numerous studies of premotor cortex, including studies of speech. They can also be interpreted as part of a mental syllabary as described by Levelt and colleagues (e.g., Levelt & Wheeldon, 1994). After a speech sound map cell has been activated, signals from the premotor cortex travel to the auditory and somatosensory cortical areas through tuned synapses that encode sensory expectations for the sound being produced. These "forward models" are hypothesized to include both cortical and cerebellar components, with the cerebellar contribution being particularly important for fine temporal details. The synapses projecting from the premotor cortex to the higher-order auditory cortical areas encode an expected auditory trace for each speech sound. They can be tuned while listening to phonemes and syllables from the native language and/or listening to correct self-productions. After learning, these synapses encode a spatiotemporal target region for the sound in auditory coordinates.

During production of the sound, this target region is compared to the current auditory state, and any discrepancy between the target and the current state, or auditory error, will lead to a command signal to motor cortex that acts to correct this discrepancy via projections from auditory to motor cortical areas. A second set of synapses, projecting from the premotor cortex to the higher-order somatosensory cortical areas, encodes the expected somatic sensation (both proprioceptive and tactile) corresponding to the active syllable. This spatiotemporal somatosensory target region is estimated by monitoring the somatosensory consequences of producing the syllable and averaging these somatosensory consequences over many successful production attempts. Somatosensory error signals are then mapped to corrective motor commands via pathways projecting from somatosensory to motor cortical areas.

Feedforward- and feedback-based control signals are combined in the model's motor cortex. Feedback control signals project from sensory error cells to the motor cortex as described above. These "inverse model" projections are tuned during babbling by monitoring the relationship between movement commands and their sensory consequences. The feedforward motor command is hypothesized to project from ventrolateral premotor cortex to primary motor cortex, both directly and via the cerebellum. This command can be learned over time by incorporating the corrective feedback commands from previous attempts to produce the sound into the feedforward motor program.

MODEL EQUATIONS

In this section, we present the equations that define cell activities in the model.

The model posits *auditory state cells* that correspond to the representation of speech-like sounds in auditory cortical areas (BA 41, 42, 22). The activity of these cells is represented as follows:

$$Au(t) = f_{AcAu}\,(Acoust\ (t - \tau_{AcAu})) \tag{2.1}$$

where f_{AcAu} is the function that transforms an acoustic signal into the corresponding auditory map representation, t the time, and τ_{AcAu} the time it takes for an acoustic signal transduced by the cochlea to make its way to the auditory cortical areas. The model also has *auditory error cells* in these same cortical regions that encode the difference between auditory target regions for the sound being produced and the current auditory state which is represented by $Au(t)$. The activity of the auditory error cells (ΔAu) is defined by the following equation:

$$\Delta Au(t) = Au(t) - P(t - \tau_{PAu})z_{PAu}(t) \tag{2.2}$$

where the vector $P(t)$ is the activity of the premotor cortex speech sound map at time t ($P_i = 1$ for sound currently being produced; $P_i = 0$ for all other sounds),

τ_{PAu} the propagation delay for the signals from premotor cortex to auditory cortex, and the matrix $z_{PAu}(t)$ consists of synaptic weights that encode auditory expectations for the sound being produced. The auditory error cells become active during production if the speaker's auditory feedback of his/her own speech deviates from the auditory target region for the sounds being produced.

The synaptic weight matrix $z_{PAu}(t)$ is "spatiotemporal" in that it encodes target regions for each point in time from the start of production to the end of production of the speech sound they encode. That is, each column of the weight matrix represents the target at one point in time, and there is a different column for every 1 ms of the duration of the speech sound in the current computer implementation of the model.

The model also includes *somatosensory state cells* that correspond to the representation of speech articulators in somatosensory cortical areas (BA 1, 2, 3, 40, 43):

$$S(t) = f_{ArS}\,(Artic\,(t - \tau_{ArS})) \tag{2.3}$$

where f_{ArS} is a function that transforms the current state of the articulators, represented by the vector $Artic(t)$, into the corresponding somatosensory map state.

Somatosensory error cells code the difference between the somatosensory target region for a speech sound and the current somatosensory state $S(t)$:

$$\Delta S(t) = S(t) - P(t - \tau_{PS})z_{PS}(t) \tag{2.4}$$

where τ_{PS} is the propagation delay from premotor cortex to somatosensory cortex, and the weight matrix $z_{PS}(t)$ encodes somatosensory expectations for the sound being produced. The somatosensory error cells become active during production if the speaker's somatosensory feedback from the vocal tract deviates from the somatosensory target region for the sound being produced.

According to the model, feedforward- and feedback-based control signals are combined in the motor cortex to form the overall motor command $M(t)$. The model's *motor cortex velocity cells* correspond to "phasic" cells found in motor cortex single-cell recording studies which are active during movement but return to baseline activity when the movement ends. The model includes two sets of motor velocity cells: One that encodes a feedforward control signal ($\dot{M}_{Feedback}(t)$) and one that encodes a feedback control signal ($\dot{M}_{Feedback}(t)$).

Feedback control signals project from sensory error cells to the motor cortex. These "inverse model" projections are governed by the following equation:

$$\dot{M}_{Feedback}(t) = \Delta Au(t - \tau_{AuM})z_{AuM} + \Delta S(t - \tau_{SM})z_{SM} \tag{2.5}$$

where z_{AuM} and z_{SM} are synaptic weights that transform directional sensory error signals into motor velocities that correct for these errors. The model's name, DIVA, derives from this mapping from sensory *directions into velocities of articulators*. Mathematically, the weights z_{AuM} and z_{SM} approximate the pseudoinverse of the Jacobian of the function relating articulator positions (M) to the corresponding sensory state (Au, S). These weights can be tuned during babbling by monitoring the relationship between movement commands and their sensory consequences.

The feedforward motor command, hypothesized to project from ventrolateral premotor cortex to primary motor cortex both directly and via the cerebellum, is represented by the following equation in the model:

$$\dot{M}_{Feedforward}(t) = P(t - \tau_{PM})z_{PM}(t) - M(t) \tag{2.6}$$

The weights $z_{PM}(t)$ encode the feedforward motor command for the speech sound being produced. This command is learned over time by integrating the corrective feedback commands from previous attempts to produce the sound into the feedforward motor program.

The model's *motor cortex position cells* correspond to "tonic" cells found in motor cortex single-cell recording studies. They represent the length of a muscle or muscle synergy, and they act as a command to the motor periphery. Their activity is governed by the following equation:

$$M(t) = M(0) + \alpha_{ff}\int_0^t \dot{M}_{Feedforward}(t)\, g(t)\, dt + \alpha_{fb}\int_0^t \dot{M}_{Feedback}(t)\, g(t)\, dt \tag{2.7}$$

where α_{fb} and α_{ff} are parameters that determine how much the model is weighted toward feedback control and feedforward control, respectively, and $g(t)$ is a speaking rate signal that is 0 when not speaking, 1 when speaking at a maximum rate, and between 0 and 1 for normal speaking rates.

Before an infant has any practice producing a speech sound, the contribution of the feedforward control signal to the overall motor command should be small since it will not yet be tuned. Therefore, during the first few productions, the primary mode of control will be feedback-based control. During these early productions, the feedforward control system is "tuning itself up" by incorporating the motor commands generated by the feedback control system (see also Kawato & Gomi, 1992). The feedforward commands get more and more accurate over time, all but eliminating the need for feedback control except when external constraints are applied to the articulators (e.g., a bite block) or auditory feedback is artificially perturbed. As the speech articulators get larger with growth, the feedback control system provides corrective commands that are eventually subsumed into the feedforward controller. This allows the feedforward controller to stay properly tuned despite dramatic changes in the sizes and shapes of the speech articulators over the course of a lifetime (see Callan et al., 2000).

The model also contains variables corresponding to the current articulatory and acoustic state. These values do not correspond to any brain cell activities;

they correspond instead to the physical positions of the articulators and the resulting acoustic signal. The articulatory state describes the positions of the articulators in the Maeda articulatory synthesizer (Maeda, 1990), and is governed by the following equation in the model:

$$Artic(t) = f_{MAr}\,(M(t - \tau_{MAr})) + Pert(t) \tag{2.8}$$

where f_{MAr} is the function relating the motor cortex position command to the Maeda parameter values, τ_{MAr} the time it takes for a motor command to have its effect on the articulatory mechanism, and *Pert* the effect of external perturbations on the articulators. The acoustic state is determined from the articulatory state as follows:

$$Acoust(t) = f_{ArAc}\,(Artic(t)) \tag{2.9}$$

where f_{ArAc} is the transformation performed by Maeda's articulatory synthesis software.

TESTING THE MODEL WITH ARTICULOMETRY

Numerous computer simulations have demonstrated that the model provides a straightforward, unified account for many aspects of speech

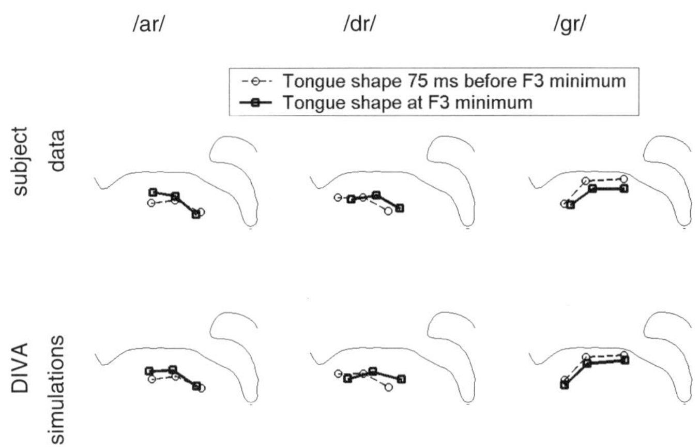

FIGURE 2.2. Average tongue movements during /r/ production in an electromagnetic articulometry study (top row) and in simulations of the DIVA model (bottom row) in three different phonetic contexts: /ar/, /dr/, and /gr/. The three tongue transducers are located approximately 1, 2.5, and 5 cm back from the tongue tip when the tongue is in a neutral configuration. The lips are located to the left in each panel (velum outline is on right).

movement kinematics (e.g., Guenther, 1994, 1995; Guenther et al., 1998, 1999). In this section we describe one such study involving American English /r/ production.

The top row of Figure 2.2 shows the results of an electromagnetic midsagittal articulometry (EMMA) study of articulations for the phoneme /r/ in different phonetic contexts for one speaker (Guenther et al., 1999). The gesture for the /r/ in each context can be deduced by looking at the progression from the dashed outline (representing the tongue shape 75 ms before the acoustic center of the /r/) to the bold, solid outline (representing the tongue shape at the acoustic center of the /r/). Two things should be particularly noted: (1) the subject uses a wide range of tongue shapes for /r/ in different phonetic contexts, and (2) the gestures used to produce these tongue shapes differ greatly across contexts.

To directly test the control scheme represented by the DIVA model, we collected structural MRI scans of one of the speakers from the EMMA study while this speaker produced different phonemes. These scans were used to build an articulatory synthesizer matching the speaker's vocal tract shape, articulatory degrees of freedom, and acoustics (Nieto-Castanon, Guenther, Perkell, & Curtin, 2005). This speaker-specific vocal tract model was then controlled by the DIVA model after a babbling stage in which the model learned to control movements of the vocal tract. We then had the model produce the same phoneme strings as the speaker in the EMMA study and compared its movements to those of the modeled speaker. The results of these simulations are provided in the bottom row of Figure 2.2.

The model's gestures in each phonetic context closely mimic those of the speaker, as do the final tongue shapes for /r/. This result occurs in the model because the sound /r/ is represented primarily by an auditory target, without a corresponding vocal tract shape target. When the model moves toward this target from different initial configurations, different gestures and tongue shapes result for /r/, and these tongue shapes closely mimic those of the corresponding speaker. We take this to be a strong evidence for the model's control scheme as a model of human movement control.

TESTING THE MODEL WITH FMRI

A major goal of this modeling work is to provide a framework for interpreting the results of neuroimaging studies of speech production, and to generate predictions to help guide future neuroimaging studies. To this end, we have identified likely neuroanatomical locations of the model's components based on the results of previous neurophysiological studies as well as the results of fMRI

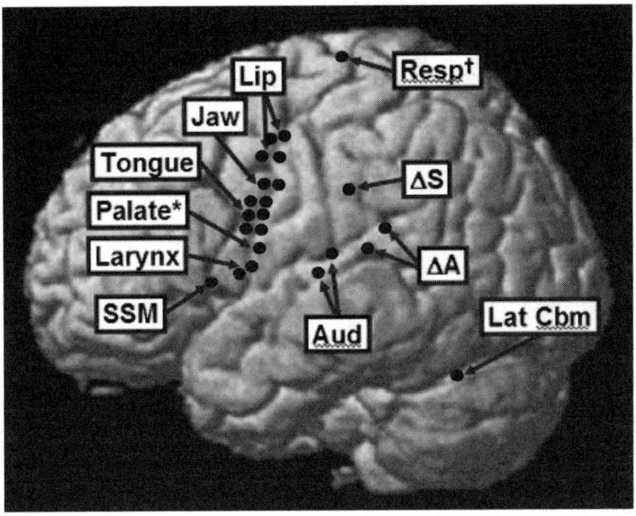

FIGURE 2.3. Locations of the model components rendered on the lateral surface of the left hemisphere. [Unless otherwise noted, labels along the central sulcus correspond to a motor (anterior) and a somatosensory (posterior) representation for each articulator. Abbreviation key: Aud = auditory state cells; ΔA, auditory error cells; ΔS, somatosensory error cells; Lat Cbm, superior lateral cerebellum; Resp, motor respiratory region; SSM, speech sound map. *Palate representation is somatosensory only. †Respiratory representation is motor only.]

experiments conducted by our laboratory. Figure 2.3 illustrates the hypothesized locations of the model's components projected onto the lateral cortical and cerebellar surface.

Because the model is specified as a neural network whose components relate closely to brain regions, it is possible to test predictions of the model using brain imaging techniques such as fMRI. Figure 2.4 summarizes preliminary results of one such study, investigating the effects of unexpected jaw perturbation on brain activity during speech production.

The DIVA model predicts that jaw perturbation should cause increased activation in the supramarginal gyrus (due to somatosensory error signals; ΔS in Figure 2.3) and tongue and lip areas of motor cortex (due to feedback-based motor commands). These areas show significant activity in the fMRI results shown in the top panel of Figure 2.4, with a slight right hemisphere bias (see also Baciu, Abry, & Segebarth, 2000). The bottom panel of Figure 2.4 shows fMRI activations derived from the model when an unexpected perturbation is applied to the model's jaw during syllable production (as compared to a baseline task of unperturbed syllable production). The

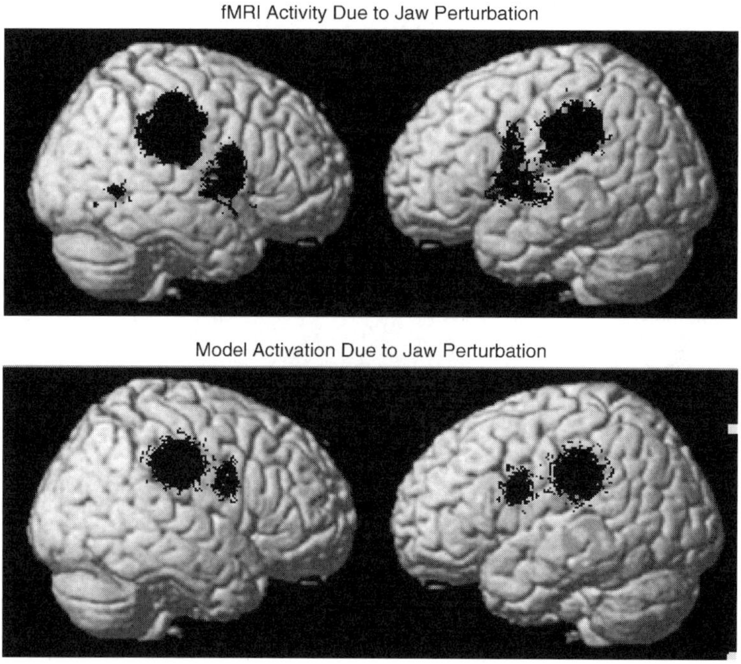

FIGURE 2.4. Top panel: Brain activity (as measured with fMRI) resulting from unexpected jaw perturbation during speech production compared to a baseline of unperturbed speech (average of three subjects). Bottom panel: fMRI activation derived from the model during jaw-perturbed speech.

pattern of activity generated by the model captures the main aspects of the fMRI data.

CONCLUDING REMARKS

This chapter has described a model of the neural processes underlying speech production. This model has been designed to provide a simple and unified account for a wide range of experimental data, including functional brain imaging, psychophysical, physiological, anatomical, and acoustic data. The model has also been used to study the effects of auditory feedback on speech in normally hearing individuals, hearing impaired individuals, and cochlear implant recipients (Perkell et al., 2000) as well as the development of speaking skills in infants and children (Callan et al., 2000).

Although the model described herein accounts for most of the activity seen in our fMRI studies of simple syllable production, it does not provide a complete account of the cortical and cerebellar mechanisms involved. In particular, as currently defined, the DIVA model is given a phoneme string by the modeler, and the model produces this phoneme string in the specified order. In actuality, the selection, initiation, and sequencing of speech movements involves brain structures not treated in the preceding discussion; these include the anterior cingulate area, the supplementary motor area (SMA), the basal ganglia, and (possibly) the anterior insula. The anterior cingulate gyrus lies adjacent to the SMA on the medial surface of the cortex in the interhemispheric fissure. This area is known to be involved in initiation of motivated behavior. Bilateral damage to the anterior cingulate area can result in akinetic mutism, characterized by a profound inability to initiate movements (DeLong, 1999). The anterior cingulate has also been implicated in the execution of appropriate verbal responses and suppression of inappropriate responses (Buckner, Raichle, Miezin, & Petersen, 1996; Nathaniel-James, Fletcher, & Frith, 1997; Paus, Petrides, Evans, & Meyer, 1993). Several researchers have posited that the supplementary motor area is particularly involved for self-initiated responses, i.e., responses made in the absence of external sensory cues, whereas lateral premotor cortex is more involved when responding to external cues (e.g., Goldberg, 1985; Passingham, 1993).

As the model is currently defined, it is not possible to differentiate between internally generated and externally cued speech. Diseases of the basal ganglia, such as Parkinson's disease and Huntington's disease, are known to impair movement sequencing (Georgiou, Bradshaw, Iansek, Phillips, Mattingley, & Bradshaw, 1994; Phillips, Chiu, Bradshaw, & Iansek, 1995; Rogers, Phillips, Bradshaw, Iansek, & Jones, 1998; Stern, Mayeux, Rosen, & Ilson, 1983), and single-cell recordings indicate that cells in the basal ganglia in monkeys and rats code aspects of movement sequences (Aldridge & Berridge, 1998; Kermadi & Joseph, 1995). The basal ganglia are strongly interconnected to the frontal cortex through a set of segregated basal ganglia-thalamo-cortical loops, including a loop focused on the SMA (DeLong & Wichman, 1993; Redgrave, Prescott, & Gurney, 1999). Like the SMA, the basal ganglia appear to be especially important when movements must be selected and initiated in the absence of external cues (Georgiou et al., 1994; Rogers et al., 1998). Also, stimulation at the thalamic stage of the basal ganglia-thalamo-cortical loops has been shown to affect the rate of speech production (Mateer, 1978).

The lesion study of Dronkers (1996) indicated that the anterior insular cortex, or insula, buried in the Sylvian fissure near the base of premotor cortex, plays an important role in speech production since damage to the insula is the likely source of pure apraxia of speech, a disorder involving an inability to select the appropriate motor programs for speech. Others have identified insula activation in certain speech tasks (e.g., Nota & Honda, 2003; Wise, Greene, Buchel, & Scott, 1999). The fMRI study of Nota and Honda (2003) suggests that the insula becomes involved when different syllables have to be sequenced in a particular order, as opposed to repetitive production of the same syllable.

Based on these studies, we hypothesize that the insula plays a role in selecting the proper speech sound map cells in the ventral-lateral premotor cortex.

ACKNOWLEDGMENTS

This research was supported by the National Institute on Deafness and other Communication Disorders (NIDCD) grants R01 DC02852 (F. Guenther, PI) and R01 DC01925 (J. Perkell, PI).

REFERENCES

Aldridge, J. W., & Berridge, K. C. (1998). Coding of serial order by neostriatal neurons: A "natural action" approach to movement sequence. *Journal of Neuroscience, 18*, 2777–2787.

Baciu, M., Abry, C., & Segebarth, C. (2000). Equivalence motrice et dominance hémisphérique: Le cas de la voyelle [u]. Étude IRMf. *Actes des XXIIIèmes Journées d'Etude sur la Parole, Aussois, France*, pp. 213–216.

Buckner, R. L., Raichle, M. E., Miezin, F. M., & Petersen, S. E. (1996). Functional anatomic studies of memory retrieval for auditory words and visual pictures. *Journal of Neuroscience, 16*, 6219–6235.

Callan, D. E., Kent, R. D., Guenther, F. H., & Vorperian, H. K. (2000). An auditory-feedback-based neural network model of speech production that is robust to developmental changes in the size and shape of the articulatory system. *Journal of Speech, Language, and Hearing Research, 43*, 721–736.

DeLong, M. R. (1999). The basal ganglia. In E. R. Kandel, J. H. Schwartz, & T. M. Jessell (Eds.), *Principles of neural science* (4th ed., pp. 853–867). New York: McGraw-Hill.

DeLong, M. R., & Wichman, T. (1993). Basal ganglia-thalamocortical circuits in Parkinsonian signs. *Clinical Neuroscience, 1*, 18–26.

Dronkers, N. F. (1996). A new brain region for coordinating speech articulation. *Nature, 384*, 159–161.

Georgiou, N., Bradshaw, J. L., Iansek, R., Phillips, J. G., Mattingley, J. B., & Bradshaw, J. A. (1994). Reduction in external cues and movement sequencing in Parkinson's disease. *Journal of Neurology, Neurosurgery and Psychiatry, 57*, 368–370.

Goldberg, G. (1985). Supplementary motor area structure and function: Review and hypotheses. *Behavioral Brain Research, 8*, 567–588.

Guenther, F. H. (1994). A neural network model of speech acquisition and motor equivalent speech production. *Biological Cybernetics, 72*, 43–53.

Guenther, F. H. (1995). Speech sound acquisition, coarticulation, and rate effects in a neural network model of speech production. *Psychological Review, 102*, 594–621.

Guenther, F. H., Espy-Wilson, C. Y., Boyce, S. E., Matthies, M. L., Zandipour, M., & Perkell, J. S. (1999). Articulatory tradeoffs reduce acoustic variability during American English /r/ production. *Journal of the Acoustical Society of America, 105*, 2854–2865.

Guenther, F. H., Hampson, M., & Johnson, D. (1998). A theoretical investigation of reference frames for the planning of speech movements. *Psychological Review, 105*, 611–633.

Kawato, M., & Gomi, H. (1992). A computational model of four regions of the cerebellum based on feedback-error learning. *Biological Cybernetics, 68*, 95–103.

Kermadi, I., & Joseph, J. P. (1995). Activity in the caudate nucleus of monkey during spatial sequencing. *Journal of Neurophysiology, 74*, 911–933.

Klein, C. A., & Huang, C. (1983). Review of pseudoinverse control for use with kinematically redundant manipulators. *IEEE*

Transactions on Systems, Man, and Cybernetics, *SMC-13*(2), 245–250.

Levelt, W. J., Roelofs, A., & Meyer, A. S. (1999). A theory of lexical access in speech production. *Behavioral and Brain Sciences, 22,* 1–38.

Levelt, W. J., & Wheeldon, L. (1994). Do speakers have access to a mental syllabary? *Cognition*, *50*, 239–269.

Liégeois, A. (1977). Automatic supervisory control of the configuration and behavior of multibody mechanisms. *IEEE Transactions on Systems, Man, and Cybernetics*, *SMC-7(12)*, 868–871.

Maeda, S. (1990). Compensatory articulation during speech: Evidence from the analysis and synthesis of vocal-tract shapes using an articulatory model. In W. J. Hardcastle, & A. Marchal (Eds.), *Speech production and speech modelling* (pp. 131–149). Boston: Kluwer.

Mateer, C. (1978). Asymmetric effects of thalamic stimulation on rate of speech. *Neuropsychologia*, *16*, 497–499.

Morasso, P., Sanguineti, V., & Frisone, F. (2001). Cortical maps as topology-representing neural networks applied to motor control: Articulatory speech synthesis. In K. A. H. Masterbroek, & J. E. Vos (Eds.), *Plausible neural networks for biological modelling* (pp. 190–216). Dordrecht: Kluwer.

Nathaniel-James, D. A., Fletcher, P., & Frith, C. D. (1997). The functional anatomy of verbal initiation and suppression using the Hayling Test. *Neuropsychologia*, *35*, 559–566.

Nieto-Castanon, A., Guenther, F. H., Perkell, J. S., & Curtin, H. D. (2005). A modeling investigation of articulatory variability and acoustic stability during American English /r/ production. *Journal of the Acoustical Society of America*, *117*, 3196–3212.

Nota, Y., & Honda, K. (2003). Possible role of the anterior insula in speech production. In *Proceedings of the sixth international seminar on speech* production, Macquarie Centre for Cognitive Science, Sydney, Australia (pp. 191–194).

Passingham, R. E. (1993). *The frontal lobes and voluntary action*. Oxford: Oxford University Press.

Paus, T., Petrides, M., Evans, A. C., & Meyer, E. (1993). Role of the human anterior cingulate cortex in the control of oculomotor, manual, and speech responses: A positron emission tomography study. *Journal of Neurophysiology*, *70*, 453–469.

Perkell, J. S., Guenther, F. H., Lane, H., Matthies, M. L., Perrier, P., Vick, J., Wilhelms-Tricarico, R., & Zandipour, M. (2000). A theory of speech motor control and supporting data from speakers with normal hearing and profound hearing loss. *Journal of Phonetics*, *28*, 233–272.

Phillips, J. G., Chiu, E., Bradshaw, J. L., & Iansek, R. (1995). Impaired movement sequencing in patients with Huntington's disease: A kinematic analysis. *Neuropsychologia*, *33*, 365–369.

Redgrave, P., Prescott, T. J., & Gurney, K. (1999). The basal ganglia: A vertebrate solution to the selection problem? *Neuroscience*, *89*, 1009–1023.

Rogers, M. A., Phillips, J. G., Bradshaw, J. L., Iansek, R., & Jones, D. (1998). Provision of external cues and movement sequencing in Parkinson's disease. *Motor Control*, *2*, 125–132.

Saltzman, E. L., & Munhall, K. G. (1989). A dynamical approach to gestural patterning in speech production. *Ecological Psychology*, *1*, 333–382.

Stern, Y., Mayeux, R., Rosen, J., & Ilson, J. (1983). Perceptual motor dysfunction in Parkinson's disease: A deficit in sequential and predictive voluntary movement. *Journal of Neurology, Neurosurgery and Psychiatry*, *46*, 145–151.

Westermann, G., & Reck, M. E. (2004). A new model of sensorimotor coupling in the development of speech. *Brain and Language*, *89*, 393–400.

Wise, R. J., Greene, J., Buchel, C., & Scott, S. K. (1999). Brain regions involved in articulation. *Lancet*, *353*, 1057–1061.

3

Distinctions Between Speech and Nonspeech Motor Control

A Neurophonetic View

WOLFRAM ZIEGLER

ABSTRACT

This chapter discusses clinical and experimental evidence for a task-specific organisation of the speech motor system. The motor actions of the facial–oral–laryngeal–respiratory musculature are classified by two criteria, i.e., voluntary vs. involuntary and learned vs. novel. A review of the literature on the dysarthrias and apraxia of speech reveals that separate organisational principles and separate neural substrates exist for different types of oral motor activities. Focussing on speech vs. voluntary nonspeech motor control, it is postulated that extensive motor learning leads to the emergence of a specific neural circuitry for the control of articulation. Indirect evidence for this view is provided by analogies from studies of sequential finger movement learning and tool-use learning. The "vertical" view of speech motor control proposed here has important theoretical and clinical implications.

INTRODUCTION

The motor mechanisms of speaking are at the end of the pipeline of spoken language production, and most serial models of speech production—with the exception of the Articulatory Phonology approach (Browman & Goldstein, 1997)—locate them outside the domain of linguistic operations. Speech motor control is considered, at least implicitly, as an information-dissipating system, which consumes the input handed down from the phonological components of the language generation apparatus, without contributing any language-related information by itself.

The input processed by the motor execution organ is conceived of as a phonetic plan (Levelt, Roelofs, & Meyer, 1999) or a motor program (Deger & Ziegler, 2002), which specifies the complete information required by the executive neuromotor system to make the speech organs move. Although the phonetic plan or motor program metaphor evokes an image of a clear-cut demarcation between linguistic formulation and motor execution, we have little knowledge about the nature and the amount of information the phonetic encoder hands-over to the muscles of the face, mouth, throat, and upper trunk for the purpose of speaking. Hence, we still have no clear understanding of how phonological encoding interfaces with speech motor execution.

Closely connected with this problem is the question of how speech motor control relates to the control of nonspeech oral movements. Theories which locate the neuromotor execution system of speaking outside the domain of language-specific processing are consistent with a "horizontal" view, according to which the speech motor system must be equally prepared to serve other purposes involving movements of the facial, oral, pharyngeal, laryngeal, or respiratory muscles (Liberman & Whalen, 2000). In the horizontal view, the oral motor apparatus is conceived of as a universal end-organ, which is implicated in all kinds of motor tasks, i.e., breathing and swallowing, laughing and crying, tongue protrusion and lip smacking, or articulation. From such a perspective, speech motor control is seen as a tool, which is not shaped by the specific task it subserves; it is only its orchestration by a linguistic conductor that transforms it into a tool for speaking.

This perspective is also prevalent in neurolinguistic theories of disorders of spoken language production, which distinguish, at a postlexical level, between disorders afflicting purely symbolic representations/operations in the linguistic domain (aphasic phonological impairment) and disorders afflicting the all-purpose motor apparatus at the bottom end of the language production system (dysarthria). While, in this view, phonemic paraphasia is entirely unrelated to the processes and representations of the speech motor system, dysarthria has no specific relation to the linguistic domain. More specifically, it is claimed that in dysarthric patients motor impairment is generally observable "for all contexts and purposes" of a movement (Rosenbek, Kent, & Lapointe, 1984, p. 13).

In this strictly dualistic world of linguistic and motor processes, it has always been difficult to find an appropriate place for a syndrome termed apraxia of speech (AOS), which counts as a disorder of speech motor programming (Darley, 1968). AOS has a hybrid position between language and movement, since, by its definition, it classifies as an impairment of the motor domain (i.e., motor programming), yet with the specification that the programming of speech movements is involved. In the past, therefore, the syndrome has alternately been allocated to either side of the language-motor rift. If a motor perspective of AOS is adopted, a strong dualistic theory entails that AOS must be considered part of a more general apraxic condition that afflicts all types of oral movements, irrespective of the goals to be achieved (Ballard, Granier, & Robin, 2000).

This chapter is focussed on the question of whether the execution of speech movements is indeed controlled by a universal neural machinery, i.e., one which is also implicated in the control of all other motor actions of the speech musculature. In the first part, clinical and experimental evidence is reviewed suggesting that neuromotor impairments of speaking are dissociated (1) from impairments of involuntary motor activities, such as metabolic breathing, swallowing, or emotional expression, and (2) from impairments of voluntary nonspeech motor activities. In the second part, I will argue for the existence of a neural network, which is specialised for the control of speech movements. The arguments raised here will be based on analogies with studies of learning-induced plasticity of motor networks.

SPEECH-NONSPEECH DISSOCIATIONS IN NEUROLOGIC CONDITIONS

Speech as a Volitional Motor Act: Distinction from Vegetative and Emotional Motor Activities

As a first step, speaking can be characterised as a volitional motor action, distinguishing it (1) from involuntary motor functions with a metabolic or vegetative basis (e.g., metabolic breathing, swallowing, yawning) and (2) from emotional expressions (e.g., laughing, smiling, crying, or sobbing). By definition, involuntary motor functions escape, at least partly, voluntary control. Metabolic breathing cannot be interrupted for more than a short time period, we often cannot suppress yawning, the swallowing reflex cannot be held up as soon as a bolus has passed the pharyngeal triggering point, and in strong emotional states we cannot suppress sobs or laughter. Involuntary motor actions of the oral–facial, pharyngeal, laryngeal, and respiratory muscles have a distinct biological significance, since they serve alimentary and metabolic purposes or protect the respiratory tract, or, as in emotional expression, signal our affective states. They rely on distinct circuitries, which are—in evolutionary terms—much older than the neocortical pathways subserving wilful control of these muscles.

Motor functions such as breathing, swallowing, or yawning are closely contingent upon vegetative or mechanical triggers. The movement patterns observed in these motor acts can be rather complex, like in swallowing, but once initiated they unfold in a remarkably constant, stereotypical way. An important clinical observation is that impairments of vegetative motor functions subsequent to brain lesions can be dissociated from impairments of voluntary motor control of the speech muscles. In a condition termed "locked-in syndrome", which may result from bilateral lesions in the ventral pontine region, patients are unable to perform virtually any volitional movement, but breathe regularly, yawn, and have a preserved swallowing reflex (Heywood, Murphy, Corfield, Morrell, Howard, & Guz, 1996; Jean, 2001; Krasnianski, Gaul, Neudecker, Behrmann, Schlüter, & Winterholler, 2003). The converse is also true: In certain clinical conditions, breathing or swallowing can be impaired while voluntary movements of oral, laryngeal, or respiratory muscles are preserved (Lee, Hwang, & Chang, 1999; Schestatsky & Fernandes, 2004; for an overview see Ziegler, 2003a, 2003b).

These observations are explainable by the fact that motor functions such as breathing, yawning, or reflexive swallowing are controlled by autonomous neural networks in the brainstem, which can be selectively affected or spared by brain lesions. The respiratory rhythm is controlled by a central pattern generator in the medulla, which consists of dorsal and ventral groups of respiratory neurons (Bianchi, Denavit-Saubie, & Champagnat, 1995). The sequential pattern of swallowing is organised by another central pattern generator, which comprises several pools of interneurons in the dorsal and ventro-lateral medulla and in the pons (Jean, 2001). With regard to yawning, no specific cerebral structure has been identified so far, but lesion studies indicate that this behavioural pattern is integrated in the caudal medulla (Töpper, Mull, & Nacimiento, 2003). In each of these behaviours the respiratory, laryngeal, and supra-laryngeal components of complex, stereotyped motor patterns are wired at a low level of the central nervous system, but they can also be orchestrated via direct motor cortical pathways. This organisation guarantees their autonomous function, but still allows for a certain degree of modulation by higher centres (Shea, 1996).

There is also clinical evidence for the existence of a separate motor network for emotional expressions, such as laughing and crying. Patients with bilateral lesions to motor cortico-bulbar fibres may develop severe dysarthria and at the same time demonstrate preserved movements of the oral and laryngeal muscles during laughing or crying (Mao, Coull, Golper, & Rau, 1989). In patients with unilateral lesions to the upper motor neurone, the lower facial musculature of the contra-lesional side can be paretic during speaking or in lip-spreading on command, but these patients may show a symmetric spontaneous smile. The opposite pattern, i.e., asymmetric spontaneous smiling with preserved wilful spreading of the lips, has been described in patients with small lesions to medial premotor cortical sites, the thalamus, or the pons (Hopf, Müller-Forell, & Hopf, 1992). This two-way dissociation, together with experimental data from nonhuman primates, is interpreted to demonstrate the existence of at least two separate motor pathways descending in a topographically organised manner to the motor nuclei in the brainstem: (1) a polysynaptic "limbic" emotional pathway originating in limbic cortical structures and terminating in the bulbar motor nuclei or the medullary respiratory complex, and (2) a "neo-cortical" voluntary pathway, which—in humans—includes a direct projection from motor cortex to the brainstem nuclei (Jürgens & Zwirner, 1996; Morecraft, Louie, Herrick, & Stilwell-Morecraft, 2001). Nonetheless, voluntary and emotional motor networks must also be interleaved, since volitional motor acts like speaking can be modulated by moods or sentiments and since emotional expressions can, to a certain extent, be inhibited (Parvizi, Anderson, Martin, Damasio, & Damasio, 2001).

Speech and Nonspeech Voluntary Motor Activities

If speech is claimed to be special (Liberman, 1982), a second criterion is needed to distinguish it not only from involuntary motor functions, but also from other wilful motor activities of the oral–facial, laryngeal, and respiratory musculature. There are not many instances of naturally occurring, wilful, nonlinguistic oral motor behaviours. Much of what we do with our lips, tongue, velum, larynx, etc. is either triggered by sensory stimuli (e.g., throat clearing), or associated with food intake (biting, chewing, bolus transport, sucking, clearing the oral cavity from food remainders, etc.). Another part of the repertoire of voluntary oral movements consists of idiosyncratic mimic or vocal habits, often contingent to some emotional or social context. Whistling and singing are further examples, but not everybody is a good whistler or singer, and still more exceptional skills are trumpet or saxophone playing. Clinical assessment batteries for the examination of cranial nerve functions or of lower face apraxia comprise a variety of oral motor activities to be performed by imitation or on command, such as lip smacking, tongue protrusion, etc., but experience with standardised assessment batteries has revealed that not all of these tasks are part of everybody's movement repertoire (Bizzozero, Costato, Della Sala, Papagno, Spinnler, & Venneri, 2000). Still more sophisticated oral motor examination techniques are based on maximum performance requirements (maximum strength, duration, or velocity) or use visuo-motor tracking devices (Robin, Solomon, Moon, & Folkins, 1997).

A useful criterion to distinguish between these types of motor functions is the degree of motor learning underlying these behaviours. Speaking is a fine motor skill which every healthy child acquires over an extensive learning period, with practice sessions on every day, and with life-long adaptation. In adolescence, the degree of mastery of this skill has reached a saturation point and has become automated, i.e., relatively uninfluenced by dual-task situations. Unlike whistling, singing, or saxophone playing, mastery of the motor skill of speaking varies only little between healthy adult individuals. Likewise, most of the nonspeech tasks used in clinical diagnosis, for instance tasks such as maximally fast repetitions of a syllable, lingual tracking of a sinusoid, or imitation of a lip smack, differ from speaking by the fact that they are untrained, uncommon, or even completely novel to many subjects.

Evidence for the exceptional nature of speaking among all these motor behaviours comes from clinical and experimental observations in patients with brain lesions (Ziegler, 2003a): (1) it is known that many dysarthric patients are still able to swallow regularly (including the oral, voluntary phase of swallowing), even when structures deep in the brainstem are lesioned (Bassetti, Bogousslavsky, Mattle, & Bernasconi, 1997; Schmahmann, Ko, & MacMore, 2004). Vice versa, not every dysphagic patient has a speech problem: even patients in whom the oral (voluntary) stage of swallowing is impaired may be free from significant dysarthria or AOS (Daniels, Brailey, & Foundas, 1999). (2) It is also known that clinical assessment batteries for cranial nerve functioning or oral apraxia have a low predictive value for the occurrence and severity of dysarthria or AOS. Nicola, Ziegler, and Vogel (2004) found that the nonspeech motor scores of 20 patients with dysarthrias of different types and different degrees of severity were not correlated with scores describing their articulatory performance. Similar observations were reported by Urban et al. (2001), who examined a large population of stroke patients for signs of dysarthria and cranial nerve dysfunction and found little overlap. (3) Although rapid syllable repetition or oral diadochokinesis is, statistically, a good predictor of dysarthria, closer investigations into the relation between maximum syllable repetition rates and speaking rates in dysarthric populations have revealed that these two parameters must be influenced by substantially different mechanisms. While patients with cerebellar lesions appear to be disproportionately vulnerable to diadochokinetic task requirements, other patient groups demonstrate a reverse relation between speech and diadochokinetic rate impairment (Figure 3.1; c.f. Ziegler, 2002).

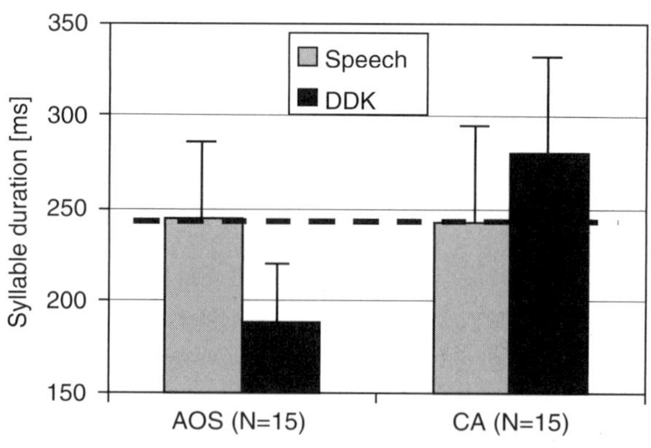

FIGURE 3.1. Average syllable durations in sentence production (grey bars) and in rapid syllable repetition (black bars). Syllables were /pa/, /ta/, and /ka/ in both tasks. In the sentence production task, syllables carried sentence stress. Patients with cerebellar atrophy (CA; $N=15$) and with apraxia of speech (AOS; $N=15$) were matched for their speaking rates (data from Ziegler, 2002).

(4) Visuo-motor tracking tasks have been considered as a sensitive indicator of speech impairments (Robin et al., 1997), but several studies have failed to detect a close relationship between the ability to speak and the ability to track a moving target on a computer screen, neither in dysarthric patients (Deger & Ziegler, 2002; McHenry, Minton, Wilson, & Post, 1994) nor in patients with AOS (Clark & Robin, 1998; McNeil, Weismer, Adams, & Mulligan, 1990).

On the whole, there is abundant clinical evidence that neurogenic impairments of speech and oral nonspeech motor mechanisms are dissociated, even if only voluntary motor aspects are considered.

What Can We Infer from Dissociations?

From a clinical viewpoint, these dissociations demonstrate that dysarthria and AOS should be distinguished from neurologic impairments of other behaviours mediated by the speech muscles. As a consequence, the diagnostic assessment of motor speech impairments should be based on speech rather than on nonspeech tasks. Asking a patient to put out his tongue or to repeat a syllable at maximum rate imposes specific requirements, which are different from the requirements of a speech task, and the patient's performance on such tasks may therefore mislead the clinician's conjectures about her/his speech impairment.

The theoretical implications of the dissociations reported here and elsewhere, however, are less straightforward, since they do not strictly imply a distinction between speech and nonspeech motor systems. If, as an example, patient A has normal speech but is unable to track a visual signal with his mandible, and patient B has a speech disorder, but is unimpaired in tracking, this result can still be consistent with a model of a common motor system used in both tasks. Since the two tasks, speaking and tracking, are complex and since each of them may include specific subcomponents, which are separable from the motor component proper, the observed double dissociation does not exclude the implication of the same motor processes in the two tasks (Dunn & Kirsner, 2003).

However, some of the findings reported in the literature make a more convincing contribution to this discussion. One such example is an observation reported by Connor and Abbs (1991), who studied mandibular movements in patients with Parkinson's disease under different task conditions, i.e., in a visuo-motor tracking task, in an isolated syllable production task, and in sentence production. Although the type of movement was the same in the three tasks, motor impairment differed grossly between conditions, and especially bradykinesia (a core symptom of Parkinsonism) was only seen in the tracking task. Such findings are consistent with physiological data demonstrating that speech and other oral motor behaviours differ basically in their underlying motor organisation. For instance, different naso-pharyngeal closure mechanisms can be observed in speaking and in swallowing (Schneider & Gross, 1997), or different movement kinematics are seen in speaking and in syllable repetition (Westbury & Dembowski, 1993). Such task-specific differences occur very early in childhood, suggesting that the development of speech movement patterns bifurcates early from motor behaviours associated with nutrition and ventilation (Moore, 2004). It should be noted, however, that this is not inconsistent with an evolutionary perspective, which traces the neurobiological roots of speaking back to chewing (MacNeilage & Davis, 2001) or to emotional-expressive behaviours (Jürgens, 1998).

IS THERE A NEURAL BASIS OF A SPEECH-SPECIFIC MOTOR ORGANISATION?

Innate Prerequisites

Experimental work on nonhuman primates has identified neocortical structures subserving voluntary control of the muscles of the lower face and mouth, and of the larynx (c.f. the section "Speech and nonspeech voluntary motor activities"). Such knowledge substantiates the distinctions between autonomous or reflexive behaviours (breathing, swallowing, yawning), emotional expression, and wilful movement. Yet, animal data cannot account for the neural basis of speaking as compared to other wilful motor actions.

As a first approach, one might therefore look at the differences between human brains and the brains of nonhuman primates to identify neural structures specifically responsible for speech motor control. Two major differences are considered relevant in the context discussed here: (1) the adult human brain disposes of a neural network based in the peri-Sylvian region of the left hemisphere, which allows the oral motor system to hook-up with auditory perception (Catani, Jones, & ffytche, 2005). It is known that the left superior temporal gyrus, a structure closely neighbouring auditory cortical areas, is activated in speech production (Hickok et al., 2000). Likewise, activity of Broca's area, which is viewed as a region relevant for speech motor planning (Hillis, Work, Barker, Jacobs, Breese, & Maurer, 2004), is associated with purely receptive phonological tasks (Hickok & Poeppel, 2004). Hence, spoken language understanding and production appear to rely on the integrity of a network that connects anterior motor with posterior acoustic centres. The connectivity between these two centres is realised through a massive fibre bundle, the arcuate fasciculus, which is absent in nonhuman primates and is not fully developed in human neonates, but myelinises progressively during the period of speech acquisition (Paus et al., 1999). The circuit connecting anterior and posterior speech centres may be considered as the structural basis of an auditory reference frame for speech movement planning (Guenther & Perkell, 2004). (2) Nonhuman primates have only limited capacity of vocal imitation and learning

(Fitch, 2000), whereas in human infants the ability to imitate vowel sounds emerges between 12 and 20 weeks of age (Kuhl & Meltzoff, 1996). The developing arcuate fasciculus, together with an indirect loop connecting anterior and posterior language centres via the inferior parietal lobe, is among the structural bases of vocal imitation and learning in humans (Aboitiz & Garcia, 1997; Catani et al., 2005). A role of parietal cortical areas can be inferred, by analogy, from visuo-motor imitation studies (Iacoboni, Woods, Brass, Bekkering, Mazziotta, & Rizzolatti, 1999).

The Role of Motor Learning

These structural prerequisites provide the basis for the ontogenesis of a neural network specialised for speaking. The major mechanism that can be made responsible for the emergence of such a network is learning-induced plasticity. Since the maturation of speech motor patterns extends over a long period during which the human brain has immense plasticity, dynamic neural changes associated with this process must lead to a reorganisation of pre-existing motor circuits for the activity of speaking. Although there is no direct evidence for such reorganisation processes in speech motor control, sufficient knowledge has been accumulated in other movement domains, which supports this view.

A first line of evidence refers to motor cortical plasticity. From observations in string players, for instance, it is known that long-term motor learning results in an increase in motor cortical representation areas of the fingers of the implied hand, the extent of which is negatively correlated with the age of inception of musical practice (Elbert, Pantev, Wienbruch, Rockstroh, & Taub, 1995). Even shorter periods of intensive motor learning are sufficient to lead to a measurable structural reorganisation of cortical networks (Draganski, Gaser, Busch, Schuierer, Bogdahn, & May, 2004). These findings and related results from animal studies demonstrate that practice-related motor improvements have a structural substrate. Ungerleider, Doyon, and Karni (2002) reviewed an extensive amount of literature documenting the dynamics of brain plasticity during motor skill learning, most of which relates to learning of sequential finger movements in humans and monkeys. One of the results of this research was that identical component movements are differentially represented in primary motor cortex when arranged in a long-term practised vs. an unpractised sequence. By analogy, one and the same mandibular movement could be represented by a firing of different subpopulations of motor neurones, depending on whether it occurs in speech (learned) or in a novel tracking task (unlearned).

A further outcome of these investigations relates to the dynamics of experience-driven changes in different brain structures: While the reorganisation in prerolandic motor cortex described above occurred only after several weeks of training, the early stages of motor learning were associated with an experience-dependent shift of activation within the cerebellum and, with extended practice, from a cerebellar–cortical to a striatal–cortical network (Doyon, Song, Karni, Lalonde, Adams, & Ungerleider, 2002; Ungerleider et al., 2002). As a consequence, nonspeech assessment techniques based on novel tasks, such as visuo-motor tracking, may predominantly probe the integrity of brain structures involved in early motor learning, whereas speech is based on motor representations acquired through long-term learning processes and is stored in distinct circuits.

Another line of research is concerned with the learning of how a moving organ interacts with the environment through the use of tools. Studies of brain plasticity related to tool use are based, for instance, on experiments including the use of a rake to retrieve objects (Iriki, Tanaka, & Iwamura, 1996) or the use of a computer mouse in a tracking task (Imamizu, Kuroda, Miyauchi, Yoshioka, & Kawato, 2003). A key aspect of tool use is that manipulation of the tool involves some more or less complex motor transformation: manipulation of a computer mouse, for instance, involves a scaling of hand movements from the size of a mouse-pad to the size of the computer screen and a rotation from a horizontal to a vertical movement plane. In a computer mouse experiment, this transformation can be made even more complex by deliberately altering the spatial and velocity relations between hand and cursor movement. Experiments have shown that such transformations can be learned within 10–20 training sessions.

Why should this research be relevant for the understanding of speech? Like in manual tool use, speaking involves a motor transformation between the geometrical space of the moving speech organs and the task-space of acoustic speech events. This articulatory-to-acoustic transformation is of a rather unique complexity, since it comprises intricate physical relations between movements, aerodynamic events, and sounds. We may assume that the use of this complex "tool", which transforms articulation into sound, is learned during babbling (Guenther, Hampson, & Johnson, 1998; Westermann & Miranda, 2004). One may further assume that the acquired tool is ultimately embodied as an "internal model", i.e., as a neural mechanism that can mimic the input–output properties of the system. Current thinking about the organisation of motor skills (Wolpert & Kawato, 1998) suggests that such an internal model would consist of a forward component predicting the acoustic result of a speech movement, and an inverse component determining the articulations to be made for the achievement of a certain acoustic goal (c.f. Perrier, this volume).

Research on the plasticity of tool-use learning has produced at least two results that are considered relevant here. The first is that learning to use a tool leads to an observable reorganisation of the sensory reference frame of the movement. For instance, learning to use a rake for the retrieval of distant objects is accompanied by an enlargement of the receptive fields of cortical neurones encoding peri-personal space, as if the representation of the tool was incorporated into the representation of the hand manipulating it

(Farnè & Làdavas, 2000; Iriki et al., 1996). Speculating about a speech analogy of this finding, one might hypothesise that the acquisition of the articulatory-to-acoustic transformation tool creates a neural encoding of an enlarged action space of the speech organs, i.e., of a space which extends into the acoustic domain and allows for direct skilful manipulations of acoustic objects by movements of the tongue, lips, etc.

A second result of the tool-use research that should be mentioned here suggests that motor learning can establish parallel neural representations of internal models for multiple tools, stored in different sites, and that we can flexibly switch between these representations. Imamizu and co-workers, for instance, were able to identify, in the lateral and posterior cerebellum, spatially segregated activations during skilful manipulations of devices with different transformation rules (Imamizu, Kuroda, Yoshioka, & Kawato, 2004; Imamizu et al., 2003). Provided that these research findings can be extended to the oral motor domain, different oral motor skills, such as whistling, speaking, or professional trumpet playing, should rely on different neural representations, since they employ different movement-to-sound transformations. Even more so, oral motor skills based on visual or tactile-sensory reference frames should be based on neural circuits distinct from those engaged in speaking.

CONCLUSION

The clinical and experimental evidence reviewed in the section "Speech–nonspeech dissociations in neurologic conditions" suggests that speech motor control is organised in a task-specific way—a view which is compatible with "verticalist" theories of the speech–language interface (Liberman & Whalen, 2000). The requirement of a task-specific organisation of the speech motor system can be motivated by a number of physiological properties specific to speaking, such as the continuous and close integration of distant subsystems (respiratory, laryngeal, naso-pharyngeal, lingual-mandibular, labial-mandibular), the motor equivalence principle governing the interplay between these subsystems, the rhythmic properties of spoken language, the role of afferent information from different sensory systems, or the embedding of speech movements into an auditory reference frame. Neurophysiologically, a separate organisation of voluntary vs. involuntary facial–oral–laryngeal–respiratory motor control can be inferred from animal studies and, at least partly, from lesion studies in humans. However, the existence of a distinct neural basis of speech vs. wilful nonspeech motor activities of this musculature is not supported by direct neurophysiological evidence. In the section "Is there a neural basis of a speech-specific motor organisation?", I have therefore collected indirect evidence for such a view, basing mainly on neuro-imaging studies of learning-induced plasticity of sequential finger movements and skilled tool use.

The verticalist view proposed here downsizes the insurmountable rift that, in the horizontalist thinking, separates linguistic from motor representational levels and aphasic from motor impairments of spoken language production. If the neural machinery controlling speech movements is specifically geared to the production of spoken language, rather than being an all-purpose vehicle, which is no more adapted to speaking than to any other activity performed by the same musculature, a more parsimonious theory of spoken language production emerges. This theory describes a stepwise transformation of motor representations from an abstract word form level to a level of concrete motor commands, and converges with existing theories of action.

REFERENCES

Aboitiz, F., & Garcia, R. (1997). The anatomy of language revisited. *Biological Research*, *30*, 171–183.

Ballard, K. J., Granier, J. P., & Robin, D. A. (2000). Understanding the nature of apraxia of speech: Theory, analysis, and treatment. *Aphasiology*, *14*, 969–995.

Bassetti, C., Bogousslavsky, J., Mattle, H., & Bernasconi, A. (1997). Medial medullary stroke—Report of 7 patients and review of the literature. *Neurology*, *48*, 882–890.

Bianchi, A. L., Denavit-Saubie, M., & Champagnat, J. (1995). Central control of breathing in mammals: Neuronal circuitry, membrane properties, and neurotransmitters. *Psychological Reviews*, *75*, 1–45.

Bizzozero, I., Costato, D., Della Sala, S., Papagno, C., Spinnler, H., & Venneri, A. (2000). Upper and lower face apraxia: Role of the right hemisphere. *Brain*, *123*, 2213–2230.

Browman, C. P., & Goldstein, L. (1997). The gestural phonology model. In W. Hulstijn, H. F. M. Peters, & P. H. H. M. v. Lieshout (Eds.), *Speech production: Motor control, brain research and fluency disorders* (1st ed., pp. 57–71). Amsterdam: Elsevier.

Catani, M., Jones, D. K., & ffytche, D. H. (2005). Perisylvian language networks of the human brain. *Annals Neurology*, *57*, 8–16.

Clark, H. M., & Robin, D. A. (1998). Generalized motor programme and parameterization accuracy in apraxia of speech and conduction aphasia. *Aphasiology*, *12*, 699–713.

Connor, N. P., & Abbs, J. H. (1991). Task-dependent variations in Parkinsonian motor impairments. *Brain*, *114*, 321–332.

Daniels, S. K., Brailey, K., & Foundas, A. L. (1999). Lingual discoordination and dysphagia following acute stroke: Analyses of lesion localization. *Dysphagia*, *14*, 85–92.

Darley, F. L. (1968). *Apraxia of speech: 107 years of terminological confusion*. Paper presented at the Annual Convention of the ASHA.

Deger, K., & Ziegler, W. (2002). Speech motor programming in apraxia of speech. *Journal of Phonetics*, 30, 321–335.

Doyon, J., Song, A. W., Karni, A., Lalonde, F., Adams, M. M., & Ungerleider, L. G. (2002). Experience-dependent changes in cerebellar contributions to motor sequence learning. *Proceedings of the National Academy of Science, USA*, *99*, 1017–1022.

Draganski, B., Gaser, C., Busch, V., Schuierer, G., Bogdahn, U., & May, A. (2004). Neuroplasticity: Changes in grey matter induced by training. *Nature*, *427*, 311–312.

Dunn, J. C., & Kirsner, K. (2003). What can we infer from double dissociations? *Cortex*, *39*, 1–7.

Elbert, T., Pantev, C., Wienbruch, C., Rockstroh, B., & Taub, E. (1995). Increased cortical representation of the fingers of the left hand in string players. *Science*, *270*, 305–307.

Farnè, A., & Làdavas, E. (2000). Dynamic size-change of hand peripersonal space following tool use. *NeuroReport*, *11*, 1–5.

Fitch, W. T. (2000). The evolution of speech: A comparative review. *Trends in Cognitive Sciences*, *4*, 258–267.

Guenther, F. H., Hampson, M., & Johnson, D. (1998). A theoretical investigation of reference frames for the planning of speech movements. *Psychological Review, 105*, 611–633.

Guenther, F. H., & Perkell, J. S. (2004). A neural model of speech production and its application to studies of the role of auditory feedback in speech. In B. Maassen, R. Kent, H. Peters, P. van Lieshout, & W. Hulstijn (Eds.), *Speech motor control in normal and disordered speech* (pp. 29–49). Oxford, New York: Oxford University Press.

Heywood, P., Murphy, K., Corfield, D. R., Morrell, M. J., Howard, R. S., & Guz, A. (1996). Control of breathing in man: Insights from the 'locked-in' syndrome. *Respiration Physiology*, 106, 13–20.

Hickok, G., Erhard, P., Kassubek, J., Helms-Tillery, A. K., Naeve-Velguth, S., Strupp, J. P., Strick, P. L., & Ugurbil, K. (2000). A functional magnetic resonance imaging study of the role of left posterior superior temporal gyrus in speech production: Implications for the explanation of conduction aphasia. *Neuroscience Letters, 287*, 156–160.

Hickok, G., & Poeppel, D. (2004). Dorsal and ventral streams: A framework for understanding aspects of the functional anatomy of language. *Cognition, 92*, 67–99.

Hillis, A. E., Work, M., Barker, P. B., Jacobs, M. A., Breese, E. L., & Maurer, K. (2004). Re-examining the brain regions crucial for orchestrating speech articulation. *Brain, 127*, 1479–1487.

Hopf, H. C., Müller-Forell, W., & Hopf, N. J. (1992). Localization of emotional and volitional facial paresis. *Neurology, 42*, 1918–1923.

Iacoboni, M., Woods, R. P., Brass, M., Bekkering, H., Mazziotta, J. C., & Rizzolatti, G. (1999). Cortical mechanisms of human imitation. *Science, 286*, 2526–2528.

Imamizu, H., Kuroda, T., Miyauchi, S., Yoshioka, T., & Kawato, M. (2003). Modular organization of internal models of tools in the human cerebellum. *Proceedings of the National Academy of Science, USA, 100*, 5461–5466.

Imamizu, H., Kuroda, T., Yoshioka, T., & Kawato, M. (2004). Functional magnetic resonance imaging examination of two modular architectures for switching multiple internal models. *The Journal of Neuroscience, 24*, 1173–1181.

Iriki, A., Tanaka, M., & Iwamura, Y. (1996). Coding of modified body schema during tool use by macaque postcentral neurones. *NeuroReport, 7*, 2325–2330.

Jean, A. (2001). Brain stem control of swallowing: Neuronal network and cellular mechanisms. *Psychological Reviews, 81*, 929–989.

Jürgens, U. (1998). Speech evolved from vocalization, not mastication. *Behavioral and Brain Sciences, 21*, 519–520.

Jürgens, U., & Zwirner, P. (1996). The role of the periaqueductal grey in limbic and neocortical vocal fold control. *NeuroReport, 7*, 2921–2923.

Krasnianski, M., Gaul, C., Neudecker, S., Behrmann, C., Schlüter, A., & Winterholler, M. (2003). Yawning despite trismus in a patient with locked-in syndrome caused by a thrombosed megadolichobasilar artery. *Clinical Neurology and Neurosurgery, 106*, 44–46.

Kuhl, D. E., & Meltzoff, A. N. (1996). Infant vocalizations in response to speech: Vocal imitation and developmental change. *Journal of the Acoustical Society of America, 100*, 2425–2438.

Lee, B. C., Hwang, S. H., & Chang, G. Y. N. (1999). Isolated dysphagia due to a medullary infarction: A new lacunar syndrome. *European Neurology, 41*, 53–54.

Levelt, W. J. M., Roelofs, A., & Meyer, A. S. (1999). A theory of lexical access in speech production. *Behavioral and Brain Sciences, 22*, 1–38.

Liberman, A. M. (1982). On finding that speech is special. *American Psychologist, 37*, 148–167.

Liberman, A. M., & Whalen, D. H. (2000). On the relation of speech to language. *Trends in Cognitive Sciences, 4*, 187–196.

MacNeilage, P. F., & Davis, B. L. (2001). Motor mechanisms in speech ontogeny: Phylogenetic, neurobiological and linguistic implications. *Current Opinion in Neurobiology, 11*, 696–700.

Mao, C.-C., Coull, B. M., Golper, L. A. C., & Rau, M. T. (1989). Anterior operculum syndrome. *Neurology, 39*, 1169–1172.

McHenry, M. A., Minton, J. T., Wilson, R. L., & Post, Y. V. (1994). Intelligibility and nonspeech orofacial strength and force control following traumatic brain injury. *Journal of*

Speech and Hearing Research, *37*, 1271–1283.

McNeil, M. R., Weismer, G., Adams, S., & Mulligan, M. (1990). Oral structure nonspeech motor control in normal, dysarthric, aphasic and apraxic speakers: Isometric force and static position control. *Journal of Speech and Hearing Research*, *33*, 255–268.

Moore, C. A. (2004). Physiologic development of speech production. In B. Maassen, R. Kent, H. Peters, P. van Lieshout, & W. Hulstijn (Eds.), *Speech motor control in normal and disordered speech* (pp. 191–209). Oxford, New York: Oxford University Press.

Morecraft, R. J., Louie, J. L., Herrick, J. L., & Stilwell-Morecraft, K. S. (2001). Cortical innervation of the facial nucleus in the non-human primate. A new interpretation of the effects of stroke and related subtotal brain trauma on the muscles of facial expression. *Brain*, *124*, 176–208.

Nicola, F., Ziegler, W., & Vogel, M. (2004). Die Bogenhausener Dysarthrieskalen (BODYS): Ein Instrument für die klinische Dysarthrie-diagnostik. *Forum Logopädie*, *2*, 14–22.

Parvizi, J., Anderson, S. W., Martin, C. O., Damasio, H., & Damasio, A. R. (2001). Pathological laughter and crying. A link to the cerebellum. *Brain*, *124*, 1708–1719.

Paus, T., Zijdenbos, A., Worsley, K., Collins, D. L., Blumenthal, J., Giedd, J. N., Rapoport, J. L., & Evans, A. C. (1999). Structural maturation of neural pathways in children and adolescents: In vivo study. *Science*, *283*, 1908–1911.

Robin, D. A., Solomon, N. P., Moon, J. B., & Folkins, J. W. (1997). Nonspeech assessment of the speech production mechanism. In M. R. McNeil (Ed.), *Clinical management of sensorimotor speech disorders* (pp. 49–62). New York, Stuttgart: Thieme.

Rosenbek, J. C., Kent, R. D., & Lapointe, L. L. (1984). Apraxia of speech: An overview and some perspectives. In J. C. Rosenbek, M. R. McNeil, & A. E. Aronson (Eds.), *Apraxia of speech: physiology, acoustics, linguistics, management* (pp. 1–72). San Diego: College-Hill Press.

Schestatsky, P., & Fernandes, L. N. (2004). Acquired Ondine's curse: Case report. *Arquivos Neuropsiquiatry*, *62*, 523–527.

Schmahmann, J. D., Ko, R., & MacMore, J. (2004). The human basis pontis: Motor syndromes and topographic organization. *Brain*, *127*, 1269–1291.

Schneider, H.-J., & Gross, M. (1997). Dysarthrische Bewegungsstörungen des Velopharynx. *HNO*, *45*, 460–465.

Shea, S. A. (1996). Behavioural and arousal-related influences on breathing in humans. *Experimental Physiology*, *81*, 1–26.

Töpper, R., Mull, M., & Nacimiento, W. (2003). Involuntary stretching during yawning in patients with pyramidal tract lesions: Further evidence for the existence of an independent emotional motor system. *European Journal of Neurology*, *10*, 495–499.

Ungerleider, L. G., Doyon, J., & Karni, A. (2002). Imaging brain plasticity during motor skill learning. *Neurobiology of Learning and Memory*, *78*, 553–564.

Urban, P. P., Wicht, S., Vukurevic, G., Fitzek, C., Fitzek, S., Stoeter, P., Massinger, C., & Hopf, H. C. (2001). Dysarthria in acute ischemic stroke. Lesion topography, clinicoradiologic correlation, and etiology. *Neurology*, *56*, 1021–1027.

Westbury, J. R., & Dembowski, J. (1993). Articulatory kinematics of normal diadochokinetic performance. *Annual Bulletin of the Research Institute of Logopedics and Phoniatrics*, *27*, 13–36.

Westermann, G., & Miranda, R. E. (2004). A new model of sensorimotor coupling in the development of speech. *Brain and Language*, *89*, 393–400.

Wolpert, D. M., & Kawato, M. (1998). Multiple paired forward and inverse models for motor control. *Neural Networks*, *11*, 1317–1329.

Ziegler, W. (2002). Task-related factors in oral motor control: Speech and oral diadochokinesis in dysarthria and apraxia of speech. *Brain and Language*, *80*, 556–575.

Ziegler, W. (2003a). Speech motor control is task-specific. Evidence from dysarthria and apraxia of speech. *Aphasiology*, *17*, 3–36.

Ziegler, W. (2003b). To speak or not to speak: Distinctions between speech and nonspeech motor control. A reply to Ballard, Robin and Folkins. *Aphasiology*, *17*, 99–105.

4

Neural Processes Underlying Speech Production of Native and Non-Native Phonetic Contrasts

DANIEL E. CALLAN

ABSTRACT

The goal of this chapter is to better understand the neural processes underlying speech production by investigating native and non-native speech. The first section outlines several behavioral findings relevant to development and acquisition of native and non-native speech. The second section gives an outline of the potential ontogeny of speech production development within the framework of a neuro-computational model. The third section reviews results of brain imaging studies of native and second-language speech production in relation to predictions of the proposed model. It is concluded that investigation of native and non-native speech production reveals aspects of the underlying control processes and the task-dependent use of perceptual target reference domains. The results of brain imaging experiments support the following hypotheses: Separate neural processes are used depending on whether acquisition of a language occurs in infancy vs. later in life. Feedforward control is used for production of well-established articulatory patterns, whereas feedback control is used for production of articulatory patterns being learned. Speech planning control relies more on orosensory information than auditory information under task constraints in which the auditory target reference domain is ambiguous. Individuals with more well-established auditory target reference domains show greater activity in brain regions involved with forward articulatory-to-auditory mapping.

NATIVE AND NON-NATIVE SPEECH PRODUCTION AND PERCEPTION

There are several issues pertinent to speech motor control that can be addressed by research into non-native speech production. The investigation of non-native speech production can help to reveal aspects of underlying control processes as well as differential use of perceptual target reference domains depending on task constraints. One issue to be explored that may be pertinent to acquisition of any motor skill is the relative contribution of feedforward and feedback control signals for articulatory patterns that are well established vs. those that are being learned. Target reference domains likely consist of time-varying auditory, orosensory (tactile-kinesthetic), and visual aspects of speech production that are acquired during development. In the case of production of a non-native category, the auditory target may be ambiguous. Investigation of non-native speech production could address the question of whether there are different neural processes reflecting differential use of target reference domains underlying speech production of the same phonetic contrast by native and non-native speakers. Additionally, an investigation of patterns of brain activity that are correlated with performance in a certain perceptual domain may reveal the brain regions involved with utilization of that target reference domain for speech articulation. A fundamental question that one could also address by investigating non-native speech production is whether there are differences in underlying neural processes that are related to the age of acquisition of particular articulatory categorical patterns.

There are differences in the speech production and perception abilities of second-language speakers from those of native language speakers that are related to the age at which the second language is learned. Individuals who acquire a second language as an adult often have accented speech throughout their life even though they may be highly proficient speakers and be immersed in the language environment for decades (Flege & Hillenbrand, 1987; Flege, Munro, & MacKay, 1995). In the realm of speech perception, individuals who acquire a second language as an adult have considerable difficulty discriminating and identifying many non-native phonetic contrasts that are not present in their native language even after years of exposure (Miyawaki, Strange, Verbrugge, Liberman, Jenkins, & Fujimura, 1975; Strange & Jenkins, 1978; Trehub, 1976; Werker, Gilbert, Humphrey, & Tees, 1981; Werker & Tees, 1999). Similar to findings for speech production, the age of acquisition of a second language is an important factor for proficiency at discriminating and identifying non-native phonetic categories (Yamada, 1995). It is possible that these similar findings for both production and perception performance may have the same underlying cause. It has been proposed that the accuracy of speech production is limited by the accuracy of speech perception (Flege, 1993).

Several studies have investigated the potential relationship between speech production and speech perception performance. The accuracy with which second-language phonemes are produced has been found in some studies to be related to the accuracy to which they are perceived (Flege, 1993; Flege, Bohn, & Jang, 1997; Flege, MacKay, & Meador, 1999). Additionally, several studies indicate improved second-language speech production performance after perceptual training of a second-language contrast even though no formal production training is given (Bradlow, Pisoni, Akahane-Yamada, & Tohkura, 1997; Rochet, 1995; Wang, Jongman, & Sereno, 2003). All of these studies suggest that auditory perception of speech contrasts play an important role in speech production acquisition and performance. This role may be to serve as a target reference domain for articulation.

Under normal speech development the auditory system is intimately involved in speech production acquisition. Speech perception performance at 6 months has been found to be correlated with subsequent word production performance as well as word and phrase understanding at 2 years (Tsao, Liu, & Kuhl, 2004). Moreover, at 9–10 months of age, infant babbling begins to become reflective of the ambient language environment (Boysson-Bardies & Vihman, 1991). It has been found that deaf infants and hearing impaired infants have abnormal patterns of babbling (Kent, Osberger, Netsell, & Hustedde, 1987; Oller & Eilers, 1988) and have considerable deficits in the production of intelligible speech (Kent et al., 1987; Wallace, Menn, & Yoshinaga-Itano, 1998). Another line of evidence that testifies to the importance of auditory representations for speech articulation comes from neural network simulation studies using the DIVA model of speech production in which it has been demonstrated that an auditory target reference space is sufficient to account for a considerable number of speech production phenomena (Guenther & Ghosh, 2003; Guenther, Ghosh, & Nieto-Castanon, this volume; Perkell et al., this volume) including adaptation to changes in vocal tract dimensions during development (Callan, Kent, Guenther, & Vorperian, 2000).

There are several studies which suggest that speech production performance in adults acquiring a second language can improve without corresponding improvement in perception performance. In a study investigating production and perception of English /r/ and /l/ by native Japanese speakers it was found that production performance was better than perception performance for some individuals but that none of the subjects had better perception performance than production performance (Yamada, Strange, Magnuson, Pruitt, & Clarke, 1994). In studies conducted by Goto (1971) and Sheldon and Strange (1982) it was found that some Japanese speakers could produce English /r/ and /l/ that was identifiable by native English speakers even though they could not reliably identify their own utterances. These studies suggest that the primary target reference domain for speech production of non-native contrasts may not be auditory in nature, but may rely more on orosensory (i.e., tactile and kinesthetic) aspects of speech production. This is consistent with reports made by subjects in the Sheldon and Strange (1982) study that they were explicitly taught to produce /r/ and /l/ using articulatory parameters (place and manner of articulation). It is important to note that unlike acquiring speech as a child through observing other speakers and listening to speech, training of production of difficult non-native contrasts often utilizes explicit orosensory targets to achieve place and manner of articulation.

Evidence that speech production influences perception comes from the results of a study conducted by Vihman and Nakai (2003) in which it was found that during development, speech production supports formation of phonological and lexical representations. In their study, it was shown that children 10.5–12 months of age perceive consonants that they produce more often (greater production frequency) as more familiar than consonants that they produce less often (less production frequency) even though they were present to the same extent in infant-directed speech. These results are consistent with the Articulatory Filter Hypothesis (Vihman, 1993, 2002a), which suggests that production of consonant–vowel syllables during babbling sensitizes infants to similar speech patterns present in the ambient speech environment. In the case of bilingual speech acquisition during infancy, the study conducted by Vihman (2002b) suggests that at first the phonological patterns of the two languages are not separated but learned holistically. As learning proceeds, two separate phonological systems emerge based on the regularities and interconnections inherent within each language (Vihman, 2002b).

SCHEMATIC MODEL OF SPEECH PRODUCTION ACQUISITION

Based on the findings reported in the previous section an outline of the potential ontogeny of speech production can be given within the framework of the DIVA model (for a detailed description of the model see Chapter 2, this volume). The DIVA model accomplishes speech production by transforming directions in an auditory and/or orosensory planning space into velocities of the articulators. Initially, auditory cortical maps are self-organized in an unsupervised manner based on statistical regularities inherent in the ambient language environment. In accordance with the DIVA model, this auditory speech mapping is thought to be encoded by auditory state cells in the STG/S (names for abbreviated brain regions are given in full in the figure legends). During the initial babbling phase, which is thought to be maturational in nature, the correspondence between the various articulatory patterns produced and their auditory and orosensory consequences are mapped cortically. These mappings are general to all vocal sounds and are thought to represent the inverse mappings responsible for auditory and orosensory feedback-based command within the DIVA model (Guenther & Ghosh, 2003; Guenther et al., Chapter 2, this volume). Some evidence suggests that auditory-based inverse mappings involve the Stp, PT area, and orosensory inverse mappings involve the SMG, BA43. Both types of mappings also involve projections with motor regions and the cerebellum.

As a result of auditory feedback of self-productions during babbling, bi-directional connections are formed between articulatory motor maps and the auditory speech map encoded by auditory state cells (reflecting speech sound regularities in the language environment) (Vihman, 2002a; Westermann & Miranda, 2003). This mapping allows for auditory speech stimulation to activate brain regions involved with articulatory motor planning. These regions include Broca's area, premotor cortex, and anterior insula. Articulatory motor plans associated with specific speech sounds are selectively reinforced (via sensorimotor coupling) based on the correspondence between the sound of the self-produced babble articulations and the speech sounds in the ambient language.

It is maintained that selective reinforcement based on sensorimotor coupling sensitizes the system to speech sounds characteristic of the ambient language. This provides the basis for the onset of selective babbling which serves to further strengthen bi-directional connections between the auditory speech map and the articulatory motor planning maps which in turn is the basis for production of word forms that constitute the beginnings of the construction of a first phonology (Vihman & Nakai, 2003; Vihman & Velleman, 2000). The sufficiency of babbling in establishing sensorimotor coupling responsible for the concurrent development of preferred motor parameters and prototypical speech perception has been demonstrated by a neural network model (Westermann & Miranda, 2003). It has been put forward that this sensorimotor coupling acts as a bridge between the mappings formed based on statistical distributional properties inherent in the ambient language environment and more stable representations of word forms that constitute the beginnings of the construction of a first phonology (Vihman & Nakai, 2003; Vihman & Velleman, 2000). This phonology is mediated by brain regions involved with articulatory motor control (Broca's area, premotor cortex, anterior insula) instantiating the "mirror neuron system" and is called the speech sound map within the framework of the DIVA model. According to the DIVA model of speech production (Guenther & Ghosh, 2003; Guenther et al., Chapter 2, this volume), during babbling when there is a correspondence between auditory feedback and representation of a phoneme in the speech sound map, projections from the speech sound map to auditory cortical regions are adapted to form an auditory target region for the corresponding phoneme. An orosensory target region can be formed based on the correspondence of the repeated orosensory outcomes of speech productions related to a phoneme in the speech sound map. These maps projecting from the premotor cortex to sensory regions constitute forward models. Auditory error cells in the same cortical regions that map auditory speech sounds are activated when the current auditory state of the sound being produced is not within the auditory target region. Activation of the auditory error cells results in an auditory feedback-based command signal to motor regions that initiates movement of the articulators in a direction toward the auditory target space based on the inverse auditory-to-articulatory mapping. Similar error cells and feedback command signals exist for orosensory targets as well.

The model proposes that initially auditory feedback is necessary for proper development of the speech production system. This is consistent with studies mentioned above regarding the relationship between initial speech perception and auditory ability and subsequent speech production ability. The model further proposes the existence of a feedforward control signal that is acquired by incorporating motor commands generated by the feedback control system for a specific speech sound being produced. The feedforward command signal is thought to project from the premotor cortex to the motor areas directly as well as via internal models instantiated in the cerebellum. It is maintained that after feedforward mappings have been established they are dominantly used as the means of speech production over that of feedback-based control except under certain conditions in which there are perturbations to the articulators or perturbations to auditory feedback (Guenther & Ghosh, 2003; Guenther et al., Chapter 2, this volume).

NEURAL PROCESSES OF SECOND-LANGUAGE SPEECH PRODUCTION

The proposed model can make certain predictions about aspects of the neural processes underlying second-language speech production. The evidence presented in the first section suggests that the age of acquisition of learning a second language is reflective of the degree of proficiency that is achieved. It has been shown that individuals acquiring two languages from infancy show interaction between speech sound categories of the two languages (Vihman, 2002b) suggesting that the first phonological patterns are learned holistically. According to the model presented above, statistical regularities of the auditory properties of the speech sounds in the environment (which may consist of more than one language) are mapped in a self-organizing unsupervised manner within auditory cortical regions. Babbling allows for selective strengthening of these representations by means of sensorimotor coupling. Separate phonological systems eventually emerge based on regularities and interconnections inherent within each language (Vihman, 2002b). The adult second-language learner with an established phonological system may have considerable difficulty acquiring the auditory speech mapping of a non-native contrast that overlaps with an established speech category that has a strong sensorimotor coupling (Westermann & Miranda, 2003). Differences in the neural processes between production and perception for native and non-native language may exist. It is predicted that brain regions involved with speech production of a second language acquired early in development will resemble that of a native speaker, whereas, different brain regions are predicted to be involved for later second-language learners.

Brain imaging studies conducted on bilingual speakers have given insight into the issue of whether there are differences in neural processes related to second-language speech production. In a positron-emission tomography (PET) study conducted by Klein, Zatorre, Milner, Meyer, and Evans (1994), it was found that individuals who acquired their second language after age 5 showed greater activity in the left basal ganglia (putamen) during a speech production task for words repeated in the second language relative to words repeated in the first language. Although the basal ganglia is not an explicit part of the model described above, it has been implicated in the value and context-dependent selection of appropriate motor control signals during articulation (Doya, 2000).

In an fMRI study conducted by Kim, Relkin, Lee, and Hirsch (1997), it was found on a covert sentence generation task that subjects who acquire their second language as adults show spatially separate brain activation in left Broca's area from that of the native language, whereas, subjects who acquired native and second language as infants show overlapping activation in left Broca's area for both languages. It should be noted that subjects in the Kim et al. (1997) study reported that they were equally fluent in both languages and used both on a regular basis. As was pointed out in the first section, it is possible for otherwise fluent speakers to have accented speech throughout their life (Flege & Hillenbrand, 1987; Flege et al., 1995). The results of the Kim et al. (1997) experiment may reflect differences in the neural processes for speech production of native and non-native phonemes that are acquired during infancy or acquired as adults.

In an fMRI study conducted by us and presented here, brain activity underlying speech production of native and non-native speech contrasts was investigated. The subjects consisted of native Japanese and English speakers. The task involved overtly reading English syllables beginning with /r/, /l/, or a vowel, presented on a screen, without excessive head movement. The English ability of the Japanese subjects varied. Some of the subjects were very proficient while others were not. All Japanese subjects began learning English in later childhood (age approximately 12 years old). Greater activity was found for non-native English speakers (native Japanese) relative to native (English) speakers for the /r/+/l/ relative to the vowel contrast in brain regions involved with auditory (STG, Stp, PT), orosensory (SMG, BA43), and articulatory (Broca's area, PMC, anterior insula) processing as well as in the cerebellum, basal ganglia (not shown), DLPFC, and PPC (Figure 4.1). These results are consistent with those investigating perception of non-native speech contrasts. Enhanced activity after relative to before training is present in brain regions

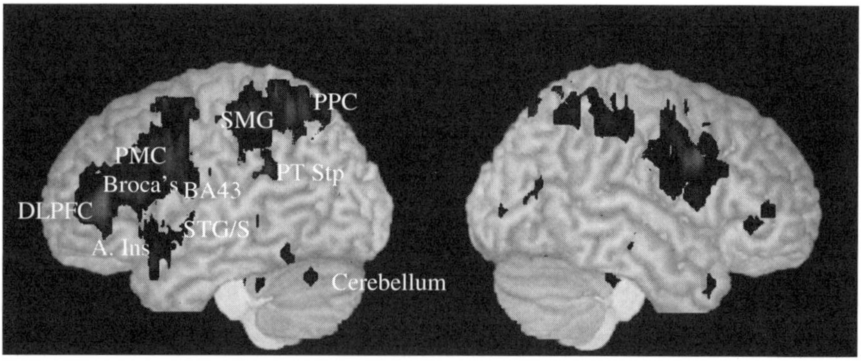

FIGURE 4.1. Neural activity rendered on the surface of the brain (depth of activation = 2 cm) for the /r/+/l/ relative to the vowel contrast that is greater for Japanese (n = 21) relative to English (n = 21) speaking subjects (activations are shown in black; $p < .05$ false discovery rate FDR (Genovese, Lazar, & Nichols, 2002) corrected for multiple comparisons across voxels in the image). BA, Brodmann area; STG/S, superior-temporal gyrus/sulcus; PT, planum temporale; Stp, superior-temporal parietal; SMG, supramarginal gyrus; PPC, posterior parietal cortex; A. Ins., anterior insula; PMC, premotor cortex; DLPFC, dorsolateral prefrontal cortex.

involved with auditory, orosensory, and articulatory processing (Callan, Tajima, Callan, Kubo, Masaki, & Akahane-Yamada, 2003; Golestani & Zatorre, 2004; Wang, Sereno, Jongman, & Hirsch, 2003). Similarly, perceptual performance on a difficult phonetic contrast has also been shown to be positively correlated with greater activity in brain regions involved with auditory, orosensory, and articulatory aspects of speech processing (Callan, Jones, Callan, & Akahane-Yamada, 2004). All of the results reported above lend some degree of support for predictions made by the proposed model that production of non-native speech learned later in life may involve different neural processes than that of native speech production. It should be pointed out that the differences in brain activity may reflect processes related to learning rather than to just processing of non-native vs. native language production. In order to specifically investigate differences between native and non-native processing, it is necessary to separate them from those processes related to learning. However, the study presented here does not make a clear distinction between non-native speakers who are already proficient in a language and non-native speakers who are less proficient and still learning the language.

As can be seen in Figure 4.1, the results of the /r/+/l/ relative to the vowel contrast for non-native speakers show considerable activity in brain regions thought to be involved with feedback-based control. These include premotor areas involved with activation of the speech sound map, auditory (STG, Stp, PT) and orosensory (SMG, BA43) areas involved with perceptual feedback of self-produced speech as well as the propagation of the inverse control signal to motor cortical regions. Also of importance to the model is the presence of activity in the cerebellum. Other brain regions that are not part of the model were also found to be active. In particular, as stated above, the basal ganglia (not shown in the figure) may be involved with value and context-dependent selection of appropriate motor control signals during articulation (Doya, 2000).

The proposed model as well as the data presented in the first section suggests that non-native speakers may differentially use target reference domains in accomplishing speech production. Several studies have reported better production performance for a non-native contrast relative to perception performance (Goto, 1971; Sheldon & Strange, 1982; Yamada et al., 1994). These studies suggest that subjects explicitly use orosensory targets when attempting to produce these non-native sounds. The fact that subjects often cannot identify their own production testifies to this account. The proposed model predicts that because establishment of an auditory target space is difficult, production of non-native contrasts may utilize an orosensory target reference domain to a greater extent than an auditory target reference domain. Consistent with this prediction the results show considerably more activity in brain regions involved with orosensory processing (SMG, BA43) than brain regions involved with auditory processing (STG, Stp, PT) for the /r/+/l/ relative to the vowel contrast for non-native speakers over that of native speakers (Figure 4.1).

The proposed model also makes predictions regarding differences in the types of control processes that are used for production of articulatory patterns that are well established vs. those that are being learned. Under normal conditions, the native speaker is expected to use the feedforward command signal instantiated by projections to the motor cortex via the premotor area or via the cerebellum. The non-native speaker is likely to use the feedback-based command signal to a greater extent because the feedforward controller has not been able to be adequately trained due to lack of a well-established auditory target domain. In the study presented here, production of /r/ and /l/ is assumed to involve more articulatory control than vowels. Therefore, a comparison of the /r/+/l/ contrast relative to the vowel contrast is expected to reveal the activity underlying the control processes of speech production that avoids some of the confounds resulting from extraneous motor, auditory, orosensory, and visual activity inherent in the task.

The results of the /r/+/l/ relative to the vowel contrast for native English speakers reveal activity localized to the left oral motor area as well as in the right cerebellum (Figure 4.2). The crossed cerebellar pattern of connectivity is consistent with what is known about anatomical pathways between the cerebellum and the cortex and is consistent with the position that a feedforward controller is responsible for differences in production relative to the vowel control condition.

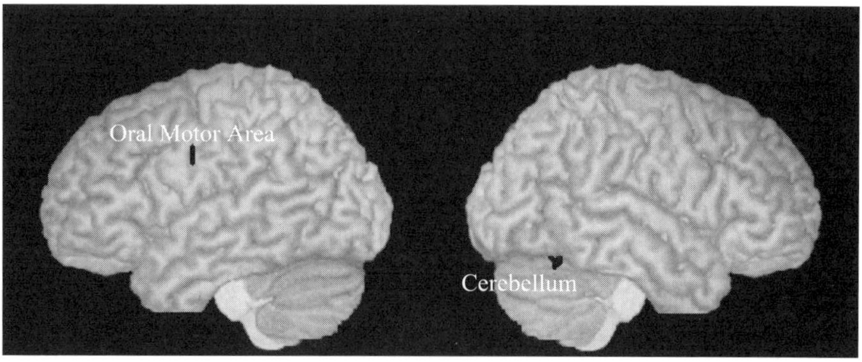

FIGURE 4.2. Neural activity rendered on the surface of the brain (depth of activation = 2 cm) for the /r/+/l/ relative to the vowel contrast for English speaking subjects (n = 21) (activations are shown in black; $p < .005$ uncorrected for multiple comparisons across voxels in the image).

The relative importance for the auditory target reference domain during production of speech can be assessed by an investigation of patterns of brain activity that are correlated with auditory performance for the non-native contrast. This type of analysis will reveal the brain regions involved with utilization of an auditory target reference domain for speech articulation. According to the

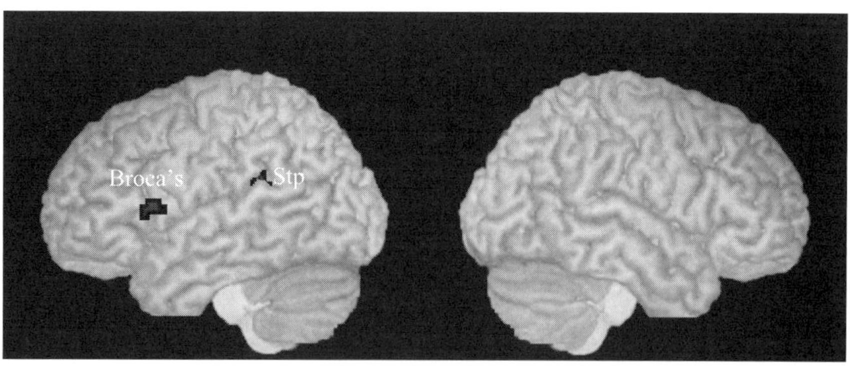

FIGURE 4.3. Neural activity rendered on the surface of the brain (depth of activation = 2 cm) for the /r/+/l/ relative to the vowel contrast for Japanese (n = 21) speaking subjects that is positively correlated with /r/ and /l/ perceptual identification performance (activations are shown in black; $p < .005$ uncorrected for multiple comparisons across voxels in the image). Stp, superior-temporal parietal. The basal ganglia (not shown) also shows significant differential activity for this contrast.

proposed model it is predicted that utilization of the auditory feedback pathway during speech production of a non-native contrast will be used to a greater extent depending on the quality of the auditory target. The results of the correlation analysis between perceptual identification performance and brain activity for the production of /r/+/l/ relative to the vowel contrast are shown in Figure 4.3. Consistent with predictions of the model, activity that is correlated with better behavioral identification performance is present in brain regions involved with feedback-based control including Broca's area and Stp, PT. Projections between Broca's area and the Stp, PT are thought to code for forward articulatory-to-auditory mappings. Other brain regions activated include the basal ganglia (not shown), which is thought to be involved with value and context-dependent selection of appropriate motor control signals during articulation (Doya, 2000).

CONCLUSION

Investigation of brain activity underlying speech production of native and non-native phonemes revealed aspects of the underlying control processes and the task-dependent use of perceptual target reference domains. Acquisition of a language in infancy vs. later in life is a factor in the degree to which separate neural processes are used for speech production. Production of articulatory patterns that are well established (native speech) utilizes predominantly feedforward control, whereas, production of articulatory patterns that are being learned (non-native speech) utilize predominantly feedback control. Greater differential use of an orosensory target domain occurs for non-native speech production because of the lack of a well-established auditory target domain. Brain regions involved with forward articulatory-to-auditory mappings are used to a greater extent in individuals with more well-established auditory target reference domains. It is likely that many of the differences found between native speech production and non-native speech production acquired later in life are a result of differences in target representations. Learning of speech during infancy is likely to be based on auditory feedback of self-produced speech, whereas, learning difficult, non-native speech contrasts likely involves achieving specific explicitly taught places and manner of articulation (orosensory targets).

ACKNOWLEDGMENTS

This research was supported in part by the National Institute of Information and Communications Technology. I would like to thank Frank Guenther for helpful comments regarding the DIVA model.

REFERENCES

Boysson-Bardies, B. de, & Vihman, M. M. (1991). Adaptation to language. *Language, 67*, 297–319.

Bradlow, A., Pisoni, D., Akahane-Yamada, R., & Tohkura, Y. (1997). Training Japanese listeners to identify English /r/ and /l/: IV. Some effects of perceptual learning on speech production. *Journal of the Acoustical Society of America, 101*, 2299–2310.

Callan, D. E., Jones, J. A., Callan, A. M., & Akahane-Yamada, R. (2004). Phonetic perceptual identification by native- and second-language speakers differentially activates brain regions involved with acoustic phonetic processing and those involved with articulatory-auditory/orosensory internal models. *NeuroImage, 22*, 1182–1194.

Callan, D. E., Kent, R. D., Guenther, F. H., & Vorperian, H. K. (2000). An auditory-feedback-based neural network model of speech production that is robust to developmental changes in the size and shape of the articulatory system. *Journal of Speech Language and Hearing Research, 43*, 721–736.

Callan, D. E., Tajima, K., Callan, A. M., Kubo, R., Masaki, S., & Akahane-Yamada, R. (2003). Learning-induced neural plasticity associated with improved identification performance after training of a difficult second-language phonetic contrast. *NeuroImage, 19*, 113–124.

Doya, K. (2000). Complementary roles of basal ganglia and cerebellum in learning and motor control. *Current Opinion in Neurobiology, 10*, 732–739.

Flege, J. E. (1993). Production and perception of a novel, second-language phonetic contrast. *Journal of the Acoustical Society of America, 93*, 1589–1608.

Flege, J. E., Bohn, O.-S., & Jang, S. (1997). The production and perception of English vowels by native speakers of German, Korean, Mandarin, and Spanish. *Journal of Phonetics, 25*, 422–470.

Flege, J. E., & Hillenbrand, J. (1987). Limits on phonetic accuracy in foreign language speech production. In G. Ioup & S. Weinberger (Eds.), *Interlanguage phonology: The acquisiton of second language sound system* (pp. 176–201), Cambridge: Newbury House.

Flege, J. E., MacKay, I. R., & Meador, D. (1999). Native Italian speakers' perception and production of English vowels. *Journal of the Acoustical Society of America, 106*, 2973–2987.

Flege, J. E., Munro, M. J., & MacKay, I. R. (1995). Factors affecting degree of perceived foreign accent in a second language. *Journal of the Acoustical Society of America, 97*, 3125–3134.

Genovese, C. R., Lazar, N. A., & Nichols, T. (2002). Thresholding of statistical maps in functional neuroimaging using the false discovery rate. *NeuroImage, 15*, 870–878.

Golestani, N., & Zatorre, R. J. (2004). Learning new sounds of speech: Reallocation of neural substrates. *NeuroImage, 21*, 494–506.

Goto, H. (1971). Auditory perception by normal Japanese audlts of the sounds 'l' and 'r'. *Neuropsychologia, 9*, 317–323.

Guenther, F. H., & Ghosh, S. S. (2003). A model of cortical and cerebellar function in speech. In M. J. Sole, D. Recasens, & J. Romero (Eds.), *Proceedings of the 15th international congress of phonetic science*, Barcelona (pp. 169–173), Universitat Autonoma de Barcelona.

Guenther, F. H., Ghosh, S. S., Nieto-Castanon, A., & Tourville, J. A. (2006). A neural model of speech production. In J. Harrington & M. Tabain (Eds.), *Speech production* (pp. 27–40). New York: Psychology Press.

Kent, R. D., Osberger, M. J., Netsell, R., & Hustedde, C. G. (1987). Phonetic development in identical twins differing in auditory function. *Journal of Speech and Hearing Disorders, 52*, 64–75.

Kim, K. H., Relkin, N. R., Lee, K. M., & Hirsch, J. (1997). Distinct cortical areas associated with native and second languages. *Nature, 388*, 171–174.

Klein, D., Zatorre, R. J., Milner, B., Meyer, E., & Evans, A. C. (1994). Left putaminal activation when speaking a second language: Evidence from PET. *Neuroreport, 5*, 2295–2297.

Miyawaki, K., Strange, W., Verbrugge, R., Liberman, A., Jenkins, J. J., & Fujimura, O. (1975). An effect of linguistic experience:

The discrimination of [r] and [l] by native speakers of Japanese and English. *Perception & Psychophysics, 18*, 331–340.

Oller, D. K., & Eilers, R. E. (1988). The role of audition in infant babbling. *Child Development, 59*, 441–449.

Perkell, J. S., Guenther, F. H., Lane, H., Marrone, N., Matthies, M. L., Stockmann, E., Tiede, M., & Zandipour, M. (2006). Production and perception of phoneme contrasts covary across speakers. In J. Harrington & M. Tabain (Eds.), *Speech production* (pp. 69–84). New York: Psychology Press.

Rochet, B. L. (1995). Perception and production of second-language speech sounds by adults. In W. Strange (Ed.), *Speech perception and linguistic experience: Issues in cross-language research* (pp. 379–410). Baltimore, MA: York Press.

Sheldon, A., & Strange, W. (1982). The acquisition of /r/ and /l/ by Japanese learners of English: Evidence that speech production can precede speech perception. *Applied Psycholinguistics, 3*, 243–261.

Strange, W., & Jenkins, J. J. (1978). Role of linguistic experience in the perception of speech. In R. D. Walk & H. L. Pick (Eds.), *Perception and experience* (pp. 125–169). New York: Academic.

Trehub, S. E. (1976). The discrimination of foreign speech contrasts by infants and adults. *Child Development, 47*, 466–472.

Tsao, F. M., Liu, H. M., & Kuhl, P. K. (2004). Speech perception in infancy predicts language development in the second year of life: A longitudinal study. *Child Development, 75*, 1067–1084.

Vihman, M. M. (1993). Variable paths to early word production. *Journal of Phonetics, 21*, 61–82.

Vihman, M. M. (2002a). The role of mirror neurons in the ontogeny of speech. In M. Stamenov & V. Gallese (Eds.), *Mirror neurons and the evolution of brain and language* (pp. 305–314). Amsterdam: John Benjamins.

Vihman, M. M. (2002b). Getting started without a system: From phonetics to phonology in bilingual development. *International Journal of Bilingualism, 6*, 239–254.

Vihman, M. M., & Nakai, S. (2003). Experimental evidence for an effect of vocal experience on infant speech perception. In M. J. Sole, D. Recasens, & J. Romero (Eds.), *Proceedings of the 15th international congress of phonetic science*, Barcelona (pp. 1017–1020), Universitat Autonoma de Barcelona.

Vihman, M. M., & Velleman, S. L. (2000). The construction of a first phonology. *Phonetica, 57*, 255–266.

Wallace, V., Menn, L., & Yoshinaga-Itano, C. (1998). Is babble the gateway to speech for all children? A longitudinal study of children who are deaf or hard of hearing. *Volta Review, 100*, 121–148.

Wang, Y., Jongman, A., & Sereno, J. A. (2003). Acoustic and perceptual evaluation of Mandarin tone productions before and after perceptual training. *Journal of the Acoustical Society of America, 113*, 1033–1043.

Wang, Y., Sereno, J. A., Jongman, A., & Hirsch, J. (2003). fMRI Evidence for cortical modification during learning of mandarin lexical tone. *Journal of Cognitive Neuroscience, 15*, 1019–1027.

Werker, J. F., Gilbert, J. H. V., Humphrey, K., & Tees, R. C. (1981). Developmental aspects of cross-language speech perception. *Child Development, 52*, 349–355.

Werker, J. F., & Tees, R. C. (1999). Influences on infant speech processing: Toward a new synthesis. *Annual Review of Psychology, 50*, 509–535.

Westermann, G., & Miranda, E. R. (2003). A new model of sensorimotor coupling in the development of speech. *Brain and Language, 89*, 393–400.

Yamada, R. (1995). Age and acquisition of second language speech sounds: Perception of American English /r/ and /l/ by native speakers of Japanese. In W. Strange (Ed.), *Speech perception and linguistic experience* (pp. 305–320). Baltimore, MD: York Press.

Yamada, R. A., Strange, W., Magnuson, J. S., Pruitt, J. S., & Clarke III, W. D. (1994). 'The intelligibility of Japanese speakers' productions of American English /r/, /l/, and /w/, as evaluated by native speakers of American English. *Proceedings of the international conference of spoken language processing* (pp. 1023–2026). Yokohama: Acoustical Society of Japan.

5

Production and Perception of Phoneme Contrasts Covary Across Speakers

JOSEPH S. PERKELL, FRANK H. GUENTHER, HARLAN LANE, NICOLE MARRONE, MELANIE L. MATTHIES, ELLEN STOCKMANN, MARK TIEDE, AND MAJID ZANDIPOUR

ABSTRACT

Two studies were performed on relations between the production and perception of sound contrasts in 19 speakers of American English. One study was of two vowel contrasts (/u-ʊ/ and /ɑ-ʌ/); the other was of the sibilant contrast, /s-ʃ/. In both studies, measures of perceptual acuity for the contrasts were obtained in ABX discrimination tests. In the vowel study, measures were made of the articulatory and acoustic distinctiveness of the produced contrast, called "contrast distance." In the sibilant study, measures were made of acoustic contrast distance and the speakers' use of a quantal biomechanical effect (called a "saturation effect") while producing the sounds. The degree to which speakers used the saturation effect in producing /s/ and /ʃ/ was assessed with a custom-made sensor that measured contact of the under side of the tongue tip with the lower alveolar ridge; such contact normally occurs during the production of /s/ but not /ʃ/. Results from each of the studies showed that subjects with higher acuity produced the contrasts more distinctly. The most distinct sibilant productions were obtained from subjects who had high discrimination scores and who also used contact in producing /s/ but not /ʃ/. Subjects who did not use contact differentially when producing the two sibilants and who also discriminated the synthetic sibilants less well produced the least distinct sibilant contrasts. Intermediate degrees of sibilant contrast were found with subjects who used contact differentially or discriminated well. The combined findings from the two studies are compatible with the DIVA model of speech motor planning, in which goals for phonemic speech movements are in auditory and somatosensory spaces.

INTRODUCTION

This chapter reports on two studies of relations between the production and perception of sound contrasts in American English. The studies are based on a theoretical framework and Guenther's DIVA model of speech motor planning (Guenther, 1995; Guenther, Hampson, & Johnson, 1998) in which phonemic goals correspond to multidimensional regions in sensory domains—auditory and somatosensory. According to the way the model functions, the goal regions are learned during speech acquisition, and phonemic speech movements are programmed to produce auditory-temporal patterns and somatosensory-temporal patterns that fall within the goal regions (c.f. Guenther & Ghosh, 2003; Guenther et al., Chapter 2 in this volume). Furthermore, according to the model, the size and spacing of the goal regions for an individual speaker depend, in part, on that speaker's perceptual acuity: Speakers with higher acuity will form goal regions that are smaller and spaced further apart.

Our experimental approach was derived from the premise that some of the widely observed inter-speaker differences in the production of speech sounds are due in part to individual differences in the implementation of the underlying sensory goals. Therefore, the primary objective of the two studies was to relate production measures that reflect speakers' phonemic goals to measures of their perceptual acuity. One study is of two vowel contrasts (Perkell et al., 2004a); the other is of the /s-ʃ/ contrast (Perkell et al., 2004b). Both studies were conducted with the same group of 19 young adult speakers of American English.

Experimental and modeling work has shown that phonemic goals may be characterized for languages in general by a combination of at least two basic principles: First, nonlinear relations between articulation and the sound output, called the "quantal nature of speech" (QNS; Stevens, 1972, 1989); second, a compromise between the listener's need for clarity and the speaker's aim to achieve an economy of effort in speech movements, called the "adaptive dispersion theory" (ADT; Lindblom, 1986, 1990). As explained below, we believe that the combined expression of these two principles also helps to account for the implementation of sensory phonemic goals in individual speakers. If the implementation of the sensory goals for sound contrasts were to vary from one speaker to the next, then that variation may be evidenced in how well the speakers produce the contrasts. Thus, demonstrating cross-speaker relations between certain measures of the production and perception of speech sounds should shed light on the nature of their hypothesized sensory goals.

According to the theory of the QNS, there are a number of speech sounds for which relatively stable acoustic cues can be produced with some variability in articulation. Such quantal effects may exist in the relation between (motor commands underlying) articulatory movements and the resulting acoustics. For example, Stevens (1972, 1989) has shown that formants of the vowels /i/, /ɑ/ and /u/ are relatively insensitive to some variation in the place of constriction of the tongue body. As described below for production of the consonant /s/, there may be a quantal relationship between motor commands and displacements of the articulators, which similarly results in a stable acoustic output over some variation in input motor commands.

Figure 5.1 is a schematic illustration of how the /s-ʃ/ contrast could be produced with the aid of a nonlinear quantal effect (Stevens, 1989), which we are calling a "saturation effect" (Fujimura & Kakita, 1979; Perkell et al., 2000). Production of a /ʃ/ is illustrated in Figure 5.1B, in which the tongue blade is positioned so that it forms a groove in the anterior palatal region and creates a space underneath the tongue that functions as a sublingual cavity. In contrast, Figure 5.1C schematizes the production of an /s/ in which the anterior part of

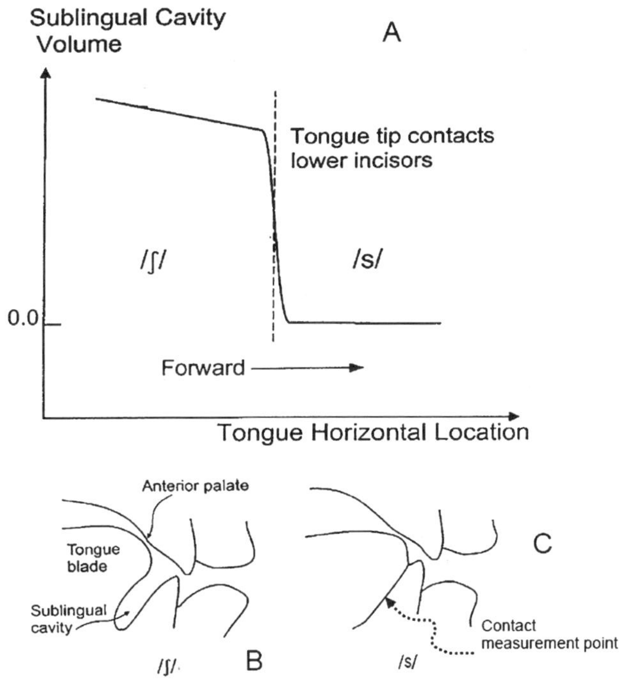

FIGURE 5.1. A hypothetical example of a saturation effect is illustrated in (A), where an abrupt change in sublingual cavity volume results from a small change in forward tongue movement. Schematized illustrations of /ʃ/ and /s/ articulation are shown in (B) and (C), respectively.

the tongue blade forms a shorter groove in the region of the dento-alveolar ridge and the under side of the tongue tip is in contact with the lingual aspect of the lower incisors. Figure 5.1A illustrates the hypothesized saturation effect that may contribute to the /s-ʃ/ contrast. As the tongue blade gradually moves forward from its position for the /ʃ/ toward the lower alveolar ridge (horizontal axis of Figure 5.1A), the volume of the sublingual cavity (vertical axis) gradually begins to decrease. Then a point is reached when the underside of the tongue blade contacts the lower incisors and alveolar ridge so that the volume of the sublingual cavity suddenly drops to zero and an /s/ is produced.

The acoustic contrast between the two sounds is likely enhanced by the presence or absence of the sublingual space (Narayanan, Alwan, & Haker, 1995; Perkell, Boyce, & Stevens, 1979). The addition of the sublingual space of /ʃ/ creates a larger and more complex resonant cavity, thereby contributing to a fricative noise with lower frequency spectral energy than /s/. For /s/ the relatively small size of the resonant cavity anterior to the constriction (formed mostly by the lips) contributes to its characteristic high-frequency fricative noise (Stevens, 1998). Approximately the same fricative noise should be generated for /s/ regardless of how hard the tongue tip is pressed against the lower alveolar ridge. Clearly, the volume of the sublingual cavity cannot decrease any further even with increasing activity of the muscles that are moving the tongue forward; therefore, the forward tongue movement for /s/ can be generated with imprecision in some of the underlying motor commands. In a preliminary study of this mechanism for the /s-ʃ/ contrast, Perkell et al. (1979) measured contact between the tongue tip and the lower alveolar ridge for four speakers of American English. They showed that /ʃ/ was generally produced with little or no contact between the tongue tip and the lower alveolar ridge, while /s/ had much more consistent contact.

As reasoned above for the QNS, the ADT also offers a principle by which phonemic goals are implemented in individual speakers: Each speaker aims to achieve an economy of effort in production while satisfying the listener's need for clarity. Producing more distinct acoustic contrasts between acoustically neighboring phonemes can make speech clearer and therefore more intelligible for the listener. The relation between the degree of produced contrast and clarity is evident in people who have speech disorders that reduce their contrasts and thus their intelligibility, but it is also measurable for people with normal speech production. For example, a study by Newman, Clouse, and Burnham (2001) noted significant variability among 20 speakers in their productions of /s/ and /ʃ/ across a range of vowel environments. The separation of the sibilants (in the centroids and skewness of their spectra) was shown to predict listeners' accuracy and speed in identifying them.

Some recent work has also shown that a speaker's production of a phoneme contrast can be related to that of the individual's perception of the contrast. Newman (2003) found significant cross-subject correlations in measures of 20 subjects' speech perception and properties of their speech productions. Speakers having perceptual prototypes with longer VOTs for the /p/ in /pɑ/ also tended to produce /pɑ/ with longer VOTs. Similarly, there was a relation between the frequency of the spectral peak of their prototypes and productions of the /ʃ/ in /ʃɑ/. Vick, Lane, Perkell, Matthies, Gould, and Zandipour (2001) found that deaf speakers who produced vowel pairs with reduced contrast (neutralized vowels) and who showed improvement in their perception of these contrasts after receiving a cochlear implant, had enhanced production of the formant contrasts in many cases. In a study of word and pseudoword imitation by children with developmental apraxia of speech, Groenen, Maassen, Crul, and Thoonen (1996) found negative, cross-subject relations between auditory discrimination of consonant place of articulation and a measure of place substitutions. High discrimination scores were associated with low proportions of place substitutions. Additional findings of relations between production and perception are reviewed in Perkell et al. (2004a, 2004b).

The goals of the present two studies follow from this background. The studies' primary objective was to determine whether the distinctiveness of speakers' produced vowel and sibilant contrasts is related to their acuity in the perception of the contrasts. A second objective was to explore speakers' use of a saturation effect for /s/, as estimated by the consistency of tongue-tip contact with the lower alveolar ridge in producing the sibilant contrast.

STUDY 1: PRODUCTION AND PERCEPTION OF TWO VOWEL CONTRASTS

This study investigated the hypothesis that subjects who have relatively higher vowel discrimination scores will produce more distinct vowel contrasts than those who do not. Because of space limitations, only a very brief summary of the methods is presented here (for details, see Perkell et al., 2004a). The study examined articulatory, acoustic, and perceptual measures of the /u-ʊ/ contrast (in the words *who'd* and *hood*) and the /ɑ-ʌ/ contrast (in the words *cod* and *cud*). In a production experiment, the test words were pronounced in a carrier phrase, and to assess the effects of speaking condition, they were produced in normal, fast, and clear conditions. Mid-vowel EMMA measurements (Perkell, Cohen, Svirsky, Matthies, Garabieta, & Jackson, 1992) were made of a position of a point on the tongue blade and $F1$ and $F2$ measurements were made from the acoustic signal. For each subject and contrast, the mean values of the x and y coordinates of the tongue-blade point were calculated for each vowel, and *articulatory contrast distance* was calculated as the Euclidean distance between the two pairs of coordinates. Correspondingly, to derive *acoustic contrast distance*, mean values of $F1$ and $F2$ were calculated for each vowel, and formant separation was calculated as the Euclidean distance between the means in the *F*1, *F*2 plane. In a perception experiment, each subject's acuity was measured as the percent correct in an ABX discrimination paradigm, in which the subject heard equally spaced, natural-sounding stimuli in seven-step continua ranging from *cod* to *cud* and *who'd* to *hood*. The A and B stimuli were spaced one, two, and three steps apart on the continua.

Results

Figure 5.2 shows an example of the EMMA data. It is a plot of transducer coil locations during all the productions of tokens containing the /ɑ/ in *cod* (+) and the /ʌ/ in *cud* (x) by one female subject in the normal speaking condition. As illustrated in this figure, the TB (tongue blade) contrast distance is the distance in mm between the centroids of the *cod* and the *cud* TB distributions.

The peak ABX discrimination score was used as a measure of acuity because it is assumed to best represent discrimination between phoneme categories. In the ABX results, the one-, two-, and three-step stimulus comparisons were not equally successful in differentiating among the subjects' perceptual performances. The peak three-step discriminations produced a ceiling effect for most subjects, and the peak one-step stimuli led to highly variable scores, many at chance level. Moreover, many one-step intervals did not cross the

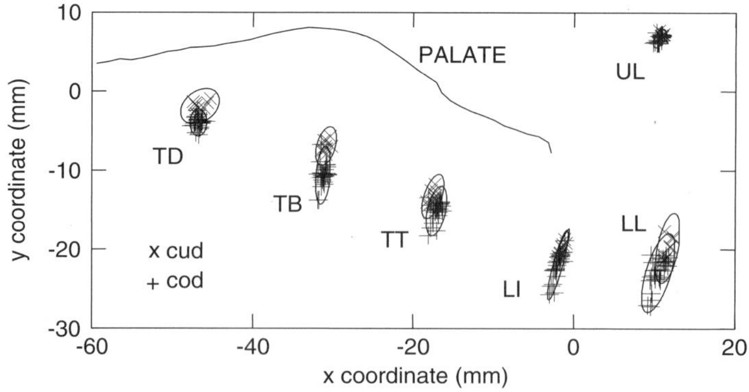

FIGURE 5.2. EMMA transducer coil locations during all the productions of tokens containing the /ɑ/ in cod (+) and the /ʌ/ in cud (x) by one female subject in the normal condition. The transducer coils are located at points on the tongue dorsum (TD), tongue blade (TB), tongue tip (TT), lower incisor (LI), lower lip (LL), and upper lip (UL). The midsagittal palatal contour (up to about the dento-alveolar junction on the right) is shown for reference.

labeling category boundary and the peak one-step scores did not correlate with any production measures. Therefore, we used the peak discrimination scores obtained with stimuli separated by two steps on the synthetic continua.

Figure 5.3 presents frequency distributions of the 19 subjects with respect to those two-step peak discrimination scores for each of the two vowel contrasts. For the following reasons, we classified subjects into two groups based on those scores. Even the two-step discrimination triads yielded substantial ceiling effects, with 37% of the subjects (*who'd-hood*) or 26% of the subjects (*cod-cud*) scoring 100%. Those subjects presumably had higher discriminative acuity than this ABX task was able to measure. Further, scores varied in increments of 6.25% because there were 16 discrimination trials per two-step stimulus comparison. As it turned out, subjects' scores fell at one of five values (*who'd-hood*) or one of four values (*cod-cud*) between 75 and 100% correct. Finally, the distribution for *who'd-hood* was right skewed. These considerations and the observation that production contrast appeared to grow nonlinearly with phoneme discrimination led us to classify all subjects who scored 100% (i.e., above the median) as "high" discriminators. Five of the subjects were ranked as high discriminators for the *cod-cud* contrast and seven as high discriminators for the *who'd-hood* contrast. All other subjects (at the median and below) were classified as "low" discriminators.[1]

Figure 5.4 plots articulatory contrast distance (for tongue-blade position) and acoustic contrast distance (for separation in the formant plane) in the

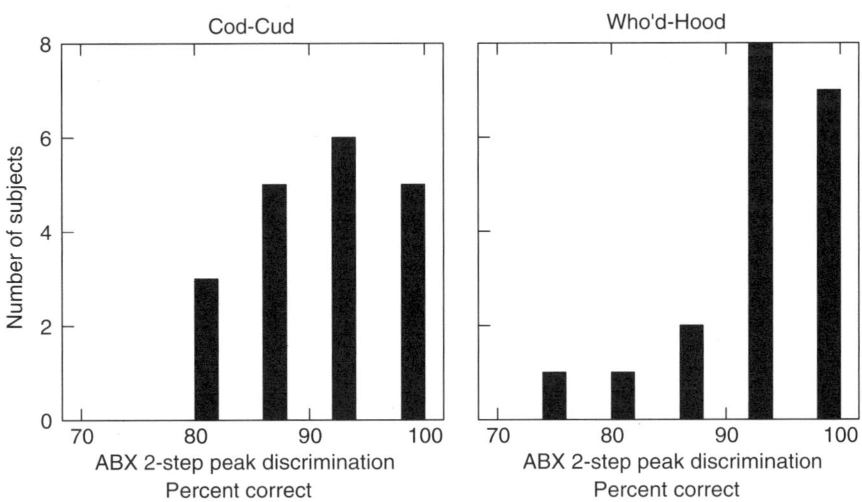

FIGURE 5.3. Frequency distributions of the 19 subjects with respect to two-step peak discrimination scores on an ABX task for each of the two vowel contrasts.

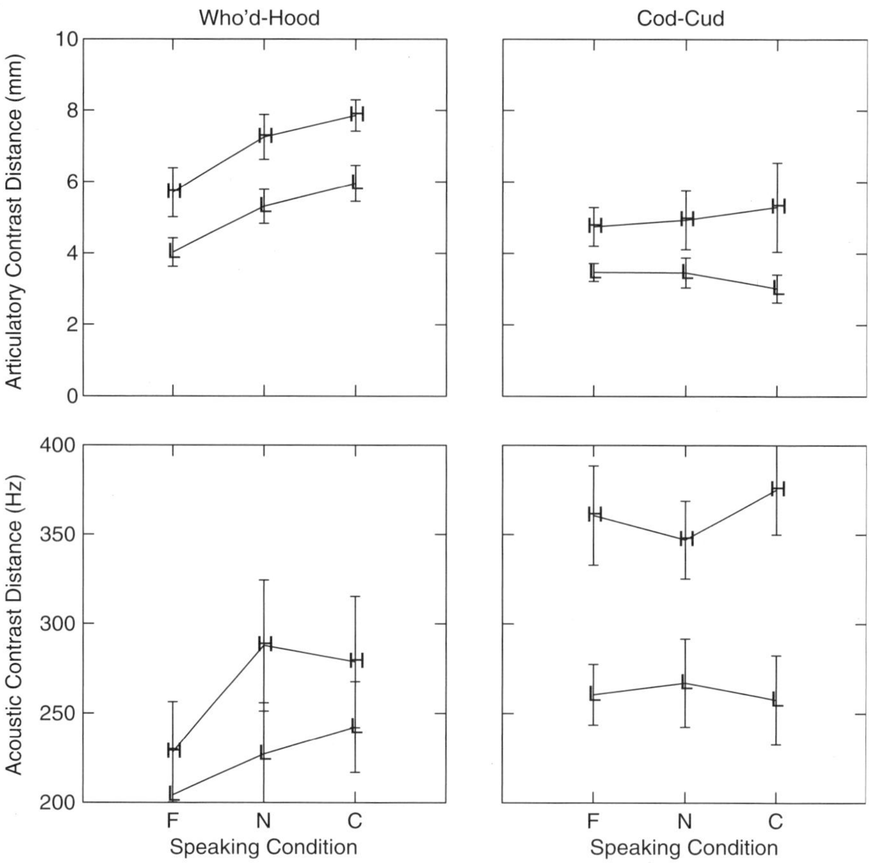

FIGURE 5.4. Articulatory contrast distance (for tongue body position—upper panel) and acoustic contrast distance (for separation in the formant plane—lower panel) as a function of the three speaking conditions. The left-hand panel gives results for *who'd-hood*, the right for *cod-cud*. Findings for high discriminators (labeled "H") and low discriminators ("L") are plotted separately. Error bars are one standard error about the mean.

upper and lower panels, respectively, as a function of the three speaking conditions. The left-hand panel gives results for *who'd-hood*, the right for *cod-cud*. For both articulatory and acoustic parameters and for both vowel contrasts, high discriminators (values labeled "H") produced greater contrast distances than low discriminators ("L") on the average. This effect was reliable for the articulatory parameter for *who'd-hood* (F = 28.6, df = 1,131, $p < .01$) and *cod-cud* (F = 17.9, df = 1,116, $p < .01$). The effect was also reliable for the acoustic parameter for *cod-cud* (F = 26.4, df = 1,70, $p < .01$) but not for *who'd-hood* where unexplained between-speaker variability was great ($F = 1.6$, df = 1,73, $p > .05$; error bars are one standard error of the mean). As inspection of Figure 5.4 reveals, articulatory and acoustic contrast distance increased from *fast* to *normal* to *clear* for *who'd-hood* (respectively, $F = 49.1$, df = 2,262, $p < .01$; $F = 5.5$, df = 2,146, $p < .01$) but not for *cod-cud* ($F = 0.5$, df = 2,232, $p > .05$; $F = 1.8$, df = 2,140, $p > .05$).

STUDY 2: PRODUCTION AND PERCEPTION OF THE /s-ʃ/ CONTRAST

Study 2 was designed to test the following hypotheses. First, speakers will vary in their ability to perceive the contrast between /s/ and /ʃ/ and this variation will also be related to how well they produce the contrast. (The reasoning is the same as with the vowels in Study 1: Speakers who are not as adept at perceiving fine acoustic differences along a /s-ʃ/continuum may be less likely to maintain a strong acoustic contrast in the production of the two sibilants.) Second, speakers will vary in the degree to which they employ contact between the tongue and the lower alveolar ridge differentially in the production of /s/ and /ʃ/ and a greater disparity (hereafter, "contact difference") will be associated with greater acoustic contrast produced. (Within the context of our theoretical framework, we consider that contact between the tongue and the lower incisors constitutes one of several possible somatosensory goals for the production of /s/.) Finally, the combination of these factors—differential use of contact and high perceptual acuity for /s/ vs. /ʃ/ will yield the largest sibilant contrasts.

As with Study 1, only a brief summary of the methods is presented; details can be found in Perkell et al. (2004b). In a production experiment, the subject pronounced the words *sod*, *shod*, *said*, and *shed* in a carrier phrase, in normal, fast, and clear conditions. A custom-made contact sensor was attached to the lingual aspect of the subject's lower incisors and alveolar ridge. The sensor was connected to the circuit from an electropalatograph, and the binary output signal (indicating contact or no contact) was used to estimate the use of an articulatory saturation effect by measuring the consistency of the contact between the tongue tip and the lower alveolar ridge during the production of /s/. Acoustic spectra were extracted from the sibilant audio signal and acoustic contrast distance was calculated as the average difference in the spectral median between /s/ and /ʃ/. In a perception experiment, each subject's acuity was measured as the percent correct in an ABX discrimination paradigm, in which the subject heard equally spaced, natural-sounding stimuli in continua ranging from *said* to *shed*. The A and B stimuli were spaced one, two, and three steps apart on the continua.

Results

To determine the use of contact for each individual subject, the proportion of the sibilant interval during which there was contact was extracted from the sibilant intervals of *said*, *shed*, *sod*, and *shod* in that subject's productions in all of the speaking conditions. The results are plotted in Figure 5.5. Repetitions across fast, normal, and clear speech conditions are pooled for each subject and phoneme.

Contact difference was computed for each speaker by calculating the mean proportion of contact pooled over the two vowel environments for each sibilant and subtracting the result for /ʃ/ from the result for /s/. The speakers were ordered with respect to this parameter (curve marked "c" in Figure 5.5) and were divided into two groups between speakers 19 and 16. (The figure shows 20 subjects; Subject 20 did not complete the perception experiment or Study 1.) This dividing point was based mainly on differences in the value of "c" and the extent of overlap of distributions of /s/ and /ʃ/ contact measures: Those for subject 16 overlapped considerably, whereas they were well separated for subject 19. The 12 subjects to the left of the vertical line were classified as

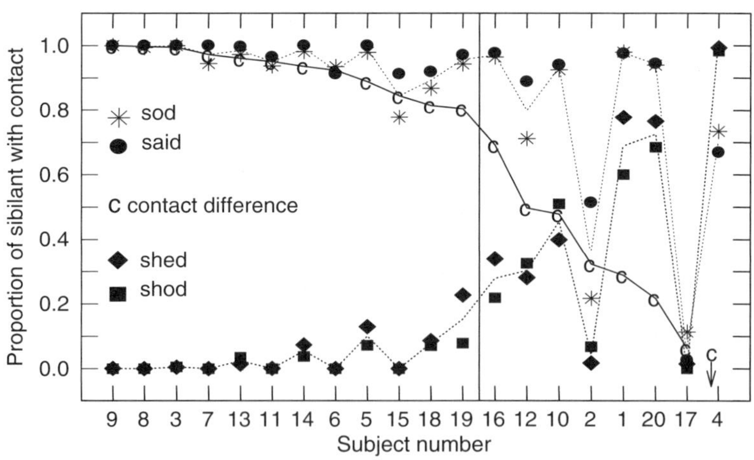

FIGURE 5.5. Response from the lower incisor/alveolar ridge contact sensor for the entire sibilant duration when the subjects were producing /s/ and /ʃ/. Each point is the mean of 45 measurements (15/speaking condition), on each of 20 subjects. The numbers on the horizontal axis identify the individual subjects. The values on the vertical axis represent the mean proportion of time during the acoustically defined sibilant interval when there was contact between the inferior aspect of the tongue tip and the lower dento-alveolar ridge. "Contact difference" (c) indicates the difference between /s/ and /ʃ/ in the proportion of contact during the sibilant interval (Subject 4 had a value of c less than 0.0). See text for further details

speakers with high contact difference: They used contact either exclusively or predominantly when producing /s/ but not /ʃ/. The remaining eight subjects, classified as speakers with low contact difference, used contact during /ʃ/ as well as /s/ or, in two cases, scarcely used contact at all. Figure 5.6 (left) plots frequency distributions of the 20 subjects with respect to contact difference; the dotted line indicates the separation into a high-contact-difference group (12 subjects) and a low-contact-difference group (8 subjects).

The analysis of subject acuity focused on two-step discrimination scores because, as in Study 1, those data showed the greatest variation across speakers and the fewest number of floor or ceiling (100%) effects. Even among the two-step ABX scores, there were numerous ceiling effects, as Figure 5.6 (right) reveals. The nine speakers with a perfect score may have had better sibilant discrimination than this task measured. The dotted line indicates the separation into a group with perfect discrimination scores, called "high," and a group called "low" (see endnote 1).

Figure 5.7 shows the effect on produced sibilant contrast of two speaker characteristics: High and low acuity on the test of sibilant discrimination (upper panels) and high and low use of differential contact in producing the sibilants (lower panels). Results are plotted in the left-hand column for *sod-shod* and in the right for *said-shed*. The pattern is evident: Those speakers who are highly acute in their sibilant discrimination and those who tend to use high differential contact produce sibilants that are more distinct (have greater contrast) acoustically. A four-way ANOVA was performed: Vowel context (two levels) and speaking condition (three levels) were within-subject variables, while discrimination score and contact difference (two levels each) were between-subject variables. The vowel context was not significant as a main effect or in any of its interactions. Speaking condition had a small but significant effect on acoustic contrast distance (F = 13.3, df = 2,484; p <.01, η^2 = .05), but none of its

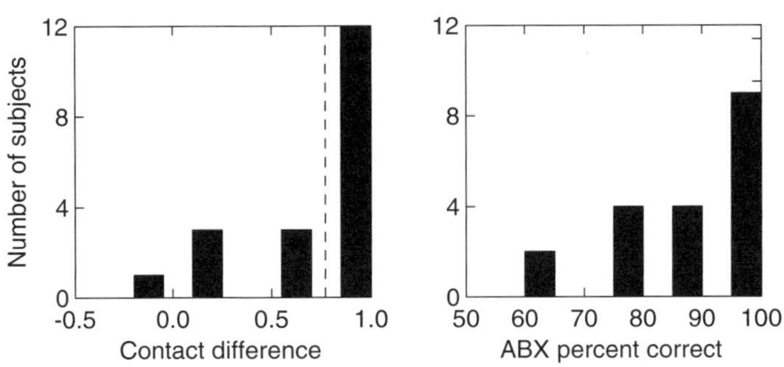

FIGURE 5.6. Frequency distributions of the number of subjects. Left: Use of differential contact (contact difference) in the production of /s/ and /ʃ/. Right: Percent correct on an ABX test of synthesized sibilant discrimination.

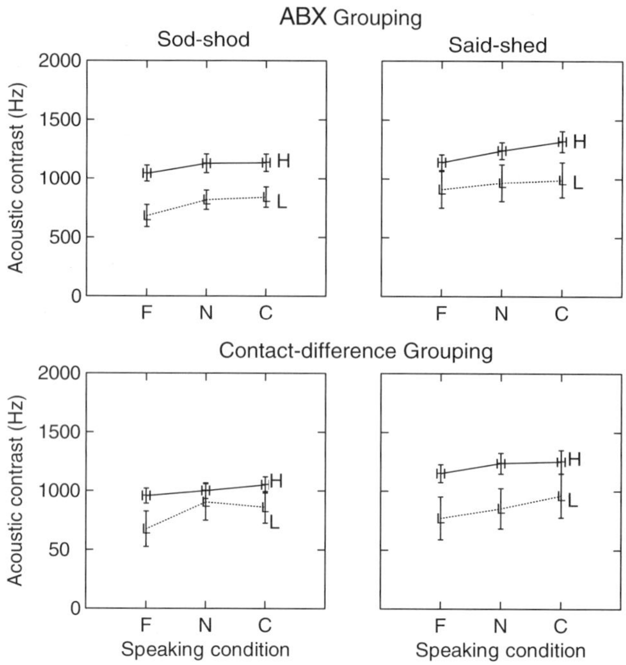

FIGURE 5.7. The effect on sibilant acoustic contrast of two binary speaker characteristics: high (H) and low (L) acuity on an ABX test of sibilant discrimination (upper panel) and high and low use of differential contact in producing the sibilants (lower panel). Results are plotted in the left-hand column for *sod/shod* and in the right for *said/shed*. Each point is the mean of values of acoustic contrast between /s/ and /ʃ/, where the number of values represented in each mean is equal to the number of subjects in the high and low groups.

two-way interactions was significant. Contact difference and discrimination groups and their interaction also had significant effects (respectively: $F = 43.7$; 72.9; 57.5; df = 1,242, $p < .01$ in each case; $\eta^2 = .15, .23, .19$). Finally, the three-way interaction of speaking condition with contact difference and discrimination was very small but statistically significant ($F = 11.7$, df = 2,484, $p < .01$, $\eta^2 = .05$). Acoustic contrast distance decreased more from normal to fast speaking conditions for the subjects in the low groups of both predictors than for the remaining subjects.

As reflected in the above-mentioned interaction, the most distinct sibilant productions were obtained from subjects who had high discrimination scores and who used contact in producing /s/ but not /ʃ/. Those subjects who did not use contact differentially when producing the two sibilants and who also discriminated the synthetic sibilants less well produced the least distinct sibilant contrasts. Intermediate degrees of sibilant contrast were found with subjects who either used contact differentially or discriminated well.

DISCUSSION

Returning to the hypotheses of the two studies, we find that speakers varied in their ability to perceive differences between synthesized tokens of vowel and sibilant continua and this variation was related to how distinctively they produced the sound contrasts. There were no significant correlations between subjects' performance in the vowel and sibilant studies, which may be due to the different nature of goals for the vowels and sibilants. We hypothesize that both vowels and sibilants have goals specified in auditory and somatosensory domains but the latter may be more prominent for the sibilants given their more extensive contact between the tongue blade and other oral structures. The relative prominence of goals in the two domains for individual speakers may also vary, depending in part on individual levels of auditory and somatosensory acuity.[2]

In addition to the relation found between acuity and contrast in the vowel and sibilant studies, in the latter study, speakers also varied in the degree to which they employed a saturation effect, as estimated by their differential use of consistent contact for /s/ in producing the /s/-/ʃ/ contrast. Finally, the combination of these factors—discriminative acuity and high contact consistency—was found among speakers who produced the largest sibilant contrasts. The significant main effect of contact difference on produced sibilant contrast is compatible with the DIVA model in its use of somatosensory goals; however, to test this idea more thoroughly within our experimental framework, it would be necessary to make measures of speakers' somatosensory acuity, which is beyond the scope of the current sibilant study.

The finding in the sibilant study that acoustic contrast distance decreased more from normal to fast conditions for the subjects in the low groups of both predictors than for the high groups is supportive of the following reasoning. At fast speaking rates there will be more neutralization of the contrast. In the tradeoff between least effort and clarity, a high-acuity speaker would resist that least-effort neutralization to maintain some intelligibility, whereas a low acuity speaker would tolerate more reduction in contrast. Thus, we would expect the interaction that was observed between acuity and clarity demands in relation to contrast reduction (see endnote 3).

Presumably, the link between perceptual acuity and productive contrast found in these studies arises in the course of speech acquisition: To learn the auditory goal regions for a phoneme, the child monitors sounds from his or her environment and constructs appropriate boundaries in acoustic–phonetic space. We hypothesize that language learners find it advantageous in their communicative interactions to be as intelligible as possible across a range of acoustic transmission conditions; therefore, children would tend to acquire auditory goal regions that are as distinct as possible. Consider two hypothetical children who are presented with approximately the same average separation of the members of a phonemic contrast, but who differ in their discriminative acuity for that contrast. In learning to maximize intelligibility, the child with higher acuity is better able to reject poor exemplars of each phoneme, and thus will adopt sensory goals for producing those phonemes that are further apart than the child with lower acuity.[3] Some indirect support for this view comes from a longitudinal study of language development (Tsao, Liu, & Kuhl, 2004), in which significant cross-subject correlations are shown between speech perception at age 6 months and language measures at 2 years, including word production. Our speculation about children's strategies would be reinforced more directly by evidence that speakers with greater acuity along a contrast dimension in fact reject more tokens of a phoneme as poor exemplars.

Although correlation results such as those presented here cannot establish causality, they are compatible with the idea that speakers' perceptual abilities influence their production mechanisms. This idea is also supported by a number of studies of speech acquisition in which perception "leads" production (c.f., Dehaene-Lambertz, & Pena, 2001; Eimas, 1999; Jusczyk & Aslin, 1995; Kuhl, Williams, Lacerda, Stevens, & Lindblom, 1992; Tsao et al., 2004).

In summary, we have presented evidence that the separation of the members of phonemic contrasts in perception and production are related. These results are compatible with the DIVA model of speech motor planning (Guenther, 1995; Guenther et al., 1998; Guenther & Ghosh, 2003). According to the way the model functions, phonemic goals are defined in auditory and somatosensory spaces; a speaker with more acute perception will acquire sensory goal regions that are smaller and spaced further apart; and the speaker is motivated by competing constraints to produce sufficiently clear speech for the listener while also minimizing the amount of effort in productions.

ACKNOWLEDGMENTS

This work was supported by Grant number DC01925 from the National Institute on Deafness and Other Communication Disorders, National Institutes of Health. We are grateful to Satrajit Ghosh and the reviewers for their helpful comments.

NOTES

1. Clearly, our procedure for measuring differences in subjects' discrimination was not sensitive enough for showing a finely graded relation; in current extensions of this work, we are replacing it with a more suitable measure.

2. It has been suggested that the observed cross-subject relations between production and perception could be due to some extraneous factor such as differences among subjects in motivation or attention. The lack of significant cross-subject correlations between measures of their performance in the vowel and sibilant studies makes such an explanation unlikely, as do the results of a variety of studies (cited in this chapter and in Perkell et al., 2004a, 2004b) that are consistent with our observations.
3. It could be argued that speakers who are not as adept at perceiving fine acoustic differences (i.e., those with low acuity) learn to produce more distinct contrasts in order to obtain a particular level of intelligibility. By the same token, speakers with relatively high acuity could be satisfied with smaller contrasts, and a smaller vowel space, to reach the same level of intelligibility, according to their own standards. However, both of those expectations are contradicted by the outcome of the present studies that find acuity and contrast positively, not inversely, related.

REFERENCES

Dehaene-Lambertz, G., & Pena, M. (2001). Electrophysiological evidence for automatic phonetic processing in neonates. *Neuroreport, 12*, 3155–3158.

Eimas, P. D. (1999). Segmental and syllabic representations in the perception of speech by young infants. *Journal of the Acoustical Society of America, 105*, 1901–1911.

Fujimura, O., & Kakita, Y. (1979). Remarks on quantitative description of lingual articulation. In B. Lindblom & S. Öhman (Eds.), *Frontiers of speech communication research*. London: Academic Press.

Groenen, P., Maassen, B., Crul, T., & Thoonen, G. (1996). The specific relation between perception and production errors for place of articulation in developmental apraxia of speech. *Journal of Speech and Hearing Research, 39*, 468–482.

Guenther, F. H. (1995). Speech sound acquisition, coarticulation and rate effects in a neural network model of speech production. *Psychological Review, 102*, 594–621.

Guenther, F. H., & Ghosh, S. S. (2003). A model of cortical and cerebellar function in speech. *Proceedings of the 15th international congress of phonetic sciences*, Barcelona, 3–9 August, pp. 169–174.

Guenther, F. H., Hampson, M., & Johnson, D. (1998). A theoretical investigation of reference frames for the planning of speech movements. *Psychological Review, 105*, 611–633.

Jusczyk, P. W., & Aslin, R. N. (1995). Infants' detection of the sound patterns of words in fluent speech. *Cognitive Psychology, 29*, 1–23.

Kuhl, P. K., Williams, K. A., Lacerda, F., Stevens, K. N., & Lindblom, B. (1992). Linguistic experience alters phonetic perception in infants by 6 months of age. *Science, 255*, 606–608.

Lindblom, B. (1986). Phonetic universals in vowel systems. In J. J. Ohala & J. J. Jeager (Eds.), *Experimental phonology* (pp. 13–44). New York: Academic Press.

Lindblom, B. (1990). Explaining phonetic variation: A sketch of the H&H theory. In W. J. Hardcastle & A. Marchal (Eds.), *Speech production and speech modeling* (pp. 403–439). Dordrecht: Kluwer.

Narayanan, S. S., Alwan, A. A., & Haker, K. (1995). An articulatory study of fricative consonants using magnetic resonance imaging. *Journal of the Acoustical Society of America, 98*, 1325–1347.

Newman, R. S. (2003). Using links between speech perception and speech production to evaluate different acoustic metrics: A preliminary report. *Journal of the Acoustical Society of America, 113*, 2850–2860.

Newman, R. S., Clouse, S. A., & Burnham, J. L. (2001). Perceptual consequences of within-talker variability in fricative production. *Journal of the Acoustical Society of America, 109*, 1181–1196.

Perkell, J. S., Boyce, S. E., & Stevens, K. N. (1979). Articulatory and acoustic correlates of the /s–sh/ distinction. In J. J. Wolf & D. H. Klatt (Eds.), *Speech communication*. Papers presented at the *97th meeting of the Acoustical Society of America*. New York: American Institute of Physics.

Perkell, J., Cohen, M., Svirsky, M., Matthies, M., Garabieta, I., & Jackson, M. (1992). Electromagnetic midsagittal articulometer (EMMA) systems for transducing speech articulatory movements. *Journal of the Acoustical Society of America, 92*, 3078–3096.

Perkell, J. S., Guenther, F.H., Lane, H., Matthies, M. L., Perrier, P., Vick, J., Wilhelms-Tricarico, R., & Zandipour, M. (2000). A theory of speech motor control and supporting data from speakers with normal hearing and with profound hearing loss. *Journal of Phonetics, 28*, 233–372.

Perkell, J. S., Guenther, F. H., Lane, H., Matthies, M. L. Stockmann, E., Tiede, M., & Zandipour, M. (2004a). The distinctness of speakers' productions of vowel contrasts is related to their discrimination of the contrasts. *Journal of the Acoustical Society of America, 116*, 2338–2344.

Perkell, J. S., Matthies, M. L., Tiede, M., Lane, H., Zandipour, M., Marrone, N., Stockmann, E., & Guenther, F. H. (2004b). The distinctness of speakers' /s-ʃ/ contrast is related to their auditory discrimination and use of an articulatory saturation effect. *Journal of Speech, Language and Hearing Research, 47*, 1259–1269.

Stevens, K. N. (1972). The quantal nature of speech: Evidence from articulatory-acoustic data. In P. B. Denes & E. E. David (Eds.), *Human communication—a unified view* (pp. 51–56). New York: McGraw-Hill.

Stevens, K. N. (1989). On the quantal nature of speech. *Journal of Phonetics, 17*, 3–46.

Stevens, K. N. (1998). *Acoustic phonetics*. Cambridge, MA: MIT Press.

Tsao, F. M., Liu, H.M., & Kuhl, P. K. (2004). Speech perception in infancy predicts language development in the second year of life: A longitudinal study. *Child Development, 75*, 1067–1084.

Vick, J., Lane, H., Perkell, J., Matthies, M., Gould, J., & Zandipour, M. (2001). Covariation of cochlear implant users' perception and production of vowel contrasts and their identification by listeners with normal hearing. *Journal of Speech, Language, and Hearing Research, 44*, 1257–1267.

6

3D Biomechanical Tongue Modeling to Study Speech Production

JEAN-MICHEL GÉRARD, PASCAL PERRIER, AND YOHAN PAYAN

ABSTRACT

The study of speech motor control from kinematic and acoustic signals collected from speakers requires an evaluation of the influence of the physical properties of the speech apparatus on the time variations of these signals. For this purpose, a 3D biomechanical tongue model is currently being developed at ICP. It is based on a 3D finite-element mesh, in which 10 different tongue muscles are represented. The nonlinear elastical properties of human tongue tissues are accounted for with hyperelastic characteristics and a large deformation modeling framework was chosen to accurately describe nonlinear geometrical changes. The model is embedded in a realistic 3D geometrical description of the jaw and of the vocal tract walls, which are both considered as fixed and nondeformable at the current stage of the model's development. In this paper, each modeling step is described and the impacts of the main tongue muscles on tongue shapes and vocal tract geometry are assessed through a number of various simulations. Their potential influences on speech motor control are discussed in the final section.

INTRODUCTION

Understanding speech motor control requires the collection and the analysis of numerous different kinds of articulatory and acoustic data from speakers. Unfortunately, experimental data cannot be the only basis for advancing our understanding of speech motor control theories for two main reasons. First, in spite of the fact that measurement devices and data-processing tools have benefited from great improvements in the recent years, experimental data analysis still has its limitations. A simple illustration of this statement can be found in the analysis of EMG signals collected in parts of the tongue where muscle fibers are highly interwoven. Under such conditions, it is quite impossible to be sure about which muscle the signal comes from (for example, in the middle of the tongue where Transversalis fibers and Posterior Genioglossus fibers are interwoven). Second, in the measured signals it is often impossible to separate what is due to the central nervous system and what is due to the physics of the speech apparatus. As concerns, for example, EMG signals, the presence of mechanoreceptors in facial and tongue muscles contributing to muscle activation, makes it impossible to know which part of the EMG activity is due to descendent inputs from the central nervous system, and which part is the result of afferent inputs. From this perspective, biomechanical models are very useful, since they describe in detail muscle anatomy, muscle mechanics, muscle force generation mechanisms, and the relations between muscle activation and tongue deformation. Thus, comparing simulations obtained with these models with experimental data provides a powerful approach to interpret the physical signals of speech production.

To our knowledge, the first biomechanical model used to study the impact of the physical properties of the articulatory system on speech production was designed by Perkell (1969). Perkell's model described the tongue in the mid-sagittal plane, and it was based on a discrete mass–spring modeling, including a distributed force model and tissue incompressibility. It also accounted for dynamics, and differentiated passive and active tissues. Simulations run with this model provided interesting insights into the relations between muscle activation and tongue deformation as well as into the constraints due to tongue and vocal tract morphology.

Kiritani, Miyawaki, and Fujimura (1976) achieved major improvements in developing the first 3D biomechanical model based on continuum mechanics and on finite-element method (FEM). This model also included a simplified lip model and was accounting for contacts between tongue and palate. Thus, the authors were able to study how tongue muscles are involved in the production of American English vowels.

The first model of the jaw and hyoid bone set was designed by Laboissière, Ostry, and Feldman (1996). They tested the influence of the jaw biomechanics on jaw displacements when constant motor command shifts were provided for different jaw positions in the mid-sagittal plane. They observed that the influence of the biomechanics was small in this specific case, and they concluded that there should be no need for the central nervous system to know precisely jaw biomechanics to control precisely this articulator.

Payan and Perrier (1997) designed the first 2D continuous biomechanical tongue model that includes elastical nonlinearities and the stiffness of the tissues varying with muscle recruitment which both contribute to a more realistic description of tongue behavior. The model is still extensively used to assess different potential impacts of tongue biomechanics on tongue movements and tongue shapes (Perrier, Payan, Zandipour, & Perkell, 2003). Sanguineti, Laboissière, and Ostry (1998) used a very similar approach to design a 2D model including the jaw, the hyoid bone, and the tongue with which they studied the muscles synergies associated with the production of movements along the main directions of deformation of the tongue. Dang and Honda (2004) designed an extended 2D model of the tongue and the jaw, representing these articulators in the mid-sagittal plane with a 2 cm thickness. This represents an intermediate step between 2D and 3D descriptions.

The most ambitious model ever built was by Wilhelms-Tricarico (1995). It is a 3D biomechanical model, featuring mechanical and geometrical nonlinearities, with both a mechanical modeling accounting for anisotropy and for interwoven fibers, and with a muscle activation model. Unfortunately, due to the conceptual complexity of the model, computational issues induced strong limitations of the use of the model in studying speech production. In spite of that, a large number of modeling principles developed by Wilhelms-Tricarico (1995) served as the basis for the development of the model that will be presented in this paper.

MODELING APPROACH

A Biomechanical Model? Why?

As discussed above, we conceive articulatory models as powerful tools to understand the control underlying the production of speech and to test hypotheses about the way physiological, articulatory, and acoustical signals of speech are likely to be influenced by the motor commands sent by the central nervous system, on the one hand, and by the physical characteristics of the articulators, on the other. From this perspective, the central question is: Which level of description of the physical reality is required for us to reach our objectives?

Articulatory models can be classified in two ways: geometrical and biomechanical. Geometrical models provide an accurate description of the relation between vocal tract geometry and positions of the articulators. The techniques underlying the design of these models are well established and reasonably simple, and this makes them very appealing. However, geometrical models cannot describe the impact of motor commands on the time course of articulatory displacements, because they do not account for the causes and the constraints of these displacements, which are typically associated with force generation principles and mechanical properties of the articulators. These phenomena are intrinsically taken into account in biomechanical models. For that reason, biomechanical models are required. However, as exemplified by Wilhelms-Tricarico's (1995, 2000) work, building realistic biomechanical models requires the use of complex mathematical techniques, which induce computational complexity with potential convergence problems and long simulation durations. The approach that was adopted during the design of the 3D biomechanical tongue model presented in this paper was guided by a constant search for compromise between accuracy of the description and computational complexity.

A Continuous Modeling Approach

In biomechanical modeling, two main approaches are possible: one of them, called the "discrete approach", is based on the use of functional discrete models while the other, the "continuous approach", uses the laws of continuum mechanics to establish the equations of movement. The latter approach is generally favored because it provides greater accuracy. The continuous approach is typically based on the FEM (Bathe, 1982; Zienkiewicz & Taylor, 1994), even though it can induce an important computational load. In this method, the mechanical continuum is divided into elements defined by nodes, and the Lagrangian equations of movement are solved at each node. Then, thanks to interpolation functions between nodes, a solution can be computed in terms of deformation, displacement or stress, at any point of the continuum.

A 3D Model

Tongue muscles are used to move and shape precisely the tongue, both in the mid-sagittal plane (determining in particular the position of the constriction) and in the coronal plane (controlling in particular the shape of the constriction). In addition, during speech production, the tongue is often in contact with palate or teeth. The contacts arising between tongue and palate in or close to the mid-sagittal plane were accounted for in previous 2D models, and this approach has allowed some aspects of stop production (e.g., Fuchs, Perrier, & Mooshammer, 2001) to be studied. However, lateral contacts could obviously not be accounted for with this kind of model. This is a drawback, since lateral contacts do influence tongue deformations in two ways: (1) there is a direct mechanical effect due to the introduction of additional friction or obstacles and (2) there is an indirect effect due to sensori-motor afference which can modify the motor commands. All those reasons led us to design a 3D model.

A Dynamical Model

Time variations of articulatory and acoustics signals are perceptually very relevant. We think that these temporal variations are the result of a combination of central and peripheral influences. Indeed, timing is an intrinsic component of the dynamics of a system due to stiffness, damping, and inertia, while motor planning can specify the timing of the commands (extrinsic component). A model of speech production has to account for both aspects. As a consequence, our model is a dynamical model.

MESH DESIGN

Design of a Tongue Generic Mesh

The mesh design process is completely described in Wilhelms-Tricarico (2000) and Gérard, Wilhelms-Tricarico, Perrier, and Payan (2003). The key points are as follows: A generic mesh was designed from the Visible Human Project™ data set (http://www.nlm.nih.gov/research/visible/visible_human.html). It specifies the shape of the elements (Figure 6.1) taking into account the main properties of muscle anatomy such as the principal orientations of muscle fibers. Then, a more precise implementation of muscles was done in the mesh, thanks to accurate anatomical data from Netter (1989), Miyawaki (1974), and Takemoto (2001) [see Gérard et al. (2003) for a comprehensive description].

Adapting the Model to a Real Speaker's Geometry (Mesh Matching)

Evaluating a model of speech production implies the comparison of simulated movements, generated by the model, with articulatory data collected on speakers. At ICP, a large amount of various kinds of data were collected for a reference speaker (PB). In order to use those data, the geometry of the tongue model was adapted to PB's geometry.

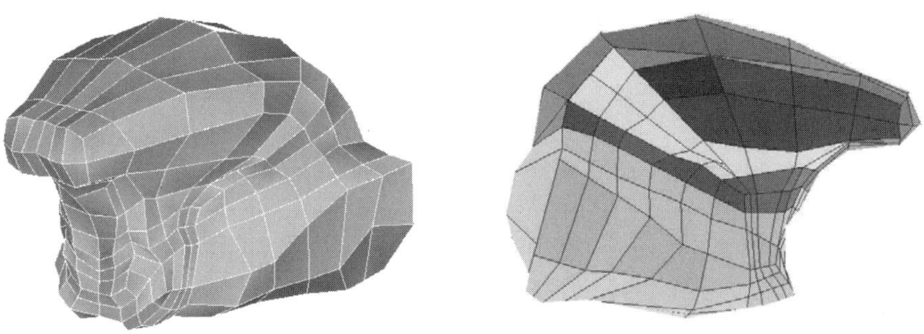

FIGURE 6.1. Generic finite-element structure: left panel, generic mesh; right panel, muscular structures within the generic mesh; each level of gray represents a specific muscle; when several muscles are present in an element, only one color is shown.

The first step consisted of measuring carefully PB's 3D tongue contours at rest position from MRI data, with manual image segmentation. Then, a mesh-matching algorithm transformed the external contours of the generic mesh into a new mesh (henceforth called target mesh) reproducing PB's characteristics. Finally, the internal structure of the mesh was interpolated with respect to the transformed external contours (see Figure 6.2).

Bony Structures and Vocal Tract Geometry

Since tongue positioning during speech production is made with reference to the vocal tract walls, a mesh of the whole vocal tract had to be designed. Once the tongue was matched to the reference speaker's geometry, meshes of the other structures such as jaw, soft and hard palate, and hyoid bone were built. Several techniques were used. The jaw and the hyoid bone were manually extracted from CT-scan images, in the coronal plane. Then, spline functions were defined on each segmented image in order to obtain continuous representations of the contours. The software stacks up all these contours, creates a surface representation, and provides a mesh using the Marching cube algorithm (Lorensen & Cline, 1987). At this stage, the mesh describing the jaw contained approximately 15,000 surface elements, which would generate, in case of contact between tongue and palate, a much too heavy computation load with unacceptable computation times. The ANSYS™ FEM package (ANSYS, Inc., Canonsburg, PA, USA, http://www.ansys.com/) was used to undersample the mesh with the constraint to carefully respect geometry in some crucial regions of the jaw, such as the region in the anterior part where the tongue is inserted in the jaw. The number of elements was reduced to 1450. The same technique was used for decimating the hyoid bone mesh.

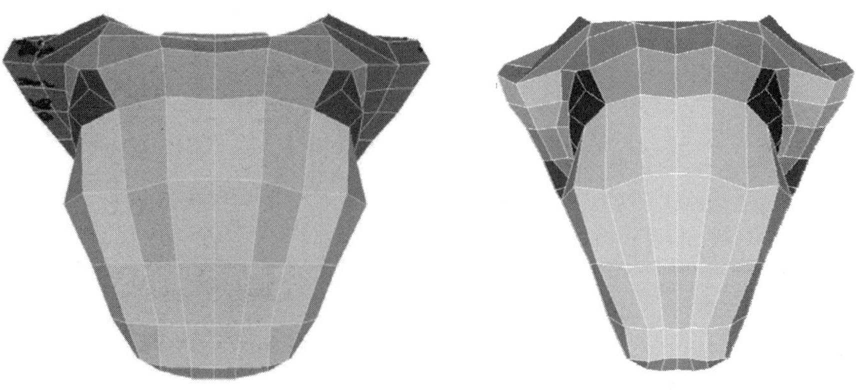

FIGURE 6.2. Top view of the tongue mesh before matching (left panel) and after matching with PB's tongue geometry (right panel).

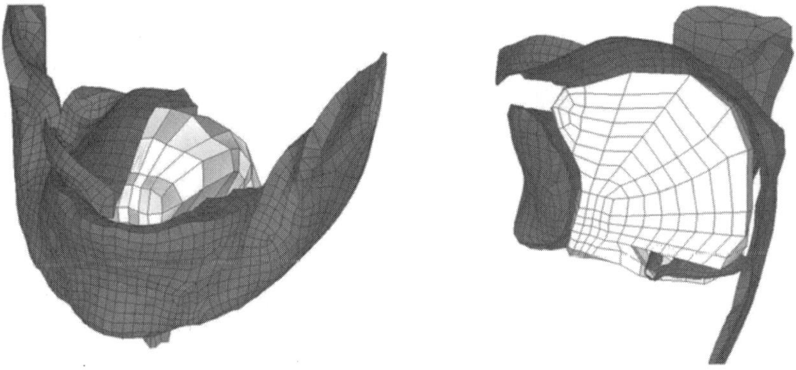

FIGURE 6.3. Complete 3D structure including tongue, hard palate, soft palate, jaw, and hyoid bone in an oblique view (left panel) and in a mid-sagittal view (right panel).

The hard palate was designed from a dental cast, which was digitized using a 3D scan. After undersampling, a 600 elements mesh was generated. The soft palate mesh was based on MRI data. A grid, made of regularly spaced planes, was used to spatially sample the vocal tract shape of PB at rest position. On each of those planes, the MRI data were interpolated and the soft palate contour was extracted. Then, using spline interpolation, a surface was created and a mesh was automatically set up.

The last step consisted of assembling all the components to make a unique mesh, associating volume and surface elements. Note again that at the current stage of the modeling only the tongue is likely to move and to be deformed (Figure 6.3).

MECHANICAL MODELING

On the basis of published force measurements during strong and sustained contacts between tongue and palate (Bunton & Weismer, 1994), and in the absence of any other kind of data, we estimated the muscle force level during speech production to be of the order of a few newtons. With this level of force, the tongue displacement associated with a two phoneme sequence has to be as short as 50–100 ms. To reproduce this order of magnitude of forces and durations with the tongue model, an accurate estimation of mechanical properties of the tongue would be very helpful. Unfortunately, there is a lack of data in the literature about these properties. In order to increase the reliability of the model, we designed a specific indentation experiment to measure tongue tissues elasticity (Gérard, Ohayon, Luboz, Perrier, & Payan, 2005).

Indentation Experiment

The goal of an indentation experiment is to obtain the constitutive law of a material, i.e., the relation between stress and strain which determines the mechanical behavior of the material. For this purpose, a human tongue was removed from the fresh cadaver of a 74-year-old woman by Professor Lebeau from Grenoble University Hospital. The indentation experiment was run less than 24 hours after death, in order to limit tissue deterioration. It was done at the Purpan Hospital in Toulouse by Vincent Luboz from TIMC laboratory.

Human soft tissues, including those of the tongue, are likely to feature nonlinear elasticity, anisotropy, plasticity, and viscoelasticity. As a first approximation, it was decided to model only nonlinear elasticity, while viscoelasticity was considered to correspond to critical damping, and no account was given of anisotropy and of plasticity. Moreover, the tongue is covered with a layer of mucosa on its surface. In order to differentiate the mechanical properties of the mucosa from those of the tongue body, two indentations were successively made: the first was applied to the whole tongue (including the mucosa); for the second, the mucosa layer was removed and the remaining body was indented. In addition, the indentation was made at the rear and at the front of the tongue in each case, in order to test the possible limits of the isotropy hypothesis, primarily used in our model for computational simplicity.

Indentation Results

The computation of a constitutive law from indentation measurements cannot be derived directly from the measurements. It was necessary to formulate hypotheses about the nature of the constitutive law and then to calculate the parameters of this law that permitted a good fit of the indentation measurements.

According to Fung (1993), hyperelastic material seems to be well adapted for a good approximation of human soft tissues. A material is said to be hyperelastic, if it is possible to find a function W, called the hyperelastic potential energy function (HPEF), whose derivative with respect to the strain equals the stress. The specification of this function determines the nonlinear elastic properties of the material. Among the various strain-energy functions, which can describe such a mechanical response (Holzapfel, 2001), we focused on the incompressible two-parameter Yeoh strain-energy function W. This strain-energy function is given by the following analytical expression:

$$W = a_{10}(I_1 - 3) + a_{20}(I_1 - 3)^2 \tag{6.1}$$

where a_{10} and a_{20} are two constants that characterize tissue properties, while I_1 is the first invariant of the right Cauchy–Green strain tensor C [I_1 = Trace(C)].

Our objective was to infer a_{10} and a_{20} values from the indentation measurements, which are compatible with the deformations measured on the cadaver tongue.

This was done by an iterative algorithm based on an analysis-by-synthesis technique. In this approach, a numerical model of the indentation experiment was designed (Figure 6.4), in which tongue tissues are modeled with a FEM structure and the indentor is simulated by the application of an external force. Starting from arbitrary initial values of the parameters determining the HPEF of the tissues, the iterative algorithm consists of (1) simulating the tissue deformations owing to a given indentor force; (2) comparing the deformations with the experimental data; (3) updating the HPEF parameters and starting again with Step (1), until a convergence criterion between simulated and experimental data is reached. This algorithm is described in more detail in Gérard et al. (2005). Figure 6.5 shows an example of the results obtained with the optimization procedure: For the rear part of the tongue and without mucosa, the dotted line depicts the measured relation between force and displacement and the solid line corresponds to the simulated relation obtained with the optimal HPEF. It can be seen that the approximation is very accurate, since the error between the measured curve and the simulated one is smaller than the variance of the measures.

Table 6.1 gives the Young modulus which is computed as the derivative of stress with respect to the strain and corresponds to the stiffness of the material in the direction of the stress, inferred at rest position in the rear and front parts of the tongue, with and without the mucosa layer. It can be seen that (1) the rear and front values are very close and (2) the mucosa does not significantly affect the global elasticity. These observations support our isotropic hypothesis.

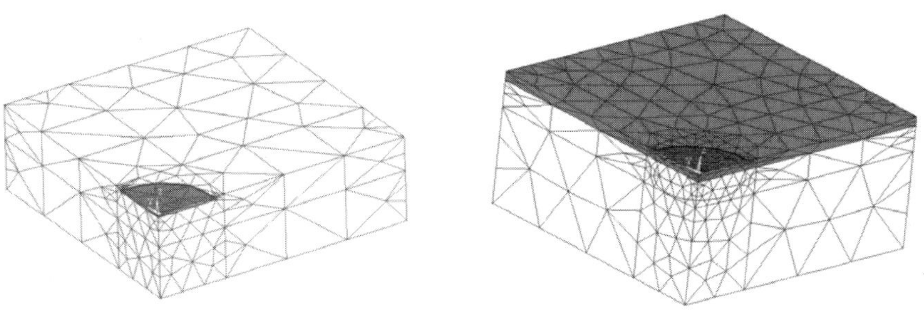

FIGURE 6.4. Meshes used for numerical simulations of indentation: left, one layer model (tissues without mucosa); right, two layers model (tissues and mucosa). The quarter circle represents the area where the indentor applies pressure.

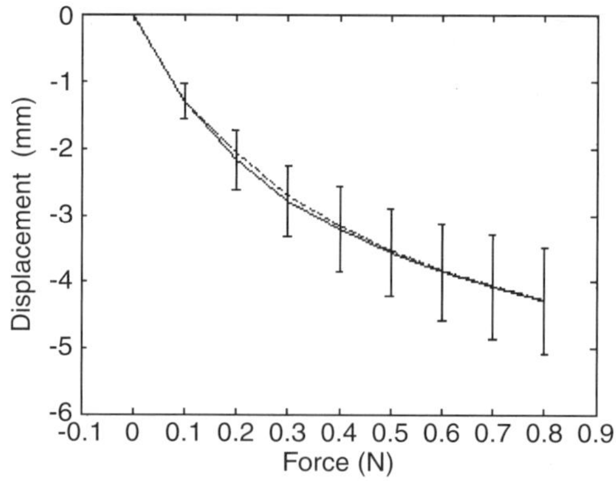

FIGURE 6.5. Measured (dotted line) and simulated (solid line) curves between indentor displacement and force. The standard deviation of the measure is depicted by vertical segments around the measured curve.

TABLE 6.1. *E* is the Inferred Young Modulus Values for the Cadaver Tongue under the Four Different Experimental Conditions

Experiment	*E* (kPa)
Rear muscular tissues without mucosa	1.16
Front muscular tissues without mucosa	1.10
Rear mucosa	1.19
Front mucosa	1.14

SIMULATIONS

The methodology described above has allowed us to build up a tongue model whose mechanical properties are realistic. This was an important challenge of the current study, since our project is to use the model to infer the motor commands underlying tongue movements in speech. In this purpose, the model has absolutely to be reliable in terms of description of the physics. Since the model is adapted to speaker PB, future works in this project will consist (1) of a comparison between predictions made with the model and data collected from speaker PB for a number of sounds whose muscle activations are well known, and (2) of attempts to infer muscle commands from tongue shapes measured during speech on speaker PB. Before that, it is necessary to determine the best approach for solving of the Lagrangian equations of movement.

Small vs. Large Deformation Framework

The step by step solving of the Lagrangian equations of movement can be made within two different theoretical frameworks, which determine how geometrical deformations and strain are related to each other. If ∇D is the deformation gradient, the strain tensor is given by

$$\varepsilon = \frac{1}{2}\left(\nabla D + (\nabla D)^T + \nabla D^T\,(\nabla D)\right) \tag{6.2}$$

If we assume that the system has small deformations, the second-order term can be neglected. In this case, the strain tensor can be simplified, and it becomes a linear function of the deformation gradient. This corresponds to the so-called "small deformation framework".

However, in some cases, the modeled continuum distorts sharply, implying higher values in the deformation gradient, and the above simplification is no longer valid. In this case, significant changes occur in the directions of loads during the movement and in stiffness values. Consequently, the stiffness matrix K and the load vector F depend on the displacement vector u. Hence, the equation to be solved for a static problem is

$$K(u) \cdot u = F(u) \tag{6.3}$$

This is the so-called "large deformation framework". Iterative algorithms must be used to solve the equations.

Napadow, Chen, Wedeen, and Gilgert (1999) measured tongue deformation rates during speech production and they found values as large as 160 percent in compression and 200 percent in stretch. Since modeling deformations beyond 20 percent are assumed to be large in soft tissues, a large deformation framework was required for our simulations.

Simulation Settings

The tongue is assumed to be incompressible and to be critically damped. Damping was accounted for in the model using the Rayleigh damping method, where the damping matrix $[C]$ is a linear combination of the mass matrix $[M]$ and the stiffness matrix $[K]$:

$$[C] = \alpha[M] + \beta[K] \tag{6.4}$$

α and β are the Rayleigh damping coefficients computed to reach critical damping. Contacts are modeled for the hard palate and for the interior part of the jaw according to a penalty method. This method allows a small interpenetration of the materials in contact, and models the contact reaction force with a damped nonlinear spring system. Contact parameters, such as contact stiffness and maximal allowed penetration were set in an *ad hoc* manner, in order to obtain an acceptable maximal penetration (0.1 mm) and to avoid numerical instabilities when contact occurs.

In the current version of the model, the jaw is fixed and displacements of the hyoid bone are limited to the horizontal plane. Muscle forces are applied as external forces on nodes using a distributed force model (Payan & Perrier, 1997). Lagrangian equations of movements are solved using the FEM package ANSYS™ with a combination of Newmark and Newton–Raphson methods (Gérard et al., 2003). All simulations presented in this paper were obtained with muscle forces applied as step functions during 120 ms.

Results

Before precise and quantitative comparisons between simulations and data collected from speaker PB can be made, the model behavior was evaluated by observing the qualitative impact of specific muscle recruitments (Posterior Genioglossus, Anterior Genioglossus, Hyoglossus, and Stylogossus) on the tongue shape. This is the purpose of this section. The results were qualitatively assessed by visually comparing the resulting tongue shape in the model with vocal tract X-ray images in the mid-sagittal plane (for French: Bothorel, Simon, Wioland, & Zerling, 1986; and for English: Perkell, 1969). To do so we selected among the X-ray images those corresponding to sounds for which EMG data (e.g., Baer, Alfonso, & Honda, 1988) have suggested that they are mainly produced with the recruitment of one of these muscles.

Figure 6.6 shows the results obtained for a 2 N force generated by the Genioglossus Posterior (GGp), which is known for its role in the production of high-front vowels such as /i/, /ɪ/, and /e/. Our simulation shows a main rear-front movement of the tongue body with an elevation of the tongue dorsum due to contact with the incisors and due to tissue incompressibility. The simulated forward displacement of the rear of the tongue was about 2 cm and the elevation of the tongue dorsum 0.9 mm. This is consistent with X-ray data on vowel /i/ in English and French.

Changes in the coronal plane were also observed owing to the fact that tongue tissues are assumed to be isotropic and incompressible. These latter changes can be limited by activating the Transversalis, since its fibers are oriented in the coronal plane. Combining an activation of GGp (2 N) with an activation of the Transversalis (0.1 N), it was possible to limit tongue expansion in the coronal plane which in turn increases the elevation of tongue dorsum from 9 mm up to 1.3 cm. This example shows how muscles are likely to influence the tongue shape in a plane, which is orthogonal to the main orientation of its muscle fibers.

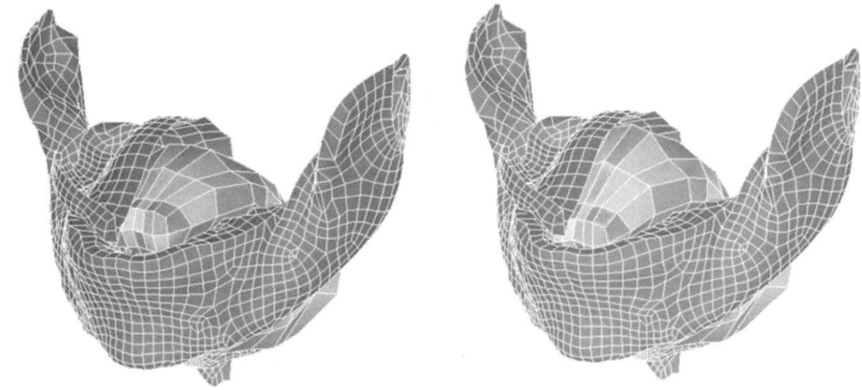

FIGURE 6.6. 3D tongue deformation (oblique front view) simulated on the model for a 1 N force produced by the GGp: left panel, tongue at rest position; right panel, final tongue position. The light gray mesh represents the tongue. The dark meshes represent the jaw (in front of the tongue and on its sides) and the right half of the hard palate (upper mesh), respectively.

Figure 6.7 shows the tongue deformation generated by a 0.5 N force produced by the Anterior Genioglossus (GGa). As expected (Baer et al., 1988), this muscle lowers the tongue tip slightly. This is in agreement with X-ray data on vowel /a/ that is known to be mainly produced with the combination of the GGa

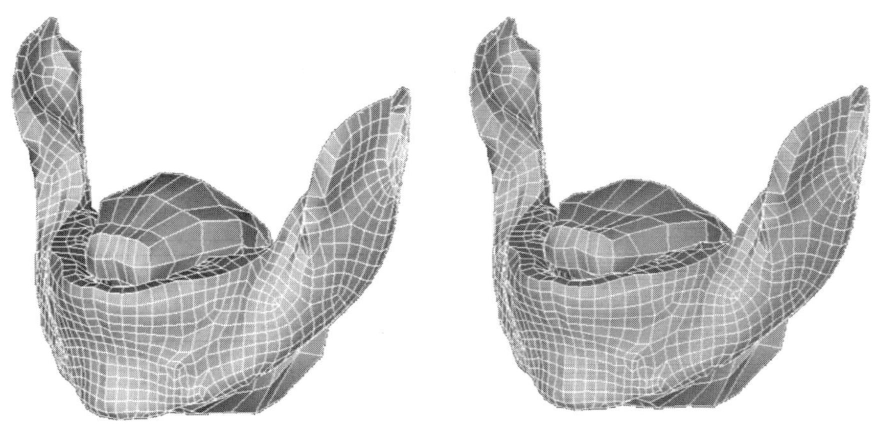

FIGURE 6.7. 3D tongue deformation (oblique front view) simulated on the model for a 0.5 N force produced by Gga: left panel, tongue at rest position; right panel, final tongue position. The mesh in front of the tongue and on its sides represents the jaw.

and the Hyoglossus. It should also be noted that, in addition, it produces a slight tongue grooving in the apical region. This grooving is similar to the one observed on speakers during the production of /i/. It suggests that a combination of the recruitment of GGa, GGp, and the Transversalis could underlie the production of /i/.

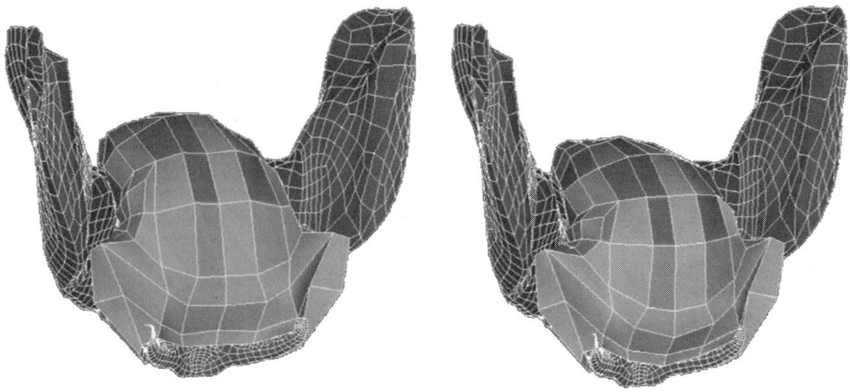

FIGURE 6.8. 3D tongue deformation (oblique view from the back) simulated on the model for a 2 N force produced by the Hyoglossus: left panel, tongue at rest position; right panel, final tongue position. The light gray mesh represents the tongue. The mesh in front of the tongue and on its sides represents the jaw.

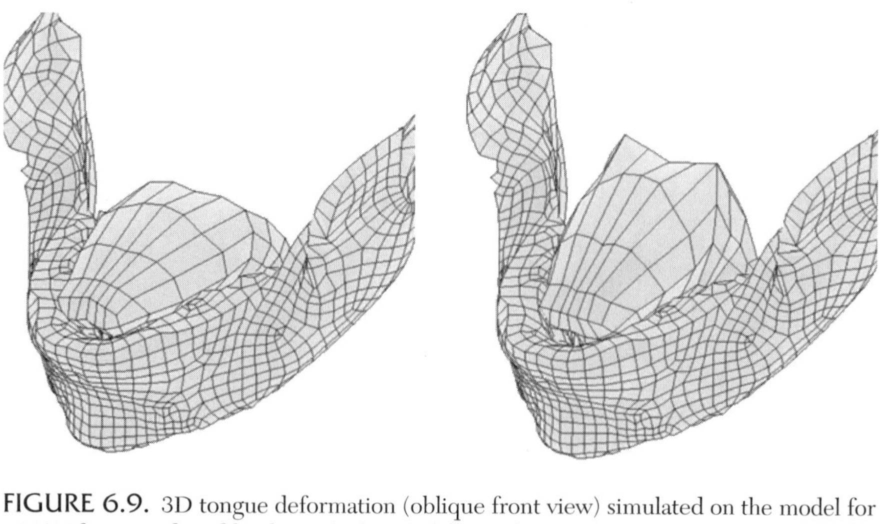

FIGURE 6.9. 3D tongue deformation (oblique front view) simulated on the model for a 0.5 N force produced by the Styloglossus: left panel, tongue at rest position; right panel, final tongue position. The mesh in front of the tongue and on its sides represents the jaw.

The consequence of an activation of the Hyoglossus in the tongue model is shown in Figure 6.8. Located at the rear of the tongue, the Hyoglossus lowers the back part of the tongue body and moves it back. As said above, this muscle is known for being involved in the production of the vowel /a/. The simulation was obtained for a 1 N force. The vertical lowering of the rear of the tongue was 1.2 cm.

Figure 6.9 shows the deformation associated with a 1 N force produced by the Styloglossus. An elevation of the tongue in its dorsal region can be observed together with a lowering of the tongue tip and a general backward displacement of the whole tongue body. This is very close to the tongue shape observed for velar vowels such as /u/. The direction of the deformation is consistent with EMG data (Baer et al., 1988) about the role of the Styloglossus in the production of velars. However, sharp edges can be observed on the top of the tongue (right panel), which is not realistic. This suggests that the muscle force could be applied too locally on specific elements of the tongue, namely the ones where the external fibers of the Styloglossus are inserted. This has to be further assessed.

CONCLUSION

A 3D tongue model was developed to study speech production and to test motor control models in speech production. Its design takes into account some complex aspects of the mechanical characteristics of tongue tissues, such as nonlinear elasticity and large deformations. An experimental indentation allows a realistic estimation of the elasticity parameters. Thus, tongue shape variations compatible with observations on human subjects during speech production have been simulated with reasonable muscle force levels and with realistic movement durations (<100 ms).

In future analyses, the model, representing a real speaker's geometry, will be validated using MRI data for French phonemes and the related acoustic output from the same speaker.

ACKNOWLEDGMENTS

The authors are very indebted to Jacques Ohayon, Professor at the University of Chambéry, for his valuable help in solving theoretical issues in biomechanical modeling; Jacques Lebeau, Professor and surgeon at Grenoble University Hospital, who provided us with the fresh cadaver tongue; Vincent Luboz, from TIMC Laboratory, and currently at CIMIT, in Cambridge, Massachusetts, who made the indentation measurements on the human tongue; Pierre Badin, from Institut de la Communication Parlée, who provided us with CT scans and MRI data for mesh design.

REFERENCES

Baer, T., Alfonso, P. J., & Honda, K. (1988). Electromyography of the tongue muscles during vowels in /əpVp/ environment. *Annual Bulletin of the Research Institute of Logopedics and Phoniatrics*, 22,7–19, Tokyo University.

Bathe, K. J. (1982). *Finite element procedures in engineering analysis*. Englewood Cliffs, NJ: Prentice-Hall.

Bothorel, A., Simon, P., Wioland, F., & Zerling, J.-P. (1986). *Cinéradiographie des voyelles et des consonnes du français*. Institut de Phonétique, Université Marc Bloch, Strasbourg, France.

Bunton, K., & Weismer, G. (1994). Evaluation of a reiterant force-impulse task in the tongue. *Journal of Speech and Hearing Research*, *37*, 1020–1031.

Dang, J., & Honda, K. (2004). Construction and control of a physiological articulatory model. *Journal of the Acoustical Society of America*, *115*(2), 853–870.

Fuchs, S., Perrier, P., & Mooshammer, C. (2001). The role of the palate in tongue kinematics: An experimental assessment in VC sequences from EPG and EMMA data. *Proceedings of EUROSPEECH 2001* (pp. 1487–1490).

Fung, Y. C. (1993). *Biomechanics: Mechanical properties of living tissues*. New York: Springer.

Gérard, J.-M., Wilhelms-Tricarico, R., Perrier, P., & Payan, Y. (2003). A 3D dynamical biomechanical tongue model to study speech motor control. *Recent Research and Developments in Biomechanics, 1*, 49–64.

Gérard, J.-M., Ohayon, J., Luboz, V., Perrier, P. & Payan, Y. (2005). Non linear elastic properties of the lingual and facial tissues assessed by indentation technique. *Medical Engineering and Physics*, *27*(10), 884–892.

Holzapfel, G. A. (2001). *Nonlinear solid mechanics*. Chichester: Wiley.

Kiritani, S., Miyawaki, K., & Fujimura, O. (1976). A computational model of the tongue, *Annual Bulletin of the Research Institute of Logopedics and Phoniatrics*, *10*, 243–252, Tokyo University.

Laboissière, R., Ostry, D. J., & Feldman, A. G. (1996). The control of multi-muscle systems: Human jaw and hyoid movements. *Biological Cybernetics, 74*(3), 373–384.

Lorensen, W. E., & Cline, H. E. (1987). Marching cube: A high resolution 3D surface construction algorithm. *ACM Computer Graphics*, *21*, 163–169.

Miyawaki, K. (1974). A study on the musculature of the human tongue. *Annual Bulletin of the Research Institute of Logopedics and Phoniatrics, 8*, 22–50, Tokyo University.

Napadow, V. J., Chen, Q., Wedeen, V. J., & Gilgert, R. J. (1999). Intramural mechanics of the human tongue in association with physiological deformations, *Journal of Biomechanics, 32*, 1–12.

Netter, F.H. (1989). *Atlas of human anatomy*. CIBA-GEIGY Corporation editor.

Payan, Y., & Perrier, P. (1997). Synthesis of V–V sequences with a 2D biomechanical tongue model controlled by equilibrium point hypothesis. *Speech Communication*, *22*(2/3), 185–205.

Perkell, J. S. (1969). *Physiology of speech production: Results and implication of a quantitative cineradiographic study*. Cambridge, MA: MIT Press.

Perrier, P., Payan, Y., Zandipour, M., & Perkell, J. (2003). Influences of tongue biomechanics on velar stop consonants: A modeling study. *Journal of the Acoustical Society of America*, *114*(3), 1582–1599.

Sanguineti, V., Laboissière, R., & Ostry, D. J. (1998). A dynamic biomechanical model for the neural control of speech production. *Journal of the Acoustical Society of America, 103*, 1615–1627.

Takemoto, H. (2001). Morphological analyses of the human tongue musculature for three dimensional modelling. *Journal of Speech, Language, Hearing Research, 44*, 95–107.

Wilhelms-Tricarico, R. (1995). Physiological modeling of speech production: Methods for modeling soft-tissue articulators. *Journal of the Acoustical Society of America*, *97*(5), 3085–3098.

Wilhelms-Tricarico, R. (2000). Development of a tongue and mouth floor model for normalization and biomechanical modelling. *Proceedings of the 5th speech production seminar and CREST workshop on models of speech production* (pp. 141–148). Kloster Seeon, Bavaria.

Zienkiewicz, O. C., & Taylor, R. L. (1994). *The finite element method* (4th ed.). New York: McGraw-Hill.

7

Prediction of Geometrical Vocal Tract Limits from Bony Landmarks

Modern Humans and Neandertalians

LOUIS-JEAN BOË, JEAN-LOUIS HEIM, DENIS AUTESSERRE, AND PIERRE BADIN

ABSTRACT

This work is part of a project in a quest of the origin of speech, and in particular aims to define possible speech prerequisites in the geometry, the musculature, and the control of the vocal tract. From classical bony landmarks of the head and jaw used in anthropology, we attempted to predict the geometric limits of the vocal tract for modern man and to apply these predictions to fossils, namely two famous Neandertal skulls: La Chapelle-aux-Saints and La Ferrassie. We defined the limits of the vocal tract by the lip extremities, pharyngeal wall, and glottis position, which are important for the prediction of the maximal acoustic space of the vocal tract. We developed a database of midsagittal X-ray images of 22 speakers uttering vowels. Then, we selected the optimal combination of the bony landmarks that predicts the vocal tract limits and yields the smallest prediction errors. A second database was constructed that included a diverse collection of 91 skulls from places spread over the world and displaying strongly diverse skull morphology. We measured, for all these modern skulls as well as for the two fossils, the bony landmarks used to predict the vocal tract limits in the first database. We found that the bony landmarks of the two fossil skulls are located near the border of the dispersion ellipses of the modern population sample. We conclude that we may predict what could have been the vocal tract limits and the hyoid bone position of the two Neandertal men.

INTRODUCTION

Mankind acquired the capability to speak as a result of anatomical and cognitive evolution. This work is part of a project that aims to define possible speech prerequisites for the geometry, the musculature, and the control of the vocal tract (Hombert, 2002; Schwartz, 2002). Do apes have a vocal tract disability, a cognitive incapability, or both? If vocal tract configuration plays an important role for speech emergence, can the study of skulls and mandibles of fossils enlighten us about the speech potentialities of our predecessors? These questions have raised terms by Lieberman and Crelin (1971) who postulated that the development of a low laryngeal position and of an enlarged pharyngeal cavity was a necessary condition for the realization of the maximal vowel contrasts existing between /a/, /i/, and /u/. In their view, Neandertals did not possess this "anatomical basis of speech" and therefore could not speak, presumably causing their extinction. We have already shown (Boë, Heim, Honda, & Maeda, 2002; Heim, Boë, & Abry, 2002) that the Lieberman theory could no longer be considered valid and that a low larynx (and large pharynx) cannot be considered to be the anatomical prerequisites for producing the full range of human speech. There is, therefore, no reason to believe that the lowering of the larynx and a concomitant increase in pharynx size are necessary evolutionary pre-adaptations for speech. The question of the emergence of speech is, however, more general and more complex. It concerns, among other things, the possibility that the evolution of the musculature of the tongue, or of the sensory innervation of the tongue–lip–palate systems could have provided a necessary basis for speech control. New observation tools of the anatomy and physiology of the orofacial system, together with the development of a new generation of articulatory and biomechanical models, will allow us to advance our knowledge about this first challenge.

In order to answer these questions, one should be able at least to reconstruct geometrical limits of the vocal tract from bony architecture. Using bony reference landmarks, we have attempted to predict palatal distance and laryngeal height. These two dimensions are important in that they reflect differences of sex, growth, stage of evolution (Boë, 1999; Boë et al., 2002; Honda & Tiede, 1998), and lead to the prediction of maximal acoustic space of the vocal tract (Boë, Perrier, Guerin, & Schwartz, 1989; Bonder, 1982). We evaluated the accuracy of this kind of reconstruction using head and neck (xero)radiographic images. This kind of images allows us to see the bony structure of the head and neck as well as soft tissues of the vocal tract. Thereafter, we will try to extrapolate our procedure to two famous Neandertal skulls: La Chapelle-aux-Saints (Boule, 1911, 1913; Heim, 1989, 1990) and La Ferrassie (Heim, 1976).

THE BONY STRUCTURES AND SOFT TISSUES

The vocal tract is essentially composed of muscles, membranes, ligaments, fibrous lamella, and adipose tissues. In manuals dealing with speech production, the laryngeal source and the vocal tract are described in terms of soft tissues without relating them to the bony architecture. The cervical vertebra (C1–C7) and hyoid bone, which are visible on X-ray images, are only referred to when it comes to describing the position of the larynx. But the hyoid bone is unique in that it is not directly attached to any other bone in the skeleton. Upper incisors constitute the only visible bony landmark for the upper part of the vocal tract, as are the lower incisors for mandible position. Goldstein's (1980) thesis exemplified for the first time the possibilities of predicting vocal tract dimensions from bony landmarks using data gathered from the medical literature. Her model incorporated data concerning influence of sex and growth on the vocal tract.

SELECTED LANDMARKS

For our prediction of the vocal tract dimensions, we have selected the following landmarks that are used in anthropology (Brothwell, 1994; Buikstra & Ublaker, 1994), radiology (Goldstein, 1980), orthodontics (Scheideman, Bell, Legan, Finn, & Reisch, 1980), and forensic analyses of the skull (Vignal, 1999; Yasar Iscan & Helmer, 1993) (Figure 7.1):

Atlas (the most anterior point of the tubercle of the): landmark of the first cervical.

Basion: the middle of the anterior margin of the great foramen of the skull.

Bregma: the point at the junction of the sagittal and coronal sutures at the top of the cranium.

Gonion: the most inferior, posterior, and lateral point of the external angle of mandible.

Incisors (upper and lower): landmarks for the delimitation of the anterior part of the vocal tract.

Infradental: the point of the superior alveolar process that project most anteriorly in the midline of the maxilla.

Inion: the most prominent point at the back of the head, just below the occipital protuberance.

Lambda: the junction of the sagittal and lamboid sutures of the skull.

Menton: the most inferior point of the chin in the sagittal plane (sometimes confused with gnathion).

Nasal spine (anterior): the tip of the bony anterior nasal spine at the inferior margin of the piriform aperture, in the midsagittal plane.

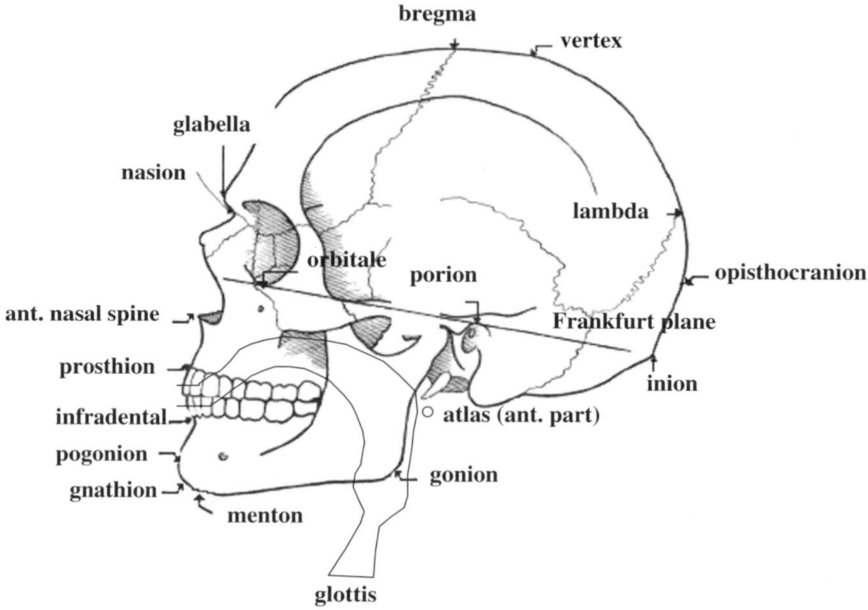

FIGURE 7.1. Anthropological landmarks.

Nasal spine (posterior): the most posterior point on the bony hard palate in the midsagittal plane; the meeting point between the inferior and the superior surfaces of the bony hard palate (nasal floor) at its posterior aspect.

Nasion: the depression at the root of the nose indicating the intersection of the internasal and frontonasal sutures, in the midsagittal plane.

Opisthion: the middle of the posterior, or dorsal, margin of the great foramen of the skull.

Opisthocranion: the point of the occiput that is the most distant from the glabella in the midsagittal plane.

Orbitale: the lowest point on the lower edge of the orbit.

Pogonion: the most anterior point of the chin in the sagittal plane.

Porion: the most superior point of the outline of the external auditory meatus. The line orbitale-porion allows to define the Frankfurt plane.

Prosthion: the point of the inferior alveolar process that project most anteriorly in the midline of the maxilla.

Sella turcica (centre of the): a transverse depression crossing the midline on the superior surface of the body of the sphenoid bone.

Vertex: the higher point of the skull in reference to the Frankfurt plane (nasion–orbitale).

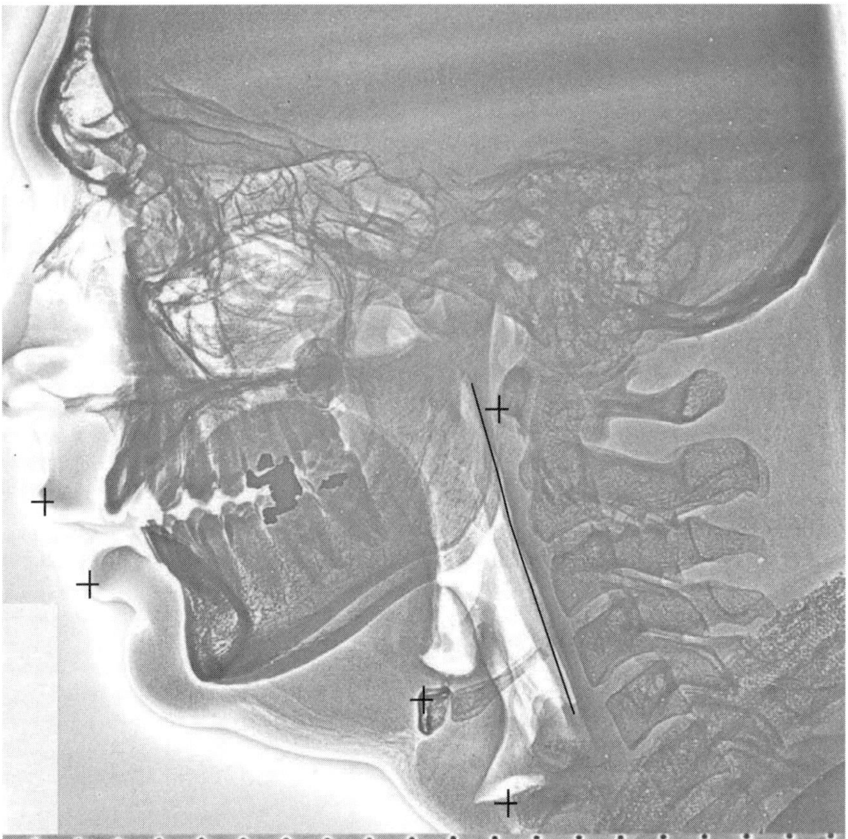

FIGURE 7.2. Xerography of an adult male uttering the /i/ vowel. The crosses and the line mark the extremities of the vocal tract (lips, pharyngeal wall, and glottis). The anterior part of the hyoid bone is a visible radiographic landmark associated to the larynx position.

For the purpose of reconstruction of the soft tissues delimiting the vocal tract from bony landmark, we added speech-related landmarks as follows (Figure 7.2):

Cervical vertebra (centre of the seven C1–C7): landmarks allowing to locate the position of the larynx.

Corporeal line: tangential line to the anterior part of cervical vertebra on which the pharyngeal wall is located.

Glottis: landmark for the delimitation of the inferior part of the vocal tract. In fact, the glottis is not identifiable on RX, only laryngeal ventricles are visible.

Hyoid bone (the most anterior point of the tubercle): visible radiographic landmark related to larynx position.
Lips (the most anterior point of the upper and lower lips): anterior extremity of the vocal tract.
Pharyngeal wall: the most posterior part of the pharynx.

XERORADIOGRAPHIC AND RADIOGRAPHIC DATABASE

Xeroradiography was well suited for visualizing bony, cartilaginous, and soft-tissue contours (Figure 7.2). It should be noted particularly that the hyoid bone, pharyngeal, and laryngeal regions, as well as the lip contours were clearly visible. Xeroradiography has since been replaced by scanners based on either X-rays or magnetic resonance. We used a part of a xeroradiographic database constituted by Denis Autesserre at the Marseille Hospital. This database contains a total of 89 high-quality images obtained from 15 French male and female adult speakers uttering sustained vowels and consonants (Autesserre et al., 1980). A second set of teleradiographic images was made at the Polyclinique de l'Essonne for a set of 22 French adult male and female subjects in rest position. All these images were digitized at ICP.

SOFTWARE

We developed *Craniomat* (Jaunais, 2000), a software tool that is specialized for skull measurements on photographic, radiographic, and MRI images. Depending on the nature of available images, the software suggests a list of landmarks that can be modified. Some landmarks are automatically determined (e.g., centre of the sella turcica from three points, glabella, and opisthocranion from a cubic spline contour), while others are acquired semi-automatically (gnathion, menton, and pogonion). Contours (mandible, corporeal line, and pharyngeal wall) are also smoothed by cubic spline interpolations. A zoom function allows the accuracy and the reliability of all the points to be increased. Altogether, the software can deliver 41 landmark coordinates, 40 distances between landmarks, 17 angles between reference planes, and 5 indices (ratios between distances). A series of evaluations allowed us to compare (1) the distances measured by the Craniomat software and those that we could obtain directly from skulls; and (2) the differences in locating landmarks between the three experts. In order to assess the accuracy of the measurements obtained by means of the Craniomat software, we have chosen the nasion–opisthocranion distance as a reference. We have compared the measures of this distance obtained with an anthropologic calliper rule for 42 skulls, with those obtained with Craniomat from photographs of the same skulls. This distance ranges between 155 and 190 mm for our set of adults; the absolute difference between the two methods of measurement reaches 4.30 mm, with an average of 1.40 mm, which amounts to 0.85% of the mean distance. We also assessed the variability related to the manual pointing: The absolute difference between all the landmarks determined with Craniomat for one skull by three different experts reaches a maximum of 2.65 mm, with a mean of 0.42 mm.

We began by predicting glottis and hyoid bone positions, and the pharyngeal wall and external lip extremities from bony landmarks. We selected as a reference the line through the nasion and sella turcica NSL, which is clearly visible on all X-ray images.

TRAINING AND PREDICTION OF LIMITS OF THE VOCAL TRACT FOR MODERN MAN

We defined the limits of the vocal tract by the lip extremities, pharyngeal wall, and glottis position. We wanted to predict these extremities as a linear combination of a selection among the measured bony landmarks. To test the possible occurrence of overlearning of the matrix of linear coefficients, we used a method inspired by the Jackknife test (Efron & Gong, 1983). For each of the 22 skulls taken one by one, we computed the prediction of the associated soft-tissue landmarks as a linear combination of the bony landmarks by multilinear regression on the remaining set of 21 skulls, for all the combinations of the available bony landmarks. We determined the best number and the best combination of bony landmark predictors that yield the smallest prediction errors. We observed the well-known phenomenon of overlearning in this kind of situation: Increasing the number of predictors decreases both the learning and test errors, but beyond a certain number (two or three in our case), the learning errors keep decreasing whereas test errors increase. Table 7.1 presents the best bony landmarks that predict the vocal tract extremities, and Table 7.2 the minimal training and prediction errors (in mm) for landmarks useful to reconstruct the vocal tract extremities. When assessing the size of errors, it is crucial to keep in mind that the set constituted by the hyoid bone and the larynx does not stay in a fixed position during phonation, but moves vertically. These height variations are due to the influence of muscles that control the positioning of the larynx, and, in a more indirect way contribute to the tongue displacement and jaw opening/closing movements (Beautemps et al., 2001). Hoole and Kroos (1998) report a range of variation of 7 mm for the vertical position of the larynx between rounded and nonrounded vowels (/y/ and /i/). During an utterance, the activity of the muscles that raise and lower this structure can also vary with the tension of the vocal folds: When the vocal fold vibration frequency increases, the larynx is observed to rise vertically (Faaborg-Andersen & Sonninen, 1960). Beautemps et al. (2001) have also observed for one speaker that the hyoid bone

TABLE 7.1. The Landmarks Related to the Vocal Tract to be Predicted and the Best Predictors

Landmarks of the vocal tract to be predicted	Bony landmarks Best predictors	Remarks
The most anterior part of upper and lower lips	Anterior nasal spine (x) Glabella (x) Orbitale (x)	Reflecting neighbouring relationships
Atlas and pharyngeal wall	Posterior nasal spine (x, y) Porion (y)	Reflecting neighbouring relationships Importance of the inclination of head
The most anterior part of hyoid bone (horizontal position x)	Nasion (x) Pogonion (x) Orbitale (x)	Reflecting skull size, jaw position, and dimension (sex related)
The most anterior part of hyoid bone (vertical position y)	Orbitale (x) Gonion (y) Pogonion (y)	Reflecting skull size, jaw position, and dimension (sex related)
The horizontal position of glottis (laryngeal ventricle)	Glabella (y) Gonion (x)	Reflecting skull size, jaw position, and dimension (sex related)
The vertical position of glottis (laryngeal ventricle)	Posterior nasal spine (y) Gonion (y)	Reflecting skull size, jaw position, and dimension (sex related)

TABLE 7.2. Mean of the Absolute Errors of Prediction and Standard Deviation (in mm) for Training and Prediction

	Training		Prediction	
(mm)	Mean	S.D.	Mean	S.D.
Upper lip (horizontal extremity)	3.7	5.7	6.6	9.3
Lower lip (horizontal extremity)	2.3	3.4	7.6	8.9
Atlas (anterior extremity)	2.3	3.0	3.4	4.2
Hyoid bone (vertical position)	4.3	5.8	12	15
Glottis (vertical position)	5.1	7.8	14	17

and the larynx can move vertically by ±6 mm around their average positions for short speech sequences (Figure 7.3).

Table 7.3 presents the range of data (difference between minimum and maximum observed values) and the mean of the absolute errors of prediction for our 22 subjects. These results confirm that it is possible to predict the extremities of the vocal tract (lips, pharyngeal wall, and glottis) and the position

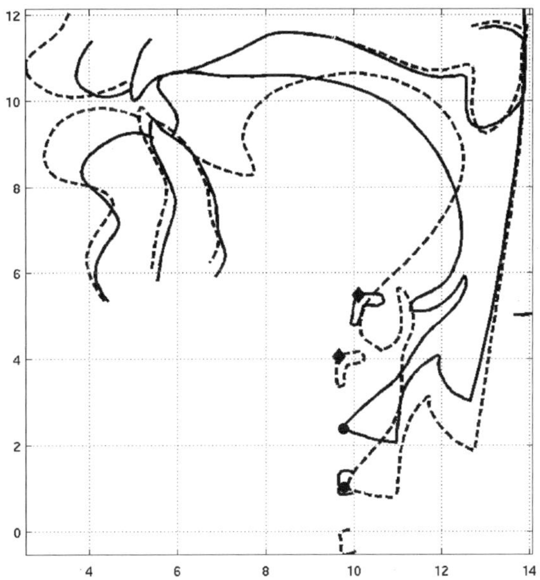

FIGURE 7.3. Two midsagittal curves drawn from cineradiographic data (50 frames per second): /d/ extracted from a /da/ syllable (solid line), /u/ extracted from a /bu/ syllable (dashed line). A variation of about 1.5 cm of the vertical position of the hyoid bone and vocal cords can be observed (Beautemps et al., 2001).

of hyoid bone given the bony structure dispersion of bony landmarks selected for predicting vocal tract limits.

The aim of the second part of the study was two-fold:

1. To evaluate the dispersion of the bony landmarks selected as the best predictors of the vocal tract extremities and of the hyoid bone position in four modern populations (I, XVII, and XIX centuries) spread over the world surface and displaying strongly diverse skull morphology.
2. To assess whether the landmarks of the two Neandertals (La Chapelle-aux-Saints and La Ferrassie) belong to these distributions.

TABLE 7.3. Range of Data and the Mean of the Absolute Errors of Prediction for 22 Subjects

	Range of the vertical position (mm)	Mean error of prediction (mm)
Hyoid bone	44	12
Glottis	50	14

Table 7.4 presents the name of the populations, their geographic location, the period of the selected skulls, the origin of collections, the number of skulls and their principal morphological differences. Figure 7.4 displays five skulls corresponding to our selection.

We began by making measurements from digital photographs of the skulls. The coordinates of the bony landmarks were determined with the help of the Craniomat software by three of the authors (D. Autessere, L. J. Boë, and J. L. Heim). In order to obtain the position of the posterior nasal spine, which is not

TABLE 7.4. The Name of the Populations, their Geographic Location, the Period of the Selected Skulls, the Origin of Collections, the Number of Skulls, and their Principal Morphological Differences

Population	Geographic origin	Period	Source	Number of skulls	Morphological characteristics
Toucouleur, Mandingue, Malinke (Maninka)	West Africa Mali Senegal Guinea	XVIII–XIX centuries	Musée de l'Homme, Paris	11	Constant dolichocephaly, skull slenderness, moderate prognathism, receding chin
Mongolian: Tchouktchi, Bouriate	Asia, Mongolia Ourga (Oulan Bator), Kobdo, Gobi desert	XIX century	Doctor Chazaud and Dumoutier collections Musée de l'Homme, Paris	15	Dominant brachicephaly, skull robustness, weak prognathism, flattening-out of the face, high cheekbones
Australian, Tasmanian	Australia Tasmania	XIX century	Dumont d'Urville and Dumoutier collections Musée de l'Homme, Paris	16	Marked skull robustness, important prognathism, receding chin
Egyptian	Egypt (Kharga: Libyan desert)	Around the first century (Roman period)	Heim and Boë scientific expedition in Kharga	31	Mediterranean type, mesocephaly, weak to marked prognathism, jutting chin
Neandertal La Chapelle-aux-Saints La Ferrassie	France Périgord	45,000 years BP (Before Present)	Musée de l'Homme, Paris	2	Neandertalian type, developed face, archaic features of the skull

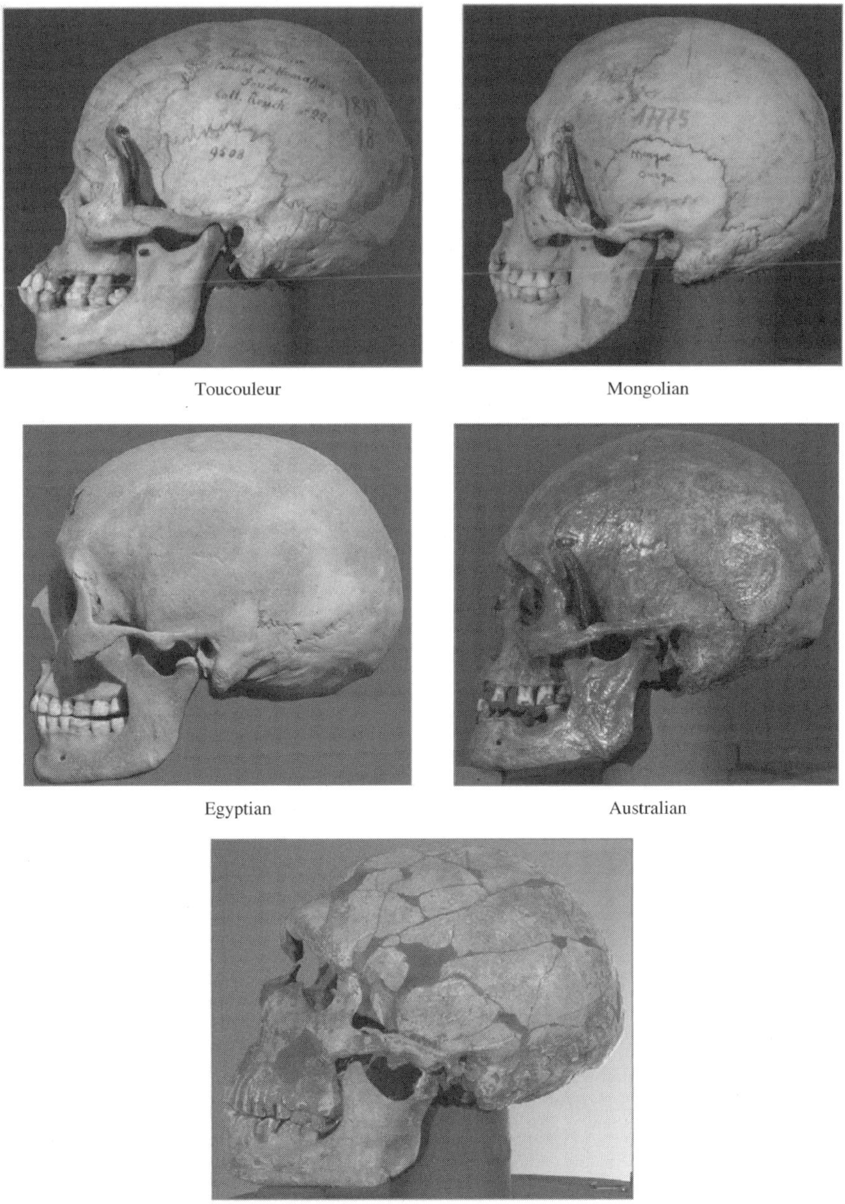

Toucouleur

Mongolian

Egyptian

Australian

Neandertal (La Ferrassie)

FIGURE 7.4. Photographs of modern men displaying morphological diversity, and of a Neandertal fossil.

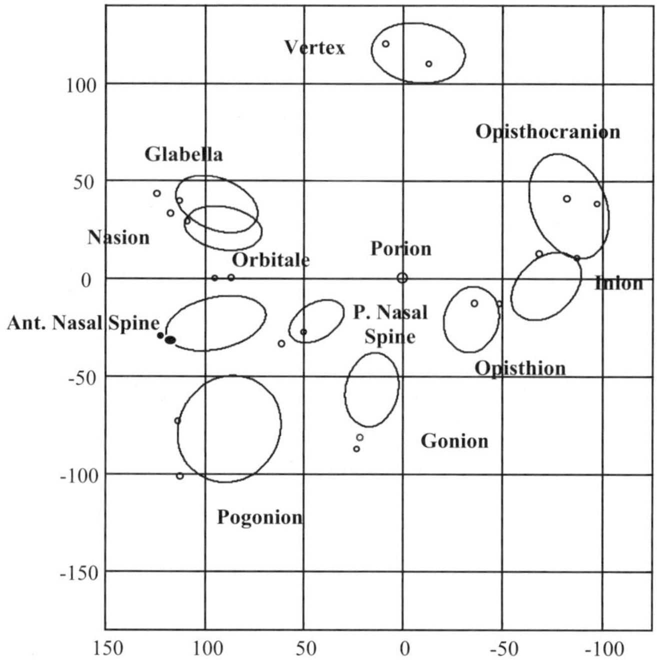

FIGURE 7.5. Ellipses of dispersion (±2.5 S.D.) of the bony landmarks for all modern skulls in the orbitale–porion coordinate space (in mm). The dots correspond to the two Neandertal men.

visible on the photographs, we used three distances manually measured on each skull between this point on the one hand and the anterior nasal spine, the nasion, and the bregma on the other. The dispersion ellipses (±2.5 S.D.) of the bony landmark points used as predictors for the vocal tract extremities and for the hyoid bone position are also presented in Figure 7.5 in the same coordinate space (orbitale, porion). One can observe that the bony landmarks of the two Neandertal men are located near the border of the dispersion ellipses of the population sample.

We can thus consider that the predictions concerning the vocal tract extremities and the hyoid bone position also apply to the two Neandertal skulls.

CONCLUSION AND PERSPECTIVES

The first part of the study has shown that it is possible to predict the vocal tract extremities and the hyoid bone position in the midsagittal plane from bony landmarks of the skull and jaw: glabella, nasion, anterior and posterior nasal spine, orbitale, porion, gonion, and pogonion. The data for training and testing were extracted from a database of X-ray images of modern living speakers. A second database was constructed that included a diverse collection of skulls from very different parts of the world. We have shown that the bony landmarks used for the predictions, are located, for two Neandertal skulls, within—though near the border of—the dispersion ellipses corresponding to this world population. We concluded that the prediction rules extracted from this modern population could thus be applied to these two Neandertals. Future research should aim to establish such predictions for other Palaeolithic fossils available at the Musée de l'Homme in Paris. These skulls, that are all well kept and possess a jaw, cover a period between 10,000 and 35,000 years BP (Before Present): Chancelade (12,000 years BP), Obercassel 2, Saint-Germain-La-Rivière, and Cap Blanc (12,000–15,000 years BP), Le Rond-du-Barry (17,000 years BP), Abri Pataud (18,000–20,000 years BP), Cromagon 1 (25,000 years BP), and Combe-Capelle (35,000 years BP). Another point of interest will be to verify whether similar measurements obtained from great apes (Dean & Wood, 2003) fall within or beyond the same dispersion ellipses.

ACKNOWLEDGMENTS

The first set of radiographic data has been acquired courtesy of Professor Chevrot and Dr. Sarrat, from the *Service Central de Radiologie Adulte* of the *CHU de la Timone*, Marseille, France. The second set of X-ray images are courtesy of Fleur Letellier-Willemin, Eric Seneterre, and Muriel Sahin, *Polyclinique de l'Essonne*, France. Philippe Mennecier, Director of the collections at the *Musée de l'Homme*, Paris, France, has kindly granted us access to all the skulls. The Egyptian skull collection has been collected by Françoise Dunand, Head of the scientific society *AlphaNecropolis* and Head of the French scientific expeditions in Kharga, Egypt. Alain Arnal has manufactured the device for the skull photographs. The Craniomat software has been developed with the help of Dimitry Obolensky, Christophe de la Brouhe, Thomas Mazur, Servan Riaud, Philippe Jaunais, Laurent Cavazzana, Sylvain Ogier, and Hassen Khenissi. Fleur Letellier-Willemin (radiologist), Roger Lichtenberg (radiologist), and Patricia Soto-Heim (anthropologist) helped us to test and improve it. Jean-Luc Schwartz and Gordon Ramsay advised us on statistical processing.

This research has been partly funded by the French CNRS (*Contrôle oro-facial dans la communication chez les primates humains et non humains: Neandertal, le singe et l'Homme*) project (managed by Jean-Luc Schwartz, ICP, since 2001), within the *Origine de l'Homme du Langage et des Langues* (OHLL) project (managed by Jean-Marie Hombert), and by the European Community EUROCORES program (*Orofacial control in communication in human and non human primates*) (principal investigator, Didier Demolin, Phonology Laboratory, Brussels, since 2002), within *The Origin of Man, Language and Languages* (OMLL project).

Finally, we are also very much indebted to Jonathan Harrington for his very careful review of the manuscript.

REFERENCES

Autesserre, D., Rossi, M., Sarrat, P., Giraud, G., Visquis, R., Demange, R., & Chevrot, L. (1980). Contrôle radiologique de l'oropharynx, de l'hypopharynx et du larynx en phonation. In *Larynx et Parole* (pp. 47–73). Grenoble: Institut de Phonétique.

Beautemps, D., Badin, P., & Bailly, G. (2001). Linear degrees of freedom in speech production: Analysis of cineradio- and labio-film data and articultory-acoustic modeling. *Journal of the Acoustical Society of America*, 109, 2165–2180.

Boë, L. J. (1999). Modelling the growth of the vocal tract vowel spaces of newly-born infants and adults: Consequences for ontogenesis and phylogenesis. *Proceedings of the 14th international congress of phonetic sciences* (Vol. 3, pp. 2501–2504).

Boë, L. J., Heim, J.-L, Honda, K., & Maeda, S. (2002). The potential Neandertal vowel space was as large as that of modern humans. *Journal of Phonetics*, *30*, 465–484.

Boë, L. J., Perrier, P., Guerin, B., & Schwartz, J. L. (1989). Maximal vowel space. *Eurospeech*, *2*, 281–284.

Bonder, L. J. (1982). The n-tube formula and some of its consequenses. *Acustica*, *52*, 216–226.

Boule, M. (1911, 1913). L'Homme fossile de La Chapelle-aux-Saints. *Annales de Paléontologie Humaine*, *6*, 111–172; *7*, 21–56, 85–172; *8*, 1–70.

Brothwell, D. R. (1994). *Digging up bones*. Ithaca: Cornell University Press.

Buikstra, J. E., & Ublaker, D. H. (1994). *Standards for data collection from human skeletal remains*. Archeological Survey, series, 44, Arkansas, Fayetteville.

Dean, C., & Wood, B. (2003). In L. Bondioli & R. Macchiarelly (Eds.), *A digital radiographic atlas of great apes. Skull and dentition*. Digital Archives of Human Paleobiology (Vol. 3). Rome: National Museum of Prehistory and Ethnography "Luigi Pigorni".

Efron, B., & Gong, G. (1983). A leisurely look at the bootstrap, the jackknife, and cross-validation. *The American Statistician*, 37(1), 36–48.

Faaborg-Andersen, K., & Sonninen, A. (1960). The function of extrinsic laryngeal muscles at different pitch. *Acta Oto-Laryngologica*, 51, 8–93.

Goldstein, U. G. (1980). *An articulatory model for the vocal tract of the growing children*. Ph.D. thesis, MIT, Cambridge, MA.

Heim, J. L. (1976). Les Hommes fossiles de La Ferrassie. *Archives de l'Institut de Paléontologie Humaine*, Mémoire (Vol. 35, p. 332), 8 planches. Paris: Masson.

Heim, J. L. (1989). Une nouvelle reconstitution du crâne néandertalien de la Chapelle-aux-Saints. *Compte Rendu de l'Académie des Sciences de Paris*, *308*(II), 1187–1192.

Heim, J. L. (1990). La nouvelle reconstitution du crâne néandertalien de la Chapelle-aux-Saints. Méthode et résultats. *Bulletins et Mémoires de la Société d'Anthropologie de Paris, 1*, 1–2, 95–118.

Heim, J. L., Boë, L. J., & Abry, C. (2002). La parole à la portée du conduit vocal de l'Homme de Neandertal. Nouvelles recherches, nouvelles perspectives. *Compte-Rendu à l'Académie des Sciences, Palevol. Paléontologie humaine et préhistoire*, *1*, *2*, 129–134.

Hombert, J. M. (2002). *Origine de l'Homme, du Langage et des Langues*. Rapports scientifiques de fin de deuxième année 2001–2002. CNRS, Paris.

Honda, K., & Tiede, M. K. (1998). An MRI study on the relationship between oral cavity shape and larynx position. *Proceedings of the 5th international conference on spoken language processing* (Vol. 2, pp. 437–440).

Hoole, P., & Kroos, C. (1998). Control of larynx height in vowel production. In R. H. Mannell & J. Robert-Ribes, (Eds.), *Proceedings of the 5th international conference on spoken language processing*, Sydney (Vol. 2, pp. 531–534).

Jaunais, P. (2002). *Acquisition de données craniométriques*, Rapport de stage, ENSERG, Grenoble.

Lieberman, P., & Crelin, E. S. (1971). On the speech of the Neanderthal man. *Linguistic Inquiry*, 2, 203–222.

Scheideman, G. B., Bell, W. H., Legan, H. L., Finn, R. A., & Reisch, J. S. (1980). Cephalometric analysis of dentofacials normals. *American Journal of Orthodontics*, 78(4), 404–420.

Schwartz, J. L. (2002). Contrôle oro-facial dans la communication chez les primates humains et non-humains: Néandertal, le singe et l'Homme. In J. M. Hombert (Ed.), *Origine de l'Homme, du Langage et des Langues* (pp. 191–198). Centre National de la Recherche Scientifique.

Vignal, J. N. (1999). *Les reconstitutions faciales assistées par ordinateur*. Paris: Artcom.

Yasar Iscan, M., & Helmer, R. P. (Eds.). (1993). *Forensic analysis of the skull*. New York: Wiley-Liss. Inc.

8

A Physiologically Based Model of Perioral Dynamics for Various Lip Deformations in Speech Articulation

HIROAKI GOMI, JYUNICHI NOZOE, JIANWU DANG, AND KIYOSHI HONDA

ABSTRACT

Elastic lip shape greatly varies in order to control speech sounds. We introduce a lip-dynamics model for exploring speech articulatory movements. The shapes of the lip-rounding muscle (orbicularis oris), jaw and maxillar bones, and skin surface were extracted from three-dimensional magnetic resonance imaging (MRI) data, and then the locations of the perioral muscles were defined based on the MRI data. To represent fine deformation patterns of lip shape, the orbicularis oris muscle was subdivided into eight regions. Nine perioral muscles and five jaw muscles were implemented to reproduce large lip deformation. Muscle dynamics consist of a force generator and visco-elastic components, and all passive dynamics are represented by a mass–spring meshed network. This model enables us to reproduce dynamical perioral movements by specifying arbitrary muscle inputs. Using this model, we have succeeded in reproducing lip protrusion only by activating peripheralis parts of the upper and lower lip muscles, the possibility of which was predicted by a previous EMG study. We also demonstrate other natural lip deformations obtained from several muscle activation patterns and discuss the important aspects of modeling studies for understanding the mechanisms of speech motor control.

INTRODUCTION

Lip shape, along with tongue shape, greatly affects speech utterances. For example, lip constriction modifies sound resonance in voiced phonemes and regulates airflow in fricative and stop consonants; lip protrusion changes vocal tract length, which also affects sound resonance (e.g., Stevens, 1999). An understanding of the mechanisms governing lip deformation is important because it will help us reveal the underlying control principles of speech production.

Owing to the complexity of muscle interdigitation and three-dimensional (3D) deformation of lip soft tissue, analytical studies (Abbs, Gracco, & Blair, 1984; Blair & Smith, 1986; Ho, Azar, Weinstein, & Bowley, 1982; Honda, Kurita, Kakita, & Maeda, 1995; Muller, Milenkovic, & MacLeod, 1985) have had limited success accessing the details of lip movement and its control mechanisms. Actually, recording the activities of each of the muscles surrounding the perioral region without signal contamination from other muscles is technically unrealistic because these muscles are highly interwoven with each other. Although recent technical advances in magnetic resonance imaging (MRI) (Takemoto et al., 2003) enable us to animate the lip internal structure, the temporal and spatial resolutions of MRI are still insufficient for observing precise and quick movements around the perioral region.

An efficient way to overcome the difficulties in investigating lip deformation mechanisms by analytical approaches may be to synthetically reproduce lip movements using a 3D physiological model of the orofacial system. Dynamical models of the tongue, the other elastic articulatory organ, whose shape is also determined by multiple muscle interactions, have been developed in several studies (Dang & Honda, 2001; Engwall, 2003; Kakita, Fujimura, & Honda, 1985; Kiritani, Miyawaki, Fujimura, & Miller, 1976; Perkell, 1974; Wilhelms-Tricarico, 1995). The most sophisticated approach to precisely describe elastic tissue deformation was proposed by Wilhelms-Tricarico (1995), but that method requires much more computation than the mass–spring method (Dang & Honda, 2001). The high computational cost can be greatly reduced by decomposing shape using a principal components analysis (Engwall, 2003), but describing the physical interactions among articulators may be difficult.

On the other hand, several facial models have been developed (King, 2001; Lucero & Munhall, 1999; Terzopoulos & Waters, 1993) for animating facial expressions. However, precise muscle mechanisms for lip deformation were not implemented, mainly because of the limited knowledge about these mechanisms, and therefore fine 3D lip deformations cannot be performed. Developing a model that can perform more realistic deformations may require the implementation of precise muscle mechanisms based on detailed knowledge of the arrangements of the perioral muscles and their functional compartmentalization.

To investigate the mechanisms of lip articulation, we have developed a lip dynamics model using 3D-MRI data and mass–spring meshed network previously used for modeling tongue dynamics (Dang & Honda, 2001) and facial dynamics (Terzopoulos & Waters, 1993). The lip region, including the orbicularis oris muscle and soft tissue, is represented by a mass–spring meshed network, and the nine perioral muscles connecting the lip with the maxillar or the mandibular bone and five jaw muscles are implemented for deforming lip shape. The multiple node positions representing lip deformation were obtained by solving a discrete second-order dynamical equation. We will demonstrate several lip deformation patterns and synthetically test a hypothesis of protrusion shaping only by activating the peripheralis part of lip muscles.

METHODS

MRI Data

We used two sets of MRI data from one male subject (51-year-old Japanese native who is not one of the authors): High-resolution MRI data of the orofacial region (boxel size: 0.25 × 0.25 × 0.5 mm; area: 128 × 128 × 106 mm; RF-FAST: TE=6.71 ms; TR=13 ms), from which we investigated the details of perioral muscles; and low-resolution MRI data of the whole head region (boxel size: 0.5 × 0.5 × 1.00 mm, area: 256 × 256 × 180 mm, RF-FAST, TE = 4.47 ms, TR = 13 ms), from which we extracted the geometric features of the maxillar and the jaw bones. Both sets of data were obtained using a Shimazu–Marconi Magnex Eclipse 1.5 T. The 3D-MRI data sets were interpolated to reconstruct different slice images, and image contrast was adjusted appropriately to enhance muscle shapes and bone or skin surface in each modeling process.

Geometrical Modeling of the Perioral Region

Figure 8.1a shows a parasagittal plane image of MRI data around the perioral region, including the upper and lower lips and tongue tip (mid-right part). In this image, the OOS (orbicularis oris superior) and the OOI (orbicularis oris inferior) muscles appear as white J-shaped regions in the upper and lower lips, respectively. The long part of the J-shape is called the peripheralis, and the curved tip part closer to the oral cavity is called the marginalis.

To model the structure of the perioral region with a wire frame, we allocated nine nodes in the vertical (Y) direction and five nodes in the front-back (X) direction for the upper and lower lips, respectively, as shown in Figure 8.1a. The nodes in the first and fifth layers (thin white lines in the figure) represent the skin and the internal mucosal surface, respectively, and the nodes in the intermediate three layers were placed at the borders of image intensity change to represent the orbicularis oris muscles.

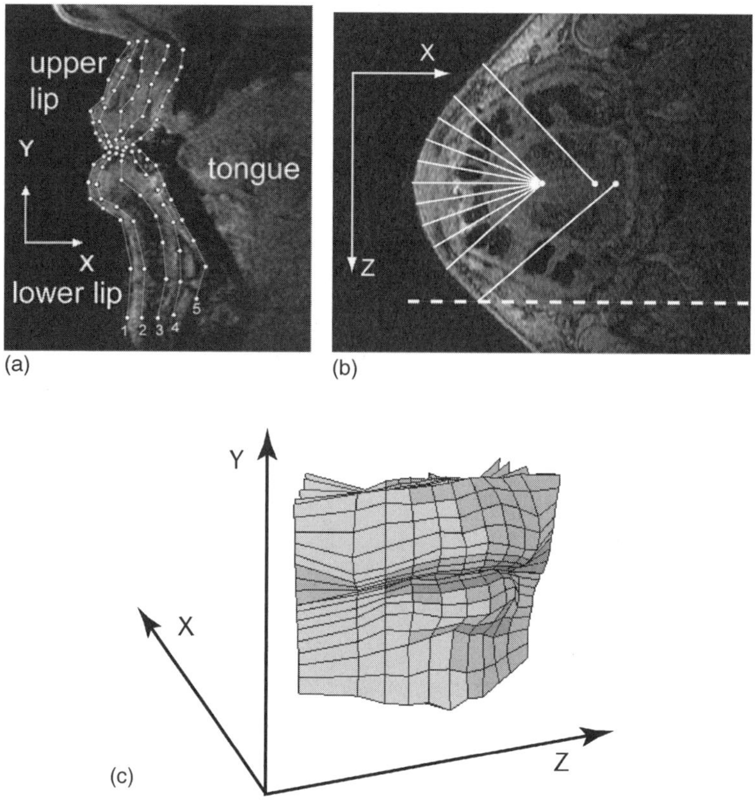

FIGURE 8.1. (a) MRI data of the parasagittal plane (*XY* plane). Each white dot denotes the arranged node-location for modeling. The thin white lines that connect nodes denote the depth layers (1–5) of the perioral region. (b) Transversal MRI image (*XZ* plane) around the upper lip. The 11 solid lines denote the locations of the reconstructed section planes in the vertical direction for arranging mesh nodes for modeling. The dotted line denotes a sample of the original sagittal plane around the corner of the mouth at which muscle cross-sectional area is hard to identify. (c) Wire-frame model extracted from defined nodes on 11 section planes. The frontal mesh plane represents the skin surface.

Figure 8.1b shows a horizontal section of the MRI around the upper lip. Because the MR image in the sagittal plane around the corner of the mouth (indicated by the dashed line) is not perpendicular to the skin nor to the muscle fibers, it is difficult to identify the inside border of the perioral soft tissue and discriminate muscle regions in the image. To solve these problems, 11 new slice images (from the left to the right corner of the mouth) were reconstructed from 3D-MRI data so as to allocate the mesh nodes perpendicular to the skin and the orbicularis oris muscle fibers. The 11 solid white lines on a horizontal MR image in

Figure 8.1b indicate the locations of the reconstructed vertical slice planes. The mesh nodes were specified on each image by the procedure explained above.

Figure 8.1c shows the 3D wire-frame model of the upper and lower lips constructed by the mesh nodes extracted in the above procedure. In total, 990 (18 × 11 × 5) nodes make up the skin surface layer and the four inside layers, and each node is connected to the adjacent nodes (except the oral cavity) by viscoelastic components that represent passive soft tissue (dermis, hypodermis, etc.).

Geometrical Modeling of Muscle Arrangement

Orbicularis Oris Muscles. It was once believed that the oral fissure was surrounded by one elliptical muscle (like a sphincter) as frequently depicted in anatomy textbooks. Further inspections revealed that the orbicularis oris muscle is functionally separated into several parts: marginal and peripheral, superior and inferior, and left and right (Blair, 1986; Goffman & Smith, 1994; Kennedy & Abbs, 1979; Wohlert & Goffman, 1994). Additionally, an EMG study (Honda et al., 1995) suggested that the marginalis and peripheralis parts of the orbicularis oris muscles are functionally distinct from each other in forming various lip shapes, such as protrusion and rounding.

Following the recent anatomical literature (e.g., Blair, 1986; Choquet, Sick, & Constantinesco, 1999; Salmons, 1999), we represented the peripheralis muscle contours of the OOS and OOI in each slice plane mainly by the nodes of the third and fourth layers, and the marginalis muscle contour mainly by the nodes in the second and third layers as shown in Figure 8.2a. Using these mesh nodes, orbicularis oris muscle fiber bundles were represented by connecting the nodes on the adjacent slice planes as shown in Figures 8.2b and 8.2c. The upper part of the upper lip and the lower part of the lower lip represent peripheralis muscles in the OOS and OOI, respectively. The lines connecting the 11 section surfaces around the oral fissure represent marginalis muscle fiber bundles. According to the above-mentioned studies, we functionally divided the orbicularis oris muscle into eight portions.

Perioral Muscles. The nine orofacial muscles connected to the perioral region [zygomaticus minor (ZMIN) and major (ZMAJ), levator labii superioris (LLS), levator labii superioris alaeque nasi (LLSAN), levator anguli oris (LAO), buccinator (BUC), mentalis (MENT), depressor labii inferioris (DLI), and depressor anguli oris (DAO)] contributing to lip shape configuration were modeled by direct linkages between the muscle origin and several nodes of the lip wire frame as shown in Figure 8.3a (in the separate color plate section). Since the insertion of these muscles into the lip regions is quite complex and since the muscles interdigitate (Blair, 1986; Blair & Smith, 1986; Kennedy & Abbs, 1979), it was not possible to identify the specific insertion positions of these muscles from MRI data. Instead, we arranged the insertion positions of these

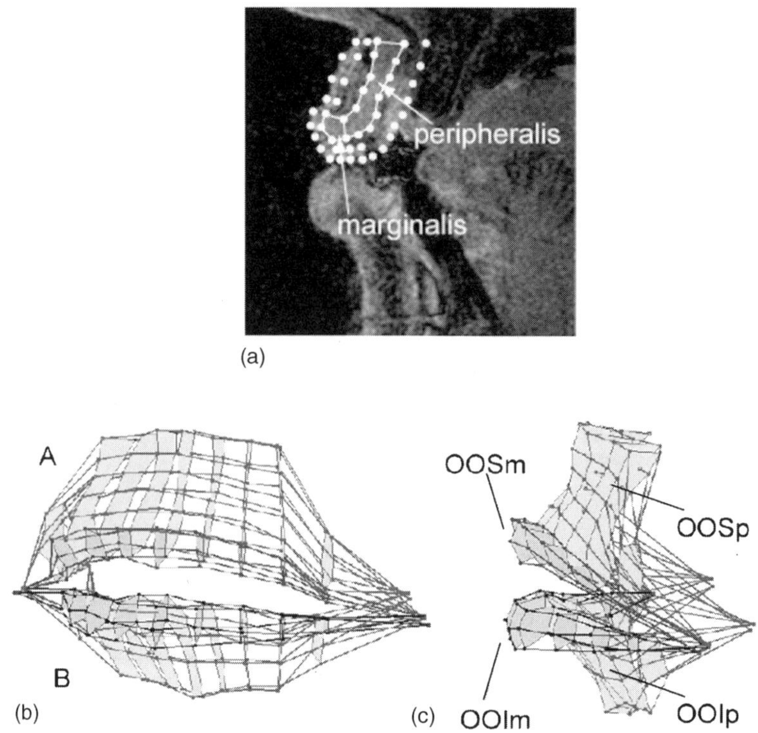

FIGURE 8.2. (a) Node arrangement for the peripheralis and marginalis parts of the OOS muscle. (b) Wire-frame model of the orbicularis oris muscles. (c) Its side view. Upper and lower parts are OOS (A) and OOI (B), respectively. Thin lines transversal to the 11 section surfaces around the oral fissure denote the muscle fiber bundles of the marginalis part of orbicularis oris muscles (OOSm and OOIm). Transversal lines around the upper region of the OOS and bottom region of the OOI denote the muscle fiber bundles of the peripheralis part of orbicularis oris muscles (OOSp and OOIp).

muscles based on previous anatomical observations (Kennedy & Abbs, 1979). The number of muscle linkages for each muscle was defined according to each muscle's width.

As shown in Figure 8.3a, the models of the ZMIN, ZMAJ, LLS, LLSAN, DLI, and DAO muscles are connected at the nodes in the third layer of the wire frame model because these muscles are inserted into the superficial part of the lip region (Kennedy & Abbs, 1979). The BUC and LAO muscles are connected at the nodes on the fourth layer because they are deep muscles. The MENT muscle connects the nodes on the second layer and on the bone. The positions of these muscle origins were specified on the bone surface reconstructed from the MRI data (explained below) as shown in Figure 8.3b (in the separate color plate section) based on anatomical studies and inspections of actual MRI data.

Jaw and Jaw Muscle Arrangement Modeling. The MRI image intensity of the maxillar and the mandibular bones were first emphasized, and then the polygon surfaces shown in Figures 8.3b and 8.4, respectively, were extracted from the MRI data by using commercial software (RapidForm). To obtain a high-resolution representation of the shape of the teeth, dental plaster casts of the subject were scanned with a 3D laser scanner (ShapeGrabber), and then these surfaces were connected to the surfaces of the maxillar and the mandibular bones, respectively.

To represent jaw dynamics, we defined the four nodes at around the mental protuberance, condylar process, coronoid process, and mandible angle based on the extracted mandibular bone shape (see Figure 8.4), according to the study by Dang and Honda (2001). Each jaw node has mass and was connected to the

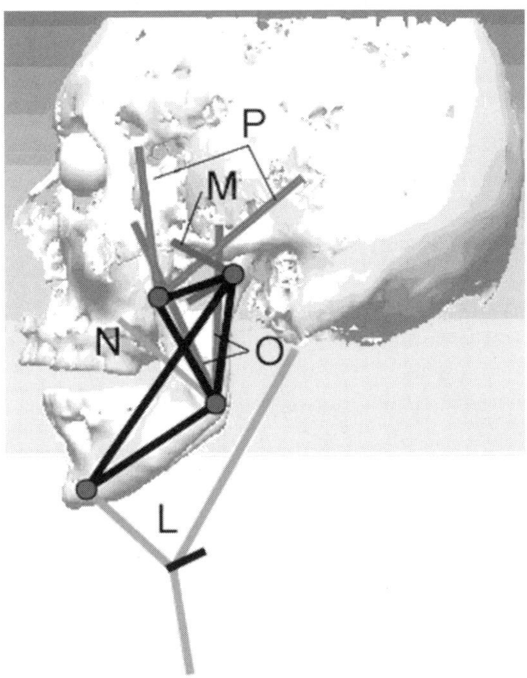

FIGURE 8.4. Maxillar and mandibular bones (side view), simplified jaw model (thick black lines), and the following jaw opening/closing muscles (thick gray lines with letters): digastric (ant. and post.) and sternohyoid (L), lateral pterygoid (M), masseter (N), medial pterygoid (O), and temporalis (P).

other jaw nodes by rigid beams. This jaw model is vertically placed between the actual left and right condylar processes. We also modeled the muscles connecting the maxillar and the mandibular bones (i.e., for jaw opening, the anterior and posterior digastric, sternohyoid, and lateral pterygoid; for jaw closing, the temporalis, masseter, and medial pterygoid) as shown in Figure 8.4. The origin and insertion of each muscle were located on the same vertical plane as in the simplified jaw model, while their sagittal locations were defined based on an anatomy textbook (Salmons, 1999) and actual MRI data.

Dynamics Representation

Lip, Jaw, and Muscle Dynamics. In the present model, the perioral passive dynamics of all nodes that represent all soft tissue and muscles are described by masses and viscoelastic elements, and the rigid body dynamics of the jaw bone are represented by masses and hard springs as in the tongue model (Dang & Honda, 2001). Note that each node was connected to neighboring nodes (7–26 points). Accordingly, all dynamics can be described by a second-order dynamical equation as follows:

$$M\ddot{X}(t) + B\dot{X}(t) + KX(t) = F(t) \tag{8.1}$$

Here, X, $\dot{X}$, $\ddot{X}$ and F denote the position, velocity, acceleration, and force vectors of the nodes, respectively. In the present model, vector size (i.e., number of nodes) is 2895×1. Matrices M, B, and K denote the mass, viscosity, and stiffness of the perioral dynamics. The mass value of each node representing lip soft tissue is calculated from the volumes in the vicinity of the corresponding node (see Dang & Honda, 2001). Since the elements in the matrices B and K are state dependent variables, this model has time-varying linear dynamics. In calculating K, the following equation was used for representing an elastic linkage between nodes in the Cartesian space:

$$k_{3i+u,3i+v} = \sum_{j=1}^{jn} kk_{ij} \cdot r_{ij}(u) \cdot r_{ij}(v),\ k_{3j+u,3i+u} = kk_{ij} \cdot r_{ij}(u) \cdot r_{ij}(v) \tag{8.2a}$$

$$u = 0,1,2, \quad v = 0,1,2 \tag{8.2b}$$

where $k_{i,j}$ is the stiffness value of the (i, j) element in the stiffness matrix K, kk_{ij} denotes the stiffness component of the linkage between node i and node j, $r_{ij}(u)$ the direction cosine from node i to node j, and u=0 for the x direction, 1 for the y direction, and 2 for the z direction. For the viscosity matrix B, the same decomposition was applied.

The unit mass for nodes was set at 1.0 g/cm^3, and the mandibular bone mass was set at 152 g, as in Dang and Honda (2001). The modulus of stiffness and modulus of viscosity were set at 14,380 dyn/cm^2 and 11,500 dyn s/cm^2, respectively, so as to obtain smooth movements with sufficient stabilization in the simulation. The stiffness parameter is in the middle range used in the previous studies (Dang & Honda, 2001; Lucero & Munhall, 1999). For simplicity, we did not consider the nonlinearities of the passive structures (e.g., differences in mechanical characteristics of skin surface and fatty part) in this model. This simplification may be the reason that the stiffness value is approximately twice greater than that used by Lucero and Munhall (1999) to produce the natural movement using our model.

The force, F, is supplied from the muscle element, which consists of a nonlinear spring, damping, and force generation components, similar to the tongue model (Dang & Honda, 2001). Each muscle force, f_m, is represented by

$$
\begin{aligned}
f_m &= f_s + f_b + f_a \\
f_s &= \begin{cases} k_1 \cdot \Delta l & \text{if} \quad \Delta l > 0 \\ 0 & \text{otherwise} \end{cases} \qquad (8.3) \\
f_b &= k_1/(2\pi \cdot f_r) \cdot \Delta \dot{l} \\
f_a(\varepsilon) &= \begin{cases} \alpha\left(\exp(-\varepsilon^2) - \exp(\varepsilon_{\max}^2)\right) & \text{if } -\varepsilon_{\max} < \varepsilon < \varepsilon_{\max} \\ 0 & \text{otherwise} \end{cases}
\end{aligned}
$$

Here, f_s, f_b, f_a denote muscle inherent stiffness, muscle viscosity, and force–length properties, respectively. Δl, ε, and α denote the muscle length change, muscle stretch ratio, and scaled muscle activity. The muscle inherent stiffness, k_1, was calculated from the Young's modulus of the perioral passive dynamics as mentioned above. The muscle viscosity was defined from the cut-off frequency, $f_r = 5$ Hz, of muscle force generation dynamics observed by Ito, Murano, and Gomi (2004). Since the lip muscle length would change greatly for producing large oral deformation (Barlow & Muller 1991; Muller et al., 1985), $\varepsilon_{\max}$ was set at 0.6. Note that the muscles and viscoelastic connections from the other nodes support all nodes except for the nodes at the border of the lip model. The upper-half nodes located at the surrounding border of the model were connected by viscoelastic elements to the fixed nodes placed just beside the surrounding border on the maxillar structure, and the lower ones were connected to the fixed nodes on the mandibular structure so that the lower lip would move with jaw motion. Using a backward-difference method, we obtained the positions of all the perioral nodes in each time step.

As a result of the muscle dynamics and lip muscle connections described above (see Figures 8.2b and c), the peripheralis muscle primarily shortens the outside of the vermilion border of the lip, and the marginalis muscle mainly shortens the vermilion part of the lip. The lip deformation, however, greatly depends on the combination of muscle activations, interactions between muscle and passive elastic elements, and movement constraints as described below; thus, the actual movement cannot be simply understood by the muscle force directions. In other words, total lip deformation is governed by the dynamics of all nodes, which interact with each other. This feature makes it more difficult to understand the lip movement compared to the limb dynamics in which the number of degrees of freedom is comparatively small and all arm muscle activation influence directly on the rigid bone dynamics.

Movement Constraints. Jaw movement is restricted by the jaw condyle joint of the maxillar bone, and lip movements are restricted by the teeth and their surrounding cervical wall. In this model (Figure 8.5a), these movement constraints are represented as follows. For the jaw condyle joint, we assumed that the joint center of the condyle slides on a curved path corresponding to the concave articular groove of the tempromandibular joint as in Dang and Honda (2001) and Laboissière, Ostry, and Feldman (1996). The curved path was modeled by a third-order polynomial of the x-position whose coefficients were adjusted to this maxillar bone. The force perpendicular to the tangent line to the curve path at the current condyle location is cancelled before solving the dynamical equation, and the force parallel to the tangent line is responsible for the movement along the curved path.

The inside of the lip frequently makes contact with the teeth and the surrounding cervical wall. Thus, it is important to model these constraints on lip movement (deformation). To reduce the computation, we simplified the contact dynamics as follows. First, we simplified the constraints of the teeth and surrounding cervical wall by using the triangular surfaces shown in Figure 8.5b and then detected the node in the lip inside surface (fifth layer) crossing the surfaces. When the node goes beyond the triangular surfaces (P) in a particular calculation step, the nodes are pushed back in the normal direction to the surface and then put on the triangle surface (P_{porj}) as shown in Figure 8.5c. Using this method in every calculation step, the lip nodes can slide on the constraint surfaces.

SIMULATIONS

In addition to modeling the perioral region as described above, we are constructing an extended model that includes the tongue and the shape of vocal tract based on the MRI data for speech generation as shown in Figure 8.6. (in the separate color plate section). Thin lines represent the muscle bundles modeled above, all of which can contribute to deformation of lip shape. We need to control all of these muscles for speech articulation and other kinds of perioral movements. By activating different combinations of muscles in the dynamical model, we can observe the difference in lip-deformation patterns. To investigate synthetically the lip-protrusion mechanism, we first focus on lip model deformations by activating the marginalis and peripheralis muscles.

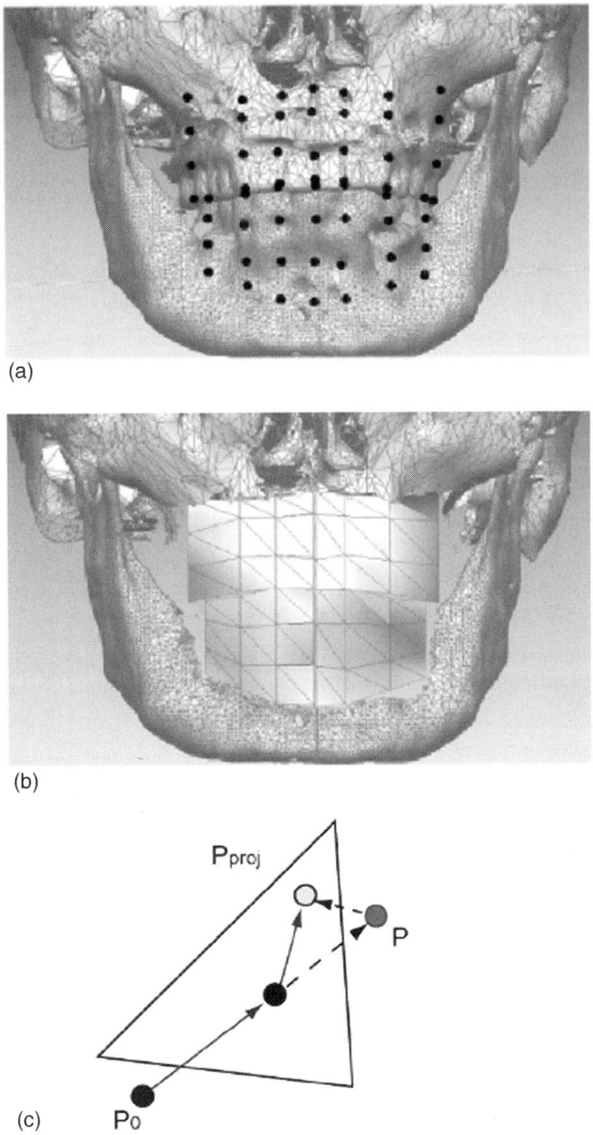

FIGURE 8.5. Modeling of surface for detecting collision between the lips and the teeth wall. The teeth and their surrounding cervical wall shown in (a) were extracted from MRI data and from a 3D scan of dental plaster casts. To simplify the detection of lip and teeth collision, those complex shapes were simplified by the triangular surfaces shown in (b). These surface apices were configured by 28 nodes [black dots in (a)], respectively, for the upper and lower teeth walls. (c) Node-motion adjustment when it goes beyond the wall surface. P_0, P, and P_{proj} denote the original position, next step position obtained by calculating the dynamics, and the projected position of the node.

Figure 8.7a (in the separate color plate section) shows the neutral lip configuration (i.e., no activation of lip muscle). By activating the peripheralis parts of the OOS and OOI, the upper and lower lips shrunk in the mid-sagittal direction and protruded in the frontal direction as shown in Figure 8.7b (in the separate color plate section). This 3D deformation was achieved by an interaction between the lip elastic passive dynamics and the constraints of the teeth and their surrounding cervical wall. This simulation result synthetically supports the hypothesis, based on EMG observation (Honda et al., 1995), that the lip protrusion is formed by the peripheralis muscle activation.

On the other hand, by activating the marginalis parts of the OOS and OOI, the mouth shut more firmly (pursed lips) as shown in Figure 8.7c (in the separate color plate section). This drastic difference in deformation by activation of the marginalis or peripheralis muscles suggests a functional control change in these subregions of the orbicularis oris muscle for lip shaping during speech articulation. We should note that, in spite of the previous prediction (Honda et al., 1995), lip rounding could not be achieved only by activating the marginalis parts of the OOS and OOI and the DLI as shown in Figure 8.7d (in the separate color plate section), suggesting that additional muscle combinations (jaw opening, peripheralis, or other perioral muscles) would be required to form rounded lips.

In addition to these movements by the orbicularis oris muscles, this model enables us to easily produce various lip deformations by activating other perioral muscles. Figure 8.7e (in the separate color plate section) shows an example of lip and perioral deformation, which has the effect of a wry smile, and which is achieved by activating one side of the zygomaticus major muscle. By activating this muscle, the region surrounding the angle of the mouth was twitched upward owing to the passive interaction among the nodes. Because of the insufficient area of the perioral model, the movement of the border of the region might be somewhat inappropriate for representing a wry smile. To fully reproduce this and other facial expressions a wider perioral region should be modeled using the meshed mass–spring network.

SUMMARY AND DISCUSSION

We presented in this paper a physiologically based model of perioral dynamics made by a mass–spring network. In addition to the complex perioral muscles and actual bone shapes and muscle locations extracted from MRI data, we modeled precisely not only the orbicularis oris muscles, whose peripheralis and marginalis parts are independently controlled, but also the constraints imposed by the teeth and their surrounding cervical wall. We used this model to examine the hypothesis that the peripheralis and marginalis contribute to lip rounding and protrusion, respectively. This hypothesis was proposed based on an EMG observation of the lower-lip marginalis and peripheralis during /u/ and /o/ productions

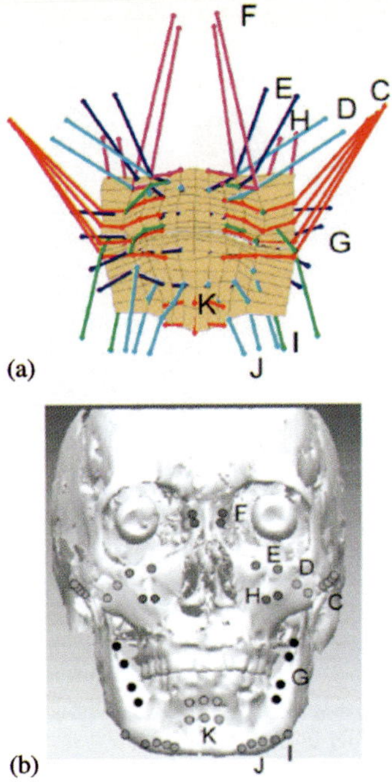

FIGURE 8.3. (a) Perioral muscle modeling. Zygomaticus minor (C) and major (D), levator labii superioris (E), levator labii superioris alaeque nasi (F), depressor labii inferioris (J), and depressor anguli oris (I) are connected to the nodes in the third (superficial) layer. Levator anguli oris (H) and buccinator (G) are connected to the fourth (deep) layer, and mentalis (K) is connected from the second layer to the mandibular bone. (b) Front view of maxillar and mandibular bones and arranged muscle origins on the bone surface.

FIGURE 8.6. Combined model of lip, tongue, and vocal tract wall. The lines represent muscle models.

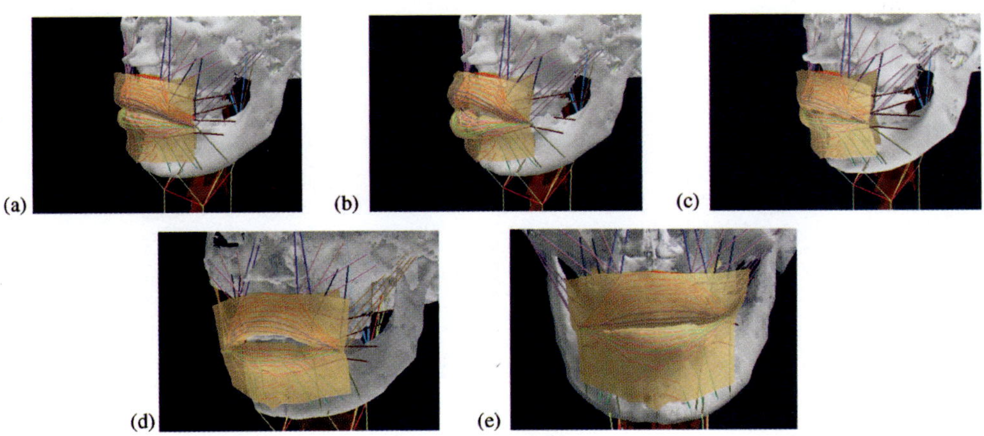

FIGURE 8.7. (a) Neutral lip configuration. (b)–(e) show various lip deformations, created as follows: (b) by activating peripheralis parts of OOS and OOI muscles, (c) by activating marginalis parts of the OOS and OOI muscles, (d) by activating marginalis parts of the OOS and OOI muscles and the DLI muscle, and (e) by activating the zygomaticus major muscle.

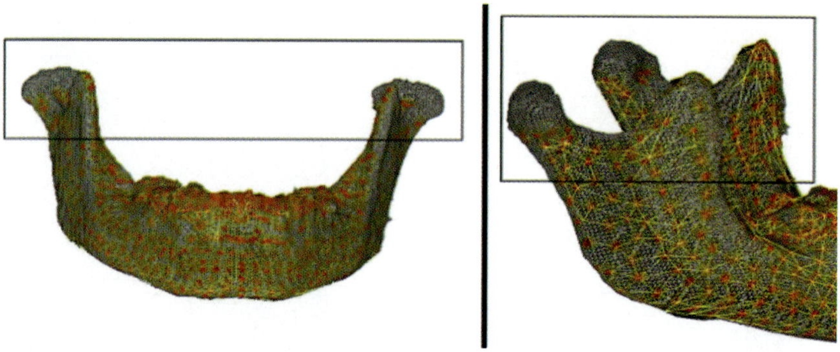

FIGURE 20.4. Projection of the transformed mesh on the original data. Except in the condyle region, each part of the mesh is well matched (red and orange less than 1 and 2 mm respectively).

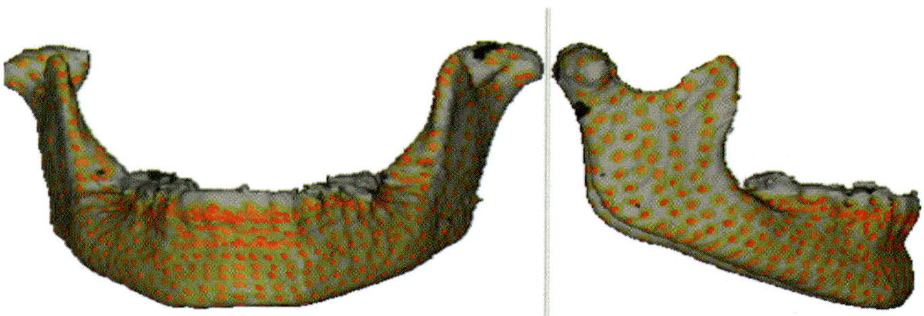

FIGURE 20.6. Projection of the transformed mesh on the original data using the symmetric matching.

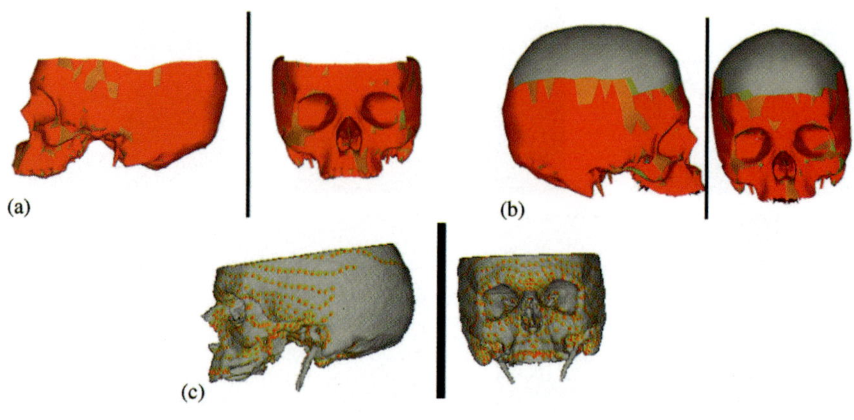

FIGURE 20.8. (a) partial transformed mesh; (b) final transformed generic mesh with its distance to the scan (red less than 1 mm, orange less than 2 mm, yellow, less than 5 mm); (c) projection of the transformed mesh on the original data. The location of the styloid processes is emphasized.

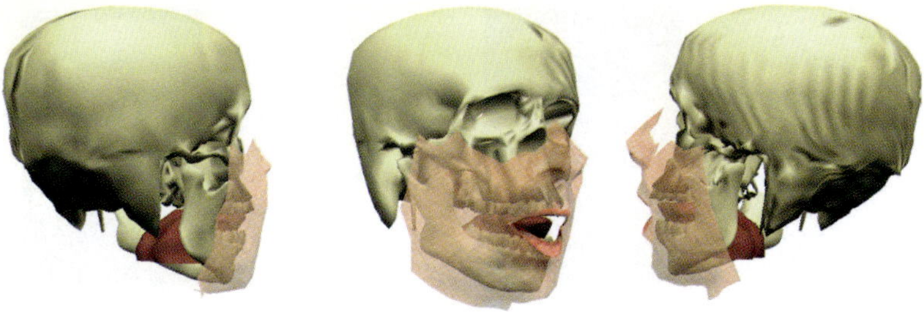

FIGURE 20.12. Augmented reality obtained by merging a speaker-specific shape model of the face and tongue with morphed generic models of the skull and the jaw.

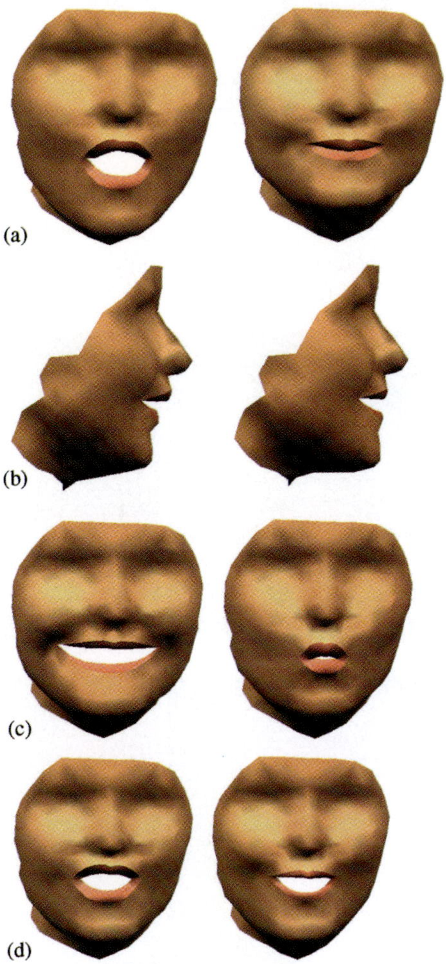

FIGURE 20.14. Elementary speech movements extracted from statistical analysis of motion capture data.

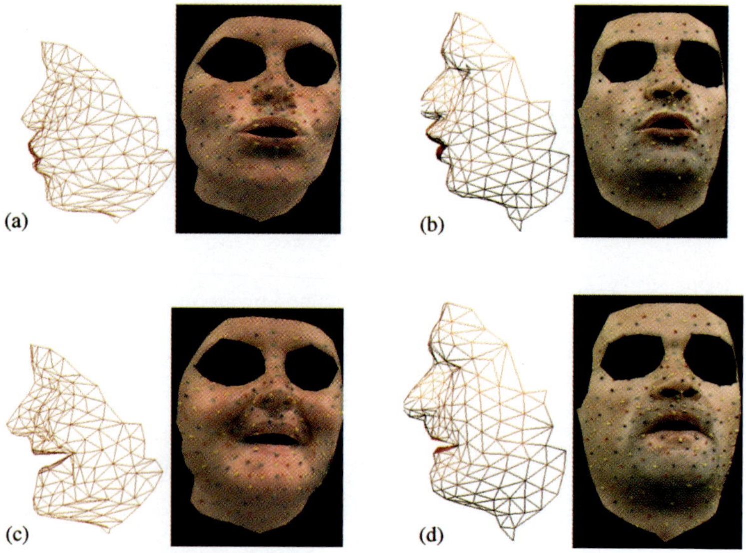

FIGURE 20.15. Shape and appearance changes associated with extreme variations along the first lip component (rounding/spreading) for two speakers. Shape-free textures (as in Cootes, Edwards et al. 2001) have been obtained from image data with colored beads.

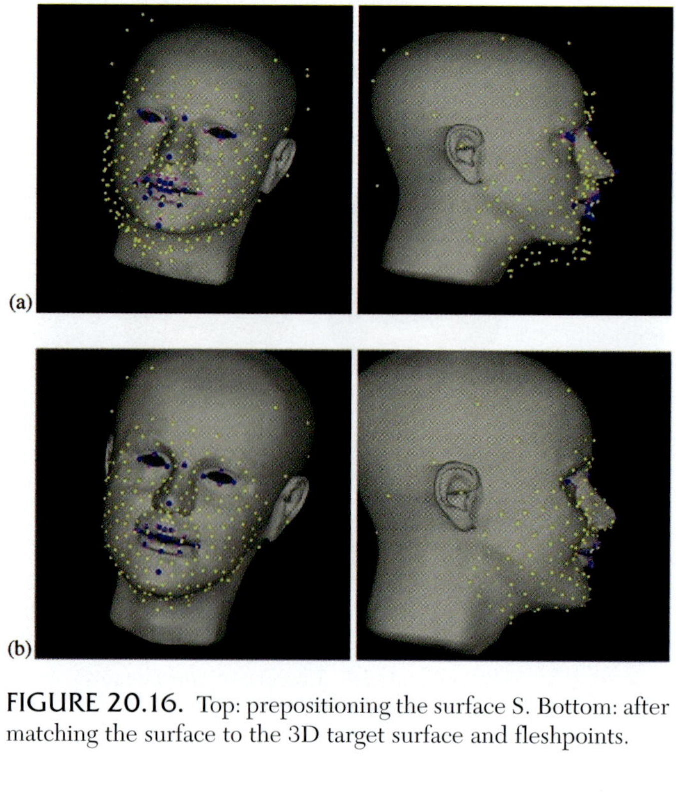

FIGURE 20.16. Top: prepositioning the surface S. Bottom: after matching the surface to the 3D target surface and fleshpoints.

(Honda et al., 1995). From the simulation using a realistic lip model, we confirmed that lip protrusion can be produced by activations of the peripheralis parts of the OOS and OOI muscles. Additionally, it is inferred that additional muscles, other than the marginalis parts of the OOS and OOI and the DLI, are activated to form the lip rounding in the real system.

In addition to the testing of the above hypothesis, this model will allow us to investigate the following important topics in speech motor control. First, we can investigate synthetically each muscle's contribution to lip deformation. As mentioned in the introduction, it is difficult to fully understand the lip shaping and muscle interaction during speech articulation only from observations, mainly because the perioral muscles are highly interwoven and because lip shape is flexibly changed. Here we demonstrated the major difference in deformation by the marginalis and peripheralis parts of the lip muscle, but other perioral muscles would also contribute to produce various lip shapes. Further synthetic analyses using a dynamical model would be beneficial in understanding the role of each muscle, or combination of muscles, in lip deformation and interaction during continuous speech movements. Additionally, delicate lip movement control may help to create rich facial expressions in facial animation.

Secondly, the physiologically based lip model enables us to examine the strategy of motor command generation for speech motor control. To make arbitrary lip shapes, we need to find the appropriate combination of muscle activations. Due to muscle redundancy, we have to use some constraints for selecting one of the many possible combinations. This problem is frequently examined as "control optimization" or "economy of efforts" in limb motor control studies. Pitermann and Munhall (2001) examined this issue in a facial dynamics model using an inverse motor command estimation. They successfully demonstrated the facial kinematics during speech tasks by feeding estimated muscle activations into the dynamics model, but there was little correlation between the estimated muscle activation patterns and the recorded ones. As they noted, one of the reasons for this difference might have been due to their insufficient optimization constraints (only a non-negative muscle force) in the inverse estimation process. Additional minimization criteria for synergistic muscle activations (Pedotti, Krishnan, & Stark, 1978; Prilutsky, Herzog, & Allinger, 1997; Yeo, 1976) could be worth examining for reducing the redundancy in the inversion process. Another possible cause of their different muscle activations is an oversimplification of the lip muscle structure. Their lip muscle model was represented by two portions (OOS and OOI), with fewer muscle elements than in our model. Since the lip is quite elastic, its deformation may be tightly coupled with muscle geometry, for which a sufficient number of muscle elements would be needed to represent elastic deformation. Their estimated negative lip muscle activation for obtaining better kinematic performance of a protrusion could have been due to an insufficient geometrical representation in muscle modeling, as they speculated, because a non-negative constraint for muscle activation should not affect the performance of kinematics reproduction. To understand the computational mechanisms of speech motor control, we need to clarify the strategy adopted by the central nervous system for controlling multiple muscles. The precise lip dynamics model would be useful for examining optimization criteria that describe the strategy of the speech articulator control.

Third, the adaptation issue in speech motor control can be examined based on the linkage between production and perception (Guenther, Hampson, & Johnson, 1998; Perkell et al., 1997). The generative speech-learning paradigm is quite attractive not only for speech science but also for speech production technology. Dynamical articulatory models provide realistic constraints for generating articulatory movements, whereas only a smoothness constraint has been considered in recent speech production studies (Hiroya & Honda, 2002; Hogden & Valdez, 2000). It should be noted that such realistic constraints would also be critical in the exploitation process in speech learning. To explore these important issues, we have to refine the lip model and develop a total articulator model as exampled in Figure 8.6. By constructing a speech production model that can produce realistic articulatory movements and speech sounds, we may be able to advance our understanding of the control mechanisms in human speech production.

ACKNOWLEDGMENTS

We thank Y. Shimada, I. Fujimoto, and S. Takano of ATR for their technical assistance in MRI, T. Ito of NTT and M. Honda of Waseda University for discussion, and M. Kashino, K. Moriya, and N. Sugamura of NTT for advice and support. This work was supported by CREST funding by the Japan Science and Technology Agency.

REFERENCES

Abbs, J. H., Gracco, V. L., & Blair, C. (1984). Functional muscle partitioning during voluntary movement: Facial muscle activity for speech. *Experimental Neurology*, *85*, 469–479.

Barlow, S. M., & Muller, E. M. (1991). The relation between interangle span and in vivo resultant force in the perioral musculature. *Journal of Speech and Hearing Research*, *34*, 252–259.

Blair, C. (1986). Interdigitating muscle fibers throughout orbicularis oris inferior: Preliminary observations. *Journal of Speech and Hearing Research*, *29*, 266–269.

Blair, C., & Smith, A. (1986). Emg recording in human lip muscles: Can single muscles be isolated? *Journal of Speech and Hearing Research*, *29*, 256–266.

Choquet, P., Sick, H., & Constantinesco, A. (1999). Ex vivo high resolution mr imaging of the human lip with a dedicated low field system. *European Journal of Dermatology*, *9*, 452–454.

Dang, J., & Honda, M. (2001). A physiological model of a dynamic vocal tract for speech production. *Acoustical Science & Technology*, *22*, 415–425.

Engwall, O. (2003). Combining MRI, EMA and EPG measurements in a three-dimensional tongue model. *Speech Communication, 41*, 303–329.

Goffman, L., & Smith, A. (1994). Motor unit territories in the human perioral musculature. *Journal of Speech and Hearing Research*, *37*, 975–984.

Guenther, F. H., Hampson, M., & Johnson, D. (1998). A theoretical investigation of reference frames for the planning of speech movements. *Psychological Review*, *105*, 611–633.

Hiroya, S., & Honda, M. (2002). *Determination of articulatory movements from speech acoustics using an HMM-based speech production model*. Paper presented at the *ICASSP 2002*, Denver.

Ho, T. P., Azar, K., Weinstein, S., & Bowley, W. W. (1982). Physical properties of human lips: Experimental and theoretical analysis. *Journal of Biomechanics*, *15*, 859–866.

Hogden, J., & Valdez, P. (2000). Bridging the gap between speech production and speech recognition. Paper presented at the *Proceedings of the 5th Seminar on Speech Production: Models and Data*, Kloster Seeon, Bavaria.

Honda, K., Kurita, T., Kakita, Y., & Maeda, S. (1995). Physiology of the lips and modeling of lip gestures. *Journal of Phonetics*, *23*, 243–254.

Ito, T., Murano, E. Z., & Gomi, H. (2004). Fast force-generation dynamics of human articulatory muscles. *Journal of Applied Physiology*, *96*, 2318–2324; discussion: 2317.

Kakita, Y., Fujimura, O., & Honda, K. (1985). Computation of mapping from the muscular contraction patterns to formant patterns in vowel space. In V. L. Fromkin (Ed.), *Phonetic linguistics*. New York: Academic Press.

Kennedy, J., & Abbs, J. (1979). Anatomic studies of the perioral motor system: Foundations for studies in speech physiology. In N. Lass (Ed.), *Speech and language: Advances in basic research and practice* (Vol. 1, pp. 211–270). New York: Academic Press.

King, S. A. (2001). *A facial model and animation techniques for animated speech*. Unpublished Ph.D. thesis, The Ohio State University, OH.

Kiritani, S., Miyawaki, K., Fujimura, O., & Miller, J. (1976). A computational model of the tongue. *Annual Bulletin Research Institute of Logopedics and Phoniatrics, University of Tokyo*, *10*, 243–251.

Laboissière, R., Ostry, D. J., & Feldman, A. G. (1996). The control of multi-muscle systems: Human jaw and hyoid movements. *Biological Cybernetics*, *74*, 373–384.

Lucero, J. C., & Munhall, K. G. (1999). A model of facial biomechanics for speech production. *Journal of the Acoustical Society of America*, *106*, 2834–2842.

Muller, E. M., Milenkovic, P. H., & MacLeod, G. E. (1985). Perioral tissue mechanics during speech production. In J. Eisenfeld & C. DeLisi (Eds.), *Mathematics and computers in biomedical applications* (pp. 363–371). North-Holland: Elsevier Science Publishers.

Pedotti, A., Krishnan, V. V., & Stark, L. (1978). Optimization of muscle-force sequencing in human locomotion. *Mathematical Biosciences*, *38*, 57–76.

Perkell, J. (1974). *A physiological-oriented model of tongue activity in speech production*. Unpublished Ph.D. thesis, MIT.

Perkell, J., Matthies, M., Lane, H., Guenther, F., Wilhelms-Tricarico, R., Wozniak, J., Guiod, P. (1997). Speech motor control: Acoustic goals, saturation effects, auditory feedback and internal models. *Speech Communication*, *22*, 227–250.

Pitermann, M., & Munhall, K. G. (2001). An inverse dynamics approach to face animation. *Journal of the Acoustical Society of America*, *110*, 1570–1580.

Prilutsky, B. I., Herzog, W., & Allinger, T. L. (1997). Forces of individual cat ankle extensor muscles during locomotion predicted using static optimization. *Journal of Biomechanics*, *30*, 1025–1033.

Salmons, S. (1999). Muscle. In P. L. Williams (Ed.), *Gray's anatomy* (38th ed., pp. 737–900). London: Churchill Livingstone.

Stevens, K. N. (1999). *Acoustic phonetics* (Vol. 30). Boston: MIT Press.

Takemoto, H., Honda, K., Masaki, S., Shimada, Y., Fujimoto, I. (2003) Measurement of temporal changes in vocal tract area function during a continuous vowel sequence using a 3D cine-MRI technique. In: *Proceedings 6th International Seminar on Speech Production* (pp. 284–289). Manly, Sydney: Macquarie Center for Cognitive Science.

Terzopoulos, D., & Waters, K. (1993). Analysis and synthesis of facial image sequences using physical and anatomical models. *IEEE Transactions. Pattern Analysis and Machine Intelligence*, *15*, 569–579.

Wilhelms-Tricarico, R. (1995). Physiological modeling of speech production: Methods for modeling soft-tissue articulators. *Journal of the Acoustical Society of America*, *97*, 3085–3098.

Wohlert, A. B., & Goffman, L. (1994). Human perioral muscle activation patterns. *Journal of Speech and Hearing Research*, *37*, 1032–1040.

Yeo, B. P. (1976). Investigations concerning the principle of minimal total muscular force. *J. Biomechanics*, 9, 413–416.

9

Analysis of Audiovisual Speech Intelligibility Based on Spatial and Temporal Filtering of Visible Speech Information

HUGO DE PAULA, HANI CAMILLE YEHIA, DOUGLAS SHILLER, GREGOIRE JOZAN, KEVIN G. MUNHALL, AND ERIC VATIKIOTIS-BATESON

ABSTRACT

This work investigates how viewers extract phonetically relevant visual information from dynamic audiovisual speech. It tests the hypothesis that low-resolution spatial and temporal information is sufficient for speech perception. Audiovisual perception studies were carried out using spatial and temporal low-pass filters applied to video image sequences for Japanese and English sentences at the rate of 30 frames/s. In the time domain, the results indicate that the information contained in the frequency band above the average rate of opening and closing the vocal tract (i.e., >6 Hz) can be removed without significant degradation of audiovisual speech intelligibility. In the space domain, it was observed that intelligibility is not degraded if spatial frequencies below 18.8 cycles/face are preserved. The tests used Gaussian filters, whose monotonic smooth attenuation prevented visual artifacts. However, the lack of a flat pass-band and the wide transition band of Gaussian filters made it difficult to analyze accurately the effects of the combination of temporal and spatial filters. For this reason, Chebyshev filters, which have a sharper attenuation and a flatter pass-band, have been used in the time domain to allow a more precise analysis of how audiovisual speech information is distributed in space and time. A detailed analysis of the frequency contents of video sequences also allows a deeper understanding of audiovisual speech perception.

INTRODUCTION

This paper addresses the issue of measuring the relevance of the frequency content of audiovisual speech in both the space and time domains. The objective is to go deeper into the problem of understanding the way auditory and visual stimuli are integrated during human speech production and perception.

The idea that speech production and perception occur in multiple modalities has been investigated in several studies. As examples, Sumby and Pollack (1954) have shown that being able to see the speaker's face enhances speech intelligibility, and Summerfield (1987) quantified this enhancement effect at an acoustic SNR of 8–10 dB. Recognizing and understanding the bimodality of speech perception are not the same. This point has been investigated by Beskow, Dahlquist, Granström, Lundeberg, Spens, and Ashman (1997), who analyzed the phonetic relevance of visible or facial events during speech readings by normal and hearing-impaired viewers.

From the speech production point of view, Yehia, Rubin, and Vatikiotis-Bateson (1998) demonstrated that speech information is distributed over the entire face, rather than concentrated on the lip region. Later, Yehia, Kuratate, and Vatikiotis-Bateson (2002) have also shown that time-varying attributes of the vocal tract, face, and head position are strongly correlated with spectral features of the speech acoustics. Implicit in the high degree of dependence between articulatory and acoustic domains there exist important time-varying properties. Specifically, the rate of speech production corresponds approximately to the average rate of opening and closing of the vocal tract, which is between 6 and 10 Hz (Munhall & Vatikiotis-Bateson, 1998). Evidence for the importance of visual information for speech communication is given by Benoît and LeGoff (1998), who have shown that speech intelligibility is improved by adding synthesized visible features, such as naturalistic lips, a skeletal jaw, or a parametric face, to the speech acoustics.

From the perception point of view, Vatikiotis-Bateson, Eigsti, Yano, and Munhall (1998) have shown that the eyes attract a significant amount of the listener's attention, even when audio is severely degraded. This can be understood as evidence from the fact that the temporal resolution necessary to acquire visual speech information is considerably below the human vision limits. An alternative explanation is that, while focusing attention on the eyes, the lower region of the face, including jaw and lips, is observed through the peripheral vision, which is the part of the vision system most sensitive to movement, at the cost of a lower spatial resolution.

Based on these interpretations, it can be hypothesized that there exists a trade-off between spatial and temporal resolutions and that visual speech information does not contribute equally in multimodal speech perception. Using band-pass-filtered face images, Munhall, Kroos, and Vatikiotis-Bateson (2001) showed that speech information is not degraded at all except the very lowest spatial frequencies.

Also, applying low-pass filters to image sequences, Munhall, Jones, Callan, Kuratate, and Vatikiotis-Bateson (2003) and Munhall, Kroos, Jozan, and Vatikiotis-Bateson (2004) have recently found full visual information recovery at a spatial cutoff frequency of only 7.2 cycles/face (i.e., 7.2 sinusoidal cycles across the face vertically or horizontally). However, there is no reason to assume that the results obtained for a particular language will be representative for all other languages. As suggested by studies of Japanese audiovisual speech perception (Sekiyama & Tohkura, 1991a, 1991b), different linguistic or cultural groups may process multimodal speech differently.

In the time domain, Vitkovich and Barber (1994) showed that intelligibility starts to degrade when the frame rate falls below 16 frames/s. Note that this is just below the standard frame rate of 18 frames/s used in silent movies. An interesting consideration here is that the spatial and temporal structures of facial motion are correlated with events in the vocal tract. That is, visible speech information can be filtered at the vocal tract rate, which is not far from 8 Hz, the Nyquist frequency of a sampling rate of 16 frames/s. Furthermore, using point-light animations, Rosenblum, Johnson, and Saldaña (1996) and Smeele (1996) have shown that facial motion preserves the temporal structure of speech even in the absence of detailed spatial information.

In this paper, spatial and temporal characteristics of speech production are analyzed from the perspective of multimodal speech perception. Specifically, the hypothesis that faces can be filtered to remove all information above the vocal tract rate without degrading the perception of visual speech information is tested. This comes in addition to the results obtained by Munhall et al. (2003, 2004), who found that Japanese and English viewers can extract full visible speech information from image sequences filtered at quite low spatial frequencies. The importance of the hypothesis that perception is tuned to the spatiotemporal resolution of vocal tract events is that it can be used to define the degree of accuracy required to construct models for the production and perception of audiovisual speech.

The analysis starts by measuring the effects of spatial and temporal filtering of video image sequences accompanying degraded speech acoustics. Next, the codependency between spatial and temporal filtering (i.e., spatial filtering affecting effective temporal resolution and vice versa) is quantified. The results are obtained through Gaussian filters, which are fully separable and, hence, can be efficiently used to process video in one temporal and two spatial dimensions. Finally, for the case of temporal resolution analysis, the results obtained with Gaussian filters are compared with those obtained with sharper Chebyshev filters.

METHODS

Two sets of stimuli were used. For the tests performed in Japanese, the stimuli consisted of a subset of 80 Japanese sentences recorded at ATR Labs

(Kyoto, Japan) by a Japanese native speaker. The sentences were constructed to be unusual or exotic, yet meaningful. In this way, sentence topics were novel to most of our subjects, thus reducing the increased predictability of words and phrases. The length of the sentences varied from 17 to 35 morae, with an average of 27.5 morae (Kubozono, 1989). For the tests performed in English, the stimuli consisted of a subset of the 100 CID everyday sentences spoken by an American English native speaker (Davis & Silverman, 1970). Owing to filter design limitations, only sentences lasting more than 2 s were used.

The sets of stimuli were recorded in standard NTSC resolution, converted into sequences of grayscale images and then low-pass filtered in space, using Gaussian filters, and in time, using both Gaussian and Chebyshev filters. Each sentence was filtered using 20 different spatiotemporal filter combinations. The resulting image sequences were transferred to a video track (30 frames/s) together with a speech audio track (48 kHz) using an ACCOM digital-videodisk array. The resulting video was then recorded to DVD (Pioneer PRV R-55) and a multispeaker babble noise (Auditec, St. Louis, MO) was added to the audio track. During the subjective measurements, a Pioneer V730 DVD player was used to present stimuli on a 20 in. Sony Trinitron HR video monitor placed 1.5 m away from the viewer. The DVD player was controlled by the experimenter via an RS-232 interface.

Filter Design

The spatiotemporal filter combinations used in the experiments are defined by the 20 possible combinations of the following sets of spatial and temporal cutoff frequencies: {150, 18.8, 9.4, 4.7, 2.4} cycles/face; and {15, 6, 4.5, 3} Hz. The first two octaves below the unfiltered images were skipped in the spatial domain because their effects on perception were undetectable. Thus, starting at 18.8 cycles/face, four filters were defined at one-octave intervals. Figure 9.1 shows the square region used to define the facial area where the number of sinusoidal cycles per face was counted. It also presents examples of low-pass-filtered facial images in order to illustrate the quality of the different spatial resolutions analyzed.

Gaussian kernels were used for both spatial and temporal domains. The expressions for 1-D Gaussian kernels in space (or time) and frequency domains are given by

$$h(n) = \frac{\omega}{\sqrt{2\pi \ln a^{-2}}} \exp\left(-\frac{n^2\omega^2}{2\ln a^{-2}}\right) \Leftrightarrow H(k) = \frac{1}{\sqrt{2\pi}} \exp\left(-\frac{k^2 \ln a^{-2}}{2\omega^2}\right) \quad (9.1)$$

where $a \in [0,1]$ is the gain at the cutoff frequency $\omega \in [0,\pi]$, π being the normalized Nyquist frequency. Therefore, the standard deviation is defined by $\sigma = \sqrt{\ln a^{-2}}/\omega$. Thus, the standard cutoff frequency attenuation of 3 dB is

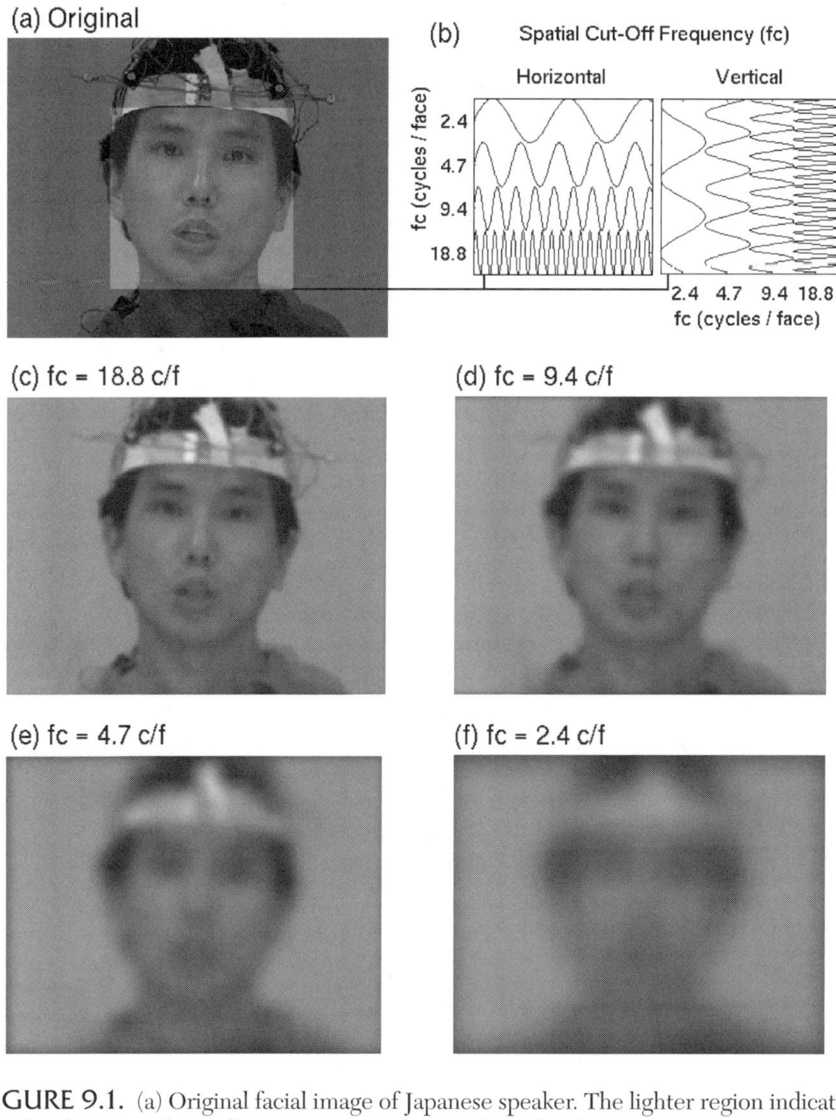

FIGURE 9.1. (a) Original facial image of Japanese speaker. The lighter region indicates the facial area used as reference to count the number of cycles per face. Its resolution is approximately 300 × 300 pixels, which corresponds to a maximum spatial frequency of 150 cycles/face. (b) Spatial cutoff frequencies of the low-pass-filtered images shown in: (c) 18.8 cycles/face; (d) 9.4 cycles/face; (e) 4.7 cycles/face; and (f) 2.4 cycles/face.

attained with $a = 1/\sqrt{2}$ and an attenuation of 6 dB with $a = 1/2$. In contrast with the Gaussian filters, designed to avoid sampling artifacts, the Chebyshev filters used were designed to be more localized, i.e., most of the kernel energy

TABLE 9.1. Kernel Order for the Designed Temporal (Left) and Spatial Filters (Right)

Cutoff frequency (Hz)	6	4.5	3	Cutoff frequency (cycles/face)	18.8	9.4	4.7	2.4
Gaussian	9	11	15	Gaussian	17	33	65	129
Chebyshev (IIR)	12	12	12					

is concentrated on only a few coefficients. IIR Chebyshev Type-I filters were used in time domain (Parks & Burrus, 1987). The orders effectively used for both Gaussian and Kuibyshev's filters are given in Table 9.1.

In order to illustrate how IIR Chebyshev filters are sharper than Gaussian filters, Figure 9.2 shows a comparison of the frequency responses of both kinds of temporal filters. While the Gaussian filters never achieve 40 dB of attenuation, the Chebyshev filters attenuate more than 60 dB in a 3 Hz transition band. This is in contrast with the case of spatial filters, where it is more convenient to approximate the frequency response of Chebyshev filters by the frequency responses of finite-filter kernels. Figure 9.3 compares the kernel shapes (left) and the frequency responses (right) of spatial Gaussian and Chebyshev filters. The Chebyshev filter has the advantage of being more

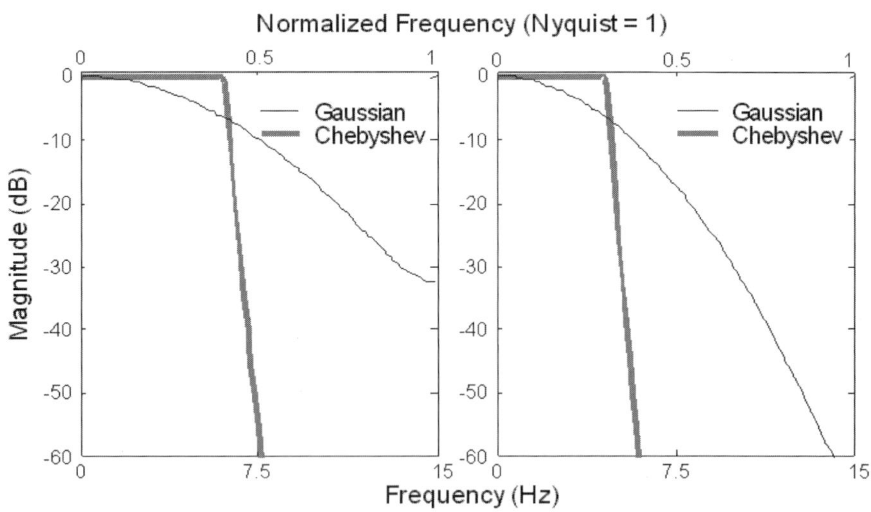

FIGURE 9.2. Temporal-filter frequency responses. The desired cutoff frequency is 6 Hz (left) and 4.5 Hz (right). For the Gaussian filters, the attenuation at the cutoff frequency is 6 dB, rather than the standard 3 dB, in order to improve the attenuation in the rejection band.

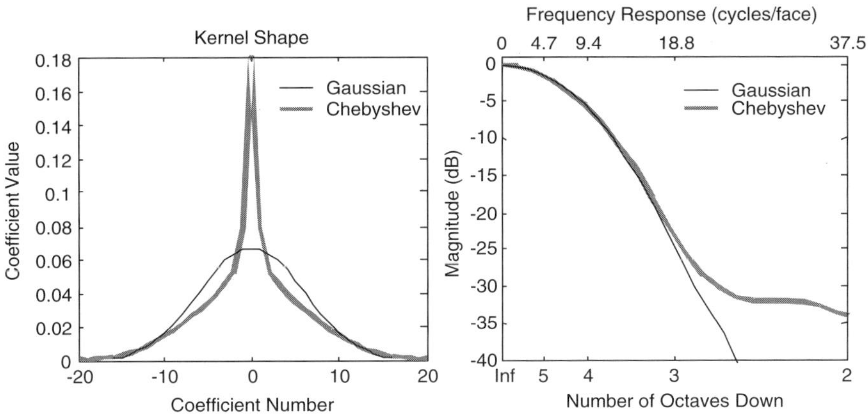

FIGURE 9.3. Kernel shapes of spatial filters (left) and their corresponding frequency responses (right). The Chebyshev kernel shape has its energy more concentrated around the central coefficient. The frequency responses are similar in the pass-band (i.e., less than 9.4 cycles/face), but in the stop-band (i.e., more than 18.8 cycles/face), the Gaussian filter exhibits superior performance.

compact, concentrating almost 35% of the coefficient energy on the central pixel and its adjacent neighbours, whereas the Gaussian filter needs seven coefficients to achieve a similar result. However, the frequency responses of both kernels are similar, with a better performance of the Gaussian filter in the stop band. For this reason, in the experiments carried out, only Gaussian filters were used in the space domain, whereas both Gaussian and Chebyshev filters were used in the time domain.

Procedure

The level of the babble noise was set for each subject so that an intelligibility of ~40% for audio-in-noise-only presentation was attained. When the speech-in-noise was combined with unfiltered video the intelligibility was always less than 100%. Throughout the study the initial setting for each subject was −1 dB, which is the average of the SNR values determined for the subjects in previous tests. During the experiments, the acoustic SNR varied between –3 and 0 dB. After each sentence presentation, subjects were asked to repeat what had been said and their answers were registered. Hiragana was used for the Japanese answers. Owing to particularities of each language, the evaluation method was different for Japanese and English: Keywords were counted for English and morae (which are, roughly, syllabic units of equally perceived duration that determine the rhythm of the Japanese language) were counted for Japanese. The use of morae for Japanese is justified by the fact that, although production data do not match perceived information, especially at higher speaking rates (Vatikiotis-Bateson, 1988), morae are perceived to be of equal duration and are clearly salient as a unit in prelexical processing (Otake, Hatano, Cutler, & Mehler, 1993) and other stages of the production and perception of Japanese (Port, Dalby, & O'Dell, 1987). An alternative for the case of English, which could allow a more direct comparison with counting morae, but that has not been carried out, would be to count stressed syllables, rather than keywords.

Results and Discussion

The results obtained are divided into four groups: (1) temporal Gaussian and Chebyshev filters for English, (2) temporal, (3) spatial, and (4) spatiotemporal Gaussian filters for Japanese. During the experiments in English, nine subjects were tested with Gaussian filters and 18 with Chebyshev filters. For Japanese, 27 subjects were tested with Gaussian filters. As expected, the intelligibility of speech-in-noise varied as a function of the video spatial and temporal frequency contents. The results are shown in Figure 9.4. For filtering in the time domain (Figure 9.4, left), no significant loss of intelligibility is observed before the cutoff frequency of 6 Hz. After that, intelligibility decreases monotonically, but differently, for the three cases analyzed. Finally, at the cutoff frequency of 1.5 Hz, the difference between the audio-in-noise-only and audiovisual conditions becomes less than 3%, indicating that, at this point, viewers no longer rely on visual information. In the space domain (Figure 9.4, right), the main change

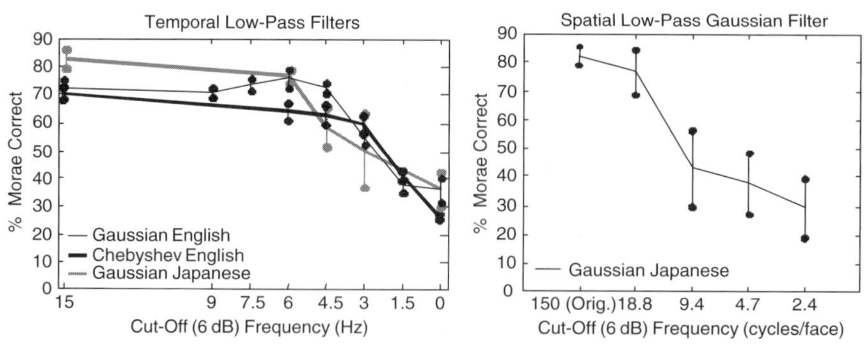

FIGURE 9.4. Left: Intelligibility scores for video low-pass filtered in the time domain. A significant loss of intelligibility occurs after the cutoff frequency of 6 Hz. Right: Intelligibility scores for low-pass Gaussian-filtered video of Japanese sentences in the space domain. The main change in speech intelligibility occurs for filter cutoff frequencies between 18.8 and 9.4 cycles/face. The vertical bars denote data standard deviation.

in speech intelligibility occurs for filter cutoff frequencies between 18.8 and 9.4 cycles/face, i.e., three and four octaves below the original 150 cycles/face (c.f. Munhall et al., 2003, 2004). There are no statistically significant differences outside this interval.

TABLE 9.2. Mean Percentage of Correct Morae for Each Filter Combination

Japanese sentences	Temporal frequency (Hz)			
Spatial frequency (cycles/face)	Original 15	6	4.5	3
Original 150	**82**	76	58	50
18.8	77	56	48	**78**
9.4	43	40	**53**	36
4.7	38	41	**54**	35
2.4	29	40	**55**	35

Note. Gray, not significantly different from the audio-in-noise-only condition. Bold, best result for each spatial filtering condition.

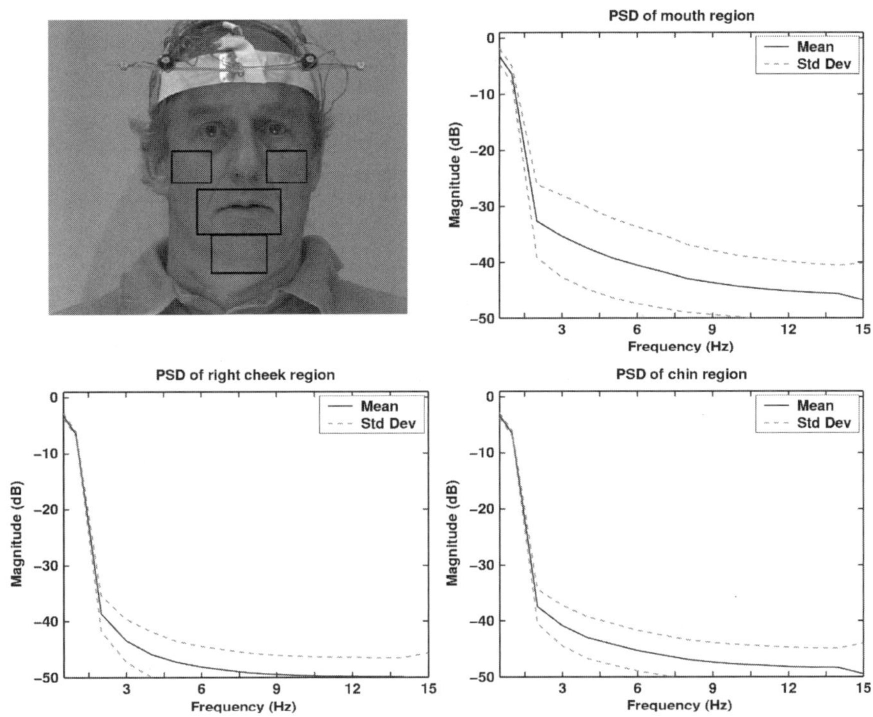

FIGURE 9.5. English speaker regions of the mouth, chin, and cheeks (photograph) followed by the respective power spectral densities. Most of the power density is concentrated in the mouth region under 6 Hz.

The co-dependence between spatial and temporal information is shown in Table 9.2, which contains the results for all combinations of filters used in the experiments. The gray area contains the results that are not significantly different from the audio-in-noise-only condition. Analyzing the columns of Table 9.2, progressive-intelligibility degradation is observed for video low-pass filtered to 15 (original) and 6 Hz, in contrast with 4.5 and 3 Hz, where the results show little variation. The combination of temporal and spatial low-pass filters rapidly removes most of the perceived visual information. Two exceptions should be noted: (1) the anomalous result obtained with video low-pass filtered to 3 Hz and 18.8 cycles/face, where 78% of the morae were correctly identified; and (2) the lack of significant degradation of the videos low-pass filtered to 4.5 Hz. Another interesting point is a tendency for some subjects to give up recovering visual information from heavily filtered sequences. These subjects attained better results by blocking out visual information (e.g., by closing their eyes) than the subjects that tried to match video and audio

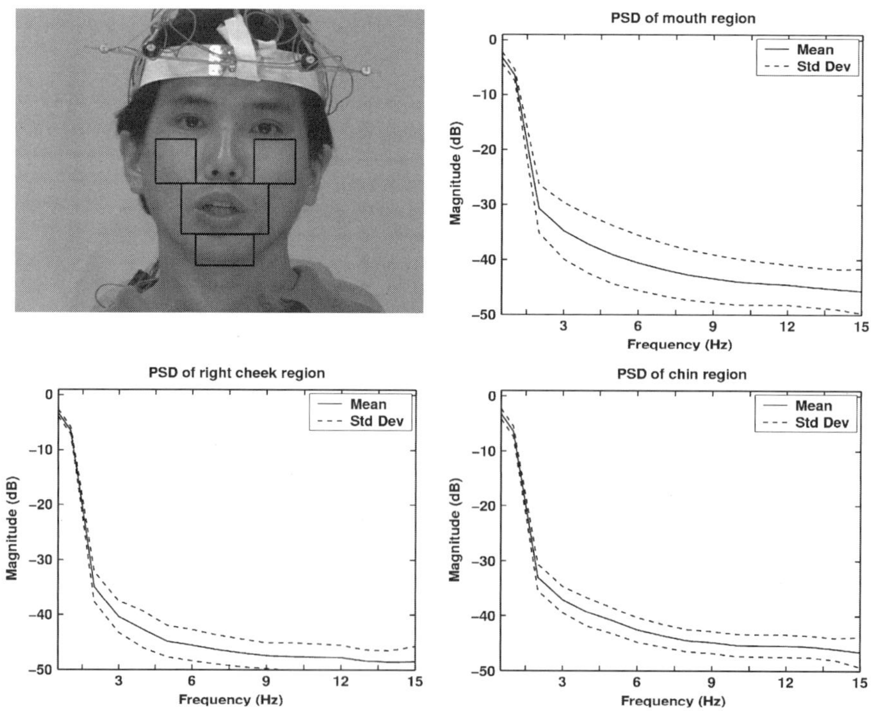

FIGURE 9.6. Japanese speaker regions of the mouth, chin, and cheeks (photograph) followed by the respective power spectral densities. Most of the power density is concentrated in the mouth region under 6 Hz.

stimuli, who ended up with percentages of correctly identified morae worse than those obtained with the audio-in-noise-only condition (~40%). This bimodality of subject strategy could account for part of the variability present in the results. More detailed experiments are necessary to explain the reasons for these specific cases.

Going deeper into the analysis of the frequency contents of facial motion, the power spectral density (PSD) of the regions of the mouth, chin, and cheeks were computed for each sentence for the English (Figure 9.5) and Japanese (Figure 9.6) speakers. The PSD was calculated for the temporal variation of the brightness of each pixel of the selected facial region using a Hanning window of 30 frames (i.e., 1 s) and a time shift of 15 frames (i.e., 0.5 s). The mean and *SD* were calculated based on all pixels of the selected facial region and all sentences recorded for each speaker. The comparable results obtained for both speakers confirm that the analysis carried out is consistent across the languages investigated. Not surprisingly, the mouth region has the highest PSD, which is, on an average, 10 and 15 dB higher than the chin and cheeks, respectively. Figures 9.5 and 9.6 show that, above 6 Hz, most of the PSD of the mouth region is more than 30 dB below the maximum. Although Gaussian temporal filters are not sufficiently sharp to remove all information above the cutoff frequency, even the weakest filter (6 Hz) reduces the PSD of the cheeks and chin regions to more than 40 dB below the maximum, making motion in these regions imperceptible.

CONCLUSION

This study investigated the effects of spatiotemporal filtering of Japanese and English audiovisual speech. It was observed that, during audiovisual speech perception, intelligibility is subject to a compromise between face temporal and spatial resolutions (see Table 9.2). This is in agreement with the fact that viewers alternate between focusing on the speaker's eyes and on the lower part of the speaker's face (Vatikiotis-Bateson et al., 1998), thus placing the face, respectively, in higher temporal and spatial resolution areas of the vision system. With respect to language dependence, the results obtained have not changed significantly for English and Japanese.

Summarizing the quantitative results, for spatially filtered video, there is no significant intelligibility loss for frames low-pass filtered to 18.8 cycles/face. From there on, a sharp degradation occurs and, at 9.4 cycles/face, the intelligibility loss is more than 30%. For frames with less than 9.4 cycles/face, the intelligibility loss does not vary significantly. At these levels, temporal filtering is ineffective. The results obtained with the temporal filters confirm that low-frequency dynamics play an important role in audiovisual speech. An intelligibility loss of 20% occurs for signals low-pass filtered to 4.5 Hz. From that point on, intelligibility degradation increases progressively and, for signals low-pass filtered to 1.5 Hz, there is no significant difference from the audio-in-noise-only condition. The two filter types used (Gaussian and Chebyshev) produced a difference of about 10% of intelligibility for signals low-pass filtered to 4.5 Hz, but converged after that. In conclusion, regarding speech intelligibility, visual information is concentrated in the temporal frequency range of 4.5–6 Hz; and in the spatial frequency range of 9.4–18.8 cycles/face. Future research should focus on these frequency bands.

The quantitative results presented here constitute only a starting point for spatiotemporal manipulation of speech visual information. A deeper analysis of the frequency ranges defined above, as well as of the phonetic and phonological contents of the speech produced, will provide the necessary information for a better comprehension of the audiovisual speech perception process.

ACKNOWLEDGMENTS

This work was supported in part by CAPES and CNPq (Brazil), NSERC (Canada), and by a grant from the Telecommunications Assistance Organization (TAO) to ATR-Human Information Science (Kyoto, Japan). The authors thank three anonymous reviewers whose work significantly improved the contents of this paper.

REFERENCES

Benoît, C., & LeGoff, B. (1998). Audio-visual speech synthesis from French text: Eight years of models, designs, and evaluation at the ICP. *Speech Communication*, *26*, 117–130.

Beskow, J., Dahlquist, M., Granström, B., Lundeberg, M., Spens, K.-E., & Öhman, T. (1997). The Teleface project—multimodal speech communication for the hearing impaired. In Proc. EUROSPEECH'97, 2003–2006.

Davis, H., & Silverman, S. R. (1970). *Hearing and deafness*. New York: Holt Rine-Hart & Winston.

Kubozono, H. (1989). The mora and syllable structure in Japanese: Evidence from speech errors. *Language and Speech*, *32*(3), 249–278.

Munhall, K. G., & Vatikiotis-Bateson, E. (1998). The moving face during speech communication. In R. Campbell, B. Dodd, & D. Burnham (Eds.), *Hearing by eye: Part 2* (pp. 123–129). *The psychology of speechreading and audiovisual speech*. London: Taylor & Francis, Psychology Press.

Munhall, K. G., Jones, J. A., Callan, D., Kuratate, T., & Vatikiotis-Bateson, E. (2003). Visual prosody and speech intelligibility: Head movement improves auditory speech perception. *Psychological Science*, *15*(2), 133–137.

Munhall, K. G., Kroos, C., Jozan, G., & Vatikiotis-Bateson, E. (2004). Spatial frequency requirements for audiovisual speech perception. *Perception and Psychophysics*, *66*, 574–583.

Munhall, K. G., Kroos, C., & Vatikiotis-Bateson, E. (2001). Band-pass filtered faces and audiovisual speech perception. *Journal of the Acoustical Society of America*, *109*(5), 2314.

Otake, T., Hatano, G., Cutler, A., & Mehler, J. (1993). Mora or syllable? Speech segmentation in Japanese. *Journal of Memory and Language*, *32*(2), 258–278.

Parks, T. W., & Burrus, C. S. (1987). *Digital filter design* (Chapter 7, Section 7.3.3). New York: Wiley.

Port, R. F., Dalby, J., & O'Dell, M. (1987). Evidence for mora timing in Japanese. *Journal of the Acoustical Society of America*, *81*(5), 1574–1585.

Rosenblum, L. D., Johnson, J. A., & Saldaña, H. M. (1996). Visual kinematic information for embellishing speech in noise. *Journal of Speech and Hearing Research*, *39*, 1159–1170.

Sekiyama, K., & Tohkura, Y. (1991a). McGurk effect in non-English listeners: Few visual effects for Japanese subjects hearing Japanese syllables of high auditory intelligibility. *Journal of the Acoustical Society of America*, *90*, 1797–1805.

Sekiyama, K., & Tohkura, Y. (1991b). Japanese listeners are less influenced by vision than Americans in speech perception. *Journal of the Acoustical Society of America*, *90*(Suppl. 1) 8SP3 2361–2362.

Smeele, P. M. T. (1996). Psychology of human speech reading. In D. G. Stork & M. E. Hennecke (Eds.), *Speech reading by humans and machines: Models, systems, and applications* (*NATO ASI series F: Computer and systems sciences*). Berlin: Springer.

Sumby, W. H., & Pollack, I. (1954). Visual contribution to speech intelligibility in noise. *Journal of the Acoustical Society of America*, *26*, 212–215.

Summerfield, A. Q. (1987). Some preliminaries to a comprehensive account of audio-visual speech perception. In B. Dodd & R. Campbell, (Eds.), *Hearing by eye: The psychology of lip-reading* (pp. 3–52). Hillsdale, NJ: Lawrence Erlbaum Associates.

Vatikiotis-Bateson, E. (1988). *Linguistic structure and articulatory dynamics: A cross-language study*. Bloomington, IN: Indiana University Linguistics Club.

Vatikiotis-Bateson, E., Eigsti, I. M., Yano, S., & Munhall, K. (1998). Eye movement of perceivers during audiovisual speech perception. *Perception and Psychophysics*, *60*(6), 926–940.

Vitkovich, M., & Barber, P. (1994). Effects of video frame rate on subjects' ability to shadow one of two competing verbal passages. *Journal of Speech and Hearing Research*, *37*, 1204–1210.

Yehia, H. C., Kuratate, T., & Vatikiotis-Bateson, E. (2002). Linking facial animation, head motion and speech acoustics. *Journal of Phonetics*, *30*(3), 555–568.

Yehia, H. C., Rubin, P., & Vatikiotis-Bateson, E. (1998). Quantitative association of vocal-tract and facial behavior. *Speech Communication*, *26*(1–2), 23–43.

10

What Role Does the Palate Play in Speech Motor Control?

Insights from Tongue Kinematics for German Alveolar Obstruents

SUSANNE FUCHS, PASCAL PERRIER, CHRISTIAN GENG, AND CHRISTINE MOOSHAMMER

ABSTRACT

By means of simultaneous electromagnetic midsagittal articulometry (EMMA) and electropalatography (EPG) recordings, we investigated tongue-tip kinematics and tongue–palate contact patterns for four German speakers in order to compare production strategies of alveolar stops with fricatives. For alveolar stops vs. fricatives, two different control strategies were hypothesized: A target above the contact location for alveolar stops resulting in a collision of the tongue tip at the palate as opposed to a precise positioning of the tongue at the lateral margins at the palate for alveolar fricatives. Additionally, we suspected differences between stops and fricatives with respect to anterior and lateral palate contacts and their influence on tongue kinematics. Results of this study confirmed two different control strategies for alveolar stops and fricatives by means of significant differences in movement amplitude, velocity, and duration of the closing gesture, the amplitude of deceleration peaks, tongue-tip movement during acoustically defined closure and constriction, and maximal anterior contact during closure. Additionally, results for speaker-dependent mechanisms were related to the subject's coronal palatal shape.

INTRODUCTION

A particular characteristic of speech production compared to other human motor systems is that the tongue moves in a narrow space delimited by the pharyngeal walls, cheeks, teeth, lips, and palate. Hence, even if the basic principles that govern arm or limb motor control might also apply to speech, it seems reasonable to assume that in speech production specific strategies are used to deal with these additional constraints. The focus of this paper is on the upper extent of the tongue's possible movement, the palate. Since tongue movements for oral consonants are most of the time produced in the presence of palatal contacts, it is hypothesized that: (1) the palate passively influences kinematic properties of speech movements, and (2) the tongue's action at the palate is taken into account in the speech motor control process in terms of limiting the degrees of freedom for tongue movement and supporting the tongue's shaping. As far as consonant production is concerned, Stone (1991) suggested that some tongue shapes, particularly those in the production of alveolar fricatives, could not be produced by a free-standing tongue position, i.e., with the palate as a spatial reference for the tongue. Stone also suggests that the palate can be used to provide tactile feedback information in order to learn and/or control specific tongue shapes. Additional evidence for the role of the palate was provided by perturbation studies. In 1978, Hamlet and Stone recorded tongue–palate contact patterns for 10 speakers wearing a dental prosthesis of 4 mm thickness in the alveolar region. Data were observed in two sessions: Immediately after the insertion of the prosthesis, when subjects were still unfamiliar with it, and 2 weeks after adaptation. Results from the first session provided evidence for tongue overshoot in /s, z, t, d, n/. Results for the second session showed compensatory movements with a similar variability as in the first session. The authors suggested that:

> The way sensory feedback is used in learning a compensatory form of speech is qualitatively similar to its use routinely. That is, all sensory information (from audition, proprioception, touch, etc.) by which the status of the oral environment and relative positions of the articulators can be assessed, is continuously being monitored, and used in planning the speech act (Hamlet & Stone, 1978, p. 246).

Baum and McFarland (1997) investigated acoustic and perceptual changes for /s/ production after structural modifications of the alveolar ridge using an artificial palate. Seven subjects were analyzed. They found that /s/ was acoustically and perceptually highly susceptible to perturbing effects in the beginning of the session. After 1 hour's practice, a significant improvement of acoustic and perceptual characteristics was observed, although compensation was not complete. The authors propose that an adaptation to articulatory perturbations could be achieved in a relatively short time period due to a recalibration of the speech motor control system taking into account the new spatial reference at the alveolar ridge. Honda, Fujino, and Kaburagi (2002) and Honda and Murano (2003) used another experimental paradigm, dynamic (time-varying) perturbations. They examined compensatory tongue movement for unexpected perturbations due to an inflatable artificial palate whose thickness could suddenly be increased or reduced; this technique was combined with or without auditory masking. Their findings suggest that incomplete compensatory movements are actively and immediately produced due to tactile feedback information, and that auditory feedback is used to complete precise articulatory adjustment, but with a longer time delay in comparison to tactile feedback.

The influence of the tongue's action at the palate on tongue kinematics was discussed in Hoole (1996) who found for German /aCa/ sequences differences with respect to the deceleration peak of the closing gesture in the following order: /t/>/d/>/n/>/s/. He assumed that in alveolar stop production, the relatively high deceleration peak of the tongue tip is mainly passive and a result of tongue's action at the palate; whereas in alveolar fricatives, the deceleration phase is actively controlled. Fuchs, Perrier, and Mooshammer (2001) showed that the onset of oral closure, defined by EPG data, coincided with the time point of the high deceleration peak for the tongue-tip sensor. It was proposed that a collision of the tongue tip against the palate could be responsible for the abrupt deceleration and the strength of the deceleration peak. These findings support the hypothesis of Löfqvist and Gracco (1997) for bilabial stops that articulatory gestures could be directed toward a target that is beyond the contact location. Thus, coronal stops are not controlled via a fine positioning of the tongue at the palate, but by the use of the palate as a reference, which automatically blocks the tongue's movement at the required location in the vocal tract. In terms of stability and simplicity, such a control strategy seems to be extremely efficient in comparison with the control of a fine positioning of the tongue at the palate. The effects of target variations in stop production on tongue kinematics (a precise positioning of the tongue without the palate and a collision between tongue and palate) were modeled in Perrier, Payan, Zandipour, and Perkell (2003) using a 2D biomechanical tongue model. They showed that the tongue's action at the palate combined with the relative articulatory target positions of the surrounding phonemes could explain some of the direction of the anticlockwise trajectories (the so-called loops) in /VkV/ sequences.

In contrast to stops, Mooshammer, Geumann, Hoole, Alfonso, van Lieshout, and Fuchs (2003) observed that fricatives have a more precise positioning of tongue and jaw. Fricatives are also often described as being difficult to produce. They are acquired later in the children's speech development in comparison to less complex sounds, cause most problems in patients who suffer from sensorimotor coordination impairments, and they seem to occur more frequently in tongue slips, especially regarding place of articulation (Boomer & Laver, 1968).

Previous studies have mainly focused on tongue kinematics by means of EMMA data and have inferred the corresponding tongue–palate contact patterns. We will take the advantage of simultaneous EMMA and EPG recordings. The aims of our study are twofold. First, we will compare alveolar stops with fricatives, because fricatives show both a fine positioning of the tongue at the lateral margins of the palate as well as tongue grooving which is not required in stop production. Thus, we suppose two different control strategies for stops vs. fricatives. Second, the tongue's action at the anterior and lateral parts of the palate were investigated separately in order to interpret their potential influence on tongue kinematics. Lateral contacts could potentially cause damping, and they might explain speaker-dependent differences in tongue kinematics based on the shape of the palate (Mooshammer, Perrier, Fuchs, Geng, & Pape, 2004; Tiede, 1998).

METHOD

Tongue-tip movements and tongue–palate contact patterns from four German speakers (all colleagues from the lab), three male (CG, DF, JD) and one female (SF, the first author of this paper), were recorded simultaneously by means of EPG (Reading EPG3) and EMMA (AG100, Carstens Medizinelektronik) systems. Tongue-tip movement was associated with the movement of a sensor placed mid-sagittally approximately 1 cm behind the tip. Two sensors served as reference points to compensate for helmet movements, one at the bridge of the nose and one at the upper incisors. All other sensors at the tongue and the jaw were not taken into account here. Speech signals were synchronously recorded on digital audio tape (DAT). The sampling frequencies were 16 kHz for the acoustic data, 100 Hz for EPG, and 200 Hz for EMMA data, respectively. The speech material consisted of the nonsense words ge/C1VC2/e and ge/C1VC2/, where C was always either /t/ or /z/. The phonologically voiced /z/ has been used instead of /s/ since it coincides most frequently with a preceding tense vowel in the German inventory whereas /s/ occurs with lax vowels. The focus of this paper is on C2 of each target word, following one of the stressed vowels /ɑː/ or /uː/. Different positions of the consonant were considered: Word medial C (henceforth med) in e.g., [gəˈ tʰ ɑːtə] corresponding to orthographic "getahte", and word final position C (henceforth fin) in, e.g., [gəˈ tʰ ɑːt], orthographically "getaht". All target words were embedded in the carrier phrase "Ich habe geC1VC2e nicht geC1VC2 erwähnt." (= I have geC1VC2e not geC1VC2 said, i.e., I said geC1VC2e not geC1VC2.) with pitch-accents on C1VC2 in both cases to convey contrastive sentence stress. A neutralization process of word final /z/ to the voiceless allophone takes place in German, i.e., word final /z/ was in most cases realized as [s]. As will be seen in the results section, supralaryngeal production mechanisms of word medial phonological /z/ (produced as [z]) and word final /z/ (produced as [s]) did not differ most of the time so that voicing distinction was not likely to be relevant for the interpretation of the tongue kinematics in our data. Thus, we maintained the phoneme description /z/.

Each sentence was repeated 10 times in a randomized order. The tongue-tip closing gesture from the stressed V to C was measured. The on- and offsets of the closing gesture were defined using a 20% threshold criterion (see Figure 10.1), i.e., closing gesture onset corresponds to the point where the tangential velocity signal of the tongue tip reached 20% by traveling from the velocity minimum to the peak. Closing gesture offset corresponds to the time landmark where the velocity signal reached 80% by traveling from the velocity peak to the next velocity minimum. The advantages of the 20% threshold criterion are described in Kroos, Hoole, Kühnert, and Tillmann (1997).

Starting from the landmarks defining the closing gesture, the velocity peak, the duration of the closing gesture, and the movement amplitude were calculated. The latter was calculated as the integral of the tangential velocity signal from onset to offset of the closing gesture, which corresponds to the area

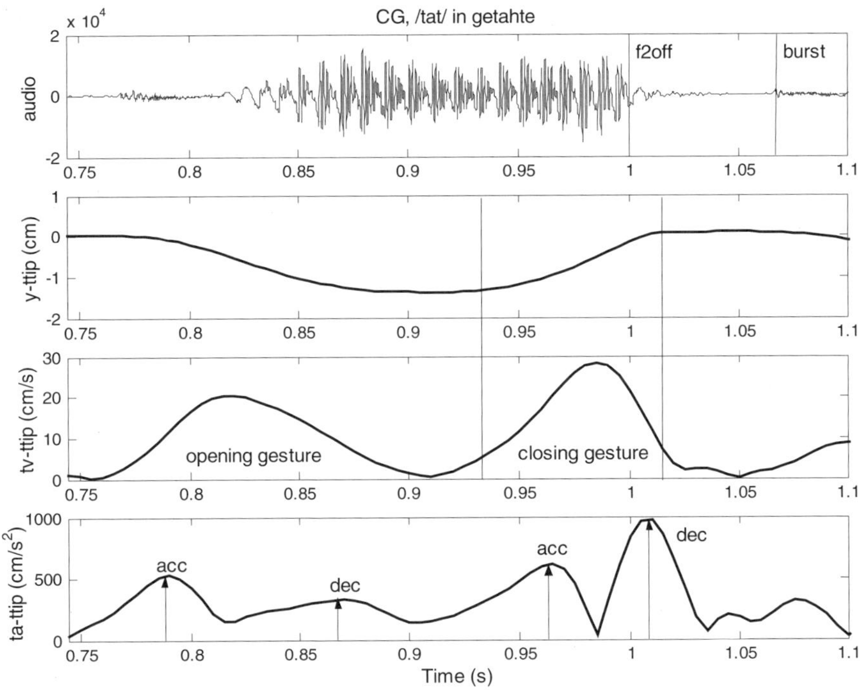

FIGURE 10.1. Articulatory and acoustic labeling criteria from CG's medial /t/ production in /a/ context: 1st track, audio signal with f2 offset and the burst; 2nd track, tongue-tip vertical movement in cm; 3rd track, tongue-tip tangential velocity signal in cm/s with closing gesture onset and offset; 4th track, tongue-tip tangential acceleration signal in cm/s^2 with acceleration (acc) and deceleration peaks (dec).

beyond the velocity signal. The measurement is generally more precise in comparison to calculations of the Euclidian distance, since it takes into account the whole curvature of the trajectory.

In order to compare stop production with fricative production in relation to previous findings in Fuchs et al. (2001) and Hoole (1996), the acceleration and deceleration peaks of the closing gesture (VC sequence) as well as of the preceding opening gesture (CV sequence) were labeled. Peaks in the preceding opening gesture were taken into account in order to have some references for the magnitude of the deceleration peaks.

Two acoustic landmarks were used for analyzing the obstruents. For the stops, the closure and burst were labeled and the closure onset was marked at the offset of F2 in the preceding vowel. The acoustic boundaries for the fricatives were marked at the on- and offset of high-frequency noise.

From each EPG pattern, the percentage of contact in the anterior region (4 most front rows) = ANT, in the posterior region (4 most back rows) = POST, and in the lateral region (2 most peripheral columns on the left and right side of the palate) = LAT were computed in order to quantify tongue–palate contact in time. Onsets of lateral and anterior contacts of the closing gesture were labeled as the landmarks where the relevant contact increased after the preceding vowel. The increase of contact was most of the time rather abrupt, particularly for stops that showed nearly no contact during the end of the vowel

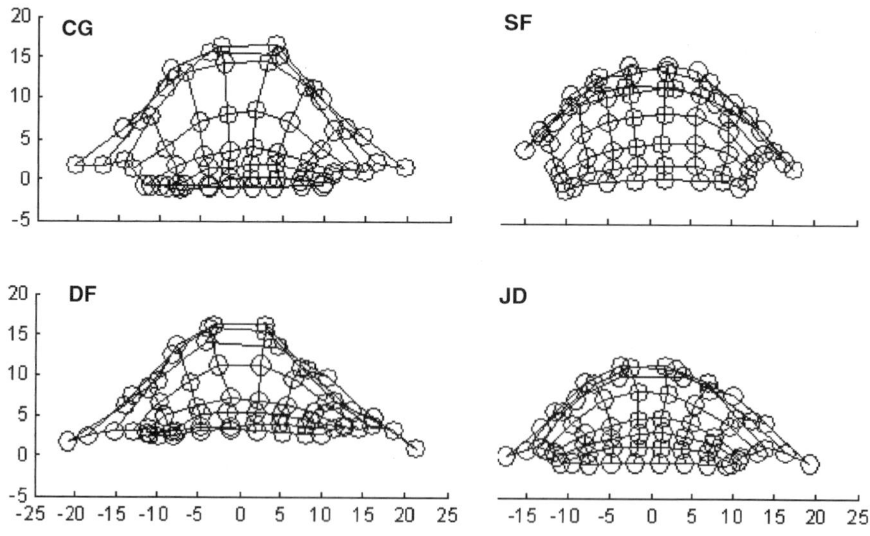

FIGURE 10.2. Coronal shapes of the artificial palates (anterior to posterior view for four speakers); positions of the 62 electrodes are marked by the open circles, lines connect open circles in the relevant row and column, x-axis (mm): left–right axis, y-axis (mm): palatal height.

and a sudden rise in the following pattern for closure onset. Additionally, the landmarks of maximal lateral and anterior contact during oral closure/constriction were marked. In order to get an impression of subject's palatal shape, for each of the 62 electrodes placed in the individual artificial palates, the x, y, and z coordinates were measured using a caliper (for a detailed description of the method see Fitzpatrick & Ní Chasaide, 2002).

Figure 10.2 exhibits the palatal shapes for all subjects based on the coordinates of the 62 electrodes. Two subjects (left column) showed coronal shapes similar to a dome and the two other subjects (right column) a rather flat palate shape in the coronal plane. The classification—flat vs. dome-shaped palates—was based arbitrarily on the individual differences in palatal height.

RESULTS

Closing Gesture Amplitude and Its Duration

A number of analyses of variance were calculated using the General Linear Model in SPSS 11.5. Closing gesture amplitude, its duration, and velocity peak were the dependent variables and consonant (/z/ vs. /t/) was the independent variable. The data were split by vowel (/a/ vs. /u/) and position in word (med vs. fin). The results showed that movement amplitudes in /t/ were significantly larger (see Figure 10.3) for all subjects in all conditions (all $p < .001$, except JD

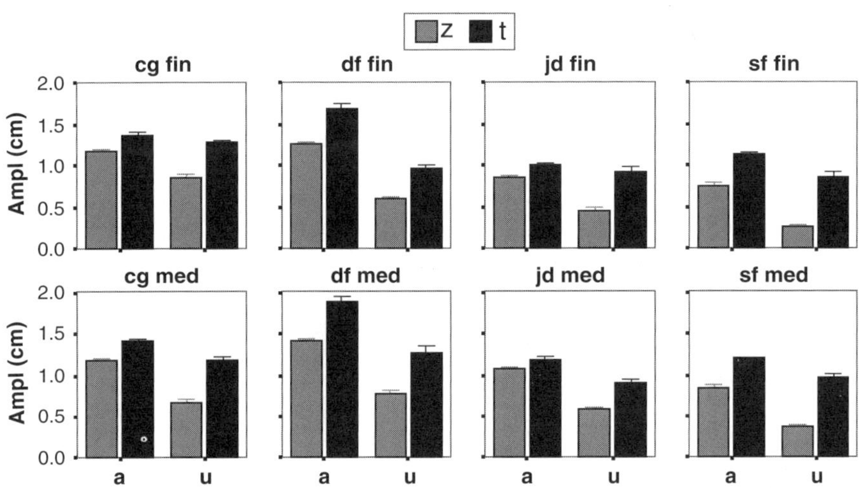

FIGURE 10.3. Bar plots showing means of closing gesture movement amplitudes in cm with ±1 S.E.; gray bars, /z/; black bars, /t/; upper row, word final position; lower row, word medial position; graphs correspond to different subjects (CG, DF, JD, SF) from left to right; x-axis: /a/ vs. /u/ context.

med /a/ context $p < .05$ at a 95% confidence interval). The same was true for the velocity peaks (all highly significant).

Similar findings have been presented by Geumann (2001), who showed a smaller movement amplitude due to a lower tongue-tip target position in /s/ and a higher tongue target position in /t/. The smaller movement amplitude for the fricative may also be a result of tongue grooving as described, e.g., in Narayanan, Alwan, and Haker (1995), and because the tongue-tip sensor was placed within the mid-sagittal groove. Tongue grooving may also be confirmed by means of maximal anterior contact during oral closure for the stops in comparison to the contacts during oral constriction for the fricatives. Results for stop production showed generally significant more percent of maximal anterior contact than in fricative production (all /a/ contexts $p < .001$, except DF fin $p < .05$, /u/ context med CG, SF $p < .001$, JD $p < .05$, fin CG, SF $p < .001$, JD $p < .05$). The smaller amount of anterior contact in /z/ should be due to the missing palatal contacts in the tongue groove.

If alveolar fricatives and stops were controlled in the same way, we would expect movement duration to be similar for both types of consonants. We would also expect larger movement amplitudes to coincide with greater velocity peaks and smaller movement amplitudes with smaller velocity peaks. Such results were generally found for the alveolars realized in /u/ context (see Figure 10.4). However, in all speakers' production of the /a/ context, the movement amplitude and the velocity peak were larger in /t/ compared to /z/, but the

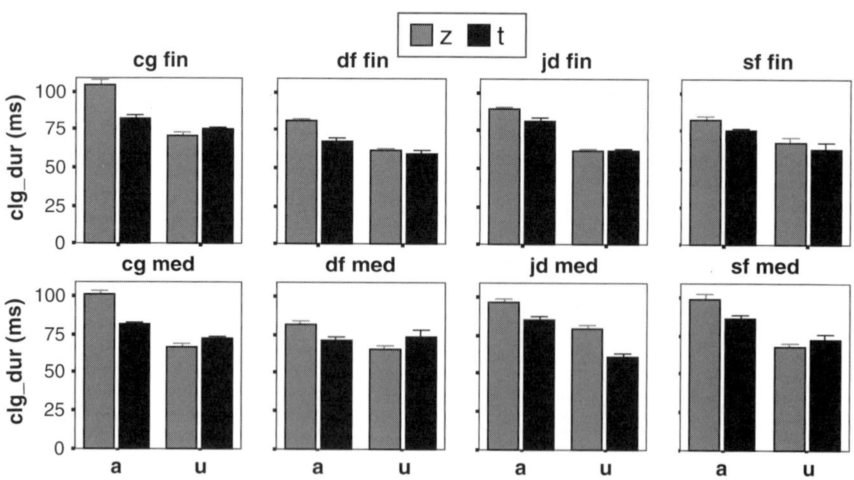

FIGURE 10.4. Bar plots showing means of closing gesture duration in ms with ±1 S.E.; gray bars, /z/; black bars, /t/; upper row, word final position; lower row, word medial position; graphs correspond to different subjects (CG, DF, JD, SF) from left to right; x-axis: /a/ vs. /u/ context.

closing gesture duration was shorter for /t/ than /z/ (med: CG $p < .001$, DF/JD/SF $p < .01$; fin: CG/DF $p < .001$, SF $p < .01$, JD $p < .05$).

The shorter duration observed for /t/ in the /a/ context gives a quantitative information about the consequence of the differences observed in peak velocity and movement amplitude between fricatives and stops. If the movement amplitude is large enough, the tongue can move in a shorter time interval for stops as compared to fricatives. In the case of the /u/ context, these differences cannot be observed since the movement amplitude was too small.

Deceleration of Tongue-Tip Movement and Movement during Closure/Constriction

Two separate measurements were made in order to further assess strategies used in stop and fricative production: first, acceleration and deceleration peaks in the opening and closing gestures were compared; and second, tongue-tip movements (movement amplitude, vertical, and horizontal movements) during the oral closure or constriction were analyzed.

As predicted from the hypothesis that the tongue's collision at the palate strongly affects movement kinematics for stops, a consistently higher deceleration peak during the closing gesture was found in comparison to the opening gesture for /t/ (see Figure 10.5). This was also true for /z/ (except for SF). Additionally, the relative differences between deceleration peaks in the opening and closing gestures were always greater for /t/ than /z/, e.g., for CG, the

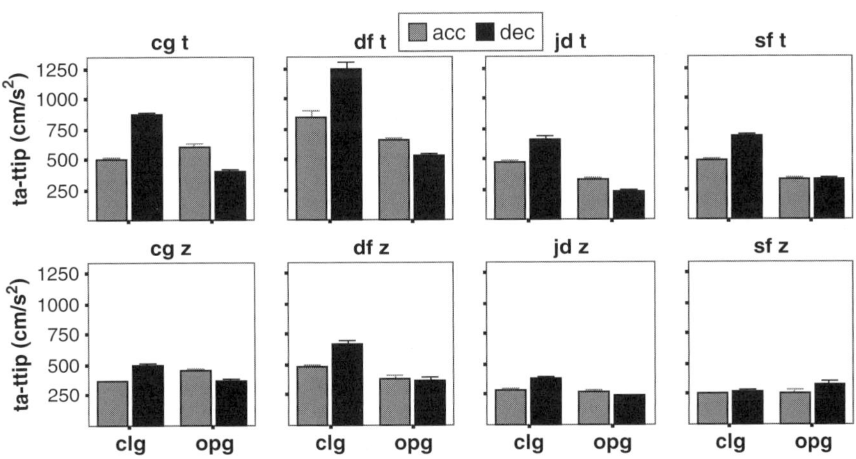

FIGURE 10.5. Bar plots showing means of acceleration (acc) and deceleration peaks (dec) in cm/s^2 with ±1 S.E., averaged over vowel context and word position; 1st row, /t/; 2nd row, /z/; CG, DF, JD, SF, from left to right; clg, closing gesture; opg, opening gesture; gray bars, acceleration peak; black bars, deceleration peak.

deceleration peak in the closing gesture for /t/ was 2.2 times greater than in the opening gesture; whereas in /z/, it was only 1.4 times greater. Acceleration peaks did not exhibit comparable relations and varied considerably between speakers. In order to rule out a possible influence of the larger movement amplitude in /t/ on the deceleration peak (this could come due to the fact that larger amplitudes are associated with larger peak velocities, and thus, they are necessarily associated with a larger deceleration, because deceleration is the velocity's derivative), a covariance analysis was calculated with deceleration peak in the closing gesture as the dependent variable, movement amplitude as the covariate, and consonant (/t/ vs. /z/) as the independent variable. Data were split by position (med vs. fin) and vowel context (/a/ vs. /u/). Significant differences for the deceleration peaks between /t/ and /z/ were found in all /a/ context (med: CG, JD $p < .001$, DF $p < .01$, SF $p < .05$, fin: CG, DF, SF $p < .001$, JD $p < .001$). In /u/ context, differences were less consistent (med: JD, SF $p < .001$, DF $p < .01$, fin: SF $p < .001$, DF $p < .05$). These findings suggest that the tongue's movement does not stop due to an active deceleration in alveolar stop production, but due to an impact at the palate. It is in general agreement with Hoole's (1996) proposal and Löfqvist and Gracco's (1997) suggestion for a planned target position beyond the contact location.

Additional evidence was derived from the results concerning tongue-tip movement during acoustically defined closure and constriction. If a target is planned beyond a contact location, the tongue's movement is reoriented due to the collision at the palate. The reorientation of the movement depends on the angle of incidence the tongue collides at the palate. For example, if the tongue moves against the palate in an obtuse angle coming from the back, it should be redirected toward the front and sliding along the palate. If the angle is around 90°, the tongue should have the greatest impact on the palate since the force cannot be redirected (for calculation of the angle of incidence by means of tongue kinematics in looping patterns, see Brunner, Fuchs, Perrier, & Kim, 2004). For a target planned at the contact location, less damping effects should occur due to the missing impact, and less movement should be produced in order to place the articulator precisely at the target location.

Figure 10.6 shows that there were larger movement amplitudes during /t/ closure compared to /z/ constriction in all cases for the /u/ context (highly significant). In the /a/ context, significant differences between /t/ and /z/ occurred particularly in the word medial position (DF, JD, SF). In word final position, a /t/-/z/ distinction was only found for DF. Results from subject CG showed generally the reverse pattern in /a/ context with larger amplitudes for /z/ than for /t/.

The larger movement amplitudes during oral closure for /t/ were mainly a result of a forward movement of the tongue tip as shown in Figure 10.7 (except for CG in /a/ context for whom differences in amplitude corresponded to vertical tongue movement, which explains the patterns observed for this speaker). Forward movements during /t/ closure (i.e., the tongue tip slides along the

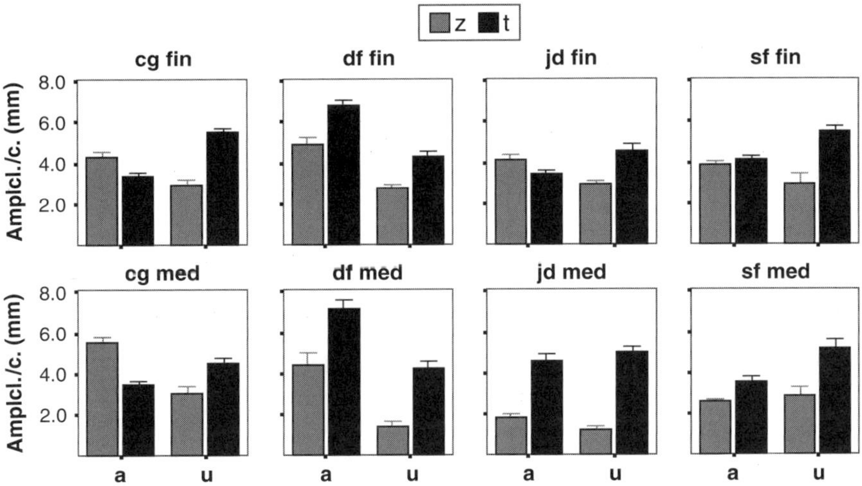

FIGURE 10.6. Bar plots showing means of movement amplitude during acoustically defined closure/constriction in mm with ±1 S.E.; gray bars, /z/; black bars, /t/; upper row, word final position; lower row, word medial position; graphs correspond to different subjects (CG, DF, JD, SF) from left to right; *x*-axis: /a/ vs. /u/ context.

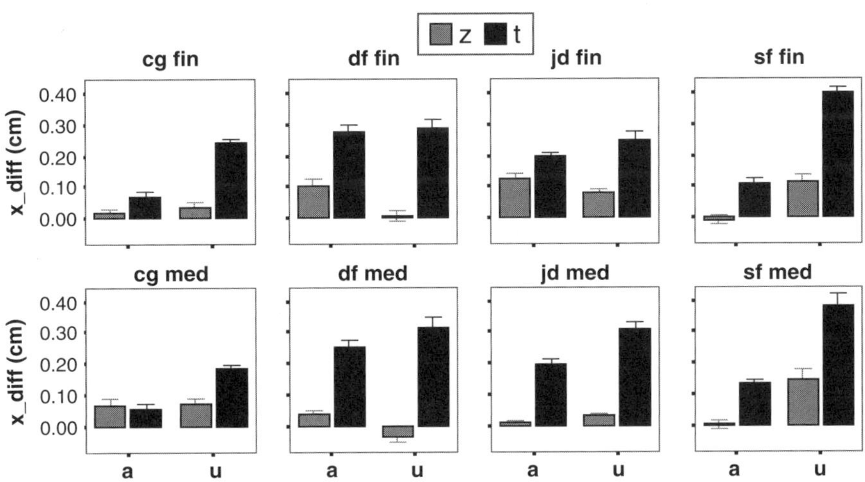

FIGURE 10.7. Bar plots showing means of the difference in horizontal tongue-tip position from closure/constriction onset to closure/constriction offset in cm with ±1 S.E.; positive values correspond to a forward movement; gray bars, /z/; black bars, /t/; upper row, word final position; lower row, word medial position; graphs correspond to different subjects (CG, DF, JD, SF) from left to right; *x*-axis: /a/ vs. /u/ context.

palate) were more pronounced in /u/ than in /a/ context, confirming the idea that a redirection of the movement depends on the planning of the target and on the angle of incidence. Brunner et al. (2004) suggested that the greater the size of the angle of incidence, determined by the target positions of the surrounding environment, the larger the movement amplitude of the sliding tongue. Although the exact angle of incidence was not calculated here, it seems reasonable to assume that the angle of incidence in /u/ context is more obtuse than in /a/ context since the tongue moves from a back high vowel toward the front.

Duration from Onset of Lateral Contacts to Velocity Peak

In a previous pilot study of one subject, we observed that the velocity peak in /t/ was well synchronized with an increase in lateral contacts, corresponding to the onset of stop occlusion. This observation raised the question whether for stop production the deceleration phase could be a result of the tongue's action at the palate only. In order to begin to test the reliability of these preliminary findings, the temporal difference between the velocity peak and the onset of lateral contact was calculated. In the /u/ context (all speakers, all conditions), lateral contacts started already during the vowel, i.e., they preceded the velocity peak. Tongue and palate were always in contact with each other since /u/ is a high vowel. Results obtained for the /a/ context are shown in Figure 10.8. They show considerably inter-speaker variation.

Differences between /z/ and /t/ are relatively small, keeping in mind that the frame rate of EPG is 100 Hz. However, results clearly reveal specific patterns (/a/ context) for speakers with a dome-shaped palate vs. speakers with a flat palatal shape. For the latter (JD and SF), tongue contact with the lateral margins of the palate occurred already during the preceding /a/ (between 15–30% LAT) and increases during the consonant. This type of pattern did not occur in speakers with a dome-shaped palate (CG and DF). Their results showed roughly a simultaneous timing of the velocity peak with the onset of lateral contacts. In contrast, for speakers with a flat palatal shape (JD and SF), the tongue is already in contact with the palate during the vowel. One consequence of this seems to be a weaker impact of the tongue at the palate during stop production, as suggested by comparing the magnitude of the deceleration peaks during /t/ for the two groups of speaker. Those with a flat palate had lower deceleration peaks, suggesting that contact with the palate caused less damping of the tongue movement than it is the case for the speakers with more dome palate shapes. In this way, the variations in the tongue–palate contact patterns during the preceding vowel affected tongue kinematics in different ways. Since lateral contacts were already produced during the acceleration phase, they cannot induce the deceleration phase alone. However, a combination of lateral and anterior contacts may cause the beginning of the deceleration, at least for stop production.

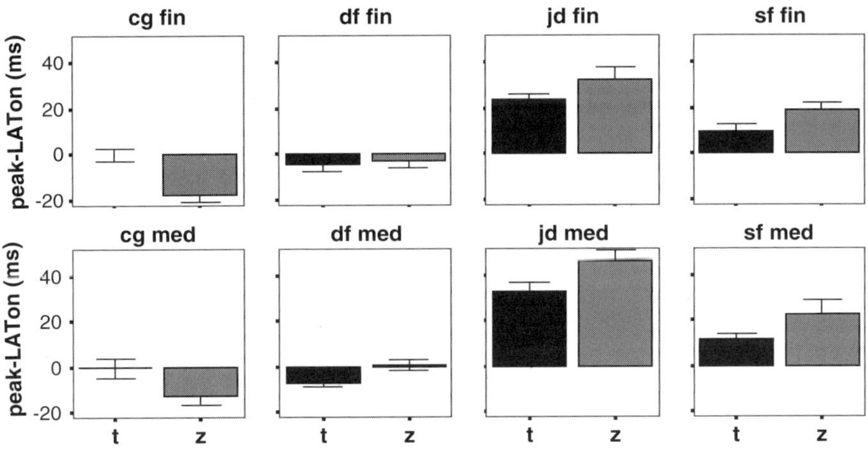

FIGURE 10.8. Bar plots with means of the difference between the time points of the velocity peak and the beginning of LAT in ms with ±1 S.E.; negative values correspond to lateral contact after the occurrence of velocity peak; positive values to lateral contacts before velocity peak; gray bars, /z/; black bars, /t/; upper row, word final position; lower row, word medial position; graphs correspond to different subjects (CG, DF, JD, SF) from left to right, /a/ context.

Contrary to our expectation that lateral contacts start earlier with respect to anterior contacts in /z/ production, we did not find reliable differences between /t/ and /z/. If differences occurred, then they were often 10 ms and therefore close to the reliability range of EPG. This means that either lateral contacts always co-occurred with anterior contacts in alveolar obstruent production or that differences between the onsets of such contacts were very tiny and should be investigated by means of a higher time-resolution technique.

DISCUSSION

We investigated tongue-tip kinematics and tongue–palate contact patterns by means of simultaneous EMMA and EPG recordings for four German speakers in order to compare production strategies of alveolar stops with fricatives. We assumed that the central nervous system incorporates the palate in speech motor control and that tongue–palate contact patterns influence the kinematics of the tongue movement. In stop production, the alveolar target is planned beyond the contact location (see Löfqvist & Gracco, 1997). In terms of stability and simplicity, such a control strategy would be efficient, since it can tolerate quite a large amount of variability in the motor commands without endangering the final tongue positioning and the corresponding auditory goal.

The tongue's collision at the palate guarantees an airtight seal corresponding to a silent closure phase in the acoustics. By contrast, fricatives are planned with a target at the lateral margins of the palate in order to create a narrow mid-sagittal constriction as a prerequisite for the production of turbulent noise, the most prominent acoustic characteristic of fricatives. To do so, a more precise tongue and jaw position is required.

Results for both strategies were evident in tongue-tip kinematics and tongue–palate contact patterns. The larger deceleration peak in /t/ production provides evidence for a collision of the tongue tip with the palate [in agreement with Hoole (1996) and Fuchs et al. (2001)]. Additionally, the movement amplitude and the velocity peak of the closing gesture were larger in /t/ whereas the duration of the closing gesture was significantly shorter, at least in the /a/ context. Movement amplitudes for /z/ were smaller, slower, and were produced with a longer duration. There was a significantly greater percentage of maximal anterior contact during closure or constriction for /t/ than for /z/, supporting two ideas: first, alveolar fricatives are produced with tongue grooving and have therefore less contact with the palate; second, an impact always produces a high amount of contact, whereas fine positioning can potentially produce either a small or a large amount of contact.

By observing the movement amplitude during the acoustically defined oral closure for stops and the oral constriction for fricatives, a larger tongue-tip movement amplitude was found for /t/ than for /z/. The tip generally moves in a forward direction which is particularly pronounced in the /u/ context and confirms the earlier work of Brunner et al. (2004). In /z/ production, less movement was produced during oral constriction, probably because of the more precise tongue positioning that is required in fricatives than in stops. We suppose that the different control strategies are used in order to create the appropriate auditory goals, i.e., a silent closure interval for stops and turbulent noise for fricatives.

Concerning the role of lateral tongue–palate contacts, differences were less consistent for the two consonants. However, speaker-dependent variations were found and interpreted with respect to differences in palate shape. Speakers with a flat palate shape exhibit lateral contact already during /a/ production; whereas for speakers with a dome-shaped palate, such contact did not occur. As far as the /a/ context is concerned, we suggest that for speakers with a flat palate shape, the impact between tongue and palate was less pronounced since the tongue was already in contact with the palate during the preceding vowel. A previous study of the token-to-token variability of all German vowels (Mooshammer et al., 2004), including the same male speakers recorded here, provided evidence for a smaller variability of tongue positioning in general, comparing JD with CG and DF. We interpreted this result partly due to differences in palate shape, since small tongue movements have larger effects on the area function for speakers with a flat palate. Thus, speakers with a flat palate may have learnt a more precise tongue positioning. Whether this also holds true for consonant production and the extent to which differences in the precision of vowel production affect consonant production need further investigation.

Johnson, Ladefoged, and Lindau (1993) proposed that palatal doming affects articulatory organization, in particular tongue and jaw coordination. In a subsequent investigation, we will also observe jaw movements, since preliminary inspections showed differences in vertical jaw movements for the two groups of speakers with smaller movement amplitudes for speakers with the flat palate (JD, SF) and larger amplitudes for the speaker with a dome-shaped palate (CG, DF).

ACKNOWLEDGMENTS

This work was supported by a grant from the German Research Council (DFG) GWZ 4/8-1, P.1. We thank Jonathan Harrington and two anonymous reviewers for their helpful comments on an earlier version of this manuscript, our subjects, and Jörg Dreyer for technical support during the recordings.

REFERENCES

Baum, S. R., & McFarland, D. H. (1997). The development of speech adaptation to an artificial palate. *Journal of the Acoustical Society of America, 102*, 2353–2359.

Boomer, D. S., & Laver, J. D. M. (1968). Slips of the tongue. *British Journal of Disorders and Communication, 3*, 1–12.

Brunner, J., Fuchs, S., Perrier, P., & Kim, H. Z. (2004). *Correlation between angle of incidence and sliding patterns of the tongue along the palate in Korean velar stops*. Poster presented at the 147th ASA meeting, New York.

Fitzpatrick, L., & Ní Chasaide, A. (2002). Estimating lingual constriction location in high vowels: A comparison of EMA- and EPG-based measures. *Journal of Phonetics, 30*, 397–415.

Fuchs, S., Perrier, P., & Mooshammer, C. (2001). The role of the palate in tongue kinematics: An experimental assessment in VC sequences from EPG and EMMA data. *Proceedings of Eurospeech*, Aalborg (pp. 1487–1490).

Geumann, A. (2001). Invariance and variability in articulation and acoustics of natural perturbed speech. *Forschungsberichte des Instituts für Phonetik und Sprachliche Kommunikation der Universität München (FIPKM), 39*, 265–378.

Hamlet, S. L., & Stone, M. (1978). Compensatory alveolar consonant production induced by wearing a dental prosthesis. *Journal of Phonetics, 6*, 227–248.

Honda, M., Fujino, A., & Kaburagi, A. (2002). Compensatory responses of articulators to unexpected perturbations of the palate shape. *Journal of Phonetics, 30*, 281–302.

Honda, M., & Murano, E. (2003). Effects of tactile and auditory feedback on compensatory articulatory response to an unexpected palatal perturbation. *Proceedings of the 6th speech production seminar*, Sydney (pp. 97–100).

Hoole, P. (1996). Theoretische und methodische Grundlagen der Artikulationsanalyse in der experimentellen Phonetik. *Forschungsberichte des Instituts für Phonetik und Sprachliche Kommunikation der Universität München (FIPKM), 34*, 3–173.

Johnson, K., Ladefoged, P., & Lindau, M. (1993). Individual differences in vowel production. *Journal of the Acoustical Society of America*, *94*, 701–714.

Kroos, C., Hoole, P., Kühnert, B., & Tillmann, H. (1997). Phonetic evidence for the phonological status of the tense–lax distinction. *Forschungsberichte des Instituts für Phonetik und Sprachliche Kommunikation der Universität München (FIPKM)*, *35*, 17–25.

Löfqvist, A., & Gracco, V. L. (1997). Lip and jaw kinematics in bilabial stop consonant production. *Journal of Speech, Language, and Hearing Research*, *40*, 877–893.

Mooshammer, C., Geumann, A., Hoole, P., Alfonso, P., van Lieshout, P., & Fuchs, S. (2003). Coordination of lingual and mandibular gestures for different manners of articulation. *Proceedings of the 15th ICPhS*, Barcelona (pp. 81–84).

Mooshammer, C., Perrier, P., Fuchs, S., Geng, C., & Pape, D. (2004). An EMMA and EPG study on token-to-token variability. *Arbeitsberichte Institut für Phonetik und digitale Sprachverarbeitung Universität Kiel (AIPUK)*, *36*, 46–63.

Narayanan, S. S., Alwan, A. A., & Haker, K. (1995). An articulatory study of fricative consonants using magnetic resonance imaging. *Journal of the Acoustical Society of America*, *98*, 1325–1347.

Perrier, P., Payan, Y., Zandipour, M., & Perkell, J. (2003). Influences of tongue biomechanics on velar stop consonants: A modeling study. *Journal of the Acoustical Society of America*, *114*, 1582–1599.

Stone, M. (1991). Toward a model of three-dimensional tongue movements. *Journal of Phonetics*, *19*, 309–320.

Tiede, M. (1998). Palate shape effects on characteristic vowel tongue postures. *Journal of the Acoustical Society of America*, *103*, 2893.

PART 2

PHONETICS AND CROSS-LINGUISTIC ANALYSES

11

Phonetic Encoding of Prosodic Structure

PATRICIA A. KEATING

INTRODUCTION

Prosody has been defined as the "grouping and relative prominence of the elements making up the speech signal" (Pierrehumbert, 1999). That is, prosody serves both a grouping function and a prominence-marking function in speech. As examples of the grouping function, some ways in which smaller units are combined to form larger ones (perhaps via intermediate groupings) include: segments combine to form syllables, syllables combine to form words, and words combine to form phrases. As examples of the prominence-marking function, there are at least two levels of prominence in English: lexical stress, or prominence at the word level, and pitch accent, or prominence at a phrasal level.

Some prosodic constituents	Some levels of prominence
• Utterance	• Nuclear accent
• Intonational phrase	• Pitch accent
• Smaller phrases: Phonological phrase/ Intermediate phrase/Accentual phrase	• Lexical primary stress
• Phonological word	• Lexical secondary stress
• Foot	
• Syllable	
• Mora	

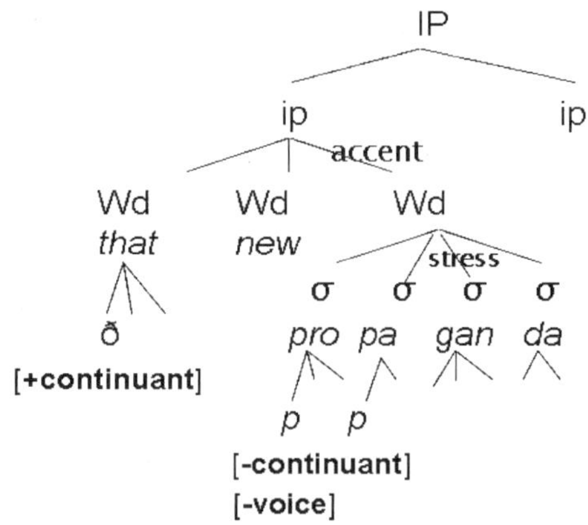

FIGURE 11.1. Sample partial prosodic tree for a phrase, "that new propaganda." Phrasal accent and lexical stress are indicated ad-hoc on the appropriate branches in the tree. Only three segments and selected feature values are shown.

The grouping function and the prominence-marking function can be seen together in a prosodic tree of an utterance. Figure 11.1 is a partial prosodic tree of the phrase "that new propaganda" as part of some larger utterance, showing four levels of prosodic domains (leaving out several other levels): it shows a single intonational phrase (IP), containing two intermediate phrases (ip), the first of which contains three prosodic words (Wd) corresponding to the three lexical words in "that new propaganda." The third word has the phrasal accent or prominence, and it contains four syllables (sigma), of which the third has the lexical stress or prominence. This partial tree has syllables as its smallest prosodic units. Each syllable contains some segments, and the features of the segments are the terminal nodes of the prosodic tree. A few of these segmental features are included in the figure. As can be seen, each segment and thus each feature has a position in the tree relative to the domains and prominences.

For the purposes of this chapter, we can consider any one interval of speech that is grouped into a single prosodic domain and ask, at what level of prosodic structure does this domain occur? What speech events occur at the beginning and end of this domain? How prominent is this domain relative to its neighbors? All of this information will be relevant phonetically.

The phonetic dimensions that are most obviously connected with prosody are pitch, duration, and loudness, which are generally thought of as the suprasegmental dimensions. But the phonetic dimensions that are typically thought of as more segmental than suprasegmental also serve to realize prosodic distinctions. For example, it is well known that vowel quality varies not only with phonemic vowel identity, but also with traditional suprasegmental factors such as stress and length (Lehiste, 1970). This classic observation can be generalized to all of prosody as now understood, including its hierarchical structure. Put generally, then, the phonetic realization of phonological properties of an individual speech segment (vowel or consonant) depends in part on that segment's position in the entire prosodic structure (Hawkins & Smith, 2001; Pierrehumbert & Talkin, 1992). The exact pronunciation of any one feature will depend on the other features in that segment, features of neighboring segments, and the position of the feature in the overall tree. Thus, segmental phonetic dimensions, though they convey segmental contrasts, are influenced by prosody in much the same way as are the traditional suprasegmental dimensions (dimensions not involved in conveying segmental contrasts).

In the Levelt, Roelofs, and Meyer (1999) important model of planning for speech production, a distinction is made between (1) phonological encoding, or generating a complete phonological representation, including prosody, from lexical entries and syntactic structure; and (2) phonetic encoding, which specifies the surface phonetic shape of the phonological representation. At each of these stages, Levelt et al., relying on the traditional distinction between segmental and suprasegmental phonological representations and speech parameters, envision segmental and prosodic planning as virtually independent. Phonetic encoding of segments is thought to operate at the level of the word, and it consists largely of retrieval of stored syllable plans. Segmental and prosodic planning interacts in only a minor fashion, at the end of the encoding process, when the results of these two independent processes are brought together.

As discussed at length in Keating and Shattuck-Hufnagel (2002), the missing ingredient from their model (and similarly, from the model in Levelt, 1989) is the close link between prosodic structure and segmental phonetic properties. We outlined instead an opposing view, according to which segmental and prosodic planning are not independent, since planning segmental articulation depends crucially on prosody. We stressed that even if phonetic encoding relies on stored syllable plans, the work of phonetic encoding has just begun with their retrieval, as adjustments to them are required on the basis of all kinds of prosodic information; and even if phonetic encoding relies on stored exemplars, then that retrieval operation itself must be highly sensitive to prosodic structure and the retrieved exemplar may still require further processing. The present chapter, like Keating and Shattuck-Hufnagel (2002), defends this claim by reviewing a variety of ways in which phonetic encoding must be sensitive to prosodic structure, focusing especially on results from my own laboratory. In particular, I will review results of experiments suggesting a strength relation between prosodic positions and phonetic realizations.

The general idea of a strength relation is that prosodic positions are stronger or weaker; segment/feature phonetic realizations are also stronger or weaker; and segment strength matches position strength, with stronger pronunciations in stronger positions. Positions of lexical and phrasal prosodic prominence seem strong due to their suprasegmental properties (e.g., greater loudness in the case of stress, and pitch excursions in the case of accent), and in these positions segment qualities can also vary. The notion of a strong position is then generalized to other positions in which the same variants are observed. For example, Donegan and Stampe (1979) observe that traditional segmental fortitions are most likely in "strong" positions, in which they include prosodically prominent positions and syllable-initial position. Similarly, Vaissière (1988) related certain prominent, domain-initial, and domain-final positions, in which velum position patterned similarly, as "[+strong]."

What exactly does strengthening mean? Our strengthening is articulatory, meaning that the articulations themselves are stronger, or more extreme. For consonants in strong positions, for example, the primary oral constriction is more extreme, meaning that the primary articulator moves farther from a neutral position into a more extreme position, which reduces the size of any mouth opening.[1] Also, any glottal opening is more extreme, giving more aspiration. Such strengthening (often called fortition in the historical linguistics literature) can be seen as the opposite of weakening (or lenition), by which, for example, a more reduced primary consonant articulation results in a greater mouth opening, or a more reduced glottal opening results in greater voicing. (However, other views are possible; for example, Donegan and Stampe (1979) define fortition as perceptual enhancement, and lenition as articulatory reduction.) In historical sound changes (e.g., Hock, 1991, 1992), "initial strengthening" as a specific process refers to something that happens to initial sonorants, in languages which also weaken medial obstruents; that is, it is a generalization to sonorants of the pattern of strong initial obstruents vs. weak medial obstruents. In our phonetic work, the term is used even more generally, to refer to increased articulatory opening or constriction in any articulation of any segment type.

Many previous studies have been concerned with the articulation of prominent vowels, including the direction of displacement for prominent high vowels, and differences between prominence and other strengthenings (e.g., Beckman, Edwards, & Fletcher, 1992; Cho, 2002; de Jong, 1995; Edwards, Beckman, & Fletcher, 1991; Erickson, 2002; Fletcher & Vatikiotis-Bateson, 1994; Harrington, Fletcher, & Beckman, 2000). Other studies (reviewed in Epstein, 2002, 2003) have been concerned with the phonation qualities associated with prominence. Strengthenings at the beginnings of prosodic domains and in prominent syllables are complemented by domain-final lengthenings, the well-known phenomenon where segments at the ends of domains have longer durations (e.g., Wightman, Shattuck-Hufnagel, Ostendorf, & Price, 1992). See Shattuck-Hufnagel and Turk (1996) and Fougeron (1999) for reviews of the articulation of prominence and final lengthening, which will not be discussed in any detail in this chapter.

The total effect, then, is that at the end of one domain there is a slowing down, and at the beginning of the next domain a strong attack, with another strong moment associated with any prominence. Such phonetic effects are also seen in synchronic phonological patterns. At the word level, languages may license or distribute inherently stronger segment types in stronger positions, e.g., a preference for initial obstruents, especially stops, as opposed to noninitial sonorants or continuants (e.g., Bell & Hooper, 1978; Martinet, 1955).[2] Overall, then, there is a tendency for prosodic domains, such as words, in a given language to have a phonological and/or phonetic shape conditioned by the prosodic structure of the language.[3]

BASIC DOMAIN-INITIAL EFFECTS

In my work (with various collaborators) I have been most interested in domain-initial articulatory strengthening, that is, strengthening associated with the beginning of prosodic domains. I have put forward a specific claim about how this strengthening works through the whole of prosodic structure: that it is cumulative, in the sense that the higher in the prosodic tree an initial position is, the stronger that position and the segment in it. The empirical support for this claim is somewhat mixed, as I will make clear below, but there is an interesting range of data that seem to work this way.

The prosodic positions we compare are generally edges of domains. A domain-initial segment (or syllable) is at the beginning of some prosodic domain. A domain-final segment (or syllable) is at the end of some prosodic domain. Because prosodic domains are hierarchically organized, a given segment (or syllable) is usually initial or final in multiple (nested) domains. To see how this works for domain-initial syllables, look at the six syllables shown in the partial tree in Figure 11.1. The first is initial in all the domains shown. We generally refer to the highest domain in which some segment or syllable is initial, so in this case the syllable is IP-initial. The second and third syllables are word-initial, but IP- and ip-medial. The other syllables are not initial in any domains. The last syllable of the six is final in the ip and in all lower domains.

Experimentally, we measure something we take to be related to segment strength, for example linguopalatal contact as a measure of oral constriction. At UCLA we have primarily used electropalatography (EPG) to infer the strength of segment articulation. With the Kay Elemetrics EPG system, a speaker wears a custom-made false palate embedded with 96 contact electrodes. When the tongue touches any electrodes, a circuit is completed, current flows, and the contact is thereby registered. Figure 11.2 shows the electrode layout, which concentrates electrodes around the inner tooth surfaces and thus registers variation in tongue height. A computer samples the contact over the entire palate every 10 ms, and each frame of data shows which electrodes were contacted at that time. Figure 11.3 shows a sample frame of contact. Our general method is to construct speech materials that put a test consonant into different prosodic

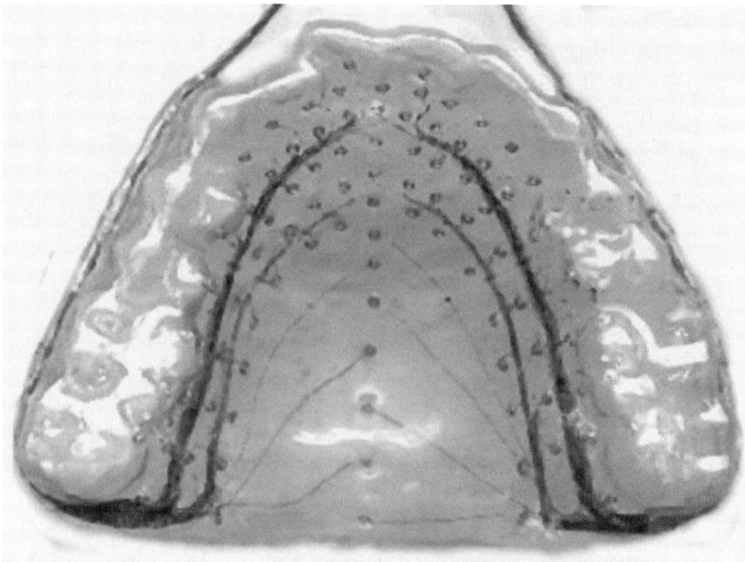

FIGURE 11.2. Sample pseudo-palate used with Kay Elemetrics Palatometer, showing arrangement of 96 contact electrodes. The front of the mouth is at the top of the picture.

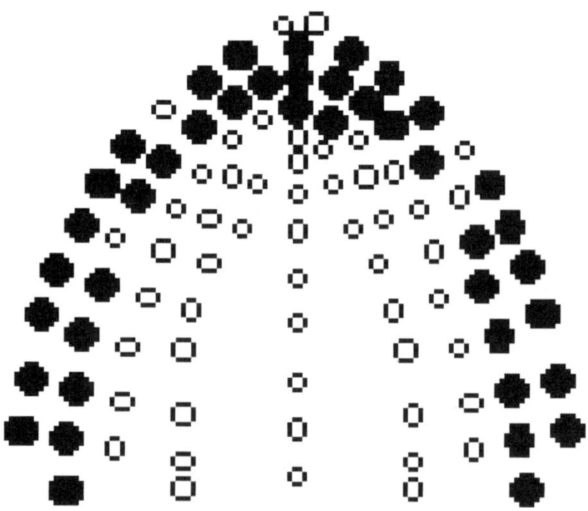

FIGURE 11.3. Sample frame showing peak linguopalatal contact for a Korean word-initial /n/. The orientation is the same as in Figure 11.2. Each circle is an electrode on the palate; filled circles have been contacted by the tongue (here, 42% contacted).

positions, and then take the simplest measure of strength, namely the maximum amount of contact between tongue and palate found during that consonant in each condition. This measure ignores where on the palate, and when during the consonant, this peak contact occurs, but those aspects can be measured as follow-ups. For stop consonants, we also generally measure the duration of the stop seal, that is, the amount of time (in number of data frames) that the vocal tract is completely sealed off by the stop occlusion.

Our first study, Fougeron and Keating (1997), looked at English /n/ and /o/ in initial and final positions in several domains. Three American speakers read reiterant versions of sentences, using the reiterant syllable /no/ to replace every syllable of the sentences. The sentences were arithmetic expressions in which the use of parentheses was crucial to the meanings of the expressions. One speaker produced a larger set of sentences in which different numerals occurred in the sentences, but the other two speakers produced only sentences with the numeral "89." This numeral was chosen because its lexical stress is generally on the last syllable, and thus should not be a factor in the articulation of the initial syllable. The prosodic phrasing of the utterances was coded post-hoc, using ToBI constituents,[4] and the prosodic position of each reiterant syllable was determined from these phrasings. The domains coded were the Utterance, the IP, the ip (or PP for Phonological Phrase, for typographical clarity), the Word, and the Syllable.

The percent contact was calculated for each frame of data; Figure 11.4 shows such data in a contact profile for a sample utterance. This figure illustrates that not only the consonants but also the vowels vary in contact across the utterance. The measured contacts for each segment are the values of the consonant peaks and vowel valleys as seen here. The temporal pattern can also be seen in this figure, though the duration measures that we took did not come from this kind of record. Articulatory seal duration (the duration of the frames in which a complete stop occlusion can be inferred) was not measured or

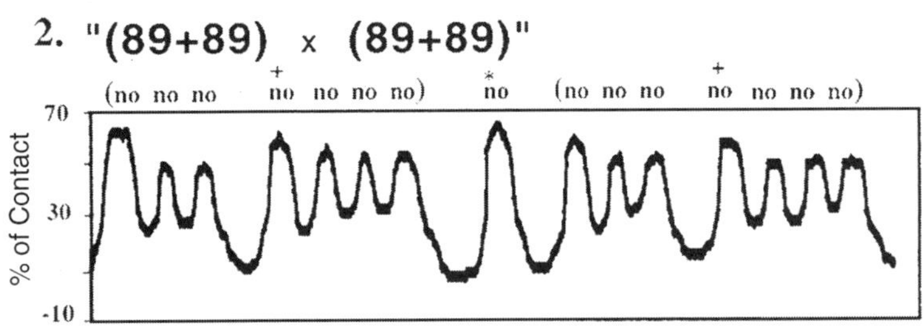

FIGURE 11.4. Sample trace of percent contact over time for a reiterant utterance. The reiterant utterance is modeled on the arithmetic expression shown at the top of the figure; the 15 reiterant syllables are indicated above the trace. High values of contact occur for /n/ while low values of contact occur for /o/.

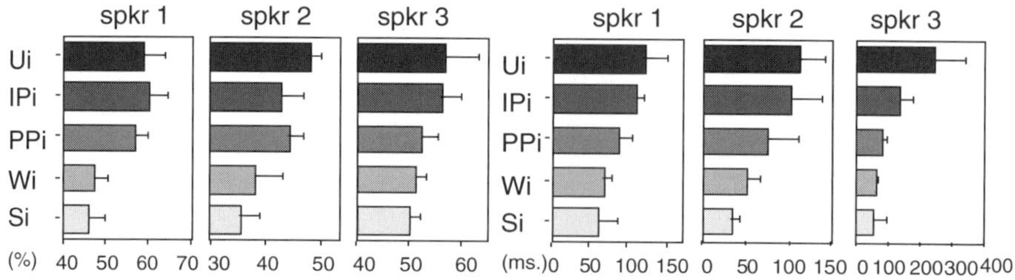

FIGURE 11.5. Mean results for three speakers of English: peak contact on the left, seal duration on the right, for /n/s initial in five prosodic domains (Utterance-initial: Ui, Intonational Phrase-initial: IPi, Phonological Phrase-initial: PPi, Word-initial: Wi, Syllable-initial: Si). From Keating et al. (2003).

reported in Fougeron and Keating (1997) but was measured subsequently and reported in Keating, Cho, Fougeron, and Hsu (2003). Figure 11.5 shows the results for both measures (peak contact on the left and seal duration on the right). This figure, like Figure 11.6 later, shows the mean peak contact for all /n/s initial in each prosodic domain, laid out like a prosodic hierarchy, with the highest domains at the top of the figure. If the prosodic positions have a cumulative effect on a measure, then the dark bars at the top will be longest and the light bars at the bottom will be shortest. And overall, this is what the figure shows, though not completely consistently.

The original hypothesis motivating this study did not involve domain-initial strengthening; we expected to see some kind of final or progressive weakening (declination), as discussed in detail in Fougeron and Keating (1997). Yet many

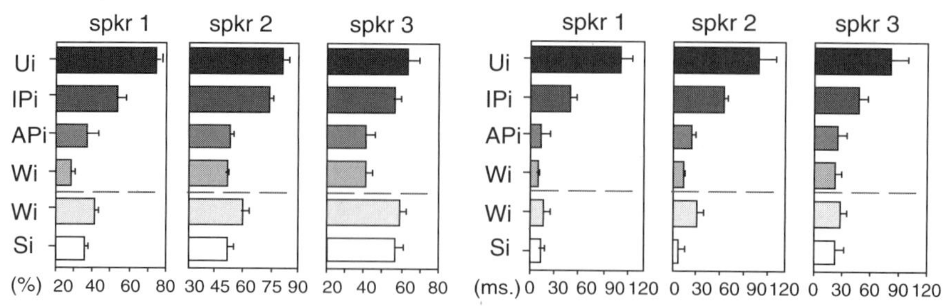

FIGURE 11.6. Mean results for three speakers of Korean: peak contact on the left, seal duration on the right, for /n/s initial in five prosodic domains (Utterance-initial: Ui, 33 Intonational Phrase-initial: IPi, Accentual Phrase-initial: APi, Word-initial: Wi, Syllable-initial: Si). The dashed horizontal line divides one set of comparisons, of levels above the Word, from another comparison, Word vs. Syllable, as explained in the text. From Keating et al. (2003).

explicit tests for declination failed to provide any evidence for it. What we found instead in our data for /n/ was fairly cumulative domain-initial strengthening: each speaker made three or four pairwise cumulative distinctions between /n/s in domain-initial positions. However, no speaker made all possible distinctions, and there was no pairwise distinction that was made by all three speakers. There was also a trend toward strengthening (meaning less contact) of the vowels in initial /no/ syllables; and strengthening of /n/ in domain-final syllables was occasionally found. Domain-final vowel strengthening was observed, but it was not as strongly cumulative, in that phrase final /o/s at different levels were not distinguished by amount of opening. Also, acoustic duration of /o/ did not vary much according to domain. In contrast, acoustic and articulatory durations of /n/ were more consistently cumulative than linguopalatal contact; nonetheless, correlations between /n/ durations and contact were minimal to modest.

We then followed up with a study of domain-initial strengthening in three other languages, which differ in their prosodic properties: French, Korean, and Taiwanese (Keating et al., 2003). None have lexical stress—French and Korean have phrasal tone patterns, and Taiwanese has lexical tones. In this study we used real-word utterances rather than reiterant speech, with test words beginning with the consonants /n/ or /t/, but similar prosodic domains as in the English study.[5] Overall, each language showed cumulative initial strengthening—as in English, contact and duration are generally greater in higher prosodic positions. In fact, the surprising result was how similar the results were for the three languages, despite their prosodic differences. The pattern was most consistent for Korean, which we had predicted could show the most articulatory strengthening, as its domain beginnings are generally thought to be prosodically strong. Figure 11.6 shows the results for Korean /n/; /t/ is similar. Here the smaller phrase is the Accentual Phrase (AP). This figure combines results for two different corpora, one for Word and above, the other for Word and below. Because the vowel contexts for the /n/s in the two corpora are different, the amount of contact for the two Word-initial /n/s is different. Indeed, it can be seen that the difference in contact between two prosodic domains is about the same size as the difference between two vowel contexts; it is furthermore about the same size as the difference between two consonant manners, such as /n/ vs. /t/ (/n/ having less contact).

A further result concerned the relation of duration to linguopalatal contact in the different languages: While all the languages had fairly consistent cumulative initial lengthening, only in Korean was strengthening (contact) strongly related to that lengthening. In our English data, the correlations of contact with duration were low to modest ($r^2 < .3$); in French there was a stronger relation ($r^2 > .6$); but in Korean the correlations were very high ($r^2 < .9$). This strong relation suggests a sort of undershoot mechanism. Strengthening in Korean seems to be related to how much time is available for the articulation: In Cho and Keating (2001), we showed that up to about 80 ms, the amount of contact is a function of the duration, with the peak contact coming at the end of the consonant and shorter consonants undershooting their target; but above about 80 ms, there is no additional contact. Thus it seems that in Korean, there is little if any independent effect of strengthening apart from lengthening. However, to the extent that the other languages are not like this, they in turn provide evidence that initial strengthening is a separate effect from lengthening—two effects, but both sensitive to prosodic position.

Other researchers have contributed to our knowledge about initial strengthening in a variety of languages, including Byrd, Kaun, Narayanan, and Saltzman (2000), Gordon (1999), Lavoie (2001), and Tabain (2003b). Most studies that have included several prosodic domains have found an overall tendency, but not a perfect pattern, of cumulative domain-initial strengthening. For example, in an EPG study of Japanese (Onaka, 2003; Onaka, Watson, Palethorpe, & Harrington, 2004), two speakers showed some effects of prosodic position on contact for /n/, but only one of the speakers showed effects for /t/. The effects on consonant duration (domain-initial lengthening), and on the preboundary vowel's openness, were perhaps more striking in this study.

A major exception is found in EMA studies in which displacement is the spatial measure. Thus, Byrd et al. (2000) found that in Tamil /m/ and /n/ lengthen but show only small differences in spatial displacement; Tabain (2003b) likewise found no effect of prosodic position on the peak displacement of French domain-initial consonants / b d g f s ʃ /. And, Byrd and Saltzman (1998) found a very different result for English than we did: Comparing lip movements at the boundaries of what were probably three different prosodic domains, they found that displacement to the postboundary consonant was highly correlated with duration.[6] It seems from these studies that displacement does not depend on prosodic position in the way that peak linguopalatal contact does. Even in Fougeron and Keating (1997), we found that the closest EPG measure to true articulator displacement, namely change (difference) in contact, is not strongly related to peak contact. Peak linguopalatal contact is probably more closely related to constriction degree, and thus to the magnitude of the articulation, than is displacement of an EMA coil.

FURTHER RESULTS

Further observations can be made about domain-initial strengthening on the basis of additional analyses in Fougeron and Keating as well as later studies at UCLA. On English: Cho (2002), Keating, Wright, and Zhang (1999); on Korean: Cho and Jun (2000), Cho and Keating (2001), and Kim (2001); and on French: Fougeron (1998, 2001).

First, some segments vary more than others; indeed some segment types show no initial strengthening. For example, Fougeron (1998, 2001) looked at EPG contact for French /n t k l s i/, and found that prosodic position had less effect on contact for /s/ and /i/ than for the other segments. For the sibilant fricative /s/, Fougeron measured several aspects of the fricative constriction, not just overall contact. By all measures, it varied very little across prosodic positions, presumably because the production of sibilance constrains the articulation. That fricative /s/ is highly constrained in its articulation is no surprise, and the same has been shown at the word level for English, e.g., Byrd (1996) and Keating et al. (1999). However, Kim (2001) did find differences in the two Korean sibilants, /s/ and /s*/, specifically in the contact in the mid-palate and the fricative channel region, across three prosodic positions, with /s/ seemingly showing more of an effect than /s*/. This result shows that sibilants in at least one language are free to vary, but no reason is offered for why Korean might be different in this respect. Perhaps it is another reflection of the strong relation in Korean between duration and articulatory contact; clear prosodically determined duration differences are seen for /s/ but not /s*/. As another example, Cho and Keating (2001) compared the four Korean coronal stops /n/, /t/, /t^h/, /t*/, and while all showed an effect of prosodic position on contact, the range of variation differed across the consonants, such that the prosodic effect was larger for some than for others.

Second, domain-initial strengthening appears to be a very local effect largely limited to the first segment after a boundary, and is thus unlike final lengthening, which extends over a larger span. For example, in the French study (Fougeron, 1998), domain-initial strengthening was limited to only the /k/ in a /kl/ cluster, and to a vowel only when there is no preceding initial consonant (/i/ in /#ip/ but not /a/ in /#na/). This very local effect is perhaps consistent with the fact that in French, final lengthening is more limited in extent than in English (Fletcher, 1991). Similarly, in our Korean study (Cho & Keating, 2001), we found no consistent domain-initial vowel lengthening in initial CVs. In English, the evidence seems more mixed, but in two studies vowels in #CV varied only somewhat with prosodic domain (Cho, 2002, in press; Fougeron & Keating, 1997).

Third, it is noteworthy that strengthening does not result in discrete phonetic categories, corresponding to the domains of the prosodic hierarchy, even though descriptions of prosody are couched in terms of these discrete domains. In Cho and Keating (2001), we compared pooled measures of acoustic domain-final lengthening and EPG domain-initial contact, as seen here in Figure 11.7. In statistical comparisons, both sets of measures support a four-way prosodic distinction. However, only the data for final duration clearly fall into discrete categories, and only two of those; in contrast, the data for initial contact belong to a single large unimodal distribution. That is, it cannot be claimed that there are four (or however many) categories of phonetic strength, each of which gets

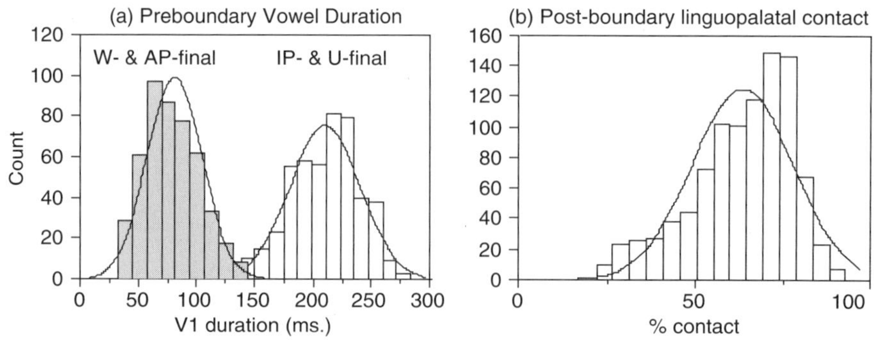

FIGURE 11.7. Histograms of all measurements of (a) domain-final vowel duration and (b) domain-initial consonant contact, pooled across consonants and speakers. From Cho and Keating (2001).

some additional increment of constriction; the effect appears instead to be continuous.

Finally, it is worth stressing that in Fougeron and Keating (1997), we were careful to distinguish initial strengthening from final weakening and declination. While these terms might sound as if they are different names for the same thing (e.g., some sort of downtrend), they in fact describe different outcomes when a large enough span of speech is considered. Fougeron and Keating called the effect initial strengthening because of explicit tests[7] that favored that interpretation. (To be sure, initial strengthening cannot be distinguished from everywhere-but-initial-weakening, but that is the only sense in which strengthening and weakening are two sides of the same coin here.) Simple comparisons of two positions cannot decide this point. For example, a comparison of initial vs. final positions by itself cannot distinguish these three possibilities, and much of the literature compares only two positions in this way. In such two-way comparisons the terms initial strengthening, final weakening, and declination all come to the same thing, and no importance can be placed on the choice of descriptive term.

Fougeron and Keating did not look at domain-final consonants, since all our test syllables were CVs. Given the historical linguistics literature, it is plausible that domain-final consonants should show some weakening. In Keating et al. (1999) we made a very limited comparison of domain-initial and domain-final consonants—four coronals / t d n l /; in the test corpus, word-initial consonants occurred utterance-initially vs. utterance-medially, while word-final consonants occurred utterance-medially vs. utterance-finally. The maximum EPG contact depended on position in both the word and the utterance. Overall, as expected, word-initial consonants had more contact than word-final, and also as expected, word-initial consonants had more contact when they were also at the beginning of an utterance. However, utterance-final consonants had more contact than other word-final consonants. That is, there appears to be no cumulative domain-final weakening of consonants; instead we see some strengthening at the end of the largest domain. The role of domain-final lengthening in this apparent strengthening deserves further study.

ACOUSTIC AND OPTICAL CORRELATES

The kinds of articulatory variation discussed above give rise to two kinds of potentially perceivable variation: acoustic and optical.[8] Two influential phonetic studies of initial strengthening, Pierrehumbert and Talkin (1992) and Dilley, Shattuck-Hufnagel, and Ostendorf (1996), were in fact acoustic, not articulatory, studies. Pierrehumbert and Talkin showed that in phrase-initial position, /h/Vs are more consonant-like by an RMS measure (lower RMS indicating less glottal excitation); and aspirated stops are more aspirated, suggesting greater magnitude of their glottal spreading gestures. Another interesting example of prosodically conditioned acoustic variation involving the glottis is Hsu and Jun's (1998) study of Taiwanese VOT. Taiwanese has voiced (often prenasalized), voiceless unaspirated, and voiceless aspirated stops. Hsu and Jun found that when /k^h/ and /b/ are initial in higher domains, the /k^h/ is more aspirated and the /b/ is more voiced. Thus the phonetic voicing categories are acoustically more distinct in stronger positions. Other acoustic studies of initial strengthening include Cho and Keating (2001) and Tabain (2003a).

The optical correlates of prosody have been studied very little to date, mainly the correlates of prominence, but since many articulations involve the face, at least some aspects of phrasing should also be visible. Certainly durational differences should be apparent, even if subtler articulatory differences are difficult to see. A study with colleagues at the House Ear Institute in Los Angeles (Auer, Kim, Keating, Scarborough, Alwan, & Bernstein, 2004) tested the visual perceptibility of prosodic boundaries.

Talkers read minimal pairs of sentences differing in the presence/absence of boundaries, while movements of reflective markers on their faces, including on the chin, were tracked by the Qualysis infrared system. Some sentences contrasted in presence/absence of a word boundary (e.g., He was noted for getting the right number vs. He just hated forgetting the right number), while others contrasted in presence/absence of a phrase boundary (e.g., When you sing, his songs are better vs. When you sing his songs, they're better). The duration of the movement of the marker on the chin was measured, and was found to be longer around a boundary. Acoustic durations were also longer across a boundary. Perceivers then saw sentence fragments and had to decide which sentence (with or without boundary) the fragment had come from. Perceivers were generally good at doing this.

IMPLICATIONS OF STRENGTHENING

Whether the acoustic correlates of prosody, of the sort discussed in the preceding section, are used in auditory perception has only recently begun to be determined. When segmental contrasts are enhanced, listeners' perception of segments might be improved.[9] And, when the acoustic correlates indicate a prosodic boundary, listeners' prosodic parsing might be improved. Cho, McQueen, and Cox (2004) review the literature so far and offer some evidence that listeners use segmental correlates in perceiving prosodic boundaries. In this section, I speculate on two possible functional implications of domain-initial strengthening, if it turns out to be useful to perceivers in these ways.

First, the information about phrase boundaries that might be conveyed by segment strength could also be seen as information about the local coherence vs. disjuncture in connected speech. A strengthened segment indicates a break and the start of a new domain, while domain-internal spans of segments are not interrupted by strengthening. We do not know whether speakers manipulate strength on purpose for the sake of listeners, but on this view, if they do, they may do so to indicate the degree of break/cohesion between words in connected speech. This suggests to me the possibility that while stronger segments may consume more calories of a speaker's articulatory energy than do weaker ones, weaker segments do not reflect laziness or inattention on the part of the speaker. Rather, we should think of the speaker's energy as constantly directed to control of the modulation of articulation, because all levels of strength carry information. To be sure, there is a general tendency in speaking toward ease of articulation, which is resisted in strong positions; and as a result, segmental cues may be weaker in weak positions. (See several chapters in Hayes, Kirchner, & Steriade, 2004 for examples.) But then this reduction in segmental information is itself information for listeners—information about juncture.

Second, if strengthening increases information about segment identity, it does so in just those positions where such information is most important. Psycholinguists (e.g., Levelt et al., 1999) have noted the special status of word-initial position in speech errors, at least in English; word-initial segments:

- Are more vulnerable to speech errors
- Are exchanged in speech errors
- Show stronger similarity effects in speech errors (Frisch, 2000)

And these word-initial segments are produced with articulatory strengthening. Is this a paradox? Phonetically, word-initial position is said to be "strong," yet much of the psycholinguistic evidence concerns errors. If these segments are strong, why do they seem so vulnerable? A possible resolution to this quandary can be found in the contributions of Dell (2000) and Frisch (2000) to the *Laboratory Phonology V*, in which they suggest that speech errors arise in word- (or in most such experiments, utterance-) initial position due to lack of a constraining prior context. Because other words are possible, other word candidates are activated and compete with the correct word, resulting in selection errors. Furthermore, word-initial position is a position of competition between many competitors, in the sense that words generally can begin with a greater variety of segments than they end with, such that there are more (different) segments in strong competition word-initially than elsewhere. That is, word-initial segments are more vulnerable to errors because there are more possibilities when context does not provide strong constraints.

This explanation seems comparable to a suggestion by Fougeron and Keating (1997) concerning phonetic strengthening. They noted that, from the perspective of the listener, initial segments are probably on average less determined by prior context, and that therefore the acoustic signal must bear a greater load in the recovery of the message in those positions. Anything that improves the perception of initial segments would compensate for their lack of predictability. Initial strengthening could thus help the listener by enhancing segmental properties in positions of uncertainty. Thus the resolution of the paradox would be that initial segments are contextually weak, that is, relatively unconstrained by their prior context. Because of this contextual weakness they are more vulnerable to competition from other lexical entries in the process of speech production, and more vulnerable to mis-hearing in speech perception; yet for the same reason they stand to benefit more from strengthening. On this view, we would expect to find a relation between predictability (on some independent measure) and degree of strengthening, with greater predictability associated with less strengthening.

Finally, as shown earlier, phonetic strengthening occurs in higher prosodic domains. The larger the phrasal domain, the more likely is the initial position to be unconstrained by context (for example, the first segment of a sentence is probably far less predictable than the first segment of most words within a sentence).[10] If contextual uncertainty is indeed the connection between the psycholinguistic phenomena and phonetic strengthening, then we would also predict that speech errors and mis-hearings should be more frequent in initial positions of higher phrasal domains. As Keating and Shattuck-Hufnagel (2002) review, errors across phonological words are far more common than errors within words, so this prediction is plausible.

CONCLUSION

This review of findings about domain-initial articulatory strengthening counters the view, espoused by Levelt et al. (1999), that segmental and prosodic planning for speech production can proceed separately. Since phonetic encoding of segments is highly sensitive to prosodic structure, prosody needs to be computed first, not last as in Levelt's model. Returning to the example phrase in Figure 11.1 ("that new propaganda"), consider the effects of prosodic position on the feature values indicated. The word "that" is in the strongest position, initial in the highest domain, so the initial continuant consonant is likely to be strengthened to a stop articulation.[11] The word "propaganda" is in a strong position because of its prominence, which will affect the stressed syllable "gan." The /p/ at the beginning of the word should be somewhat stronger than the /p/ in the second syllable, and thus should have a closer oral consonant constriction, while its glottal abduction should be larger. Phonetic plans for those, and all other, aspects of the utterance must refer to prosody.

How might such prosody-dependent phonetic encoding of features be modeled? One possibility would be Byrd et al.'s (2000) π-gestures, gestures associated with prosodic boundaries, by which the prosody could modulate precompiled syllable scores. Another possibility is a window-style model, in which prosody could modulate articulatory targets. Window models (Keating 1990, 1996) posit ranges, rather than fixed points, as the targets of articulatory movements. Guenther (1995) first suggested that such target ranges could be sensitive to prosody, expanding or contracting over the course of an utterance; Cho (2002, 2004) in contrast proposes that prosody specifies a subrange within the window. Either way, at an edge or a prominence, target ranges would shift toward extreme values. While such proposals remain to be worked out, they have the potential advantage of extending readily to other kinds of variability, on other timescales, that are not accounted for by fixed windows, or by Byrd et al.'s gestures. In addition to shifts that are local to a prosodic position, target ranges could shift at the word level, as a function of lexical difficulty due to competition, and more globally, as a function of discourse factors.

In summary, when a speaker plans for the phonetic aspects of speech production, prosodic structure organizes the treatment of possibly every feature in every segment, and the interactions of segments. One aspect of this dependence is the relation between the strength of a prosodic position, and the phonetic strength of a segment in that position. A theory of phonetic encoding that incorporates this basic fact is a major challenge, but an important one.

ACKNOWLEDGMENTS

This research was supported by an NSF Linguistics grant to P. Keating (#95-11118), an NSF dissertation improvement grant to P. Keating and T. Cho (#BCS-0001716), and an NSF KDI grant to L. Bernstein et al. (#99-96088). Collaborations with all my co-authors on the various papers cited here, the contributions of the former students cited, and helpful comments on the manuscript by the editors and reviewers, are gratefully acknowledged.

NOTES

1. Possibly the articulations are more forceful, with greater muscular contraction—see Fougeron (1999, 2001) for discussion.
2. See Zhang (2004, pp. 167–168) for a phonological effect of domain-final lengthening, namely on the distribution or licensing of contour tones in languages.
3. This is not to say that synchronic phonological patterns or sound changes across languages uniformly illustrate initial strengthening. It seems clear that in some languages, at least at the word level, the stem, root, or some other part of a word is more important than the beginning. A striking example is provided by Australian languages, as described by Butcher (this volume) and Tabain, Breen, and Butcher (2004).
4. ToBI transcription uses the acoustic signal, particularly fundamental frequency and durations, to determine the phrasing of a spoken utterance. This phrasing is thus potentially different from a prosodic parse assigned by a theory of prosodic phonology, e.g., Nespor and Vogel (1986). In effect, ToBI transcription gives up a concern with predicting the different factors that could influence phrasing, in favor of a more veridical account of surface phonological form, after any restructurings. (Prosodic theories must allow for restructuring, or its nonderivational equivalent, since most sentences have multiple possible prosodic phrasings.) For a review of the correspondences between these two types of representation, see Shattuck-Hufnagel and Turk (1996). For a proposal about how they might be related in production planning, see Keating and Shattuck-Hufnagel (2002). For discussion of transcription practice for boundaries, see de Pijper and Sanderman (1994).
5. Two points deserve mention in this connection. First, there is no reason that the prosodic domains should be exactly comparable across the languages; the small phrases in particular seem to vary across languages. Second, the speakers of the different languages differed in their use of pauses; the French speakers sometimes paused at IP boundaries, while the Korean and Taiwanese speakers were instructed not to do so.
6. This result might seem to suggest that English is in fact like Korean, with a relation between strengthening and lengthening, contrary to our own result. However, our correlations are with peak contact, not displacement.
7. Because our test utterances contained many syllables we were able to compare initial vs. medial vs. final syllables in the various domains. For example, final weakening would have meant that the final syllable consonants had less contact, and declination would have meant a decrease in contact across consonants in the domain.
8. The term "optical," as opposed to "visual," is perhaps surprising, but it is parallel to "acoustic" in the sound domain. That is, acoustic:auditory::optical:visual—optical and acoustic properties of signals lead to auditory and visual percepts. Characterization of the stimuli used in visual perception experiments involves optical phonetics.
9. It must be noted that the hypothesis that strengthening serves an enhancing function for listeners is controversial. Various views on the nature and possible function of segmental enhancement in domain-initial positions can be found in, for example, Pierrehumbert and Talkin (1992), Fougeron and Keating (1997), Hsu and Jun (1998), Fougeron (1998, 1999, 2001), and Cho and McQueen (2005).

10. We do not know of any evidence about segment predictability by prosodic position. If large domains were more likely to begin with th- function words, then our assumption would be wrong.
11. Although not generally noted in the literature (though see Pierrehumbert and Talkin 1992 for one mention), stopping of nonsibilant fricatives, both labiodental and dental, seems to be common in at least American English. In the case of the dentals, the interdental articulation means that these stops do not sound like alveolars. By hypothesis, the stopped variants are in prosodically strong positions.

REFERENCES

Auer, E. T. Jr., Kim, S., Keating, P., Scarborough, R. A., Alwan, A., & Bernstein, L. E. (2004). *Optical phonetics and visual perception of lexical and phrasal boundaries in English*. Paper presented at the 148th meeting of the Acoustical Society of America, San Deigo. Abstract in *Journal of the Acoustical Society of America, 116*, 2644.

Beckman, M. E., Edwards, J., & Fletcher, J. (1992). Prosodic structure and tempo in a sonority model of articulatory dynamics. In G. J. Docherty & D. R. Ladd (Eds.), *Papers in laboratory phonology II: Gesture, segment, prosody* (pp. 68–86). Cambridge, UK: Cambridge University Press.

Bell, A., & Bybee Hooper, J. (1978). Issues and evidence in syllabic phonology. In A. Bell & J. Hooper (Eds.), *Syllables and segments* (pp. 3–24). Amsterdam: North-Holland Publishing.

Butcher, A. (2006). Australian Aboriginal languages: Consonant-salient phonologies and the "place-of-articulation imperative". In J. Harrington & M. Tabain (Eds.), *Speech production* (pp. 187–210). New York: Psychology Press.

Byrd, D. (1996). Influences on articulatory timing in consonant sequences. *Journal of Phonetics, 24*, 209–244.

Byrd, D., & Saltzman, E. (1998). Intragestural dynamics of multiple prosodic boundaries. *Journal of Phonetics, 26*, 173–200.

Byrd, D., Kaun, A., Narayanan, S., & Saltzman, E. (2000). Phrasal signatures in articulation. In M. B. Broe & J. B. Pierrehumbert (Eds.), *Papers in laboratory phonology V: Acquisition and the lexicon* (pp. 70–87). Cambridge, UK: Cambridge University Press.

Cho, T. (2002). *The effects of prosody on articulation in English*. New York: Routledge.

Cho, T. (2004). Prosodically-conditioned strengthening and vowel-to-vowel coarticulation in English. *Journal of Phonetics, 32*, 141–176.

Cho, T. (2005). Prosodic strengthening and featural enhancement: Evidence from acoustic and articulatory realizations of /a,i/ in English. *Journal of the Acoustical Society of America, 117*, 3867–3878.

Cho, T., & Jun, S.-A. (2000). Domain-initial strengthening as enhancement of laryngeal features: Aerodynamic evidence from Korean. In J. Boyle, J.-H. Lee, & A. Okrent (Eds.) (Vol. 36, pp. 31–44). *CLS 36-1: The main session*. Chicago Linguistic Society. (Also in *UCLA Working Papers in Phonetics, 99*, 57–69.)

Cho, T., & Keating, P. (2001). Articulatory and acoustic studies on domain-initial strengthening in Korean. *Journal of Phonetics, 29*, 155–190.

Cho, T., & McQueen, J. (2005). Prosodic influences on consonant production in Dutch: Effects of prosodic boundaries, phrasal accent and lexical stress. *Journal of Phonetics, 33*, 121–157.

Cho, T., McQueen, J., & Cox, E. (2004). *Prosodically driven phonetic detail in speech processing: The case of domain-initial strengthening in English*. Unpublished manuscript, Max Planck Institute for Psycholinguistics.

de Jong, K. (1995). The supraglottal articulation of prominence in English: Linguistic stress as localized hyperarticulation. *Journal of the Acoustical Society of America*, *97*, 491–504.

de Pijper, J. R., & Sanderman, A. A. (1994). On the perceptual strength of prosodic boundaries and its relation to suprasegmental cues. *Journal of the Acoustical Society of America*, *96*, 2037–2047.

Dell, G. (2000). Commentary: Counting, connectionism, and lexical representation. In M. B. Broe & J. B. Pierrehumbert (Eds.), *Papers in laboratory phonology V: Acquisition and the lexicon* (pp. 335–348). Cambridge, UK: Cambridge University Press.

Dilley, L., Shattuck-Hufnagel, S., & Ostendorf, M. (1996). Glottalization of word-initial vowels as a function of prosodic structure. *Journal of Phonetics*, *24*, 423–444.

Donegan, P., & Stampe, D. (1979). The study of natural phonology. In D. A. Dinnsen (Ed.), *Current Approaches to Phonological Theory* (pp. 126–173). Bloomington: Indiana University Press.

Edwards, J., Beckman, M. E., & Fletcher, J. (1991). The articulatory kinematics of final lengthening. *Journal of the Acoustical Society of America*, *89*, 369–382.

Epstein, M. (2002). *Voice quality and prosody in English*. Unpublished UCLA dissertation.

Epstein, M. (2003). Voice quality and prosody in English. *Proceedings of the 15th international congress of phonetic sciences* (pp. 2405–2408).

Erickson, D. (2002). Articulation of extreme formant patterns for emphasized vowels. *Phonetica*, *59*, 134–149.

Fletcher, J. (1991). Rhythm and final lengthening in French. *Journal of Phonetics*, *19*, 193–212.

Fletcher, J., & Vatikiotis-Bateson, E. (1994). Prosody and intrasyllabic timing in French. *Ohio State University Working Papers*, *43*, 41–46.

Fougeron, C. (1998). *Variations articulatoires en début de constituants prosodiques de différents niveaux en français*. Thèse de doctorat, Université Paris III.

Fougeron, C. (1999). Prosodically conditioned articulatory variations: A review. *UCLA Working Papers in Phonetics*, *97*, 1–74.

Fougeron, C. (2001). Articulatory properties of initial segments in several prosodic constituents in French. *Journal of Phonetics*, *26*, 45–69.

Fougeron, C., & Keating, P. (1997). Articulatory strengthening at edges of prosodic domains. *Journal of the Acoustical Society of America*, *101*, 3728–3740.

Frisch, S. (2000). Temporally organized lexical representations as phonological units. In M. B. Broe & J. B. Pierrehumbert (Eds.), *Papers in laboratory phonology V: Acquisition and the lexicon* (pp. 283–298). Cambridge, UK: Cambridge University Press.

Gordon, M. (1999). The effect of stress and prosodic phrasing on duration, acoustic amplitude and air flow of nasals in Estonian. *UCLA Working Papers in Phonetics*, *92*, 151–159.

Guenther, F. (1995). Speech sound acquisition, coarticulation, and rate effects in a neural network model of speech production. *Psychological Review*, *102*, 594–621.

Harrington, J., Fletcher, J., & Beckman, M. (2000). Manner and place conflicts in the articulation of Australian English consonants. In M. B. Broe & J. B. Pierrehumbert (Eds.), *Papers in laboratory phonology V: Acquisition and the lexicon* (pp. 40–51). Cambridge, UK: Cambridge University Press.

Hawkins, S., & Smith, R. (2001) Polysp: A polysystemic, phonetically-rich approach to speech understanding. *Journal of Italian Linguistics – Rivista di Linguistica*, *13*, 99–188.

Hayes, B, Kirchner, R., & Steriade, D. (Eds.). (2004). *Phonetically based phonology*. Cambridge, UK: Cambridge University Press.

Hock, H. H. (1991). *Principles of historical linguistics* (2nd ed.). Berlin: Mouton de Gruyter.

Hock, H. H. (1992). Initial strengthening. In W. U. Dressler, H. C. Luschutzky, O. E. Pfeiffer, & J. R. Rennison (Eds.), *Phonologica 1988* (pp. 101–110). Cambridge, UK: Cambridge University Press.

Hsu, C.-S., & Jun, S.-A. (1998). Prosodic strengthening in Taiwanese: Syntagmatic or paradigmatic? *UCLA Working Papers in Phonetics*, *96*, 69–89.

Keating, P. (1990). The window model of coarticulation: Articulatory evidence. In J. Kingston & M. Beckman (Eds.), *Papers in laboratory phonology I* (pp. 451–470). Cambridge, UK: Cambridge University Press.

Keating, P. (1996). The phonology-phonetics interface. In U. Kleinhenz (Ed.), *Interfaces in Phonology* (pp. 262–278). Studia grammatica, 41. Berlin: Akademie Verlag.

Keating, P., Cho, T., Fougeron, C., & Hsu, C.-S. (2003). Domain-initial strengthening in four languages. In J. Local, R. Ogden, & R. Temple (Eds.), *Phonetic interpretation: Papers in laboratory phonology VI* (pp. 143–161). Cambridge, UK: Cambridge University Press.

Keating, P., & Shattuck-Hufnagel, S. (2002). A prosodic view of word form encoding for speech production. *UCLA Working Papers in Phonetics, 101*, 112–156.

Keating, P., Wright, R., & Zhang, J. (1999). Word-level asymmetries in consonant articulation. *UCLA Working Papers in Phonetics, 97*, 157–173.

Kim, S. (2001). Domain initial strengthening of Korean fricatives /s/ and /s*/. *Harvard Studies in Korean Linguistics, IX*, 164–173.

Lavoie, L. (2001). *Consonant strength: Phonological patterns and phonetic manifestations*. New York: Garland.

Lehiste, I. (1970). *Suprasegmentals*. Cambridge, MA: MIT Press.

Levelt, W. J. M. (1989). *Speaking: From intention to articulation*. Cambridge, MA: MIT Press.

Levelt, W. J. M., Roelofs, A., & Meyer, A. S. (1999). A theory of lexical access in speech production. *Brain and Behavioral Sciences, 22*, 1–38.

Martinet, A. (1955). *Economie des changements phonétiques: Traité de phonologie diachronique*. Berne: Francke SA.

Nespor, M., & Vogel, I. (1986). *Prosodic phonology*. Dordrecht: Foris Publications.

Onaka, A. (2003). Domain-initial strengthening in Japanese: An acoustic and articulatory study. *Proceedings of the 15th international congress of phonetic sciences* (pp. 2091–2094).

Onaka, A., Watson, C., Palethorpe, S., & Harrington, J. (2004). *Prosodic boundary effects on domain-initial segments in Japanese: An acoustic and articulatory study*. Unpublished manuscript, Macquarie University.

Pierrehumbert, J. (1999). Prosody and Intonation. In R. A. Wilson & F. Keil (Eds.), *The MIT encyclopedia of the cognitive sciences* (pp. 479–482). Cambridge, MA: MIT Press.

Pierrehumbert, J., & Talkin, D. (1992). Lenition of /h/ and glottal stop. In G. J. Docherty & D. R. Ladd (Eds.), *Papers in laboratory phonology II: Gesture, segment, prosody* (pp. 90–117). Cambridge, UK: Cambridge University Press.

Shattuck-Hufnagel, S., & Turk, A. E. (1996). A prosody tutorial for investigators of auditory sentence processing. *Journal of Psycholinguistic Research*, 25, 193–247.

Tabain, M. (2003a). Effects of prosodic boundary on /aC/ sequences: Acoustic results. *Journal of the Acoustical Society of America, 113*, 516–531.

Tabain, M. (2003b). Effects of prosodic boundary on /aC/ sequences: Articulatory results. *Journal of the Acoustical Society of America, 113*, 2834–2849.

Tabain, M., Breen, G., & Butcher, A. (2004). CV vs. VC syllables: A comparison of Aboriginal languages with English. *Journal of the International Phonetic Association, 34*, 175–200.

Vaissière, J. (1988). Prediction of velar movement from phonological specifications. *Phonetica, 45*, 122–139.

Wightman, C., Shattuck-Hufnagel, S., Ostendorf, M., & Price, P. (1992). Segmental durations in the vicinity of prosodic phrase boundaries. *Journal of the Acoustical Society of America, 91*, 1707–1717.

Zhang, J. (2004). The role of contrast-specific and language-specific phonetics in contour tone distribution. In B. Hayes, R. Kirchner, & D. Steriade (Eds.), *Phonetically Based Phonology* (pp. 157–190). Cambridge, UK: Cambridge University Press.

12

Australian Aboriginal Languages

Consonant-Salient Phonologies and the "Place-of-Articulation Imperative"

ANDREW BUTCHER

ABSTRACT

Australian languages typically have small vowel inventories and very unusual consonant systems. They have no close vowels, no voicing contrast, and no manner-of-articulation contrasts among the obstruents but they have an unusually large number of places of articulation. Observation of spontaneous speech and acoustic measurements of laboratory speech indicate an overwhelming imperative to preserve place of articulation distinctions, especially in medial consonants. Controlled experiments on the articulatory dynamics and micro-prosody of these languages indicate that many of the durational contrasts and nearly all of the spectral contrasts are found in the medial consonants rather than in the vowels. This phonetic enhancement of the acoustic and perceptual salience of intervocalic consonants is manifested synchronically at the phonetic level in most currently spoken Australian languages. It has become phonologised to varying degrees in a number of these languages, whose phonological structure is now arguably VC(V), rather than the universally accepted CV(C). However, languages that have reached this stage may not retain this structure, but show signs of moving towards a CV(C) pattern once more. Thus this may be a cyclical process, possibly driven by a tension between a universal linguistic preference for CV(C) structure in the human brain on the one hand and the unique phonetic characteristics of Australian languages on the other. These characteristics appear to be motivated by the "place-of-articulation imperative", which strongly favours the VC(V) structure as a means of maximising the perceptual distinctions between consonants. I conclude with some speculations as to what might be the motivation for the place-of-articulation imperative.

INTRODUCTION

It is estimated that at the time the First Fleet sailed into Botany Bay in 1788, over 200 different languages were spoken in Australia. Today, less than 100 have any surviving speakers (and less than 20 are "living" languages, used in everyday life and being transmitted to the next generation). Figure 12.1 indicates approximately where those languages referred to in this paper are spoken. The indigenous languages of Australia are as different from one another in their lexicon and in their grammar as to be mutually unintelligible. However, they share a number of striking similarities in their phonology and in their phonetics, which set them apart from most other languages of the world.

To begin with, almost all Australian languages have a rather small system of vowel contrasts (Butcher, 1994). In the north, the majority of languages have a five-vowel system, but over the continent as a whole, over 50% of languages distinguish just three vowel categories—though there may be an additional length contrast with limited distribution. In most accounts, these have been

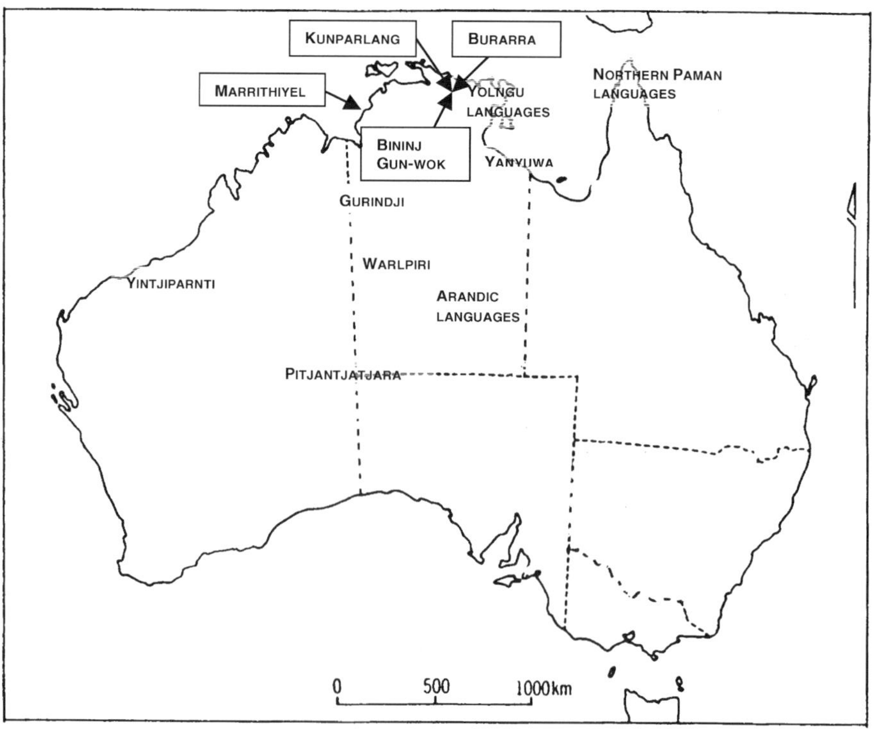

FIGURE 12.1. Approximate location of Australian languages referred to in this chapter.

described as two high vowels—one front unrounded and one back rounded—and one low central vowel.

Figure 12.2 shows a formant plot of the vowels of a speaker of Warlpiri—a typical Australian three-vowel language—and gives an indication as to where

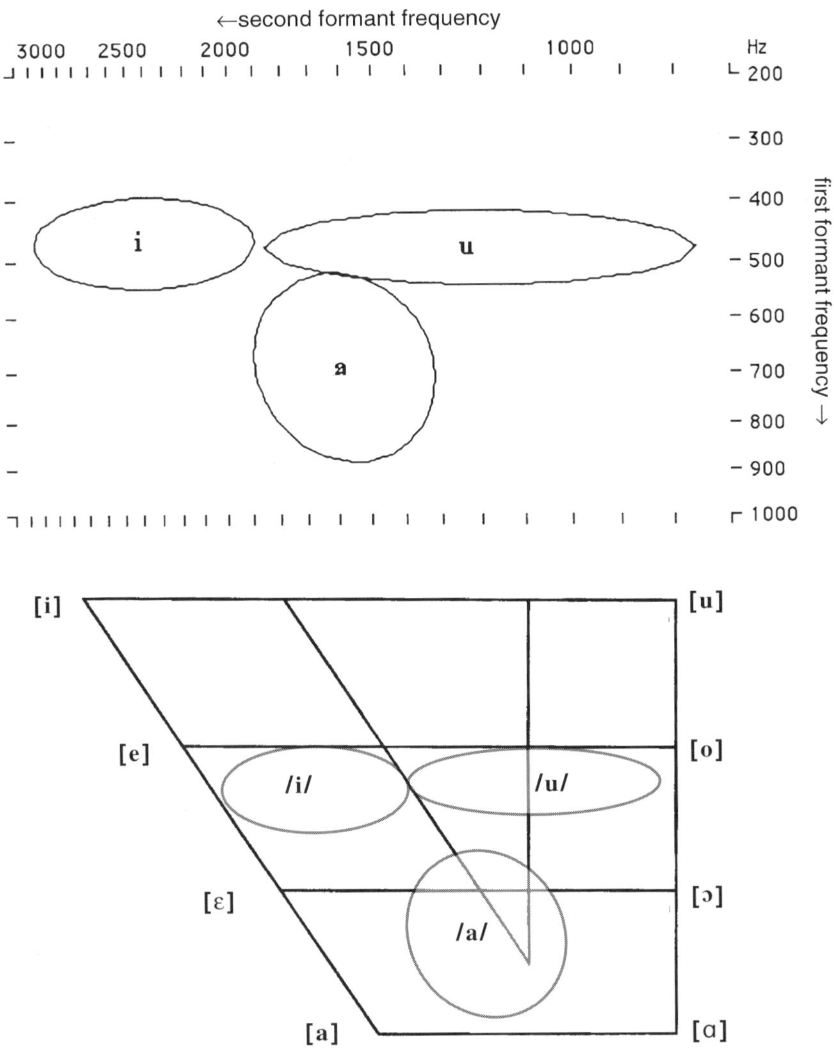

FIGURE 12.2. Warlpiri vowels. Above: Plot of mean first and second formant frequencies of approximately 600 vowels in various contexts, from a list of isolated words (Speaker BP ♀). Ellipses indicate two standard deviations from the means. Below: Indication of vowel positions relative to Cardinal Vowel quadrilateral. Suggested phonetic values: /i/ = [e], /u/ = [o], /a/ = [ɐ].

the phonetic qualities of these vowel realisations would lie in relation to the Cardinal Vowel reference system. With a rather consistent realisation in an area of the vowel space centred on F_1 = 800 Hz and F_2 = 1500 Hz, the /a/ does indeed lie in the region between half-open and open central vowels and could be symbolised as raised and centralised [ä̝] or perhaps more simply as [ɐ]. The mean values for /i/, however, suggest that this vowel is not pronounced by these speakers with a quality approaching very near to [i]. F_1 values of over 450 Hz strongly indicate a half-close vowel, even in female speakers, and in general the quality is of a lowered half-close front vowel [e̞]. Similarly, with F_1 values centred in the area of 450–500 Hz, /u/ would also appear to be a mid-vowel, most accurately described as a lowered half-close back-rounded [o̞]. Furthermore, a wide range of second formant values extending beyond 1000 Hz indicate a fair degree of centralisation for some allophones. This could be because the tongue is not very retracted for these variants, but probably a more important factor is the lack of lip rounding, which has been remarked upon in the literature (e.g., Dixon, 1980, p. 130).

Even more striking than this, however, are the unusual "long flat" consonant systems of these languages (Butcher, 1996). The unusually large number of place-of-articulation distinctions and reduced number of manner-of-articulation distinctions mean that the consonantal phoneme chart for a typical Australian language has more columns and fewer rows than most languages elsewhere in the world (Table 12.1). In addition to the more familiar bilabial and velar categories, all Australian languages have at least two coronal sounds—one made with the tongue tip (apical) and one with the tongue blade (laminal). This distinction, in terms of the active articulator, is a very important and basic one in these phonologies (Butcher, 1995; Dixon, 2002, p. 548ff). Only a small number of languages have this minimal system of contrasts however, as the majority of Australian languages split the apical category further into an alveolar and a retroflex class. A substantial minority of languages additionally contrast dental and alveopalatal sounds within the laminals, while a few have the laminal contrast without the apical one. Examples of these four coronal articulations are shown in Figures 12.3 and 12.4. (For more details of the phonetics of these contrasts, see Butcher, 1995.)

Thus, the vast majority of Australian languages have five or six phonologically distinct places of articulation. There are even some languages which have been analysed as having seven places of articulation—one group with an additional "palatalised" alveolar category (Breen, 2001) and another with a distinction between front and back velar sounds (Butcher & Tabain, 2004). There are also a number of languages in northern Australia with phonemic glottal stops in addition to the other five or six categories.

The relative lack of manner distinctions is entirely within the domain of the obstruents: The vast majority of Australian languages have a single series of these, with no [voiced] ~ [voiceless] contrast and no [stop] ~ [fricative] contrast.

TABLE 12.1. Prototypical Australian Phonological Inventory, Arranged According to Natural Class

				PERIPHERAL		CORONAL			
						APICAL		LAMINAL	
				LABIAL	VELAR	ALVEOLAR	POSTALV	DENTAL	ALVEOPAL
OBSTRUENT	STOP			p	k	t	ʈ	t̪	c
	NASAL			m	ŋ	n	ɳ	n̪	ɲ
SONORANT		LIQUID	LATERAL			l	ɭ	l̪	ʎ
	APPROX		RHOTIC			r	ɹ		
		GLIDE		w				j	
	VOWELS	FRONT		BACK					
	HIGH	i (iː)		u (uː)					
	LOW		a (aː)						

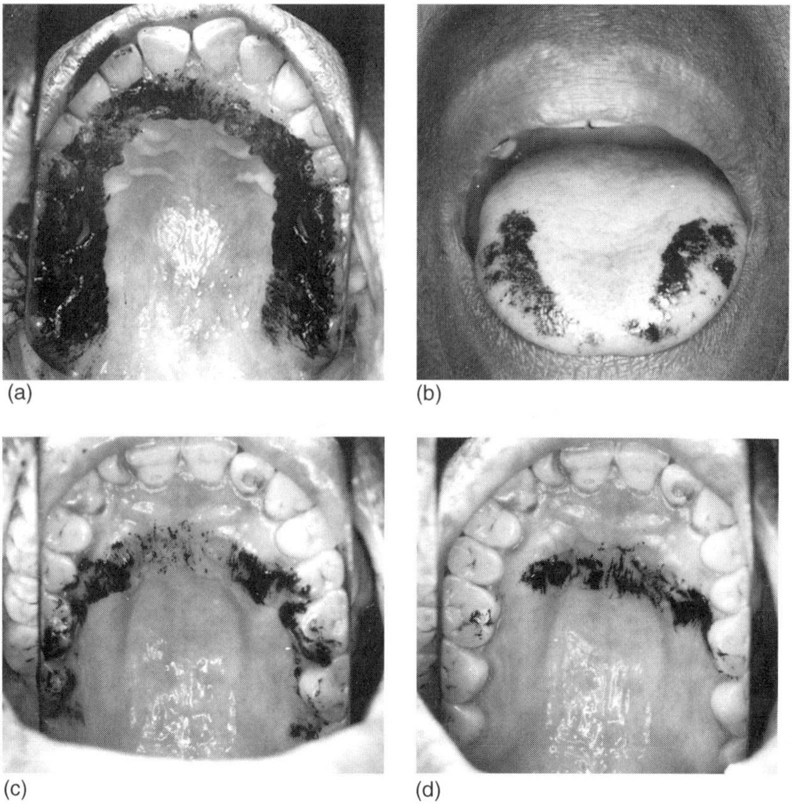

FIGURE 12.3. Apical articulations in Australian languages. Above: Alveolar stop in Eastern/Central Arrernte /a'tʷəm/ = [ɐ'tʊmɐ] *"hit"*(ν) (Speaker MM ♀) (a) normal palatogram and (b) linguagram. Below: Retroflex stop in Warlpiri /'miʈa/ *"narrow shield"* (Speaker CW ♀) (c) normal palatogram (with entire superior surface of tongue painted) and (d) palatogram with inferior surface of tongue tip and blade painted.

On the other hand, these languages have as rich a system of sonorant contrasts as any language in the world—and richer than most. This means that these systems have precisely the opposite proportion of obstruents to sonorants to that proposed as the normal tendency among the languages of the world (Lindblom & Maddieson, 1988). A typical Australian inventory may consist of 70% sonorants and only 30% obstruents. This implies that the perception of oppositions within Australian phonological systems is heavily reliant on systematic differences in formant transition patterns at vowel–consonant boundaries.

It is, then, perhaps not surprising that the phonological structure of Australian languages also appears to be quite unusual. It has been suggested that the phonological word, rather than the syllable, may be the more appropriate

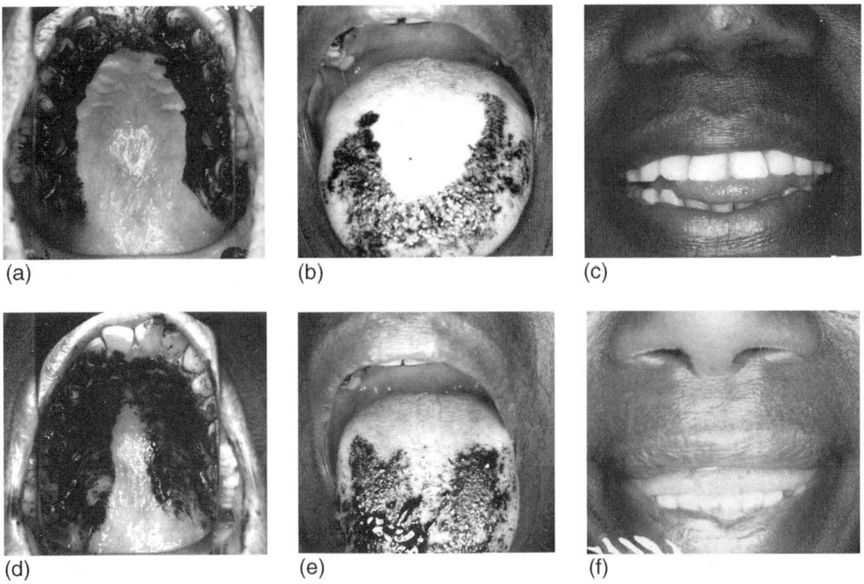

FIGURE 12.4. Laminal articulations in Australian languages. Above: Dental stop in Eastern/Central Arrernte /a'ţəm/ = [ɐ'ţɐmɐ] *"grind"*(*v*) (Speaker MM ♀) (a) normal palatogram, (b) linguagram, and (c) frontal photograph of mouth. Below: Alveopalatal stop in Eastern/Central Arrernte /a'cəməj/ = [ɐ'cɐmeɪ] *"grandfather"* (Speaker MM ♀) (d) normal palatogram, (e) linguagram, (f) Alveopalatal nasal in Warlpiri /'maɲa/ *"soft"* (Speaker CW ♀) frontal photograph of mouth.

unit in terms of which to describe the phonotactics and lower-level prosody (such as vowel harmony and suffixal allomorphy) of Australian languages (Baker & Harvey, 2003; Dixon, 2002; Hamilton, 1996; Pentland, 2003). A prototypical phonological word would be of the form

$$C_{INIT}VC_1(C_2)V\ (C_{FIN})$$

In both the C_{INIT} and C_2 positions, obstruents are less marked than sonorants and peripherals (labials and velars) less marked than coronals, while in the C_{FIN} and C_1 positions, precisely the opposite trends are observed. The most favoured manner combination in the C_1C_2 position is thus sonorant+obstruent. The most favoured place combinations are coronal+peripheral and apical+laminal. In the C_{INIT} position, the apical contrast is usually neutralised. In the C_{FIN} position, the laminal contrast is often neutralised (for a detailed account, see Hamilton, 1996). Note that only in the $C_1(C_2)$ position are all consonantal segments in contrast—precisely the position where we might expect the spectral changes so crucial to place-of-articulation distinctions to be perceptually optimised.

THE PLACE-OF-ARTICULATION IMPERATIVE

But what happens to this system of contrasts when the structures are put together to form connected speech? As with all languages, the phonetic distinctiveness of speech sounds is reduced by the constraints of "economy of effort" and the requirements of co-production. Thus, in common with many other languages of the world, most Australian languages may reduce unstressed vowels to a schwa or a syllabic consonant:

(1)
Warlpiri: /'calaŋuɭucu/ *"today"* pronounced as ['cɐlɐŋəɭəɟɵ][1]

Burarra: /kun'menama ku'para/ *"he ate pandanus"* pronounced as [kən'mɛnmə ɡə'bɐɾə]. A second almost universal connected speech process, which is extremely common in Australian languages is the lenition of consonants. This is generally seen as a "weakening" of the articulation of an obstruent. Since in most Australian languages, stops are undifferentiated in terms of voicing and aspiration, the range of allophonic variation is quite wide. Stop allophones that are voiceless in citation forms may become voiced and stops that are voiced may become continuants—usually without any appreciable degree of friction—while intervocalic apicals are commonly "flapped".

(2)
Warlpiri: /'waca kanpa/ *"are you going?"* pronounced as ['wɐɟɐ ɰɐb]
Kunbarlang: /ŋa'ttakitaɲ 'paɹpuŋ/ *"we went fishing"* pronounced as ['ŋəːɾɐɲ 'β̞ɐɹwʊŋ]
Pitjantjatjara: /'jaːlcikutun/ *"where are you going?"* pronounced as ['jɐːlcɪɡʊɾʊn]

(For a fuller discussion and more examples, see Butcher, 1996.)

Most of the world's languages also manifest connected speech processes, which come under the general heading of assimilation. Probably, the commonest type is what is generally known as anticipatory assimilation of place of articulation. In many languages, the earlier consonants in a sequence will show a strong tendency to assume the place of articulation of later ones. Thus, as any introductory phonetics text will tell you, in English "fat boy" may commonly be pronounced as [fæp bɔɪ] and "thin girl" as [θɪŋ ɡɜl]. In Australian languages, however, assimilation of place of articulation as a historical process seems to have affected consonants only within the apical and laminal categories (and in many cases has left its mark in the form of synchronic morphophonemic processes—see Dixon,

2002, p. 619ff). There is very little evidence of synchronic assimilation between the four major categories of labial, apical, laminal, and dorsal. As indicated earlier, the two most favoured heterorganic consonant sequences in Australian languages are coronal+peripheral and apical+laminal. In view of the anticipatory assimilation of coronals to noncoronals which is so widely attested in Germanic languages (e.g., Kohler, 1975), one might assume that there would be plenty of scope for similar processes in Australian languages. In historical terms, however, these sequences seem to show a remarkable stability. O'Grady and Fitzgerald (1997, p. 347), for example, draw attention to the /-nk-/ in the etymon /kunka/ "*raw*", which occurs in both Nyangumarta and Dyirbal, "languages spoken on opposite sides of Australia, [which] cannot have been in contact for several millennia at least. Amazing as it may seem to the outsider to Pama-Nyungan studies, the **-nk-** sequence in the words for 'raw' (…leading in the case of most languages of the world to the **n** assimilating to the **k**) must be seen as having descended from the identical sequence *__-nk-__, in the immediate common ancestor of Nyangumarta and Dyirbal, and in fact in proto-Pama-Nyungan itself". Moreover, this unusual stability of heterorganic nasal+stop clusters in Australian languages persists in contemporary connected speech (Butcher, 1996):

(3)

Warlpiri:			
/'caɳpa/	"*sorcerer*"	**NOT**: ['cɐmbɐ]	**BUT:** ['cɐɳbɐ]
/'jinka/	"*laughter*"	**NOT**: ['jɪŋgɐ]	**BUT:** ['jɪngɐ]
/'manca/	"*mulga tree*"	**NOT**: ['mɐɲɟɐ]	**BUT:** ['mɐnɟɐ]
Marrithiyel:			
/'gumun kupa/	"*it went soft*"	**NOT**: ['ɰʊmʊŋ kʊpɐ]	**BUT:** ['ɰʊmʊn kʊpɐ]
/'ŋumut belwa/	"*I will pick it up for you*"	**NOT**: ['ŋʊmʊp bɛlwɐ]	**BUT:** [ŋʊmʊt bɛlwɐ]

Figure 12.5 shows the EPG record of a /n/+/k/ sequence (in the place name *Ankabadbirri*) pronounced in connected speech by a speaker of the Kune dialect of Bininj Gun-wok. There are two clearly distinct articulations for the /n/ (frames 58–63) and the /k/ (frames 64–71), with no visible overlap between the two. That the overwhelming majority of examples from our data show a similar pattern, suggests that there is a general resistance to anticipatory assimilation of place of articulation in Australian languages. Both intramorphemically and across word and morpheme boundaries it seems that speakers tend to preserve the distinctiveness of the place of articulation in the $C_1(C_2)$ position.

An equally common form of anticipatory assimilation in the languages of the world is that of nasality (Kawasaki, 1986, p. 83). It is quite usual, even in citation forms, for the velum to lower during a segment (usually a vowel) not specified in the phonology as [+nasal], when this segment is followed by a nasal

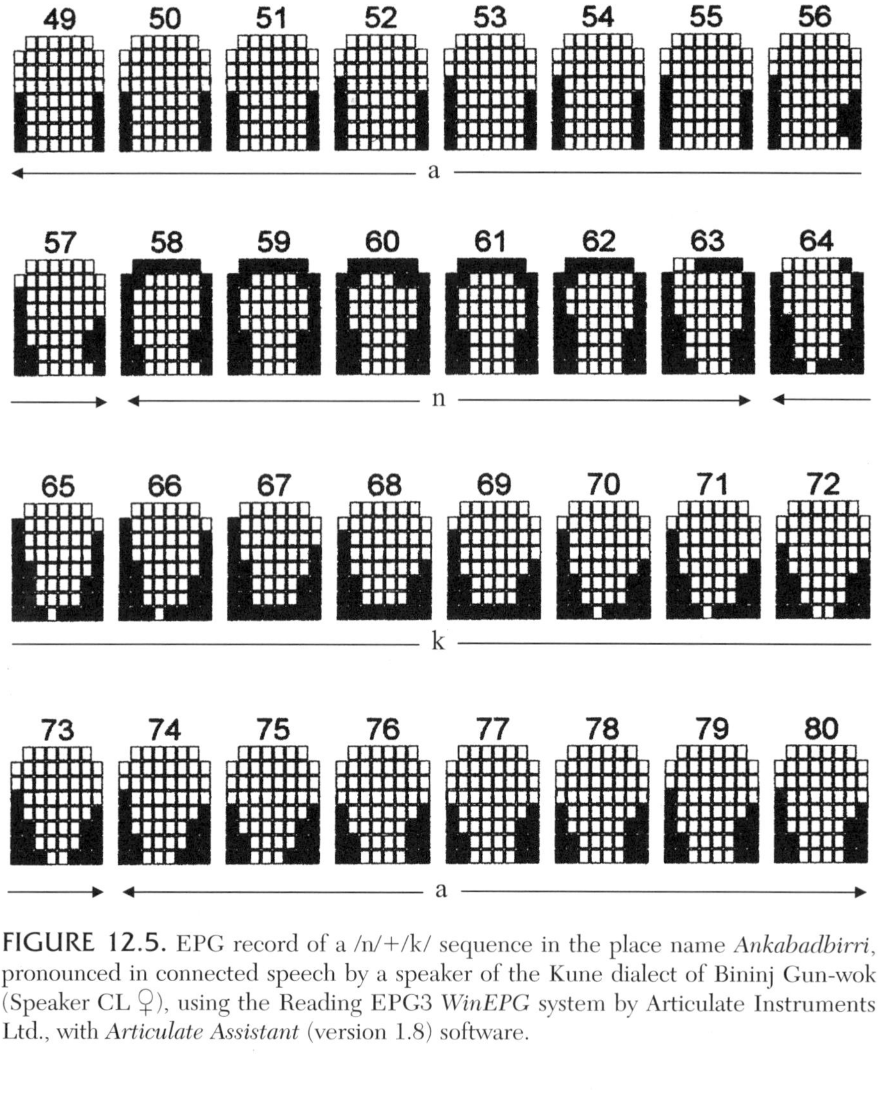

FIGURE 12.5. EPG record of a /n/+/k/ sequence in the place name *Ankabadbirri*, pronounced in connected speech by a speaker of the Kune dialect of Bininj Gun-wok (Speaker CL ♀), using the Reading EPG3 *WinEPG* system by Articulate Instruments Ltd., with *Articulate Assistant* (version 1.8) software.

consonant. Thus, many speakers of English realise phonological sequences of vowel+nasal as phonetically nasal throughout, more especially when the preceding vowel is low (e.g., AusEng *barn dance* as [ˈbɐ̃ːndɐ̃ːns], GenAm *long time* as [lɑ̃ŋ ˈtʰɑ̃ẽm]). This type of realisation is generally regarded as a universal phenomenon and historically has led to the development of nasalised vowels from V+N sequences in languages such as French and Portuguese. However, it seems that Australian languages are again an exception to the rule.

Historically, only one language—Anguthimri—appears to have developed nasalised vowel phonemes (Crowley, 1981) and indeed two well-documented historical processes provide evidence of an opposite trend. Firstly, denasalisation (sometimes referred to as "nasal dissimilation") is a process (Dixon, 2002, pp. 625–627) whereby a nasal has been lost from a C_1C_2 nasal+stop cluster in many Australian languages, if C_{INIT} was itself a nasal; and a number of languages across the continent still have morphophonemic alternations whereby the initial consonant (or cluster) of a suffix is denasalised if there is a nasal or (in some cases) a nasal+stop cluster in the stem:

(4)
Gurindji (McConvell, 1988):

/lucu-ŋka/ *"on the ridge"*	**BUT**	*/wiɲɟi-ŋka/→/wiɲɟi-ka/ *"at the spring"*
/ɟalŋak-kumpalŋ/ *"to avoid riding"*	**BUT**	*/ɲin-kumpalŋ/→/ɲin-kupalŋ/ *"to avoid drowning"*

Secondly, pre-stopped nasals, either as phonemes, or as major allophones of nasal consonants, are a well-documented feature of certain Australian languages—mostly concentrated in the southern and central areas of the continent:

(5)
Eastern/Central Arrernte (Henderson & Dobson, 1994):

/apˈəɹ/ *"gum tree"*	/aˈməl/ *"nest"*	/aˈᵖməɹ/	*"camp"*
/aˈkək/ *"cut"*	/aˈŋəp/ *"crow"*	/aˈᵏŋək/	*"carried"*
/aˈtəm/ *"bursting"*	/aˈnəm/ *"staying"*	/aˈᵗnəm/	*"yamstick"*

Synchronically, there is a very strong phonetic tendency in most Australian languages to delay lowering the velum in vowel+nasal sequences until the latest possible instant. This tendency is apparent both auditorily and through the visual inspection of spectrograms and airflow data. Figure 12.6 (from Butcher, 1999) compares the nasal airflow produced during a sequence of stressed low vowel+nasal in English and in an Australian language.

The avoidance of premature velum lowering results in two phenomena which parallel the above historical processes—pre-stopping and denasalisation. The (phonetic) pre-stopping of (phonologically) plain nasals has also been noted (and illustrated) by Ladefoged and Maddieson (1996, pp. 129, 240) in Eastern Arrernte, where, as we have seen, the plain nasals are already in contrast with a full set of (phonologically) pre-stopped nasals. In fact, the pre-stopping of nasal consonants is a widespread phenomenon at the synchronic phonetic level in many Australian languages, and is certainly not restricted to central Australia.

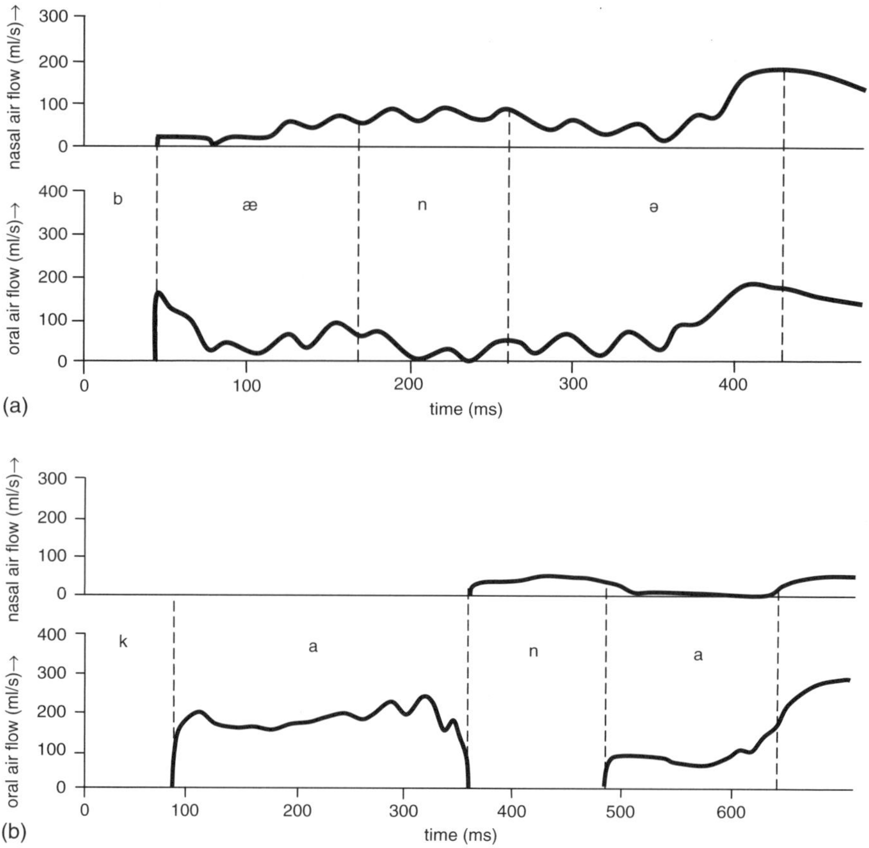

FIGURE 12.6. Oral and nasal airflow (volume velocity) during the production of the words (a) *banner* in British English (Speaker AB ♂) and (b) /ˈkana/ *"with the eyes open"* in Burarra (Speaker PM ♂).

Figure 12.7 (from Butcher, 1999) gives an illustration of phonetic pre-stopping in the Yolŋu language Gupapuyŋu, spoken in north-eastern Arnhem Land, some 1000 km further north than the Arandic languages, and not closely related to them. In this example the word /ˈcinaka/, *"inside; underneath"* is pronounced as [t̪^{ç}ɪ^{d}nɐk^{h}ɐ]. Complete denasalisation of underlying nasal consonants is also found in a wide range of Australian languages in rapid casual speech. Peripheral nasals in particular (especially the velars) can be realised phonetically as oral stops, oral approximants, or may be elided altogether:

(6)

Warlpiri: /ˈwacaˈkanpaˈjaniɳi *"are you coming?"* pronounced as [ˈwɐɟɐ ˈɰɐb jənəɳ]

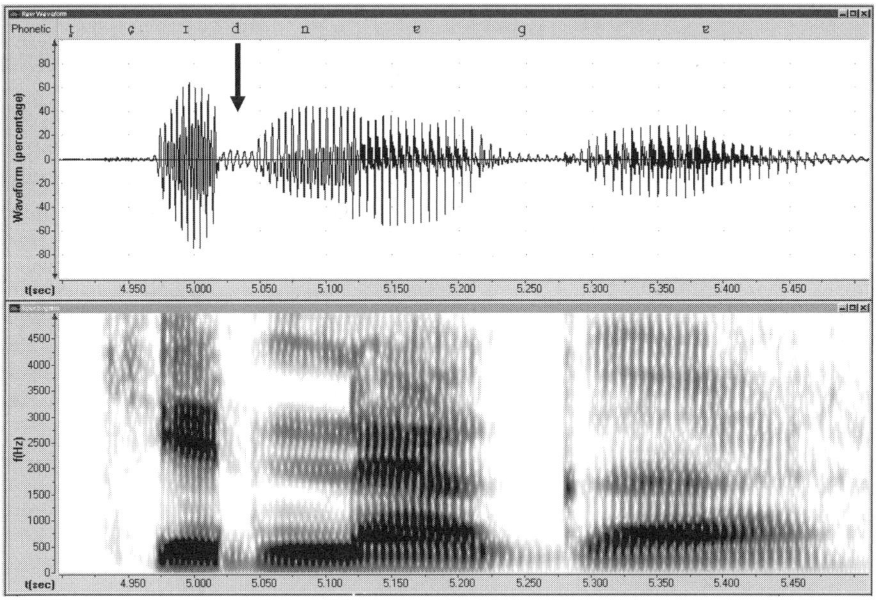

FIGURE 12.7. Waveform and spectrogram of the Gupapuyŋu word /'cinaka/ (*"inside; underneath"*), spoken in isolation (Speaker BT ♀). The arrow indicates the epenthetic oral "pre-stop".

Yolŋu (Djapu): /'n̪aamir 'ŋarat̪u/ *"How about I (erg.)"* pronounced as ['d̪ɐːmə'ɾɐed̪ʊ]

It has been shown that perceptual information on the place of articulation of postvocalic nasals is conveyed by the formant transitions out of the vowel and by the nasal murmur itself (Harrington, 1994). Thus it would seem essential for a language with half a dozen places of articulation contrasts among the nasals to maintain clearly distinctive vowel transitions in the preceding vowels. As nasalisation of vowels produces extra nasal formants and antiresonances, which flatten the spectrum and lower the overall amplitude, rendering place of articulation cues much less distinct (Repp & Svastikula, 1988), it seems reasonable to suppose that delaying the lowering of the velum for the nasal consonant for as long as possible would facilitate the maintenance of clear spectral cues to place of articulation in the pre-nasal vowel.

Thus we find that, despite their "long flat" sound systems, speakers of these languages conflate manner contrasts rather than place contrasts in connected speech, thereby "flattening" the system still further. It appears that there is an overwhelming imperative to preserve the rich system of place of articulation distinctions.

THE SALIENCE OF INTERVOCALIC CONSONANTS

It is notable that the two major types of assimilation which are inhibited in Australian languages (place of articulation and nasalisation) are both examples of anticipatory assimilation. It is equally notable that the inhibition applies to the coda consonant (C_1), rather than to the onset of the syllable. A view that has come to be fairly widely accepted in recent years is that these kinds of anticipatory coarticulation effects are timing effects, reflective of articulatory preprogramming, whereas left-to-right (carry-over) coarticulation effects are largely due to biomechanical inertia. Recasens (1989), for example, has argued that anticipatory coarticulation reflects planning of the speech sequence, and that carry-over coarticulation reflects lingering effects from the preceding segment, and is therefore not planned or controlled. The evidence for this claim is based on the assumption that, if coarticulation between consonant and vowel is at a minimum, the speaker has planned that sequence carefully, attempting to maximise the identity of both segments—i.e., by minimising coarticulation the hearer is provided with as much information as possible regarding the syllable onset. This in turn implies that formant values for the consonant and vowel are maximally distinct and stable and the duration of the formant transition is longer, thereby giving the hearer more time to integrate the sequence of phonemes. By contrast, with a high degree of coarticulation, formant values for the individual segments are likely to be less distinct and more variable, while the duration of the transition between the two phonemes is more likely to be reduced. There is an increasing amount of phonetic evidence from European languages which supports the view that speakers of those languages show greater stability in syllable onset gestures (see Krakow, 1999 for a review). Most recently, Kochetov (in press) has presented electromagnetic midsagittal articulometry data, which demonstrate clear differences in the nature and organisation of articulatory gestures in syllable onset and coda positions in Russian. Onset gestures are more tightly controlled—greater in magnitude and sometimes in duration. Coda gestures are more variable and often reduced in magnitude and duration. The corollary of these articulatory findings is that from a perceptual point of view, syllable-initial consonants are expected to be more easily identifiable and distinguishable than syllable-final ones—and in English this turns out to be the case (Benki, 2003; Redford & Diehl, 1999).

In a recent study that compared the variability of F_2 onsets and offsets for intervocalic consonants in three Australian languages, Tabain, Breen, and Butcher (2004) confirmed the earlier findings that English speakers show less variability in these parameters in CV contexts than in VC contexts. However, as Figure 12.8 shows, in all three Australian languages studied (Arrernte, Yanyuwa, and Yintjiparnti), speakers showed an equal amount of variability in CV and VC contexts. This suggests that, whereas in English, spectral cues to

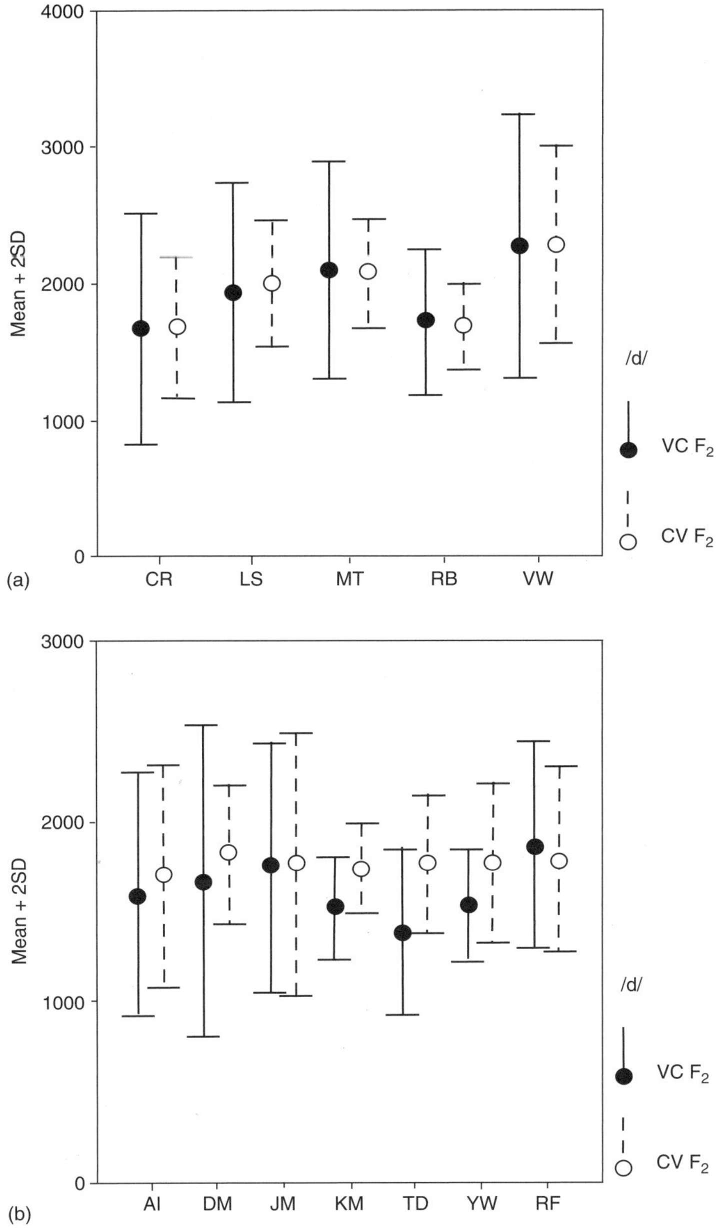

FIGURE 12.8. Plots showing means and two standard deviations for F_2 in VC context and CV context for alveolar stops. Values are in Hertz. (a) English speakers (309 tokens). CR and RB are ♂; LS, MT, and VW are ♀. (b) Aboriginal language speakers (123 tokens). AI ♀, JM ♀, and DM ♂ are Yanyuwa speakers; KM ♀, TD ♀, and YW ♂ are Yintjiparnti speakers; and RF ♀ is an Arrernte speaker.

place of articulation are more tightly controlled at the CV boundary than at the VC boundary, in Aboriginal languages, spectral cues are controlled in both these contexts to the same extent. The result is that acoustic distinctiveness is preserved equally at both edges of the intervocalic consonant.

Over recent years various experimental analyses (e.g., Harrington, Fletcher, & Beckman, 2000) have shown that prosodically accented words are typically hyperarticulated—i.e., they are accompanied by a durational and supralaryngeal expansion, the main consequence of which is phonetically more peripheral vowels. Other studies (e.g., Keating, Fougeron, Cho, & Hsu, 2003) have demonstrated that the presence or absence of word boundaries and the difference between word-initial, syllable-initial, and word-medial consonants are accompanied by phonetic differences in English and other languages. Cho's (2001) analysis of consonants in Korean also shows that speakers' articulatory patterns are influenced by morphological structure in that language—and there is an implicit assumption that these effects are universal. However, most of our knowledge of the articulatory and acoustic effects, both of focus and accent and of junctural differences at word and morpheme level, is restricted to Germanic languages.

A recent acoustic and electro-magnetic articulography (EMA) study by Butcher and Harrington (2003) looked at the effects of varying focus and grammatical boundary in segmentally identical sequences in the Australian language Warlpiri. Figure 12.9 shows some tongue trajectory data from this study, illustrating one speaker's productions of the word /kuju/ in four different conditions. This shows that in the focused context with a following word boundary (F#) there is a more anterior tongue position for the /j/ of /kuju/ than in the other three contexts. As far as tongue height is concerned, there is a much greater degree of tongue raising in the focused (F) than in the unfocused (U) contexts, but again this difference in tongue raising reaches a peak at about the midpoint of the /uju/ sequence. Overall, the results show that this language signals focus and distinguishes boundary types using F_0, supralaryngeal expansion and duration as do many other languages. What sets Warlpiri apart, however, is that most of the duration differences and all of the pitch peaks and supraglottal expansion are found in the coda consonants (C_1) rather than in the preceding vowels.

Historically, the salience of intervocalic consonants has been enhanced by a number of related processes, which have shaped the phonological structure of Australian languages. Possibly the most striking of these has been the weakening and deletion of initial consonants (and, in some cases, whole syllables)—a process that has affected upwards of one-third of Australian languages, to a greater or lesser extent (Blevins, 2001). This process has typically been facilitated (or perhaps simply accompanied) by a stress shift from the first to the

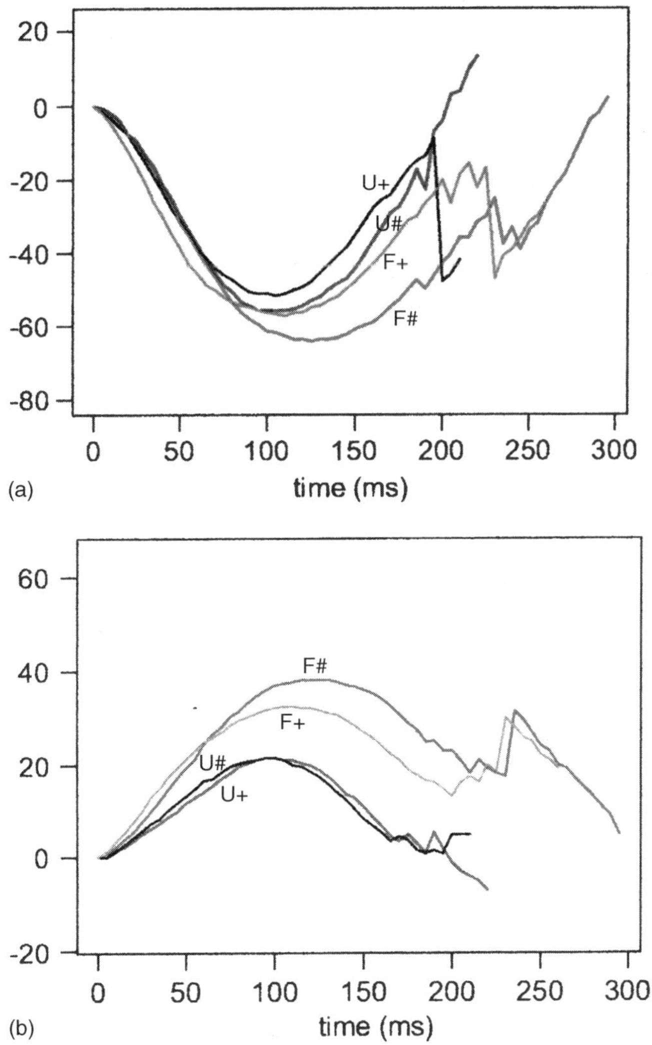

FIGURE 12.9. EMA traces of (a) tongue backness and (b) tongue height in the word /kuju/ "*animal*; *game*", as pronounced by a speaker of Warlpiri (BP ♀). Trajectories are the average of 10 repetitions in a sentence frame, synchronised in time (0 ms) and amplitude (0) at the acoustic onset of /uju/. In (a), higher values mean a more retracted tongue position; in (b), higher values mean a higher tongue position. F, focussed position; U, unfocussed position; #, single word; +, first element of compound noun.

second vowel. The following examples are from widely separated areas of the continent:

(7)

Northern Paman (Hale, 1976)

proto-Paman			Uradhi	Lut̪iɣ Ntraʔŋit̪ Linŋit̪iɣ	Yinwum	Alŋit̪ Awŋt̪im	Ngkot̪	Aritinŋit̪iɣ	Mbiywom
*kami	*mother's mother*	→	'ami	mi	me	may	may	may	me
*mara	*hand*	→	'mata	'aʔa	^{n}t^{r}a	ʔa	t^{r}a	ta	ta
*calan	*mouth, tongue*	→	'lalan	lan	lin	lan	ʎan	lan	lin

Arandic (Koch, 1997)

pre-Arandic			E/C Arrernte	Kaytetye
*kuna	*excrement*	→	a'tnə	a'tnə
*muŋa	*night*	→	i'ŋwə	ə'ŋwə
*cilika	*prickle*	→	'ʎəkə	a$^{'y}$ləkə

As the above examples show, initial consonant loss and stress shift is often followed by a weakening (and in extreme cases, loss) of the first vowel. However, most initial-dropping concerns only certain types of consonant—most frequently velars, labials, glides, and nasals. It is worth noting that all of these might be characterised as consonants with rather weak perceptual cues at the "right edge." In many languages, initial consonants are not entirely lost, but (stops in particular) have lenited to become glides. This weakening of the initial consonant is mirrored by a "strengthening" of the post-tonic $C_1(C_2)$ consonants. In its most basic manifestation, this consists of a lengthening of this consonant (which is often longer than the preceding vowel). In the case of stops, C_1 typically has heightened intraoral pressure—in the case of Warlpiri, for example, roughly twice that of corresponding initial stops (Butcher, 2004). Nasals—and in a few languages, laterals—may be pre-stopped in the C_1 position (and *only* in the C_1 position). In almost all those languages that have a fortis/lenis contrast, that contrast is also restricted to the C_1 position. This is the case for all of the Gunwinguan and Yolŋu languages (south and east of Darwin) with a stop contrast. The only languages with a contrast in initial position are the Daly languages (south-west of Darwin).[2] A further process which has been noted in a number of languages is the rightward migration of prosodies, such as lip-rounding, palatalisation, and possibly tongue retroflexion. Rounding in Arandic dialects, for example, appears to have moved within a few generations from the first syllable to the second and, in at least one documented case, on to the third (Breen, 2001):

(8)

E/C Arrernte:	utyene	*"sore"*	[ʊ'cɐnɐ] > [cʊn]
E/C Arrernte:	unte	*"you"*	[ʊn'dɐ] > [ndwɐ]
Alyawarr:	tywerrk	*"fig"*	[ʊ'cɐrkɐ] > ['cʊrkɐ] > ['cɐrk^{w}ɐ]

CV, VC, OR VCV?

Thus, on the one hand, we have identified a number of processes in Australian languages which tend to increase the acoustic and perceptual salience of the $C_1(C_2)$ position in the word, all of which are manifested synchronically at the phonetic level in most currently spoken Australian languages. These include resistance to $V \leftarrow C_1$ nasal coarticulation, resistance to $C_1 \leftarrow C_2$ place assimilation, with spectral cues to consonant identity as tightly controlled in VC_1 as in $C_{1/2}V$. We have also seen that consonants in this intervocalic position tend to be "strengthened" durationally and in other ways and that they usually carry the major lower-level prosodic cues. At the same time, a number of historical processes have led to the weakening of initial consonants and whole syllables and the corresponding increased salience of the $C_1(C_2)$ consonant position within the phonological structure of these languages: As a result this is usually the only position in which the full range of consonants can appear and often C_1C_2 is the only position allowing consonant sequences. The Arandic group of languages seems to have taken these processes furthest and now has a basic phonological structure, which may well be most appropriately analysed as VC. Evidence for this claim comes from a number of areas of the language, including stress assignment, prosodically conditioned allomorphy and reduplication, but one of the most striking illustrations comes from the language game known as "Rabbit Talk", which involves transposing initial portions of words to the end.

(9)

(Breen & Pensalfini, 1999; Tabain, Breen, & Butcher, 2004)

/arac/	→	/acar/	"right"
/itirəm/	→	/irəmit/	"thinking"
/akəʎ/	→	/ʎak/	"small"
/itəcək/	→	/cəkit/	"to light (fire)"
/kəɹ/	→	/ɹək/	"meat"
/n̪t̪əm/	→	/mən̪t̪/	"giving"
/waɹ/	→	/aɹəw/	"only"
/jan̪/	→	/an̪əj/	"that (nearby)"

As Breen and Pensalfini (1999) point out, if we formulate rules for these changes in terms of CV syllables, they turn out to be rather cumbersome:

1. Shift the first consonant(s) plus any preceding vowel to the end of the word.
2. If this leaves /ə/ at the beginning, delete it.
3. If the moved part does not include /ə/, insert one to separate the two consonants.

If we formulate the rule for this and other morphophonological processes in terms of VC syllables, however (and assume an underlying /ə/ which surfaces only between consonants), the statement becomes simple and elegant:

Transpose the first syllable to the end of the word.

There appears, then, to be some evidence that the unit of articulatory programming in some Australian languages may be VC (or VCV?), rather than the universally assumed CV. Phonetic indications of this trend are certainly to be found in many widely separated Australian languages. On the other hand, there is some evidence that languages which have reached the putative VC stage do not retain this structure, but, either by dropping the initial vowel or by replacing a previously dropped initial consonant, show signs of moving towards a CV(C) structure once more (Breen, 2001; Dixon, 1970). There is thus a possibility that this is a cyclical process, with different languages at different stages of the cycle.

CONCLUSIONS

If it were indeed the case that the phonological structure of some Australian languages is changing from CV(C) to VC(V) and back again, what might be the driving forces underlying such a process? One possibility is that this cycle might be driven by a tension between a universal linguistic preference for CV(C) structure in the human brain on the one hand and the unique phonetic characteristics of Australian languages on the other. These characteristics appear to be motivated by the "place-of-articulation imperative", which strongly favours the VC(V) structure as a means of maximising the perceptual place distinctions between consonants. This imperative, in turn, is the consequence of the unusual phonemic inventories of these languages, with their large range of place of articulation contrasts. This brings us to the final question: What motivates and perpetuates the unusual phonemic inventories and hence the place-of-articulation imperative? By this point we are well into the realm of speculation, but I will conclude with the following remarks. Middle ear infection [more precisely chronic *otitis media* (COM)] develops in almost all Aboriginal infants within a few weeks of birth and up to 70% of Aboriginal children consequently have a significant conductive hearing loss (Coates, Morris, Leach, & Couzos, 2002). This commonly affects the low-frequency end of the scale (under 500 Hz), but may also affect the upper end of the scale (above 4000 Hz). As we have seen, the vowel systems of Australian languages are in general quite small and the majority of them lack any true close vowels. In other words, these systems have no vowel quality distinctions which depend on formant frequencies below about 400 Hz. The consonant systems of Australian languages are also lacking in contrasts which depend on low-frequency acoustic cues (voicing), but in addition lack contrasts which depend on cues at the high-frequency end of the spectrum (friction and aspiration). On the other hand, Australian sound systems are rich in contrasts which depend on rapid spectral changes in the middle of the frequency range. Sounds with high-amplitude lower formants can make use of large areas of the basilar membrane of the inner ear, whereby neurons primarily tuned to higher frequencies may nevertheless phase-lock their firing to these lower frequency sounds because of their high intensity. Sounds of this type therefore have a temporal representation in terms of the firing pattern of neurons over a broad span of the basilar membrane and are therefore highly resistant to noise (Greenberg, 1996). Thus it appears that Aboriginal languages are rich in sounds whose differentiation exploits precisely that area of hearing ability which is most likely to remain intact in sufferers of chronic middle-ear infection.

A hypothesis that the phonetics and phonology of a language have been shaped by the hearing status of the speakers is not easily falsifiable, but we can at least identify two major types of *prima facie* counterevidence that would be a problem for such a hypothesis: Firstly, evidence that the cause of the hearing impairment had not existed in the population long enough for it to have had the postulated effect and secondly, evidence that there are other languages with "long flat" phonologies whose speakers do not show a high prevalence of COM and/or populations with a high prevalence of COM whose languages do not have "long flat" phonologies. As to the first point, it is probably a reasonable assumption that the kinds of atypical phonological characteristics we are dealing with here would take longer than 200 years to develop. However, recent research has produced evidence that diseases of nonindigenous origin may have already been introduced and spread in precolonial Australia (Campbell, 2002). Furthermore, the possibility that the continent may have been visited by explorers from the northern hemisphere at a much earlier date than the 18th century cannot be entirely discounted (Menzies, 2002). We know nothing about the middle-ear health of Aboriginal Australians prior to 1788, but we have at least one contemporary reference to the widespread presence of chronic upper respiratory tract infection (Worgan, 1788/2003, p. 36).[3] As to the second point, there are very few languages elsewhere in the world with a system of contrasts anything like those found in Australia. While the consonant systems of New Guinea and Polynesian languages typically lack a voicing distinction (and in some cases a fricative series), the number of places of articulation is invariably restricted to /p t k/ (with the occasional /ʔ/) and almost all of these languages have at least five vowels. Eskimo-Aleut languages, such as Inuktitut, typically have four places of articulation, no voicing contrast and only three vowels (although they do have fricatives). On the other side of the Arctic, Chukokto-Kamchatkan languages, such as Chukchee, arguably have five or six places of articulation, no voicing distinction, and a minimal fricative contrast (but six or seven vowels). Perhaps most similar to Australian languages are the Dravidian languages of southern India. Tamil, for example, has five places of articulation in a single series of stops, paralleled by a series of nasals, and no fricatives (thus approaching the Australian proportion of sonorants to obstruents of 70–30%).

Approaching the question from the opposite direction: According to the latest WHO data on the prevalence of COM (Acuin, 2004, p. 14ff), Aboriginal Australians have the highest prevalence in the world—10–54%, according to Coates et al. (2002), up to 36% with perforations of the eardrum. They are followed—at some distance—by the Tamils of southern India (7.8%, down from previous estimates of 16–34%), Eskimos (Greenland, 8% COM; Alaska, 9.7% perforations); and Pacific Islanders (Solomon Islands, 6.1% otorrhoea; Guam, 2.2–8.3% perforations).[4] Thus it seems clear that (1) the Aboriginal population of Australia has a prevalence of COM, which is an order of magnitude greater than any other population and (2) no other group of languages combines quite all of the features of the "long flat" Australian phonologies. It is also clear that in order to test this hypothesis, a great deal more research would be needed into the phonetics of these languages and the hearing status of their speakers.

ACKNOWLEDGMENTS

I would like to thank my fellow investigators, Gavan Breen, Janet Fletcher, Jonathan Harrington, and Marija Tabain, who have been jointly responsible for much of the research on which the above musings are based. Thanks are also due to Bob Dixon for starting me on this path many years ago and, more recently, providing the environment for me to continue along it. I am also grateful to John Henderson for first pointing out to me the widespread occurrence and potential significance of "medial consonant strengthening" in Australian languages and to Geoff Plant and Terry Nienhuys for alerting me to the possibility of a relationship between hearing impairment and Aboriginal phonologies. Thanks finally to Nick Evans, who made many constructive suggestions in the course of reviewing this paper. None of these people should be held responsible for the views expressed herein.

NOTES

1. Note that, for the sake of simplicity, the palatal symbols [c, ɟ, ɲ, ʎ] are used throughout this paper to denote laminal alveopalatal sounds, as shown in Figure 12.4 (d,e,f).
2. The Daly languages are also atypical in having a fricative-stop contrast at some places of articulation. Also the nature of the stop contrast appears to be one of voicing rather than fortition—at least in Murrinh Patha, Ngan'gikurunggurr, and possibly Marrithiyel.
3. George Worgan, ship's surgeon with the First Fleet, in his journal for 24 May 1788, calls attention to "the constant Appearance of the excrementitious Matters of the Nose which is collected on the upper Lip, in rich Clusters of dry Bubbles, and is kept up by fresh Drippings."
4. The remaining populations for which figures are given are: South-East Asia, 0.9–4.7%; Sub-Saharan Africa, 0.4–4.2%; China, 4%; Central and South America, 1.5%; Arab countries, 1.5%; Europe and North America, 0.4%.

REFERENCES

Acuin, J. (2004). *Chronic suppurative otitis media. Burden of illness and management options*. World Health Organisation Report. Geneva: WHO.

Baker, B., & Harvey, M. (2003). Word structure in Australian languages. *Australian Journal of Linguistics, 23*, 1–33.

Benki, J. R. (2003). Analysis of English nonsense syllable recognition in noise. *Phonetica, 60*, 129–157.

Blevins, J. (2001). Where have all the onsets gone? Initial consonant loss in Australian Aboriginal languages. In J. Simpson, D. Nash, M. Laughren, P. Austin, & B. Alpher (Eds.), *Forty years on: Ken Hale and Australian languages* (pp. 481–492). Canberra: Pacific Linguistics.

Breen, J. G. (2001). The wonders of Arandic phonology. In J. Simpson, D. Nash, M. Laughren, P. Austin, & B. Alpher (Eds.), *Forty years on: Ken Hale and Australian languages* (pp. 45–69). Canberra: Pacific Linguistics.

Breen, J. G., & Pensalfini, R. (1999). Arrernte: A language with no syllable onsets. *Linguistic Inquiry, 30*, 1–25.

Butcher, A. R. (1994). On the phonetics of small vowel systems: Evidence from Australian languages. In R. Togneri (Ed.), *Proceedings of the 5th Australian international conference on speech science and technology* (Vol. I, pp. 28–33). Canberra: Australian Speech Science and Technology Association.

Butcher, A. R. (1995). The phonetics of neutralisation: The case of Australian coronals. In J. Windsor Lewis (Ed.), *Studies in general and English phonetics. Essays in honour of Professor J.D. O'Connor* (pp. 10–38). London: Routledge.

Butcher, A. R. (1996). Some connected speech phenomena in Australian languages: Universals and idiosyncrasies. In A. P. Simpson & M. Pätzold (Eds.), *Sound patterns of connected speech: Description, models and explanation. Proceedings of the symposium*, Kiel University on 14–15 June (pp. 83–104). (= Arbeitsberichte 31, Institut für Phonetik der Universität Kiel).

Butcher, A. R. (1999). What speakers of Australian aboriginal languages do with their velums and why: The phonetics of the nasal/oral contrast. In J. J. Ohala, Y. Hasegawa, M. Ohala, D. Granville, & A. C. Bailey (Eds.), *Proceedings of the XIV international congress of phonetic sciences* (pp. 479–482). Berkeley: ICPhS.

Butcher, A. R. (2004). 'Fortis/Lenis' revisited one more time: The aerodynamics of some oral stop contrasts in three continents. *Clinical Linguistics & Phonetics, 18*, 547–557.

Butcher, A. R., & Harrington, J. M. (2003). An acoustic and articulatory analysis of focus and the word/morpheme boundary distinction in Warlpiri. In S. Palethorpe & M. Tabain (Eds.), *Proceedings of the 6th international seminar on speech production*, Sydney, 7–10 December (pp. 19–24). [CD-ROM].

Butcher, A. R., & Tabain, M. (2004). On the back of the tongue: Contrasting dorsal sounds in Australian languages. *Phonetica, 61*, 22–52.

Campbell, J. (2002). *Invisible invaders: Smallpox and other diseases in Aboriginal Australia 1780–1880*. Carlton: Melbourne University Press.

Cho, T. (2001). Effects of morpheme boundaries on intergestural timing: Evidence from Korean. *Phonetica, 58*, 129–162.

Coates, H. L., Morris, P. S., Leach, A. J., & Couzos, S. (2002). Otitis media in Aboriginal children: Tackling a major health problem. *Medical Journal of Australia, 177*, 177–178.

Crowley, T. (1981). The Mpakwithi dialect of Anguthimri. In R. M. W. Dixon & B. J. Blake (Eds.), *Handbook of Australian languages* (Vol. 2, pp. 146–194). Canberra: ANU Press.

Dixon, R. M. W. (1970). Olgolo syllable structure and what they are doing about it. *Linguistic Inquiry, 1*, 273–276.

Dixon, R. M. W. (1980). *The languages of Australia*. Cambridge: Cambridge University Press.

Dixon, R. M. W. (2002). *Australian languages: Their nature and development*. Cambridge: Cambridge University Press.

Greenberg, S. (1996). Auditory processing of speech. In N. J. Lass (Ed.), *Principles of experimental phonetics* (pp. 362–407). St Louis: Mosby.

Hale, K. (1976). Phonological developments in particular Northern Paman languages. In P. Sutton (Ed.), *Languages of Cape York* (pp. 7–40). Australian Aboriginal Studies, Research and Regional Studies 6.

Hamilton, P. J. (1996). *Phonetic constraints and markedness in the phonotactics of Australian Aboriginal languages*. Ph.D. thesis, University of Toronto.

Harrington, J. (1994). The contribution of the murmur and vowel to the place of articulation distinction in nasal consonants. *Journal of the Acoustical Society of America, 96*, 19–32.

Harrington, J., Fletcher, J., & Beckman, M. E. (2000). Manner and place conflicts in the articulation of accent in Australian English. In M. Broe & J. Pierrehumbert (Eds.), *Papers in laboratory phonology V: Language acquisition and the lexicon* (pp. 40–51). Cambridge: Cambridge University Press.

Henderson, J., & Dobson, V. (1994). *Eastern and Central Arrernte to English dictionary*. Alice Springs: IAD Press.

Kawasaki, H. (1986). Phonetic explanations for phonological universals: The case of distinctive vowel nasalisation. In J. J. Ohala & J. J. Jaeger (Eds.), *Experimental phonology* (pp. 81–103). Orlando, FL: Academic Press.

Keating, P., Fougeron, C., Cho, T., & Hsu, C.-H. (2003). Domain-initial articulatory strengthening in four languages. In J. Local, R. Ogden, & R. Temple (Eds.), *Papers in laboratory phonology VI: Phonetic interpretation* (pp. 145–163). Cambridge: Cambridge University Press.

Koch, H. (1997). Pama-Nyungan reflexes in Arandic languages. In D. Tryon & M. Walsh (Eds.), *Boundary rider: Essays in honour of Geoffrey O'Grady* (pp. 271–302). Canberra: Pacific Linguistics (C-136).

Kochetov, A. (in press). Syllable position effects and gestural organization: Articulatory evidence from Russian. In L. Goldstein, D. Whalen, & C. Best (Eds.), *Papers in laboratory phonology VIII: Varieties of phonological competence*. Berlin: Mouton de Gruyter.

Kohler, K. J. (1975). Die Instabilität wortfinaler Alveolarplosive im Deutschen: Eine elektropalatographische Untersuchung. *Arbeitsberichte des Instituts für Phonetik der Universität Kiel, 5*, 47–79.

Krakow, R. (1999). Physiological organization of syllables: A review. *Journal of Phonetics, 27*, 23–54.

Ladefoged, P., & Maddieson, I. (1996). *The sounds of the world's languages*. Oxford: Blackwell.

Lindblom, B., & Maddieson, I. (1988). Phonetic universals in consonant systems. In L. M. Hyman & C. N. Li (Eds.), *Language, speech and mind. Studies in honour of Victoria A. Fromkin* (pp. 62–78). London: Routledge.

McConvell, P. (1988). Nasal cluster dissimilation and constraints on phonological variables in Gurindji and related languages. *Aboriginal Linguistics, 1*, 135–165.

Menzies, G. (2002). *1421: The year China discovered the world*. London: Transworld.

O'Grady, G., & Fitzgerald, S. (1997). Cognate search in the Pama–Nyungan language family. In P. McConvell & N. R. Evans (Eds.), *Archaeology and linguistics: Aboriginal Australia in global perspective* (pp. 341–355). Melbourne: Oxford University Press.

Pentland, C. (2003). *Stress in Warlpiri: Stress domains and word-level prosody*. Masters thesis, University of Queensland.

Recasens, D. (1989). Long range coarticulatory effects for tongue dorsum contact in VCVCV sequences. *Speech Communication, 8*, 293–307.

Redford, M., & Diehl, R. (1999). The relative perceptual distinctiveness of initial and final consonants in CVC syllables. *Journal of the Acoustical Society of America, 106*, 1555–1565.

Repp, B. H., & Svastikula, K. (1988). Perception of the [m]-[n] distinction in VC syllables. *Journal of the Acoustical Society of America, 83*, 237–247.

Tabain, M., Breen, J. G., & Butcher, A. R. (2004). VC vs. CV syllables: A comparison of Aboriginal languages with English. *Journal of the International Phonetic Association, 34*, 175–200.

Worgan, G. B. (1788/2003). *Journal of a First Fleet surgeon*. Sydney: University of Sydney Library. Available online at http://purl.library.usyd.edu.au/setis/id/worjour

13

Devoicing of Word-Initial Stops

A Consequence of the Following Vowel?

DANIEL PAPE, CHRISTINE MOOSHAMMER, PHIL HOOLE, AND SUSANNE FUCHS

ABSTRACT

The aim of the current study is to investigate the contextual conditions of devoicing of phonologically voiced stops (bilabial and velar). Articulatory and acoustic data from four male speakers were recorded by means of EMMA and EPG. Devoicing was observed more frequently for the velar stops than for the bilabials. The highest occurrence of devoicing was observed when the voiced stop was followed by a low or mid-vowel. To test whether articulatory positions are affected by the identity of the following vowel ANOVAs were computed. All subjects showed significant effects on positional data varying with place of articulation of the stop. Percentage of devoicing was significantly correlated with vertical and horizontal tongue positions for the velar and with the vertical jaw position for both stops. Stepwise regression models were computed to achieve an objective measure of the relevance of the measured parameters. We assume that in German, movement economy, i.e., co-articulation is more important than the maintenance of voicing during the closure, which is in agreement with the view that the voicing distinction in German is primarily produced by a longer VOT for the voiceless stops.

INTRODUCTION

Devoicing of stops can be attributed to the fact that, due to the accumulation of air behind the oral closure, the transglottal pressure drop decreases and the vocal folds stop vibrating (see e.g., Ohala & Riordan, 1980).

Accordingly, devoicing of stops is generally a natural consequence of an oral closure, assuming the velar port is closed and the speaker does not produce an active or passive mechanism to overcome the transglottal pressure drop. A passive mechanism for this maintenance of voicing would be soft-tissue compliance, e.g., for the cheeks during the production of bilabials. A possible active strategy to counteract the effect of air accumulation behind the closure is to enlarge the intraoral cavity. This so-called cavity enlargement was investigated by Westbury (1983), who found that, depending on the place of articulation, tongue, jaw, larynx, and the soft palate can contribute to an increase in oral volume.

Thus there seems to be a trade-off between consequences of the physical properties of our speech apparatus, i.e., devoicing as a consequence of oral closure on the one hand and language-dependent demands related to the voicing contrast on the other: In Romance languages voicing is often found to be maintained throughout the complete stop closure, therefore mechanisms like cavity enlargement are necessary. In contrast, for Germanic languages the distinction between phonologically voiced and voiceless stops is mainly based on differences in aspiration, i.e., no additional strategy for the maintenance of voicing is required. This language contrast was experimentally examined by Shih, Möbius, and Narasimhan (1999) using "voicing profiles," which trace voicing status frame by frame from the beginning of stop closure until stop release. Shih et al. found a language-dependent contrast for Italian and Spanish vs. German with almost no devoicing for the former languages and lower devoicing probability for the latter. Fischer-Jørgensen (1968) found similar results examining the voicing patterns of French vs. Danish stops.

However, in both language families velar stops are more prone to devoicing in comparison with bilabial stops. This phenomenon can be attributed to aerodynamics: For velar stops the back cavity is rather small and probably allows only restricted use of enlargement strategies, whereas in bilabial stops such mechanisms could be applied rather easily. Maddieson (2003) provided evidence that the "missing /g/" patterns in the phoneme inventories of the sounds of the world's languages occur rather frequently; this he attributed to the morphology of the vocal tract in combination with aerodynamic factors.

Several factors have been found to influence devoicing of phonologically voiced stops:

1. *Place of articulation.* Ohala and Riordan (1980) found empirically that velar stops are more often subject to devoicing due to less volume behind the point of constriction. This limits their capacity for passive enlargement, which is necessary to keep the pharyngeal pressure low. Keating, Linker, and Huffman (1983) found that the duration of voicing into closure varies with

place of articulation in English and Swedish, with higher durations for bilabials and shorter durations for velars.

2. *Position in utterance.* To examine the likelihood of voiced and devoiced stops in different positions in an utterance, Westbury and Keating (1985) computed the different aerodynamic conditions given by different positions of a stop in an utterance. They found that, from an aerodynamic point of view, a voiced stop is more likely to be produced in medial position. However, in utterance initial and final position aerodynamic demands are more likely to produce a voiceless stop.
3. *Voicing status of context.* Shih et al. (1999) found strong contextual influences on the devoicing patterns of stops in different languages, i.e., the devoicing of phonologically voiced German stops was dependent on whether the preceding context was voiced (vowels and sonorants) or voiceless (voiceless stops and voiceless fricatives), with lower percentage of devoicing if the preceding phone was voiced.
4. *Vowel context.* Ohala and Riordan (1980) observed that stops coarticulated with high vowels permitted voicing to continue longer than those coarticulated with low vowels, due to the enlarged pharyngeal cavity for high vowels.
5. *Stress.* Keating et al. (1983) found that stress increased the duration of closure voicing for Swedish.
6. *Duration of the stop.* The longer the stop closure the higher the probability that voicing will cease. Ohala (2003) found in a vented-valve experiment controlling the oral air pressure artificially that voicing during stop production could not be maintained for longer than about 60 ms. Kawahara (2004) examined Japanese singleton stops in comparison to geminates and found that voiced singleton stops showed voicing for almost 100 per cent of closure duration whereas voiced-geminate stops showed voicing for only 30–40 per cent of stop closure.

The general aim of the current investigation is to study the dependency of devoicing effects on the following vowel. Therefore, we extend the work of Ohala and Riordan (1980) to a greater variety of vowel contexts, i.e., to the whole German vowel inventory. The second aim is to test their hypothesis that coarticulatory influences cause the vowel-specific distribution of devoicing occurrence by means of articulatory and acoustic measurements. Therefore, we conducted a combined EMMA, EPG, and acoustic experiment to investigate the causes for devoicing of phonologically voiced word-initial stops in German.

In particular, we were interested in (1) whether the patterns of devoicing in German resembled the patterns in American English, (2) whether the articulatory configuration at the onset of the consonantal constriction is already influenced by the following vowel, and (3) whether the patterns of devoicing can be explained by these anticipatory effects.

METHOD

Experimental Setup

We investigated tongue and jaw movements together with tongue–palate contact patterns by means of synchronized EPG (Reading EPG3), EMMA (AG100, Carstens Medizinelektronik) and acoustic recordings of four male subjects (CG, DF, JD, RW). Four sensors were attached mid-sagittally to the tongue spaced equally from 1 to 5 cm behind the tongue tip, one to the jaw (lower incisors) and one to the lower lip. Two sensors, one at the bridge of the nose and the other at the upper incisors, served as reference coils to compensate for helmet movements during the recording session. The audio signal was simultaneously recorded on DAT. The final sampling frequency for the articulatory data was 200 Hz (low-pass filtered with a cut-off frequency of 20 Hz) and 16 kHz for the acoustic data.

The speech material consisted of nonsense words /gVkə/ for the velars and /bVpə/ for the bilabials, where V consisted of the 14 German tense and lax stressed vowels /iː yː uː ɪ ʏ ʊ eː øː oː ɛ œ ɔ ɑː a/. The target words were embedded in the carrier phrase "Sage __ bitte." (/za:gə __ bɪtə/, "Say __ please."). Since the devoicing of stops occurs only rarely in word-medial position we chose the word initial position to examine devoicing. Following Shih et al. (1999) a lower percentage of devoicing could be expected since the investigated stop was preceded by a vowel. Obviously a word boundary preceding the stop occurred and could introduce variation in stop duration. Each sentence was repeated 10 times in randomized order, except for speaker RW whose sensors came off after eight repetitions. Speakers were instructed to speak at a comfortable speaking rate and loudness.

Acoustic and Articulatory Measurements

For this study of vowel-specific influences on articulatory positions during the stop, we chose the acoustically defined onset of the stop closure as our reference point. The reasons for this choice were: (1) we assumed that if the patterns of devoicing can be explained by anticipation, then articulatory positions should differ before devoicing occurs and (2) it is guaranteed that for all tokens voicing is still maintained at this time point. The onset of stop closure is usually labelled as the offset of higher formants (Klatt, 1975), preferably the second formant.

Two problems occurred during labelling of the data: First, it was found that frequently the offset of the different higher formants did not occur at the same point in time, thereby introducing wide measurement variability. Secondly, even when concentrating on the offset of the second formant, one speaker showed strong nasalization during the preceding vowel, which was the speaker's anticipatory strategy to maintain voicing throughout the following closure (this nasalization was clearly audible and confirmed by informal perceptual tests). This frequently resulted in a pronounced weakening of the second formant of the vowel to be measured, due to the interference of resonances of the nasal cavity (Stevens, 1998). The resulting increased variability led us to a different labelling technique in order to get a more reliable measurement: A relevant decrease of the sound intensity (intensity settings: 0.047 s Kaiser20 window) was operationally labelled as –6 dB, measured from the point of maximal intensity of the preceding vowel. Since there is no aerodynamic (or linguistic) reason to assume that at this acoustic landmark the speaker is actively decreasing the acoustic intensity of the glottal output, the –6 dB decrease of global intensity indicates the beginning of the stop closure and was in about 95 per cent of the cases identical with the offset of the second formant of the vowels. Figure 13.1 illustrates the procedure. The intensity decrease

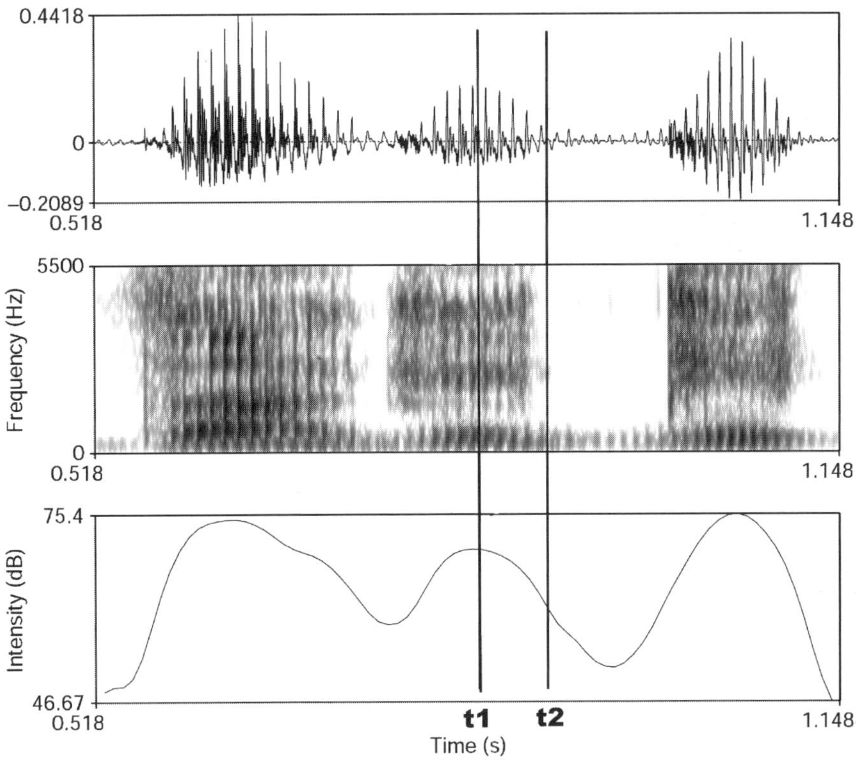

FIGURE 13.1. Procedure for acoustic labelling. Upper panel: the oscillogram; middle panel: the spectrogram; lower panel: the intensity contour. The left black bar (t1) indicates the landmark of the maximal intensity of the vowel. The right bar (t2) indicates the 6 dB intensity decrease measured from the point of maximal intensity.

was automatically measured using a script with the standard intensity settings (0.047 s Kaiser) of the software PRAAT (Boersma & Weenink, 1999).

At this acoustically defined landmark of closure onset, we measured the horizontal and vertical positions of the tongue dorsum (TDORS), tongue back (TBACK), jaw (JAW), and lower lip (LLIP) sensors. From the EPG data, the centre of gravity index (COG) and the percentage of contacts in the posterior palatal region (POST) were calculated by using the formula given in Gibbon and Nicolaidis (1999):

[$COG=(0.5^*R8+1.5^*R7+2.5^*R6+3.5^*R5+4.5^*R4+5.5^*R3+6.5^*R2+7.5^*R1)/(R8+\ldots+R1)$], where *R*s are the number of activated contacts per row (*R*8: posterior row...*R*1: anterior row). POST is computed as the sum of the activated electrodes of the four posterior rows divided by the number of electrodes of the four posterior rows.

The stop was labelled as devoiced if there was no visible periodicity in the oscillogram for more than one glottal period (about 10 ms for male subjects, corresponding to one phonatory cycle at a fundamental frequency of 100 Hz) preceding the burst. The alternative method would be to measure the ratio of the devoiced part to the complete closure duration. This method was disfavoured because the aim of this investigation was to find the causal relationships between devoicing and articulatory configurations and not the temporal patterns. Therefore, we judged categorically the stop as voiced or devoiced by applying the criterion mentioned above. Closure duration (DurC) was measured as the temporal distance between the beginning of the stop closure (see above) and the stop release (burst).

RESULTS

Occurrence of Devoicing

Figure 13.2 shows the percentages of devoicing for all speakers split by place of articulation and following vowel. As was expected the velar stop is more often subject to devoicing than the bilabial stop (46.3 vs. 26.4 per cent). The percentage of devoicing clearly increases with decreasing vowel height, e.g., the bilabial stop was more often devoiced when followed by the mid- and low vowels /ɑː, a, ɛ, ɔ/ compared to the high vowel /iː, yː, uː, eː/. These findings are generally in agreement with previous studies. Also shown in Figure 13.2 is a tense-lax effect for mid- and high vowels, with lax vowels more likely to induce devoicing. This could be attributed to the fact that lax vowels are produced with a more open vocal tract compared to their tense counterparts (Hoole & Mooshammer, 2002) and therefore shows the same tendency as described above.

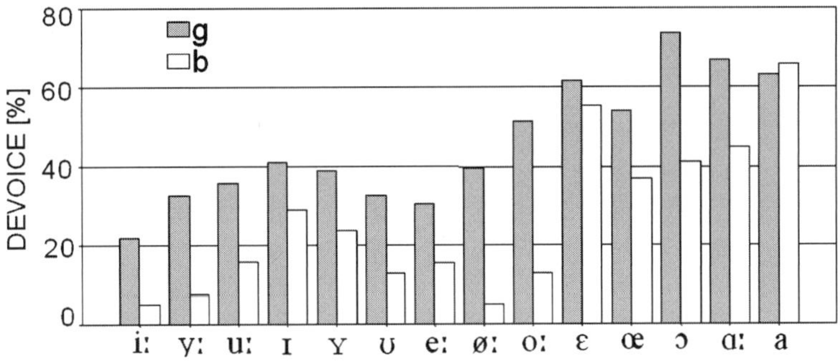

FIGURE 13.2. Percentage of devoicing, shown for each vowel and the contexts /b/ and /g/. The vowels are ordered by their phonological vowel height. Mean values are 46.3 per cent for the velar and 26.4 per cent for the bilabial.

Table 13.1 shows the percentage of stop devoicing for each vowel, split by speaker and stop. Data for each speaker show similar relationships between devoicing and vowel height, but the overall amount of devoicing varies according to the speaker, e.g., speaker DF is more prone to devoice the bilabial than speaker CG. Speaker JD's devoicing pattern for the bilabial is exceptional, with almost no instances of devoicing. This speaker avoids devoicing by prenasalizing the bilabial but not the velar stop.

TABLE 13.1. Percentage of Stop Devoicing Split by Speaker and Following Vowel

	Bilabial stop				Velar stop			
Vowel	CG	DF	JD	RW	CG	DF	JD	RW
iː	0.00	20.00	0.00	0.00	0.00	50.00	0.00	25.00
yː	0.00	18.18	0.00	12.50	20.00	66.67	10.00	37.50
uː	10.00	0.00	10.00	50.00	20.00	63.64	20.00	37.50
ɪ	20.00	60.00	0.00	37.50	11.11	63.64	40.00	44.44
ʏ	10.00	70.00	0.00	12.50	10.00	80.00	25.00	37.50
ʊ	20.00	18.18	0.00	12.50	0.00	63.64	10.00	55.56
eː	0.00	27.27	20.00	12.50	0.00	60.00	22.22	37.50
øː	0.00	18.18	0.00	0.00	10.00	80.00	50.00	12.50
oː	0.00	18.18	0.00	37.50	40.00	100.00	10.00	50.00
ɛ	50.00	100.00	10.00	62.50	20.00	81.82	66.67	77.78
œ	20.00	70.00	0.00	62.50	40.00	90.91	30.00	50.00
ɔ	30.00	72.73	0.00	62.50	70.00	100.00	80.00	37.50
ɑː	40.00	70.00	10.00	62.50	80.00	81.82	40.00	62.50
a	70.00	100.00	0.00	100.00	60.00	100.00	33.33	50.00

Anticipatory Effects on Duration and Articulatory Positions at Consonantal Closure Onset

As mentioned in the introductory section, closure duration plays a major role for the devoicing of phonologically voiced stops. Therefore, in Table 13.2 the means and *SD*s of the closure durations and in Table 13.3 the significant effects are shown. For two speakers we found longer closure durations when the bilabial stop was followed by a lax vowel, but no consistent effects for the other two speakers. For all speakers the duration of the velar was either not affected or only slightly affected by the following vowel.

The vowel-specific distribution of devoicing suggests that the following vowel influences the volume of the oral cavity during occlusion. To test whether tongue, jaw, and lip positions are also affected by the identity of the following vowel at the moment of the acoustically defined consonant onset ANOVAs were calculated with vowel identity as independent variable and position of the articulators and EPG measures as dependent variables, split by speaker and consonant. The results are shown in Table 13.3. Since vowel identity is a factor with 14 levels we used the highly conservative Scheffé post-hoc test, which requires very large differences between means in order to detect different groups. Therefore in some cases, the ANOVA gives significant effects where the Scheffé test shows no significantly different groups. These cases are marked in Table 13.3 by brackets around the asterisks, whereas when both the ANOVA and the Scheffé test yielded significant effects and groups, the *F* values are

TABLE 13.2. Mean Closure Durations for the Bilabial and Velar Stop, Split by Speaker and Following Vowel

	Bilabial stop				Velar stop			
Vowel	CG	DF	JD	RW	CG	DF	JD	RW
iː	106 (11)	102 (08)	124 (17)	87 (24)	76 (31)	78 (09)	136 (50)	106 (24)
yː	95 (16)	104 (20)	108 (12)	121 (28)	104 (14)	85 (10)	145 (18)	132 (22)
uː	93 (13)	74 (23)	107 (19)	112 (17)	97 (16)	98 (22)	108 (29)	124 (13)
ɪ	93 (10)	125 (10)	161 (24)	110 (16)	89 (16)	112 (24)	132 (21)	122 (14)
ʏ	88 (07)	125 (17)	135 (13)	110 (14)	85 (21)	107 (17)	130 (20)	135 (13)
ʊ	92 (11)	112 (23)	129 (14)	105 (15)	84 (17)	110 (28)	108 (23)	134 (29)
eː	100 (09)	116 (15)	127 (21)	102 (31)	89 (24)	85 (12)	121 (37)	116 (15)
øː	80 (12)	106 (23)	112 (17)	114 (32)	95 (13)	92 (17)	124 (19)	115 (35)
oː	93 (12)	99 (14)	123 (11)	122 (39)	87 (22)	92 (09)	90 (32)	108 (37)
ɛ	99 (17)	141 (34)	144 (15)	129 (23)	81 (19)	104 (31)	110 (20)	121 (29)
œ	82 (12)	125 (09)	136 (19)	127 (22)	83 (16)	119 (16)	118 (26)	129 (24)
ɔ	95 (10)	124 (18)	136 (08)	119 (28)	68 (15)	105 (23)	119 (22)	112 (35)
ɑː	102 (08)	108 (18)	116 (12)	110 (17)	74 (18)	79 (13)	78 (19)	95 (21)
a	95 (07)	110 (12)	136 (10)	127 (27)	69 (12)	99 (19)	114 (12)	108 (25)

Note. The corresponding standard deviations are given within parentheses.

TABLE 13.3. ANOVAs Showing the *F* Values, the Degrees of Freedom, and the Significance Levels

	Bilabial stop							
	CG $F(13, 126)$		DF $F(13, 123)$		JD $F(13, 126)$		RW $F(13, 98)$	
POST	**6.8**	***	**17.6**	***	**5.0**	***	**34.6**	***
COG	0.4		0.6		3.7	(***)	2.3	(**)
TBACKX	5.1	(***)	**8.5**	***	**12.9**	***	**4.4**	***
TBACKY	**5.2**	***	**7.7**	***	2.0	(*)	3.1	(***)
TDORSX	**15.3**	***	**7.5**	***	**5.6**	***	**10.0**	***
TDORSY	**11.0**	***	**23.5**	***	**7.3**	***	**8.8**	***
JAWX	0.3		0.6		1.8		1.5	
JAWY	**4.1**	***	**5.2**	***	**10.0**	***	1.4	
LLIPX	3.3	(***)	1.5		**11.4**	***	1.6	
LLIPY	2.5	(***)	**6.1**	***	**9.8**	***	1.0	
DURC	**3.8**	***	**5.9**	***	**8.2**	***	1.5	
	Velar stop							
	CG $F(13, 119)$		DF $F(13, 133)$		JD $F(13, 120)$		RW $F(13, 101)$	
POST	**3.6**	***	**7.5**	***	**19.0**	***	**5.4**	***
COG	0.8		0.6		**12.7**	**	1.7	
TBACKX	1.7		0.8		2.0	(*)	0.8	
TBACKY	2.1	(*)	**6.1**	***	1.0		1.1	
TDORSX	**4.3**	***	1.9	(*)	1.0		2.3	(***)
TDORSY	**5.1**	***	**18.1**	***	**11.0**	***	3.2	(***)
JAWX	2.0	(*)	3.6	(***)	1.7		1.8	
JAWY	4.2	(***)	5.2	(***)	3.0	(***)	3.0	(***)
LLIPX	**47.2**	***	**27.2**	***	**37.1**	***	**13.7**	***
LLIPY	**13.3**	***	**31.9**	***	**4.3**	***	**10.4**	***
DURC	2.94	(**)	**4.6**	***	**4.1**	***	1.6	

Note. The significant levels are *** $p < .001$; ** $p < .01$; * $p < .05$ for each speaker split by bilabial and velar context. The asterisks in parentheses indicate cases where the ANOVA yielded significant effects, but the more conservative Scheffé-post-hoc test could not separate groups. *F* values printed in bold indicate significantly different vowel groups obtained by Scheffé-post-hoc test.

printed in bold. In the following section, anticipatory effects will only be considered for articulators if the Scheffé test showed significant groups.

For the EPG measures, the COG was insensitive for vowel context (except for speaker JD) but the POST increased significantly for all speakers and both consonants comparing front high vowels with low back vowels. At the onset of the velar, the position of the most posterior tongue sensor (TBACK) was not affected by the vowel but the vertical positions of the more fronted sensor (TDORS) varied significantly with vowel height for three speakers (not significant for RW). Jaw positions for velars tended to be higher for following closed vowels for speaker CG and higher for rounded vowels for speaker DF (both almost significant).

In contrast to the velar, for the bilabial both tongue sensors varied significantly according to the following vowel in the expected direction (the TDORS sensor was affected more consistently). The jaw tended to be significantly more closed when the following vowel was rounded for speakers DF and JD (for speaker CG the jaw was influenced by vowel height but not by rounding). The horizontal lip position at the onset of the bilabial was affected by rounding for three speakers but significant only for speaker JD, the speaker who maintained voicing most effectively for the bilabials. This speaker also showed a peculiar pattern for the vertical lip position, with lower values following rounded vowels, whereas the other speakers tended to lower the lower lip for unrounded vowels (not significant).

To summarize the results so far, significant vowel effects could be detected at the onset of the consonant. As might have been expected, those articulators, which do not directly contribute to the production of the stop, vary most consistently with vowel identity, e.g., lip position for the velars and tongue position for the bilabials. For the jaw, whose position during phonologically voiced bilabial and velar closures is highly influenced by vowel context (see, e.g., Keating, Lindblom, Lubker, & Kreiman, 1994), we assume a helping function, which is probably more pronounced in the bilabial stop. For both contexts, the vertical jaw position varied for all speakers (except RW) but no consistent pattern could be extracted: For speaker CG the jaw height is influenced by vowel height whereas for speaker DF the jaw is elevated for rounded vowels (only for the bilabials for speaker JD). The presumably active articulator, namely the lower lip for bilabials and both tongue sensors for the velars, also varied for three speakers but the effects were weaker and less consistent compared to the nonactive articulators.

Relationship Devoicing–Articulatory Positions

To analyse which of the articulators might have an influence on the occurrence of devoicing, we computed correlations between average positional data and the percentage of devoicing calculated over 10 repetitions of each item. Since it is well known that the occurrence of devoicing is also influenced by closure duration (see the Introduction section) we added this variable (DurC) to our analyses. Table 13.4 shows the correlation coefficients and the level of significance.

For the bilabial stop, the devoicing pattern can only be related to the vertical jaw position for two speakers with a highly significant negative correlation, i.e., the lower the jaw position the higher the percentage of devoicing. This is also captured by Figure 13.3 (in the left panels), which shows scatter plots of the percentage of devoicing and the averaged vertical jaw position, split by speaker and consonant. The jaw positions of speakers CG and DF also varied significantly with vowel height. Speakers JD and RW showed no significant

TABLE 13.4. Correlation Coefficients Between Devoicing and Articulatory Measurement Points

	Bilabial stop				Velar stop			
	CG(B)	DF(B)	JD(B)	RW(B)	CG(G)	DF(G)	JD(G)	RW(G)
TBACKX	.291	−.113	−.273	.173	−.577	.593	−.483	−.386
TDORSX	.354	−.050	−.345	.353	−.167	.544	−.664	.090
JAWX	.214	.276	−.096	−.258	.009	−.250	.610	−.017
LLIPX	.433	.156	.175	−.133	.053	−.234	.348	.366
TBACKY	−.399	−.129	−.168	−.499	−.425	−.638	−.571	−.292
TDORSY	−.478	−.071	−.075	−.533	−.465	−.665	.173	−.553
JAWY	**−.669**	**−.700**	−.401	−.469	**−.715**	−.038	−.647	−.639
LLIPY	.058	−.475	.313	−.165	−.388	.143	.109	−.551
COG	.201	−.183	.143	−.181	−.029	−.349	.024	−.632
POST	−.149	.073	−.088	−.489	−.642	−.570	.002	−.481
DurC	.176	**.738**	−.152	**.664**	−.586	.309	−.134	−.010

Note. Significant values (p = .05) are marked with a grey cell background. Highly significant values (p = .01) are in bold.

correlations at all for the bilabial. For speaker JD, obviously this can be attributed to the very rare instances of devoicing. Lip rounding (LLIPX) was never significantly related to the percentage of devoicing. The duration of the bilabial (DurC) was positively correlated for two speakers, i.e., the longer the stop the higher the likelihood for devoicing.

For the velar stop, the devoicing pattern is also related to the vertical jaw position for three speakers, for CG with a highly significant correlation. For two speakers, the POST and for speaker RW the COG was significantly negatively correlated with the percentage of devoicing. The vertical tongue sensors showed a negative correlation, i.e., the lower the tongue, the higher the percentage of devoicing (not significant for speaker CG). For the two posterior tongue sensors, which are assumed to capture the velar articulator best, opposing patterns could be observed for speakers CG and JD on the one hand and speaker DF on the other. The latter fronted the place of articulation before front vowels. Because of the curved shape of the palate the tongue was also higher before front vowels. Furthermore, speaker DF tended to devoice the velar more frequently when the stop was followed by a back vowel which was not the case for speakers CG and JD. The latter two speakers showed no fronting of the velar with a following front vowel but significant negative correlations between horizontal tongue position and devoicing, i.e., the more fronted the tongue the more frequently devoicing occurred. No significant correlations between devoicing and horizontal tongue position could be found for speaker RW.

To achieve an objective measure of the relevance of the measured parameters for the occurrence of devoicing SPSS, stepwise regression models were

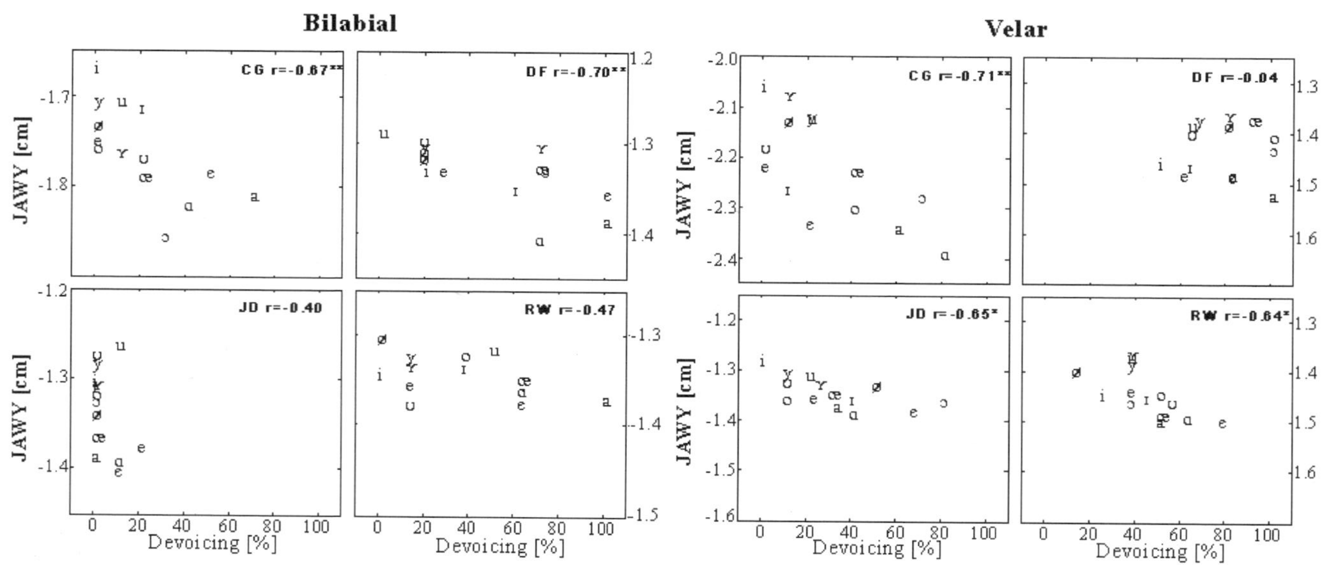

FIGURE 13.3. Scatter plots of the percentage of devoicing and the mean vertical jaw position at consonant onset for bilabials (left) and velars (right) for each speaker.

TABLE 13.5. Regression Models Computed by the SPSS Procedure Linear Stepwise Regression

CONS	VP	Model	R^2	F	Probability
Bilabial	CG	JAWY	.448	9.73	.0089
	DF	DurC	.545	14.37	.0026
		DurC, JAWY	.774	18.83	.0003
	RW	DurC	.442	9.51	.0095
		DurC, JAWY	.611	8.64	.0056
Velar	CG	JAWY	.511	12.53	.0041
		JAWY, JAWX	.767	18.12	.0003
	DF	TDORSY	.442	9.50	.0095
	JD	TDORSX	.441	9.46	.0096
		TDORSX, JAWX	.636	9.60	.0039
	RW	JAWY	.408	8.27	.0139

Note. Degrees of freedom are always (1, 13). The dependent variable is percentage of devoicing and the independent variables are articulatory positions and EPG measures at the onset of the stop as well as stop duration.

computed with percentage of devoicing as dependent variable and articulatory positions of tongue back, tongue dorsum, jaw, and lower lip sensors. The EPG measures POST, COG, and stop duration as independent variables. Table 13.5 shows the extracted regression models with the predictors selected by stepwise regression models, explained variance (R^2), F values, and probability. As can be seen no model could be extracted for speaker JD for the devoicing pattern of bilabials. Closure duration (DurC) only played a significant role for the bilabials (speakers DF and RW) but not for the velars. The inclusion of the vertical jaw component improved the prediction considerably for speakers DF and RW whereas for speaker CG the vertical jaw position was actually the only variable that met the criterion for inclusion ($F > 3.84$) and explains about 45 per cent of the variance. The occurrence of devoicing of velar stops was best predicted by the vertical jaw position for speakers CG and RW. In two cases, the horizontal jaw position was included in the models. The inclusion for speaker CG can be attributed to a suppression effect of JAWX (Bortz, 1979) because it did not correlate with the criterion variable but significantly improved the model due to the high correlation between JAWX and JAWY ($r = -.586^*$). This was not the case for speaker JD whose pattern of devoicing significantly varied with jaw retraction (see Table 13.4). The main predictor variable for this speaker was the horizontal tongue dorsum position. Speaker DF, as can be seen in Figure 13.3, produced the velar stop with a higher jaw position when followed by a rounded vowel. Therefore, the jaw was not selected as a predictor variable for devoicing but the vertical tongue dorsum position was selected.

CONCLUSION AND DISCUSSION

In this study, we investigated the occurrence of devoicing in phonologically voiced stops and its dependence on the following vowel in German. We measured articulatory data (EMMA and EPG) at the acoustically defined closure onset. Depending on the place of articulation of the stop, devoicing was more frequently found for the velar with 46.3 per cent compared to the bilabial with 26.4 per cent. In accordance with earlier studies on American English (Ohala & Riordan, 1980), we found that the percentage of stop devoicing increases with increasing vowel openness. Ohala and Riordan attributed this devoicing pattern to the decreased pharyngeal volume in anticipation of following lower vowels. The presence of anticipatory effects at the onset of the stop closure was confirmed by ANOVAs and varied with place of articulation of the stop. However, one speaker showed no vowel effects in bilabial context because he used a different strategy to avoid devoicing, i.e., he prenasalized the stop. Another speaker-dependent pattern could exist due to the different palatal coronal shape of the speakers. In Mooshammer et al. (2004), the palatal shape of the speakers CG and DF is shown to be dome-shaped, whereas the palate of speaker JD is more flat. This morphologically different shape may influence the size of the oral cavity during a stop closure with a smaller cavity more prone to devoicing than a larger cavity. However, our speaker-dependent devoicing patterns (see Table 13.1) do not reflect this hypothesis.

Correlation between articulatory data and percentage of devoicing revealed significant correlations for the vertical jaw position for both stops. In the stepwise regression model, this articulator was selected as a predictor variable for all speakers who showed a devoicing pattern for the bilabial and two speakers for the velar. For the velar, significant correlations with vertical and horizontal tongue positions were found for three speakers. Closure duration showed a significant effect on the percentage of devoicing for the bilabial for only two of the four speakers. Since passive compliance of the walls plays a greater role for bilabials (see Ohala, 2003), occurrences of devoicing might be more strongly affected by closure duration, i.e., the cavity enlargement due to lax cheeks provides a sufficient pressure drop only for shorter closure durations. This possibility of cavity enlargement does not exist for velars.

Obviously not all relevant factors explaining devoicing patterns were captured by our experimental set-up, which can be seen in the low explained variances in the stepwise regression models. Aerodynamic factors such as the volume of the pharyngeal cavity, transglottal, and intraoral pressure were not captured nor were positions of articulatory structures such as larynx height or velum which contribute to the size of the oral cavity (see Westbury, 1983). Ohala and Riordan's hypothesis that pharyngeal volume plays the major role for vowel-specific devoicing patterns can only be tested indirectly with our data: As was found by Tiede (1996) tongue dorsum height and pharyngeal volume are highly positively correlated for English vowels. In our regression models tongue dorsum height was relevant only for one speaker in velar context whereas jaw height was one of the major factors. One possible explanation is that the jaw captures vowel height more consistently compared to the two tongue sensors, which are strongly influenced by vowel frontness (e.g., /i:/ is produced with a higher tongue dorsum position than /u:/ due to the shape of the palate). Since the jaw and the tongue are biomechanically linked and therefore highly correlated, an alternative possibility would be that one of these articulators is therefore more consistently selected in the regression analysis.

Another vowel-specific anticipatory effect, which also enlarges the cavity and therefore might be involved in maintenance of voicing, is larynx height, which has been shown to be significantly lower for rounded vowels (for German see, e.g., Hoole & Kroos, 1998). The hypothesis here would be that if larynx height is adjusted already at the beginning of the stop then stops followed by rounded vowels should be less frequently devoiced compared to unrounded vowels with the same vowel height. This pattern of devoicing was only found for one speaker (DF) in bilabial context (see Table 13.1) whose jaw position was also mainly dependent on rounding (see Figure 13.3). Since this pattern was only found for one speaker and one context larynx height does not seem to play a major role. The other possibility to control vocal tract length is lip rounding, but this strategy was not used by our speakers (i.e., no significant correlations between devoicing and lip position for the bilabials, as can be seen in Table 13.4).

However, even with our limited data set we are tempted to conclude that cavity enlargement does not seem to play a major role in the production of German stops. Our results are in accordance with the results of Jessen (2001) and others who stated that in Germanic languages other features for voiced/voiceless stop distinction, mainly aspiration duration, are of greater importance than the maintenance of voicing throughout the complete stop closure. Even though anticipatory effects of the following vowel on the occurrence of stop devoicing vary speaker-dependently, requirements for economy of movement play a more important role than the maintenance of voicing in German.

ACKNOWLEDGMENTS

This work was supported by a grant from the German Research Council GWZ 4/8-1, P.1. We would like to thank Jörg Dreyer at the ZAS for technical setup and maintenance, especially for the realization of the synchronized recording of EMMA, EPG, and acoustic data. Thanks to Christian Geng for advice regarding the regression statistics.

REFERENCES

Boersma, P., & Weenink, D. (1999). *PRAAT, a system for doing phonetics by computer*, Report of the Institute of Phonetic Sciences of the University of Amsterdam (pp. 132–182).

Bortz, J. (1979). *Lehrbuch der statistik—für sozialwissenschaftler*. Berlin: Springer.

Fischer-Jørgensen, E. (1968). Voicing, tenseness and aspiration in stop consonants, with special reference to French and Danish. *ARIPUC*, *3*, 63–115.

Gibbon, F., & Nicolaidis, K. (1999). Palatography. In W. J. Hardcastle & N. Newlett (Eds.), *Coarticulation* (pp. 229–245). Cambridge: Cambridge University Press.

Hoole, P., & Kroos, C. (1998). Control of larynx height in vowel production. *Proceedings of the 5th international conference on spoken language processing* (Vol. 2, pp. 531–534).

Hoole, P., & Mooshammer, C. (2002). Articulatory analysis of the German vowel system. In P. Auer, P. Gilles, & H. Spiekermann (Eds.), *Silbenschnitt und tonakzente* (pp. 129–252). Tübingen: Niemeyer.

Jessen, M. (2001). Phonetic implementation of the distinctive auditory feature [voice] and [tense] in stop consonants. In T. A. Hall (Ed.), *Distinctive feature theory* (pp. 237–294). Berlin: Mouton De Gruyter.

Kawahara, S. (2004). *An acoustic and perceptual study of Japanese voiced geminates*. Manuscript for UMASS Mini-Conference.

Keating, P., Lindblom, J., Lubker, J., & Kreiman, J. (1994). Variability in jaw height for segments in English and Swedish VCVs. *Journal of Phonetics*, *22*, 407–422.

Keating, P., Linker, W., & Huffman, M. (1983). Patterns in allophone distribution for voiced and voiceless stops. *Journal of Phonetics*, *11*, 277–290.

Klatt, D. H. (1975). Voice onset time, frication, and aspiration in word-initial consonants clusters. *Journal of Speech and Hearing Research*, *18*, 686–706.

Maddieson, I. (2003). Phonological typology in geographical perspective. *Proceedings of the 15th ICPhS*, Barcelona, (Vol. 1, pp. 719–722).

Mooshammer, C., Perrier, P., Fuchs, S., Geng, C., & Pape, D. (2004). An EMMA and EPG study on token-to-token variability. *AIPUC*, *36*, 47–63.

Ohala, J. (2003). Effects on speech of introducing aerodynamic perturbations. *Proceedings of the 15th ICPhS*, Barcelona (Vol. 1, pp. 2913–2916).

Ohala, J., & Riordan, C. (1980). *Passive vocal tract enlargement during voiced stops*. Report of the Phonological Laboratory UC Berkeley (Vol. 5, pp. 78–87).

Shih, C., Möbius, B., & Narasimhan, B. (1999). Contextual effects on consonantal voicing profiles: A cross-linguistic study. *Proceedings of the 14th ICPhS*, San Francisco (Vol. 2, pp. 989–992).

Stevens, K. N. (1998). *Acoustic phonetics* (p. 512). Cambridge: The MIT Press.

Tiede, M. K. (1996). An MRI-based study of pharyngeal volume contrasts in Akan and English. *Journal of Phonetics*, *24*, 399–421.

Westbury, J. R. (1983). Enlargement of the supraglottal cavity and its relation to stop consonant voicing. *Journal of the Acoustical Society of America*, *73*, 1322–1336.

Westbury, J. R., & Keating, P. (1985). On the naturalness of stop consonant voicing. *Journal of Linguistics*, *22*, 145–166.

14

Articulatory and Acoustic Correlates of Contrastive Focus in French Children and Adults

LUCIE MÉNARD, HÉLÈNE LŒVENBRUCK, AND CHRISTOPHE SAVARIAUX

ABSTRACT

This chapter deals with the articulatory and acoustic correlates of contrastive focus in French, in both children and adults. Ten speakers (three 4-year-old, three 8-year-old children, and four adult males and females) were recorded while producing repetitions of the [baba] sequence in two prosodic contexts: in neutral condition and under contrastive focus. The opening (from the consonant into the vowel) lip gestures were video recorded and monitored using the Institut de la Communication Parlée (ICP) tracking system. Lip area and its first derivative were described under both prosodic conditions, in the first and second [ba] syllables. Analyses of formant frequencies and root mean square (RMS) amplitude were also carried out on the acoustic signal. Results show that the effect of contrastive focus on articulatory measurements is smaller for children compared to adults. Results are discussed with respect to motor control development during childhood.

INTRODUCTION

The development of speech entails the control of various components of the vocal tract. The sequential mastery of the larynx, jaw, and tongue, for instance, shapes the vocal repertoire of the young speaker (Vihman, 1996). Learning to speak also means embedding a sequence of segments within a hierarchically organized prosodic structure. It has been shown in various languages that adult speakers signal prosodic structure by acoustic and articulatory cues both realized by the glottal and supraglottal articulators (e.g., Beckman, Edwards, & Fletcher, 1992). As detailed below, in English and French, for example, it is reported that syllables produced with contrastive focus are uttered with increased values of fundamental frequency (*F*0), duration, or intensity, compared to their unfocused counterparts (e.g., Ladd, 1996; Selkirk, 1984; Touati, 1987), and are also associated with changes in the kinematics of the supralaryngeal articulators (e.g., De Jong, 1995; Dohen, Lœvenbruck, Cathiard, & Schwartz, 2004b; Erickson, 2002; Lœvenbruck, 1999). In typically developing children, glottal and supraglottal mechanisms are controlled at different stages during development (Vihman, 1996). Hence, it is possible that different articulatory strategies are involved in prosodic marking for adults and children. This paper aims at examining production differences between 4-year-old, 8-year-old, and adult French speakers in marking focus-induced prominence at the articulatory and acoustic levels.

CONTRASTIVE FOCUS IN ADULTS

Contrastive focus is one type of narrow focus defined as involving the selection by the speaker of a given constituent of the message to be underlined as opposed to another constituent in a paradigmatic comparison (Bartels & Kingston, 1994; Dahan & Bernard, 1996; Di Cristo, 2000; Ladd, 1996; Pierrehumbert & Hirshberg, 1990; Selkirk, 1984; Touati, 1987). In French, contrastive focus can either be signalled syntactically (the prominent word or phrase X is put forward through a syntactic focus construction, such as a syntactic extraction: “c’est X qui”, “it’s X who”) or prosodically (the prominent word or phrase is put forward through the manipulation of prosodic features such as fundamental frequency (*F*0), duration or intensity), or both (e.g., Di Cristo, 2000). The present paper deals with contrastive focus conveyed by both syntax and prosody, which will be referred to simply as “contrastive focus”. Studies carried out in English have shown that this prosodic prominence is associated with larger, faster, and longer lip opening gestures for /a/ and /i/ (Cho, 2002; 2005) and lower jaw positions for /a/ (Erickson, 1998). Lœvenbruck (1999) also reports that tongue position is lower for [la] syllables produced under contrastive focus, compared to the neutral condition. These articulatory correlates are often related to spectral changes, with low vowels being more peripheral in the acoustic space (Cho, 2005). It is important to note that between-speaker variability is reported with respect to the articulatory and acoustic effects of prominence.

This study is concerned with contrastive focus in French. Unlike English, French is usually described as a fixed-accent language in which an obligatory primary accent is assigned to the final full syllable of a prosodic phrase. This demarcative accent, referred to as H* in Jun and Fougeron (2000, 2002), marks the right edge of a prosodic phrase (see also e.g., Di Cristo, 2000; Jun & Fougeron, 2000, 2002; Lacheret-Dujour & Beaugendre, 1999; Pasdeloup, 1990). When carrying a primary accent, in French, syllables are longer and higher in intensity than the preceding syllables. In addition, if the phrase is not utterance final, the primary-accented syllable bears a rise in *F*0. In addition to the phrase-final primary accent, French features an optional phrase-initial secondary accent, referred to as Hi in Jun and Fougeron (2000, 2002). The location of the secondary accent is variable: it generally occurs on one of the first syllables of the phrase [see Welby (2003) for data and hypotheses on the alignment of the initial rise]. Contrary to the primary accent, the secondary accent is not always accompanied by syllabic lengthening or increased intensity and its associated *F*0 peak is generally lower than that of the primary accent.

The intonational correlates of contrastive focus in French have been widely studied (e.g., Clech-Darbon, Rebuschi, & Rialland, 1999; Delais-Roussarie, Rialland, Doetjes, & Marandin, 2002; Di Cristo, 1998; Dohen & Lœvenbruck, 2004; Jun & Fougeron, 2000; Rossi, 1999; Touati, 1987). They include a large and sharp rise in *F*0 or intensity on the focused constituent, an increased duration of the focused syllables and a global *F*0 and intensity compression in the post-focus sequence, with either a low plateau or a steady fall until the end of the utterance. The *F*0 peak, or Hf, most often replaces Hi; that is, Hf is usually located on one of the initial syllables. But Hf can also sometimes replace H* or even both Hi and H* (the rise in *F*0 can be borne by all the syllables and culminates on the last syllable). The post-focal sequence is usually deaccented, i.e., it is realized as a low-plateau in which all tones are deleted but phrase boundary lengthening is still present (no dephrasing).

Although the terminology used may differ, a number of articulatory studies deal with what we consider as contrastive focus, in several languages. In order to explain the effects of contrastive focus on the kinematic patterns of the supraglottal articulators, two models are proposed. In a first model, the mechanism involved in the variation of the supraglottal articulation associated with the prominence would be a local hyperarticulation of the focused syllable, evidenced by reduced coarticulation (de Jong, 1995). A similar hyperarticulation account is also proposed by Lœvenbruck (1999) for the tongue movements, in a study of the strategies used by two speakers to achieve contrastive focus in French. Note however that a recent study by Erickson, Iskarous, and Whalen (2005) has shown that hyperarticulation and contrastive focus differ in terms of the relationship between the jaw and the tongue. In a task involving hyperarticulation of vowels in English, the tongue and jaw were lower and positively correlated. On the contrary, in the contrastive focus task, no linear relationship was found between the tongue and the jaw, the tongue moving independently from the jaw. According to this result, hyperarticulation and contrastive focus do not involve the same articulatory reorganization. In a second account of the articulatory correlates of contrastive focus, the speaker would lower the jaw and the tongue dorsum in order to increase the area of the oral passage, and thus, to increase the loudness of the vowel. This model is referred to as the "sonority expansion" model (Beckman et al., 1992). For low vowels, both hypotheses lead to the same predicted articulatory correlates: lowering of the jaw and the tongue, and larger lip area.

THE DEVELOPMENT OF PROSODIC CORRELATES

From a developmental point of view, since the laryngeal and supralaryngeal mechanisms involved in the focused vs. unfocused contrast are mastered at different growth stages (Vihman, 1996), it is possible that children recruit different articulatory strategies compared to adults when signalling contrastive focus. For instance, it is likely that the supralaryngeal articulators are not as finely tuned in young children (in speed or in magnitude of displacement) as they are in adults. Young children would then not be able to exploit the full-scale articulatory dimension, like adults seem to do, as suggested by the hyperarticulation hypothesis discussed above. If this were the case, adult-like articulatory and acoustic correlates of contrastive focus would gradually emerge with age.

The ability to signal contrastive focus using syntax and prosody has been found in children from 3 years old (Hornby & Hass, 1970). However, correlates of prosodic prominence have mainly been studied, in English, for lexical stress. For instance, Connaghan, Moore, Reilly, Almand, and Steeve (2001) report that children of 2 and 3.6 years of age use pitch and intensity values comparable to adults in stressed syllables. Allen and Hawkins (1980) report that the magnitude of the contrast along each of these acoustic dimensions is reduced for 2- to 4-year-old children, compared to adult speakers. (For a review of supporting data, see Kehoe, Stoel-Gammon, & Buder, 1995.) The ability to realize adult-like pitch movements is also observed early in French (Konopczynsky, 1986). In French also, it has been shown that adult-like syllable lengthening is realized by young children (from 2 years of age) on accented vowels (Konopczynsky, 1986).

By contrast, adult-like control of the supraglottal articulators is not achieved until the end of the first decade of life (Green, Moore, & Reilly, 2002; Vihman, 1996). Besides the overall greater within-speaker variability across repetitions revealed by these studies, the articulatory gestures are realized in children with a reduced velocity, even though they do not differ in magnitude from the adults (Smith & Goffman, 1998). Considering the smaller size of the articulators in children, articulatory movements are expected to have smaller amplitudes. As concerns duration, children have been reported to produce longer segments (Kent & Forner, 1980). Very few studies have attempted to find articulatory correlates of linguistic prominence in children, with the exception of

Connaghan et al. (2001), in English, who reported that in the production of trochaic and iambic stressed patterns of [baba], lip distance was not correlated with intensity for the children (from 3.6- to 6.5-year-old), whereas these two parameters were correlated in adults. However, this study was concerned with lexically stressed syllables, and not with focused syllables. Goffman and Malin (1999) studied the kinematic differentiation of articulatory movements across iambic and trochaic stress patterns in 3-year-old English-speaking children. Results showed that children produce adult-like iambs where the first syllable (unstressed) is smaller in amplitude and duration compared to the second syllable (stressed). However, trochees are produced in children with undifferentiated kinematic patterns over both syllables, even though the first one is supposed to be stressed. This pattern contrasts with the adult pattern, for which the first syllable is larger in amplitude and duration compared to the second syllable.

These globally large movements, reduced velocities, and increased durations, for children compared to adults, can be seen as characteristics of slowly and carefully articulated speech. In line with this interpretation, a few studies report an inability in children to reduce vowels in unaccented syllables, therefore leading to a constantly carefully articulated speech style. Allen and Hawkins (1980) studied English-learning children from 1 to 3 years of age and describe the lexically unstressed vowels as more peripheral than those produced by adults. Thus, Allen and Hawkins (1980) propose that learning to put lexical stress for children means learning to reduce unstressed syllables. In this paper, we test the hypothesis that French-speaking children will not differentiate articulatory and acoustic patterns across accented and unaccented syllables as much as adult speakers will do, under contrastive focus compared to the neutral condition. As a result, the articulatory contrast in lip area as well as the acoustic contrast, in the $F1$ vs. $F2$ space, will be reduced for the child. Since we relate the kinematic differentiation between the focus and unfocused conditions to motor control, this study will attempt to test whether supralaryngeal motor control is fully acquired or not by the age of 8.

METHOD

The present study was designed to determine the acoustic and articulatory correlates of contrastive focus in standard metropolitan French, in children and adults. Acoustic correlates include formant values and RMS amplitude. In the articulatory domain, lip area data were obtained.

Speakers and Corpus

Six children (three 4-year-olds and three 8-year-olds) and four adult speakers were audio-visually recorded. All subjects were native speakers of French. The six children were evaluated as normal for language development by a vocabulary test (EVIP-P Body). Furthermore, they did not show any hearing or articulatory disability, as evaluated by a brief conversation with the child. The target word was [baba], produced in two prosodic conditions: in a neutral condition and under contrastive focus. The target word was embedded in two carrier sentences: "J'ai vu Baba qui mange un gâteau" (I saw Baba eating a cookie), in which [baba] is in the neutral condition, and "Non, c'est Baba qui mange un gâteau" (No, it's Baba who is eating a cookie), in which [baba] is focused. These two utterances were part of a story told by the experimenter. In both conditions, the speaker was asked to say what one of the characters of the story had said. In the focus condition, the experimenter asked a question to the speaker, while replacing the target word [baba] by another word. The speaker was asked to correct the wrong utterance by using a syntactic extraction ("No it's … ") and producing the word [baba] with contrastive focus.[1]

Between five and ten repetitions of each sentence were obtained, for each subject. It is reported that deixis, conveyed here by contrastive prosodic focus, is well mastered by preschool children (Hornby & Hass, 1970). In the neutral condition, a high pitch accent (the primary accent) was expected to occur on the second syllable of the target word [baba]. In the contrastive focus condition, a prominence was predicted most likely on the first syllable, but might also occur on the second, or on both syllables of the word [baba], as explained in the previous section. Furthermore, as mentioned previously, it was expected that the second syllable should bear a final lengthening (compared to the initial syllable) in both conditions. Previous studies have shown that when focus falls on an initial syllable, although the post-focal sequence is deaccented, it is not dephrased, i.e., it keeps durational properties (Jun & Fougeron, 2002). The pitch-accented syllable in the neutral condition and the prominent syllable(s) in the focused condition will be simply referred to as "accented" in the following, to remain theory-neutral about their actual prosodic status (pitch accent, insistence accent, focus accent, stress, etc.).

Experimental Procedure

Audio and visual data were recorded using the Lip-track system developed at ICP. The images were recorded via one fixed camera and stored on a betacam-ST tape. The speakers wore glasses with two calibration pellets, and sat on a chair. Their head was maintained by a helmet, fixed to the chair. Their lips were painted in blue. The images were digitized at 50 Hz, which corresponds to the standard sampling rate of PAL video format (one video image consists of two interleaved frames). The acoustic signal was also digitized at a frequency of 22,050 Hz. Using a program designed at ICP (Audouy, 2000), the external and internal lip contours were automatically detected from the video signal, for the total duration of the target word [baba], after using a chroma-key on blue pixels and filtering the data. Lip area is defined as the area (in cm^2) of the surface inside the internal lip contour. The number of pixels inside the internal contour was thus converted into a surface in cm^2 to obtain lip area (S). The zone shaded by diagonal lines in Figure 14.1 represents the lip area parameter on a typical video image. Each image was examined by the experimenter, in order to detect computation errors. For some children, the lip contours were hand-corrected, when part of the blue make-up had inadvertently been removed from the lips.

Perceptual Analysis of Accent Patterns

All target words were transcribed by five trained phoneticians (four graduate students and one professional phonetician). Following previous studies, each listener had to identify the "accent" (or rather prominence) pattern of the [baba] sequence among three patterns: (1) the first syllable is accented; (2) the second syllable is accented; or (3) both syllables are accented. For the current study, only sequences perceived by at least four judges as bearing an accent on the second syllable, in the neutral condition, and those bearing an accent on the first syllable, in the focus condition, were analysed. This last pattern is the most frequently observed for contrastive focus in French, as explained previously. Table 14.1 summarizes the number of sentences produced by each speaker in each condition. It can be seen that the neutral condition is always realized with a final accent. In the focused condition, only three speakers produced some occurrences of the target word with an accent on the second syllable. The percentage of tokens produced with an accent on the first syllable is always higher

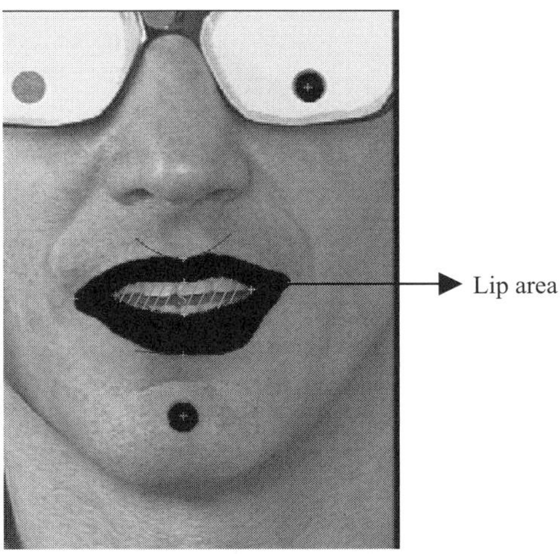

FIGURE 14.1. Example of a video image with the lip area represented by the zone shaded by diagonal lines.

TABLE 14.1. Number of Sentences Produced by Each Speaker, in Each Prosodic Condition (Neutral and Under Contrastive Focus), and for Each Perceived Accent Pattern

	Neutral	Contrastive focus		
	baBA	BAba	baBA	Total
AR, adult	11	6	3	9
CB, adult	17	11		11
PH, adult	12	9		9
LA, adult	12	8		8
JU, 8	5	5		5
LR, 8	9	5		5
SY, 8	6	5	1	6
CA, 4	6	6		6
MA, 4	5	5		5
NE, 4	6	5	1	6

Note. Syllables in capital letters are those perceived prominently by at least four judges among five.

than the reverse pattern (67% for AR and 83% for SY and NE). Thus, the utterances with a rare prominence pattern (baBA) constituted a very small subset, and since no statistical analysis was possible on this subset, they were not included in the analysis. In all cases, syllables perceived as accented (second syllable in neutral condition and first syllable in focus condition) were produced with a $F0$ peak. In the focus condition, the typical deaccented $F0$ pattern on the post-focus sequence was observed. Despite the variation in prominence patterns, all sentences produced in this prosodic condition were perceived as focused by all listeners.

Analysis of Articulatory and Acoustic Data

For each target sequence [baba], the recorded data were analysed as follows. Three synchronous signals were available: the acoustic signal, the evolution of lip area S, and the first derivative of S (referred to as velocity). Figure 14.2 shows labelled articulatory events based on minimal values, maximal values, and zero-crossing values of S and velocity. For the present study, the following parameters were studied based on the various events shown in Figure 14.2:

- The maximal lip area reached for [a] (value of S at the time of $v3$ and $v8$).
- The peak velocity of the opening gesture (values of $v2$ and $v7$).
- The duration of the opening gesture (the duration between $v3$ and $v1$ and $v8$ and $v6$).

In addition, formant frequencies at the time of maximal lip area of the vowel were extracted, using LPC algorithms integrated in the Praat software

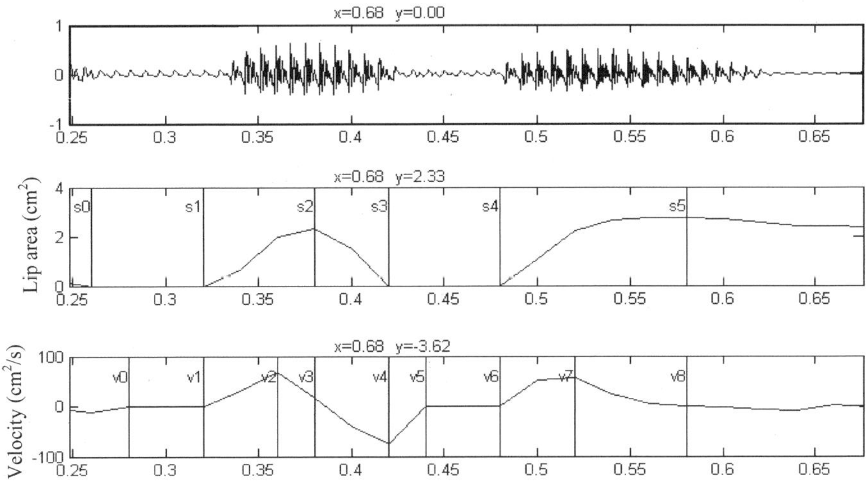

FIGURE 14.2. Labelling points on the [baba] sequence. Upper panel: acoustic signal; middle panel: lip area (*S*) (in cm^2); lower panel: velocity (first derivative of the *S* values). These events correspond to the zero-crossing, minimal and maximal values of the two signals. Note that due to the sampling rate (50 Hz) of the video signal, one sample occurs every 20 ms.

(http://www.fon.hum.uva.nl/praat/). The number of poles varied from 10 to 14. We used a 14-ms Hamming window, with a pre-emphasis factor of 0.98 (pre-emphasis from 50 Hz for a sampling frequency of 22,050 Hz). For all vowels, the results were compared to formant values based on a visual inspection of the spectrogram. In case of important discrepancies between the two methods, parameters for the detection algorithm were readjusted and the analysis was performed again. RMS amplitude was also extracted at the time of maximal lip area.

Statistical Analyses

First, for each articulatory and acoustic parameter, repeated-measures ANOVAs were carried out, with age as the between-subject factor. The prosodic condition (neutral or focus) and the syllable position (first or second syllable) were the within-subject factors. Theoretically, this design requires that each speaker is represented by one cell in each experimental condition. In line with Cho (2005), in this procedure, a factor has a significant effect if all speakers contribute to this effect. It is thus not possible to determine whether a non-significant effect is simply due to between-speaker variability, which is often observed in articulatory prosody. Based on Max and Onghena (1999), we included the different trials in each condition as a within-subject factor. This resulted in three-way repeated-measures ANOVAs, with prosodic condition, syllable position, and trial as the within-subject factors. Age group (adult, 8-year-old, 4-year-old) was the between-subject factor. It is to be noted that in order to make this analysis possible, a balanced model, in which each speaker contributes an equal number of repetitions, is necessary. Thus, five repetitions were randomly selected among the set of tokens, in each prosodic condition, and for each speaker.

Moreover, because of the important between-speaker variability often reported in previous studies (Erickson, 1998; Tabain, 2003), individual subjects' behaviour is described. Finally, linear regression analyses were carried out on articulatory (as the independent variable) and acoustic values (as the dependent variable).

RESULTS

Articulatory Data

The following section groups the values of the maximal lip area, peak velocity of the opening gesture, and duration of the opening gesture, in both syllable position (1st or 2nd syllable in words) and prosodic condition (neutral or focus).

Maximal Lip Area. Mean values and standard deviations of the maximal lip area reached during the production of [a] are plotted in Figure 14.3, for each speaker. Detailed statistical results are provided in Table 14.2 (repeated-measures ANOVAs). It is striking to observe that the global values of maximal lip area do not show a tendency to decrease with speaker age. If one considers the size of the articulators for children relative to adults, one could expect that the maximal lip area should be reduced for children. However, according to the results of repeated-measures ANOVAs, the differences related to age as a main effect do not reach significance $F(2, 7) = 0.15$; $p > .05$. This result might be considered as an evidence that children hyperarticulated the target syllables more than adults. Concerning the main effect of position, the lip area is significantly larger in the second position than in the first position, $F(1, 7) = 21.19$; $p < .05$. This is consistent with the final lengthening effect observed in French speakers. If the second syllable is longer, more time is available for the lips to reach their open configuration. The interaction of position and condition is significant, $F(1, 7)=18.15$; $p < .05$, and planned comparisons reveal that in the first position, lip area is larger for [a] when articulated under contrastive focus, compared to the neutral condition, which is consistent with the perceptual analysis reported previously. No significant difference is observed for the second position. However, as suggested by the significant effect of the interaction of position, condition, and age, $F(2, 7)=4.68$; $p < .05$, a developmental trend is observed. According to the results of planned comparisons, the increased value of lip area in contrastive focus, compared to the neutral condition, in the first syllable position, is significant only for the adult group. Thus, the pattern of variation in lip area shows that all speakers produce larger lip areas in the second position, compared to the first position, and that in the first position, only adult speakers increase the lip area values under contrastive focus, compared to the neutral condition.

Figure 14.3 also reveals important between-speaker variations. Three adult speakers (CB, PH, and LA) produce [a] with a smaller lip area under focus, compared to the neutral condition, in the second position. Even though this did not reach significance for the adult group, it can be seen as a strategy exploited to enhance the prominence of the first syllable, similarly to the post-focal deaccenting observed in the acoustic domain (as explained previously). Recall that the chosen focus sequences are all perceived as bearing acoustic prominence on the initial syllable. No such pattern is observed for children. One 4-year-old speaker (MA) produces very broad lip areas in the second position, although the standard deviation values are rather large. Concerning the effects of condition, one child out of six (CA, 4) produces much larger values of lip area for both syllables, under contrastive focus, compared to the neutral condition. In other words, this speaker produces decreased values of lip area in the neutral condition compared to the focused condition. The maximum magnitude of lip area for this child is comparable to the mean maximum achieved

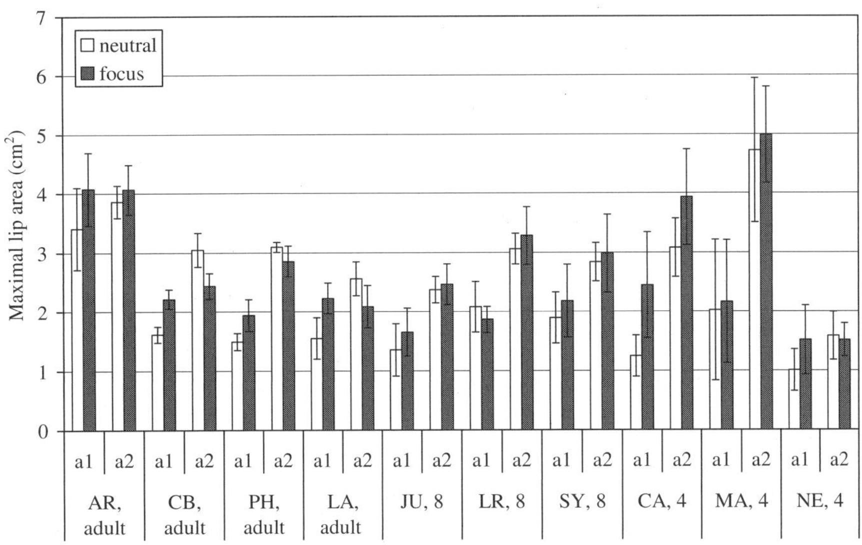

FIGURE 14.3. Mean values and standard deviations of the maximal lip area for the 10 speakers, in neutral condition (light bar) and under contrastive focus (shadow bar), for the first vowel (labelled "a1") and the second vowel (labelled "a2") in [baba].

for the other children, but the minimum (reached in the neutral condition) is lower than the mean for the other children (especially a1 in neutral condition). Therefore, this speaker seems to better exploit the lower range of possible mouth opening for the /a/ vowel.

Peak Velocity of the Opening Gesture. Larger lip area may not always characterize focused syllables. When speaking rate increases, independent of the degree of focus, the amount of time devoted to opening the lips decreases, and the movement may be reduced. Peak velocity can be a better correlate of focus (De Jong, 1995; Kelso, Vatikiotis-Bateson, Saltzman, & Kay, 1985; Lœvenbruck, 1996). Our prediction was that higher peak velocities should mark focused syllables. The mean values of the peak velocity of the opening gesture from [b] to [a] are plotted in Figure 14.4. According to this figure, the peak velocities show a tendency to decrease with decreasing age, except for the 4-year-old speaker CA. However, this global tendency is not significant, based on the results of the repeated-measures ANOVA, reported in Table 14.2. By contrast, the condition factor has a significant effect on peak velocity ($F(1, 7)=9.36$; $p < .05$), opening movements being faster under contrastive focus than in neutral condition. The interaction between position and condition is also significant ($F(1, 7)=25.96$; $p < .05$), and planned comparisons

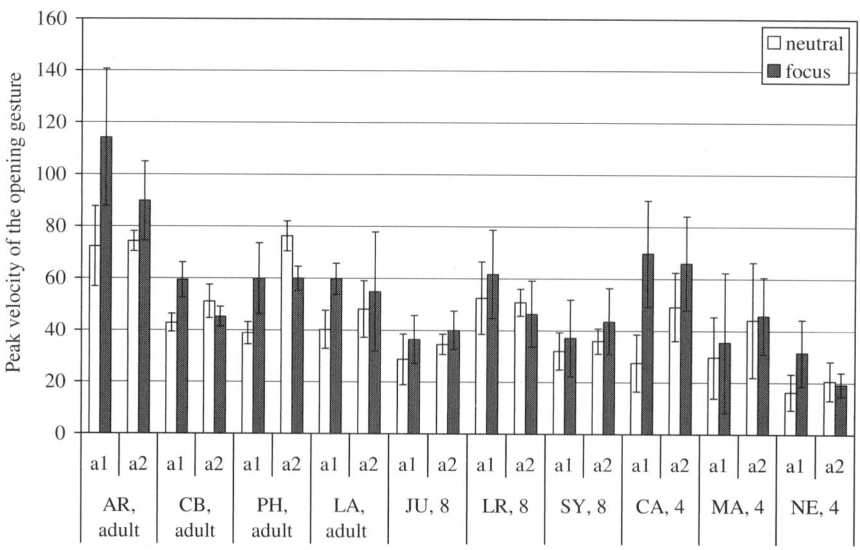

FIGURE 14.4. Mean values and standard deviations of the peak velocity of the opening gesture (first derivative of the lip area) for the 10 speakers, in neutral condition (light bar) and under contrastive focus (shadow bar), for the first vowel (labelled "a1") and the second vowel (labelled "a2") in [baba].

reveal that peak velocity is increased in focus compared to neutral condition for the first position only. No effect of interaction with age is found, suggesting that all speakers produce the same pattern.

However, within-speaker variability is observed in Figure 14.4. Two adult speakers (CB and PH), decrease the values of peak velocity under focus, for the second syllable only. These adults produce a velocity profile in line with the strategy observed previously for lip area: Under contrastive focus, the velocity of the opening gesture is increased for the first syllable, whereas the values of the peak velocity for the second position decrease or do not differ according to the prosodic condition. As regards the young speakers, the 4-year-old CA produces much faster opening gestures under contrastive focus than in neutral condition. The very large difference between focus and neutral for this child may be responsible for the lack of significant effect of the Age factor, in the repeated-measures ANOVAs reported in Table 14.2. This difference is indeed comparable to the difference in velocity produced by the adult speaker AR. Furthermore, unlike what was observed on lip area values, the peak velocities for CA are not just lower for unfocused syllables. For focused syllables they are much higher than they are in the other children. As mentioned above, peak velocity is considered as a good correlate of focus and has been related to articulatory effort or precision. The fact that this speaker is able to increase the

TABLE 14.2. *F* values of Repeated-Measures ANOVAs, with Condition (Neutral or Focus), Position (First or Second Syllable), and Trial (One of Five Trials) as the Within-Subject Factors

Factor	Maximal lip area	Peak velocity open. gesture	Duration of the open. gesture	*F*1 (Hz)	*F*2 (Hz)	RMS amplitude
Age						
$F(2, 7)$	0.15	2.93	**25.60***	**10.91***	**6.75***	1.38
Pos						
$F(1, 7)$	**21.19***	0.58	**154.40***	1.71	2.84	**15.87***
Cond						
$F(1, 7)$	3.95	**9.36***	5.60	**6.19***	0.67	**6.16***
Pos*Cond						
$F(1, 7)$	**18.15***	**25.96***	1.00	**6.79***	3.57	2.94
Pos*Age						
$F(2, 7)$	0.93	0.23	3.10	0.31	5.25	**6.45***
Cond*Age						
$F(2, 7)$	0.87	0.51	1.30	0.46	0.02	0.62
Pos*Cond*Age						
F(2, 7)	4.68*	4.05	1.30	0.23	0.11	1.37

Note. The between-subject variable was age. For all speakers, five tokens were randomly selected in each prosodic condition, in order to obtain a balanced model and to make the analysis possible. Values in bold characters and followed by * are those for which $p < .05$.

velocity of the opening gesture to a degree comparable to the adults' is another argument for concluding that this child is articulatorily more mature.

Duration of the Opening Gesture. Mean duration values (in ms) of the opening gesture are plotted in Figure 14.5. The global tendency of increasing mean values of duration with decreasing age is significant, based on the results of repeated-measures ANOVA (Table 14.2), $F(2, 7)=25.60$; $p<.05$. The significant effect of the position factor, without interaction with age, $F(1, 7)=154.40$; $p<.05$ reveals that all speakers significantly increase the duration of this gesture for the second [a], compared to the first [a]. This pattern is presumably due to final lengthening of accentual phrase in both conditions, as explained above. No significant effect of condition is observed. Thus, unlike the pattern revealed by the maximal lip area, duration is not always increased for [a] in the first syllable, under contrastive focus, compared to the neutral condition. Interestingly, this pattern contrasts with English, for which it has been shown that under contrastive focus, the opening gesture is longer, faster, and larger (Cho, 2005). This result may be an artefact of the relatively low sampling rate (one sample every 20 ms). Another possible interpretation is that increasing the duration of the opening gesture is not necessary to signal prosodic prominence coming from contrastive focus in French. Increasing articulatory magnitude and movement

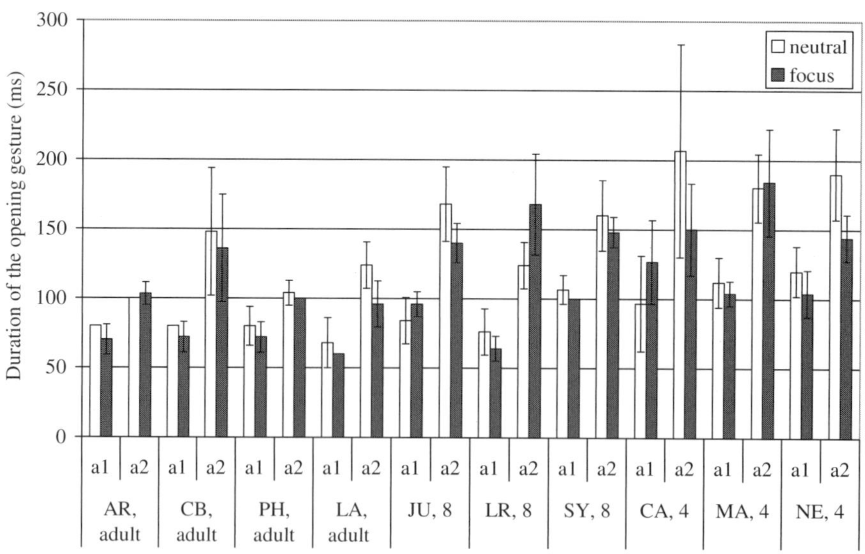

FIGURE 14.5. Mean duration values and standard deviation for the opening gesture for the 10 speakers, in neutral condition (light bar) and under contrastive focus (shadow bar), for the first vowel (labelled "a1") and the second vowel (labelled "a2") in [baba].

velocity could be the strategy used to reach the more articulated lip configuration, rather than increasing movement duration.

Figure 14.5 shows that different durational patterns are produced by speakers. Indeed, some speakers reduce the duration of the opening gesture under focus, in the second position (the adult LA and the children JU, CA, and NE). The difference in duration between the focus and neutral conditions for CA and NE, in the second position, is even larger than the difference found for adults. Note however the large token-to-token variability associated with these values for CA and NE, as revealed by the standard deviations. By contrast, the 8-year-old child LR increases the duration of this movement under focus, in the second position.

Acoustic Results

These reinforced articulatory gestures, observed for adults, and sometimes for children, have acoustic consequences in the speech signal. It was predicted that a hyperarticulated [a] (increased lip area, increased tongue lowering and backing) should result in a more peripheral (lower and more back) position of this vowel in the acoustic $F1/F2$ space, i.e., in a higher $F1$ and a lower $F2$. This section investigates the effects of position and prosodic condition on the formant patterns and RMS amplitude values of the vowels in [baba].

Formant Values. Dispersion ellipses of the formant values (in Hertz), in the $F1$ vs. $F2$ space, are plotted in Figure 14.6, for both conditions and positions. As reported in other studies (Sharkey & Folkins, 1985; Smith & Gartenberg, 1984),) children show a larger token-to-token variability than adults, as depicted by the size of the dispersion ellipses. As can be seen from Table 14.2, age has a significant effect on $F1$ values, adult speakers producing lower values than 4- and 8-year-old speakers $F(2, 7) = 10.91; p < .05$. This pattern is a consequence of the shorter cavities in the child's vocal tract, compared to the adult's vocal tract. Prosodic condition has a significant effect on $F1$, the low vowel having higher $F1$ values under contrastive focus than in neutral condition $F(1, 7) = 6.19;$ $p < .05$. This contrast is however not significant in the second position, as revealed by planned comparisons of the interaction of position and condition $F(1, 7) = 6.79; p < .05$. This is in line with the perceived initial prominence in the focus condition. The effect of age, in interaction with position or condition, is not significant, suggesting that all speakers increase the value of $F1$ for [a], in the first position. This result is particularly interesting since it does not exactly reflect the articulatory effects of prosodic condition. Indeed, it has been shown, in a previous section, that lip area was not increased in focus, compared to the neutral condition, for the 8- and 4-year-old groups. An inspection of Figure 14.6 however shows between-speaker variability in the acoustic space, suggesting that some children do not contrast prosodic conditions along the $F1$ dimension as

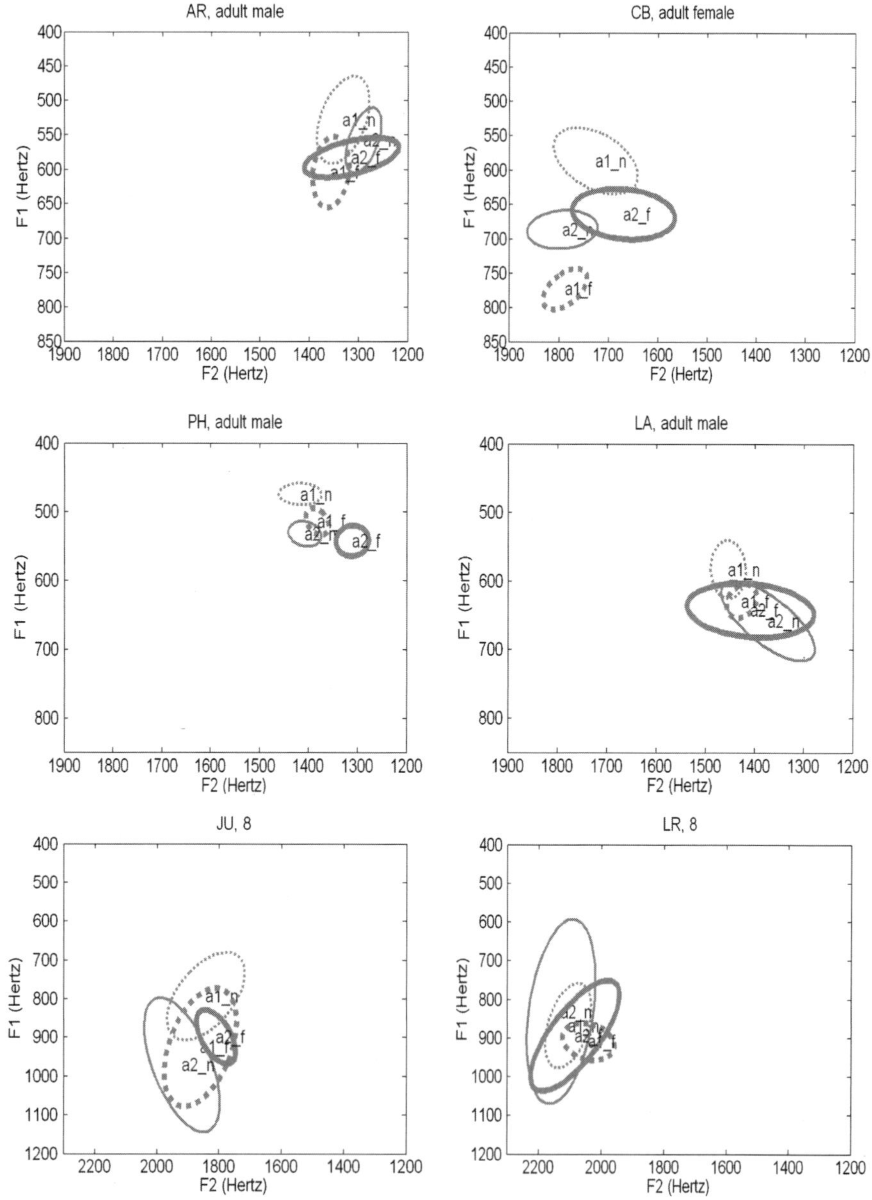

FIGURE 14.6. Dispersion ellipses, in the $F1$ vs. $F2$ space, enclosing ±1.5 standard deviations from the mean, for the 10 speakers [thin dotted line: first vowel in neutral condition (a1_n); thin solid line: second vowel in neutral condition (a2_n); thick dotted line: first vowel in contrastive focus (a1_f); thick solid line: second vowel in contrastive focus (a2_f)].

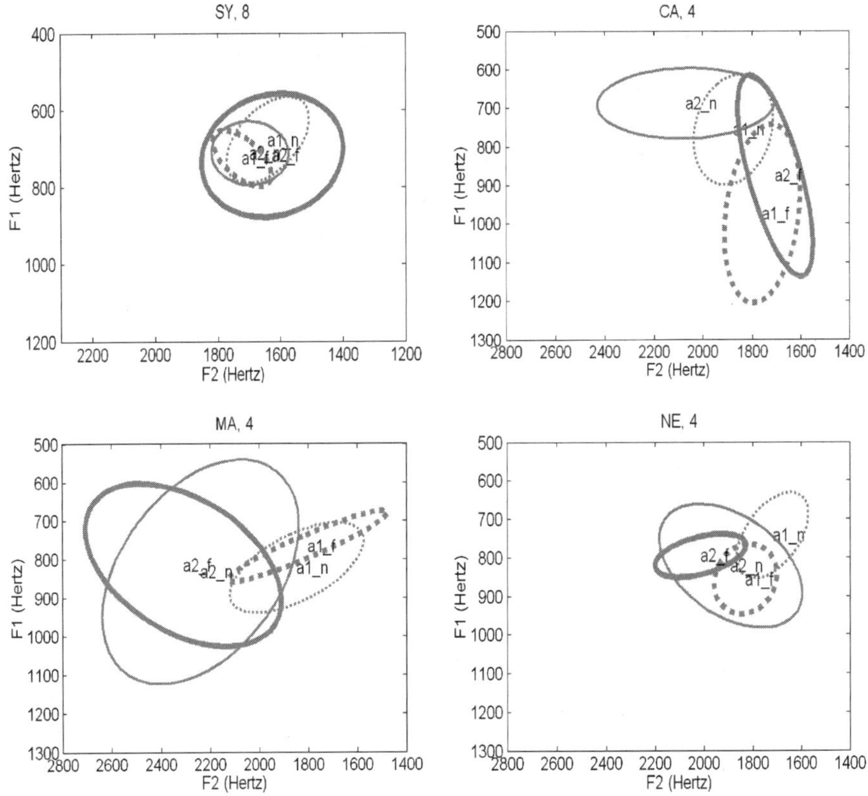

FIGURE 14.6. (Continued)

much as adults do. Indeed, the dispersion ellipses for the first position are much more peripheral under focus (labelled "a1_f") than in neutral condition (labelled "a1_n") for three adults out of four (CB, PH, and LA) and one child out of six (the 4-year-old CA). In line with what has been observed in the articulatory domain, speaker CA seems to better exploit the *F*1 dimension compared to the other children. Child CA uses a wider range of *F*1 values than any other child and has an adult-like use of *F*1 differences to convey differences in focus. Among the five remaining children, speaker NE (4-year-old) produces a pattern similar to CA (and to the adult AR), but to a lesser extent. This child was not characterized by increased lip area on the first [a] under focus. Thus, strategies other than increasing lip area are likely exploited to increase *F*1. The four remaining children produce ellipses associated with "a1_n" and "a1_f" that greatly overlap. The relationships between articulatory and acoustic parameters will be discussed in a further section.

As concerns the variation of $F2$, Table 14.2 shows that this formant is significantly higher with increasing age, $F(2, 7) = 6.75$; $p < .05$. This effect can be ascribed to the shorter cavities of the children, compared to the adults. No significant effects of position and condition are found. Figure 14.6 shows that, among the adult speakers, CB and PH produce lower values of $F2$ for [a] in the second position (ellipses labelled "a2_f" and "a2_n") under focus than in neutral condition, resulting in a further back position in the vowel spaces. This pattern is also found for English by Cho (2005) who reports that under accent, $F2$ is lower for [a], i.e., further back in the vowel space. Note that $F2$ values for [a], produced by the 4-year-old MA, are higher in the second position than in the first position.

RMS Amplitude. It has been noted that intensity can sometimes be used to signal contrastive focus. In order to compare this acoustic parameter across syllable positions and prosodic conditions, we calculated the RMS amplitude produced for [a] by each speaker. Data are presented in Figure 14.7, and p values associated with ANOVAs are grouped in Table 14.2. Based on the results of Table 14.2, position has a significant effect on RMS values $F(1, 7) = 15.87$; $p < .05$. The interaction of position and age is also significant $F(2, 7) = 6.45$; $p < .05$. Planned comparisons aimed at further exploring this interaction effect revealed that smaller RMS values for the second position, compared to the first

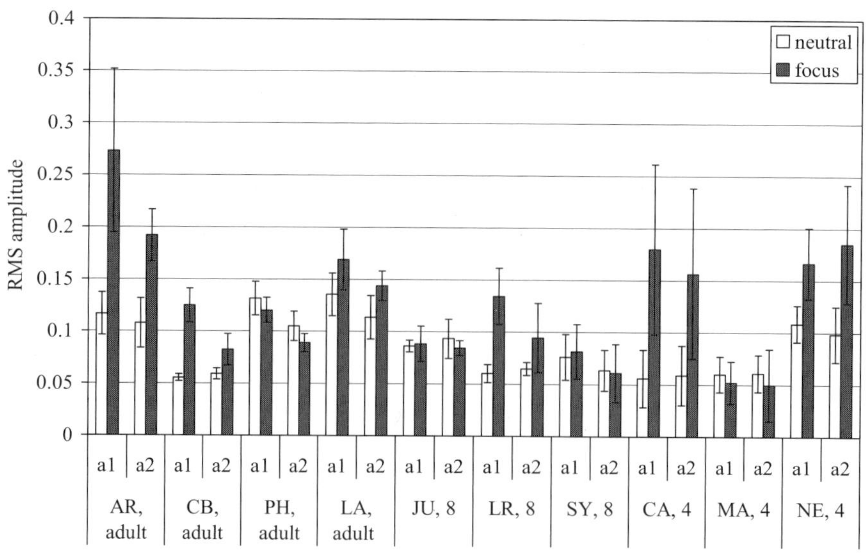

FIGURE 14.7. Mean values and standard deviations of the RMS amplitude, for the 10 speakers, in neutral condition (light bar) and under contrastive focus (shadow bar), for the first vowel (labelled "a1") and the second vowel (labelled "a2") in [baba].

position, are found for the adult group only. Concerning prosodic condition, for both syllable positions, Table 14.2 suggests that [a] is produced with larger RMS values under focus than in neutral condition, $F(1, 7) = 6.16$; $p < .05$.

However, individual speakers' data, depicted in Figure 14.6, suggest that increasing RMS values is an optional strategy to signal contrastive focus, in all age groups. As noted for articulatory measurements, child CA produces maximal RMS values, which are higher than any other child, and minimal values (in the neutral condition) comparable to those of adults.

Relationships between Articulatory and Acoustic Parameters. According to the predictions stated above, increased articulatory movements should be related to increased $F1$ values and decreased $F2$ values for /a/, resulting in a more peripheral position in the acoustic space. A significant increase in lip area for the first syllable was found for the adult group, only under focus compared to the neutral condition. By contrast, in the acoustic domain, increased $F1$ values are found for all age groups, without any significant interaction of age. It is likely that other articulatory strategies, such as tongue movements, allowed some speakers to produce a more peripheral [a], in the acoustic space. Furthermore, under the effect of position, speakers produce broader lip areas without any effect in the $F1$ or $F2$ dimension (see the F-values grouped in Table 14.2). In order to explore the relationship between lip area and acoustic parameters, results of linear regression analyses for each speaker are grouped in Table 14.3. The correlation coefficients r and the slope are presented only for significant correlations. Lip area values have been regressed against $F1$, $F2$, and RMS. It can be seen that significant correlations between maximal lip area and

TABLE 14.3. Correlation Coefficient (r) and Slopes Obtained from Linear Regression Analyses between Maximal Lip Area and $F1$, Maximal Lip Area and $F2$, and Maximal Lip Area and RMS Values

	Maximal lip area vs. $F1$		Maximal lip area vs. $F2$		Maximal lip area vs. RMS	
Speaker	r	Slope	r	Slope	r	Slope
AR, ad.	.84	71.28	-	-	.60	0.09
CB, ad.	.48	52.99	.30	40.53	-	-
PH, ad.	.83	40.93	-	-	.67	-0.02
LA, ad.	.62	55.82	-	-	-	-
JU, 8	.60	103.91	-	-	-	-
LR, 8	-	-	-	-	-	-
SY, 8	.62	66.10	-	-	-	-
CA, 4	.46	61.93	-	-	.58	0.04
MA, 4	-	-	.69	75.88	-	-
NE, 4	.60	106.17	-	-	-	-

Note. Analyses were performed for each speaker, across position and condition. Only significant correlations are shown.

$F1$ are obtained for all speakers but two (the 8-year-old LR and the 4-year-old MA). Even though no developmental pattern can be found in the values of the slope, it is noteworthy that the three adult speakers CB, PH, and LA are associated with the shallower slopes, suggesting that an increase in lip area is related to a smaller increase in $F1$ for these speakers, compared to the other speakers. Lip area and $F2$ are significantly correlated for the 4-year-old speaker MA and the adult CB, in line with Cho (2005). Note that RMS is correlated with lip area for two adults (AR and PH) and one 4-year-old child (CA). The slope values for these correlations are however very small. No developmental pattern emerges. Overall, $F1$ seems to be correlated with lip area in adults and children, even though the strength of the correlation varies across speakers.

DISCUSSION

The results presented so far have shown that the articulatory effects of contrastive focus for /a/ are smaller for 4- and 8-year-old children compared to adults. Indeed, repeated-measures ANOVAs reveal that in the first syllable position, maximal lip area values are larger under contrastive focus than that in neutral condition for the adult group only. This result is in line with previous studies showing that children by 4 years of age have not yet mastered the full scale of articulatory contrast related to prosodic prominence. A possible explanation could be that children did not understand the task or signalled contrastive focus using only syntactic extraction. However, as described in the Method section, prosodic focus was very well signalled by an $F0$ rise on the first syllable, followed by a typical deaccented post-focus sequence. Thus, children as well as adults used prosody to convey focus and the observed differences cannot be ascribed to attention or to linguistic abilities. As far as peak velocity is concerned, opening movements from /b/ to /a/ are faster in focus than in neutral condition, for the first syllable. Opening movements are globally longer for children than for adults, and their duration is not significantly related to condition. For all age groups, $F1$ is higher in the first position under focus than in neutral condition. In order to better describe each speaker's behaviour, individuals' data were presented and discussed. First, it was found that for three adult speakers, lip area is wider on the first syllable, as predicted, but lip area decreases in the second syllable, under contrastive focus. This pattern has been interpreted as a strategy used by the adult speakers to enhance the prominence of the first syllable, by hypoarticulating the second syllable, similarly to the post-focal $F0$ reduction observed in the acoustic domain. This lip area pattern is accompanied by an increased velocity of the opening gesture, and by a reduced duration of the opening gesture (for two adults). The latter result contrasts with English for which it was observed (Cho, 2005) that contrastive focus is related to longer opening gestures. Nonetheless, considering lip area and velocity values, these results suggest that adult speakers of French contrast focused and unfocused syllables along the articulatory dimension of lip area [see Lœvenbruck (1999) for similar findings with tongue gestures and Dohen et al. (2004a, 2004b) for further results on lip area and jaw opening]. Such a pattern was not observed in children, suggesting that they do not exploit the lower range of articulatory contrasts.

The case of the 4-year-old speaker CA is particularly interesting. Unlike other children, this speaker shows focus-induced variations in lip area and opening peak velocity (c.f. Figures 14.3 and 14.4). As mentioned earlier, CA even seems to better exploit the full scale of articulatory contrasts along the lip area dimension. Indeed, the maximum magnitude of lip area for this child is comparable to the mean maximum achieved for the other children, but the minimum (reached in the neutral condition) is much lower than the mean for the other children (especially a1 in neutral condition). Note that the mean values of opening peak velocity are even higher for this child compared to adults, and could be responsible for the lack of significant results as concerns the effect of age in interaction with condition. The fact that this speaker is able to increase the velocity of the opening gesture to a degree comparable to the adults' is another argument for concluding that this child is articulatorily more mature.

In the formant domain, besides a significant effect of age on $F1$ and $F2$, no significant developmental trends were found. For all speakers, $F1$ is significantly higher under focus than in neutral condition, in the first position. These effects are in line with previous works carried out on articulatory and acoustic effects of focus in English (Cho, 2005; Erickson, 1998) An inspection of individual strategies however suggested that the acoustic effects of contrastive focus are less consistent in children compared to adults. Indeed, four children produced overlapping dispersion ellipses, in the $F1$ vs. $F2$ space, while two 4-year-olds produced a pattern in line with the one produced by the adult speakers. Further experiments are currently in progress to support this finding, since the small number of repetitions (five) and the large variability could have affected the results.

It was also found that for some children, maximal lip area could be increased while $F1$ was not significantly affected. This dissociation between articulatory and acoustic correlates is not reflected by smaller correlation coefficients between lip area and $F1$. The correlation coefficients in fact suggest that $F1$ is as much related to lip area for children as it is for adult speakers. Some children do not show any significant correlation between lip area and $F1$, whereas some others are characterized by high correlation coefficients and slopes. It is likely that other articulatory strategies than lip area, such as tongue movements, allow the production of a more peripheral /a/, in the acoustic space. Previous work has shown that adult-like control is acquired earlier for the jaw than for the lips (Green et al., 2002), mature control of the tongue being reached even later (Nittrouer, 1993). Thus, whereas adults can generate differentiated jaw, lip, and tongue movements to produce a more peripheral [a], children would not differentiate jaw, lip, and tongue movements to the same extent. According to Erickson et al. (2005), contrastive focus is characterized by independent movements of the tongue and the jaw. Some of the young speakers could not have differentiated jaw, lip, and tongue movements, resulting in an overall reduced effect of prosodic prominence on articulatory and acoustic parameters. This highly complex differentiation phase would be an important step in motor control development (Green et al., 2000). By contrast, some children could be in the process of differentiating jaw, lip, and tongue movements, resulting in a more important effect of prosody on one articulator (the tongue, for instance), compared to the others (the jaw and the lips). The necessity of increasing contrasts between prosodic conditions could thus be seen as a factor leading to fine-tuning of different articulatory movements.

On the basis of the global patterns reported here, a hasty conclusion could be that the smaller effects of focus for children are related to the inability of the children to hyperarticulate in this condition. However, the greater values of lip area depicted in Figure 14.3 suggest that, in line with Smith and Goffman's (1998) observations , children produce relatively large articulatory movements considering the size of their oral structures, compared to adults. Thus, the observed undifferentiated kinematic patterns according to condition could rather be due to the inability to reduce unfocused syllables (Allen & Hawkins, 1980). Children have generally learned to exploit the higher range of the hyper-hypoarticulation scale, but the ability to reduce the magnitude of articulatory movements (i.e., exploiting the lower range of the scale) comes later in the acquisition of motor control, presumably because it may require fine-tuning of articulation. The differences between children and adults may be even more obvious in more complex sequences. Indeed, according to Smith and Goffman (1998), it might be hypothesized that certain phonetic goals (rather than specific articulator controls) may mature earlier than others (/b/ mastered earlier than /v/). The /baba/ sequence involves the combined action of the lips and jaw and it may be that this sequence is acquired earlier, relative to sequences involving tongue movements (such as /tata/) or tight controlled lip movements (such as /vava/). Further articulatory and acoustic analyses are currently in progress in order to further investigate this hypothesis.

CONCLUSIONS

This paper dealt with the articulatory and acoustic correlates of contrastive focus in three 4-year-old and three 8-year-old children, and four adult French speakers. Using video recordings, lip area and its first derivative were studied during the production of the [baba] sequence in neutral condition and under contrastive focus. Results show that the effects of contrastive focus on lip area are less important for children compared to adults. These results suggest that children at age 8 do not contrast the vowels along the hypo-hyperarticulation dimension according to the prosodic condition, as adults do. Learning the articulatory correlates of prosodic contrasts could involve the integration of multiple articulatory movements in order to better exploit the acoustic space.

ACKNOWLEDGMENTS

This work was supported by a grant from the Social Sciences and Humanities Research Council of Canada and a grant from the Fonds Québécois de Recherche sur la Société et la Culture. We thank the reviewers for constructive comments on an earlier version of this paper. This work benefited from fruitful discussions with Christian Abry and Pascal Perrier.

NOTES

1. Due to the design of the corpus (which was highly constrained by the fact that we were recording young speakers), contextual effects can be noted. In a pilot study, we had tried to use a similar context for the two conditions, with the sentence "c'est Baba qui mange" in the neutral condition. But this construction generally leads to an unwanted focused intonation on /baba/. We, therefore, chose to use two different carrier sentences for the two prosodic conditions. As a consequence, the first /a/ in the neutral condition was preceded by a /y/, whereas the first /a/ in the focused condition was preceded by a /e/, or /ɛ/. /y/ and /e, ɛ / differ in the amount of lip protrusion, /y/ being more protruded and thus having a lesser lip area than /e, ɛ/. If there were no inserted consonant between /y/ and the following /a/, persevatory co-articulation effects could certainly influence the amount of protrusion in the /a/, and thus probably decrease lip area for /a/. However, /y/ is followed by a closed consonant /b/, which tends to reset the amount of lip protrusion. Although we cannot certify that /y/ has absolutely no influence on the following /a/, with the inserted /b/, we believe that this influence is much reduced compared to the possible influence of prosodic condition.

REFERENCES

Allen, G. D., & Hawkins, S. (1980). Phonological rhythm: Definition and development. In G. Yeni-Komshian, J. F. Kavanagh, & C. A. Ferguson (Eds.), *Child phonology, vol. 1: Production* (pp. 227–256). New York: Academic Press.

Audouy, M. (2000). Traitement d'images video pour la capture des mouvements labiaux, Final engineering report, Institut National Polytechnique de Grenoble.

Bartels, C., & Kingston, J. (1994). Salient pitch cues in the perception of contrastive focus. In P. Boach, & R. Van der Sandt (Eds.), *Focus & natural language processing* (pp. 94–106). *Proceedings of* Journal of Semantics *conference on focus*, IBM Working Papers, TR-80.

Beckman, M. E., Edwards, J., & Fletcher, J. (1992). Prosodic structure and tempo in a sonority model of articulatory dynamics. In G. J. Docherty & D. R. Ladd (Eds.), *Papers*

in laboratory phonology II: Segment, gesture, prosody (pp. 968–986). Cambridge: Cambridge University Press.
Cho, T. (2002): *The effects of prosody on articulation in English*. New York: Routledge.
Cho, T. (2005). Prosodic strengthening and featural enhancement: Evidence from acoustic and articulatory realizations of /ɑ, i/ in English. *Journal of the Acoustical Society of America, 117, 3867–3878.*
Clech-Darbon, A., Rebuschi, G., & Rialland, A. (1999). Are there cleft sentences in French? In L. Tuller & D. Rebuschi (Eds.), *The grammar of focus* (pp. 83–118). Amsterdam: Benjamins.
Connaghan, K. P., Moore, C. A., Reilly, K. J., Almand, K. B., & Steeve, R. W. (2001). *Acoustic and physiologic correlates of stress production across systems*. Poster presented at the American Speech-Language-Hearing Association, New Orleans, LA.
Dahan, D., & Bernard, J.-M. (1996). Interspeaker variability in emphatic accent production in French. *Language and Speech*, *39*, 341–374.
De Jong, K. (1995). The supraglottal articulation of prominence in English: Linguistic stress as localized hyperarticulation. *Journal of the Acoustical Society of America*, *97*, 491–504.
Delais-Roussarie, E., Rialland, A., Doetjes, J., & Marandin, J. M. (2002). The prosody of post focus sequences in French. *Proceedings of Speech Prosody 2002*, Aix-en-Provence.
Di Cristo, A. (1998). Intonation in French. In D. Hirst & A. Di Cristo (Eds.), *Intonation systems: A survey of twenty languages* (pp. 195–218). Cambridge: Cambridge University Press.
Di Cristo, A. (2000). Vers une modélisation de l'accentuation du français (deuxième partie). *Journal of French Language Studies*, *10*, 27–44.
Dohen, M., & Lœvenbruck, H. (2004). Pre-focal rephrasing, focal enhancement and post-focal deaccentuation in French. *Proceedings of international conference on spoken language processing (ICSLP)* (Vol. 1, pp. 785–788) Jeju Island, Korea, 4–8 October.
Dohen, M., Lœvenbruck, H., Cathiard, M.-A., & Schwartz, J.-L. (2004a). Visual perception of contrastive focus in reiterant French speech. *Speech Communication*, *44*, 155–172.
Dohen, M., Lœvenbruck, H., Cathiard, M.-A., & Schwartz, J.-L. (2004b). Identification of the possible visible correlates of contrastive focus in French. *Proceedings of speech prosody 2004* (pp. 73–76), Nara, Japan, 23–26 March.
Erickson, D. (1998). Effects of contrastive emphasis on jaw opening. *Phonetica*, *55*, 147–169.
Erickson, D. (2002). Articulation of extreme formant patterns for emphasized vowels. *Phonetica*, *59*, 134–149.
Erickson, D., Iskarous, K., & Whalen, D. (2005). Production of hyperarticulated vs. contrastively accented vowels. *A century of experimental phonetics: Its history and development*, Grenoble: Institut de la Communication Parlée.
Goffman, L., & Malin, C. (1999). Metrical effects on speech movements in children and adults. *Journal of Speech, Language, and Hearing Research*, *42*(4), 1003–1015.
Green, J. R., Moore, C. A., Higashikawa, M., & Steeve, R. W. (2000). The physiologic development of speech motor control: Lip and jaw coordination. *Journal of Speech, Language and Hearing Research*, *43*, 239–255.
Green, J. R., Moore, C. A., & Reilly, K. J. (2002). The sequential development of lip and jaw control for speech. *Journal of Speech, Language, and Hearing Research*, *45*, 66–79.
Hornby, P. A., & Hass, W. A. (1970). Use of contrastive stress by preschool children. *Journal of Speech and Hearing Research*, *13*, 395–399.
Jun, S.-A., & Fougeron, C. (2000). A phonological model of French intonation. In A. Botinis (Ed.), *Intonation: Analysis, modelling and technology* (pp. 209–242). Dordrecht: KAP.
Jun, S.-A., & Fougeron, C. (2002). Realizations of accentual phrase in French intonation. *Probus*, *14*, 147–172.
Kehoe, M., Stoel-Gammon, C., & Buder, E. H. (1995). Acoustic correlates of stress in young children's speech. *Journal of Speech, Language, and Hearing Research*, *38*, 338–350.

Kelso, J. A. S, Vatikiotis-Bateson, E., Saltzman, E. L., & Kay, B. (1985). A qualitative dynamic analysis of reiterant speech production: Phase portraits, kinematics, and dynamic modeling. *Journal of the Acoustical Society of America*, *77* (1), 266–280.

Kent, R. D., & Forner, L. L. (1980). Speech segment durations in sentence recitations by children and adults. *Journal of Phonetics*, *8*, 157–168.

Konopczynsky, G. (1986). *Du prélangage au langage: Acquisition de la structuration prosodique*. Thesis, University of Strasbourg.

Lacheret-Dujour, A., & Beaugendre, F. (1999). *La prosodie du français*. Paris: CNRS Langage.

Ladd, D. R. (1996). *Intonational phonology*. Cambridge: Cambridge University Press.

Lœvenbruck, H. (1996). *Pistes pour le contrôle d'un robot parlant capable de réduction vocalique*. Ph.D. dissertation, INPG, Grenoble, France.

Lœvenbruck, H. (1999). An investigation of articulatory correlates of the accentual phrase in French. *International Congress of Phonetic Sciences*, San Francisco (Vol.1, pp. 667–670).

Max, L., & Onghena, P. (1999). Some issues in the statistical analysis of completely randomized and repeated measures designs for speech, language, and hearing research. *Journal of Speech, Language, and Hearing Research*, *42*, 261–270.

Nittrouer, S. (1993). The emergence of mature gestural patterns is not uniform: Evidence from an acoustic study. *Journal of Speech and Hearing Research*, *36*, 959–972.

Pasdeloup, V. (1990), *Un modèle de règles rythmiques appliqué à la synthèse de la parole*. Ph.D. thesis, Aix-en-Provence.

Pierrehumbert, J., & Hirshberg, J. (1990). The meaning of intonational contours in discourse. In P. Cohen, J. Morgan, & M. Pollack (Eds.), *Intentions in communication*. Cambridge: MIT Press.

Rossi, M. (1999). *L'intonation, le système du français: description et modélisation*. Paris: Ophrys.

Selkirk, E. O. (1984). The grammar of intonation. In E. O. Selkirk (Ed.), *Phonology and syntax: The relation between sound and structure* (pp. 197–296). Cambridge: MIT Press.

Sharkey, J., & Folkins, J. W. (1985). Variability of lip and jaw movements in children and adults: Implications for the development of speech motor control. *Journal of Speech and Hearing Research*, *28*, 8–15.

Smith, A., & Goffman, L. (1998). Stability and patterning of speech movement sequences in children and adults. *Journal of Speech, Language, and Hearing Research*, *41*, 18–30.

Smith, B. L., & Gartenberg, T. E. (1984). Initial observations concerning developmental characteristics of labio-mandibular kinematics. *Journal of the Acoustical Society of America*, *75*, 1599–1605.

Tabain, M: (2003). Effects of prosodic boundary on /aC/ sequences: Articulatory results. *Journal of the Acoustical Society of America*, *113*, 2834–2849.

Touati, P. (1987). *Structures prosodiques du suédois et du français*. Working Paper 21, Lund University Press.

Vihman, M. M. (1996). *Phonological development*. Cambridge/Oxford: Blackwell Publishers.

Welby, P. (2003). *The slaying of Lady Mondegreen, being a study of the association and alignment of French intonational rises and their role in speech segmentation*. Ph.D. thesis, The Ohio State University, OH.

15

Temporal and Spatial Correlates of Quantity Contrasts in Wolof Acoustic, Kinematic, and X-Ray Data

RUDOLPH SOCK, BÉATRICE VAXELAIRE, JOHANNA-PASCALE ROY, VÉRONIQUE FERBACH-HECKER, AND FABRICE HIRSCH

ABSTRACT

The present investigation, based on acoustic, kinematic, and X-ray data, focuses on the use of vowel quantity for lexical distinctions in Gambian Wolof. This dialect has a contrast between two lengths and such a contrast occurs only in the first syllable, which is the lexically stressed syllable. The vowel is either referred to as being short or long and both short and long vowels are followed by a single consonant, i.e., VC vs. VVC. The main questions addressed here are: (1) How will the phonological feature of quantity be reflected in the timing characteristics of acoustic and movement signals? (2) Will this distinction be further cued by differences in vocal tract geometry of sagittal profiles? (3) How robust will these vowel quantity linguistic distinctions be?

INTRODUCTION

Wolof, an African language belonging to the Northern branch of the West Atlantic subgroup of the Niger-Congo family, is spoken in Senegal, in the Gambia, and in Mauritania. It uses quantity for lexical and grammatical distinctions. The present investigation focuses on the use of vowel quantity for lexical distinctions in Gambian Wolof. There are two degrees of quantity in this variant of Wolof, establishing the phonemic distinction between pairs such as /nit/ "a person" and /niit/ "to scrutinize", /laka/ "burn" and /laaka/ "language", and /mut/ "ripe" and /mut/ "lick". Quantity contrast only occurs in the first syllable, which is the lexically stressed syllable. In the traditional phonological analysis, both short and long vowels are followed by a single consonant, i.e., Vowel–Consonant (VC) vs. VVC.

The vowel system of this language contains seven short and seven corresponding long vowels. The distinctiveness of the quantity feature is illustrated by the following contrasts:

/fit/ "courage"	vs.	/fiit/ (also /fiiɾ/) "trap"
/cat/ "tip"	vs.	/caat/ "cadet"
/muɲ/ "bear"	vs.	/muuɲ/ "enjoy"
/deg/ "thorn"	vs.	/deeg/ "pond"
/sɛt/ "clean"	vs.	/sɛɛt/ "look"
/mbot/ (a co-verb of quantity)	vs.	/mboot/ "cockroach"
/pɔt/"bowl"	vs.	/pɔɔt/ "short-cut"

The ATR feature is not attested in the Gambian dialect as compared with Senegalese Wolof. Vowel harmony, said to be based on the [ATR] feature in Senegalese Wolof, is discussed extensively by Ka (1993). In the Senegalese dialect, the ATR feature distinguishes words like:

[−ATR]	vs.	[+ATR]
/bɛj/ "to cultivate"	vs.	/bej/ "goat"
/rɛɛr/ "to have dinner"	vs.	/reer / "to be lost"
/tɔɔj/ "to be wet"	vs.	/tooj/ "to be shy"
/baɲ/ "to refuse"	vs.	/ bəɲ/ "tooth"

Note that the [+ATR] vowel corresponding to /a/ is /ə/. It should also be noted (Ka, 1993) that the high vowels (/i, ii, u, uu/) do not have [−ATR] counterparts, and that the low long vowel (/aa/) does not have an [+ATR] counterpart. However, the [ATR] distinction is equated in structuralist descriptions of

Senegalese Wolof with a distinction in aperture. Details on the treatment of this feature are given in Ka (1993); although the notion of ATR/RTR will be briefly discussed later in this work, phonological details concerning this feature go beyond the scope of the present research.

Let us return to the main issues in this study, which are the acoustic and articulatory analyses of the phonological contrast of quantity in Gambian Wolof. Previous research has shown that vowel quality does not vary with quantity in Gambian Wolof. In one of a series of acoustic studies that were carried out, prior to movement investigations for Wolof (described in Sock, 1999), the corpus (given under Method) consisted of the same six words that will be examined in the present investigation. Each word was uttered 10 times, by two speakers, in two speaking rates: normal conversational and fast. The 120 analysed segments for one speaker (RS, also first author) are shown in Figure 15.1, where *F*1 values are plotted on the *Y*-axis and *F*2 values on the *X*-axis. The spectral data, depicted in this figure, bear evidence that formant values, measured (in Hertz) for short and long extreme vowels /i, a, u/, did not differ significantly, as a function of quantity contrasts, at normal (left) and fast (right) speaking rates. See Table 15.1 also for mean values and standard deviations.

The data in the figure do not show any significant target undershoot for the short vowels. Formant values do not reveal any remarkable undershoot in fast speech either. Slight tendencies for undershoot should not be considered, due to high standard deviation values.

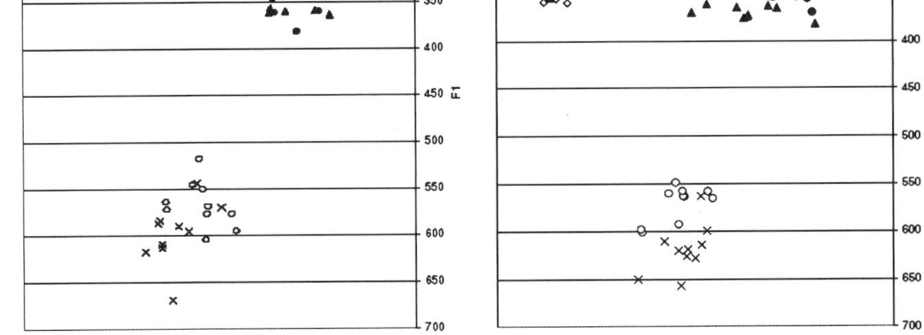

FIGURE 15.1. Formant frequencies of Gambian Wolof long and short extreme vowels, in normal and fast speech.

TABLE 15.1. Average Formant Frequencies of Gambian Wolof Long and Short Vowels, in Normal and Fast Speech

	Normal		Fast	
	*F*1	*F*2	*F*1	*F*2
i	300 (11)	1883 (52)	341(14)	1894 (56)
ii	285 (08)	1938 (24)	338(11)	1908 (36)
a	567 (25)	1436 (106)	571(19)	1374 (93)
aa	598 (33)	1485 (91)	619(26)	1349 (82)
u	349 (13)	1002 (150)	368(09)	1094(142)
uu	339 (25)	801 (73)	353(07)	961(104)

Standard deviations are within parentheses.

Similar spectral results, showing the nonrelevance of quality differences while quantity is varied, have also been verified in movement studies comprising a simultaneous acquisition of acoustic data. Consequently, the present research work will focus on quantity contrasts, although quality differences will also be examined later, when the X-ray data will be discussed in terms of potential spatial correlates of vowel quantity contrasts.

Several studies (see, e.g., Delattre, Jomaa, Al Dossari, Worley, & Sock, 1990; Sock & Löfqvist, 1995; Adu Manyah & Sock, 2002) have demonstrated the relevance of some temporal measures, mainly in terms of latencies, on both the acoustic and movement levels, as domains where phonological contrasts emerge distinctly. Owing to the well-known elasticity of speech signals, such studies have judiciously examined proportional values of target vocalic and consonantal intervals, within defined temporal VC and CV domains (Elert, 1964; Lehiste, 1970). The present investigation is in line with such research, and presents new data on the articulatory correlates of quantity in Wolof that to our knowledge have been unavailable previously. Thus, the two specific questions that are addressed here are related to the spatiotemporal aspects of quantity in this language:

1. How will the phonological feature of quantity be reflected in the timing characteristics of acoustic and movement signals? It will be interesting to know, for example, when speaking rate increases, what portions of the speech signal undergo compression and what portions resist compression, so as to preserve quantity contrasts.
2. Will such contrasts be accompanied by differences in vocal tract geometry of sagittal profiles? If so, it could be relevant to know how differences in vocal tract geometry may serve to reinforce quantity contrasts, in terms of more or less pronounced amplitudes of specific gestures, without necessarily provoking noticeable vowel quality changes.

Speech rate is varied to test for the robustness of emerging temporal patterns and vocal tract configurations to changes in the tempo of utterances. Such timing patterns and vocal tract shapes will be analysed and discussed in terms of linguistic constraints, i.e., in terms of incompressibility limits, due to required minimum durations that ensure appropriate identification of a category, and also avoidance of phonological class confusion. Biomechanical constraints may also help in understanding the behaviour of an articulator, especially under increased speaking rate. This investigation, based on acoustic, kinematic, and X-ray data, is thus a contribution, hopefully, to pinpointing articulatory and acoustic factors that signal quantity contrasts.

METHOD

Acoustic and Movement Data

The corpus consisted of six Wolof words: /fitam/ "his courage" vs. /fiitam/ "his trap"; /fatam/ "its filling up" vs. /faatam/ "its expiration"; and /futam/ "his blister" vs. /fuutam/ "his Fouta (Guinea)". Two male speakers of Gambian Wolof (SN and RS) uttered these CVCV(m) words that were chosen to vary vowel quantity and quality. Each token was embedded in an interrogative carrier sentence: /lum ne_____?/, meaning "What did he/she say_____ ?"

To obtain *acoustic data*, the speakers were instructed to produce the randomized list of utterances at a normal conversational rate, and at a self-selected fast rate, at least 14 times in each speech condition. Thus, there were three conditions in all: two speech rates (conversational or normal and fast) × 2 vowel lengths (short and long) × 3 vowel types (/i, a u/).

The *movement data* were recorded for one subject (RS), using a three-coil transmitter system with five transducers, the Electro Magnetic Articulograph (AG 100, *Carstens Medizinelektronik*) as described by Perkell, Cohen, Svirsky, Matthies, Garabieta, and Jackson (1992). Receivers were placed on the vermilion borders of the upper and lower lips, the lower incisors for the jaw, and at a median position on the tongue body. In addition, a receiver placed on the upper incisors was used for correction of head movements relative to the helmet. Checks were made to ensure that head rotation was not a major source of error. A simultaneous audio recording was carried out, using a helmet-incorporated microphone.

X-Ray Data

Digital X-ray data obtained for one speaker (RS), under medical care, together with a simultaneous recording of the acoustic signal were extracted from the Phonetics Institute of Strasbourg's database. Note that only two repetitions (one per speech rate) of each word were recorded.

Measurement Procedures for Acoustic and Movement Data

On the basis of articulatory and acoustic events in the velocity and audio signals, respectively, one interval (among several possible intervals) was identified in the movement of each articulator, and another interval (among several other intervals) was also measured in the acoustic waveform, for all repetitions. Movement and acoustic durations, within the relevant intervals, were then determined by specific articulatory and acoustic timing relations, respectively (see, e.g., Abry, Benoit, Boë, & Sock, 1985). Figure 15.2 is a representative example of the acoustic signal and the position curve for the vertical displacement of the tongue body (Sock, 1999), for one of the words extracted from the corpus: /fatam/.

The acoustic *vowel-to-vowel* duration, measured in the VC domain, is defined in the audio signal as the interval from onset of a clear formant structure for the first vowel (V1on) to onset of the same formant structure for the

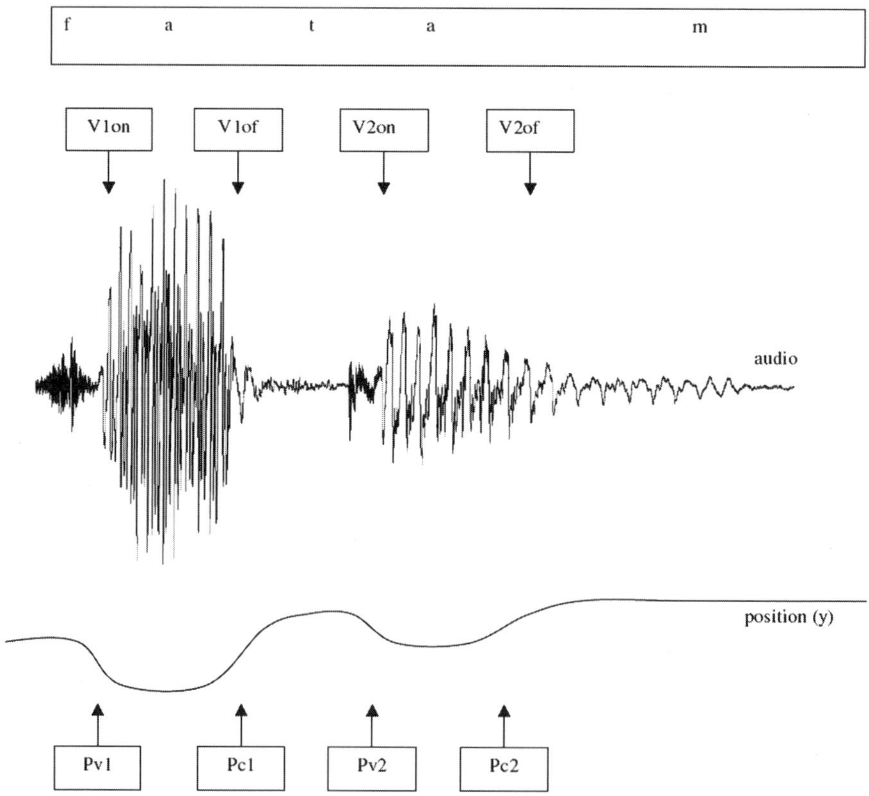

FIGURE 15.2. A representative signal of the audio for the word /fatam/ and the position signal of the tongue body (adapted from Sock, 1999). See text for measurement procedures.

subsequent vowel (V2on). This *vowel-to-vowel* duration thus includes the consonant closure of the medial consonant. A *vowel* interval is determined within the *vowel-to-vowel* span, as the steady-state portion between onset of a clear formant structure of the first vowel (V1on) and offset of the formant structure, due to closure (V1of) of the following consonant /t/. VOT values for the medial consonant /t/ did not vary across the short and long categories.

The *peak-to-peak Velocity* interval, measured in the VC domain, for the lower lip, the jaw and the tongue body, is defined in the position signal, with the help of the velocity curve, as the duration between successive negative peaks, associated with lowering movements in the production of the vowels. This interval goes from the first negative peak, for the production of the first vowel (PV1), to the second negative peak (PV2), associated with the production of the second vowel, which is always /a/. An articulatory measure, referred to as *Vowel* duration in the position signal, is determined for each articulator, within the *peak-to-peak Velocity* duration, as the interval between the first negative peak (PV1) and peak velocity (PC1), in the raising movement associated with the production of the medial apical consonant /t/.

It should be mentioned that the acoustic vowel-to-vowel interval and the articulatory peak-to-peak Velocity span, both specified in the VC domain, had proven useful in portraying quantity contrasts for various languages, examined in previous studies (see, e.g., Delattre et al., 1990). Moreover, the kinematic peak-to-peak Velocity interval seems to coincide best, in terms of timing characteristics, with the acoustic vowel-to-vowel duration, compared with other intervals (such as movement onsets) that could also be defined on a position signal. Results obtained for several quantity languages, and reported in Sock (1999), have shown that articulator movements are efficient in portraying quantity contrasts, for both vowels and consonants, only when the peak velocity of the movement of the articulator is attained, and not at its onset.

Regarding the movement data, one relevant question that cropped up during analyses of movement patterns, related to vocal tract opening gestures, in producing quantity contrasts, was the appropriateness of placing the pellet at a median position on the tongue body. Such a position may not necessarily cue tongue strategies for vowel quantity contrasts. Thus, it was hypothesized that tongue constriction information, furnished by the X-ray data, would give better insights into the contribution of this organ in cueing quantity.

Measurement Procedures for the X-Ray Data

Measurement parameters were specified on sagittal profiles, with the help of an interface, INTRIC (Roy, 2003), a software developed under Matlab®, using a semi-polar coordinate system (adapted from Maeda, 1989). This semi-polar coordinate system serves to monitor tongue movements and to extract sagittal functions (Perrier, Boë, & Sock, 1992). First, a reference system is specified for

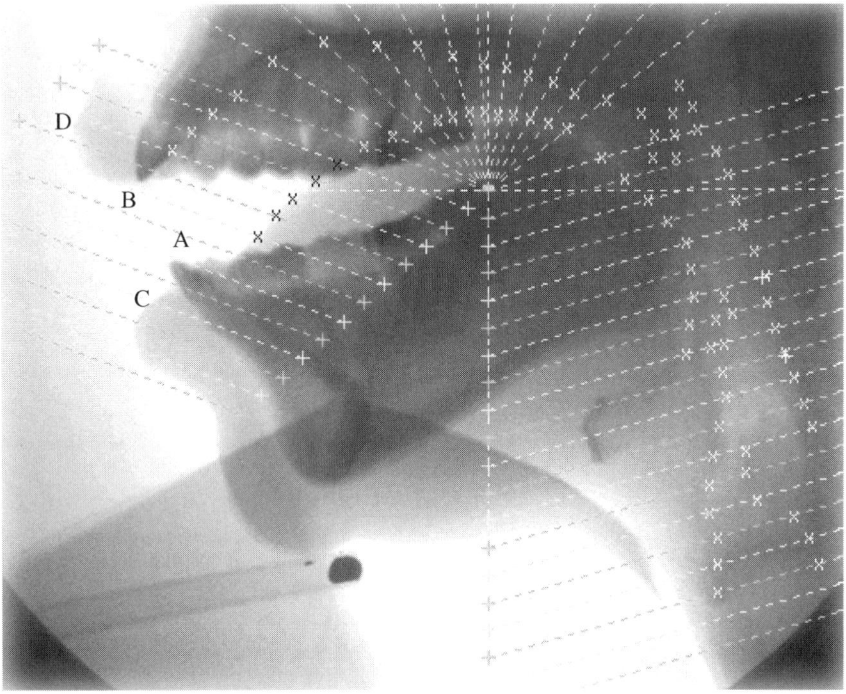

FIGURE 15.3. A semi-polar grid (adapted from Maeda, 1989) showing the articulators monitored for vowel quantity contrasts: jaw lowering (A), lip opening (the distance between C and D) and tongue constriction width, from the larynx to the alveolar ridge. Upper-lip protrusion (D) was also acquired for the rounded vowels /u/ and /uu/.

the images. It consists of two perpendicular axes that divide each frame into four parts. The intersection of the two axes corresponds to the centre of rotation of the semi-polar coordinate system (Figure 15.3). In addition, reference points, located on fixed bony structures and easy to identify, allow aligning the X-ray images. More detailed information concerning X-ray measurement procedures can be found in Roy (2003).

Articulators monitored for vowel quantity contrasts, using the reference system described above in the interface were jaw lowering, lip opening, and tongue constriction width, from the larynx to the alveolar ridge. Upper-lip protrusion was also acquired for the rounded vowels /u/ and /uu/.

RESULTS

After having discarded defective productions due to the inherent difficulty in acquiring movement data, the main body of statistical data corresponds to 10 out of 14 repetitions of the 6 words uttered at 2 speech rates. Further data processing is based on the *proportion* of time taken by the acoustic vowel duration in the acoustic vowel-to-vowel interval. Also in the movement domain, the *proportion* of time occupied by the articulatory interval defined as vowel duration in the kinematic peak-to-peak Velocity span is also examined. Results reported here, only focus on acoustic data and movement data for the *tongue*. Owing to significant variability in the jaw and lip data and consequently to no regular behaviour, it is inferred that, for at least these speakers, such articulators do not play a *critical timing* role in the production of these words that vary vocalic quantity and quality. If the irregular behaviour of the jaw cannot be explained in terms of the nature of the sequences examined, inconsistent results obtained for the lips are not very surprising, in view of the fact that the medial consonant is not labial. However, it is noteworthy that the jaw has demonstrated a significant contribution to the production of vocalic quantity contrasts in various timing studies (see, e.g., Delattre et al., 1990). As regards lip data and quantity contrasts, results obtained for Swedish, show significant timing patterns for the lower lip in the production of vowel quantity contrasts (Sock, Löfqvist, & Perrier, 1996).

Three-way analyses of variance (ANOVAs) were performed on measures of *vowel-to-vowel durations*, *peak-to-peak durations*, and on the *percentages* of their component *vowel* portions, for both the acoustic speech signal and for the tongue body (y) signal. Factors were vowel (for vowel quality differences), Quantity (for quantity contrasts), and Rate (for the two speaking rates). In determining the statistical significance of main and interaction effects, only significant results with <1% probability of having been obtained by chance ($p<.01$) are reported here. Note that, because of space limitations, only acoustic results from subject RS are given here. However, acoustic patterns are strikingly similar to those obtained from speaker SN, and only minor variability was observed in absolute durations (Sock, 1999). Moreover, as consonantal patterns, in the CV interval, in both the acoustic and movement domains did not reflect vocalic quantity contrasts in a previous study (Delattre et al., 1990) only data in the VC interval will be presented in this work.

Acoustic Data

Vocalic Patterns in the Acoustic Vowel-to-Vowel Interval. For the /i/ vs. /ii/ contrast (see Figure 15.4), in normal speech rate, phonological quantity contrasts emerge distinctly in this acoustic temporal domain.

Figure 15.4 shows stacked bar charts of absolute durations (left), along with percentage bar graphs (right) for the /i/ vs. /ii/ contrast, in normal and fast speech rates. This figure highlights the importance of considering relative values when dealing with quantity contrasts and durational values.

It can be seen from the charts that long vowels (94 ms), as expected, have significantly longer durations than their shorter counterparts (29 ms) in normal speech, and also in fast speech (55 vs. 15 ms for long and short vowels,

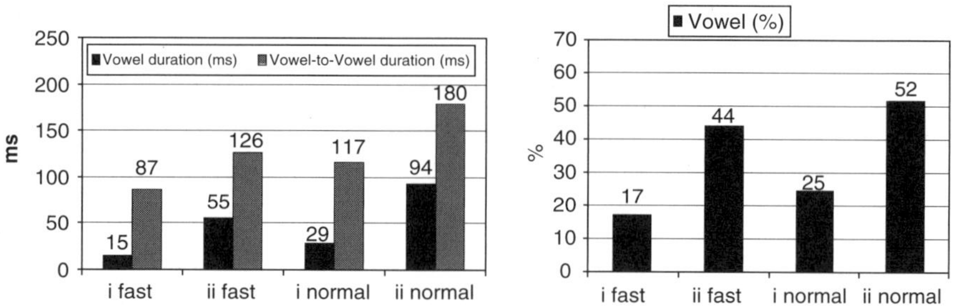

FIGURE 15.4. Stacked bar charts (left) and % bar graphs for Wolof /i/ vs. /ii/ in normal and fast speech rates. Acoustic data.

respectively). Such an observation is also true for vowel-to-vowel durations. However, the complementary distribution of the quantities, i.e., short vowels being followed by long consonants and long consonants by short vowels is not a feature of Gambian Wolof as it is of Swedish (Elert, 1964). This means that if short vowels are followed by significantly longer consonants (88 ms after short /i/ in normal speech and 72 ms in fast speech), the consonants that follow long vowels (86 and 71 ms in normal and fast speech, respectively) are not always shorter than the vowels (see also similar data reported for Twi in Adu Manyah & Sock, 2002).

Examining the proportion of time taken by the vowel interval in the vowel-to-vowel span should give us some additional insights into how quantity contrasts emerge within a defined domain, and if temporal relationships across speaking rates are differently affected by phonological identity. If durations in general seem to be compressed when speaking rate is increased, the compression of vocalic and consonantal intervals, for short and long vowels, may not scale linearly.

The percentage value of acoustic vowel patterns for short vowels (that make up 25% of the vowel-to-vowel interval) are significantly different from their longer counterparts (52% of the vowel-to-vowel duration). These contrasts, that are in fact clear-cut, are also due to highly significant vowel-to-vowel durational differences (117 ms for short vowels vs. 180 ms for long vowels). In fast speech, the scenario is the same: Quantity contrasts are maintained not only along the vowel interval (17% of the vowel-to-vowel span for short vowels vs. 44% for long vowels), but also along the duration of the vowel-to-vowel interval (87 and 126 ms for short and long vowels, respectively).

The complementary distribution of the quantities is confirmed, here also, for short vowels but it is only a tendency for long ones: Consonants take up 48 and 56% of the vowel-to-vowel interval for /ii/ in normal and fast speech rates, respectively.

Figure 15.5 shows data for absolute durations (left), along with percentage bar graphs (right) for the /a/ vs. /aa/ contrast, in normal and fast speech rates.

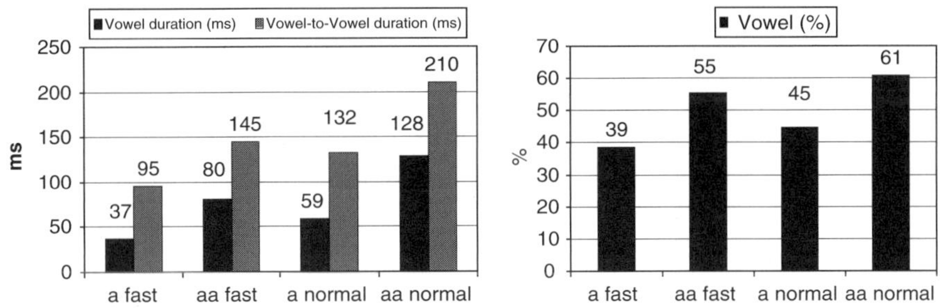

FIGURE 15.5. Stacked bar charts (left) and % bar graphs for Wolof /a/ vs. /aa/ in normal and fast speech rates. Acoustic data.

The charts show that long vowels (128 ms) have significantly longer durations than their shorter counterparts (59 ms) in normal speech, and also in fast speech (80 vs. 37 ms for long and short vowels, respectively). Vowel-to-vowel durations are also longer for long vowels. In this vowel-to-vowel span, the consonants take up 82 ms for the long vowel in normal speech and 65 ms in fast speech and 73 ms for the short vowel in normal speech and 58 ms in fast speech. The complementary distribution of the quantities, in this VC domain, seems to be verified.

The vowel duration of the short category /fatam/ takes up 45% of the vowel-to-vowel interval, at a normal speaking rate, while that of the long category /faatam/ occupies 61% of the vowel-to-vowel interval, at this same speaking rate. This significant difference in average percentage values of the vowels (16%) is coupled with a mean vowel-to-vowel durational difference of 78 ms between short vowels (132 ms) and long vowels (210 ms). In fast speech, the vocalic portion of the short vowel takes up 39% of the vowel-to-vowel interval, while that of the longer vowel is reduced to 55% of its vowel-to-vowel interval. However, the difference in mean percentage values, in fast speech, is comparable with that observed in the normal speaking condition: it comes up to 16% here also. In relative terms, both short and long vowels undergo the same degree of compression, as they are both reduced by 6%, with respect to the vowel-to-vowel interval, when speaking rate is increased. Although both short and long vowels have their vowel-to-vowel durations compressed in fast speech, the short and long phonetic classes are still separate, due to differences in both vowel-to-vowel durations (50 ms) and vowel proportions (16%) in the VC domain. Thus, quantity contrasts do emerge clearly in this acoustic vowel-to-vowel interval, with a complementary distribution of the quantities in relative terms.

As regards the /u/ vs. /uu/ contrast (see Figure 15.6), vocalic patterns for quantity contrasts can be seen here clearly as in the previous contexts.

The duration of long vowels (102 ms) is significantly higher than that of their shorter counterparts (31 ms) in normal speech, and also in fast speech (46 vs. 16

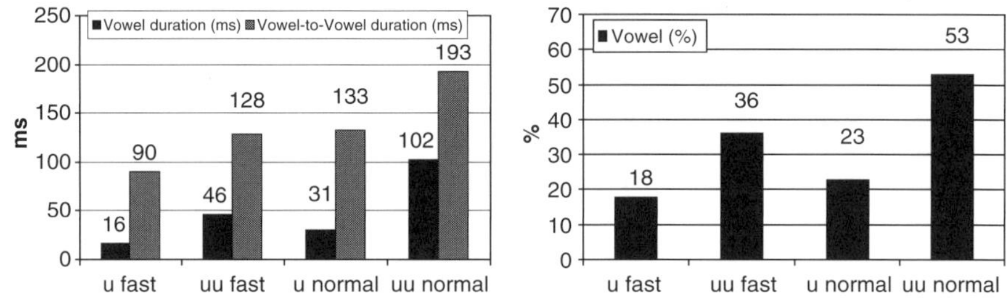

FIGURE 15.6. Stacked bar charts (left) and % bar graphs for Wolof /u/ vs. /uu/ in normal and fast speech rates. Acoustic data.

ms for long and short vowels, respectively). This is also true for vowel-to-vowel durations. Durations for consonants are: 91 ms for /uu/ in normal speech and 82 ms in fast speech; 102 ms for /u/ in normal speech, and 74 ms in fast speech. There is no complementary distribution of the vowel and consonant quantities here.

In normal speech rate, the vowel interval for long vowels that takes up 53% of the vowel-to-vowel span is significantly different from that of their shorter counterparts, which occupies only 23% of their vowel-to-vowel duration. There is also a noticeable vowel-to-vowel durational difference between the two classes, with 193 ms for long vowels and only 133 ms for the shorter class. The distinction between the two classes is maintained in fast speech, regardless of a pronounced vowel percentage and vowel-to-vowel duration compression: The vowel interval for the long vowels now takes up 36% of their vowel-to-vowel span, while that of the short vowels is reduced to 18% of the vowel-to-vowel duration. The vowel-to-vowel durational difference also contributes to ensuring the maintained difference between the two classes: The vowel-to-vowel duration for the long vowels is 128 ms, as opposed to that of the shorter ones that becomes 90 ms in fast speech. Here also, quantities are not distributed in a complementary way.

Movement Data

Vocalic Patterns in the Peak-to-Peak Velocity Interval. In its vertical displacement, the tongue body shows fairly coherent patterns that correspond to the different phonological classes. Let us focus on two of the three extreme vowel contexts: /i/ and /a/. Of the three vowels, /u/ seems to present less-defined quantity contrast kinematic patterns. Although this finding may be related, partially, to the use of a single sensor that might not have captured the relevant constriction location and the horizontal movement component, in the production of the contrasts, results reported elsewhere (Sock, 1999) show, for several speakers (including Senegalese speakers) that /u/ seems to present the most fragile quantity contrast patterns as distinctions between classes (not well defined in normal speech rate) systematically disappear in fast speech rate. Sock (1999) hypothesizes that such contrasts, because of their fragility, are likely to disappear earlier than others in the vowel system of the dialect examined.

The stacked bar charts and percentage graphs in Figure 15.7 indicate that long vowels have significantly longer articulatorily defined vowel durations and peak-to-peak Velocity durations than their shorter counterparts, in both normal and fast speech. However, the distribution of quantities between vowels and consonants is not complementary as short vowels do not have longer consonants: 89 ms for the vowel vs. 60 ms for the consonant in normal speech, and 60 ms for the vowel vs. 59 ms in fast speech.

Here also, due to the elasticity of temporal speech signals, it is worthwhile analysing the behaviour of the measured vocalic segments, relative to the defined peak-to-peak Velocity interval, when speaking rate is increased (see percentage graphs in Figure 15.7).

For the /i/ vs. /ii/ contrast, in normal speech, the distinction is based solely on the peak-to-peak Velocity interval (149 ms for the short class vs. 201 ms for the longer class, a 52 ms mean difference that is significant at $p < .01$). As speech rate is increased, this distinction along the peak-to-peak Velocity interval is reduced to a 25 ms difference between the two classes, that is, statistically significant only at $p < .05$ (119 ms for the short vowel vs. 144 ms for the long vowel). It is clear from the figure that the distribution of the quantities is not observed here.

The manoeuvre used to distinguish the classes is simple: (1) As the vocalic interval is not relevant in distinguishing short vowels from long vowels in either speech rate, it is the peak-to-peak Velocity duration that ensures the distinction in both speech rates; (2) The nonrelevance of the articulatorily defined vowel in this vocalic /i/ context may have been an artefact, as in the /u/ context, caused by using a single pellet on the tongue body to monitor quantity contrasts. The X-ray data should provide a better understanding of constriction locations and sizes for this vowel, in particular, and the two other vowels in general.

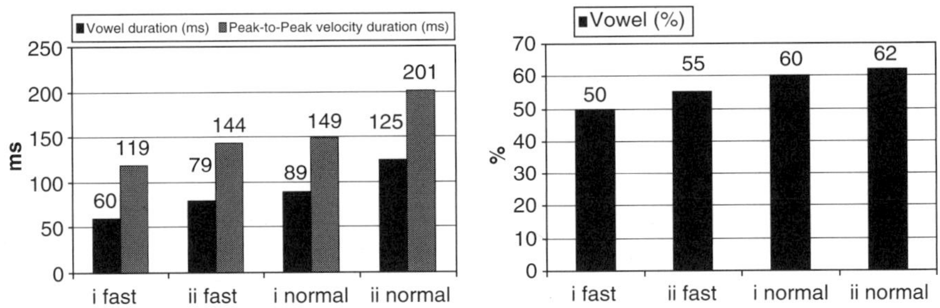

FIGURE 15.7. Stacked bar charts (left) and % bar graphs for Wolof /i/ vs. /ii/ in normal and fast speech rates. Movement data.

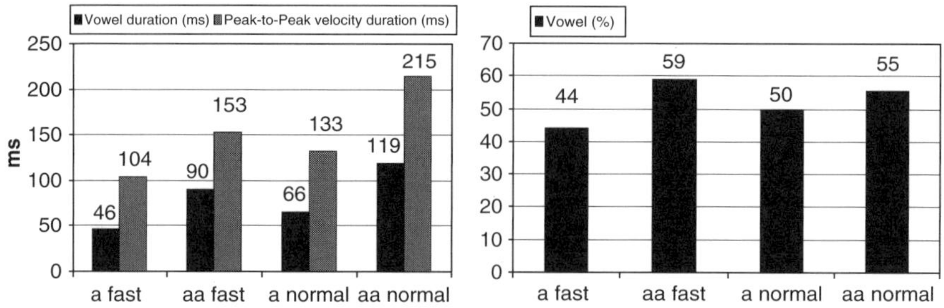

FIGURE 15.8. Stacked bar charts (left) and % bar graphs for Wolof /a/ vs. /aa/ in normal and fast speech rates. Movement data.

It can be seen in Figure 15.8 that articulatorily defined vowel durations and peak-to-peak Velocity durations are longer for the long /aa/ vowels, compared with the short ones, in both normal and fast speech. The complementary distribution of the quantities is not verified for the short vowel in normal speech, with a duration of 66 ms for the vowel and of 67 ms for the consonant.

As regards relative values for this /a/ vs. /aa/ contrast, in normal speech rate, the distinction relies more on an 82 ms peak-to-peak Velocity durational difference (133 ms for the short vowel vs. 215 ms for the long vowel, $p < .01$) than on the 5% vowel proportion difference. However, when speech rate is increased, the length difference along the peak-to-peak Velocity interval (a 49 ms difference between the two classes, with 104 ms for short vowels vs. 153 ms for long vowels) is reinforced by a 15% vowel difference that now becomes significant (59 and 44% for long and short vowels, respectively, $p < .01$). As can be seen in the figure, quantities are not distributed in a complementary way. Strategies adopted to preserve the phonological contrasts under speech rate increase are the following: (1) when the long category increases the proportion of its vowel under speech rate increase, while reducing its peak-to-peak Velocity duration, its shorter counterpart reduces the proportion of its vowel while compressing its peak-to-peak Velocity duration; the result is a maintained peak-to-peak Velocity interval difference in fast speech, coupled with an enhanced vowel percentage difference; (2) long vowels in this /a/ context are limited, in the compressibility of their vocalic portions, for reasons related to linguistic coherence (avoidance of phonological class confusion) but have the possibility of increasing the proportion of the vowel, which is finally the strategy adopted.

Note that Klatt (1976) provides data suggesting that an incompressibility limit prevents further temporal reduction in English, so as to ensure sufficient time for the execution of articulatory gestures and thereby avoid excessive vowel undershoot. Wolof movement data analysed here seem to be in line with such findings. As the articulatorily defined vowel interval in the present study is quite similar to the peak-to-peak ratio used in works by Harrington, Fletcher, and

Roberts (1995) on de-accentuation, and in Hoole, Mooshammer, and Tillmann (1994) and Mooshammer, Fuchs, and Fischer (1999) on the tenseness contrast in German, it should be useful, at this point, to summarize results given in such studies. As opposed to the Wolof data described here in normal speech, results found in the above-mentioned investigations showed a systematic reduction of the ratio, which was interpreted as a truncation of the opening gesture by the closing gesture; such a truncation also reduced the movement amplitude. In the case of Gambian Wolof, where long and short vowels seem to contrast on purely quantity bases, vowel truncation by the consonant is apparently not significant, thus avoiding unwanted reductions in movement amplitudes that may provoke remarkable quality differences between short and long vowels.

X-Ray Data

Les us recall that X-ray and acoustic data were simultaneously acquired. Each word was uttered once, in each speech rate. Acoustic analyses were carried out, in this experiment also, in order to ensure that quality differences did not vary with quantity contrasts. The spectral data (Figure 15.9) show again that formant values, for short and long extreme vowels /i, a, u/, were similar, regardless of differences in quantity at normal (left) and fast (right) speaking rates.

In this spatial domain, vocal tract measurements were then carried out on frames that correspond, more or less, to the acoustic mid-region of the phonologically short or long vowel. Thus, all frames that are compared in order to analyse vowel quantity contrasts refer, not only to the acoustic steady-state portion of target vowels, but also to open configurations of the vocal tract, flanked by labiodental and apical contacts for the production of /f/ and /t/, respectively.

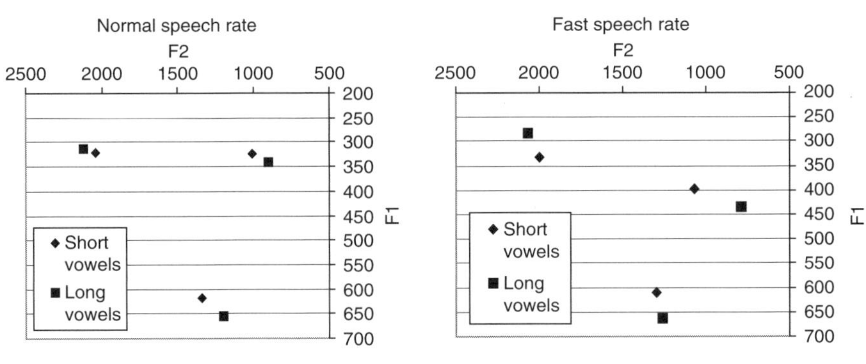

FIGURE 15.9. Formant frequencies (one repetition for each vowel) of Gambian Wolof long and short extreme vowels, in normal and fast speech. Acoustic data obtained during X-ray acquisition.

In the /i/ vs. /ii/ context, in normal speech (Figure 15.10), the data show that *lip opening* is noticeably wider (10.7 mm) for the long vowel, at frame 427 (in the right panel) than for its shorter counterpart (2.98 mm) at frame 327 (in the left panel). Lip-opening (and jaw) values to the right of frames 327 and 427 in the left and right panels, respectively, correspond to configurations associated with the production of the medial consonant /t/, followed by the subsequent vowel /a/. The difference in degree of lip-opening width is maintained in fast speech and is still significantly pronounced; it is 10.13 mm for the long vowel compared with a 1.93 mm value for the short one. As concerns *jaw lowering*, jaw position for the long vowel and the short vowel is comparable in normal speech (c.f. frames 327 and 427 again), with a tendency for a lower jaw position for the long vowel in fast speech. When *speech rate* is increased, amplitudes of lip opening and jaw lowering are slightly reduced.

At a normal speaking rate, *tongue constriction* width (Figure 15.11), in this /i/ context, is greater for the long vowel, compared with the short one, in the entire pharyngeal cavity (lower and upper pharynx) and in the velar region, with a 5 mm difference on average. This is due to a noticeable fronting of the tongue body in the production of the long vowel. It should be mentioned that constriction size is similar for both vowels in the palatal–alveolar region, presumably a critical zone for the required acoustic quality of the vowels. Moreover, the overall tongue shape is similar for the production of both vowels. Although, phonologically, the [ATR] feature is not attested in Gambian Wolof, such a difference in vocal tract configuration, between the long and the short vowels, resembles an ATR/RTR distinction. This difference in the pharyngeal region does not, however, provoke significant acoustic consequences (lowering of F1, due to enlargement of the pharynx), as revealed by spectral data. In fast speech, no consistent difference in constriction size is observed between the two vowel categories, seemingly revealing the nonrobustness of the ATR/RTR phonetic distinction. As regards the ATR feature, remember that in all cases, when this

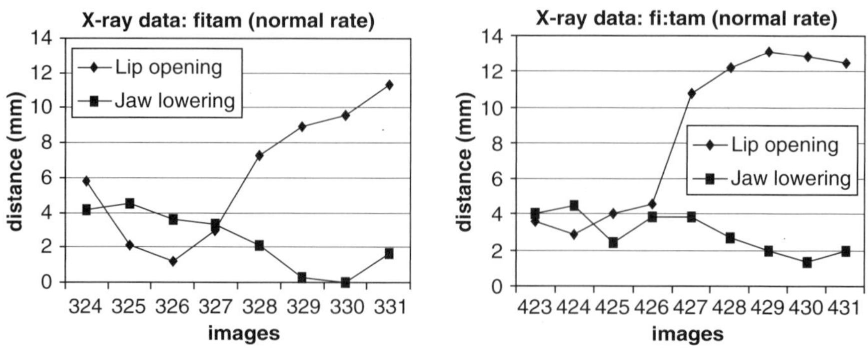

FIGURE 15.10. Frame-by-frame analysis of lip-opening variations and jaw lowering for sequences /fitam/ and /fi:tam/ at a normal speaking rate (see text for details).

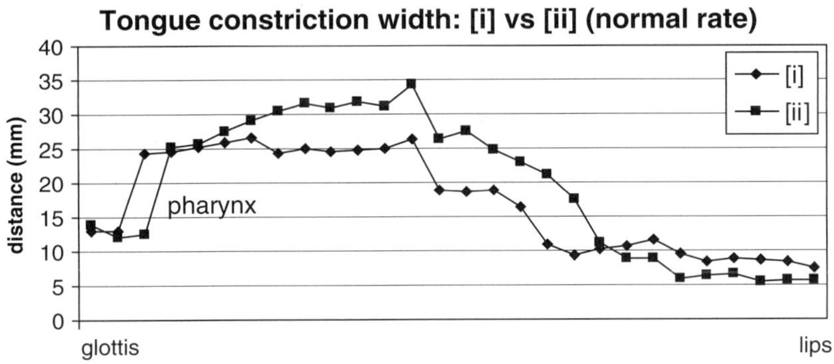

FIGURE 15.11. Changes in tongue constriction width for /i/ and /ii/ from the glottis to the lips.

feature is attested, as in Senegalese Wolof, the high vowels studied here do not have [-ATR] counterparts.

As regards the /a/ vs. /aa/ context (Figure 15.12), results indicate that *lip opening* is wider for the long vowel in both normal and fast speech, with a distance of 12.20 mm for /aa/ vs. 6.70 mm for /a/ in the normal speech rate. Compare frame 460 (in the right panel), that corresponds to the open vocal tract configuration for vowel /aa/, with frame 360 (in the left panel), that is associated with the open configuration for the short vowel /a/. All frames to the right of frames 360 and 460 in the left and right panels depict configurations for the production of /t/, /a/, and /m/. An opening of 13.56 mm for /aa/ vs. 8.05 mm is registered in the fast speech rate. *Jaw lowering* is also more defined for the long vowel compared with its shorter counterpart in the two prosodic conditions: 8.49 mm for /aa/ (frame 460) vs. 4.62 mm for /a/ (frame 360) in normal speech and 8.94 mm for /aa/ vs. 4.47 mm for /a/ in fast speech.

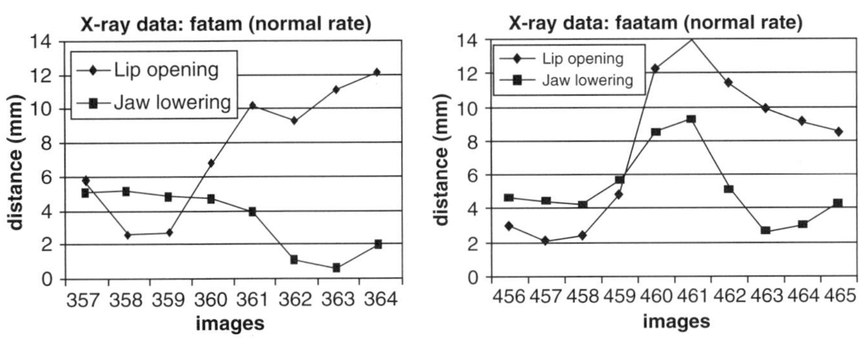

FIGURE 15.12. Frame-by-frame analysis of lip-opening variations and jaw lowering for sequences /fatam/ and /faatam/ at a normal speaking rate (see text for details).

In this /a/ context (Figure 15.13), where tongue body and jaw coupling is usually rather tight, it is the long vowel that has a smaller *constriction* than the short one in the pharyngeal region (a difference of 2.5 mm), but a much larger constriction in the velar region, in normal speech. The small difference between the two vowels in constriction size in the pharyngeal region is due, to a large extent, to a more pronounced lowering (and consequently backward translation) of the jaw for the long vowel. However, in fast speech, both vowels have a comparable constriction size throughout the vocal tract, despite the significant lowering of the jaw for the long vowel; a relative uncoupling of the tongue body and the jaw is predominantly responsible for this similarity in constriction size.

Speech rate does not seem to have any coherent influence on the amplitude of gestures in this case.

In the /u/ vs. /uu/ context (Figure 15.14), the data for *lip opening* and *jaw lowering* do not seem to suggest any clear-cut and consistent behaviour for the measured parameters, as far as these pairs are concerned. Moreover, an additional control of lip *protrusion* did not reveal any defined amplitude difference between the two phonological categories.

Constriction size in normal speech (Figure 15.15) is similar for the long and short vowels throughout the vocal tract except in the pre-palatal region, where the long /uu/ has a larger constriction size than the short one (a 5 mm difference). In fast speech, the above-mentioned difference in the pre-palatal region is reduced (2.5 mm) but maintained. Moreover, the long vowel in fast speech rate has a larger constriction size than the short one in the pharyngeal region (a difference of 2.5 mm on average). Such a result, observed in fast speech and compared to that obtained in normal speech, seems to suggest that no consistent behaviour of the tongue root, in terms of advancing and retracting, may be related to quantity contrasts.

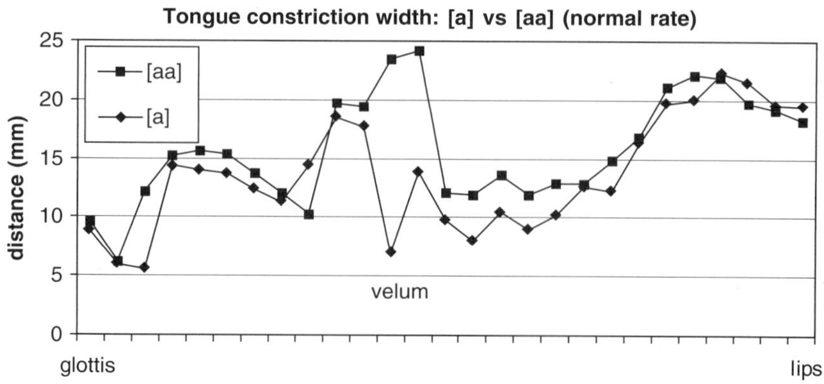

FIGURE 15.13. Changes in tongue constriction width for /a/ and /aa/ from the glottis to the lips.

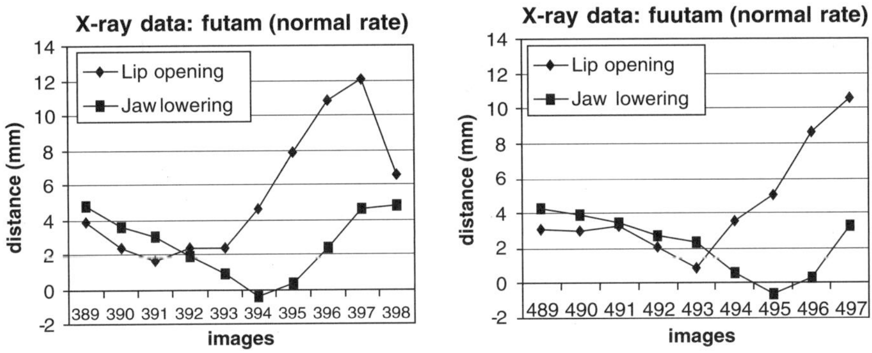

FIGURE 15.14. Frame-by-frame analysis of lip-opening variations and jaw lowering for sequences /futam/ and /fuutam/ at a normal speaking rate (see text for details).

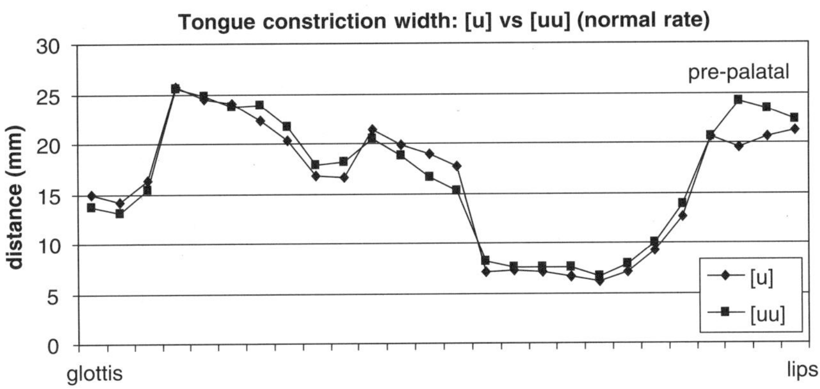

FIGURE 15.15. Changes in tongue constriction width for /u/ and /uu/ from the glottis to the lips.

SUMMARY AND CONCLUSION

On the *acoustic level*: (1) the acoustic vowel-to-vowel duration span is an efficient temporal domain where quantity contrasts are exemplified. Such results are in line with data reported by Delattre et al. (1990). The vocalic patterns, i.e., the proportion of time taken by the vowels in this acoustic vowel-to-vowel interval, and corresponding to different linguistic entities, emerge clearly in this temporal span in normal speech, and are more or less maintained in fast speech, thus confirming the relevance of such measurements in speech-timing studies on quantity contrasts. (2) No systematic complementary distribution of the quantities is observed.

On the *movement level*: (1) the peak-to-peak Velocity interval of the tongue body's vertical displacement is a relevant temporal span in which to observe for vocalic quantity contrasts. Articulatorily defined vocalic patterns, measured in this kinematic domain, and corresponding to the different linguistic entities, rely mainly on peak-to-peak Velocity durational differences. Thus long vowels, compared with their shorter counterparts, have longer peak-to-peak Velocity durations, associated with the tongue gestures in producing quantity contrasts. This movement interval also proved efficient for the jaw in its vertical displacements to produce vocalic quantity contrasts (Delattre et al., 1990). (2) In this domain also, there is no consistent distribution of the quantities.

In the *spatial domain*, differences in the amplitude of lip opening and jaw lowering reflect quantity contrasts for /i/ and /a/: Lip opening is wider for the long vowels and jaw lowering tends to be greater for the latter compared with the short ones. Differences in the diameter of tongue body constriction are also spatial correlates of quantity contrasts for all vowels examined. Thus, the constriction is wider for the long vowel compared with the short one for: (1) /i/ in the pharyngeal region but not in the sensitive acoustic zone, i.e., the palatal region; (2) /a/ in the velar region and to a much lesser degree in the pharyngeal region where variation in this constriction is quite constrained; (3) /u/ in the pre-palatal region but not in the critical velar region.

In conclusion, if quantity contrasts indeed rely more on timing factors than on spatial considerations, differences in vocal tract geometry serve, nevertheless, in reinforcing durational correlates of quantity. Formant values do not vary significantly from one phonological category to the other, as differences in vocal tract constrictions are much more related to quantity contrasts than to sensitive acoustic regions that portray vowel quality differences.

Future work will try to explain why differences in constriction size between the two phonological categories, although significant in some instances, do not provoke noticeable qualitative differences. Remarkable differences in vocal tract configurations may, however, be portrayed in the amplitude (root mean square (RMS)) of the acoustic signals. Perception tests will finally be carried out in order to determine the auditory effects of these spatial and kinematic differences between short and long Wolof vowels.

ACKNOWLEDGMENTS

This work was funded by a French Ministry of Research grant to the Phonetics Institute of Strasbourg E.A. 3403, Programme "Cognitique" ACT1B 2001–2003. Support also came from the Fonds québécois de la recherche sur la société et la culture ("Concourse" 2002–2003). We are grateful to Dr. Marija Tabain, Dr. Phil Hoole, Dr. Tine Mooshammer, and one anonymous reviewer, for invaluable comments on an earlier version of the manuscript.

REFERENCES

Abry, C., Benoit, C., Boë, L. J., & Sock, R. (1985). Un choix d'événements pour l'organisation temporelle du signal de la parole. *14èmes Journées d'Etudes de la Parole du GCP du GALF,* 133–137.

Adu Manyah, K., & Sock, R. (2002). La quantité vocalique en twi. Quelques considérations phonologiques et analyses acoustiques préliminaires. *XXIV Journées d'Etudes sur la Parole de l'Association Francophone de la Communication Parlée*, 41–44.

Delattre, C., Jomaa, M., Al Dossari, A., Worley, C., & Sock, R. (1990). Comparaison articulatori-acoustique des structures temporelles en arabe et en français. Où peut-on séparer les classes dans les VC?. *18èmes Journées d'Etudes de la Parole du GCP de la SFA*, 113–118.

Elert, C. C. (1964). *Phonological studies of quantity in Swedish*. Uppsala: Almqvist and Wiiksell.

Harrington, J., Fletcher, J., & Roberts, C. (1995). Coarticulation and the accent/unaccented distinction: Evidence from jaw movement data. *Journal of Phonetics*, *23*, 305–322.

Hoole, P., Mooshammer, C., & Tillmann, H. (1994) Kinematic analysis of vowel production in German. *Proceedings of the international conference of spoken language processing*, Yokohama, Japan, 19–22, September (pp. 305–322).

Ka, O. (1993). *Wolof phonology and morphology*. Lanham, MD: University Press of America.

Klatt, D. (1976). Linguistic uses of segmental duration in English: Acoustic and perceptual evidence. *Journal of the Acoustical Society of America*, *59*, 1206–1221.

Lehiste, I. (1970). *Suprasegmentals*. Cambridge: MIT Press.

Maeda, S. (1989). Articulation compensatoire des voyelles: Analyses des données cinéradiographiques avec un modèle linéaire. Mélanges de Phonétique Générale et Expérimentale offerts à Péla Simon, t. 2., Strasbourg Publications de l'Institut de Phonétique de Strasbourg (pp. 545–562).

Mooshammer, C., Fuchs, S., & Fischer, D. (1999). Effects of stress and tenseness on the production of CVC syllables in German. *Proceedings of the 14th international congress of phonetic sciences* (pp. 409–412).

Perkell, J. S., Cohen, M. H., Svirsky, M. A., Matthies, M. L., Garabieta, I., & Jackson, M. T. (1992). Electromagnetic midsagittal articulometer systems for transducing speech articulatory movements. *Journal of the Acoustical Society of America*, *92*, 3078–3096.

Perrier, P., Boë, L.-J., & Sock, R. (1992). Vocal tract area function estimation from midsagittal dimensions with CT scans and a vocal tract cast: Modelling the transition with two sets of coefficients. *Journal of Speech and Hearing Research*, *35*, 53–67.

Roy, J.-P. (2003). INTRIC, une interface de traitement d'images cinéradiographiques. *Travaux de l'Institut de Phonétique de Strasbourg (TIPS)*, *33*, 163–177.

Sock, R. (1999). *Organisation temporelle en production de la parole. Emergence de catégories sensori-motrices phonétiques*. Presses Universitaires du Septentrion. Collection Thèses à la carte, Villeneuve d'Ascq.

Sock, R., & Löfqvist, A. (1995). Quantity contrasts in Swedish: Kinematic and acoustic patterns. *XIIIth International congress of phonetic sciences* (pp. 580–583), Stockholm, 13–19, August.

Sock, R., Löfqvist, A., & Perrier, P. (1996). Kinematic and acoustic correlates of quantity in Swedish and Wolof: A cross-language study. *First European Speech Communication Association (ESCA) tutorial and research workshop*, Autrans-France (pp. 81–84).

16

Laryngeal Adjustments in the Production of Voiceless Obstruent Clusters in Berber

RACHID RIDOUANE, SUSANNE FUCHS, AND PHIL HOOLE

ABSTRACT

Laryngeal adjustments in voiceless obstruent clusters in Tashlhiyt Berber were examined by means of simultaneous transillumination, fibre-optic films and acoustic recordings. This language allows a rich variety of voiceless clusters naturally. Several combinations of /s/ and /k/ clusters including singleton and geminate consonants were examined. We focused on the number of glottal-opening gestures, the influence of manner of articulation and effects of word boundaries. Results of this study provide evidence that the manner of articulation of segments and their position in the clusters have a major impact both on the number and on the location of glottal abduction movements. Word boundaries did not influence laryngeal adjustment to the same extent.

INTRODUCTION

A number of studies have investigated laryngeal articulation in the production of voiceless consonant clusters in order to study coarticulation patterns at the laryngeal level. The first main objective of these works is to compare laryngeal adjustments observed in voiceless singleton obstruents with those attested in consonant clusters. A second objective is to understand the way laryngeal adjustments are coordinated with supralaryngeal events in complex sequences and the mechanisms, which might determine the number, amplitude, and location of glottal-opening gestures. Most of these studies used a similar methodology—photoelectroglottography combined with fibre optics—and a speech material consisting of different /s/-stop combinations. Germanic languages (English, German, Icelandic, and Swedish) are by far the most studied languages. Pétursson (1977), Fukui and Hirose (1983), and Jessen (1999), for example, observed glottal adjustment and the number of glottal abduction gestures in fricative-stop clusters in some of these languages. One general aspect that comes out from these studies is that laryngeal adjustments can be organized into one or more continuous opening and closing gestures.

In Pétursson (1977), Icelandic [s#t^h] and [s+t^h][1] clusters show two glottal-opening peaks whereas only one peak occurs in [#st] cluster. The author concludes that there are discrete phoneme commands for glottal abduction although the intervening boundary might have influenced the pattern too. In Fukui and Hirose (1983), the two-peakedness observed in Danish [s#p^h] clusters was rather speaker-dependent. One explanation of these differences could be that two different glottal abduction gestures are underlyingly present; in a fast speech-rate condition they overlap, whereas no overlap would be found in a slow speech-rate condition. Munhall and Löfqvist (1992) investigated this issue based on English [s#t^h] clusters and simulated gestural overlap as a sum of the two underlying movements. Their simulations fit the transillumination data with respect to timing characteristics, but differences were found concerning glottal-opening amplitudes. The simulations showed higher amplitudes than the experimental data. They explain these differences in terms of the non-calibration possibility of the transillumination technique as well as in terms of rate effects, which can decrease movement amplitudes. Jessen (1999) raised the question of whether the monomodal vs. bimodal distribution of glottal-opening movements would be an effect of the word boundary or whether aspiration of the stop in the fricative-stop cluster could explain the distinction. His findings drawn from German confirm the latter idea, initially based on results from Löfqvist and Yoshioka (1980a), and Yoshioka, Löfqvist, and Hirose (1981) on Swedish and English, respectively. These authors observed that glottal opening is characterized by one-, two-, or three-peaked patterns according to the nature of the voiceless obstruents and the way they are combined. Each voiceless obstruent or geminate accompanied by aspiration or frication noise tends to require a specific separate peak glottal opening. They interpret these independent glottal apertures as assuring the aerodynamic requirements for turbulent noise production during aspirated stops or fricative segments.

Laryngeal adjustments in voiceless obstruent production will be examined here in Berber voiceless clusters and compared to the organization of the laryngeal adjustment in other languages, mainly some of the Germanic languages mentioned above. We will present some general properties that appear to be commonly shared by speakers of different and unrelated languages.

Berber is an Afro-Asiatic language spoken in North Africa. Tashlhiyt Berber (henceforth TB), which is a variety of Berber analysed in this article is a dialect spoken in the Southern part of Morocco. Even if some variation is pervasive across the Tashlhiyt domain, it does not hinder mutual comprehension. TB uses both voicing and gemination distinctively. Both singleton and geminate velar and dental stops may be aspirated. Following a commonly accepted view, we consider a geminate as a single melodic unit associated with two prosodic positions (Clements & Keyser, 1983). Such a representation accounts for the dual behaviour of the geminate, which behaves in some respects as a consonant cluster and, in others, as a single consonant. Heteromorphemic geminates are a sequence of two identical segments separated by a morpheme boundary. They are generally homophonous with tautomorphemic geminates. In certain contexts, however, as is the case of /k#k/, the first velar stop may either be released or spirantized. Spirantization is an optional phonological process affecting simple noncoronal stops, which become fricatives (i.e., /k/ is realized as [x][2]). TB is of special interest in contributing to a better understanding of the organization of laryngeal adjustment, since this language allows an unusually rich combination of voiceless sounds, large series of voiceless words, and different types of geminates in initial, medial, and final positions (Ridouane, 2003).

The aim of this study is to improve our understanding of laryngeal adjustment in voiceless consonant cluster production and the mechanisms underlying the temporal coordination of laryngeal and oral articulations in sequential voiceless sounds. Our data can provide additional evidence for the interpretation that a static glottal-opening position of the glottis is unlikely to occur (e.g., Munhall & Löfqvist, 1992; Yoshioka et al., 1981), since we included combinations of up to six voiceless consonants in our data (various combinations of /s/ and /k/). In this study, we will focus on laryngeal adjustments during the production of different voiceless clusters and examine:

1. The influence of manner of articulation (stops and fricatives) or of gemination (tautomorphemic and heteromorphemic)
2. The effect of preceding, following, or intervening word boundaries
3. The presence or absence of aspiration in stops preceded by /s/.

METHOD

Two male native speakers of TB, RR, the first author, and RF were recorded by means of simultaneous transillumination (hereafter PGG), fibre-optic filming (hereafter FF), and acoustic recordings in the ZAS Laboratory in Berlin. A standard endoscope (Olympus ENF type P3) was inserted in the subject's pharynx and a photosensor was glued externally on the subject's neck. The endoscope was attached to a camera and connected to a video recorder with a monitor. The video images enabled the otorhinolaryngologist to control the position of the tip of the endoscope throughout the experiment. The video signals were taped to enable qualitative interpretation of the transillumination data. To provide the relevant amount of cold light for the tip of the endoscope, an external light source was attached to the endoscope.[3]

Acoustic and transillumination data have a sampling frequency of 24 kHz, PGG data were further downsampled to 200 Hz, and the FF data have the standard video format of 25 i/s. The velocity signal of the PGG signal was calculated as the first derivative. By analysing the velocity signal, we defined the beginning and end of glottal opening and closing using a 5% threshold criterion (i.e., the point where the signal crossed 5% of the corresponding movement segment). In the acoustic data, we labelled for /k/ closure onset (clon) as the second formant offset of the preceding vowel, burst (b), aspiration offset (aspoff) as the end of high-frequency energy, and for /s/ frication onset (fricon) and frication offset (fricoff).[4] An example of our data is presented in Figure 16.1. The top panel shows the acoustic waveform of the cluster /s#ks/. The second panel shows the glottographic pattern, which indicates the duration, degree, and number of glottal-opening peaks. The vertical axis shows the amount of light in arbitrary unit. In this figure, we can see that two glottal-opening peaks were produced, being located during the production of the two fricatives. The third panel indicates the velocity of glottal-opening and -closing gestures (i.e., the derivative of the transillumination data).

Both the transillumination technique and fibre-optic filming require a wide pharyngeal cavity, which was taken into consideration in selecting the linguistic material. The real word speech material consisted of several combinations of singleton and geminate /s/ and /k/ consonants. All the clusters were preceded and followed by the vowel /i/. Forms indicated in Table 16.1 were produced by two subjects (RR and RF). RR participated in two experimental sessions.[5] The results of the two sessions have been merged. The second subject (RF) participated in the second session. The number of repetitions for each subject is indicated between brackets, RR produced 160 tokens and RF 77 tokens. "#" indicates word boundary.

The number of glottal-opening peaks was calculated algorithmically as the number of (negative) zero crossings in the velocity signal. To guard against counting spuriously large numbers of local maxima (e.g., due to noise during periods of low velocity), we defined a noise band as 5% of the average peak velocity over all utterances (separately for each speaker), and only counted those zero crossings falling in movement segments that crossed this noise band above and below zero velocity. To obtain some further basic information on the shape

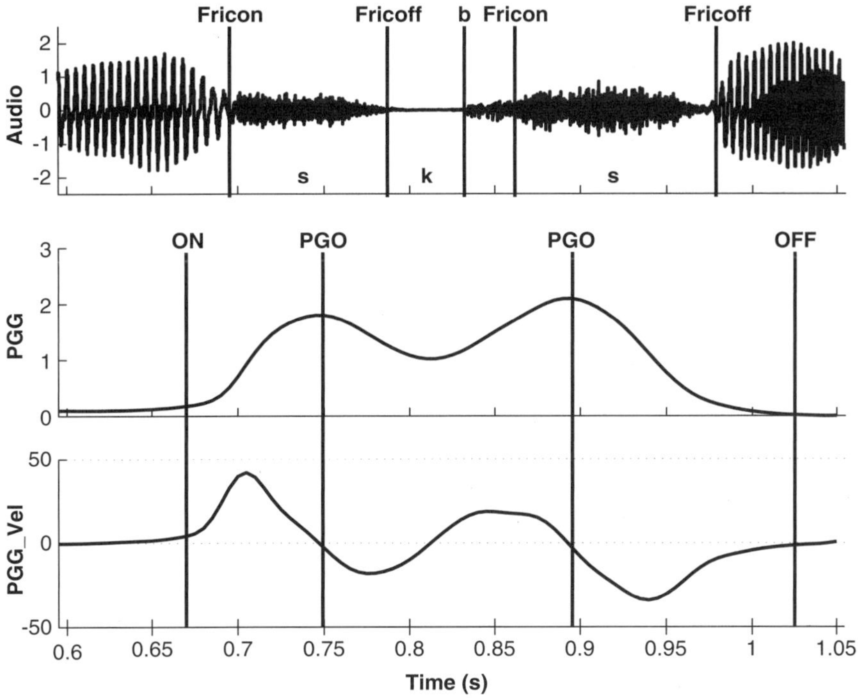

FIGURE 16.1. Example of defined time landmarks concerning acoustic and PGG data in /s#ks/. Fricon = frication onset, Fricoff = frication offset, b = burst; ON = glottal-opening onset, PGO = peak glottal opening, OFF = glottal-opening offset.

TABLE 16.1. The Linguistic Material

2 Consonants	3 Consonants	4 Consonants	5 Consonants	6 Consonants
#ks (10,5)	s#sk (3,-)	sk#sk (10,4)	ssk#kk (10,5)	ssk#ssk (7,4)
k#s (10,5)	ss#k (3,-)	ks#ks (7,5)	kk#skk (10,5)	ssk#skk (7,5)
ks# (10,5)	k#ks (3,-)	k#sks (7,5)		ssk#sks (7,5)
#sk (10,5)	kk#s (3,-)	k#kss (3,-)		
s#k (10,5)	s#ks (7,5)	kk#ss (3,-)		
sk# (10,5)	k#sk (7,4)	k#kks (3,-)		

Note. # marks a word boundary; numbers within parentheses indicate the number of repetitions, first value for subject RR and second value for subject RF.

of the glottal movements, we also counted the number of positive velocity peaks during opening movements and the number of negative velocity peaks in closing movements.[6] In the labelling of Figure 16.2, these velocity peak counts are referred to as "Vel. peaks (ab)" and "Vel. peaks (ad)", respectively (i.e., for abduction and adduction phases). The simplest movements are those in which

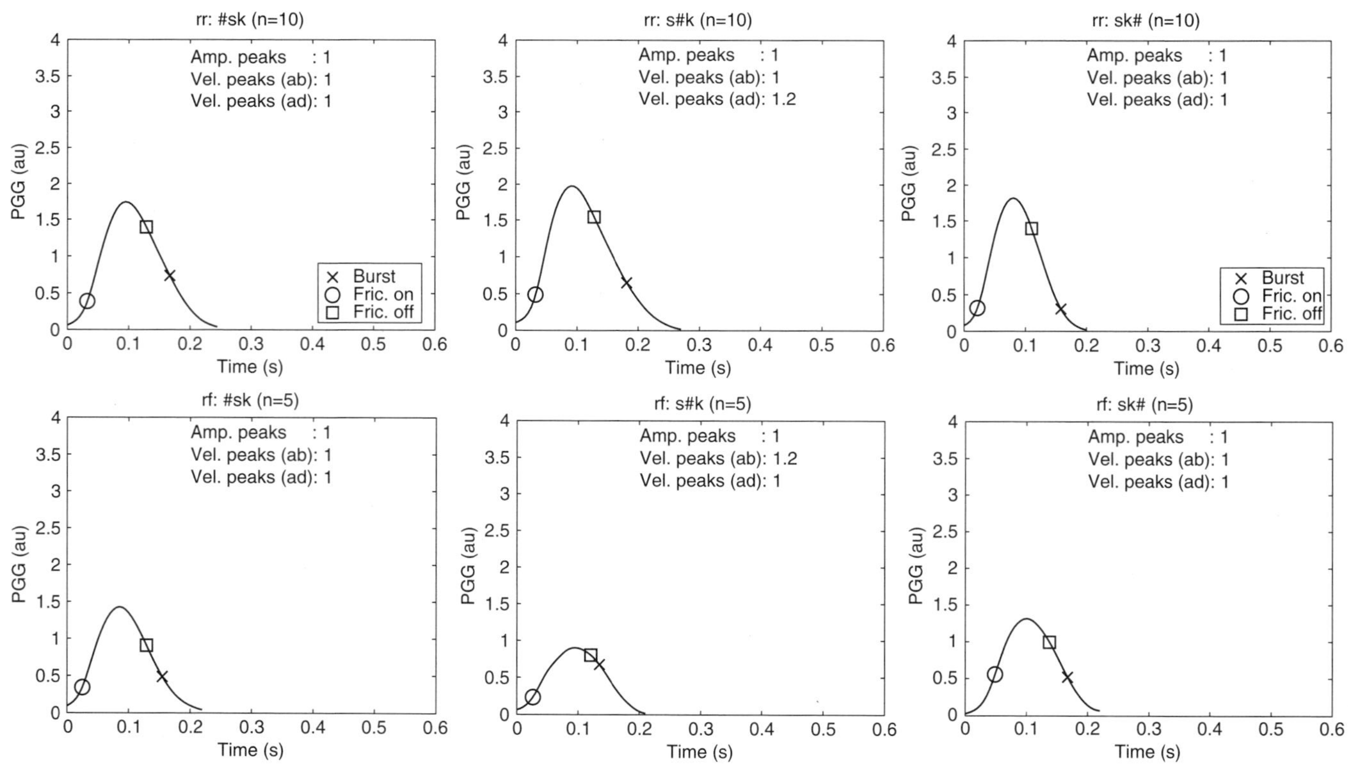

FIGURE 16.2. Averaged glottal abduction pattern for /sk/ clusters with different word boundary locations: #sk (left), s#k (middle), sk# (right), subject RR (top), subject RF (bottom). Circles correspond to frication onset, squares to frication offset for the fricatives, and crosses correspond to stop release. Each figure displays the number of amplitude peaks as well as the number of abduction and adduction velocity peaks. The number of repetitions of each sequence is indicated between parentheses.

each glottal-opening peak is associated with exactly one positive and one negative velocity peak. While there can never of course be less velocity maxima than amplitude maxima, if either the number of positive velocity maxima or negative velocity maxima exceeds the number of amplitude maxima, then this indicates a more complex—generally more gradual—movement pattern for abduction or adduction movements, respectively.

In Figure 16.2, which shows the movement pattern for each linguistic category, we have included the average counts of the amplitude and positive and negative velocity maxima. For clarity, we have omitted any measure of variability from the figures (e.g., standard deviation). In most cases, particularly for amplitude peaks, this information is redundant as it can be derived from the average peak counts. For example, a peak count of 1.1 with $n=10$ indicates nine tokens with one peak and one token with two peaks.

To generate plots of the average movement pattern for each utterance type, the transillumination signal was normalized with respect to both time and amplitude. For the time normalization, the average duration of each utterance type was calculated over the interval from the start to the termination of glottal abduction (ON to OFF in Figure 16.1), and then each individual token was time-warped to this duration.[7] Amplitude normalization was designed to take account of gross changes in signal gain, which may be caused, for example, by shifts in endoscope position over the course of the experiment. To this end, first, the minimum amplitude preceding glottal abduction in each item was subtracted from the signal, then the average signal amplitude between ON and OFF labels was calculated for all items in a block of repetitions, and the transillumination signal was then normalized by this value. Ensemble averages for each utterance type were then calculated from this time- and amplitude-normalized data. On the basis of the amplitude-normalized data, we believe that statistical comparison of glottal-opening amplitude between utterance types is justified if carried out cautiously, e.g., by using nonparametric tests.

RESULTS AND DISCUSSION

Clusters with Two Consonants

Results for two-consonant clusters are shown in Figures 16.2 and 16.3. Figure 16.2 shows clusters with /s/ in first position, while Figure 16.3 shows those with /k/ in first position. As can be seen from these figures, two-consonant clusters for both subjects exhibit a clear single-peaked pattern in the averaged traces regardless of the placement of word boundaries.[8] The peak almost always occurs during the fricative.

This is in agreement with results from Löfqvist and Yoshioka (1980a) based on data from Swedish language. Two different strategies can explain the

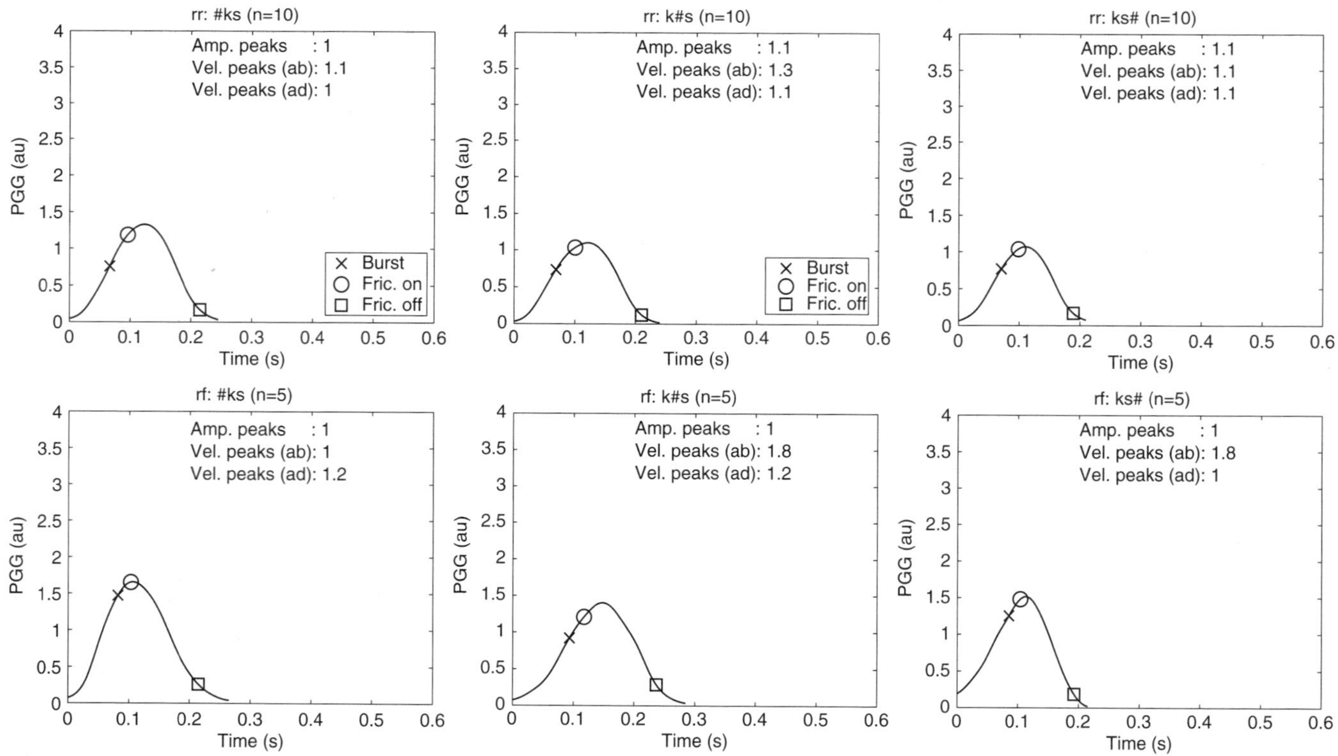

FIGURE 16.3. Averaged glottal abduction pattern for /ks/ clusters with different word boundary locations.

fact that the location of peak glottal opening follows the location of the fricative in the cluster. First, this is caused by aerodynamic conditions. The fricative requires a higher oral airflow than the stop and hence the peak glottal abduction occurs during the /s/. Second, this might be caused by two underlying glottal-opening gestures which overlap—a larger one for /s/ and a smaller one for /k/. This latter view is advocated by Munhall and Löfqvist (1992) on the basis of an experimental exploration of gestural aggregation, showing that such clusters consist underlyingly of two gestures. For Browman and Goldstein (1986), the single-peaked glottal opening observed in word initial fricative-stop clusters is a phonological regularity of syllable-initial position in English, suggesting that the single peak is a property of the whole syllable onset. They capture the relevant timing of laryngeal–oral coordination in the following rule:

If a fricative gesture is present, coordinate the peak glottal opening with the midpoint of the fricative. Otherwise, coordinate the peak glottal opening with the release of the stop gesture.

This rule, tested over various voiceless clusters in different languages, does not appear to be completely accurate (see Hoole et al., 2004). Berber material also shows that the peak glottal opening is not systematically coordinated with the midpoint of the fricative. The generalization that can be drawn from our data is that peak glottal opening is almost always located within the fricative both for stop-fricative and for fricative-stop sequences. The timing of this opening peak tends to shift to a relatively earlier point in the fricative when it follows a stop (at 23.49% of the fricative) and to a later point in the fricative when it precedes a stop (at 66.06% of the fricative), regardless of the word boundary location. Figure 16.4 illustrates these timing patterns for each subject.

Contrary to what has been observed in different languages (e.g., English and Swedish), in TB, /k/ can be acoustically aspirated after /s/ whether separated or

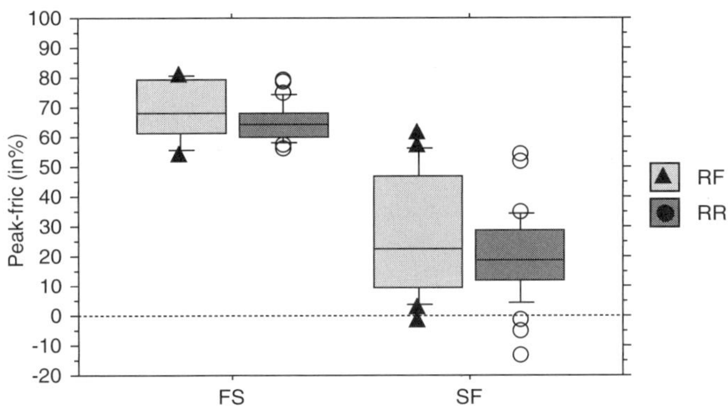

FIGURE 16.4. Timing of peak glottal opening during the fricative in two-consonant clusters: fricative+stop (FS) and stop+fricative (SF) sequences. Results are presented as a percentage of the total fricative duration (on the y-axis).

not by a word boundary. Previous work (e.g., as summarized by Löfqvist, 1980) suggests that typically each fricative and aspirated plosive require a separate laryngeal peak. In Swedish (Löfqvist & Yoshioka, 1980a) and English (Yoshioka et al., 1981), a sequence of voiceless fricative + voiceless aspirated stop usually contain two separate peak glottal openings located during the fricative and just before stop release. In TB, this generalization has to be qualified since, interestingly, the language shows aspirated plosives following fricatives in initial position, but nevertheless the results, as illustrated in Figure 16.2, make clear that only one opening peak occurs.

This pattern may well be related to the fact that voiceless geminates also show aspiration—in fact a very similar amount of aspiration to the singleton consonants. It was shown in Ridouane (2003) that aspiration duration, based on an acoustic study for seven subjects, is not a significant criterion for distinguishing between singleton and geminate stops.[9] Both are produced with virtually identical aspiration durations. For dentals aspiration duration varies between 45 and 65 ms for singletons and between 35 and 50 ms for geminates. For velars, aspiration duration varies between 45 and 70 ms for singletons and between 45 and 65 ms for geminates.

A photoelectroglottographic study, based on one subject, showed however important differences between singletons and geminates both in terms of timing and amplitude of glottal opening (c.f. Ridouane, 2003). The maximum glottal opening, measured in arbitrary units, shows clearly that geminates are systematically produced with larger glottal opening than singletons. The interval between peak glottal opening and oral release is longer for geminates than for single stops. For dentals, this interval varies between 0 and 10 ms for singletons and between 55 and 120 ms for geminates. For velars, the interval varies between –10 and 20 ms for singletons and between 55 and 70 ms for geminates.

Laryngeal abduction for geminates is much larger in amplitude and longer in overall duration compared to singletons. However, the glottal opening at stop release appears to be similar for both. Figure 16.5, which is arranged so as to show the glottal opening of a minimal pair involving a geminate and a singleton stop, shows that the size of glottal opening at stop release is nearly identical for both singletons and geminates which may thus explain the fact that aspiration duration for both stops is virtually identical.

Löfqvist (1980) has argued rather persuasively for the importance of laryngeal–oral timing in contrasting aspirated and unaspirated plosives, but the present results for TB provide a striking example of the contrary phenomenon, namely radically different timing patterns (of peak glottal opening relative to closure release) leading to similar degrees of aspiration duration. One might speculate that the somewhat atypical aspiration in initial fricative-plosive clusters is using the same timing pattern that has emerged for the geminates, suggesting that aspiration, as was defined by Kim (1970), is essentially a function of the degree of glottal opening at stop release.

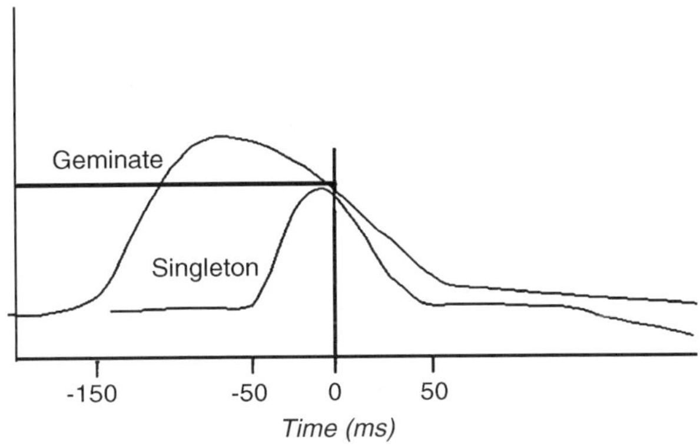

FIGURE 16.5. Illustration of the glottal opening during the production of the stops in [ittili] and [itili]. The vertical bar indicates the onset of oral release (adapted from Ridouane, 2003).

Clusters with Three Consonants

Tautomorphemic vs. Heteromorphemic Geminates. Figure 16.6 contains the glottographic patterns of three-consonant clusters produced by RR. These clusters are composed of two types of geminates, tautomorphemic and heteromorphemic ones. As was outlined above, one of the main topics of this study was to determine the possible influence of gemination on glottal adjustments. Comparisons between /kk#s/ and /k#s/ (middle column of Figure 16.3) on the one hand and between /ss#k/ and /s#k/ (middle column of Figure 16.2) on the other show that all these clusters are always produced with one peak glottal opening. This suggests that the presence of a geminate, instead of a singleton, is not accompanied with an additional separate laryngeal peak. There is some increase in movement complexity; however, the opening phase of /kk#s/ and the closing phase of /ss#k/ are rather gradual (indicated by velocity peak counts of 1.67 for the former and 1.33 for the latter). A major difference is nonetheless worth noting. The cluster with the velar geminate stop is systematically produced with larger glottal-opening amplitude than the singleton counterpart, in fact approximately double on the basis of the ensemble averages.[10] This seems to correspond to a systematic difference, as already mentioned above, observed between singleton and geminate stops in intervocalic position. By contrast, peak amplitude is practically identical for the singleton and geminate fricatives.[11]

The comparison between tautomorphemic and heteromorphemic geminates indicates that the number and the location of peak glottal opening vary according to the phonetic nature of the voiceless obstruents and the way they are combined. The glottographic patterns for the form with the velar tautomorphemic geminate /kk#s/ show that the peak glottal opening is most often

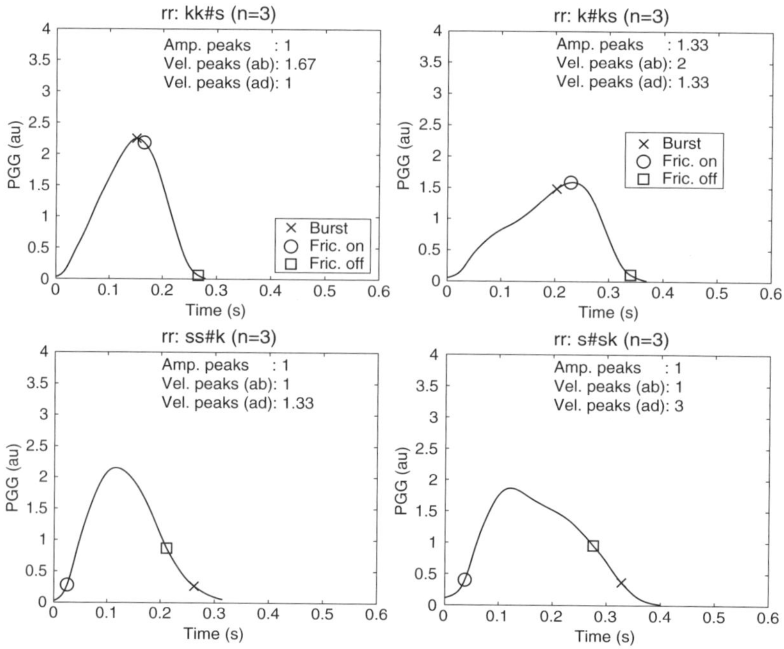

FIGURE 16.6. Averaged glottal abduction pattern for /kk#s/, /k#ks/ (top row), and /ss#k/, /s#sk/ (bottom row) produced by one subject (RR).

located during the geminate (towards the burst). The three realizations of the form /k#ks/ were not produced with the same number of amplitude peaks. One repetition was realized with two glottal openings, and two repetitions were realized with only one. A closer examination of the three repetitions shows that for the bimodal realization, the first velar was pronounced as a fricative [x]; the additional peak was thus located during this first velar fricative.[12] This configuration, as we shall show in the following section, is identical to the one attested in the three-phone combinations where the first segment and the third are dental fricatives. Regardless of the number of observable amplitude peaks, all repetitions of /k#ks/ had two velocity peaks on the opening phase, which, accordingly, is much more gradual than the closing phase.

/ss#k/ and /s#sk/ are similar to the extent that both sequences always have only one amplitude peak. Peak glottal opening for /ss#k/ is always located during the geminate /ss/. The cluster with a heteromorphemic geminate /s#sk/, produced with an uninterrupted frication noise during the two fricatives, is also produced with only one large glottal opening located during the geminate fricative. The two sequences differ in that the closing phase is longer for /s#sk/ (which has three velocity peaks, compared to a count of 1.33 for /ss#k/).

Overall, one might say that there is some indication for greater movement complexity in the heteromorphemic compared to the tautomorphemic sequences, the former having a greater number of velocity peaks.

Clusters without Geminates. Figure 16.7 compares two three-phone combinations /s#ks/ and /k#sk/. Looking first at /s#ks/ (right panels, Figure 16.7), one finds a very clear two-peaked pattern for RR. Word final /s/ in /s#ks/ is produced with a single opening peak and word initial /ks/ is produced with another one. Again, peak glottal abduction is always located during the fricatives. The same configuration was also observed for identical clusters in Swedish (Löfqvist & Yoshioka, 1980a), Icelandic (Löfqvist & Yoshioka, 1980b), and American English (Yoshioka et al., 1981). The glottis is only slightly adducted without complete closure between the two opening maxima. This transitory glottal-closing movement is not necessarily a consequence of a pause due to a word boundary. No specific opening gesture is observed for the velar stop /k/. This segment is rather produced within the closing phase of the glottal gesture for the preceding fricative and within the opening phase for the following /s/ segment.

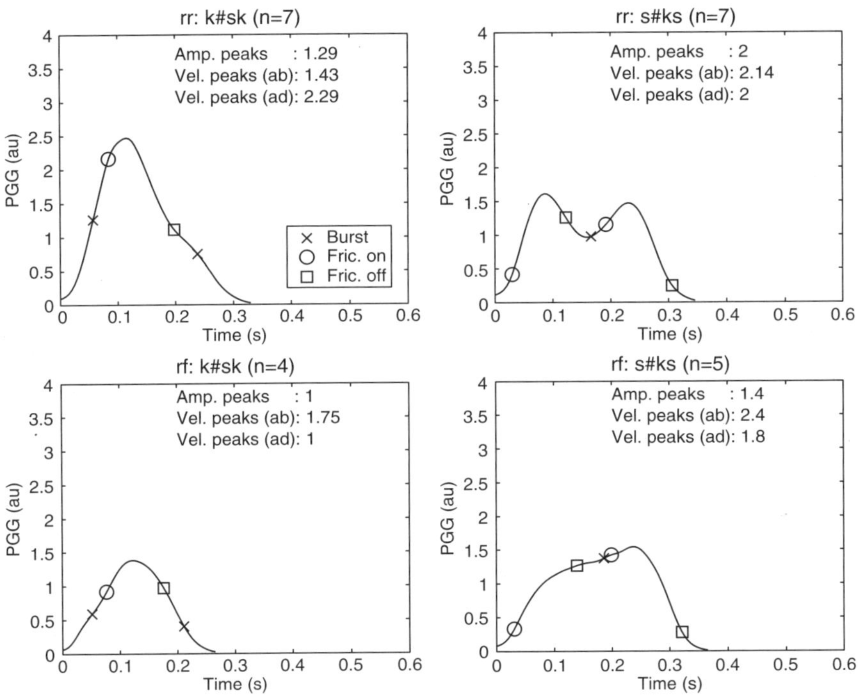

FIGURE 16.7. Averaged glottal abduction pattern for /k#sk/ and /s#ks/.

The pattern for RF is at first sight more ambiguous: The amplitude peak count of 1.4 indicates that two repetitions were monomodal and three bimodal. Closer inspection indicates that the monomodal patterns had shorter durations. Taking into account that the velocity peak counts are very close to 2 for both opening and closing, this suggests that an underlyingly bimodal amplitude pattern changes into a monomodal one as the duration of the cluster decreases. This seems to correspond to what has been observed by Löfqvist and Yoshioka (1980b) in their analysis of voiceless clusters in Icelandic. For the production of the Icelandic sequence [s#sp], for example, where the duration is less than 300 ms, there is only a single glottal-opening movement. For the longer productions two glottal-opening movements occur during the cluster.

On average, the /k#sk/ cluster is realized with one single opening peak located during the /s/ for both subjects as is shown in Figure 16.7. Only two repetitions out of seven for RR were realized with two peak glottal openings, one during the fricative /s/ and the second during the following velar consonant. Closer examination of the phonetic nature of these bimodal forms shows that this velar consonant was also produced as a fricative [x] in both cases, presumably thus favouring two peaks.[13]

Clusters with Four to Six Consonants

Figure 16.8 contains the glottographic patterns of the three clusters /sk#sk/, /ks#ks/, and /k#sks/. All these sequences contain two dental fricatives. They are most often produced with two glottal-opening peaks located during these two fricatives.

These results are, once again, in accordance with results drawn from various languages. Yoshioka et al. (1981), for instance, observed that American English fricative + stop + fricative + stop sequences were also produced with two peak glottal openings located during the fricatives. The same laryngeal adjustments were produced during the Icelandic sequence [st#sp] (Löfqvist & Yoshioka, 1980b). Similar configurations observed in different unrelated languages provide a striking illustration of the tight temporal coordination of laryngeal and oral articulations in voiceless obstruent production: A sequence with two nonadjacent fricatives is most of the time produced with two glottal-opening gestures. Another important observation is that /ks#ks/ and /k#sks/ are produced with virtually the same laryngeal adjustments for both subjects, showing once again that word boundaries are quite transparent as far as laryngeal gestures are concerned.

Figure 16.9 firstly compares two similar four-phone combinations with different word boundary locations: /k#kss/ (left panel) and /kk#ss/ (middle panel). These clusters are produced with only one glottal-opening peak achieved during the fricative. This always held true despite the placement of the word

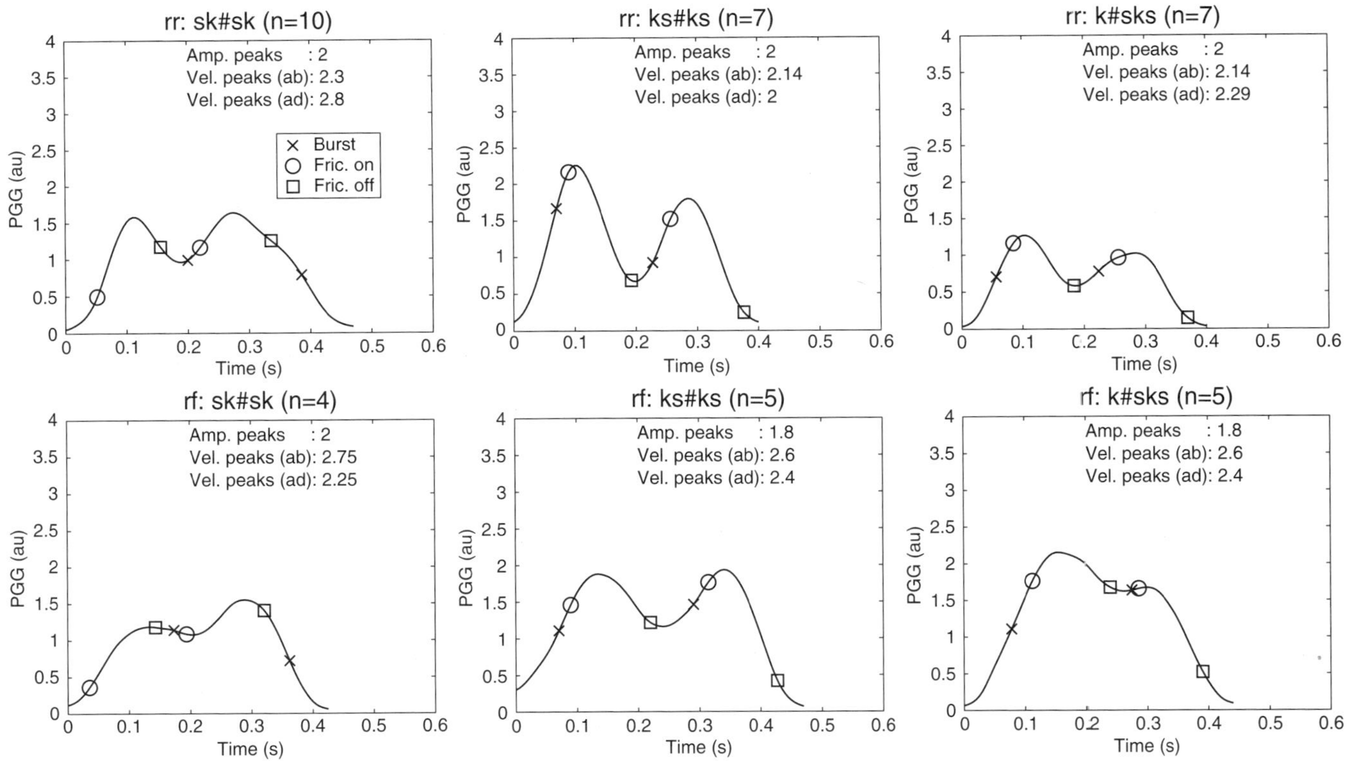

FIGURE 16.8. Averaged glottal abduction pattern for /sk#sk/, /ks#ks/, and /k#sks/.

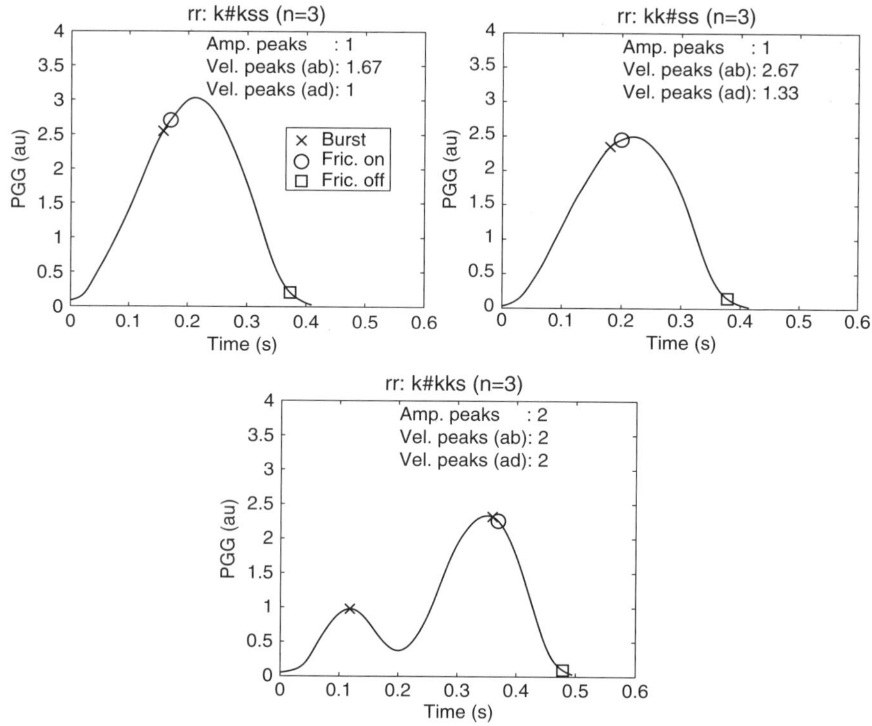

FIGURE 16.9. Averaged glottal abduction pattern for /k#kss/, /kk#ss/, and /k#kks/ produced by one subject (RR).

boundary and despite some slight differences in the number of velocity peaks in the opening and closing phases. Compared to the three-consonant clusters /kk#s/ and /k#ks/ (see Figure 16.6, top left and right, respectively), these clusters exhibit quite similar movements but the location of the peak shifts slightly more into the fricative in the sequences with geminate fricatives. The comparison here between Figures 16.9 and 16.6 also in effect compares geminate with singleton fricatives. It was already mentioned that geminate fricatives do not increase the glottal-opening amplitude as much as geminate plosives do (compared to corresponding singletons). Here, too, there is not much indication that fricative gemination results in a strong increase in amplitude. /k#kss/ does not appear larger than /k#ks/ but the small number of tokens effectively precludes statistical testing.[14]

/k#kss/ and /kk#ss/, as realized here by RR, are homophonous, both forms being produced with a long closure duration followed by a release, i.e., in the first half of the heteromorphemic geminate the oral closure was maintained and the release follows in the second half of the geminate. Similar pronunciations are not produced in adjacent identical consonant sequences in which one segment is a geminate (e.g., /k#kk/ or /kk#k/). In such sequences, the geminate stop must be released and the singleton is either produced as a released stop or, if the optional spirantization rule operates, as a spirant. The sequence /k#kk/, for example, is phonetically distinct from /kk/, the first singleton velar being produced either as a stop or as a fricative (i.e., [x#kk]). This latter pronunciation was the one produced during the three realizations of /k#kks/ (bottom panel, Figure 16.9). These forms are always produced with two glottal-opening peaks, the first being generally produced during the fricative [x] and the second either during the burst of the geminate /kk/ or at the onset of the fricative /s/.

Figure 16.10 contains clusters of five consonants. The sequence /ssk#kk/ (right panels) is produced either with two or three glottal abduction gestures. The first peak is always produced during the dental fricative /ss/. RR produced seven repetitions with three peak glottal openings and three repetitions with two peaks. The second peak in the bimodal productions is always located during the closure of the geminate stop /kk/. The third peak in the trimodal production is

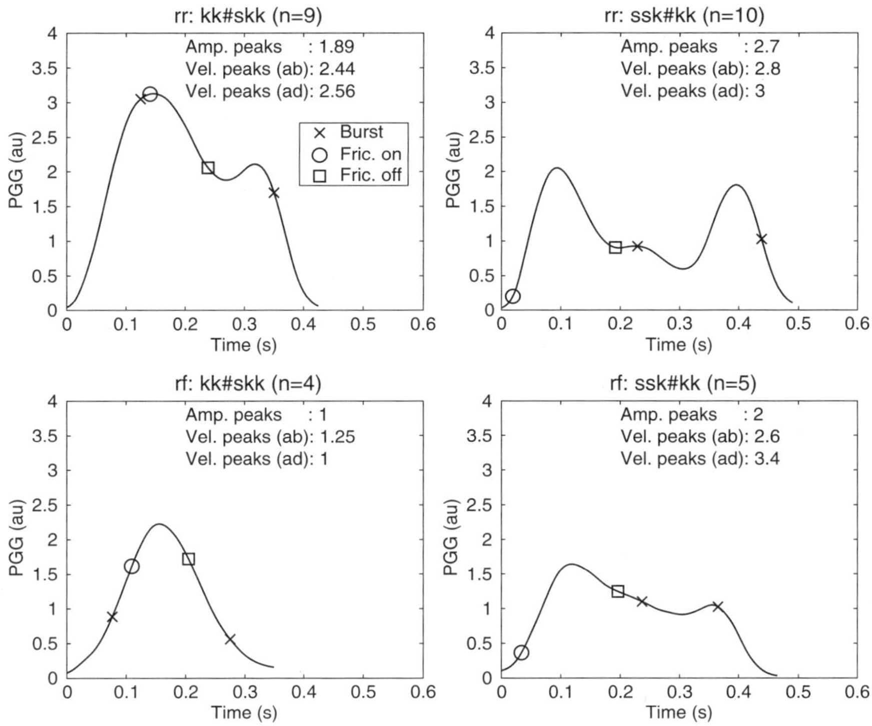

FIGURE 16.10. Averaged glottal abduction pattern for /kk#skk/ and /ssk#kk/.

located during the singleton velar segment, generally realized as a spirant [x]. RF always produced this cluster with a bimodal gesture. The second peak is either realized during the spirantized singleton velar stop [x] (in one repetition) or during the occlusion of the geminate stop /kk/.

The glottographic pattern of the /kk#skk/ cluster (left panels) also varies according to the subjects. For RR, the overall pattern shows two amplitude peaks. The second peak is rather weak, and in two cases only one peak was detected based on our criteria. In one case, a very weak third peak was detected. The velocity peak counts are consistent with the idea that the basic pattern has two glottal-opening movements, but with both opening and closing being somewhat more gradual than in the simplest two-peaked patterns. The first opening peak was located roughly at the boundary between the first geminate and the following fricative, the second peak during the second geminate.[15]

All the realizations of RF, by contrast, are characterized by one opening gesture. A closer examination of this monomodal pattern reveals that this configuration is presumably related to the very short closure duration for the two velar geminates. Peak glottal opening is always located during the fricative /s/. This was thus the linguistically longest sequence in our material with a clearly monomodal pattern.

The glottographic patterns for the six-consonant clusters are presented in Figure 16.11. For /ssk#ssk/ (left panels) the clearly predominant pattern for both subjects is for two glottal-opening peaks, located during the first and second geminate fricatives, respectively (note, however, that both opening and closing velocity peak counts are well above two for both subjects). The movement pattern for this 6-consonant sequence is quite similar to the corresponding singleton pattern /sk#sk/ in the left panels of Figure 16.8. In the longer sequence, however—with the usual caveat because of the small number of tokens—there was significantly greater opening amplitude for both subjects for the sequence containing geminate fricatives—perhaps because the double change from singleton to geminate has an amplifying effect.

The remaining sequences /ssk#skk/ and /ssk#sks/ exhibit much variability even within the same subject. Taking the simplest case first, namely /ssk#skk/ for RF, it is observed that this has a fairly clear two-peaked pattern. The most instructive sequence for comparison is once again /sk#sk/ from Figure 16.8 (i.e., reducing each geminate to a singleton). The overall movement pattern is very similar, supported by similar peak counts for amplitude and velocity, and there is a similar location of the opening peaks in the fricative segments. The linguistically longer sequence simply, and not surprisingly, has longer duration (464 ms for the longer sequences and 360 ms for the shorter on average) and also significantly greater opening amplitude. For RR, on the other hand, inspection of the curve as well as the high values for all the peak counts indicates substantially more movement complexity in this sequence than in either /ssk#ssk/ just discussed above, or the comparison singleton sequence /sk#sk/.

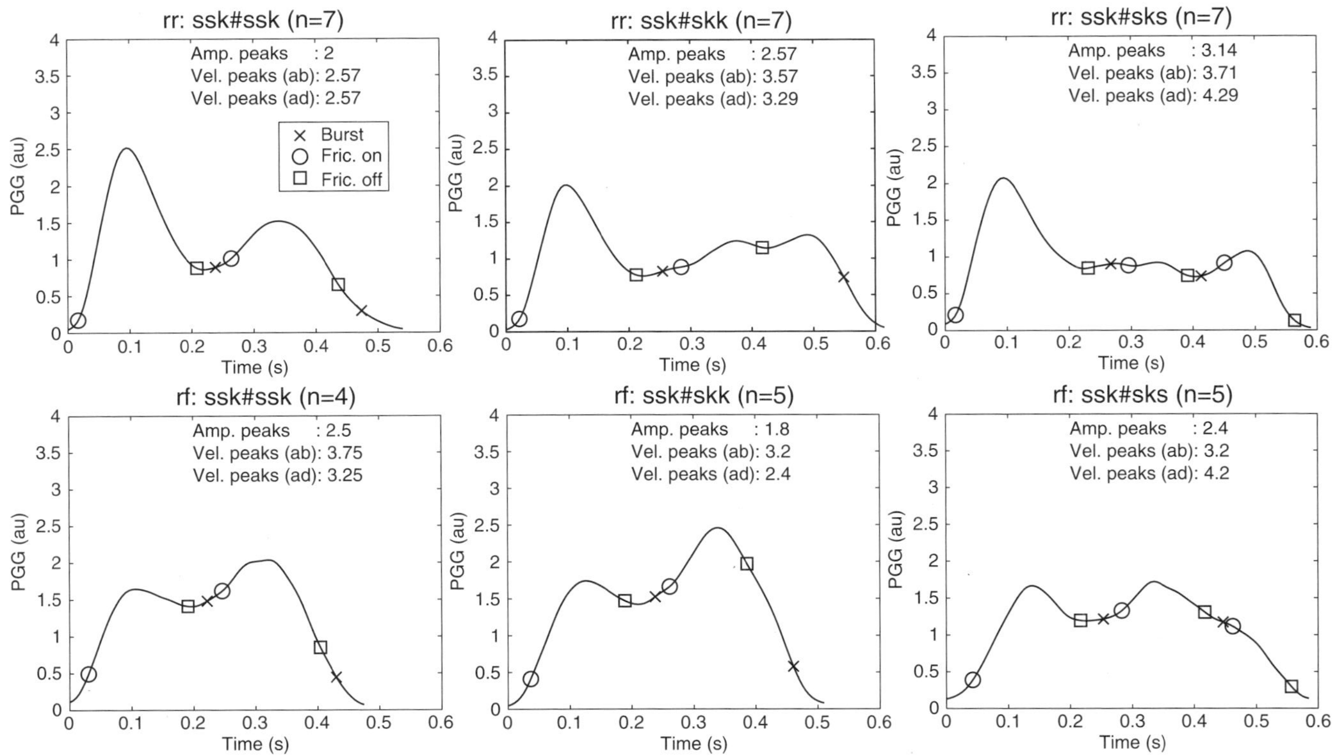

FIGURE 16.11. Averaged glottal abduction pattern for /ssk#ssk/, /ssk#skk/, and /ssk#sks/.

Turning finally to /ssk#sks/, this is the sequence where greatest movement complexity might be expected as it is the only sequence in the material with three separate fricative segments. By and large, this expectation is borne out. RR had a clear preference for three opening peaks, quite clearly associated with each of the three fricative segments (albeit rather different in amplitude). This was the only occasion in the whole material where the mean amplitude peak count went above three (caused by one exception where four peaks occurred). For RF the amplitude peak count was more evenly balanced: three repetitions with two peaks, and two repetitions with three. In the averaged trace, peaks are found associated with the first two fricative segments. For both subjects, the complexity of the movement pattern is made clear by the very high count for closing velocity peaks (4.29 for RR and 4.2 for RF), which is substantially higher than for any other sequence.

CONCLUSION

The main results of the present study are in general agreement with those obtained from some Germanic languages. We thus have further evidence from different unrelated languages that laryngeal activity during the production of voiceless obstruent clusters is organized in one, two, or more glottal-opening peaks. The manner of articulation of obstruents and their position in the clusters have a major impact on the number of glottal-opening peaks and their locations. A major generalization that comes out from this study is that sequences produced with *n* fricative segments are most often produced with *n* peak glottal openings; these peak glottal openings are located during the production of these fricatives. In other words, segments produced with a high rate of oral airflow are produced with a separate laryngeal-opening gesture. Geminates, mainly stops, are usually produced with larger glottal amplitude than their singleton counterparts. But the presence of a geminate in a cluster, instead of a singleton, is not accompanied with an additional separate laryngeal peak, although the geminate sequences exhibit an increase in movement complexity (i.e., the opening and closing phases during these sequences are rather gradual).

Another topic of interest in this article was to determine if there are laryngeal correlates of word boundaries. From the data analysed here, it appears that when a word boundary is marked by a long silent pause, it is associated with glottal adduction. According to Löfqvist and Yoshioka (1980a), such an adduction gesture is made to prevent airflow and waste of air during an ongoing utterance. Another possible interpretation would be that word boundaries are in themselves accompanied by glottal adduction. TB material, however, shows that glottal adduction is not necessarily associated with linguistic boundaries. Recall that adduction gestures are usually found in clusters without apparent word boundaries. Another piece of evidence showing that word boundaries are transparent as far as laryngeal gestures are concerned is illustrated by the numerous cases where two clusters with two different word boundary locations are often produced with similar laryngeal adjustments. Glottal adduction found in these sequences seems better ascribed to segmental properties.

In addition to TB, other languages present aspirated stops after /s/. The absence of aspiration in such segments is thus not a universal phonetic feature, contrary to what was assumed by Lindqvist (1972). Pétursson (1976) cited cases observed in some Indian languages as well as in some Colombian Spanish dialects. This aspiration is rather exceptional, not only because it is not attested in the most widely studied languages, but also, at least in the case of TB, because it seems totally independent of word boundaries. The TB case is thus typologically interesting, making it possible to determine the two possible laryngeal mechanisms accounting for stop aspiration after /s/: on the one hand, a large amplitude and a delay in peak glottal opening relative to fricative onset; on the other, two peak glottal openings, each corresponding to one of the two obstruents. The second realization is the one produced in /s/-stop heteromorphemic sequences in some Germanic languages. In sum, different combinations of interarticulatory timing and glottal-opening size can result in similar amounts of aspiration.

Löfqvist and Yoshioka (1980a, p. 800) in their analysis of long voiceless consonant clusters noted that: "There is little, if any evidence that the glottis ever opens and maintains a static open position in speech." TB material, which included up to six voiceless consonant clusters, provides further evidence that the glottis does not simply remain open for voiceless utterances. These results can be combined with those obtained from an earlier study on TB voiceless words (Ridouane, 2004). Here the whole utterances, which contain up to 10 obstruents, were voiceless, and one might have expected that the devoicing gesture might be regarded as superfluous and simply eliminated, leaving the glottis in respiratory position. However, just as in the present experiment, the results showed clearly that the glottal aperture is continuously modulated in a manner that can be related quite systematically to the individual segments in the voiceless sequence. This gives a compelling demonstration of how intimately laryngeal and supralaryngeal articulations are linked.

ACKNOWLEDGMENTS

We would like to thank Dr. Klaus Dahlmeier for his expertise during the transillumination recording, Jörg Dreyer for technical support, and Christine Mooshammer for help with post-processing of the data. This work was supported by a grant from the German Research Council (DFG) GWZ 4/8-1, P.1.

NOTES

1. [#] and [+] symbols indicate word and morpheme boundaries, respectively.
2. In our transcriptions, forms enclosed between slashed lines are intended to represent the underlying structure of these forms. When a form has a phonetic output different from its underlying structure, the phonetic form is enclosed between brackets.

3. Detailed discussion on the transillumination procedure and the factors affecting its reliability is given in Hoole (1999).
4. The labelling of the acoustic data was done by visual and perceptual inspection of the signals and spectrograms.
5. The second experiment took place in Berlin about a year after the first one.
6. This was done analogously to the amplitude peaks by counting zero crossings in the acceleration signal.
7. One item was excluded from this procedure as being highly untypical (one repetition of /kk#skk/ with a duration more than 50% longer than the average duration).
8. The mean count of amplitude peaks indicates only two tokens that did not conform to the overall pattern: one token each of /k#s/ and /ks#/ for speaker RR.
9. For dentals and velars. TB lacks voiceless bilabial stops. The other voiceless stops (the dental emphatic and the uvular and their geminate counterparts) are not aspirated.
10. A nonparametric test of this difference proved highly significant, though note that we have only three tokens for the geminate.
11. The absence of systematic differences in terms of laryngeal amplitude between singleton and geminate fricatives has also been observed in Ridouane (2003), where intervocalic labiodental and dental singletons were compared to their geminate counterparts.
12. The symbol indicating the burst for stops is maintained for forms realized as aspirants. In this case, the symbol indicates the offset of the velar consonant.
13. This displays the same pattern observed in some repetitions of /k#ks/ discussed above. Note also that all /k#sk/ repetitions for RR are characterized by a very gradual closing phase, with a high number of velocity peaks.
14. If /k#kss/ and /kk#ss/ are merged to a geminate group, and /k#ks/ and /kk#s/ to a singleton group (with six tokens in each group), no significant difference in amplitude is found.
15. One of the 10 repetitions of this form by RR was not included in the average curve or the peak counts. The first repetition of the five recorded by RF was not considered further as it was much longer than the others (720 ms instead of 280 ms for the other realizations which are also shorter than expected probably due to degemination). The longer duration of this form is due to a long silent pause maintained during the word boundary. This silent pause was associated with clear glottal adduction (without complete closure).

REFERENCES

Browman, C. P., & Goldstein, L. (1986). Towards an articulatory phonology. *Phonology Yearbook*, *3*, 219–252.

Clements, G. N., & Keyser, S. J. (1983). *CV phonology: A generative theory of the syllable*. Cambridge, MA: The MIT Press.

Fukui, N., & Hirose, H. (1983). Laryngeal adjustments in Danish voiceless obstruent production. *Annual Report of the Institute of Phonetics, University of Copenhagen*, *17*, 61–71.

Hoole, P. (1999). Techniques for investigating laryngeal articulation. Section A: Investigation of the devoicing gesture. In W. Hardcastle & N. Hewlett (Eds.), *Coarticulation: Theory, data and techniques* (pp. 294–300). Cambridge: Cambridge University Press.

Hoole, P., Fuchs, S., & Dahlmeier, K. (2004). Interarticulator timing in initial consonant clusters. In S. Palethorpe & M. Tabain (Eds.) *Proceedings of the 6th international seminar on speech production*, Macquarie University, Sydney, Australia (pp. 101–106).

Jessen, M. (1998). Word boundary marking at the glottal level in the production of German obstruents. In A. Alexiadou, N. Fuhrop, U. Kleinhenz, & P. Law (Eds.), *Papers on Morphology and Phonetics. ZAS Papers in Linguistics*, *11*(9), 147–166.

Kim, C.-W. (1970). A theory of aspiration. *Phonetica*, *21*, 107–116.

Lindqvist, J. (1972). *Laryngeal articulation studied on Swedish subjects*. Quarterly Progress and Status Report, Speech Transmission Laboratory (Vol. 2/3, pp. 10–27). Royal Institute of Technology, Stockholm.

Löfqvist, A. (1980). Interarticulator programming in stop production. *Journal of Phonetics*, *8*, 475–490.

Löfqvist, A., & Yoshioka, H. (1980a). Laryngeal activity in Swedish obstruent clusters. *Journal of the Acoustical Society of America*, *68*(3), 792–801.

Löfqvist, A., & Yoshioka, H. (1980b). Laryngeal activity in Icelandic obstruent production. *Haskins Laboratories: Status Report on Speech Research*, *SR-63/64*, 275–292.

Munhall, K., & Löfqvist, A. (1992). Gestural aggregation in speech: Laryngeal gestures. *Journal of Phonetics*, *20*, 111—126.

Pétursson, M. (1976). Aspiration et activité glottale [Aspiration and glottal activity]. *Phonetica*, 33, 169–198.

Pétursson, M. (1977). Timing of glottal events in the production of aspiration after /s/. *Journal of Phonetics*, 5, 205—212.

Ridouane, R. (2003). *Suite de consonnes en berbère: phonétique et phonologie* [*Consonant clusters in Berber: Phonetics and phonology*]. Thèse de Doctorat, Université Paris III.

Ridouane, R. (2004). Les mots sourds en berbère chleuh: analyses fibroscopiques et photoglottographiques. Actes des **25**[e] Journées d'Etudes sur la Parole. In B. Bel & I. Marlien (Eds.), Fès, Maroc (pp. 425–428).

Yoshioka, H., Löfqvist, A., & Hirose, H. (1981). Laryngeal adjustment in the production of consonant clusters and geminates in American English. *Journal of the Acoustical Society of America*, *70*(6), 1615—1623.

PART 3

TECHNIQUES

17

Assessing Magnetic Resonance Imaging Measurements

Effects of Sustenation, Gravitation, and Coarticulation

OLOV ENGWALL

ABSTRACT

Magnetic resonance imaging (MRI) is well suited for studying the three-dimensional (3-D) shape of the vocal tract and tongue. However, when MRI is used for speech production measurements, it does not measure normal speech, as the subject lies in supine position and often has to sustain the articulation artificially due to very long acquisition times. In this chapter, MRI is used to estimate the effects of the sustained articulation. Coarticulation in real-time and sustained articulations are compared in particular. The subject was further positioned facing downwards during one part of the acquisition in order to evaluate the effect of gravitation. Finally, a 3-D tongue model, derived from sustained articulations was tested regarding its ability to replicate real-time midsagittal tongue contours.

INTRODUCTION

Ever since Rokkaku, Hashimoto, Imaizumi, Niimi, and Kiritani (1986) proposed to apply magnetic resonance imaging (MRI) to analyze speech production, it has been used widely to study three-dimensional (3-D) articulations in many different languages: English (e.g., Baer, Gore, Gracco, &

Nye, 1991; Story, Titze, & Hoffman, 1996); French (e.g., Apostol, Perrier, Raybaudi, & Segebarth, 1999; Badin, Bailly, Revéret, Baciu, Segebarth, & Savariaux, 2002); Japanese (e.g., Matsumura, Niikawa, Shimizu, Hashimoto, & Morita, 1994); Norwegian (Foldvik, Kristiansen, & Kvaerness, 1993), etc. The popularity of MRI in speech production research is a result of several qualities of the method. One is that as MRI has no known harmful side effects for the subject, no ethical constraints need to be put on the amount of data that can be collected. Another is that images can be collected in arbitrarily oriented, approximately two-dimensional (2-D) slices, which means that 3-D shapes can be reconstructed with a high level of detail. The method is, moreover, less obtrusive on the subject's articulations than electropalatography (EPG), electromagnetic articulography (EMA), or X-ray microbeam, as no special measurement equipment is needed inside the vocal tract.

MRI consequently provides researchers with unique possibilities for gathering articulatory data. The technique has, however, several disadvantages for speech production measurements as well, such as the high-amplitude noise that makes sound recordings difficult, the long acquisition times and the supine position of the subject. This chapter aims to give an indication of the effects of the latter two by comparing MRI data for one reference subject collected using different measurement protocols. As only one subject was used, it would be premature to claim that the observations below are universal, but they, nevertheless, point out issues that should be considered when using MRI in speech production research.

The problem of using measurements of sustained sounds or articulations to model running speech is a well-known issue. Speech sounds are often measured in isolation or at a slow speaking rate and some transformation is subsequently needed to adapt it for continuous speech. In acoustic synthesis, Klatt's (1979) rule-based approach to account for higher speaking rates by compressing the phonetic segments based on their inherent and minimal duration has been used extensively. Cohen and Massaro (1993) proposed a similar influential method to model speaking rate variations in visual speech synthesis. The Cohen–Massaro model defines target positions for all articulators in each phoneme, and the extent to which the target is reached depends on the phoneme duration. Speech production modeling based on MRI measurements has the same theoretical ground; the sustained articulations are considered as prototype targets that will be reached if the phoneme duration is long enough. For shorter durations, these targets define what the speaker aims for, even if the higher speaking rate means that the articulator positions are not reached. However, as the articulations have to be sustained over very long periods of time in 3-D MRI, it is not certain that they actually represent valid targets for running speech—the subject may have to use a different articulation strategy to be able to hold the articulation during the entire acquisition.

In the study by Baer et al. (1991), 30 min were required to obtain the full set of images for a given vocal tract configuration and the subjects had to produce a sustained monotone for the 3.4 min that it took to acquire each image, breathing in briefly every 15 s. The technical progress, allowing the entire vocal tract to be imaged in 3-D with high resolution in around 30 s, is hence very important for speech production research. Perhaps even more important is that slowly produced speech can be imaged in the midsagittal plane in real-time using dynamic MRI. The acquisition rate of MRI is a compromise between temporal and spatial resolution; Demolin, Hassid, Metens, and Soquet (2002) acquired 5 images/s with a thickness of 6 mm and Mády, Sader, Zimmermann, Hoole, Beer, Zeilhofer, and Hanning (2001) acquired 8 images/s with a thickness of 10 mm. The rate, fortunately, also increases continuously with improvements of MRI scanners and acquisition set-up. Indeed, Narayanan, Nayak, Lee, Sethy, and Byrd (2004) recently proposed a new approach permitting to collect 5 mm thick images at an acquisition rate of 8–9 images/s, but a reconstruction rate of 20–24 images/s.

Real-time imaging of 3-D vocal tract shapes is, however, still far away and the options for 3-D imaging are either using many repetitions or asking the subject to sustain the articulation artificially. If repetitions are used, it is possible to generate a real-time image sequence through postprocessing (Foldvik et al., 1993; Shadle, Mohammad, Jackson, & Carter, 1999), but the large number of repetitions may also introduce variability. There is hence a risk that the generated averaged articulatory movement does not correspond to any of its constituent repetitions. With sustained articulation, on the other hand, it is possible to collect high-resolution images that give detailed data on one production, but the long acquisition time may introduce artifacts that make the measured articulation qualitatively different from the realization in normal speech. The first question to be addressed is the consequences of the artificial sustained articulation.

Shadle, Tiede, Masaki, Shimada, and Fujimoto (1996) and Engwall and Badin (2000) have shown that different vowel contexts produce coarticulatory effects on sustained fricative articulations. However, when the static MRI data in Engwall and Badin (2000) was compared to real-time EMA and EPG measurements, Engwall (2000) concluded that the sustained articulations did show similar coarticulatory effects (on the place of constriction, cross-sectional area, protrusion, and jaw and larynx height) as the real-time data, but also that they were hyperarticulated.

The sustained coarticulation has thus already been partially assessed using EMA and EPG, but as these techniques give discrete spatial data rather than continuous, the evaluation was based on a limited part of the articulations. MRI with short acquisition time, on the other hand, provides the opportunity to compare the entire vocal tract shapes. The second issue is whether static coarticulated articulations are representative of real-time coarticulation.

The construction of commonly available MRI scanners requires that the subjects are imaged in supine position. Upright MRI scanners (such as Fonar's 0.6-T scanner) are beginning to appear, but are still very rare. The subjects hence lie on the back during MRI studies, and it is implicitly assumed that gravitation has a negligible effect on their speech production. However, several MRI studies, notably Badin et al. (2002) and Engwall (2003), have noted a backward displacement of the tongue and Tiede, Masaki, and Vatikiotis-Bateson (2000) found postural differences between speech produced in sitting and lying position when mimicking an MRI acquisition protocol with X-ray microbeam. The effect of gravity on the tongue has further been investigated by Stone, Crouse, and Sutton (2002) using ultrasound images. Shiller, Ostry, and Gribble (1999) have modeled the effect of posture on jaw movements mathematically and showed that the first two formant frequencies of two vowels varied systematically depending on subject position. There is hence evidence that gravitation does indeed affect the articulation. The advantage of using MRI to investigate the influence of gravitation is that it can provide an overall view of the effect on the entire vocal tract, rather than on specific articulators. The third question to be addressed is how much MRI data is affected by the supine position.

MR images are often not used merely to make speech production measurements, but to create articulatory models using both MRI and real-time measurements (e.g., Badin et al., 2002; Engwall, 2003). The most crucial point is then no longer if the articulations in the MR images are influenced by the measurement set-up, but if the created model can be accepted as a good representation of normal speech production. That is, as long as real-time data are able to compensate for the artificial sustained articulation so that the model replicates the articulatory positions and movements of running speech, deviations in the MRI data upon which the model is based are of minor importance for the model. EMA data have been used previously (Engwall, 2003) to reproduce articulatory movements with the model, but real-time MRI has the benefit that information of the entire tongue contour is available, whereas EMA only provides data of the movement of a few points on the front part of the tongue. The fourth evaluation part is focused on whether a model derived from artificially sustained articulations can reproduce real-time speech motion.

METHOD

Image Acquisition and Analysis

The data were collected on two separate occasions, 2.5 years apart, but using the same subject, a male native speaker of Swedish (the author), for all acquisitions. Set 1 consists of high-resolution images of articulations that were artificially sustained (Engwall, 2003). In order to address the questions outlined in the introduction, the same articulations were acquired again in Set 2, using shorter acquisition times. Table 17.1 summarizes the technical data of the two sets. From Table 17.1, it should be noted that Set 2 could not replace Set 1 for detailed speech production modeling, as the level of detail that can be extracted is lower due to both the lower spatial resolution and the orientation of the images (the 3-D data

TABLE 17.1. Technical Data of the Acquisition Set-Up and Images

	Set 1	Set 2
Scanner	Philips GyroScan T10-NT	Philips CompactPlus, PowerTrak 6000
Magnetic field strength	1 T	1.5 T
Image size (pixels)	256 × 256	128 × 128
3D		
Number of slices	54 (3 sets of 18 parallel slices)	16 sagittal, 22 coronal
Image resolution (mm/pixel)	1	2.1875
Slice thickness (mm)	3.6	4
Interslice distance (mm)	4	4
Acquisition time (s)	43	5
Midsagittal		
Resolution (mm/pixel)	1	2.34275
Thickness (mm)	4	6
Acquisition time	11 s	9 images/s

in Set 1—18 axial pharyngeal images, 18 oblique velar and 18 coronal oral images—gives both a more complete coverage of the vocal tract and a better air-tissue boundary detection, as the images are approximately perpendicular to the vocal tract cross-section in each part). Set 2 is, however, able to indicate qualitatively problems that may occur in Set 1 due to the longer acquisition time.

In order to avoid unwanted head movements, the subject's head was fixed with solid foam cushions when he was facing upward. For a part of the acquisition in Set 2, the subject was facing downward. He was then positioned with his lower arms together in front of the face (upper arms parallel to and lower arms vertical to the body) and rested the forehead against the lower arms for steady support. For all acquisitions in which the subject was facing upward, a quadrature neck coil was used as receiver coil, whereas a syn-body coil was used when he was facing downward. The real-time data in Set 2 were T1-weighted images collected with a Turbo Spin Echo (TSE) Zoom (Buecker, Adam, Neuerburg, Glowinski, van Vaals, & Guenther, 1998).

In Set 1, the 3-D vocal tract shape was reconstructed from the air-tissue border that was traced in each image (c.f. Engwall, 2003). The 3-D data in Set 2 were reconstructed from the sagittal images, while the coronal images served as reference for the contour extraction. The contours of the upper and lower lip, the velum, the posterior and anterior pharyngeal walls, and the tongue were traced in each sagittal image. Three-dimensional reconstructions of the palate and jaw created from dental casts were positioned manually based on the midsagittal image. A semipolar grid (Beautemps, Badin, & Bailly, 2001) with 37 gridlines was used for the 3-D reconstructions. The 2-D data of both Sets 1 and 2 were extracted from each midsagittal image using semiautomatic boundary detection and manual positioning of the jaw and palate. In all the comparisons below, Sets 1 and 2 were aligned based on the midsagittal palate contour.

Corpus

The corpus collected in the two sets is given in Table 17.2, divided into four different subcorpora depending on which part of the evaluation each subcorpus was used in. The effects of the sustained articulation were studied on Subcorpora 1 and 2. Differences between coarticulation in real-time and sustained articulations were evaluated based on Subcorpus 2. The effect of subject position was investigated using Subcorpus 3, imaged both when the subject was facing upward and downward. Finally, the statistical articulatory model was derived from Subcorpus 4 of Set 1 and evaluated on Subcorpus 4 of Set 2. In both the 3-D and the 2-D part of Set 1 and in the 3-D part of Set 2, all articulations were sustained during the acquisition time. The vowels were imaged in isolation and for the consonants, the VC and CV transitions were made prior to and after the acquisition sequence, respectively. The 2-D part of Set 2, on the other hand, included transitions between vowels and vowels and consonants. The vowel sequences in Subcorpora 1 and 4 of Set 2 were produced without any pause between vowels. The aCa ɪCɪ ʊCʊ/ sequences in Subcorpus 4 of Set 2 were produced in the same vowel context order for all consonants and with a short pause between each VCV word.

TABLE 17.2. The Corpora Collected in the Two Sets

	Set 1		Set 2	
	3D at = 43 s	2D at = 11 s	3D at = 5 s	2D 9 images/s
Subcorpus 1	/ɑː, iː, uː/	/ɑː, iː, uː/	/ɑː, iː, uː/	/ɑː, iː, uː/
Subcorpus 2	C=/s, f, ɕ, ʂ, ɧ/ in $^{V}C^{V}$ context, V=/a, ɪ, ʊ/	C=/s, f, ɕ, ʂ, ɧ/ in $^{V}C^{V}$ context, V=/a, ɪ, ʊ/	C=/s, f, ɕ, ʂ, ɧ/ in $^{V}C^{V}$ context, V=/a, ɪ, ʊ/	VCV with V=/a, ɪ, ʊ/, C=/s, f, ɕ, ʂ, ɧ/
Subcorpus 3	/eː, yː, oː, øː/		Subcorpus 1 + /eː, yː, oː, øː/	Subcorpus 1
Subcorpus 4	Subcorpus 1–3 + /a, æː, ʉː, uː, ɔː, œː/, C= /p, t, k, l, r/ in $^{V}C^{V}$ context, V=/a, ɪ, ʊ/			/ɑeiuʉyɔɛøœ/, /aCa ɪCɪ ʊCʊ/ with C=/p, t, k, l, r, n, m, s, f, ɕ, ʂ, ɧ/

Note. The division into subcorpora indicates which part of the evaluation the different corpora were used for (refer to the text for details). 3-D, multislice acquisition; 2-D, midsagittal acquisition; at, acquisition time.

Combining Static and Dynamic Data in a Statistical Tongue Model

Using a statistical analysis of the 43 articulations in Subcorpus 4 of Set 1, a 3-D tongue model was created (Engwall, 2003) with the articulatory parameters jaw height (JH), tongue dorsum (TD) raise, body raise (TB), tip raise (TT), tip advance (TA), and tongue width (TW). All parameters except TW were defined in the midsagittal plane, and they can hence be used directly in an attempt to resynthesize the articulations in Subcorpus 4 of Set 2 with the model. The correspondence between measured and synthesized midsagittal data gives an indication of the model's validity for running speech.

The articulatory parameters of the tongue model were recovered from the midsagittal contours of the tongue and the position of the maxilla. The JH was estimated directly from the jaw position as the normalized value of the vertical distance between the upper and the lower incisor. The parameters TB, TD, TT, and TA were determined by simultaneously adjusting the parameters using a Matlab optimization function to minimize the Euclidean distance between the model's midsagittal contour and the tongue contour in the MR images.

RESULTS

Sustained Articulation

The midsagittal contours in Figure 17.1 indicate that the sustained articulations had a much narrower lower pharynx and less difference in tongue contour between different vowels. The midsagittal tracings further suggest that different articulation strategies were used in the two conditions. While the jaw opening

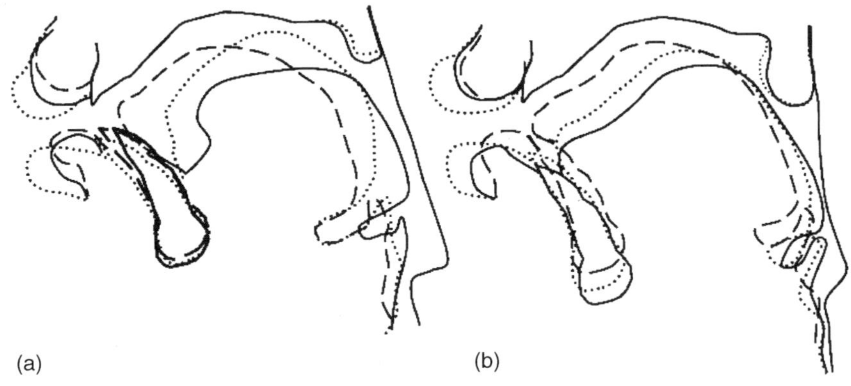

FIGURE 17.1. Midsagittal tracings of the vowels /ɑː/ (———), /iː/ (- - - - -), /uː/(············) in (a) real-time and (b) sustained production.

was used to achieve the difference in tongue body height in the sustained articulation, its role was taken over by alterations in the tongue shape when the vowels were produced in sequence. A similar difference can be found in Figure 17.3, where the constriction in /s/ was achieved by raising the tongue tip in the real-time production, but the entire tongue blade in the sustained. The real-time and sustained articulations were hence qualitatively different, with more important independent tongue movements in the former.

When the articulation was sustained even further for the 3-D acquisition, the result was a significantly narrower pharynx for /i, u/, as shown by the smaller cross-sectional areas in Figures 17.2b and c, whereas /ɑ/ was unaffected (Figure 17.2a), as it should have a constricted pharynx. The fricatives /f, ṣ, ɧ/ had the same type of decrease as the vowels in the pharynx section (as exemplified by Figure 17.2d), whereas the two fricatives with a more forward lingual constriction, /s, ç/, were less affected. The bracing against the alveolar ridge may provide more support and proprioceptive feedback than for the vowels and other fricatives, allowing the tongue position to be maintained for a longer duration. All fricatives also showed effects of hyperarticulation, with a narrower constriction in the artificially sustained condition (exemplified in Figure 17.2d, by the smaller cross-sectional area around 9–10 cm from the larynx, and in Figure 17.3) as the tongue edges were pressed more firmly against the palate.

It should be acknowledged that the pharynx in Set 1 was narrower than reported in other MRI studies using sustained articulation. This is in part

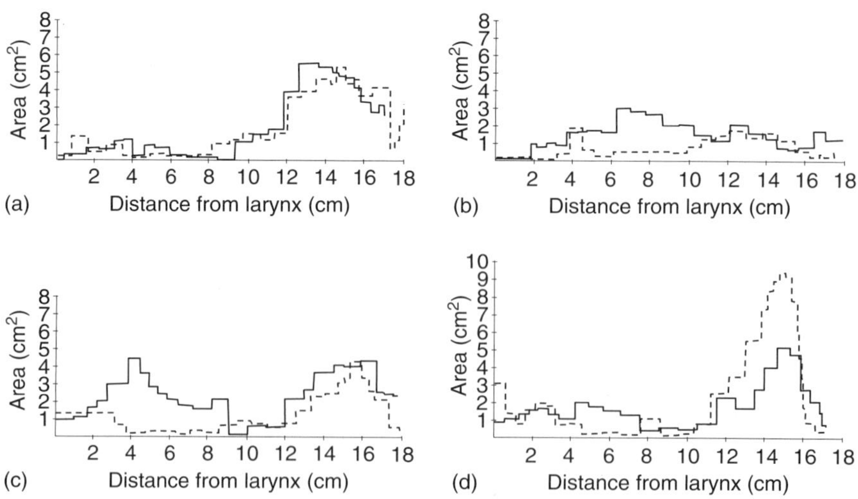

FIGURE 17.2. Cross-sectional area as a function of distance from the larynx for (a) /ɑː/, (b) /iː/, (c) /uː/, and (d) /ᵘɧᵘ/, in the sustained (———) and artificially sustained production (- - - - -).

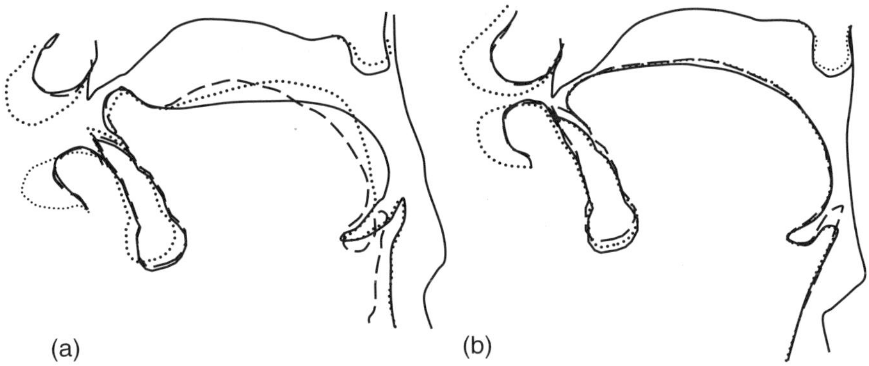

FIGURE 17.3. Midsagittal tracing of /s/ in /a/ (———), /ɪ/ (---------), /ʊ/ (············) context, during (a) real-time and (b) sustained production.

explained by the exclusion of the sinus piriforms and subject variability, but it may in part also be due to differences in the subjects' ability to maintain the articulation during the acquisition. Apostol et al. (1999) used the same acquisition protocol and setup as in Set 1 and the pharynges of their three subjects were less constricted. Their pharyngeal data were, however, narrower than in e.g., Baer et al. (1991) (for both /i, u/) and Story et al. (1996) (mostly for /u/), two MRI studies where the subjects used a normal phonation and were allowed to breathe after around 10 s of each acquisition. The pharyngeal cross-sectional areas in the latter two studies were in turn smaller than in the area functions estimated from X-rays by Fant (1960) and Woods (1979). This may well be due to the anatomical differences of the subjects, but may also result from differences in acquisition time and position between the two methods.

Coarticulation

The coarticulatory effects of the vowel context were much larger on the tongue contour, but smaller on the jaw and lips in the real-time production than in the sustained, as exemplified by the midsagittal tracing of /s/ in Figure 17.3. The sustained articulations had in turn larger differences between vowel contexts than the artificially sustained ones, especially in the pharynx. Whereas the area functions of the artificially sustained fricatives differ little between contexts in the pharynx, the normally sustained articulations had differences of 2–3 cm^2 between the most constricted (generally in the /ʊ/ context) and the most open (often in the /ɪ/ context). An effect of hyperarticulation in the artificially sustained condition is shown in Figure 17.2d: /ʊɧʊ/ had a much larger cavity in front of the tongue, because the subject tried to hold a good example of the coarticulated fricative for a prolonged time, which meant that the contrast between vowel contexts was reinforced. These conclusions replicate and extend those in Engwall (2000), by showing that there are differences not only at the EMA and EPG measurement points, but also along the entire tongue contour.

Gravitational Effects

The effects of the supine position were investigated using a standard MRI scanner, but with the subject facing both downward and upward. The midsagittal contour of the pharynx was narrower in the face-up condition, slightly for the back vowels /ɑː, uː/ and substantially for the front vowel /iː / (c.f. Figure 17.4), as the jaw was more advanced in the face down condition.

The area functions of the sustained articulations differed for /ɑː, iː/ (c.f. Figures 17.5a and b), but the difference was much smaller than the effect caused by the artificial sustained articulation. For /uː/ (Figure 17.5c), the face down areas were slightly smaller, because the epiglottis was positioned differently and the lips were more protruded. The protrusion decreased the cross-sectional areas by drawing the cheeks inward. The difference between the two conditions was hence small, but observable in the real-time acquisition, and moderate when the articulations were sustained over 5 s. In order to investigate the combined effects of artificial sustained articulation and the posture, area functions from Set 1 were compared with face down area functions from Set 2. The difference between the two measurement conditions was large (as exemplified in Figure 17.5d), but the difference was not qualitatively different from

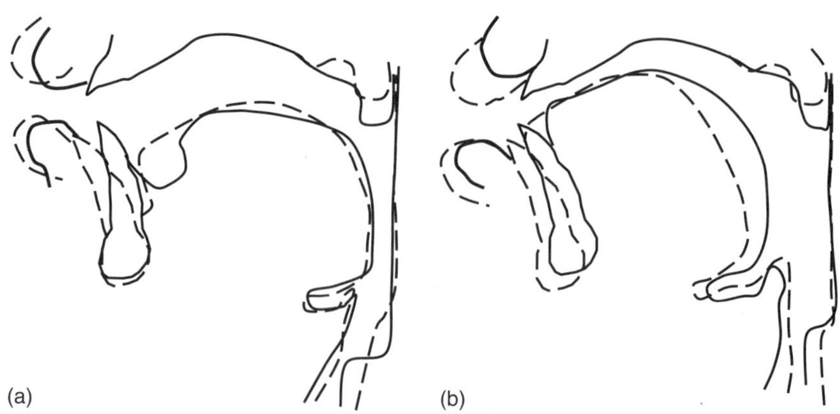

FIGURE 17.4. Midsagittal tracing of real-time production of (a) /ɑː/ and (b) /iː/ when the subject was facing upward (———) and downward (- - - - -).

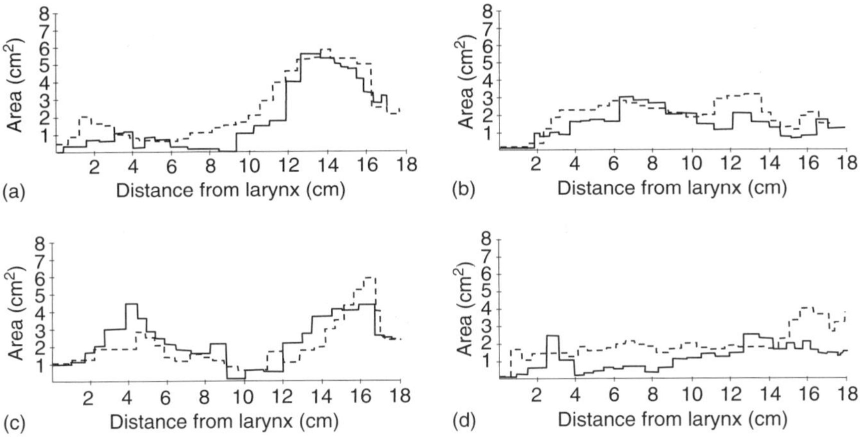

FIGURE 17.5. Area functions for (a) /ɑː/, (b) /iː/ (c) /uː/, and (d) /øː/ when the subject was facing upward (———) and downward (- - - - -). For (a)–(c), the acquisition time was equal in both positions; for (d), the face-up articulation was artificially sustained.

the effect of the artificial sustained articulation alone. The pharynx was constricted and the air passage was too small at the velum, because of the lack of control over the velum when the articulation was sustained for a long duration without phonation.

Replicating Real-Time MRI Data

The statistical model derived from the sustained articulations in Set 1 was in general able to reproduce the real-time articulations in Subcorpus 4 of Set 2. The total RMS error of 0.13 cm is quite acceptable considering that it is lower than the spatial resolution in the real-time MR images and of the same level as the accuracy of the reconstruction of the articulations in the 3-D corpus (sagittal RMS error of 0.13 cm; Engwall, 2003). Table 17.3 indicates that the error was lower for vowels than for the VCVs, which is an effect of the tongue shape being more neutral for the vowels and therefore easier to replicate. The RMS error was larger where the tongue differed the most from a neutral position, i.e., at the tongue tip for consonants with a raised (C=/t, l, r, n, s, ç, ʂ/) or lowered (C=/k, ɧ/) tip or blade. The same tendency was found in Engwall (2003), where more neutral vowels had lower sagittal reconstruction error than either more open or closed vowels. There is hence no qualitative difference between the reconstruction of the real-time tongue contours and that of the static 3-D shapes. The model was capable of reproducing the general shape of the entire real-time tongue contour, with the exception of the tongue root, where it was unable to follow the larger movements of the real-time articulations. This is an

TABLE 17.3. The RMS Error (mm) for the Resynthesis of Real-Time Movements with a Statistical Model

	All	Vowels	VCV
Total	**1.3**	**1.1**	**1.3**
Pharynx	1.2	1.0	1.2
Dorsum	1.2	1.0	1.3
Blade and tip	1.3	1.2	1.3

effect of the backward displacement of the tongue in Set 1. As the movement of the tongue root became hidden by the epiglottis, the statistical model has a parameter definition with the false notion that the tongue root hardly moves at all.

CONCLUSIONS

It is certainly not possible to draw general conclusions about the use of MRI that is applicable to all subjects in all prior MRI studies based on this evaluation of one measurement setup with one subject. It can, nevertheless, serve as an indicator of possible problems introduced when static MRI is used for speech production measurements. In general, the MR images give adequate information on the 3-D shape of the vocal tract, but this evaluation suggests that: (1) the artificial sustained articulation is more difficult to hold for the subject, inducing a backward movement of the tongue and a lack of velum control; (2) sustained productions are hyperarticulated compared to real-time productions, especially as far as coarticulation is concerned; and (3) the supine position, with the subject facing upward, does affect the position and shape of the tongue, often decreasing the passage in the pharynx, especially when the articulation has to be sustained artificially. In itself, the gravitational effect is, however, moderate.

Consequently, the acquisition time should be kept as short as possible, as differences can be observed not only between real-time and static articulations, but also depending on how long the articulation is sustained and if the subject could use a normal phonation. The static MR images further have to be complemented with other measurements to correctly replicate not only movements but also positions of running speech.

At the same time, the evaluation does show that real-time articulations can be achieved, with reasonable accuracy, by a statistical model derived from artificially sustained articulations. Using static MRI data for speech production modeling is hence still valid, if it is complemented with real-time data.

ACKNOWLEDGMENTS

This research was carried out at Laboratoire de Phonologie, Université Libre de Bruxelles (ULB), during the author's post-doctoral stay funded by the Wenner–Gren foundation and Hans Werthén-fonden. The MR images were acquired by Thierry Metens, Unité de résonance magnétique, hôpital Erasme, ULB. The author also wishes to thank Didier Demolin for the invitation to ULB and Jonathan Harrington and Eric Vatikiotis-Bateson for their very valuable comments and suggestions on this chapter.

REFERENCES

Apostol, L., Perrier, P., Raybaudi, M., & Segebarth, C. (1999). 3D geometry of the vocal tract and inter-speaker variability. *Proceedings of the 14th ICPhS*, San Francisco (pp. 443–446).

Badin, P., Bailly, G., Revéret, L., Baciu, M., Segebarth, C., & Savariaux, C. (2002). Three-dimensional linear articulatory modeling of tongue, lips and face based on MRI and video images. *Journal of Phonetics, 30*, 533–553.

Baer, T., Gore, J. C., Gracco, L. W., & Nye, P. W. (1991). Analysis of vocal tract shape and dimensions using magnetic resonance imaging: Vowels. *Journal of the Acoustic Society of America, 90*, 799–828.

Beautemps, D., Badin, P., & Bailly, G. (2001). Linear degrees of freedom in speech production: Analysis of cineradio- and labio-film data and articulatory-acoustic modeling. *Journal of the Acoustical Society of America, 109*, 2165–2180.

Buecker, A., Adam, G., Neuerburg, J. M., Glowinski, A., van Vaals, J. J., & Guenther, R. W. (1998). MR-guided biopsy using a T2-weighted single-shot zoom imaging sequence (Local Look technique). *Journal of Magnetic Resonance Imaging, 8*, 955–959.

Cohen, M., & Massaro, D. (1993). Modeling coarticulation in synthetic visual speech. In N. M. Thalmann, & D. Thalmann (Eds.), *Models and techniques in computer animation* (pp. 139–156). Tokyo: Springer.

Demolin, D., Hassid, S., Metens, T., & Soquet, A. (2002). Real-time MRI and articulatory coordination in speech. *Comptes Rendus Biologies, 325*, 547–556.

Engwall, O. (2000). Are static MRI data representative of dynamic speech? Results from a comparative study using MRI, EMA and EPG. *Proceedings of the 6th ICSLP*, Beijing, China (pp. 17–20).

Engwall, O. (2003). Combining MRI, EMA & EPG in a three-dimensional tongue model. *Speech Communication, 41*, 303–329.

Engwall, O., & Badin, P. (2000). An MRI study of Swedish fricatives: Coarticulatory effects. *Proceedings of the 5th Seminar on Speech Production: Models and data*, Seeon, Germany (pp. 297–300).

Fant, G. (1960). *The acoustical theory of speech production*. The Hague: Mouton.

Foldvik, A-K., Kristiansen, U., & Kvaerness, J. (1993). A time-evolving three-dimensional vocal tract model by means of magnetic resonance imaging (MRI). *Proceedings of Eurospeech93*, Berlin, Germany (pp. 557–558).

Klatt, D. (1979). Synthesis by rule of segmental durations in English sentences. In B. Lindblom, & S. Ohman (Eds.), *Frontiers of speech communication research* (pp. 287–299). London: Academic Press.

Mády, K., Sader, R., Zimmermann, A., Hoole, P., Beer, A., Zeilhofer, H. F., & Hanning, C. (2001). Use of real-time MRI in assessment of consonant articulation before and after tongue surgery and tongue reconstruction. *Proceedings of the 4th International speech motor conference*, Nijmegen, the Netherlands (pp. 142–145).

Matsumura, M., Niikawa, T., Shimizu, K., Hashimoto, Y., & Morita, T. (1994). Measurement of 3D shapes of vocal tract, dental crown and nasal cavity using MRI: Vowels and fricatives. *Proceedings of the 3rd ICSLP*, Yokohama, Japan (pp. 619–622).

Narayanan, S., Nayak, K., Lee, S., Sethy, A., & Byrd, D. (2004). An approach to real-time magnetic resonance imaging for speech production. *Journal of the Acoustical Society of America, 115*, 1771–1776.

Rokkaku, M., Hashimoto, K., Imaizumi, S., Niimi, S., & Kiritani, S. (1986). Measurements of the three-dimensional shape of the vocal tract based on the magnetic resonance imaging Technique. *Annual Bulletin of Research Institute of Logopedics and Phoniatrics, 20*, 47–54.

Shadle, C., Mohammad, M., Jackson, P., & Carter, J. (1999). Multi-planar dynamic magnetic resonance imaging: New tools for speech research. *Proceedings of the 14th ICPhS*, San Francisco (pp. 623–626).

Shadle, C., Tiede, M., Masaki, S., Shimada, Y., & Fujimoto, I. (1996). Articulatory effects of vowel context on fricatives: A magnetic resonance image study. *Journal of the Acoustical Society of America, 100*, 2660.

Shiller, D. M., Ostry, D. J., & Gribble, P. L. (1999). Effects of gravitational load on jaw movements in speech. *Journal of Neuroscience, 19*, 9073–9080.

Stone, M., Crouse, U., & Sutton, M. (2002), Exploring the effects of gravity on tongue motion using ultrasound images. *Journal of the Acoustical Society of America, 111*, 2476–2477.

Story, B., Titze, I., & Hoffman, E. (1996). Vocal tract area functions from magnetic resonance imaging. *Journal of the Acoustical Society of America, 100*, 537–554.

Tiede, M., Masaki, S., & Vatikiotis-Bateson, E. (2000). Contrasts in speech articulation observed in sitting and supine condition. *Proceedings of the 5th Speech Production Seminar: Models and Data*, Seeon, Germany (pp. 25–28).

Woods, S. (1979). A radiographic analysis of constriction locations for vowels. *Journal of Phonetics, 7*, 25–43.

18

Predicting 3D Tongue Shapes from Midsagittal Contours

MAUREEN STONE, MELISSA A. EPSTEIN, MIN LI, AND CHANDRA KAMBHAMETTU

ABSTRACT

This study is interested in whether there exists a predictable relationship between the midsagittal tongue contour and its related 3D tongue surface shape during speech. The assumption is that for any single language, a limited set of phonemically based 3D tongue shapes are used. If these shapes can be delineated and mapped to specific midsagittal displacements and cross-sectional (coronal) shapes, then predictions from midsagittal displacements to coronal shapes and then to 3D shapes can be made for specific speech sounds. The present study examined two ultrasound data sets: (1) the 3D static tongue surface reconstructions from a single subject (Stone & Lundberg, 1996), and (2) five coronal slices for two sentences spoken by a second subject (Yang & Stone, 2002). The midsagittal-to-coronal relationship for the 3D surfaces was extracted and applied to the continuous speech data. The predicted midsagittal-to-coronal relationship was well captured. This result supports the idea that a knowledge of the 3D shapes of a language, even based on a single speaker, can then be used to transform 2D midsagittal data into a 3D surface for other data sets.

INTRODUCTION AND BACKGROUND

Any single language has a finite number of lingual phonemes and thus a limited set of 3D static tongue surface shapes. An inventory of these 3D tongue surface shapes can be made for all the lingual phonemes of the language. Each 3D surface can be deconstructed into a "chain" of 2D coronal contours, and a complete map of 2D-contour to 3D-surface shapes can be made. The number of coronal contours required to adequately represent the 3D surface can be fairly small; it has been found that six coronal contours well represent 3D surface shapes in English (Stone & Lundberg, 1996).

Although the relationship between 3D surfaces and 2D coronal contours is straightforward, only a few instruments are able to directly collect coronal contours and thus reconstruct 3D tongue surface motions (c.f. Yang & Stone, 2002). Many instruments, however, can collect midsagittal displacement data. Midsagittal contours can be deconstructed into a chain of midsagittal points in the same way that 3D surfaces can be deconstructed into a chain of coronal contours. Five to six appropriately placed points well represent the midsagittal contour (Lundberg & Stone, 1999). Moreover, coronal contours measured at these points can be reconstructed into low-error representations of the 3D surface. Therefore, the first goal of this paper is to determine whether there is a straightforward relationship between 2D coronal tongue shapes and their 1D midsagittal displacements (hereafter, midline heights).

The second goal of this work is to determine whether the 1D to 2D mapping of steady-state sounds can be used to estimate a continuous speech data set. Tongue shapes are more variable for continuous speech than steady-state sounds, due to coarticulation, prosody, and speaking rate, to name a few effects. However, if the extreme tongue shapes are known, it is possible that the transitional shapes will be contained within that range. Figure 18.1 (top) shows four

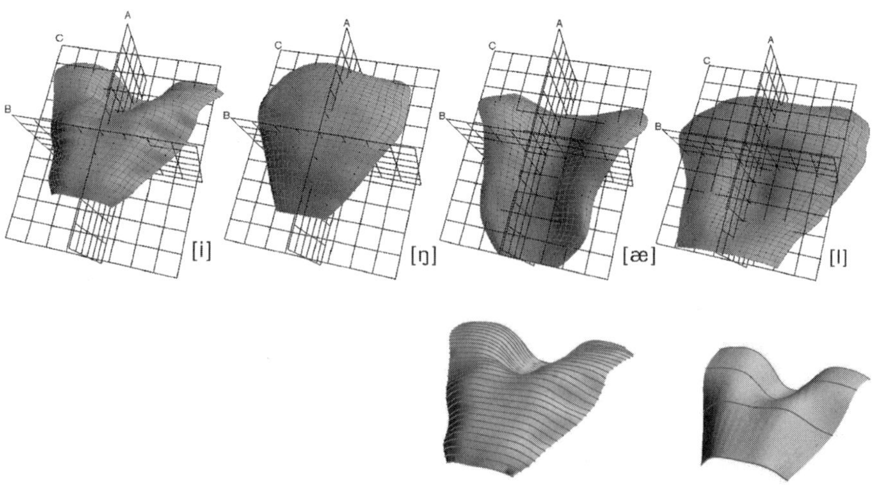

FIGURE 18.1. Top: Representative 3D tongue surface shapes based on 55 coronal contours for the four shape-based categories: front-raising (/i/), back-raising (/ŋ/), continuous groove (/æ/), and two-point displacement (/l/); Bottom: reconstructions for /i/ based on 55 slices and 4 slices.

extreme tongue shapes for US English. The surfaces can each be described, or mapped, as a chain of assorted coronal arches and grooves. The key to using these maps in a predictive manner is the relationship between the midline heights and the coronal shapes at each tissue slice. The relationship needs to be physiologically constrained, which would create universal limits, or linguistically constrained so that it holds for all data in the language. Badin, Bailly, Reveret, Baciu, and Segebarth (2002) found that tongue surface shape was linked to midsagittal contour shape as well as to jaw height. They studied the tongue tip, body, dorsum, root (advancement), and jaw height using 3D tongue surfaces reconstructed from MRI data. Using Linear Component Analysis they found that jaw height had a predictable effect on tongue surface shape because a higher jaw increases tongue–palate contact. In addition, they found that 72% of the variance of the 3D geometric features was accounted for by midsagittal contours.

In the present study, Experiment 1 used 18 3D static tongue surfaces, represented by six coronal contours, to map the relationship between midline heights and related coronal shapes (data from Lundberg & Stone, 1999; Stone & Lundberg, 1996). Coronal shape was represented by two quantities: (1) left slopes and (2) quadratic fits. Correlations between midline height and these two quantities determined whether there was a sufficient relationship to justify using this map in Experiment 2. Experiment 2 explored whether the map could be used to estimate coronal shapes from midline heights for continuous speech from a second speaker (data from Yang & Stone, 2002). Root mean square (RMS) errors in Experiment 2 were calculated between the coronal contour, the true quadratic fit, and the estimated quadratic fit, and were used to determine the quality of the estimations.

EXPERIMENT 1: MAPPING MIDLINE HEIGHTS TO CORONAL SHAPES FOR STATIC 3D SURFACES

In order to determine the relationship between midline height and coronal shape, it is useful to understand the nature of coronal shapes. Coronal shapes primarily follow a continuum from midsagittal groove to midsagittal arch, with some lateral asymmetry (Slud, Smith, Stone, & Goldstein, 2002; Stone, 1990, 1995; Stone, Faber, Raphael, & Shawker 1992; Stone, Goldstein & Zhang, 1997; Stone, Shawker, Talbot, & Rich, 1988; Stone & Vatikiotis-Bateson, 1995). Arches are typically quadratic (concave down) in shape, sometimes with a level or grooved centre. Anterior arches occur when the tongue contacts the hard palate and the sides deform against it. Posterior arches are due to muscle activity that elevates the tongue upward and backward as in vowels, or when it contacts and takes the shape of the velum (/ŋ/). Grooves are usually characterized by a bimodal shape. Maximum tongue height of the two peaks is reached some distance lateral to midline after which the tongue typically angles downward

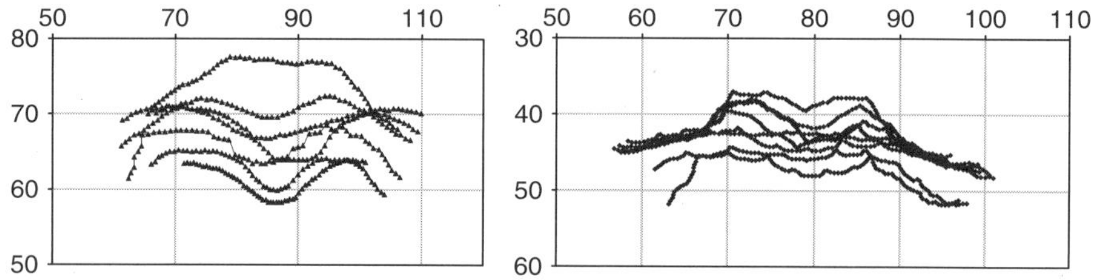

FIGURE 18.2. Representative contours for the third coronal slice for the static data set (left) and for the sentence "it ran a lot" (right).

(see Figure 18.2). Anterior grooves occur when genioglossus anterior contracts and lowers the anterior tongue, as in low vowels (/æ/,/ɛ/), or when the tongue is high and braced against the palate as in grooved fricatives (/s/,/θ/). Posterior grooves are muscularly determined as when genioglossus posterior pulls the tongue forward or when styloglossus pulls it up. Lateral asymmetries can occur because of palatal asymmetry, asymmetrical tongue shape, or motion.

The lateral tongue margins have a slightly different function in speech from the midsagittal tongue: They stabilize the tongue as well as shape the airstream. Therefore, lateral tongue motion may not correlate well with midsagittal motion. Alternatively, it may correlate very well because of the physiological linkages between the surface tissue points and the invariant boundary conditions of the vocal tract, especially the hard palate.

Methods–Experiment 1

Data set 1, spoken by a 24-year-old white, female, native of Baltimore, MD, consists of 3D tongue surfaces for 18 static sounds of US English. These 18 surfaces represent all the lingual sounds of English; for example, homorganic sounds like /t,d,n/ are represented by /n/. The original surfaces consisted of 55 coronal ultrasound slices. Figure 18.1 (bottom) shows the 55 slice and the 4 slice reconstruction for /i/, which is a short surface contour with no data in Slices 1 and 6. Full methodology and additional detail can be found in Stone and Lundberg (1996). To determine a small, but efficient number of slices to be used in future reconstructions, that experiment examined sparse data sets consisting of three to nine slices, which were optimized to maximize surface coverage and minimize error and improvement in the cost function asymptoted at five to six slices. The six slice reconstructions had 80% coverage, a mean error of 0.21 mm, and a maximum error of 1.40 mm. Since additional slices added very little improvement to the cost function and added considerable time to collect, we used six-slice coronal sets for 3D surface reconstructions. Some phonemes had shorter tongue surfaces than others and were not captured in the first or last slices, usually the first.

Therefore, for Experiment 1, Slices 2–5 were used from the sparse data set, hereafter called Data set 1.

Four shape-based categories were defined from the data: front-raising (FR) /i, ɪ, e, ɝ, n, ʃ/, back-raising (BR) /u, ʊ, o, ɔ, ɑ, ŋ/, continuous-groove (CG) /æ, ɛ, s, θ/, and two-point displacement /l/ (see Figure 18.1, and Stone & Lundberg, 1996). The original study found that low front vowels, which at midline appear to be weak versions of FR (Harshman, Ladefoged, & Goldstein, 1977), actually have a midsagittal groove for the entire tongue.

Three measurements were made on each coronal contour of the sparse data set: midsagittal height, left slope, and quadratic fit. The midsagittal height was chosen at the same x-value in every contour in the data set to simulate a single midsagittal slice, even those whose midpoints appeared off centre (see Figure 18.2). For Data set 1, the midline x-value is the plane made by axis A in Figure 18.1. For the left slope, the tongue contours were cut to a uniform length that captured the arching and grooving features. The end point was determined by overlaying the coronal contours for all the phonemes and slices (see Figure 18.2). The best value was about 1 cm from midline in the x-projection. Some phonemes, with wider or narrower grooves, would have been better represented by different lateral points, particularly in the posterior tongue. However, the chosen lengths captured the key shape features. The left slope was calculated by applying the equation $y = a_1x + a_0$ to the line connecting the midline point and left point.

The quadratic functions were fit to the entire contour length. It is not possible to estimate asymmetries when generalizing from midline contour to coronal shape, so only the arching/grooving features are considered here. In this way, for a given quadratic fit, where $y = a_2X^2 + a_1x + a_0$, the a_2 term represents contour shape, the quantity of interest in this study. The sign and magnitude of a_2 indicate, respectively, the direction and degree of global arching or grooving of the contour.

Pearson product moment correlation coefficients were calculated to determine the relationships between (1) midline height and a_2 and (2) midline height and left slope, for all five slices.

Results and Discussion–Experiment 1

The question asked by this study was whether correlations exist between midsagittal height and coronal shape at each segment of the tongue. In each of the slices, greater midline height accompanied an arched coronal shape, and lower heights a grooved shape. For each coronal segment, a specific midline height demarcated the difference between an arched and grooved shape. Correlations for Slices 1–3 were consistent and fairly strong. The three anterior slices may have been more easily mapped because palatal contact causes shape constraints that increase the correlation between shape and height (see Table 18.1).

TABLE 18.1. Pearson Product Moment Correlation Coefficients between Midline Height/Left Slopes and between Midline Height/a_2 of the Quadratic Function ($n = 18$)

	Correlations—Data set 1	
Slice	Mid- to left slope	Mid to a_2
1	.67	.65
2	.79	.73
3	.71	.70
4	.51	.65
5	.64	.44

This experiment was also designed to determine whether there was a unique map between each 3D's category shape and its coronal shape chain; that is, whether shape differences were smaller for phonemes within than between categories. The shapes in Figure 18.1 represent category shapes measured for a single speaker of US English and observed in many others. Although phonemes within these categories differ somewhat, they form a family of similar shapes (Stone & Lundberg, 1996). Figure 18.3 graphs each phoneme in each category on the basis of midline height and left slope. Fairly good correlations can be observed at each slice. In addition, the data can be further grouped by shape category. In Slice 2, FR is distinguished from CG, on the basis of height and shape. In Slice 3, CG is distinguished from BR and in Slice 4, BR is distinguished from FR and CG. Thus at any single slice, some categories clustered on the basis of left slope and/or midline displacement. In addition, some within-category patterns emerged. BR was distinguished from the other groups by very displaced midlines and little-to-no grooving at Slices 3–5. FR was high only anteriorly. Thus, the chains of contour shapes define 3D shape for each category, and further indicate 1D to 2D relationships that could be used for estimation. Similar patterns were seen for the quadratic functions; however, the left-slope data had slightly better correlations with midline height (Table 18.1); as a result the estimations in Data set 2 were done with cropped contours.

Data set 1 suggests that the information provided by midline height and category affiliation combine to provide substantial information about 3D shape. A higher anterior tongue (above 82 mm for this subject) indicates arching, a lower one grooving. Knowledge of shape category and slice position may further detail the steepness of the groove or arch. For example, midline displacement at Slice 4 was 70.8 mm for both /ɛ/ and /o/. Both are grooved (i.e., below 82 mm) but, as predicted by category affiliation, there is a steeper slope for the front-raised /ɛ/ (0.60) than the back-raised /o/ (0.21). In addition, back-raised sounds had a global coronal shape that was arched. This was not captured by the cropped contours; instead, the central groove was measured (see Figure 18.2).

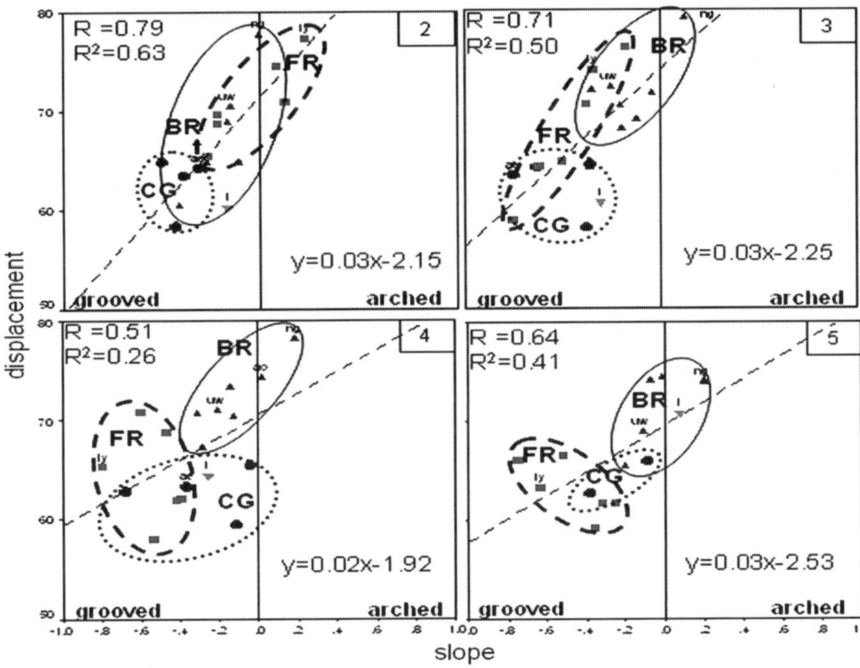

FIGURE 18.3. Correlations between left slope (x-axis) and midline height (y-axis) at the five tongue slices for all the static sounds. Categories are circled: front-raising (squares); back-raising (upright triangles); continuous-groove (circles); two-point displacement (inverted triangle).

For certain categories and slices, particularly BR and the velar slices, quadratic fits of the entire contour are a valuable shape supplement to left slopes.

EXPERIMENT 2: PREDICTING CORONAL SHAPES FROM MIDLINE HEIGHTS USING A PREDETERMINED MAPPING

There is more variability in tongue surface motions than in static shapes due to nonlinear tongue motion, and nonuniform front back timing (c.f. Yang & Stone, 2002). These factors make time-varying data sets more complex than static ones. Experiment 2, therefore, considered whether coronal shapes could be estimated, rather than mapped, from midline heights. In other words, whether the left slope or quadratic fits derived from 3D static shapes could be used in continuous speech to estimate coronal shapes from midsagittal heights. The strong correlations for the left-slope data suggested that the estimation should be for the medial 2 cm of the data. However, because the left-slope data were based on only two points (midline and 1 cm to the left), "cropped" data sets were made from Data set 1. The cropped data sets contained all the intervening points between the midline and left point, which was 2.0 cm long in the x projection. Quadratic functions were calculated for this cropped data set. The contours of Data set 1 were made symmetrical by measuring the points on the left side of the cropped contour and creating a mirror image on the right side. The symmetric contour was transformed so that its centre was 0, which means that its quadratic fit, $y = a_2X^2 + a_1x + a_0$, will have a midline height (a_0) and a midline slope (a_1) of 0. This transformation made it possible to represent the quadratic fit entirely by its a_2 value.

Estimating coronal shape for Data set 2 from the cropped a_2 terms would be more successful if the height/shape correlations are strong and in the same direction for both data sets. In Data set 1, the relationships were strong anteriorly and moderate posteriorly between specific midline heights and left slopes. Given linguistic or physiological constraints as contributors to this relationship, it should be possible to take the new cropped a_2 values for Data set 1, insert the midline heights of Data set 2, and solve the equations to get estimated a_2 values for Data set 2. The transitional movements occurring in the sentences would hopefully follow the same height/shape relationships as the extreme positions.

Methods–Experiment 2

The speaker was a 31-year-old white, female, native of Toronto, Canada. The sentences "it rang a lot" and "it ran a lot" were spoken six times each while coronal ultrasound data sets were collected at six coronal slices of the tongue. The slice angles were not optimized, but were roughly equidistant. The coronal video sequences were temporally aligned using the acoustic wave so that comparable moments in the speech event would occur in the same frames (Yang & Stone, 2002). As in Data set 1, the anterior most slice had incomplete data due to occasional tongue retraction. In addition, the most posterior slice moved little and appeared to be the jaw muscles. Therefore, the medial four slices (2–5) were used in the experiment. Tongue segments 2–5 of Data set 2 corresponded roughly to Segments 2–5 of Data set 1 and estimations were made accordingly.

For Data set 2, the left tongue point was about 0.7 cm from the midline in the x projection. Differences from midline to left points between the two studies (0.7 cm vs. 1.0 cm) are probably due to different tongue sizes, speech tasks, subject/dialect, and possibly transducer locations.

The midline height was measured for each symmetrical contour at each slice, and left slopes and cropped quadratic fits were calculated. Correlations determined that the relationship between midline height and the two shape measures were quite similar since they covered the same end points (see Table 18.2). Subsequent analyses, therefore, were done on the quadratic fits only since they used the intervening points. The estimated quadratic fits were

TABLE 18.2. Pearson Product Moment Correlations between Midline Height and Coronal Shape Measures for both "Ran" and "Rang"

Ran	Correlations—Data set 2	
Slice	Mid- to left slope	Mid to a_2
2	.66	.63
3	.05	.04
4	.94	.94
5	.88	.87
Rang		
2	.76	.72
3	.44	.44
4	.86	.84
5	.82	.80

calculated using $y = a_2X^2 + a_1x + a_0$, where the a values were from Data set 1. To determine the quality of the estimated shapes for Data set 2, the following RMS errors were calculated for each frame in the two sentences:

RMS1: the true quadratic fit and the true symmetric contour
RMS2: the estimated quadratic fit and the true quadratic fit
RMS3: the estimated quadratic fit and the true symmetric contour

Results and Discussion–Experiment 2

Table 18.2 shows a strong relationship between midline height and a_2, except at Slice 3. The relationship, as with Data set 1, was that a high tongue was more arched and a low tongue more grooved. At Slice 3, however, the correlations were weak, especially for the 'ran' data set. Figure 18.4 shows the poor correlation between midline height and a_2 for Slice 3 of "ran" and the strong correlation for Slice 4 of "ran". The dashed line is the best-fit line and the solid line represents the linear formula obtained from Data set 1 and used to estimate the a_2 values from the midline heights of Data set 2.

Two features may contribute to poor correlations for Slice 3; both are due to its location in the palatal vault/velar region of the vocal tract where there is space for much tongue elevation. The first feature is that, posterior tongue elevation, which is critical to creating high back sounds, is usually overlaid by a flat or grooved region at midline. The tongue is checked from its upward motion, probably by genioglossus, which creates this flat or grooved region (see Figure 18.2). Contact with the palate will also flatten out the upper surface. The cropped a_2 values captured the central shape features, which did not correlate with midline height. A full-contour quadratic might have better correlated with the globally arched shapes.

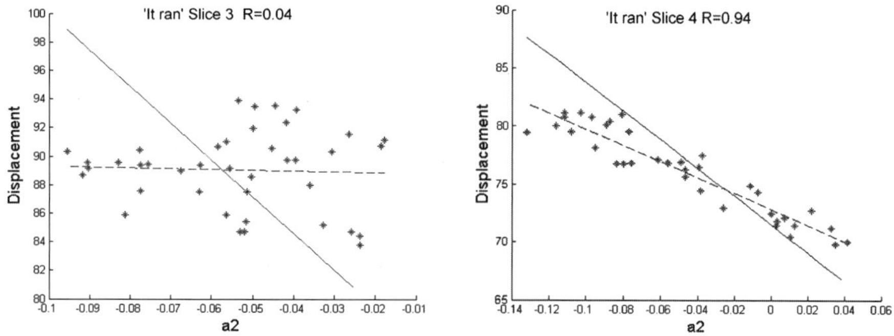

FIGURE 18.4. Correlation between midline height and a_2 for Slices 3 and 4 of "ran".

The second reason for low height/shape correlation at Slice 3 may be due to the inclusion of motion in Data set 2. The region of the third slice often is the pivot point for front–back tongue rotation (Iskarous, 2001; Unser & Stone, 1992). As the pivot point, Slice 3's heights and shapes are influenced by Slices 2 and 4, whose oppositional motions may create a more variable height-to-shape relationship. Front–back rotation occurs in continuous speech, but not in static data, so Slice 3 had stronger correlations in Data set 1 (see Table 18.1).

Estimated shapes correlated strongly with the true shapes if the height/shape correlations in Data set 2 were high (Table 18.2). Figure 18.5 details the variability in the quality of the estimations. Slice 3 had a very low height/a_2 correlation for "ran" (see Figure 18.4) and a somewhat better one for "rang" (r=.44). The a_2 values for the individual frames show that for "rang" the

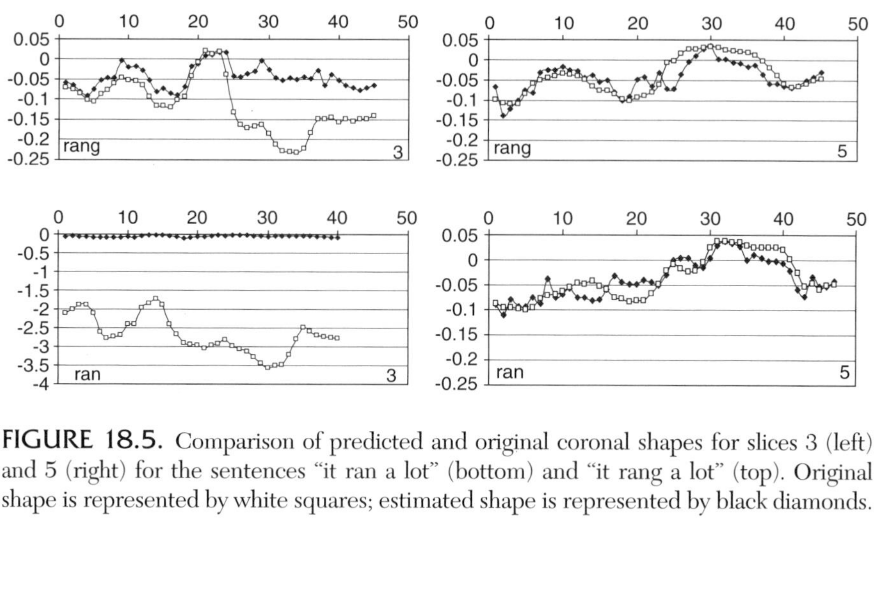

FIGURE 18.5. Comparison of predicted and original coronal shapes for slices 3 (left) and 5 (right) for the sentences "it ran a lot" (bottom) and "it rang a lot" (top). Original shape is represented by white squares; estimated shape is represented by black diamonds.

latter frames had little shape variation in the true data, but large variation in the estimated shapes. This means that the shapes were similar for these frames, but the midline heights varied considerably resulting in similar shape estimates (see Figure 18.2). Slice 5 had stronger correlations, and the similarity between true and estimated a_2 values is apparent.

RMS errors of Slices 2–5 for "ran" are shown in Figures 18.6–18.8, and Slices 2–5 for "rang" are shown in Figures 18.9–18.12. The low RMS1 errors indicate that the true quadratic fit is a good representation of the true symmetric contour. The similarity between true quadratic and true contour explains the similarity of the RMS2 and RMS3 errors, which respectively compare these two measurements to the estimated quadratic. Maximum RMS2 and RMS3 errors are about 2.2 mm for both data sets. The time frames with maximum RMS errors seem to be random. Mean RMS2 and RMS3 errors, shown in the figure legends, is less than 1 mm, which indicates fairly successful estimation of shape from height.

The goal of this study was to determine whether 3D surfaces could be predicted from midline contours, since midline data are so much more prevalent than coronal or 3D data. To do this for any specific language one would collect a static 3D corpus, determine shape measurements at reasonably placed (if not

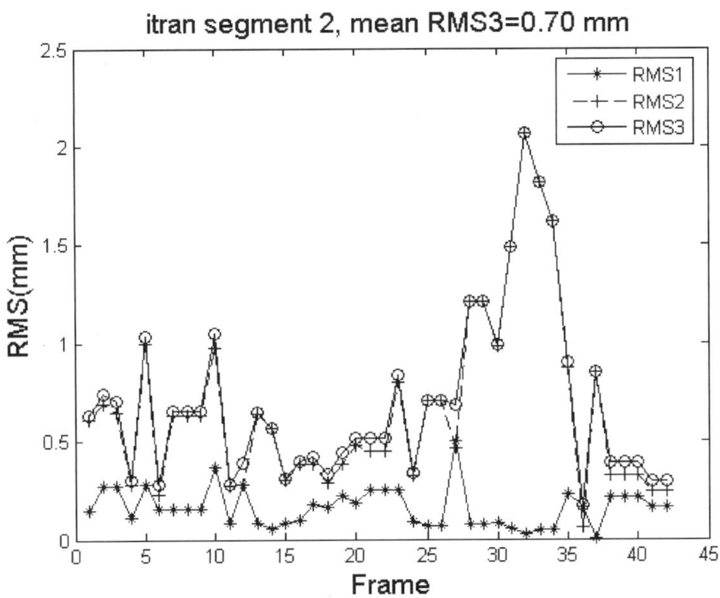

FIGURE 18.6. RMS errors of Segment 2 of "ran". RMS1 error compares the true symmetric contour to the true quadratic fit. RMS2 error compares the estimated quadratic fit to the true quadratic fit. RMS 3 error compares the estimated quadratic fit to the true symmetric contour.

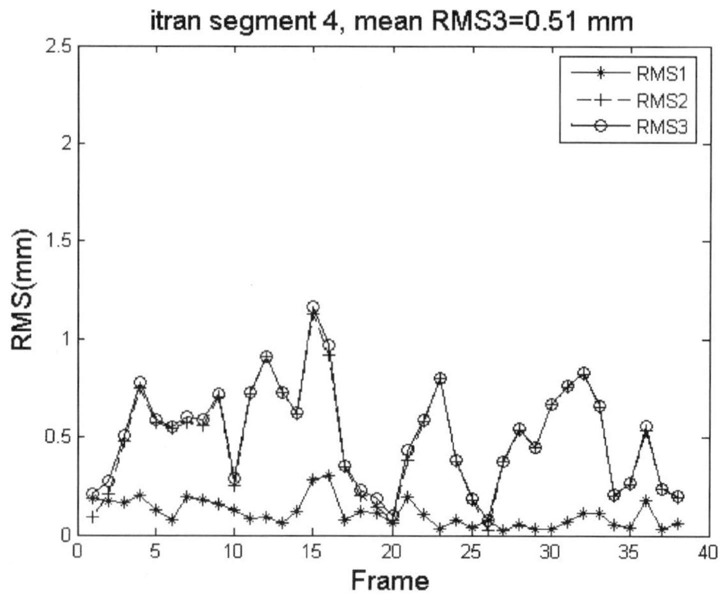

FIGURE 18.7. RMS errors of Segment 4 of "ran".

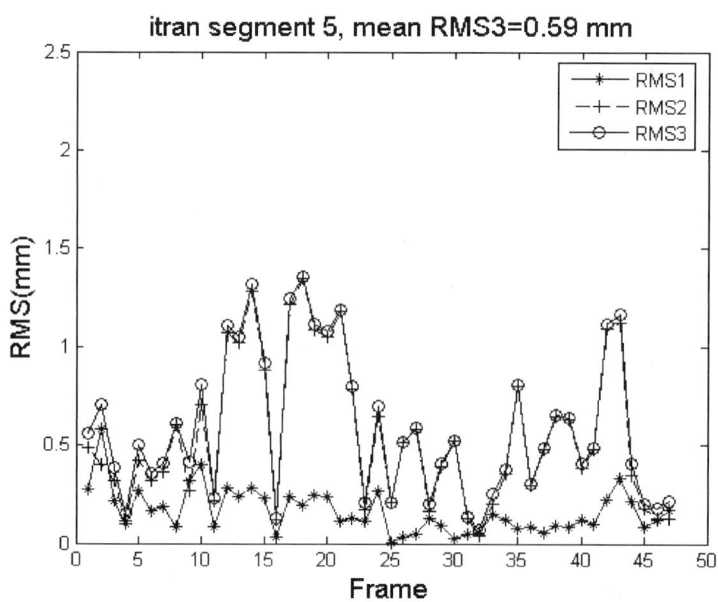

FIGURE 18.8. RMS errors of Segment 5 of "ran".

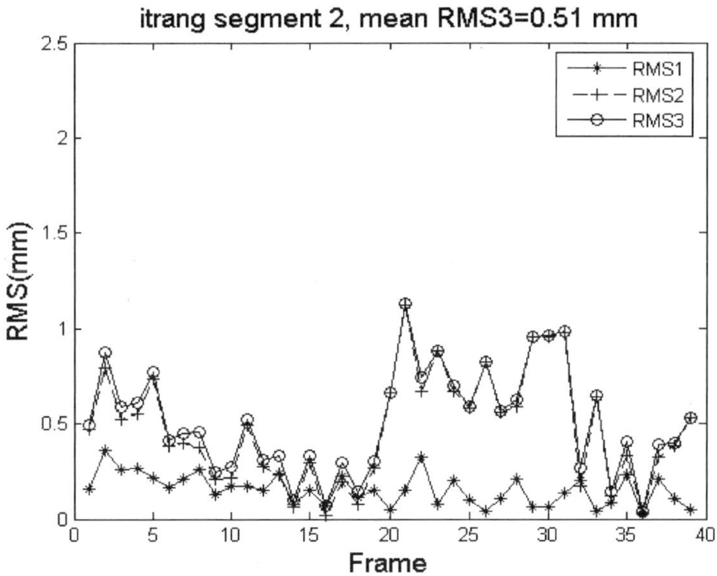

FIGURE 18.9. RMS errors of Segment 2 of "rang".

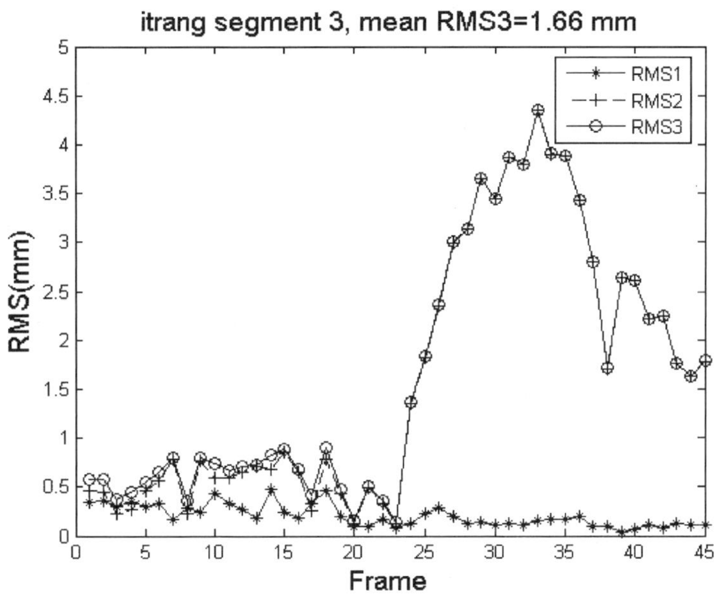

FIGURE 18.10. RMS errors of Segment 3 of "rang".

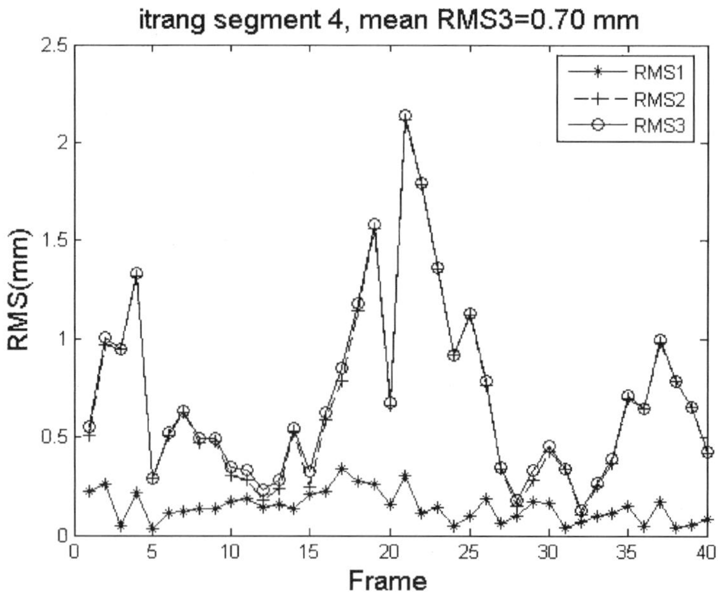

FIGURE 18.11. RMS errors of Segment 4 of "rang".

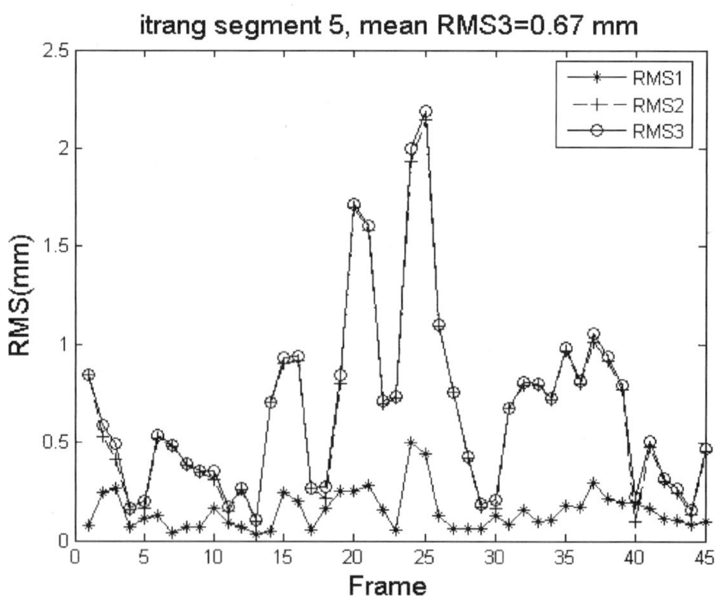

FIGURE 18.12. RMS errors of Segment 5 of "rang".

optimized) coronal slices, and calculate the linear relationships between midline height and left slope or quadratic fit. These linear and quadratic correlations could be used to predict coronal shapes at similar locations for other subjects for whom only midsagittal data are available. Chaining of these coronal shapes from front-to-back would yield a 3D tongue surface. Part of the convenience of this prediction is that the initial data set is static and can be collected via ultrasound or MRI using off-line and, if necessary, time-consuming 3D reconstructions. The subsequent data sets can be collected at midline using time-varying speech materials. The good correlations for most slices indicate that knowing the shape category of the initial sounds may not be critical.

CONCLUSIONS

This study asked whether coronal shapes could first be mapped to and then estimated from midline height data, and whether chains of coronal shapes characterized the four tongue shape categories. It was found that, in general, there was a transitional *y*-value at each coronal slice, above which the tongue shape was arched and below which it was grooved. Thus, general estimation of shape could be made. Better estimations are possible with better correlations in both data sets. At the hard palate, there was a strong correlation between midline height and groove shape due to the tongue taking the palate's shape on contact. In the velar region, however, tongue rotation and large elevations reduced the accuracy of shape estimation and quadratic fits of the entire contour are recommended as a supplementary shape parameter. Considering that these predictions were based on two different subjects, nonidentical tongue slices and different speech materials, the results are very promising for 3D tongue shape estimation from midline height.

ACKNOWLEDGMENTS

This study was supported in part by Grant No. R01-DC01758 from the National Institute of Deafness and Other Communication Disorders, NIH.

REFERENCES

Badin, P., Bailly, G., Reveret, L., Baciu, M., & Segebarth, C. (2002). Three dimensional articulatory modeling of tongue, lips and face, based on MRI and video images. *Journal of Phonetics*, *30*, 533–554.

Harshman, R. A., Ladefoged, P., & Goldstein, L. (1977). Factor analysis of tongue shapes. *Journal of the Acoustical Society of America*, *62*, 693–707.

Iskarous, K. (2001). *Dynamic acoustic–articulatory relations*. Ph.D. dissertation, University of Illinois at Urbana-Champaign.

Lundberg, A., & Stone, M. (1999). Three-dimensional tongue surface reconstruction:

Practical considerations for ultrasound data. *Journal of the Acoustical Society of America, 106*, 2858–2867.

Slud, E., Smith, P., Stone, M., & Goldstein, M. (2002). Principal components representation of the two-dimensional coronal tongue surface. *Phonetica, 59*, 108–133.

Stone, M. (1990). A three-dimensional model of tongue movement based on ultrasound and x-ray microbeam data. *Journal of the Acoustical Society of America, 87*, 2207–2217.

Stone, M. (1995). How the tongue takes advantage of the palate during speech. In F. Bell-Berti, & Raphael, L. J. (Eds.), *Producing speech: Contemporary issues: A festschrift for Katherine Safford Harris* (pp. 143–153). New York: American Institute of Physics.

Stone, M., Faber, A., Raphael, L. J., & Shawker, T. H. (1992). Cross-sectional tongue shapes and linguopalatal contact patterns in [s], [ʃ], and [l]. *Journal of Phonetics, 20*, 253–270.

Stone, M., Goldstein, M., & Zhang, Y. (1997). Principal component analysis of cross-sectional tongue shapes in vowels. *Speech Communication, 22*, 173–184.

Stone, M., & Lundberg, A. (1996). Three-dimensional tongue surface shapes of English consonants and vowels. *Journal of the Acoustical Society of America, 99*, 3728–3737.

Stone, M., Shawker, T., Talbot, T., & Rich, A. (1988). Cross-sectional tongue shape during the production of vowels. *Journal of the Acoustical Society of America, 83*, 1586–1596.

Stone, M., & Vatikiotis-Bateson, E. (1995). Trade-offs in tongue, jaw and palate contributions to speech production. *Journal of Phonetics, 23*, 81–100.

Unser, M., & Stone, M. (1992). Automated detection of the tongue surface in sequences of ultrasound images. *Journal of the Acoustical Society of America, 91*, 3001–3007.

Yang, C. S., & Stone, M. (2002). Dynamic programming method for temporal registration of three-dimensional tongue surface motion from multiple utterances. *Speech Communication, 38*, 199–207.

19

Observation of Tongue–Larynx Interaction Using Improved MRI Techniques

SAYOKO TAKANO, KIYOSHI HONDA, AND SHINOBU MASAKI

ABSTRACT

The tongue and larynx interact with each other during speech because they are connected with connective tissues via the hyoid bone. This biomechanical interaction derives small but consistent vowel-dependent variations of the voice fundamental frequency (*F*0) known as the "intrinsic vowel *F*0." This study aims to explore the chain of mechanisms of the tongue–larynx interaction using high-resolution MRI with a custom larynx coil and phonation-synchronized method. Experiments were performed on two male subjects during the production of sustained vowels /a/ and /i/ with high, mid, and low *F*0 values, with the result demonstrating both individual differences and similarities among them. The differences were found in jaw position and vertical position of the hyoid–larynx complex, while the similarities were in tight hyoid–larynx linkage. The tongue root and the hyoid bone were more advanced in vowel /i/ than in vowel /a/. At a higher *F*0, the hyoid–larynx complex was more forward and upward, while jaw position varied between subjects. It was suggested that the movement of the hyoid–larynx complex is caused by contraction of the genioglossus and geniohyoid muscles, but not by jaw position.

INTRODUCTION

The tongue and larynx are mechanically connected by muscles, ligaments, and membranes, which allows mutual interactions mediated by the hyoid bone and jaw. Figure 19.1 shows the anatomical structure of the

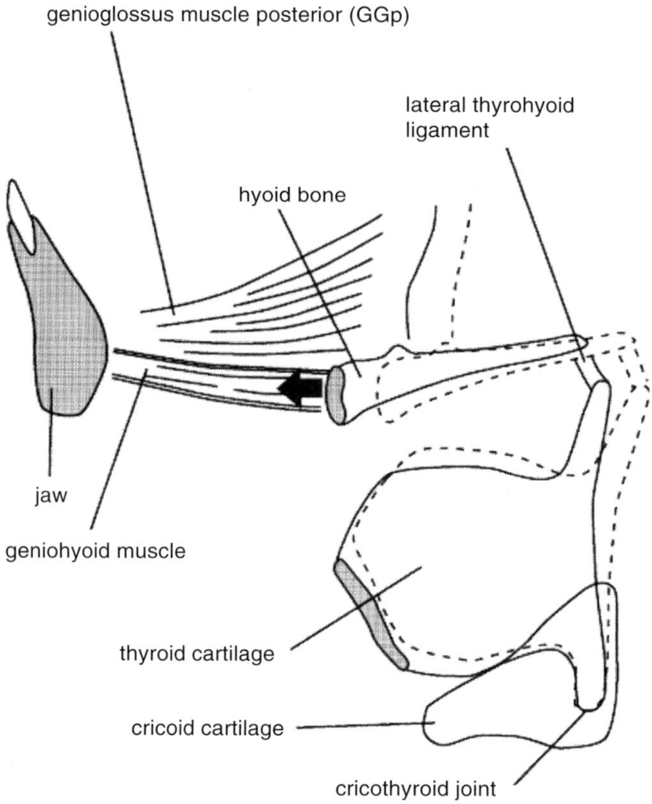

FIGURE 19.1. Geometrical relationship of the jaw, tongue, hyoid bone, and larynx. The mid-sagittal outline of the mandibular symphysis, hyoid bone body, and thyroid lamina were observed by MRI.

tongue and larynx to illustrate their possible interactions. The hyoid bone is located between the tongue and larynx, and its position varies depending on both vowel articulation and *F*0 control. The jaw supports the tongue and laryngeal framework, and its movements can also modulate the tongue–larynx interaction. The tongue and hyoid bone are connected by many muscles, such as the geniohyoid muscle, the inferior part of the genioglossus posterior (GGp) muscle, and the main fibers of the GGp via the connective tissue in the tongue root. The thyroid cartilage and hyoid bone are also mechanically constrained with each other by means of ligaments, membranes, and muscles between them.

Because of these connections, articulatory movements of the tongue influence the function of the larynx, resulting in small but consistent acoustic variations in speech signals. It is well known that higher vowels have a higher fundamental frequency (*F*0) and that lower vowels have a lower one (House & Fairbanks, 1952). This tendency, called "intrinsic vowel *F*0," has been investigated by many researchers. Whalen and Levitt (1995) reviewed the literature of the intrinsic vowel *F*0 cross-linguistically and concluded that the phenomenon is universal. Causal factors of the intrinsic vowel *F*0 have also been studied by many researchers. The mechanism of the intrinsic vowel *F*0 has long been explained by the tongue-pull hypothesis (Lehiste, 1970). This hypothesis has been advanced by an experimental study on hyoid bone movement (Honda, 1983): The hyoid bone moves forward in high vowels, which causes rotation of the thyroid cartilage toward the direction that stretches the vocal folds.

This account, however, lacks empirical support as to whether the thyroid cartilage moves in accordance with the displacement of the hyoid bone. In fact, a few X-ray studies have raised questions about such an interaction mechanism. Vilkman, Aaltonen, Raimo, Arajarvi, and Oksanen (1989) pointed out that intrinsic vowel *F*0 is not dependent on the position of the hyoid bone because their patient, with an inborn anomaly of the hyoid–larynx column, demonstrated that intrinsic *F*0 was instead correlated with cricothyroid muscle activity. Zawadzki and Gilbert (1989) observed a correlation between jaw height and *F*0 using cineradiographic data recorded during running speech, and Beautemps, Badin, and Bailly (2001) also showed that jaw height is strongly correlated with the horizontal position of the hyoid bone.

In this study, we aim to ascertain the biomechanical interaction among the jaw, hyoid bone, and the thyroid cartilage using MRI during productions of /a/ and /i/ with different *F*0 levels. An analysis is performed to examine whether the thyroid cartilage varies in position and orientation due to hyoid bone movement in vowel articulation and *F*0 adjustment in producing sustained vowels.

METHOD

The subjects in our experiments were two Japanese male speakers of middle age. Male subjects are beneficial for MRI study of the laryngeal cartilages because their larynges are larger than females', and the cartilage tends to be ossified with age. Conventional whole-body MRI is excellent for three-dimensional imaging of large organs; on the other hand, there are a few problems with imaging the larynx, such as insufficient image resolution and motion artifacts, which arise both because the larynx is small (Selbie, Gewalt, & Ludlow, 2000) and because it fluctuates in position during respiration and phonation. To solve those problems, we have developed a combined technique with a custom MRI coil designed for imaging the larynx and a synchronized scan method to collect data only during phonation (Takano, Honda, Masaki, Shimada, & Fujimoto, 2003).

While various types of MRI coils are available for imaging the brain, spine, back, and/or joints, there is no appropriate coil for imaging the larynx. For this reason, we made a custom coil by replacing the circular antenna of a small joint coil with an oval one. The antenna of the modified coil has long and short axes of 140 and 75 mm, respectively, and a slightly bent form, as shown in Figure 19.2. This coil can be placed close to the larynx without causing any discomfort to head and neck positions. A preliminary experiment revealed that the coil is capable of capturing anatomical images with a pixel resolution of 0.25 mm × 0.25 mm for a slice thickness of 1.0 mm.

Because the larynx moves vertically for respiration and phonation during long scan periods, static MRI suffers from motion artifacts. To avoid this problem, we developed a phonation-synchronized technique to allow a subject to breath and phonate during MRI experiments. This technique has been modified from a

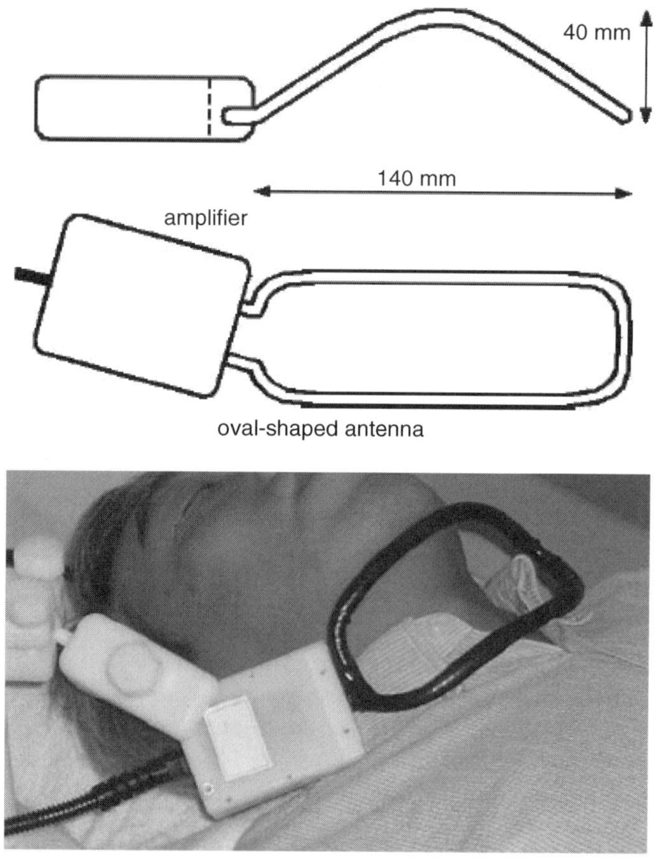

FIGURE 19.2. Custom MRI coil for high-resolution imaging of the larynx; oval-shaped antenna of the coil (top) was designed to be placed in front of the subject's neck (bottom).

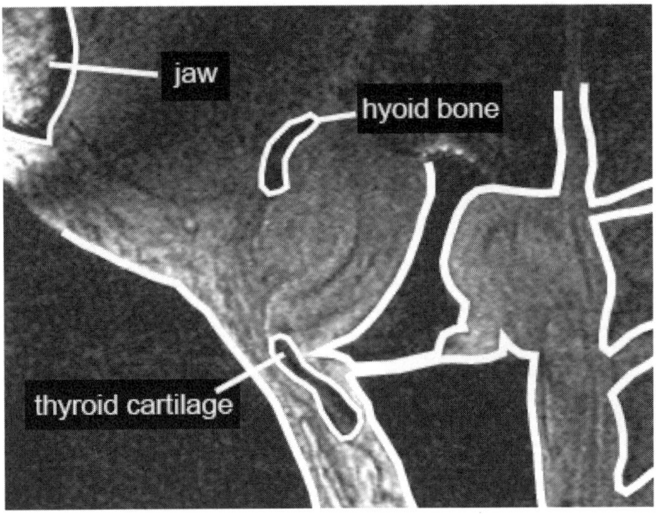

FIGURE 19.3. Tracing of the jaw, hyoid bone, and thyroid cartilage with the laryngeal cavity from a mid-sagittal image.

motion-imaging technique using an external trigger device (Masaki, Tiede, & Honda, 1999) to be applied to static imaging. A program on a personal computer generates trigger pulse trains to initiate MRI scan bursts, and it also outputs noise-burst and sine-wave trains to the subject via a headset. The subject listens to the noise-burst and sine-wave signals as a guide to adjust the onset of phonation with the intended *F*0 and the following breathing, while scans are performed only during the subject's phonation. The two subjects were instructed to produce /a/ and /i/ matching their *F*0 to target tones of 110 Hz (henceforth "low"), 136 Hz (henceforth "middle"), and 165 Hz (henceforth "high").

Figure 19.3 shows a high-resolution MRI in the mid-sagittal slice of the larynx and its tracings. In this MRI sequence, all of the tissues, including muscles and fatty tissue, show up as high signals (white), while the calcified tissue without protons appears dark. Therefore, the hyoid bone and thyroid cartilage are relatively dark in comparison to the surrounding tissues for this subject. The cricoid cartilage is barely visible in the mid-sagittal slice, and is less obvious than the thyroid cartilage.

RESULTS

The positions of the jaw, hyoid bone, and thyroid cartilage traced from the mid-sagittal images were compared in two sets of figures (Figures 19.4 and 19.5 for *F*0

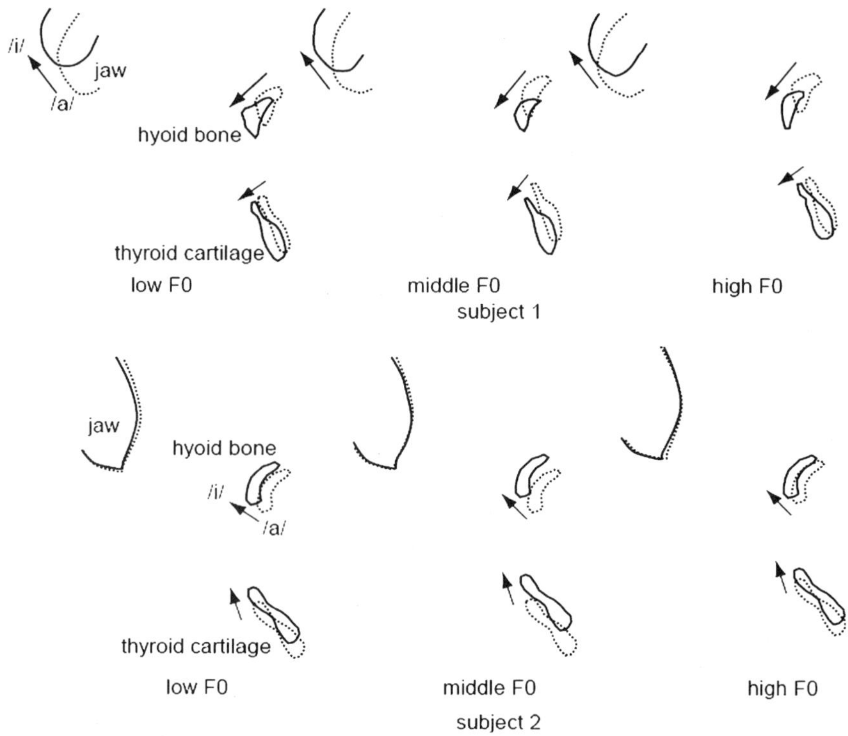

FIGURE 19.4. Displacement of the jaw, hyoid bone, and thyroid cartilage between vowel /a/ and /i/ at each *F*0.

and vowels, respectively). In Figure 19.6, landmark positions of the jaw, hyoid bone, and thyroid cartilage were plotted for the two vowels as a function of the *F*0.

Figure 19.4 shows positions of the jaw, hyoid bone, and thyroid cartilage between /a/ and /i/ at three *F*0 levels for the two subjects. In this figure, the hyoid bone and the thyroid cartilage show similar displacements in both subjects, while the jaw demonstrates a tendency different to the hyoid bone. Horizontal displacement of the hyoid bone and thyroid cartilage was consistent between the two subjects: The hyoid bone position was forward in /i/ and backward in /a/. In contrast, vertical displacement of the hyoid bone and thyroid cartilage differed between the two subjects. In Subject 1, the hyoid bone was lower in /i/ and higher in /a/, while in Subject 2, it was higher in /i/ and lower in /a/. Similarly, the jaw position was higher in /i/ than /a/ in Subject 1, whereas its position was almost constant in Subject 2.

Figure 19.5 shows positional changes of each organ between high and low *F*0 values for each vowel. In this figure, the positional relationship between the

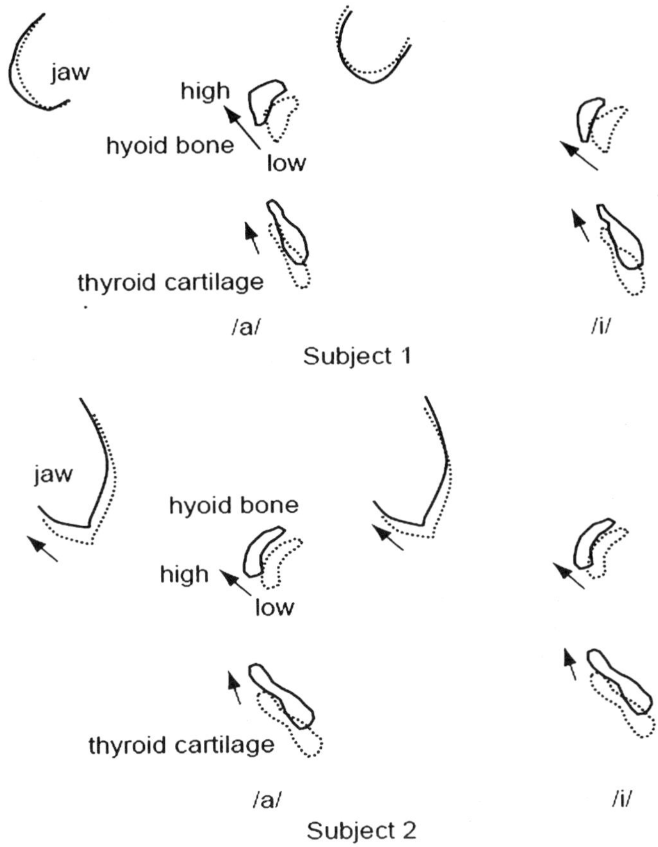

FIGURE 19.5. Displacement of the jaw, hyoid bone, and thyroid cartilage between low and high *F*0 in each vowel.

hyoid bone and thyroid cartilage is nearly constant for low *F*0. In both subjects, the positions of the hyoid bone and thyroid cartilage were higher and more advanced at a higher *F*0. The jaw position was almost constant across all *F*0 levels in Subject 1, though it was raised at a higher *F*0 in Subject 2.

Figure 19.6 summarizes changes in vertical and horizontal positions of the landmarks on the jaw (lowest point), hyoid bone (lowest point), and thyroid cartilage (lowest point) at the three *F*0 levels. The major difference between the two subjects is the jaw position both in vowel articulation and *F*0 control. Between two vowels, the jaw is lower in /a/ than in /i/ in Subject 1, while it is almost constant in Subject 2. As for the *F*0, the jaw falls as *F*0 rises in Subject 1, while the jaw rises as *F*0 rises in Subject 2. Contrarily from such an individual difference in jaw position, the mutual relationship between the hyoid bone

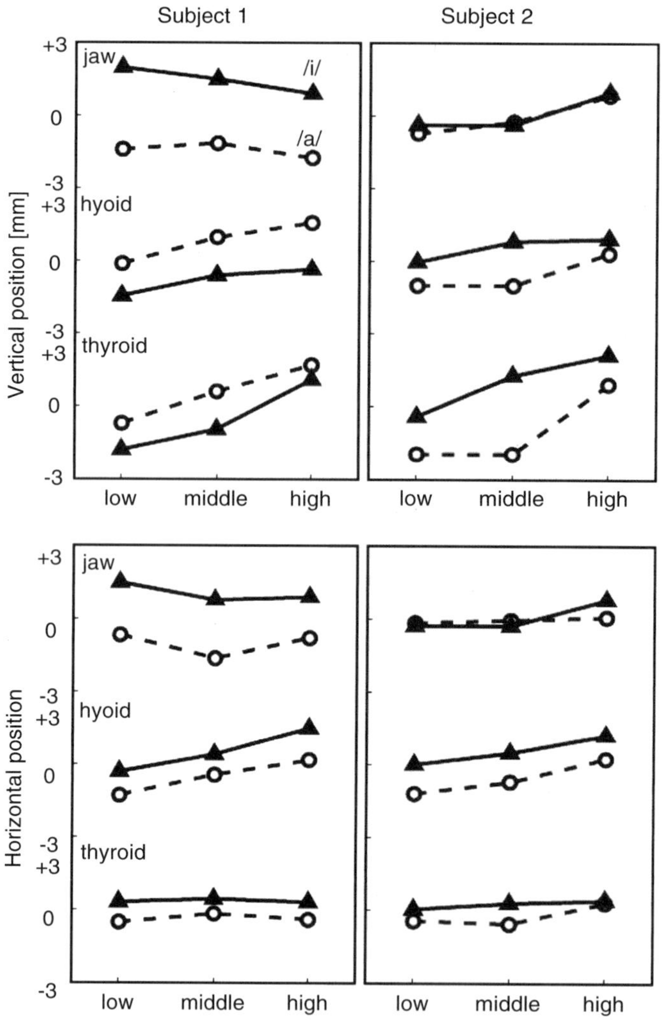

FIGURE 19.6. Horizontal and vertical coordinates of the landmarks on the jaw, hyoid bone, and thyroid cartilage. The landmark points are the bottom of the jaw, hyoid bone, and thyroid cartilage.

and thyroid cartilage is relatively constant, except for the vertical positional difference between the vowels. In the two subjects, the hyoid bone and thyroid cartilage shift in the same direction as the *F*0 changes. It may be summarized from the figure that the jaw is used for vowel articulation in Subject 1 while it is employed for *F*0 control in Subject 2. In both subjects, the hyoid bone and thyroid cartilage appear to function together in *F*0 control, and the thyroid cartilage shows remarkable elevation and slight advancement as the *F*0 rises.

DISCUSSION

In this study, the biomechanical interaction among the jaw, hyoid bone, and thyroid cartilage was investigated to explore its effects on the position of the thyroid cartilage. Observation of the larynx was accomplished with two new techniques for high-resolution MRI: a laryngeal coil and a phonation-synchronized scan. In the result described above, both differences and similarities are found between the two subjects regarding the positional relationship among the jaw, hyoid bone, and thyroid cartilage. The discrepancies between the subjects were in the jaw position and vertical position of the hyoid–larynx complex for /a/ and /i/. The similarities were movement of the hyoid–larynx complex across *F*0 levels and its horizontal component between vowels.

The major difference between the data from the two subjects was the contrast between the two vowels in the degree of jaw opening, and the height order of the hyoid–larynx complex. The jaw position was higher in /i/ and lower in /a/ in Subject 1, while there were no jaw height differences in Subject 2. Furthermore, the hyoid–larynx complex was higher in /a/ in Subject 1, while it was higher in /i/ in Subject 2. Possible explanations for the difference may be given as follows: The large jaw movement in vowel articulation in Subject 1 involves activity of the supra-hyoid muscle for jaw opening, which results in a higher position of the hyoid–larynx complex in /a/. On the other hand, the stationary jaw position in vowel articulation in Subject 2 requires a large excursion of the tongue body for contrasting vowels, which is accompanied by a large movement of the hyoid–larynx complex possibly caused by the strap muscles such as the sternohyoid and sternothyroid muscles.

The similarity between the data from the subjects is the positional relationship between the hyoid bone and thyroid cartilage. In both subjects, when the hyoid bone was higher, the thyroid cartilage was also higher, regardless of vowels and *F*0 levels. Also, when the hyoid bone was more advanced, the thyroid cartilage was also more advanced, which suggests that the mechanical connection between the hyoid bone and thyroid cartilage is tighter than between the jaw and hyoid bone. As a result, the hyoid–larynx complex moves in unison in vowel articulation and *F*0 control, and advancement of the hyoid bone results in horizontal movement of the thyroid cartilage. These observations imply that, in the articulation of /i/, advancement of the hyoid bone due to contraction of the genioglossus muscle can apply a force on the thyroid cartilage. This mechanism of biomechanical interaction between the tongue and larynx is consistent with the notion that hyoid bone movement in vowel articulation is the causal factor of the intrinsic vowel *F*0 (Honda, 1981).

A problem remaining in this study is whether the thyroid cartilage does rotate in /i/ in a direction that stretches the vocal folds as speculated by Honda (1981). In our MRI study reported elsewhere on rotation and translation of the cricothyroid joint in *F*0 control (Takano et al., 2003), the thyroid cartilage is observed to displace without rotation, and joint translation does occur horizontally. Considering the results of the present study and our previous study on cricothyroid joint movement, it may be suggested that the advancement of the hyoid bone in higher vowels contributes to vowel-to-vowel variation in *F*0 through advancement of the thyroid cartilage, possibly with translation of the cricothyroid joint.

ACKNOWLEDGMENTS

We would like to give special thanks to the members of the ATR Brain Activity Imaging Center. We also deeply appreciate the kind comments of Dr. Beautemps at the conference. This work was conducted while the first author belonged to the CREST of JST (Japan Science and Technology). This research was also supported in part by the National Institute of Information and Communications Technology.

REFERENCES

Beautemps, D., Badin, P., & Bailly, G. (2001). Linear degrees of freedom in speech production: Analysis of cineradio- and labio-film data and articulatory-acoustic modeling. *Journal of the Acoustical Society of America*, *109*, 2165–2180.

Honda, K. (1983). Relationship between pitch control and vowel articulation. In D. M. Bless & J. H. Abbs (Eds.), *Vocal fold physiology* (pp. 286–297). San Diego: College-Hill Press.

House, A. S., & Fairbanks, G. (1953). The influence of consonant environment upon the secondary acoustical characteristics of vowels. *Journal of the Acoustical Society of America*, *25*, 105–113.

Lehiste, I. (1970). *Suprasegmentals*. Cambridge: MIT Press.

Masaki, S., Tiede, M., & Honda, K. (1999). MRI-based speech production study using a synchronized sampling method. *Journal of the Acoustical Society of Japan* (E), *20*, 375–379.

Rossi, M., & Autesserre, D. (1981). Movement of the hyoid and the larynx and the intrinsic frequency of vowel. *Journal of Phonetics*, *9*, 233–249.

Selbie, W.S., Gewalt, S.L., & Ludlow, C. (2002). Developing an anatomical model of the human laryngeal cartilages from magnetic resonance imaging, *Journal of the Acoustical Society of America*, *112*, 1077–1090.

Takano, S., Honda, K., Masaki, S., Shimada, Y., & Fujimoto, I. (2003). Translation and rotation of the cricothyroid joint revealed by phonation-synchronized high-resolution MRI. *EuroSpeech 2003*, Geneva, Switzerland (pp. 2397–2400).

Vilkman, E., Aaltonen, O., Raimo, I., Arajarvi, P., & Oksanen, H. (1989). Articulatory hyoid–laryngeal changes vs. cricothyroid muscle activity in the control of intrinsc *F*0 of vowels. *Journal of Phonetics*, *17*, 193–203.

Whalen, D. H., & Levitt, A. G. (1995). The universality of intrinsic *F*0 of vowels. *Journal of Phonetics*, *23*, 349–366.

Zawadzki, P. A., & Gilbert, H. R. (1989). Vowel fundamental frequency and articulator position. *Journal of Phonetics*, *17*, 159–166.

20

Morphing Generic Organs to Speaker-Specific Anatomies

MAXIME BÉRAR, GÉRARD BAILLY, MATTHIEU CHABANAS, MICHEL DESVIGNES, FRÉDÉRIC ELISEI, MATTHIAS ODISIO, AND YOHAN PAYAN

ABSTRACT

We present here a framework for developing a generic talking head capable of reproducing the anatomy and the facial deformations induced by speech movements with only a few parameters. Speech-related facial movements are controlled by six parameters. We characterize the skull and mandible variability by six and seven free parameters, respectively. Speaker-specific skull, jaw, and face data are normalized using generic meshes of these organs and a robust 3D-to-3D matching procedure. Further analysis of these normalized data is performed using a decomposition of the 3D variance based on iterative principal component analysis aimed at identifying and predicting kinematic consequences of anatomical settings.

INTRODUCTION

Speech articulation has clear visible consequences. While the movements of the lips and the cheeks are immediately visible, the movements of the underlying musculo-skeletal structure (jaw, larynx, and tongue) also have visible consequences on the skin. Building biomechanical/statistical models that can reproduce/capture the visible characteristics of speech articulation is a prerequisite for comprehensive models of audiovisual integration, multimodal speech production, and control. Most models of articulatory control of speech articulators (see Badin, Bailly, Revéret, Baciu, Segebarth, & Savariaux, 2002, for a review) are based on data from only a few subjects, sometimes only one. The main challenge of speech production studies now is to consider the problem of inter-speaker variability: If we share the same underlying anatomical structures, speakers differ in the way they recruit and coordinate speech organs. Part of this variability is effectively due to the anatomical differences (Hashi, Westbury, & Honda, 1998) but part is also due to different control strategies exploiting articulatory degrees of freedom in excess. Besides understanding inter-speaker variability in articulation, there is also a clear technological need for generic models that can be adapted to speaker-specific anatomy and movements: Systems such as model-based computer vision (Eisert & Girod, 1998; Pighin, Szeliski, & Salesin, 1999) or MPEG-4/SNHC coding scheme (Pandzic & Forchheimer, 2002) require a generic mesh to be adapted to a real speaker via separate conformation and animation parameters. MPEG-4 facial animation parameters (FAP) and facial definition parameters (FDP) constitute a tentative separation between speaker-independent articulation parameters and speaker-specific conformation parameters. FAP (resp. FDP) describe movements (resp. neutral position) of facial/lingual fleshpoints in terms of normalized values related to five FAP units, i.e., reference lengths for nose length, lip width at rest, etc. This normalization scheme that shapes both conformation (FDP) and articulation (FAP) has no real experimental grounds and should be tested using real data.

The first aim of this work is to relate free dimensions of speaker anatomy—supposed to be mainly due to bony structures such as shape of the skull and jaw—to free dimensions of its facial appearance and movements. Static relations are primarily of interest for anthropology and forensic medicine (see, e.g., Kähler, Haber, & Seidel, 2003) when there is only access to dry bones for building hypotheses about subjects' appearance. For this purpose, statistical models can effectively provide reconstructions together with statistical precision. Kinematic relations, by contrast, are of interest not only for vision applications but also for maxillofacial surgery, where prediction of functional behavior from anatomical changes is crucial for presurgical planning.

Another challenge of this work is to relate these detailed shape models to the dimensions of feature points—such as cephalometric points (e.g., glabella and porion for the skull) or to motion capture data typically restricted to a few hundred dots glued on the speaker's face—that can be rapidly and easily acquired using simple 3D measurements.

Our approach consists of building an articulated atlas that can be adapted to the speaker's anatomy via conformation parameters. These conformation parameters relate both to free parameters of the underlying bony structure (skull, jaw, hyoid bone, etc.) and their relative positioning but also to mean shape of skin tissues (lips, cheeks, etc.). These conformation parameters further determine how basic speech-specific articulatory movements (jaw rotation, lip

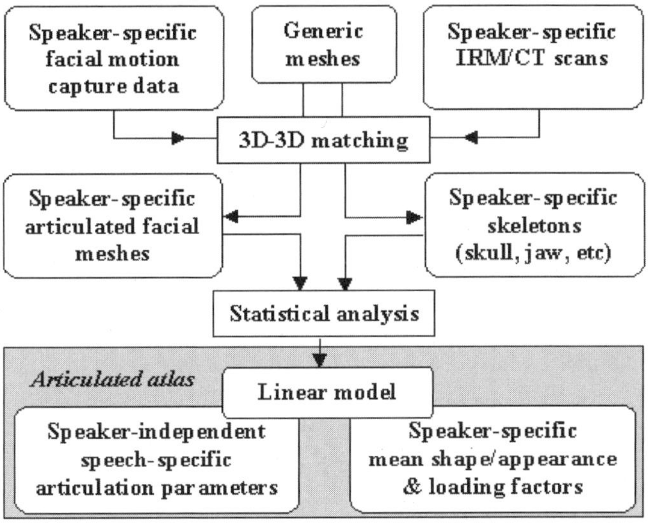

FIGURE 20.1. Building an articulated atlas dedicated to speech articulation from speaker-specific data. A 3D-to-3D matching procedure delivers meshes with the same number of vertices. The matched vertices should refer to identical—in structural terms—facial and bony landmarks. A further statistical analysis then identifies the speaker-specific impact of basic speech-specific articulations (jaw rotation, lip rounding, etc.).

rounding, etc.) deform the speaker's facial shape and appearance. An articulated atlas is built using a collection of speaker-specific data and intensive statistical analysis (see Figure 20.1). The paper focuses here on the key component of the system: the 3D-to-3D matching procedure.

This paper describes our approach for building shape models by adapting a static generic model to speaker-specific static raw X-ray tomography (see sections Building normalized shapes for the skull and A generic shape model for the skull) and motion capture data (sections Speaker-specific talking heads and Shaping a generic model to speaker-specific data). An extension of this approach to appearance models is also sketched. The section Building normalized shapes for the skull describes how we obtain a normalized speaker-specific skull and mandible using a 3D-to-3D matching procedure. The section A generic shape model for the skull explores the free dimensions of skull and mandible shape models using CT scans from 12 subjects. The section Speaker-specific talking heads presents how fine-grained speaker-specific facial movements have been collected and modeled for five subjects and the section Shaping a generic model to speaker-specific data focuses on how the 3D-to-3D matching procedure that has been extended to speaker-specific shape models is able to reproduce faithfully speech-related facial movements of our five subjects. Finally, the section Speaker-independent articulatory parameters vs. speaker-specific shape model presents the guidelines for further linking kinematic degrees of freedom to morphological parameters.

BUILDING NORMALIZED SHAPES FOR THE SKULL

In order to quantify the anatomical differences between speakers, we would like to construct a statistical model of the variability of the morphology of the skull. As each skull shape should share the same mesh structure with the same number of vertices (see the section Speaker-independent articulatory parameters vs. speaker-specific shape model), we need to register all the meshes in a subject-shared reference system. In our system, a generic mesh is mapped to the surface of the skull for several subjects. The mapping is done in such a way that each triangle of the mesh is associated with the same region of the skull, while the variability in the position of the vertices reflects the anatomical characteristics of each subject. The vertices of these shared meshes can be considered as semi-landmarks, i.e., as points that do not have names but that correspond to each other across all the cases of a data set under a reasonable model of deformation from their common mean (Bookstein, 1997). The shared meshes are obtained by matching generic meshes of the skull and the jaw (see Figure 20.2c) to several speaker-specific meshes (see the section Data collection protocol and Figure 20.2b) using our 3D-to-3D matching algorithm.

3D-to-3D Matching

The basic principle of the 3D-to-3D matching procedure developed by Couteau, Payan, and Lavallée (2000) consists basically of the deformation of the initial 3D space by a series of trilinear transformations T_l (see Wolberg,

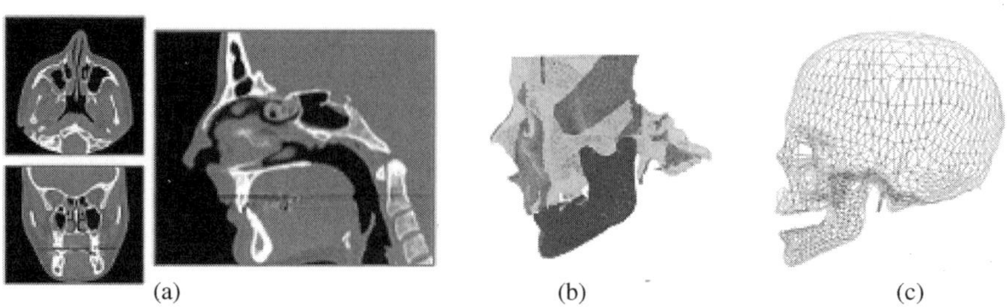

FIGURE 20.2. (a) Raw scan data (only coronal slices were collected; midsagittal and axial have been reconstructed here by image processing); (b) shape reconstructed using the marching cubes algorithm (Lorensen and Cline, 1987); and (c) generic mesh obtained from the Visible Human Project®.

1990, for more details) applied to all vertices q_i of elementary cubes (see also Figure 20.3):

$$T_l\,(q_i, p) = \begin{bmatrix} p_{00} & p_{01} & & p_{07} \\ p_{10} & p_{11} & \cdots & p_{17} \\ p_{20} & p_{21} & & p_{27} \end{bmatrix} [1\ x_i\ y_i\ z_i\ x_iy_i\ y_iz_i\ z_ix_i\ x_iy_iz_i]^T \qquad (20.1)$$

The parameters p of each trilinear transformation T_l are computed iteratively using the minimization of a cost function (see Eq. [20.2] below). The elementary

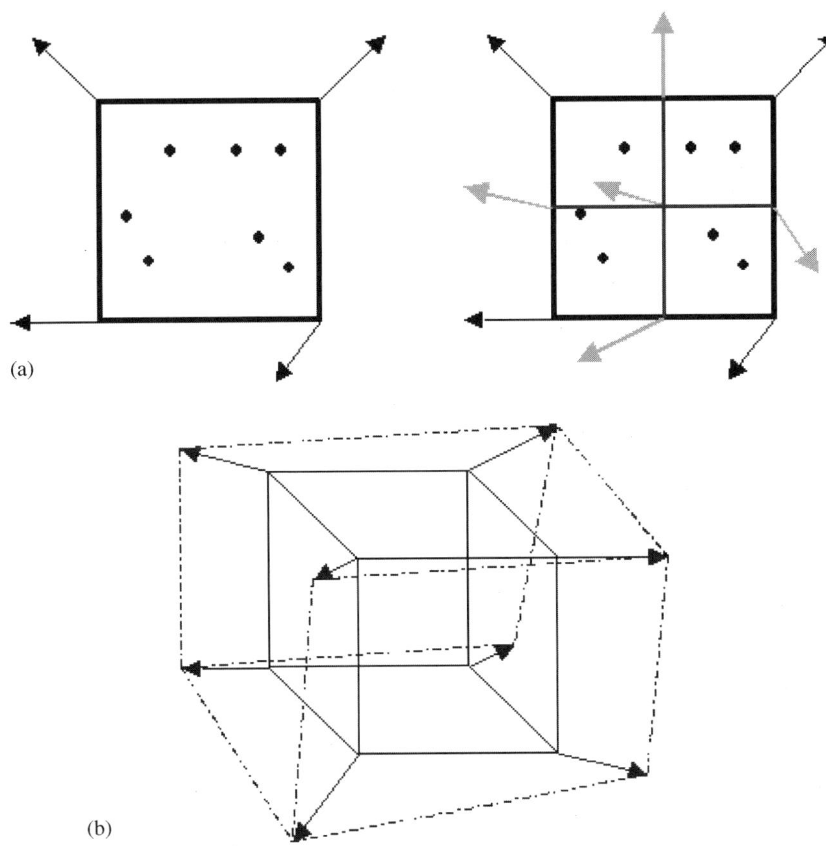

FIGURE 20.3. Applying a trilinear transformation to a cube. (a) 2D simplification of a subdivision into $n = 4$ elementary volumes of the original space and new transformation vectors; and (b) elementary 3D transformation within a cube.

cubes are determined by iteratively subdividing the input space (see Figure 20.3) in order to minimize the Euclidian distance between the 3D surfaces:

$$\min_{p}\left[\sum_{i=1;i\notin \text{Paired}(S_S,S_T)}^{\text{card}(S_S)}[d(T(s_i,p),S_T)]^2+Rw\sum_{k\in \text{Paired}(S_S,S_T)}[d(T(s_k,p),t_k)]^2+P(p)\right] \quad (20.2)$$

where S_S is the source surface to be adjusted to the set of points $\{t_i\}$ of the target surface S_T, p the parameters of the transformations T (six parameters of the initial roto-translation of the reference coordinate system plus 3×8 parameters for each embedded trilinear transformation) applied to the set of points $\{s_i\}$ of S_S. $P(p)$ is a regularization function that guarantees the continuity of the transformations at the limits of each subdivision of the 3D space and that allows larger deformations for smaller subdivisions. The second term weighted by the factor Rw deals with feature points and was added for this study. Rw compensates for the few paired points usually available. Its value is set with a high value at the first mapping for forcing pairing. It can then be decreased once transformed and target surfaces are close enough. In Eq. (20.2), the first term deals with the distance between the points and the surface (considering the projection of each point onto the deformed surface). The second term deals with point-to-point distance: A set of 3D feature points $\{t_k\}$ of the target surface S_T are identified and paired with $\{s_k\}$ vertices of the source surface S_S. The minimization is performed using the Levenberg–Marquardt algorithm (Szeliski & Lavallée, 1996).

Data Collection Protocol

Data Collection. Coronal CT slices (see Figure 20.2a) were collected for the partial skulls of 12 subjects (helical scan with a 1 mm pitch and slices reconstructed every 0.31 or 0.48 mm). The Marching Cubes algorithm (Lorensen & Cline, 1987) has been implemented to reconstruct the skull from CT slices on isosurfaces (see Figure 20.2b). The mandible and the skull are separated before the beginning of the matching process, our subjects having different mandible apertures. Speaker-specific meshes for the skull and jaw have respectively around 180,000 and 30,000 vertices. The respective generic meshes recovered from the female speaker of the Visible Human Project (Banvard, 2002) have 3473 and 1100 vertices (see Figure 20.2c). We then use our 3D-to-3D matching algorithm, obtaining separate normalized meshes of these organs.

Mandible Registration. The transformed mandible is well matched to the closest surface but the correspondence between the two surfaces is false (see Figure 20.4 in the separate color plate section). The "single distance" approach leads to many mismatches in the condyle and gonial angle regions: This is due to the necessary difference of density between the source and target meshes (number of vertices, respectively, 30 and 70 times larger in the source meshes

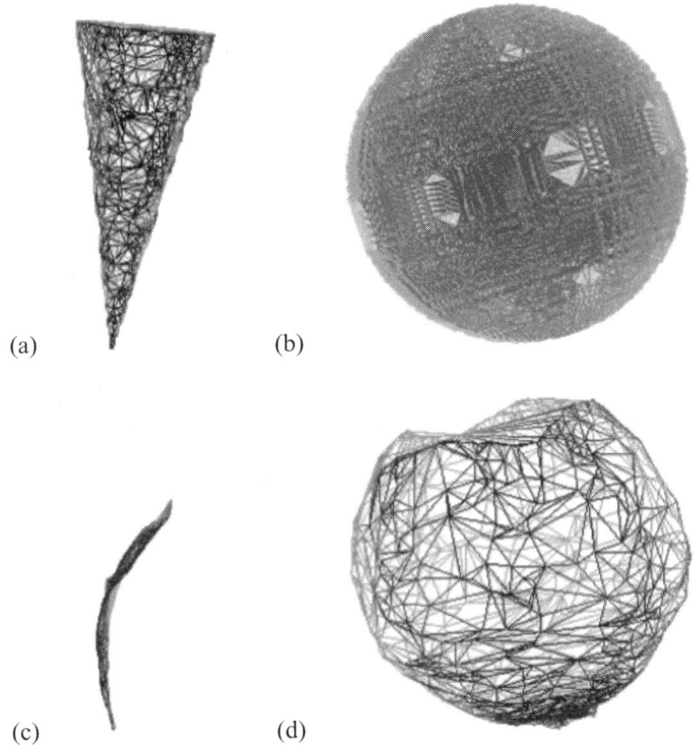

FIGURE 20.5. Matching a cone (a) to a sphere (b). (c) Mismatched cone using the standard matching method. (d) Matched cone using the symmetric matching method.

than in the target meshes). In this case, the distance from the transformed source to the target $d(T(s_i, p), S_T)$ is very low, whereas the adaptation of the target to the source may result in a much larger distance $d(T(t_i, p), S_S)$ (see Figure 20.5). Part of this mismatch is due to the problem of identification of the internal vs. external surfaces from CT scans. This could be solved by exploiting more intensively surface normals if reliable. Paired feature points could also have been used (as for the skin in the section Matching a neutral configuration) but the dramatic disproportion between the number of vertices and feature points cause, for instance, too many problems of convergence: Point-to-point pairing in this case should be replaced by the association of a target point with an entire region of the source. However this point-to-region pairing should be adapted during the matching process and often results in too many local deformations.

The problem of matching symmetry can be better observed using very different synthetic shapes. In Figure 20.5, the mismatched cone is well matched considering the first distance but is flattened on one border of the sphere.

We therefore symmetrize the minimization function of Eq. (20.2) (as in Moshfeghi, 1991) by adding a term that computes also the distance of the target mesh to the transformed source mesh using the pseudo-inverse transform T-1 in the following way:

$$\min_{p}\left[\sum_{i=1;i\notin \mathrm{Paired}(S_S)}^{\mathrm{card}(S_S)}[d(T(s_i,p),S_T)]^2+\sum_{j=1;j\notin \mathrm{Paired}(S_T)}^{\mathrm{card}(S_T)}[d(T^{-1}(t_j,p),S_S)]^2+Rw\right.$$

$$\left.\sum_{k\in \mathrm{Paired}\,(S_S,\,S_T)}[d(T(s_k,p),t_k)]^2+P(p)\right] \tag{20.3}$$

Using such a symmetric matching to mandible meshes (see Figure 20.6 in the separate color plate section), the maximal distances are located now on the teeth and on the coronoid process. The mean distances can be considered as the registration noise, again due to the difference of density (see Table 20.1).

Skull Registration. We possess complete skull volume data for only two of our subjects (since these data were collected during regular medical exams and excitation of the brain volume is avoided if not necessary). We therefore choose to first register a partial mesh of each skull, using cutting planes adjusted by hand. Symmetric matching insures better registration, as the partial mesh and the original data have equivalent shapes.

We then register the whole mesh to its transformed part ensuring a transformation with low noise as each vertex of the transformed partial mesh has an equivalent in the whole mesh. During this step, the cranial vault is (most of the time) inferred from the border of the skull, using the continuity of the transformation; hence, it cannot be considered accurate.

The maximal distances found in the resulting mesh are situated in the spikes beneath the skull, where the individual variability is large and the surface noise too high to be fitted even with elastic transformations. Moreover calcified styloid processes are only partially recovered from the scans. The nasal bone and the back of the skull are often matched to the internal scan contour (which should be corrected using normal information). At the end of the process, the mean and maximum absolute distances between the target and transformed

TABLE 20.1. Mean Distances between Transformed and Target Jaw Meshes

	Generic →Scan		Scan→Generic	
Distances (mm)	mean	max.	mean	max.
Single	1.27	9.28	5.80	56.87
Symmetric	1.33	8.42	2.57	22.78

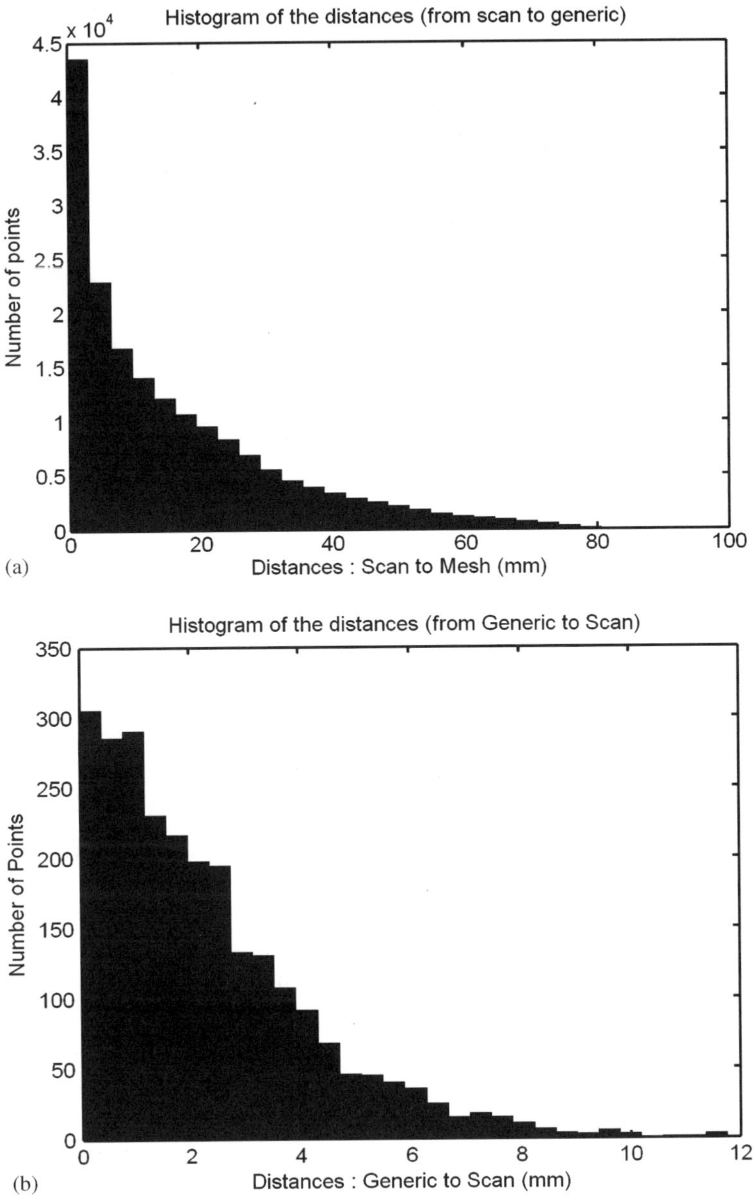

(a)

(b)

FIGURE 20.7. Histogram of distances (mm) between points of the transform mesh to the target mesh: left, for the jaw; right, for the skull.

meshes—cumulated across subjects—are, respectively, 2 and 8 mm for the jaw and 4 and 36 mm for the skull (see distance histograms for one subject in Figure 20.7). The mean RMS noise level at the end of the process is 5 mm. The large maximal error for the skull is due to the high variable shape (or more exactly the length) of the styloid processes (see Figure 20.8 in the separate color plate section). This part of the skull is too small and thin—like the anterior nasal spine and teeth—to be exactly morphed by a trilinear transformation of the space without any further surface pairing. When these regions are discarded, the maximum error is less than 6 mm.

A GENERIC SHAPE MODEL FOR THE SKULL

We first fit the 12 matched skulls and jaws on mean configurations using Procrustes normalization (Dryden & Mardia, 1998). Seven degrees of freedom due to initial location and scale are retrieved by this fit (three due to translation along three axes, three due to rotations about three axes, and one for scale adjustment). We then perform a principal component analysis (PCA) on the normalized data to build a linear model of shape variation. We compress the model to six principal modes of deformation for the skull and seven principal modes of deformation for the mandible. These principal modes of deformation represent 95% of the variance of the data and explain a large amount of shape variation.

Skull

In the case of the skull, six principal dimensions explain over 95% of the variability of the shapes (see Table 20.2). Figure 20.9 displays these dimensions. The first parameter influences variations of the volume of the skull (this should not be considered since part of this skull is obtained by extrapolation using the T transform outside of the fitting volume) together with the advance of the lacrimal and nasal bones. The second parameter acts upon the relative width of the skull and the prominence of the maxilla. The third parameter is linked to the size of the temporal bones. The fourth parameter is correlated to the height of the orbita. The fifth parameter is linked to the shape of the forehead. The sixth parameter deals with an asymmetry of the left part of the skull (temporal bone and orbita).

TABLE 20.2. Percentage (Cumulative) of Variance Explained for the 3D Skull and Jaw Data Explained

Factors	F1	F2	F3	F4	F5	F6	F7
Skull	46.1	19.9 (66.0)	14.4 (80.4)	6.2 (86.6)	4.8 (91.4)	3.7 (95.1)	
Jaw	28.4	25.3 (53.7)	14.8 (68.5)	9.2 (77.7)	8.0 (85.7)	6.3 (91.9)	4.2 (96.1)
Jaw by skull factors	5.7	10.8 (16.5)	19.8 (36.2)	22.6 (58.9)	9.5 (68.4)	10.1 (78.5)	

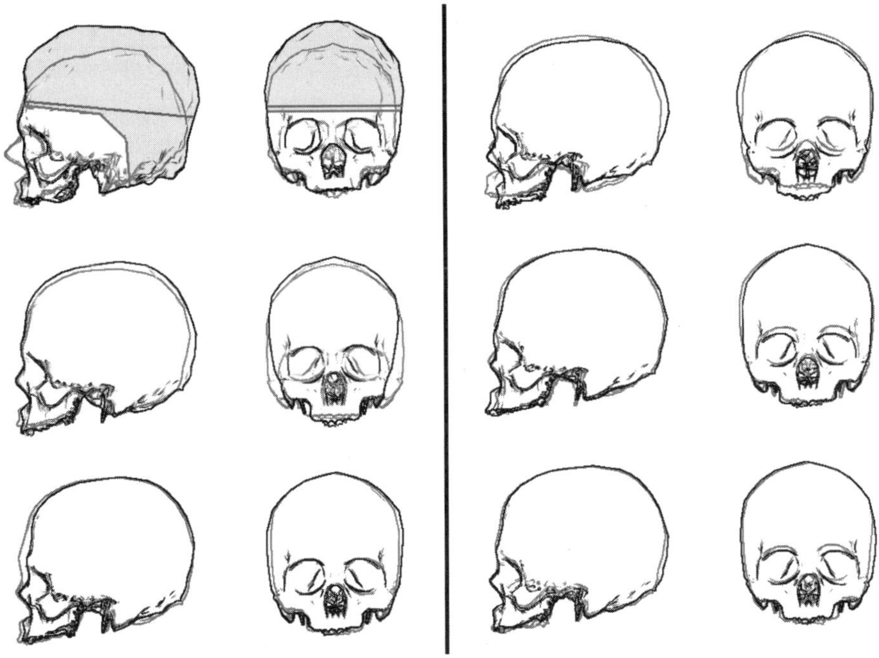

FIGURE 20.9. Variations of the skull shape according to the six modes for parameters varying between +3 and −3 times the standard deviation. Maximum and minimum fitting volume (which depends on available CT scan data) is indicated on the first mode.

The accuracy of the reconstruction (see Figure 20.10) is under the millimeter in the shape space (after rigid registration) even for the "worst" individual. Before Procrutes registration, the mean reconstruction accuracy is less than 1 mm but the worst individual is at 3 mm.

We processed scan data from two test individuals not included in the training database. Mode values obtained by regression are less than 3 standard deviation (see Table 20.3) and in most cases less than 1 standard deviation. The mean accuracy of their reconstruction is 4 mm for the skull, which is less than the RMS registration noise.

Mandible

Seven principal modes (see Table 20.2) emerge from PCA performed on the mandible data. Figure 20.11 displays these dimensions. The first parameter explains the variation of the goniac angle and the size of the alveolar region, while the second parameter controls the relative size of the condylar and coronoid processes and correction of the goniac angle.

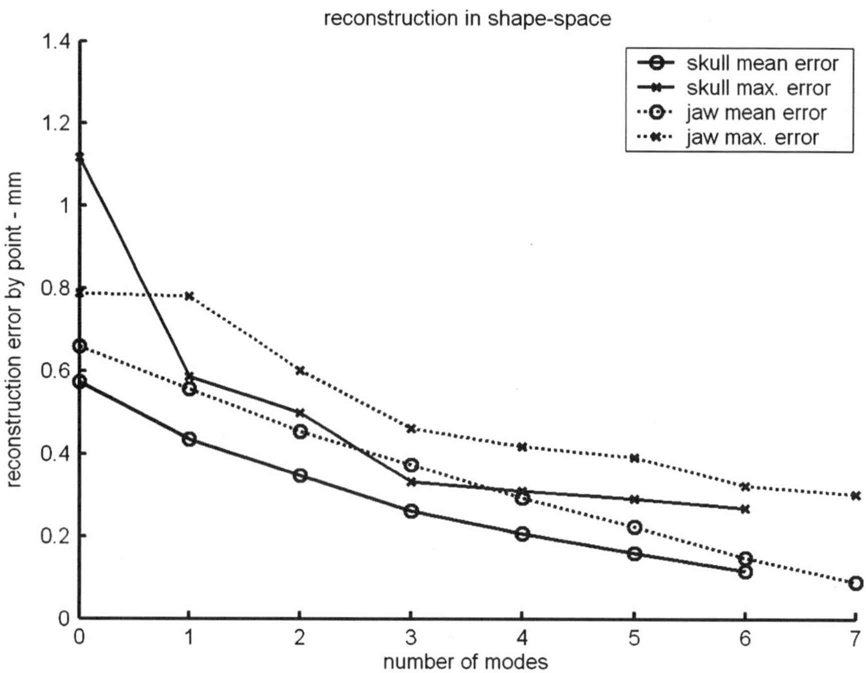

FIGURE 20.10. Mean and maximum reconstruction errors of the skull and jaw using an increasing number of modes.

TABLE 20.3. Mode Values of Two Test Subjects (Normalized by Standard Deviation)

Factors	F1	F2	F3	F4	F5	F6	F7
Skull	−1.2/−0.7	0.4/−0.5	0.4/ 0.0	0.3/−3.0	0.6/−0.7	0.6/−0.3	
Mandible	0.1/0.4	0.3/−0.4	0.1/−0.8	0.2/−1.8	1.3/0.3	0.0/−0.1	0.9/−0.1

Co-Dependency of Mandible and Skull

If we perform regression analysis on the mandible data using the shape parameters found for their skull counterparts, we can explain up to 78% of the variability of the shape of the mandibles (see Table 20.2). The parameters with strong influences are the third and first skull parameters, which are responsible for the relative width of the skull and the shape and size of the maxilla.

Discussion

This enhanced 3D-to-3D matching procedure has been intensively used for regularizing and morphing meshes to patient's data in the context of medical

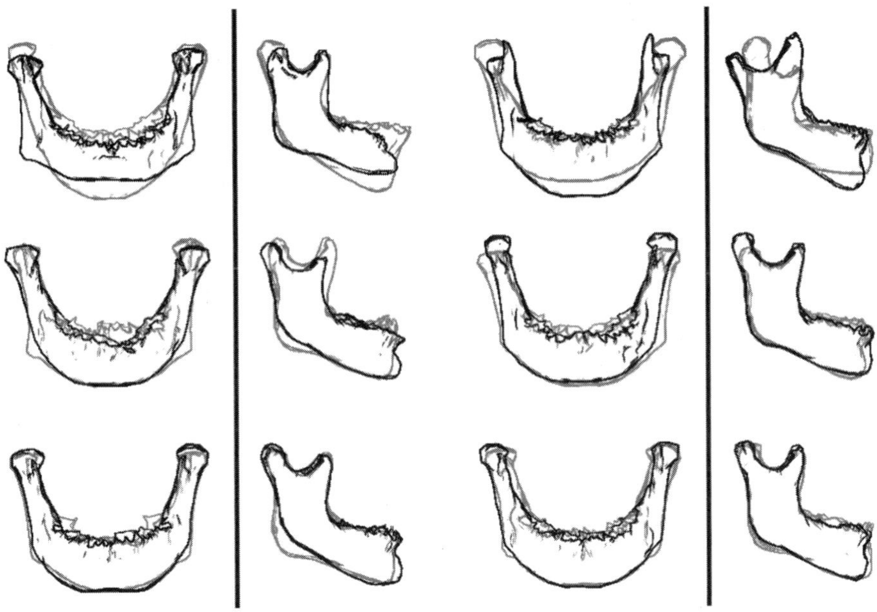

FIGURE 20.11. Variations of the mandible shape according to the six modes for parameters varying between +3 and −3 standard deviation.

applications. The transformed meshes registered from static scans are then often used to track organs in motion. This is of particular interest for non-rigid organs such as soft tissues. (Bio-)mechanical properties bound to the generic mesh can effectively be used to restrict deformations. These properties can be inherited from biomechanical models (Couteau et al., 2000). We propose here to build generic models of soft tissues that can be adapted to the target subject. We follow the same procedure as above, relying on intensive collection of motion capture data. The ultimate aim of this work is to be able to morph generic models of rigid and soft tissues to a target speaker (see Figure 20.12 in the separate color plate section) while predicting as much as possible the mechanical properties of the transformed articulations and soft tissues.

SPEAKER-SPECIFIC TALKING HEADS

When using video rewriting (Bregler, Covell, & Slaney, 1997b; Ezzat, Geiger, & Poggio, 2002) or 3D animation models (Guenter, Grimm, Wood, Malvar, & Pighin, 1998; Pighin et al., 1999), all systems use a speaker-specific shape that computes the displacement of key facial fleshpoints. Motion capture devices (e.g., Qualisys and Vicon) deliver in real time and with excellent precision (typically less than half a millimeter) the 3D positions of pellets or beads glued on the subject's face. Due to the technique used (retro-luminescent markers illuminated with infra-red light), the number and density of facial fleshpoints is actually quite limited. Moreover, lip shape could not be tracked this way: Beads could only be glued onto the dry part of the lips and such a setting would strongly affect the speaker's performance.

Speaker-Specific Shape Models

Using a very simple photogrammetric method and up-to-date calibration procedures, we recorded several dozen prototypical configurations of our speakers whose faces were marked with $n>200$ colored beads (on the cheek, mouth, nose, chin, and front neck areas), as depicted in the leftmost image of Figure 20.13a. In a coordinate system linked with the bite plane, every viseme is characterized by a set of n 3D points including positions of the lower teeth and of 30 points characterizing the speaker's lip shape (for further details see Elisei, Odisio, Bailly, & Badin, 2001; Revéret, Bailly, & Badin, 2000). Although these shapes have potentially 3^*n geometric degrees of freedom (DOF), we showed

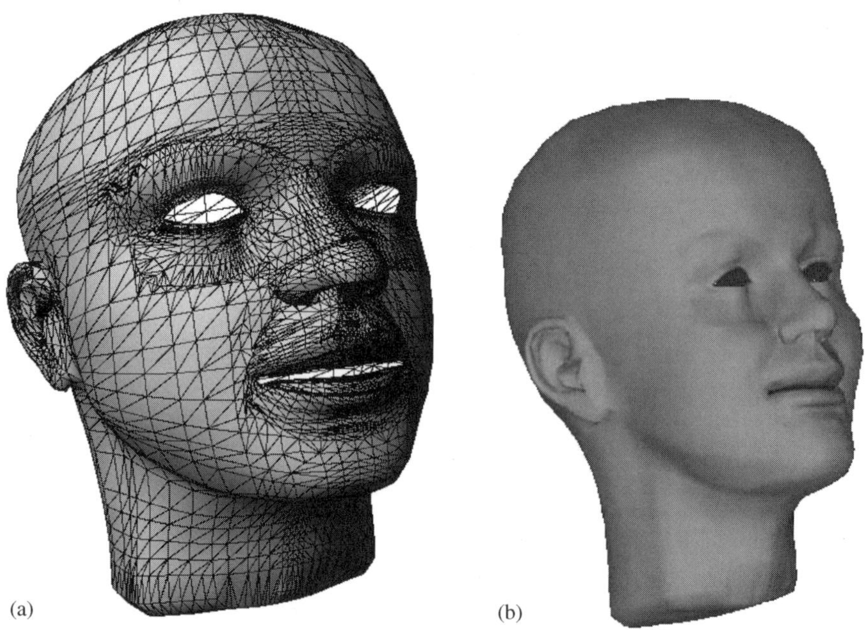

FIGURE 20.13. Combining a low-definition articulated mesh with a static high-definition facial mesh developed by Pighin et al. (1998).

that six DOF already explain over 95% of the variance of the data. Using PCA, Yehia, Rubin, and Vatikiotis-Bateson (1998) have also obtained similar results. In our case, the DOFs are derived by successive PCA applied to residual data of specific regions. The DOFs thus have a clear articulatory interpretation and can be labeled *a priori*. For jaw opening, the first component of a PCA applied to the feature points along the jaw line and the chin is extracted. Lip protrusion and lip opening DOF are also identified considering only the movements of the lips. Although determined using only a subset of the residual data, a linear regression between each DOF and the entire residual is performed and the residual for the next DOF computed for a further reduction of the explained variance. More subtle parameters such as lip raising, jaw advance, or independent vertical movements of the throat clearly emerge from this guided linear analysis. In Eq. (20.4) below, M is the mean position of the facial points and A a matrix containing the set of linear regressions successively performed using the DOFs α:

$$P = M + A \cdot \alpha \tag{20.4}$$

The control parameters α influence independently the movements of the whole lower face (e.g., the grooving of the nasogenian wrinkles and the expansion of the nose wings accompanying lip spreading in Figure 20.14c) (see the separate color plate section). These influences are sometimes subtle and distributed all over the face, but should not be neglected since interlocutors should be quite sensitive to laws governing biological motion (e.g., the experiments of Runeson & Frykholm, 1981, 1983 with body movements when carrying imaginary vs. real loads). Although its crude linear assumptions do not take into account, for now, saturation due to tissue compression, this technique nevertheless renders nicely the subtle interaction between speech organs and facial parts (such as the formation of wrinkles or movements of the nose wings mentioned above). Furthermore these "subtle" movements are necessary for rendering faithfully certain visemes: labiodentals (e.g., [v], [f]) require both retraction of the jaw and raising of both lips to ensure contact between the lower lip and the upper teeth, whereas palatal fricatives (e.g., [ʃ] [ʒ]) require both lip rounding and large aperture. Similarly, jaw protrusion is required in all allophonic variations of [s] for carrying the tongue front and upward.

Speaker-Specific Appearance Models

Shape changes are obviously accompanied by texture changes. We thus computed shape-free textures associated with all configurations used for estimating the shape model (by warping all images to the neutral configuration). Instead of combining *a posteriori* separate shape and appearance models as in Cootes, Edwards, and Taylor (2001), we estimated a simple linear model that relates RGB colors of each pixel of the shape-free images to shape parameters.

Figure 20.15 (in the separate color plate section) illustrates the change of shape-free appearance accompanying the rounding/spreading gesture: The grooving nasogenian wrinkle results clearly in a change of skin color and shades. We thus clearly need to use texture blending to properly render these changes of appearance. If the optimal statistical appearance model typically requires 6+1 textures (number of shape parameters + one average shape-free texture), 3 textures are sufficient to guarantee the most important changes of appearance around the lips: one rounded viseme with close lips (e.g., [u]), one rounded viseme with open lips (e.g., [ʃ]), and one spread viseme with open lips (e.g., [i]).

Toward a Generic Shape and Appearance Model

The parameters of all our speaker-specific models have a common semantics: open/close or advance/retract jaw, spread/round lips. These pseudo-articulatory parameters drive both the shape and appearance of the face. The way and the extent to which they affect face shape is speaker-dependent, but their number and their main actions are universal since we share the same facial musculoskeletal structure; i.e., speakers and languages differ only in the way they exploit and synchronize these same elementary gestures.

We can thus use PARAFAC analysis (Harshman & Lundy, 1984) or more directly a simple linear regression to determine the speaker's specific scaling of these universal commands. Prior to this analysis, each speaker-specific shape model should be characterized not only by the same number of commands but also drive the same mesh structure with the same number of vertices. Moreover the number of fleshpoints recorded during a motion capture session is limited to a few hundred and does not entirely cover the whole head. Using the mesh-matching algorithm described in the section 3D-to-3D matching with paired feature points, we are able to scale a generic high-definition talking face to the low-resolution surface defined by the fleshpoints characterizing each viseme of a session (see Figures 20.13a and Figure 20.16) (Figure 20.16 is in the separate color plate section).

SHAPING A GENERIC MODEL TO SPEAKER-SPECIFIC DATA

The 3D-to-3D matching algorithm described in the section 3D-to-3D matching is now applied to the facial data. The generic 3D facial mesh used here (Pighin et al., 1999) has 5826 vertices connected by 11,370 triangles (see Figure 20.13b). The 3D articulatory model of the female speaker used here drives 304 fleshpoints: 245 beads for the face, 30 control points of the lip model, and 29 markers for the skull as shown in Figure 20.13a.

Matching a Neutral Configuration

The 3D-to-3D matching algorithm is applied to the articulatory configuration that provides the same neutral articulation as the static generic model. A minimal set of obvious paired fleshpoints $\{s_k, t_k\}$ is first identified in order to constrain the global deformation in Eq. (20.3). Thirty paired fleshpoints have been selected: the nasion, the pogonion, the tip of the nose, and fleshpoints around the eyes and the lips.

Table 20.4 shows the distances (average and maximum) between the 3D data and the deformed mesh for two iterations of the matching procedure for different weighting factors Rw: The use of fleshpoints also improves the surface match. The matching converges typically after two iterations of the algorithm.

Matching All Configurations

We consider the transformed surface S_n obtained after matching the reference surface S_s to the neutral configuration. S_n is further transformed toward all articulatory configurations of the speaker-specific motion capture data. To further force the algorithm to mimic the biomechanical deformation, all fleshpoints are first paired by creating new vertices of the transformed surface S_n. These new vertices are just the projection of the remaining 3D points $\{q_i\}$ on S_n. The points $\{q_j\}$ are already paired (see the section Matching a neutral configuration) with existing vertices: the first term of Eq. (20.3) thus disappears since all 3D points are paired with vertices that will now behave as fleshpoints.

Articulating

Once all configurations have been matched and the vertices added in the procedure above removed from the generic mesh, vertices P_s of the transformed surface S_n are collected and a step-by-step linear regression is performed using the articulatory parameters α identified on the low-definition data (see the section Speaker-specific shape models). This results in Eq. (20.4). Figure 20.17a shows the effect of the jaw parameter on the deformation of the speaker-specific high-definition generic mesh.

SPEAKER-INDEPENDENT ARTICULATORY PARAMETERS VS. SPEAKER-SPECIFIC SHAPE MODEL

These operations can be iterated using motion capture data from several speakers. Up to now, low-definition facial models have been developed for five speakers (three French speakers, a German speaker, and an Algerian speaker). All models share the same set of six articulatory parameters that in all cases

TABLE 20.4. Average (Maximum) Distances in mm between the 3D Data and the Deformed Mesh

	Iteration 1			Iteration 2		
Constraints	All points	Feature points	Time (s)	All points All	Feature points	Time (s)
No FP	0.86 (4.54)	5.49 (14.51)	18.23	0.62 (3.74)	5.25 (13.24)	12.6
FP − Rw = 1	0.74 (5.85)	1.97 (5.22)	15.33	0.56 (3.47)	1.35 (3.78)	15.1
FP − Rw = 10	0.79 (3.94)	2.05 (5.05)	14.95	0.56 (3.50)	1.35 (3.78)	15.2

Note. FP, paired feature points; Rw, weighting factor of Eqs. (20.2) and (20.3).

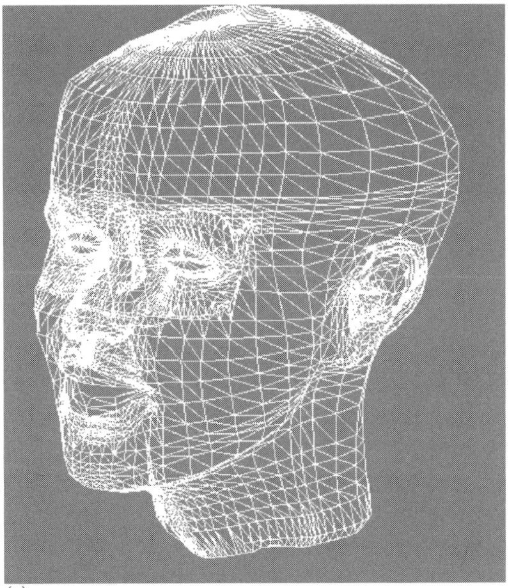

(a)

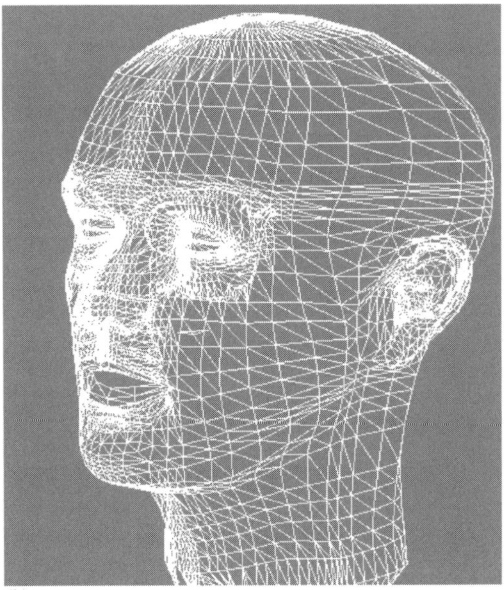

(b)

FIGURE 20.17. Building a generic talking face. Using the 3D-to-3D matching algorithm, a generic "high-definition" but static face mesh (see Figure 20.13b) is scaled to multiple "low-definition" motion capture data from each speaker. A "high-definition" articulated clone for each speaker is then developed: (a) the neutral shape for two speakers; and (b) the shape deformation resulting from setting to +1 the "jaw opening" parameter.

explain more than 95% of the variance of the 3D motion data. Compare, in Figure 20.17, the speaker-specific action of the same speaker-independent jaw rotation parameter for the female French speaker and the male German speaker.

So, by simply using parameters of the low-resolution motion capture data as linear predictors of the deformation of the high-definition mesh, we have sketched the first step toward a generic talking face where conformation and animation parameters (analog to the MPEG-4 FDP and FAP outlined in the Introduction section) are separated out.

CONCLUSIONS AND COMMENTS

The current proposal gives access to normalized speaker-specific articulatory models of facial deformations. With reference to a generic face these models describe the speaker-specific consequences of six universal actions of essential speech segments i.e., jaw, lips, and larynx. The dimensionality of the speaker-dependent variance of these actions can be further studied by collecting and analyzing the speaker-specific characteristics $\{M, A\}$ in Eq. (20.4). We plan to explain these characteristics using predictors of the skull and jaw morphology (see the section Skull). A similar scheme can then be envisaged for building appearance conformation and animation parameters using shape-free textures such as those shown in Figure 20.15.

Explaining mean face M from predictors of the skull/jaw morphology is quite helpful when facial shape and appearance are to be reconstructed from the bony structure. Similarly, the inverse transform should enable the skull/jaw model to be calibrated from external measurements of the subject, to avoid the need for an MRI scan.

Explaining the motion patterns A from predictors of the skull morphology will also help in reconstructing or planning functional behavior from static measurements. Our data-driven generic models are expected to achieve such extrapolations more reliably than *ad hoc* morphing procedures (Bregler, Covell, & Slaney, 1997a). Of course, only speech movements are considered here but this study could be extended to facial expressions, chewing, to name but two possibilities.

The global aim of this work is to first identify sources of variation in facial shape and kinematics and secondly to investigate their contributions to observed speech movements. More speech organs can be taken into account (notably the tongue and velum) in this investigation and we hope to gather sufficiently precise and spatially dense 3D motion capture data for several speakers (see some efforts in this direction in Badin et al., 2002). Biomechanical models (such as the one developed by Gérard, Wilhelms-Tricarico, Perrier, & Payan, 2003) will provide generic meshes with built-in elastic constraints that should satisfactorily replace the *ad hoc* grids (Badin et al., 2002; Engwall, 2000) or deformation models (Stone, Dick, Douglas, Davis, & Ozturk, 2000) used in the literature.

ACKNOWLEDGMENTS

Many thanks to Marija Tabain and Hani Camille Yehia for their thoughtful comments and suggestions on the early version of this paper. This work has been financed by the RNRT (TempoValse and Artus projects) as well as the CNRS (Robea project HR+). Motion capture as well as MRI data have been collected for several dozen subjects thanks to a grant from the BQR/INPG "Vésale". We acknowledge Praxim SA for the use of the initial 3D-to-3D matching software.

REFERENCES

Badin, P., Bailly, G., Revéret, L., Baciu, M., Segebarth, C., & Savariaux, C. (2002). Three-dimensional linear articulatory modeling of tongue, lips and face based on MRI and video images. *Journal of Phonetics, 30*(3), 533–553.

Banvard, R. A. (2002). *The Visible Human Project® Image Data Set From Inception to Completion and Beyond. CODATA 2002: Frontiers of Scientific and Technical Data, Track I-D-2: Medical and Health Data*, Montréal, Canada.

Bookstein, F. L. (1997). Landmark methods for forms without landmarks: Morphometrics of group differences in outline shape. *Medical Image Analysis, 1*(3), 225–243.

Bregler, C., Covell, M., & Slaney, M. (1997a). VideoRewrite: Driving visual speech with audio. *Proceedings of SIGGRAPH'97*, Los Angeles, CA (pp. 353–360).

Bregler, C., Covell, M., & Slaney, M. (1997b). Video rewrite: Visual speech synthesis from video. *Proceedings of the international conference on auditory-visual speech processing*, Rhodes, Greece (pp. 153–156).

Cootes, T. F., Edwards, G. J., & Taylor, C. J. (2001). Active appearance models. *IEEE Transactions on Pattern Analysis and Machine Intelligence, 23*(6), 681–685.

Couteau, B., Payan, Y., & Lavallée, S. (2000). The mesh-matching algorithm: An automatic 3D mesh generator for finite element structures. *Journal of Biomechanics, 33*(8), 1005–1009.

Dryden, I. L., & Mardia, K. V. (1998). *Statistical shape analysis*. London, UK: Wiley.

Eisert, P., & Girod, B. (1998). Analyzing facial expressions for virtual conferencing. *IEEE Computer Graphics & Applications: Special Issue: Computer Animation for Virtual Humans, 18*(5), 70–78.

Elisei, F., Odisio, M., Bailly, G., & Badin, P. (2001). Creating and controlling video-realistic talking heads. *Auditory-visual speech processing workshop*, Scheelsminde, Denmark (pp. 90–97).

Engwall, O. (2000). A 3D tongue model based on MRI data. *Proceedings of the international conference on speech and language processing*, Beijing, China (pp. 901–904).

Ezzat, T., Geiger, G., & Poggio, T. (2002). Trainable videorealistic speech animation. *ACM Transactions on Graphics, 21*(3), 388–398.

Gérard, J.-M., Wilhelms-Tricarico, R., Perrier, P., & Payan, Y. (2003). A 3D dynamical biomechanical tongue model to study speech motor control. *Recent Research Developments in Biomechanics, 1*, 49–64.

Guenter, B., Grimm, C., Wood, D., Malvar, H., & Pighin, F. (1998). Making faces. *Proceedings of SIGGRAPH*, Orlando, FL (pp. 55–67).

Harshman, R. A., & Lundy, M. E. (1984). The PARAFAC model for three-way factor analysis and multidimensional scaling. In H. G. Law, C. W. Snyder, J. A. Hattie, & R. P.

(Eds.), *MacDonald research methods for multimode data analysis* (pp. 122–215). New York: Praeger.

Hashi, M., Westbury, J. R., & Honda, K. (1998). Vowel posture normalization. *Journal of the Acoustical Society of America, 104*(4), 2426–2437.

Kähler, K., Haber, J., & Seidel, H.-P. (2003). Reanimating the dead: Reconstruction of expressive faces from skull data. *ACM Transactions on Graphics, 22*(3), 554–561.

Lorensen, W. E., & Cline, H. E. (1987). Marching cubes: A high resolution 3D surface construction algorithm. *Computer Graphics, 21*(4), 163–169.

Moshfeghi, M. (1991). Elastic matching of multimodality images. *Graphical Models and Processing, 53*(3), 271–282.

Pandzic, I. S., & Forchheimer, R. (2002). MPEG-4 facial animation. *The standard, implementation and applications*. Chichester, England: Wiley.

Pighin, F., Hecker, J., Lischinski, D., Szeliski, R., & Salesin, D. H. (1998). Synthesizing realistic facial expressions from photographs. *Proceedings of Siggraph*, Orlando, FL (pp. 75–84).

Pighin, F. H., Szeliski, R., & Salesin, D. (1999). Resynthesizing facial animation through 3D model-based tracking. *Proceedings of the international conference on computer vision* (Vol. 1, pp. 143–150).

Revéret, L., Bailly, G., & Badin, P. (2000). MOTHER: A new generation of talking heads providing a flexible articulatory control for video-realistic speech animation. *Proceedings of the international conference on speech and language processing*, Beijing, China (pp. 755–758).

Runeson, S., & Frykholm, G. (1981). Visual perception of lifted weight. *Journal of Experimental Psychology: Human Perception and Performance, 7*, 733–740.

Runeson, S., & Frykholm, G. (1983). Kinematic specification of dynamics as an informational basis for person and action perception: Expectation, gender recognition, and deceptive intention. *Journal of Experimental Psychology: General, 112*, 585–615.

Stone, M., Dick, D., Douglas, A. S., Davis, E. P., & Ozturk, C. (2000). Modelling the internal tongue using principal strains. *Proceedings of the 5th seminar on speech production: Models and data & CREST workshop on models of speech production: Motor planning and articulatory modelling*, Kloster Seeon, Germany (pp. 133–136).

Szeliski, R., & Lavallée, S. (1996). Matching 3-D anatomical surfaces with non-rigid deformations using octree-splines. *International Journal of Computer Vision, 18*(2), 171–186.

Wolberg, G. (1990). *Digital image warping*. Los Alamitos, CA: IEEE Computer Society Press.

Yehia, H. C., Rubin, P. E., & Vatikiotis-Bateson, E. (1998). Quantitative association of vocal-tract and facial behavior. *Speech Communication, 26*, 23–43.

Author Index

Subject Index